D0886819

CHILDREN
OF THE
KIBBUTZ

CHILDREN

OF THE

KIBBUTZ

MELFORD E. SPIRO

With the assistance of AUDREY G. SPIRO

REVISED EDITION

Harvard University Press
Cambridge, Massachusetts and London, England
1975

To Ashel and Kochevet
and of course to their sabras

Library of Congress Catalog Card Number 74-21689

ISBN 0-674-11606-2

Printed in the United States of America

CONTENTS

PART III · THE FIRST YEAR

PART IV · "THE TENDER AGE"

PART V · SCHOOL YEARS

Appendixes

Index   525

PREFACE TO THE 1965 EDITION

I

As originally conceived, this study of child training and personality was intended to achieve two ends. First, it was hoped that, as a detailed case study of "collective education" in the *kibbutz* which I have called "Kiryat Yedidim," it would provide an understanding of the unique socialization system that characterizes the kibbutz movement in Israel. The second aim of this study was to test the predictive value of ontogenetic culture-and-personality theory by attempting to relate selected personality characteristics of the *sabras* of Kiryat Yedidim to selected aspects of its socialization system. In short this study had both descriptive and theoretical aims. Since the relevance of the former aim for students of modern Israel, of socialist communities, and of comparative education is fairly obvious, I should like, before examining the extent to which the aims of this study have been achieved, to comment briefly on the relevance of the latter aim for students of social anthropology.

If the main tasks of social anthropology are the construction and testing of theories which explain social and cultural systems, it is scientific folly to neglect the central role of personality in maintaining sociocultural stability and in promoting sociocultural change. The investigation of these sociocultural functions of personality is, as I see it, the most important task of culture-and-personality research. Within this framework, socialization studies can make three important contributions. First, if techniques of problem solving and conflict resolution which characterize adult behavior are acquired in childhood, studies of socialization can discover the causal (ontogenetic) conditions of a great deal of social and cultural behavior. Second, if social and cultural systems are man's most important instruments for, as well as obstacles to, the satisfaction of his drives and needs, studies of socialization can discover the (ontogenetic) conditions which produce the psychological bases both for cultural conformity and change. Third, if early experience provides those perceptual-cognitive sets, and especially those projective sets,[1] by which individual actors structure their world, socialization studies are crucial for an understanding of those cultural systems which constitute the projective systems of communities and societies.

If these three aims constitute the *raison d'être* of socialization research within anthropology, *Children of the Kibbutz,* it must be admitted, is a truncated study in this *genre.* Because Kiryat Yedidim was still too young in 1951-52 to have raised an entire generation of adult sabras, the research on which this book is based was unable to focus on the sociocultural functions of personality. Instead it was devoted almost exclusively to the effects of socialization on personality formation. Now, however, that Kiryat Yedidim has raised a generation of adult sabras, who are not only living in the kibbutz, but who are centrally responsible for the viability of its institutions, it has become possible to investigate the sociocultural functions of sabra personality. It is to be hoped that the data obtained in this research can and will be used by others as the basis for such an investigation which, when completed, will have provided us with a rounded culture-and-personality study of the kibbutz.

The present volume, then, is narrower in scope, carrying out only the first part of my charter for culture-and-personality studies. Containing some discussion of the relationship between sabra personality and the major features of kibbutz society and culture, it is primarily concerned to present a structural (institutional) description of kibbutz socialization, a structural (psychological) description of sabra personality, and a systematic analysis of the causal relationships between them, the former system taken as the set of antecedent, the latter as the set of consequent, conditions. Although an author is hardly the best critic of his own work, I should like, nevertheless—from the perspective and psychological detachment provided by the six years which have elapsed since the publication of this volume—to evaluate these three aspects of *Children of the Kibbutz.*

[1] Abram Kardiner, *The Psychological Frontiers of Society,* New York, 1945.

II

"Collective education," the term used by the kibbutz to refer to its method of rearing children, finds few parallels in the annals of comparative education. To be sure, the upper-class educational system in Britain, for example, with its nannies, governesses, and public schools, contains structural features similar to those found in the kibbutz system of socialization. Even closer in structure, in certain respects, are the age-graded living arrangements found in certain parts of the primitive world—unisexual, among the Nyakyusa of Tanganyika, for example; bisexual, among the Muria of India. Nevertheless, it is probably fair to say ·that, structurally viewed, the system of collective education, when combined with the kibbutz marriage and family systems, comprises a cross-culturally unique institution which, together with the marriage and family systems of the Nayar of India, constitutes a crucial case for students of comparative institutions. For these students (and for those interested in contemporary Israeli society) a description of collective education should be of more than passing importance. After re-reading the present volume, I see no reason to alter or to modify its description of this institution.

Although there are some statements I would have made differently, and others on which I would have elaborated, I believe, too, after re-reading this book, that its analysis of the relationships *between* kibbutz socialization and sabra personality is essentially sound. Concerned, however, with only *selected* personality variables, the description of sabra personality presented in this book is necessarily incomplete; and being incomplete it might convey a somewhat distorted picture to the reader. Distortion can derive, I believe, not from what it says, which seems to me to be reasonably accurate, but from how it is said, and from what is left unsaid. I should like, therefore, to point to some of these possible distortions, and to indicate their probable sources. I would hope that the portrait contained in this volume might be viewed by the reader in the light of these comments.

III

A first possible source of distortion consists, as I have indicated, in what is left unsaid. In general the portrait of kibbutz sabras which is sketched in this volume tends to emphasize their negative qualities—"negative," that is, from the standpoint of generally accepted criteria of emotional adjustment—and it is this emphasis which, for those who would take the part for the whole, is the basis for possible distorted impressions. For, whereas this book attempts to trace the ontogenetic roots of sabra introversion, hostility, insecurity, and inferiority, there is no analogous treatment of the ontogenetic bases of sabra cooperation, achievement, creativity, and responsibility. That our psychodynamic personality theories, with their emphasis on conflict and defense mechanisms, make it much easier to analyze "negative" than "positive" characteristics, and to trace their early experiential roots, is one (but not the main) reason for this imbalance in treatment. The theoretical, in contrast to the pragmatic, rationale for this emphasis seemed, at the time of writing, both important and fairly obvious. Since we already knew a great deal about the structurally-induced tension and conflict inherent in the typical nuclear family, it appeared desirable to uncover their bases in a system with quite dissimilar structural features, a system which, as conceived by its founders, was intended to preclude the development of some of the personality traits alluded to above. That some of these traits were to be found among kibbutz sabras was, in itself, an important finding, and their ontogenetic explanation seemed to be one of the more urgent requirements of this research.

Obvious as this strategy was at the time of writing, it is now equally obvious to me that the positive attributes of sabra personality should have been afforded similar systematic treatment. For, although it is emphasized in this book that the ontogenetic analysis is but a partial one, and although there is some discussion of "positive" sabra qualities, the absence of any systematic treatment of these positive attributes inevitably leads to a distorted picture. Unhappily, I cannot attempt to redress the balance in this Preface. Concerned with entirely different research interests over the past six years, I am no longer capable of executing this task. It is urgently to be hoped, however, that other investigators, recognizing the importance of kibbutz personality studies, will be stimulated to undertake such a program of research.

The relative neglect of positive attributes of sabra personality, then, is one possible source of distortion. A second source of distortion may arise from the interpretation of, and the weight properly to be assigned to, their negative attributes. That these attributes exist, and that they are characterologically important, are, I believe, clearly supported findings of this study. There are, nevertheless, at least two reasons why their importance might be distorted. One reason may be found in the theoretical bias of this book; the other, in the limitations inherent in kibbutz research. I should like, by means of examples, to examine each of these reasons in turn.

IV

In re-reading this volume, it became obvious that the psychoanalytic orientation, which served to guide my observations and to cast my interpretations, was an unwitting source of two important biases, both in the research and in the writing. In the first place, this orientation led to a bias in favor of genetic, to the relative neglect of situational, determinants of behavior, a bias which can be illustrated by one simple example. There can be no question, I think, about the high incidence of aggressive and acting-out behavior in the junior and senior high school, nor of their social-ization-based—hence characterological—importance. To attribute adolescent aggressiveness, however, to exclusively characterological determinants is surely questionable in view of the fact—and this fact is pointed out in the chapter on the high school—that a significant percentage of the students are non-kibbutz, urban, children, many of whom are emotionally disturbed. It is not difficult to imagine how a small number of such disturbed students, by providing the emotional climate within which less disturbed students can be provoked into aggressive behavior, might have disrupted a classroom. The chapter describing adolescent behavior does not attempt, however, to assess the importance of this variable, either for its consequences for classroom behavior or for behavior in other situations. The point, then, is that in neglecting situational determinants of sabra aggressiveness, their characterological roots, for which there is abundant evidence, may have nevertheless been unduly emphasized.

Although one's intellectual errors can never be entirely justified, there was, I believe, some justification for the second theoretical bias of this volume, *viz.*, an undue emphasis on unconscious, to the relative neglect of conscious, motivation. Much of social science research seemed to me at the time of writing this book—and this continues to be my opinion—superficial, when not wrong, because of its neglect of unconscious determinants of behavior. Given this feeling, it was natural, if not inevitable, to have emphasized unconscious variables in this study. Although I did not assume, as some depth personality theorists would have it, that only unconscious motives and attitudes are really "real," and that conscious motives and attitudes are merely ideological superstructures and rationalizations, possessing little motivational or characterological significance, the emphasis in this research was most certainly "clinical," and not—as is typically the case in social research— "social psychological."

For this clinical approach to personality, with its emphasis on conflict and on the motivational importance of conflict resolution, I make no apology. It is the only approach which, in my opinion, even attempts to make sense of the complexity of human behavior. Since such an approach, however, places a heavy emphasis on unconscious dimensions of personality, the description and analysis of the sabras in this volume is, in large measure, a description and an analysis of the sabra unconscious; and the sabra unconscious— like the unconscious in any society—is composed essentially of "negative" features. It is not the case, then, that this study, by an undue emphasis on unconscious dimensions of personality—thereby highlighting its negative attributes—presents a distorted picture of sabra personality. It is rather in not placing these attributes in some comparative perspective, that this study provides a basis for inter- pretative distortions on the part of non-clinically oriented readers. What is required, in short, is some scale, absolute or comparative, by which the significance of these sabra traits can be properly assessed.

Thus, for example, if the observations discussed in the chapter on sabra personality are accurate—and I believe that they are—the sabras exhibit many signs of "hostility." Without further discussion, however, and especially without some comparative perspective, it might be concluded that they are uniquely hostile or that, at the least, they are more hostile than products of alternative socializa- tion systems. This is most certainly not the case, nor did I intend to convey the impression that it was the case. Although the *forms* of sabra hostility and its sociocultural *determinants* are different from the forms and determinants of hostility in other societies, its *intensity* is surely no greater than that found in any normal popula- tion, and, in my opinion, it falls well within a normal cross-cultural range. In attempting, however, to ferret out the uniquely kibbutz aspects of hostility, the obverse impression may have been con- veyed. I wish to emphasize here that this is not the case.

One further observation, related to this last point, must be made. Although Utopians may believe—and perhaps it is important that some should hold this belief—that a social system might be devised which would preclude the development of emotional conflict and tension, there are, in my opinion, neither evidential nor theoretical grounds for such an expectation. Although different social systems exact tolls of different types and magnitudes, any social system exacts a psychological toll from its members; and—what is more germane to this volume—any socialization system exacts a toll from the children whom it attempts to raise up to live in accordance with the structural arrangements and cultural values of their society. The system of collective education has successfully reared such children: the sabras of Kiryat Yedidim, like those of hundreds of other kibbutzim, now comprise its adult generation, occupying its leadership and managerial positions, operating its institutions, transmitting its values to their own children. To have achieved this end, collective education — like any socialization system—has exacted a psychological price from its products. That price, which is described in this volume, is, as I have already indicated, no larger than the price which the products of most systems must pay for the privilege of becoming human—and it is smaller than many.

In any event, and whatever one's judgments might be concerning the fairness of the price, every reader of this volume would do well to ponder the wise words of David Rapaport. The kibbutz experience, he suggests,

> may show us that it is inherent in the 'human condition' that all societies' education will inevitably exact, and thus all societies will pay, a price—a necessary sacrifice—in the coin of developmental crises and pathology, for their successes in adapting their successive generations to their ways of life.[2]

If one believes, as I do, that Rapaport's words are profoundly true, his conclusion concerning research strategy follows ineluctably. It is the strategy which this book attempted to execute.

> The scientific problem is not whether collective education is good or bad ... The problem is: *What* traditional, historical, organizational, institutional and economic forces find their unnoted expression in the forms of collective education, and *how* do these forms of upbringing induce behavior forms (social modalities) and behavior problems which in their genetic sequence result in individuals who perpetuate the way of life of the kibbutz?[3]

v

In addition to its theoretical biases, there is another reason why

[2] David Rapaport, "The Study of Kibbutz Education and its Bearing on the Theory of Development," *American Journal of Orthopsychiatry* 28: 587-597, 1958, p. 597.
[3] *Ibid.*

this volume might lead to distortion in interpreting sabra personality. This reason consists in certain objective limitations inherent
in kibbutz research, the most important being the youth of the
kibbutz movement. At the time that we conducted our field work
(1951-52), Kiryat Yedidim was only thirty years old. One potential
source of error, given the youth of the kibbutz, derives from the
sampling problem. During our field work, there were only eleven
"adult" (arbitrarily defined as twenty-one years and older) sabras
in Kiryat Yedidim, all of them under thirty. Much of the description
of the end-product of collective education—the mature sabra—was
based, therefore, on behavioral observations of very young adults,
scarcely out of adolescence. Since kibbutz adolescence, like
that in Euro-America, is a period of *Sturm und Drang*—in itself a
valuable finding—we cannot be sure from this study alone what
the sabra is like when he passes from this psychologically transitional period into one of stable maturity. Although only a follow-up
study will provide us with a complete answer, I should record here
the impressions received from a short visit to Kiryat Yedidim in the
summer of 1962. My impressions of the sabras—subjects of the
1951-52 study—whom I met during this brief encounter were un-
exceptionally favorable. They struck me as mature, purposeful
individuals, carrying out the tasks which were now theirs with
responsibility and, withal, with good humor.

A second source of interpretative error, occasioned by the youth
of the kibbutz, is that none of the adult sabras at the time of the
study were, themselves, the children of sabras. Since kibbutz
parents play a vital role in the emotional development of their
children, it can be assumed that sabra parents—since very few
exhibit either the anxious love toward their children which their
parents exhibited toward them, or their parents' nagging doubts
concerning the desirability of collective education[4]—will influence
their children differently from the way in which they were influenced by their parents. Until we can observe the effects of
collective education on children whose parents are products of the
system, we can only suspend judgment concerning its long term
psychological consequences.

The youth of the kibbutz poses still a third obstacle to any
psychological assessment of the sabras. All social systems, as I have
already indicated, not only engender conflict and anxiety in their
members, but these conflicts and anxieties are reduced, if not

---

[4] On the latter point, see A. I. Rabin, "Kibbutz Mothers View 'Collective
Education,'" *American Journal of Orthopsychiatry* 34: 140-142, 1964.

resolved, by various aspects of the cultural systems of these societies. The psychological function of these systems is to serve as culturally constituted defense mechanisms.[5] In its brief thirty years of existence, Kiryat Yedidim, at the time of this study, had evolved only a few of these cultural vehicles, by means of which kibbutz-instigated conflicts and tensions might have been resolved. For the most part, therefore, the sabras whom we studied—unlike the products of almost all other socialization systems—had to create their own techniques of conflict resolution, their own defenses. It is not that non-sabras, too, do not have private defense mechanisms —we all have our private defenses—but these latter defenses, in my opinion, play a relatively minor role in the psychological economy of the typical member of the typical society. (In our own society we are most acutely aware of the importance of private defenses because we all share many of the same culturally-constituted defenses, and because many of us are unaware of the ego-defensive functions of our cultural systems). In fact, however, it is only when culturally-constituted defenses become non-viable—and this can happen for a variety of, partially understood, reasons—that private defenses loom as the major elements in the personality's total defensive system; and when this happens the individual exhibits the kind of behavior that requires treatment by a healer, be he psychiatrist or shaman. Until the kibbutz has had sufficient time to develop a cultural system which, delicately calibrated with its social system and the personality it creates, can provide the sabras with a variety of culturally-constituted defense mechanisms, it will be premature to evaluate sabra personality or the psychological effects of collective education.

VI

We may conclude with a few additional remarks. Although a third volume, dealing with the results of the projective tests, is promised in the Introduction of this volume, it is highly improbable —for a variety of complicated reasons—that such a volume will appear.[6]

It should be noted that all statements concerning kibbutz political beliefs and attitudes refer to the period 1951-52, in which field work was carried out. Kiryat Yedidim has since undergone

---

[5] Melford E. Spiro, "An Overview and a Suggested Reorientation," in F. L. K. Hsu (ed.), *Psychological Anthropology*, Homewood, Illinois, 1961.

[6] Rorschach data on kibbutz sabras may be found in A. I. Rabin, "Kibbutz Adolescents," *American Journal of Orthopsychiatry* 21: 493-504, 1961.

important changes in its political ideology, notably in its attitude toward the Soviet Bloc and the international Communist movement.

Finally, the anthropologist will recognize a somewhat amorphous use of "culture" in this volume. This term is used for what now I would wish to break down into the three concepts of cultural system, social system, and social structure. I hope that in each case the context is sufficient to indicate to which of these concepts the omnibus term, "culture," is intended to refer.

THE UNIVERSITY OF CHICAGO
October, 1964

PREFACE

The importance of the kibbutz for the behavioral sciences — as a stimulus for new hypotheses and fresh insights, and as a laboratory for the testing of old hypotheses — is inestimable. Anthropologists have conventionally turned to non-Western societies as the locales for research, not only to increase the size of the sample from which our generalizations are ultimately derived, but also — and more important — to widen the range of discoverable variation in behavior. In short, we try to discover in nature (and history) those social conditions which in our own society can be duplicated only in an artificial experimental situation.

Within this anthropological perspective, the kibbutz stands in bold relief. Though a part of Western society, its culture in many aspects is as radically different from Western culture as the latter is from Iroquois or Arunta. The kibbutz, unlike most societies known to ethnography or history, practices comprehensive collective living, communal ownership, and cooperative enterprise. Many communistic and utopian communities, including those established in the United States during the last century, were founded on principles of comprehensive collective living. But few adopted all the features characteristic of the kibbutz, and — more important — none has survived. The importance of kibbutz culture for social science is not only that its collectivism is much more comprehensive than that found in most other communistic societies, but that it has succeeded — that is, survived, in over three hundred separate communities. And, in my opinion, the movement will continue to survive and to grow, albeit with some changes and modifications.

My curiosity about the kibbutz was first aroused while I was engaged in research on the atoll of Ifaluk in the Central Caroline Islands of Micronesia. Impressed with the functioning of this highly cooperative society,[1] I wished to observe at firsthand a society at the (cooperative) polar extreme of the competitive-cooperative continuum. But my scientific interest in the kibbutz was in its functional, rather than in its structural, aspects. Specifically, I was curious about the personality produced by such a culture. Since the adults (those in their middle years and older) had come to the kibbutz from the outside, my interest was in the younger people and the children — those born in this collective society and reared in its unique socialization system of collective education.

Thus, the kibbutz was chosen for a study in culture and personality. But the relatively brief duration of the kibbutz precluded the execution of more than a truncated study. For, though it was possible to study the effect of kibbutz culture on personality, it was not possible to study (except in a limited way) the effect of kibbutz personality on culture. If personality is viewed as the intervening variable between the culture of a prior and that of a succeeding generation, then, in the ideal research design, personality is studied as both a consequent and an antecedent condition. This was hardly possible in a community as young as Kiryat Yedidim. My research problem, therefore, was restricted to the relationships between kibbutz child training and *sabra* (one born and raised in a kibbutz) personality.

The present book is the second in a three-volume study devoted to this problem. The first, *Kibbutz: Venture in Utopia*, presents the socio-cultural setting within which socialization and personality development, the concerns of this volume, occur. The third volume will be devoted to the structure and dynamics of sabra personality as revealed by projective tests. Because the latter instruments are, allegedly, uniquely qualified to reveal a rounded and holistic picture of personality funtioning, the present volume is less concerned with total personality than it is with selected personality variables. A synthetic or inclusive personality description is neither intended nor achieved.

The field work on which this book is based was carried out during 1951–1952. Since many changes have occurred since that time, in both Israel and the kibbutz, the reader is cautioned that all factual statements in the book, unless otherwise indicated, refer exclusively to the period of our research. The locale for this

[1] For a description of Ifaluk culture, see Edwin G. Burrows and Melford E. Spiro, *An Atoll Culture*, Human Relations Area Files, New Haven, Conn., 1953. For a more detailed account of its cooperative ethos, see Melford E. Spiro, "The Problem of Aggression in a South Seas Culture" (Ph.D. thesis).

research was a (then) thirty-year-old kibbutz which permitted us to live in its midst, work in its fields and orchards, participate in its social life, and study its children. We have chosen to name this kibbutz *Kiryat Yedidim.* Further to preserve its anonymity — as well as that of its individual members — all names and terms which might serve as clues to its identity are rendered pseudonymously. Thus, the federation of kibbutzim with which Kiryat Yedidim is affiliated is, simply, The Federation; the political party which expresses its political and ideological views is The Party. Quotations from journals and books, both in Hebrew and in English, which might facilitate identification are cited without proper reference either to author or to title. I can only hope that the various authors who are quoted without credit will respect my motives. The identity of all anonymous materials, needless to say, will be made available to interested research scholars.

Perhaps even more important than maintaining the anonymity of the kibbutz is the necessity for respecting the privacy of its individual members. Therefore, the names of *all* children and adults referred to have been changed. Where the assignation of a pseudonym was not deemed sufficient, liberties were taken with sex, age, family affiliation, and other potentially identifying characteristics. It is most unlikely — and this sentence is addressed primarily to Kiryat Yedidim — that any person referred to in the text can be identified by even the most perceptive chaver. My desire to respect the privacy of the objects of this study has in a few instances precluded the possibility of making some of the data public. It is to be doubted, however, if this has importantly reduced the bulk of the evidence.[2]

In the foreword to *Kibbutz: Venture in Utopia,*[3] I pointed out that few of the more rigorous techniques of social research contributed to the findings of that book; that it was based for the most part on personal impressions derived from a year's participant-observation in Kiryat Yedidim; and that, consequently, though its author was a professional anthropologist, the book did not necessarily warrant the appellation of a "scientific" report.

[2] This concern with privacy may be deemed overly obsessive by some. I would remind them that Kiryat Yedidim is not an isolated, nonliterate community — the conventional object of anthropological study — but a highly literate community in a much publicized area of the world. Its members, moreover, will most certainly read this monograph, and they will probably be visited by others of its readers.

[3] For a synoptic description of the kibbutz in which I conducted my research, see Melford E. Spiro, *Kibbutz: Venture in Utopia,* Harvard University Press, Cambridge, Mass., reissued 1975.

Hence, I was amazed when many reviewers chose to make personal pronouncements on the kibbutz movement, which, they claimed, were "proved" by the incontrovertible findings of "science" — that is, by statements found in *Kibbutz.*

If the "scientific" findings of that volume were used to support opinions — both favorable and unfavorable — about the kibbutz, I shudder to think of what pronouncements these reviewers may make about the sabras on the basis of this second volume. For, though some will exclude the present volume, too, from the category of "science," it would be dishonest for me to do so; this book represents the product of my scientific skills. Hence, though an author cannot disclaim responsibility for what he has written, I feel that I should point out the limits and limitations of this volume.

The first point to be noted is that the methods available to the type of research essayed in this study are still somewhat crude. These methods and their rationale are described in Appendix A, Methods of Research. Though they yielded highly consistent results — that is, the *reliability* of the data is high — the *validity* of the findings remains an open question. Moreover, other methods available to social research, methods which provide different and more precise types of data (data which are amenable to sophisticated techniques of quantitative analysis) were not employed in this study — because of my unfamiliarity with, or incompetence in, their use, or because of my skepticism concerning their validity. These methods, it should be remarked, might have produced quite different results. Finally, the projective tests, which occupy an important part in the research design, are still being analyzed, and their results may importantly alter the picture of the sabras presented in this volume.

A second basis for caution in interpreting the results is the size of the sample. Although pains have been taken to indicate the variability inherent in the data, there are nevertheless many modal statements allegedly characteristic of the group. But, since the description of the adult sabras — the end products of collective education — is derived from the study of a small number of individuals, it is entirely possible that the mode would have shifted had the sample been larger — and, indeed, it might still shift as the number of adult sabras increases with the passage of time. The population of adult sabras (persons over the age of twenty-one) available for study consisted of only eleven individuals. Thus, even if the generalizations concerning these eleven are veridical, they may, in their totality, represent a snapshot taken at a specific — and not necessarily representative — moment in a highly fluid field.

A third reason for caution is due to the brief duration of the study. Ideally a research project is terminated when the investigator believes he has collected sufficient data either to describe the phenomenon in which he is interested or to confirm or disconfirm a hypothesis. This project, however, was terminated before either of these conditions had been satisfied, because the year's leave from my teaching post had expired. Knowing in advance that we had only eleven months in which to conduct the study, my wife and I budgeted our time so that some data could be collected on each of the various age-grades — infancy, early childhood, middle childhood, adolescence, adulthood. When we turned our research efforts from one of these age-grades to the next, we did so only because of our keen awareness of the passing of time, and not necessarily because sufficient data had been collected for the age-grade in question.

There are, consequently, many gaps in the data, and in some instances they may be of sufficient magnitude to distort at least some of the generalizations. It is to be hoped that these gaps will be filled by future researchers. Until that time, it is important to observe that many of the generalizations to be found in this book rest on partial data only.

The above *caveats* are methodological in nature. There are other potential sources of error, however, which are primarily substantive in nature. Although collective education constituted the configuration of "antecedent conditions" for this study, its influence as a determinant of sabra personality is contaminated by a number of uncontrolled variables, of which but two might be singled out for discussion.

In the first place, the sabras represent the first generation of a revolutionary experiment. Those who founded the kibbutz, and who instituted and administered its system of collective education, were dislocated persons. Alienated from the world of their parents, they were yet not attracted by another, alternative world except that of their own creative fantasy. Privileged (and gifted), as few people are, to transmute fantasy into reality, they had to face the psychological burdens entailed by this privilege. There were no well-trodden paths they could follow, no time-honored prescriptions they could fall back on, no traditions they could adhere to. The doubts and uncertainties, the conflicts and anxieties which are resolved in other parents by the "wisdom" of tradition, find no such resolution in these parents. Their questioning is resolved by further experimentation, by artificial rigidity, and by hope. But is it too much to suggest that their children are what they are because (among other things) of the unmapped educational terrain of their parents? To judge this system, either positively or negatively, on the basis of one generation would be rash in the extreme. A judicious, if not definitive, evaluation of collective education must wait upon two or three generations of sabra children of sabra parents. Only then will the integrative processes, whereby personality needs are satisfied through those very cultural institutions which, in turn, produce those personality needs, have an opportunity to do their work. And only then will we truly be able to discover the predictable personality consequences of collective education.

A second important contaminating factor, whose effect has not been "controlled," is extrinsic to the system of collective education, but it is very much intrinsic to the entire context of kibbutz life. The older sabras described in this book not only were born and raised in an experimental situation best characterized as a social frontier, but most of their formative years were lived in a material situation best described as a physical frontier. Malarial swampland, substandard physical conditions, physical isolation — these were characteristic features of the *early* kibbutz. And as these impediments were progressively removed, others soon supervened — Arab riots, the emotional pressures induced by Naziism, absorption of refugee children, the dislocations of war. The latter left a deep impression, particularly on the younger sabras. Many of them recall the bombings from the air, the necessity to seek shelter, and, in some instances, the impossibility of seeking shelter. It is no wonder that peace — or, as many of them put it, the absence of war — is, even for the young children, one of the "best things" that can happen to them (as is indicated by the Emotional Response Test). That all these factors have contributed to sabra personality would seem obvious; yet neither the nature nor the magnitude of this contribution has been assessed in this study — because we do not know how to assess it.

This study is not intended as an example of what is termed "area research." I am not an area specialist; I am not an expert on the Middle East, Israel, or the kibbutz movement. Although I am deeply interested in the kibbutz movement and its future, my research interest in it stemmed rather from theoretical concerns in the problems of culture and personality. This distinction entails at least two important consequences for the nature of this study.

One is that this study was more concerned with testing current theory in culture and personality, and in discovering new theoretical relationships between culture and personality, than in explaining sabra personality by means of current culture and personality theory — although the latter was also done. But my primary intention was to discover what the kibbutz could contribute to the advancement of scientific theory, not what scientific theory could contribute to an understanding of the kibbutz.

A second consequence following from the first concerns the intended provenience of the book's generalizations. Since this is intended as a scientific rather than as an historical study — to employ a distinction made by some anthropologists — it is primarily interested in generalizing *about* the relationships between analytic variables rather than in generalizing *from* Kiryat Yedidim to the kibbutz movement. The extent to which Kiryat Yedidim is representative of a population of kibbutzim, the extent to which findings concerning its sabras can also be said to hold for other sabras, and similar questions are beside the point. This book is concerned with "socializer," not *metapelet;* with "frustration," not "Rachel's refusal to give Yaakov some candy"; with "group security," not the "obvious satisfaction which Rachel and Yaakov derive from being with their *kevutza.*" Kiryat Yedidim was chosen, not because it is representative of other kibbutzim (though it may be), but because certain relationships between culture and personality could be better studied there than in many other kibbutzim — or in most other societies.[4]

This book represents in almost all its aspects the collaboration of my wife, Audrey Goldman Spiro, and me. Neither the field work on which it is based nor the writing of the book itself could have been executed without her assistance. Information on the

[4] Though my primary interest in the kibbutz was theoretical, the theoretically oriented reader should be warned that theory testing is not the primary content of this book. It is a truism that in order to test a series of hypotheses about the relationship between socialization and personality — viewed as antecedent and consequent conditions, respectively — it is necessary that the available data constitute evidence, confirming or disconfirming, for the hypotheses to be tested. It would be pointless, for example, to test predictions about the effects of maternal deprivation on adult personality if maternal deprivation were not found in the society under study. Thus, since kibbutz socialization had not been systematically studied prior to this investigation, our first task was to study in as fine detail as possible the parameters of this system. Only after the system was studied, and its various aspects properly described and classified, did the data necessary for the formulation of personality predictions become available. Only in the last section of this book, therefore, does our primary interest in theory testing become evident.

first two years in the life of a kibbutz child derives primarily from her research in the Nursery and the younger Toddlers' Houses. Her participation in field work was not restricted, however, to formal research with young children. Her interaction with parents, nurses, and adult sabras provided much of the data and many of the hypotheses of this study. Her role in the analysis of the data was as marked as the part she played in field work, and she participated in the laborious job of coding and tabulating the behavioral protocols. Finally, she wrote the first draft of some of the chapters in Parts II and III, rewrote the unintelligible sections written by me, and edited the entire manuscript.

An author is indebted, not only to his collaborator, but also to those whose intellectual influence has become an essential part of his own thought and manner of work. For myself, the paramount influence on my intellectual development has been the work of Professor A. Irving Hallowell. It was he who first stimulated my interest in the study of culture and personality, opened my eyes to the important theoretical questions it must attempt to answer, and introduced me to many of the techniques of research and analysis that I have tried to use in this study. And it was he who taught me, by his own continuous example, that the proper method of anthropological research is to begin (but not to end) with concrete human beings, in their dialectical relationships with their environment.

Professor Melville J. Herskovits is responsible not only for awakening my interest in anthropology, but for sensitizing my scientific superego to the pitfalls in my natural penchant for speculation, by insisting that I acknowledge the importance of cold fact. Professor Jules Henry convinced me of the importance of direct observation of interaction as a primary task of anthropological field work; and Professor Richard Rudner — in the course of many stimulating discussions — is primarily responsible for whatever comprehension I may have of the methodological issues inherent in social research.

In addition to these scholars whose influence has been of a personal nature, I would be remiss if I did not mention at least a few others whose influence has been mediated primarily or exclusively through their published work. My interest in the ontogenetic approach to the study of culture and in the application of psychoanalytic theory to the study of socialization and adult character is due, in no small part, to the pioneering work of Erik Homburger Erikson, Abram Kardiner, and Margaret Mead. The work of Professors John Dollard and Neal Miller first impressed me with the importance of an adequate theory of learning for the understanding of cultural behavior. Professors Irvin Child and John Whiting have contributed greatly to the organization of this book and to much of the thinking that lies behind it, as will be apparent to anyone who has read their stimulating *Child Training and Personality.*

The content of this book and its style have been improved by many criticisms and suggestions of the following persons who were kind enough to read it in typescript: Professor William Brinner, Professor Irvin Child, Professor and Mrs. A. Irving Hallowell, and Professor Jules Henry. Professor Brinner not only eliminated from the manuscript serious errors concerning kibbutz and Hebraic culture, but served as an unofficial co-worker in the field. His help in collecting data was of inestimable value.

The foregoing list would be incomplete without the name of Miss Ann Louise Coffin of the Harvard University Press whose editorial counsel in preparing both volumes of this study for publication has not only enhanced their quality, but has served to mitigate much of the pre-publication travail that an author usually dreads.

Finally, I acknowledge my indebtedness to Professor James H. Barnett, my former administrative head at the University of Connecticut. It was his wise and skillful administration, as well as his personal encouragement, that provided the tension-free intellectual climate so necessary for scholarly work.

It is a pleasure to be able to express my appreciation to the Social Science Research Council for its encouragement and support. A Post-doctoral Fellowship enabled me to conduct the field work in Kiryat Yedidim, and a Faculty Research Fellowship provided the necessary leisure for analyzing the data and writing this book.

Though I have expressed my gratitude to the people of Kiryat Yedidim in the first volume of this study, I cannot refrain from reiterating my sentiments. The warm hospitality which they extended to my wife and me, and the patience they displayed toward us as scientists prying into their affairs, was a constant source of encouragement, not only in the field, but in that long interval during which it seemed that this book would never reach completion. To their children — the primary objects of our prying — I am similarly grateful. Though it was my scientific responsibility to perceive them as *subjects*, I have always cherished them as personal *chaverim*, and I can only hope that this sentiment is reciprocated.

Glossary

Hebrew Terms and Other Names Frequently Used

chaver (chaa-vare'),° f., *chavera;* pl., *chaverim:* comrade, a member of a kibbutz.

chevra (chev-raa'): society. It is used in this volume to refer, as does the kibbutz, to the various children's groups that inhabit a common dwelling.

chevrat yeladim (chev-raat' ye-laa-deem'): children's society. The entire population of kibbutz children.

ganenet (gaa-ne'-net): nursery teacher.

hashkava (hash-kaa-vaa'): the evening period during which the children are put to bed.

kevutza (ke-voo-tzaa'): the children's peer-group that inhabits a common living quarter.

kibbutz (kee-bootz'), pl., *kibbutzim:* a collective settlement.

Kiryat Yedidim (Keer-yaat' Ye-dee-deem'): the fictitious name of the kibbutz described in this volume.

metapelet (me-taa-pe'-let): the woman ("nurse") in charge of a kevutza.

mosad (mo-saad'): kibbutz junior-senior high school.

sabra (saa'-bra): used in this volume to refer, exclusively, to anyone born in Kiryat Yedidim.

The Federation: the fictitious name for the federation of kibbutzim with which Kiryat Yedidim is affiliated.

The Movement: the fictitious name for the youth movement of which the youth of Kiryat Yedidim are members.

The Party: the fictitious name for the left-wing political party to which the members of Kiryat Yedidim belong.

° "ch" at the beginning of a word or syllable is pronounced as in the German guttural.

PART I · KIBBUTZ EDUCATION

CHAPTER 1 · THE NATURE OF A KIBBUTZ

From the deserts of the Negev to the mountains of the upper Galilee, the Israeli landscape is dotted with over 300 *kibbutzim* (collective agricultural settlements). Divided into several federations on the basis of varying ideological and structural criteria, their similarities are fundamental enough to permit us — and them — to refer to them collectively as "the kibbutz movement." This movement, comprised of less that 5 per cent of the total Israeli population, is of much greater importance than its numerical strength would indicate. Its ideals were instrumental in bringing the young state into being; from its manpower the country obtained its most valiant fighters for defense against a foreign attack which threatened its very existence; its representatives occupy important positions of leadership in almost all phases of contemporary Israeli life. It is no coincidence that the present premier of Israel lists as his permanent address a young kibbutz in the Negev, or that many of his ministers are members of kibbutzim.

Kiryat Yedidim, the kibbutz whose children are described in this volume, was founded thirty years prior to this study by a small group of Eastern European Jews. Motivated by the desire to escape from the anti-Semitism to which European Jewry was heir, by the dream of reconstituting the Jewish people as a Nation in its ancient homeland, by the conviction that physical — and, particularly, agricultural — labor was the noblest means to self-expression, and by the zeal to establish a society based on freedom and equality, this band of intellectual youths migrated to Palestine and, after a few years, began their experiment in what was then a malarial swampland. At the time of this study, Kiryat Yedidim was a prosperous and attractive village of five hundred. Its original membership had been augmented, not only by natural increase, but by the inclusion of two later adult contingents. The members of the second, and younger, contingent married the adult children of the kibbutz.

As an agricultural village, Kiryat Yedidim is characterized by group living, communal ownership, and cooperative enterprise. All land is owned by the Jewish National Fund, an arm of the Jewish Agency, which rents it to the kibbutz on a long-term lease for a nominal fee; and all capital goods are owned by the kibbutz, although individuals possess a few personal effects. Though a most efficient instrument in the agricultural colonization of a barren and malaria-infested land, kibbutz collectivism is predicated on moral rather than on pragmatic grounds. Zealously devoted to the ideals of brotherhood, equality, and freedom, the kibbutz believes that these can best be implemented in a collectivistic community. Communal ownership, it is believed, prevents the development of economic classes and the inevitable social inequality that seems to characterize societies stratified by class. Similarly, cooperative enterprise is believed to promote brotherhood and freedom by muting the more vicious aspects of a competitive economy, by precluding the rise of entrenched power and of the exploitation which, it is believed, accompanies the conjunction of power and privilege. Hence, labor is performed in work crews under the leadership of a foreman who, perceived as a *primus inter pares,* serves his tenure of office at the pleasure of his peers.

Kibbutz opposition to exploitation extends to non-kibbutz members as well. Thus, despite the shortage of manpower in Kiryat Yedidim, it will not hire workers from the outside since this would entail the reaping of profit from another's labor. This means, of course, that all who live in the kibbutz are members of it,[1] and as kibbutz members all are comrades (chaverim).

Having abolished money within the kibbutz both as a medium of exchange and a symbol of wealth, the kibbutz has also eliminated the profit motive as a stimulus for economic production. The distribution of goods is determined by the principle of "from each according to his ability, to each according to his needs," the latter being determined to a great extent by the entire group assembled in Town Meeting. This biweekly Meeting is the ultimate authority on all other matters which affect the kibbutz or any of its individual members. Authority is delegated by the Meeting to democratically elected officials who carry out policy determined by the Meeting, and who administer the various

---

[1] There are some exceptions to this generalization. Elderly parents of kibbutz founders who have been brought there from their European homes are residents, but not members. Similarly, various youth groups — either refugees or children from urban, economically depressed homes — are taken into the kibbutz for both training and rehabilitation.

economic and social institutions of the kibbutz. Tenure of office is brief — never more than three years — which, it is believed, prevents the rise of a leadership caste or an entrenched bureaucracy.

Despite the absence of a highly developed formal system of authority, the kibbutz exhibits a remarkably high degree of congruence between its social norms and the behavior of its members. Group pressure, expressed in public opinion and in the ultimate threat of expulsion, is a sufficient deterrent to deviant behavior.

Unlike a few kibbutzim, Kiryat Yedidim has tenaciously opposed the introduction of industry into its economy, persisting in maintaining the generic kibbutz emphasis on the primacy of the land. Its agricultural economy is diversified, comprising eight distinct branches: dairy, field crops, vegetable gardens, fishery, fruit orchards, flocks, poultry, and fodder. Its agriculture is not only diversified, it is highly rationalized and mechanized. The resulting efficiency has produced a prosperous agricultural economy.

Although they have been highly successful farmers, the members of Kiryat Yedidim are not merely farmers. And, despite its peasant-like devotion to the land, Kiryat Yedidim is not a village of peasants either in fact or in its self-image. On both scores the members of the kibbutz comprise a landed intelligentsia. In the fields one hears discussions not only of crops and machinery, but of books and music, of politics and literature. At the end of the working day, the interest of a chaver may turn to a class in English, a lecture on genetics, a chamber-music concert, a discussion of politics, a dramatic performance. This is not to say that all chaverim turn their attention to such intellectual pursuits, nor that all who do, display equal zeal in them. It is to say, however, that these activities are available, that they are valued by many, and that the kibbutz self-image demands at least lip-service devotion to them. It is this same self-image, and not merely kibbutz prosperity, which accounts for the attractive kibbutz landscaping, the lovely private gardens, the tasteful interior decor that impress even the most casual visitor.

But Kiryat Yedidim is not content with merely a prosperous economy and the opportunity to enjoy the pleasures of the mind and heart. And this brings us to still another component of its self-image. As a kibbutz, Kiryat Yedidim is not only an agricultural village. As a kibbutz it perceives itself as the vanguard of man's quest for the ideal society, part of the shock troops in the future social revolution. The kibbutz, together with the urban proletariat with whom it identifies, will — it is hoped — bring socialism and, ultimately, the classless society to the entire country. These political convictions, stemming from an avowedly Marxist ideology,[2] have led Kiryat Yedidim to join with other kibbutzim of like mind in a large kibbutz federation. In turn, The Federation has joined with urban workers of similar political persuasion to form a political party.[3]

If the kibbutz has still to achieve its goal of external political revolution, it has already achieved a major internal revolution: it has revolutionized the structure of the family and the educational system. Love is not only the basis for the kibbutz marriage; it is the sufficient solemnizer of the relationship. Nevertheless, since marriage is also a social relationship, the kibbutz confers social sanction on the relationship by granting a common room to the couple. This room is their home. Since meals are cooked in the communal kitchen and eaten in the communal dining room, and since children live in the various children's houses, a combined bedroom-sitting room is sufficient for their needs.

Marriage entails few changes in the life of either spouse. The woman, whose membership in the kibbutz is legally distinct from that of her husband, changes neither her name nor her work when she marries. She is supported, not by her husband, but by the entire kibbutz to whose economic well-being she, in turn, contributes by her labor. Women, like men, work a nine-hour day, although relatively few women today work in the agricultural branches of the kibbutz economy. If the wife is economically independent of her husband, so is the husband independent of his wife for domestic services. These — meals, laundry, mending, and so forth — are provided in the various communal institutions of the kibbutz. Should either become ill, he is assured of complete and continuing economic support, not by dint of special initiative on the part of his spouse, but because the kibbutz continues to provide for his needs. Having a child poses no economic problems

---

[2] Though opposed to and opposed by the tiny communist party in Israel, the Marxism of The Federation has been Stalinist in conception and pro-Soviet in practice. Disquieting events in the Soviet Union subsequent to the death of Stalin — disquieting both to its socialist and its Zionist convictions — has led to much soul searching. The future Marxist orientation of the Federation, however, is not, at the time of this writing, entirely clear.

[3] The Party has been only mildly successful in the Israeli political arena, polling less than 10 per cent of the votes in the last national elections. Though opposed to much of the platform of the leading party in the present coalition government, The Party has joined the Government after some years of steadfast refusal. It currently holds two portfolios in the cabinet.

for the couple. The kibbutz assumes complete responsibility for its economic welfare. In brief, economic factors play no role in cementing the relationship between husband and wife. The marital bond is compounded of emotional, sexual, and social ties exclusively. The advent of children does not alter this generalization; the kibbutz family is not an economic unit.

Marriage in the kibbutz almost inevitably results in children. And it is in the care and training of children that the kibbutz has instituted one of its crucial social revolutions. It is this educational revolution which is the subject of this monograph.

CHAPTER 2 · COLLECTIVE EDUCATION

The educational system of Kiryat Yedidim is known as *chinuch meshutaf*, or collective education. Its characteristic feature is the fact that the children live in communal nurseries with age peers, where they are reared by "nurses," nursery teachers, and teachers, rather than by their parents. Since parents of both sexes work in the kibbutz economy, the daily interaction between parent and child is in general restricted to the interval between the parents' return from work in the afternoon and the child's bedtime.

When a child is born in Kiryat Yedidim, he becomes an official member, not of the kibbutz, but of the Children's Society (*chevrat yeladim*); and in this Society he remains until, upon graduation from high school, he is elected to membership in the kibbutz. Kiryat Yedidim is similar to a religious sect in that membership is not a right conferred upon an individual at birth, but is, rather, a privilege that the group confers upon an adult who, at the age of consent, knowingly and willingly accepts its values and its way of life. Thus it is that, although the children live in and are raised by Kiryat Yedidim, they are not viewed as members of the kibbutz until their candidacy is announced and they are formally elected as chaverim.

The children do not live in one immense institution-like dwelling. They are organized into small peer groups — the number of children in a group varying and increasing with age — which occupy scattered dwellings or "cottages" within the kibbutz. All the houses are designed for the convenience of the particular age groups occupying them. Until they enter high school, the children's houses, as well as their communal kitchen, lie within the living area of the kibbutz, although they all lie to one side of this area. While in general these houses may be said to form a separate community from their parents' dwellings, they are in actuality not isolated from the rest of the kibbutz, for adult dwellings are scattered throughout the children's area, and, indeed, some of the nurseries are actually parts of adult dwellings that have been converted.

When the children enter the junior-senior high school (*mosad*), however, they do move to a separate community — for the land occupied by the high school lies across the road from the kibbutz living area. The high school has its own dwellings, classrooms, dining room and kitchen, and library.

An infant enters the kibbutz educational system when he returns with his mother from the hospital at the age of four or five days. The Nursery is designed to care for a maximum of sixteen babies, who are in the care of kibbutz women who qualify as infants' "nurses." Thus, the responsibility for the kibbutz child is assumed immediately by some one or more persons other than his parents. This is not to say that the kibbutz infant never sees his parents; he is visited at least once a day by his father and many times a day by his mother, who comes not only to play with him but to nurse him.

The first important change in the infant's life occurs at the age of six months, when he may be taken to his parents' room in the afternoon for approximately one hour. The second important change occurs at the age of about one year, when he is moved from the Nursery to the Toddlers' House (*beth peutot*). In the Toddlers' House, which consists of two nurses and eight children, the infant is gradually toilet trained; he is taught to feed himself; and he learns to interact with his age-mates. At this age the infant may remain in his parents' room for approximately two hours in the evening, and he may be taken to their room not only on Saturdays, but on other days when they may be free.

In some instances the group of eight children in the Toddlers' House remain with the same nurse or nurses until they enter the Kindergarten (*gan*), at which time they not only change buildings, but nurses as well. In most instances, however, the group remains with its nurses until it reaches nursery age — between two and three — at which time a nursery teacher (*ganenet*) generally replaces one of the nurses.

Sometime between their fourth and fifth birthdays, the children encounter another important change. At this time the group passes into the Kindergarten. This not only involves a new building and sometimes a new nurse and Kindergarten teacher, but it also involves the enlargement of their original group to include sixteen members. This is accomplished by merging two nursery groups into one Kindergarten. This merger is an important event in the lives of the children, for this enlarged group, or *kevutza,* will remain together as a unit until its members reach high school age. This kevutza is in many ways the child's most important social group, not only because of its long duration, but also because of the frequency and intensity of interaction within it.

Between the ages of five and six the children in the Kindergarten pass into a new dwelling, where they receive their first formal intellectual instruction, including the study of reading and writing; when they have completed a year in this "Transitional Class" (*kitat ma'avar*), they are ready to enter the primary school and its dormitory. For the first time children live in a building that includes not only their own (approximate) age-peers, but other children whose ages span a wide range — from seven to twelve. Each kevutza, or group of sixteen children, remains distinct in that it has its own teacher, classroom, and bedrooms. But the entire student body eats together, plays together, and participates in the same extracurricular activities. Hence, the functional "children's society" for these children includes not only their kevutza, but the entire school population, known as their *chevra.*

The completion of the sixth grade, when the children are twelve, marks another turning point in their lives. They enter the high school, an event which is important not only for its intellectual implications, but for other reasons as well. They are physically separated from the rest of the kibbutz; their kevutza is split up; for the first time they encounter male educational figures (except for their fathers) in the person of the teacher; and they begin to work in the kibbutz economy.

Upon graduation from high school the students are expected to live outside the kibbutz for approximately one year, so that their decision to become kibbutz members may be based on the experience of non-kibbutz living. After election to membership, they become full-fledged *chaverim.*

PHILOSOPHY

This socialization system did not merely evolve as an adaptation to a pioneering mode of living; it was deliberately fashioned on the basis of certain ideological convictions of the founders of Kiryat Yedidim who delineated its major features while still members of a Youth Movement in Europe. Perceiving the society about them as decadent and degenerate, these youths aimed to regenerate society by first regenerating the individual. Since they considered the individual a product of his education, they devoted much of their efforts to formulating an ideal educational system. This, said a founder, "was our main interest. For three or four years thousands of our people struggled with this problem. It was then that the educational philosophy and structure of the kibbutz was formulated." This educational philosophy continues to inform the system to this very day.

Discussions with chaverim and a careful reading of the educational literature of The Federation point to four primary motives for the establishment of the system of collective education. These are the abolition of the patriarchal authority of the father, the emancipation of the female from her traditional social impediments, the desire to perpetuate kibbutz values, and the concern with achieving a democratic education.

The patriarchal authority of the father. The founders of Kiryat Yedidim believed patriarchal authority to be characteristic of the traditional Western family. Over and over again, as a *leitmotiv* running through all discussions of the family in the literature of The Federation, occurs the theme of emancipation from the authoritarian father. And it is the proud claim of The Federation that kibbutz society has succeeded in achieving this emancipation, as the following quotation, taken from an official educational journal of The Federation, reveals.

The changes in the family, whose economic foundations have been uprooted, have brought about a change in the status of the man and woman in the kibbutz society, and with that a change in the status of the father and mother in the family. This is most pronounced with respect to the function of the father, for all his ruling privileges, the source of his formal authority, are destroyed . . . (And one of the results of this change is the freedom from) the ambivalence and hatred that were the special characteristics of the traditional family.

Nor is this opposition to paternal authoritarianism confined to official publications whose function it is to revive a forgotten youth movement past. Living near Kiryat Yedidim was a family which was almost universally disliked by the chaverim. When questioned about this dislike, a chavera retorted:

We dislike them because of the way they raise their children. When they ask their son to do something, and he asks why, they say, "because father says so." What kind of reason is that? There isn't a single person in the kibbutz who would ever say a thing like that to his child. Moreover the father even spanks his children. It is a scandal.

So, too, when the parents were asked on the Questionnaire if children should blindly obey their parents, they responded overwhelmingly with, "Definitely no."

Instead of an authoritarian-submissive father-child relationship, the kibbutz aimed to establish an egalitarian relationship in which fathers and children were to be peers. This may be inferred from what The Federation claims as an accomplishment of its educational system. The only relations between parents and children in the kibbutz, according to an educational leader of The Federation, are "emotional." Parents have no formal or legal authority over their children, he continues, so that their authority must depend solely on such qualities as personality and character.

The father is now only a friend of his sons, and only by the strength of his friendship can he win their love and their respect.

This same educational expert, writing in another publication, observes:

The relationships between the child and his parents are different in the kibbutz from that found where the child is socialized in the family. In the kibbutz the relationships are, in the main, based on love, and not on the commandment to "obey thy father."

One way in which the child could be freed from an authoritarian father was by physically separating him and entrusting his care to some other person or institution. Actually, however, the emancipation of the child from the father's authority is not, according to kibbutz educational theory, merely a function of physical separation. By rearing the child in communal dormitories it would be possible, the founders believed, to abrogate the economic nexus that traditionally exists between child and father. Since the father traditionally is the provider, the child is economically dependent upon him; and it is this dependence, according to kibbutz ideology, which is the greatest source of the father's authority in the traditional family.

This dependence, however, is destroyed as a result of collective education, for now the father has no specific economic responsibilities for his children. The kibbutz is charged with satisfying the child's economic needs; it provides him with food, clothing, housing, and medical care. Thus, according to a publication of The Federation, in the kibbutz

. . . the child is emancipated from the rule of the father of the family . . . In the patriarchal family the child is dependent economically and legally on the father as provider, on the "master of the household," which is not true in the kibbutz. The child is not dependent, in any objective sense, except on the kibbutz as a whole.

Again, the book which describes the official educational philosophy of collective education states:

The authoritarian (parent-child relationship has declined in the kibbutz because) the child does not feel himself dependent upon his parents economically or legally . . . The child of the kibbutz does not recognize at all a feeling of economic dependence. The kibbutz as a whole, which assumes this economic burden, cannot create this feeling.

It is clear that the elimination of the authoritarian character of the father was motivated, not only by a desire to ensure the emotional well-being of the child, but also by the desire of the parents to achieve and maintain his love. The founders had themselves rebelled against their parents. The question, "Did you rebel against your parents?," was answered:

Definitely yes	9
Perhaps yes	3
Perhaps no	1
Definitely no	2
Total	15

The three who felt that they might not have rebelled against their parents are members, not of the founding, but of the youngest generation of parents. All the kibbutz founders who responded to the Questionnaire reported that they had rebelled against their parents. And, indeed, this was one of the psychological bases for the establishment of the kibbutz. The intensity of this rebellion may be gauged by the statement of one woman who, when asked about the kibbutz educational system, replied: "The basis for our system is very simple; to do the opposite of what we ourselves experienced or were taught (as children)."

Over and over again, both in kibbutz educational literature and in conversations with chaverim, a dominant theme is the maintenance of amicable parent-child relationships. "We want our children to be our pals," is the way in which this desire may be summed up, "and to destroy the barrier that conventionally exists between parents and children. We don't want our children to duplicate our own experiences. We had little in common with our parents and, indeed, we rebelled against them. We don't want our children to rebel against us."

In a very perceptive paper Elizabeth Irvine suggests a motive for the establishment of the kibbutz educational system which, though consistent with what the chaverim say, points to a deeper psychodynamic basis. It is her hypothesis — in which I concur — that collective education is an effective resolution of the conflicts about parenthood that are experienced by individuals who rebelled against their own parents.

It is apt to be difficult for the rebellious child confidently to assume the responsibilities of parenthood, since this involves identification with the rejected parent; so the delegation of parental function is a natural and welcome solution of a dilemma. By vesting authority in professionals, parents are relieved of the necessity of asserting it themselves, and of the fear that by doing so they would alienate the children as their parents alienated them.[2]

But human behavior, whatever its motives, is seldom free from paradox, and it is of some theoretical importance to point out that this desire on the part of the chaverim to retain the affection of their children represents the preservation of an important value of the parents against whom they so strongly rebelled. In the *shtetl* culture of the Eastern European villages in which most of the founders were born,

The shining reward a parent expects for all his care and sacrifice is that he should "gather joy," *klaybn nakhes,* from his children, or "draw joy," *shepn nakhes* . . . It is hard to be a parent but it is good to be a parent. Just because it is so hard there is constant insistence on the compensatory *nakhes.* Because parenthood is so important *nakhes fun kinder* is the epitome of joy.[3]

That collective education can achieve the goal of establishing and maintaining parent-child comradeship is explained in the

[2] Elizabeth E. Irvine, "Observations on the Aims and Methods of Childrearing in Communal Settlements in Israel," *Human Relations,* 5:247-275 (1952), p. 250.
[3] Mark Zborowski and Elizabeth Herzog, *Life Is with People* (New York: International Universities, 1952), p. 297. (Also available as a Schocken Paperback)

following way in the book containing the official philosophy of collective education.[4] Ambivalence generally characterizes the attitude of the child toward his parents because the latter play the conflicting roles of loving and caring for him, on the one hand, and of disciplining and punishing him on the other. Since the negative aspect of this ambivalence is a function of the latter role of the parents — "disappointments coming from the parents hurt seven-fold" — it can be eliminated entirely by abolishing the disciplinary role of the parents. And this, say the educational theorists, is what collective education has done. Collective education results in a division of labor in which the nurse and nursery teacher institute the basic childhood disciplines and are, therefore, the sources of most of the child's frustration. (But "since the nurse is more objective towards the child, his reaction to the discipline is not so acute" — and hence, he does not suffer seriously from her discipline.) The "most important function of the parents," on the other hand, "is to give of their love to the child." And this they can do unqualifiedly, not only because they are not his disciplinarians, but because their meeting with the child occurs under "most favorable" conditions — they are rested, they have no other responsibilities at that time, they can devote themselves exclusively to the child. Hence the child's relationship to his parents, if not entirely unambivalent, is "much more harmonious" than it is in other educational systems.[5]

In any event, The Federation's educational authorities believe that the system of collective education has served to eliminate those ambivalent aspects of the parent-child relationship which characterize the Oedipus Complex. The reasons for this success, which are summarized in The Federation's journal of opinion, are: (1) the child does not feel himself economically dependent upon his parents, for the family is not an economic cell in society — the kibbutz as a whole is his "provider"; (2) there is no

---

[4] Although many psychoanalysts may disagree with its application, it should be noted that the influence of psychoanalytic theory on the thinking of kibbutz educational theorists is marked.

[5] It is interesting to observe that this "division of labor" between affection and discipline in the rearing of children is found in many other societies, and is interpreted by Radcliffe-Brown in much the same way. In many societies "there is something of a division of function between the parents and other relatives on the two sides. The control and discipline are exercised chiefly by the father and his brothers . . . these are relatives who must be respected and obeyed. It is the mother who is primarily responsible for the affectionate care; the mother and her brothers and sisters are therefore relatives who can be looked to for assistance and indulgence." A. R. Radcliffe-Brown, *Structure and Function in Primitive Society* (Glencoe: Free Press, 1952), p. 98.

patriarchate in the kibbutz, for husbands and wives are equal; (3) the kibbutz does not treat the "animal instincts" as inferior; (4) the importance of the nurse in the child's life means that his love is not focused exclusively on his parents; (5) the nurses, rather than the parents, are the primary disciplinarians, and the daily period of child-parent interaction therefore takes place under ideal conditions; (6) unlike the child in the traditional system whose position in the family is like "Gulliver among the Giants," the kibbutz child lives in age-graded nurseries and, therefore, interacts primarily with peers.

The subjugation of the female. One of the original and primary goals of the kibbutz was equality of the sexes. This equality, the kibbutz founders believed, could be achieved only if the female were emancipated from the shackles responsible for her subjugation. The two most important shackles — the woman's economic dependence on her husband, and her "biological tragedy" — could be broken, it was believed, by the system of collective education.

The kibbutz founders claimed that the objectionable patriarchal role of the male in the traditional family was characteristic not only of the child-father relationship, but of the husband-wife relationship as well. In the traditional family the wife was economically and socially dependent upon her husband and, hence, was subjugated by him. The equality of the sexes could be achieved by conferring economic equality upon the woman — thus freeing her from economic dependence upon her husband, and depriving him of the basis for his traditional authority. But this economic independence of the wife could be achieved only if she earned her own living, so that the husband were no longer the "provider"; and this meant that women, like men, must work in the economy rather than remain at home as housekeepers.

If women were to become "providers" like their husbands, they must first be freed from one of the important responsibilities of the woman in the traditional family — the caring for and rearing of children. Only if she were relieved of this task could the wife be free to work, and only if she were assured of adequate care for her children could she work with peace of mind (hence, with efficiency). Thus the emancipation of the woman from the traditional patriarchal husband became a vital factor in the development of collective nurseries which could, in effect, free the woman from the responsibilities of child-rearing.

But it was the aim of the founders of the kibbutz not only to emancipate the woman from the authority of her husband, but also to emancipate her from her generalized subjugated position in society and to permit her to become the equal of men in all aspects of life — social, political, intellectual, and artistic. The traditionally inferior position of women in these creative areas of life was attributed by the founders to what they termed, "The biological tragedy of the woman" (*ha-tragediya ha-biyologi shel ha-ishah*). That is, since the woman must bear, and hence rear, children she has little time or opportunity for other than domestic activities. Once freed from the responsibility of rearing children and the manifold domestic chores (cleaning, cooking, laundering, and so on) attendant upon such care, she could devote her energies to these more creative areas of life.

The "biological tragedy of the woman" is a function not only of the woman's sex, but of the social structure. If the social structure could provide for what is termed, in the rhetoric of kibbutz ideology, "the emancipation of the woman from the yoke of domestic service" (*shichrur ha-ishah me-ol ha-sherut*), the worst feature of this biological tragedy could be eliminated. This end could be achieved, it was believed, by instituting a series of communal "service" institutions whose function it would be to relieve the woman of these various domestic duties. One of these institutions was collective education, an institution which would not only free the woman for economic activities during the day but which would also free her at night for political, intellectual, and artistic activities.

Two important factors then in the establishment of collective education were the strong desires of the kibbutz to free the woman from domination by her husband and to emancipate her from the "yoke of domestic service." That these twin desires have been satisfied is proudly acclaimed in an official pronouncement of The Federation:

We have given her equal rights; we have emancipated her from the economic yoke; we have emancipated her from the burden of rearing children; we have emancipated her from the feeling of "belonging" to her husband, the provider and the one who commands; we have given her a new society; we broke the shackles that chained her hands.

The perpetuation of kibbutz values. The kibbutz is concerned that its communal-agricultural values be perpetuated by its children. As one chavera put it, from the very beginning,

We realized that without children we had nothing to do here (*i.e.*, children were the *raison d'être* for the entire kibbutz enterprise) . . .

What is our goal? That our children should follow in our way. This is the only thing we have . . . Every other utopia has failed, and maybe here too there will be changes. But we shall succeed if we can train our children at least to follow in our way.

Hence the kibbutz educational system, in the words of The Federation's Education Director, can have but one aim:

. . . to raise a generation which will perceive as its vision the fortification, perfection, and glorification of the commune, and which will be prepared to lend a shoulder and to dedicate its life to the continuation of the work of the founders with love and with conscious purpose . . . In the "tender years" it is the function of education to lay the emotional and psychological foundations on which the deliberate education of the future can be built . . .

But the kibbutz is perceived by its founders as more than an agricultural commune. It is "a cell in the social revolutionary movement." Indeed it is this political-ideological characteristic of the kibbutz, including "its solidarity with the entire working class," that, according to a leader of The Federation, "prevents it from becoming another *petit bourgeois* society." If this be so, then an important aim of the kibbutz educational system is to rear its children to identify with the entire revolutionary movement. It is not surprising then to read in a publication of The Federation that collective education serves as a

. . . link in the attempts of a revolutionary movement to change the ways of life and the institutions of human society. . . . (Its historical purpose is) to establish the foundation for the reproduction of the kibbutz ideology in the coming generations, and to raise a human type that will be prepared and willing to implement it (the ideology) in life.[6]

If the kibbutz, in its twin role as agricultural commune and revolutionary movement, is to transmit its values to its children, it is necessary, so its founders believed, that the entire kibbutz rather than the parents educate the children. Only if the children were *reared* communally, they insisted, could they be trained to *live* communally as adults. For only the commune itself could

[6] Even the parents, who in a sense are external to the system of collective education, are to play the role (among others) of ideological mentors. For the parents, according to the Director quoted above, are not only parents "who love their children, but they are also the representatives of a movement for which they are being educated."

transmit its communal values, and only by identifying with the commune would the children come to introject its values. The communal rearing of children, then, is indispensable for the perpetuation of kibbutz values. For it is in this system that the children

> ... from the earliest childhood ... grow up with the knowledge ... that their future and fate are not determined by their parents (alone), but by the kibbutz as a whole.

This could not be achieved in the conventional child-rearing situation in which

> ... the family is the cell of society, and the child's education is in its hands. In the kibbutz the family is but one of many foci for the children, and society has taken over the main job of education.

It is true, of course, that specific socializing agents, rather than the entire kibbutz, rear the children. But these socializing agents are appointed by the kibbutz and, in theory, *represent* the kibbutz. Moreover, in the early years of Kiryat Yedidim when this conception of the entire kibbutz as socializer was taken much more seriously, the special relationship that obtained between a child and his biological parents was deliberately deëmphasized. When, for example, parents would visit their children in the nurseries they would deliberately refrain from singling out their own children for special attention, but would attempt to interact with all the children with equal frequency and intensity. In this way, it was felt, the child would come to perceive the entire kibbutz, rather than just his parents, as his primary group. Even today the chaverim refer to "our child" or "our children," as if they indeed belonged to the entire group.

Democratization of society. In a Marxist journal, a Federation educational authority writes,

> Collective education is a necessary consequence of the collective society ... The principle: from each according to his abilities to each according to his needs — finds its complete realization (in the kibbutz). This social equality requires educational equality for each child ...

The principle of equality is a primary value in kibbutz culture. One of the ways in which children could be assured of equality, it was thought, was through a system of collective education. In such a system there could be no inequalities. All the children would be reared by the same nurses so that there could be no difference among the children as a function of the differential abilities, intelligence, skills, and so forth found among parent socializers. Nor could there be any material inequalities in communal education, for every child, regardless of the social or economic position of his parents, would receive the same clothes, food, toys, instruction, as every other child.

Hence, in the early years of the kibbutz, "equality" in education was taken most seriously and came to mean *literal* equality. In the early years of the kibbutz, for example, "equality" meant that all infants of the same age were expected to have the same weight; or, if a mother had no milk, her baby was nursed by another nursing mother (because it was believed that mother's milk was more nutritious than cow's milk).

These, then, are the ideological foundation stones upon which the educational edifice of the kibbutz was erected. Collective education was to destroy the patriarchal authority of the father, and thus establish a warm and affectionate parent-child relationship; it was to lead to the emancipation of the woman and to her full social equality; it was to serve as the efficient means of transmitting kibbutz values; and it was to guarantee educational equality to all children.

GOALS

Although this educational system stems from, and is related to, many of the values upon which the kibbutz itself was founded, its aims — like those of any educational system — are educational. What are the goals of collective education? For what is the kibbutz educating?

In the questionnaire administered to parents they were asked to rank in order of importance a series of values which they hoped to inculcate in their children. Since parents are only one part of the educational process, it may be assumed that their responses not only reflect the values which they personally wish to transmit to their children, but those which they expect the entire educational system to transmit as well. These values, ranked in order of importance, are as follows.

1. Work
2. Love of humanity
3. Responsibility to kibbutz
4. Good character

5. Intellectualism
6. Socialism
7. Zionism
8. Social participation
9. Patriotism
10. Cooperation
11. Private initiative
12. Good manners
13. Respect for parents

This list should not be understood to imply that those values that are low in order of importance are necessarily unimportant in the kibbutz. On the contrary, the thirteen values that the respondents were asked to rank were selected because they were the most frequently mentioned in interviews and discussions. It does mean, however, that the chaverim consider work and the love of humanity to be more important values than, for example, good manners.[7]

The respondents were also asked to rank in order of importance certain ambitions which they hoped might be achieved by their children. The results were as follows.

1. Good chaver
2. Good worker
3. {Active in kibbutz / Well-liked
4. Ideologically sound
5. Creative
6. Cultured
7. Respected

An examination of these values and ambitions reveals that the goal of education, as perceived by the parents, is the creation of what the kibbutz terms, the "synthetic personality," and this goal is identical with that envisioned by the Department of Education of The Federation. The synthetic personality, according to The Federation's educational director, is:

. . . possessed of an ideological-political backbone on the one hand, and of a highly technical-vocational level, on the other; who strives for

[7] It is of interest to note that respect for parents was ranked as the least important value, in view of the twin facts that most of the respondents indicated that they had rebelled against their own parents, and that their avowed aim is to achieve family egalitarianism.

a maximal combination of spiritual and physical labor . . . a person of deep and embracing culture, who will be capable of contributing to the ideational, economic, and cultural elevation of kibbutz society.

Finally, the person reared in the kibbutz is:

. . . independent, original in his ideas, insists on his opinion but tries to understand everything before he accepts it; he will be revolutionary, a negator. It will not be easy to lead him, although he will be amenable to reason. He will love the collective and will be ready to do a great deal for it. He will be forceful and will want to take his fate in his own hands. No external, ruling authority will have an influence on him. He will do nothing out of fear, and will not recognize the authority of any person except from an inner attitude . . .

PART II · AGENTS OF SOCIALIZATION

Certain persons, responsible for the socialization of the infants and young children, are, presumably, the most important social influences on their development. These agents of socialization fall into three groups: the nurses and nursery teachers, with whom the children interact in the children's houses; the parents, with whom the children interact primarily in their rooms; and other individuals who play some role in the children's development.

The adult with whom the young child has most frequent contact and who is directly responsible for his well-being and his education is his "nurse" (*metapelet*), the official representative of the kibbutz, as it were. It has been noted that the children are organized into small peer-groups, each kevutza with its own nurses. In general, each kevutza has two permanent full-time nurses, although both may not always be present in the house at the same hours of the day. One of the two nurses is regarded as the "chief" or "head" nurse of the group, and the kevutza is designated by her name; the kibbutz refers, for example, to "Shlomit's kevutza," or "Rosa's kevutza." At the age of approximately three years, the children of a kevutza are assigned a nursery teacher (*ganenet*), in addition to one of their regular nurses, and she then becomes the "head" nurse of the group. With a few exceptions, nursery teachers and nurses fulfill generally the same functions, therefore both will be referred to as "nurse."

The use of the singular does not imply that the child has but one nurse and one nursery teacher from infancy until he enters the grammar school. Nurses receive specialized training for work with certain age groups so that, according to the formal structure of collective education, the child has at least two nurses in his first six years — one in the Nursery, and one during the long interval between infancy and his entry into the grammar school — and one nursery teacher. In practice, however, this continuity almost never exists. Nurses resign because they wish to leave the kibbutz temporarily for further training, because they are pregnant, or because they wish to work elsewhere in the kibbutz — in the fields, for example. They resign when their charges become older because they feel unable to cope with them and think that the children should have a nurse who is better trained to deal with children at these older ages. And, finally, a nurse may resign because her relationship with the parents has deteriorated to the point that her work is affected. Therefore the young child may be exposed to many nurses.

When, at the age of seven, the child enters the grammar school, his kevutza is assigned a new nurse and a teacher, both of whom will remain with the same kevutza (unless they resign) until the children graduate to the high school, at the approximate age of twelve. In either event, whether his experience with individual nurses is continuous or discontinuous, the child in Kiryat Yedidim is reared solely by females throughout the formative years of his life.

QUALIFICATIONS

Nurses and teachers are almost always chosen from the general kibbutz membership and from those women who voluntarily wish to work with children. With rare exceptions these women are married and have children of their own.[1] These volunteers must be acceptable to the Education Committee of the kibbutz, the Nurses' Committee, and the work assignment chairmen. The Education Committee must pass on the candidate's educational qualifications; the nurses, on her ability to work with them on a basis of congeniality and compatibility — as well as on her training and personality; and the work assignment chairmen (who are concerned with the over-all kibbutz economy) wish to be sure that the chavera is assigned to the position that will utilize her abilities to the fullest extent.[2]

[1] Assistant nurses need not be members of the kibbutz. An adolescent from one of the youth groups residing in Kiryat Yedidim may be assigned to help in a kevutza, for example, or a girl from the Army group stationed in the kibbutz may work with the children. Older children of the kibbutz — high school girls who work a few hours each day — may also help with these younger groups. A child may thus have contact with women of many ages, ranging from adolescents to grandmothers.

[2] Generally speaking, chaverim may choose to work in that branch of the economy that is most congenial to their own interests, but if the kibbutz feels that talent is being wasted, or if there is a great need for workers in a particular branch, pressure may be applied to recruit individuals into or out of work assignments. For a detailed discussion of work assignment, see Spiro, *Kibbutz*, ch. 4.

Few women have any professional training before volunteering to work as nurses. Some, however, had studied in teachers' colleges in Israel, a few had received training before migrating to Palestine, and one had had the opportunity of working with Anna Freud in England. But for the most part, nurses are not selected on the basis of formal training, but on the basis of personality qualifications. Specifically, the kibbutz, represented by the Education Committee, wants to know if the candidate likes to work with children, if she has patience, if she is good-tempered and, most important, if she genuinely likes children. One of the most respected nurses in the kibbutz evaluated two other nurses succinctly: "Ruth is a good nurse because she loves babies. Obviously, she doesn't love them all equally, but she loves babies. Rachel is not a good nurse because she does not have this love." She also felt that to be a nurse, one must be devoted, not only to the children, but also to the ideals of medicine and nursing: "It is more than an eight-hour-a-day job, and it means continued study and learning."

Parents and educators attempt to maintain high standards in their selection of nurses, but sometimes they are compelled to accept a candidate of whom they disapprove. The manpower shortage within the kibbutz is perhaps the most important reason for this compromise with standards. If a nurse is needed and all the women who might have been acceptable are permanently assigned to other positions, the committee may be forced to accept one who does not meet their standards. Similarly, if a woman is not permanently assigned, and the work assignment chairmen can find no other suitable position for her, they may insist that the nurses accept her to fill a vacancy. On one occasion during the course of this study a woman who was felt to be unqualified for the position insisted on becoming a nurse and threatened to leave the kibbutz if she did not gain her goal. Faced with this ultimatum, the committees acceded.

If there is time the neophyte nurse will be sent to an inter-kibbutz seminar for instruction in child psychology, educational theory, and practical advice in the handling of children's groups and in dealing with common behavior problems. If there is no time for her to attend such a seminar, her training will have to come through experience and from advice and information that more experienced nurses share with her. Nurses who work with infants always receive special training. Two, for example, received nurses' training in Israeli hospitals and one had studied at the American University in Beirut.

Although many nurses begin their work without formal training, it is not accurate to describe them as naïve in the field of child development. Education is a primary concern of the kibbutz and, as such, constitutes a ubiquitous topic of conversation and concern among the members, as well as a subject of speeches by visiting lecturers. Almost everyone, therefore, knows the official kibbutz attitude and approach to such things as aggression, masturbation, sharing, feeding, and toilet training. Once a woman becomes a nurse, moreover, she has a number of opportunities for study and training. The Federation arranges special short courses and refresher courses for nurses at regular intervals which they must attend. In addition, formal courses in psychology, education, and so forth are offered in the inter-kibbutz teacher's college, and many nurses are granted periodic leaves in order to complete a semester of work. The Federation arranges conferences for nurses of children of different age levels in which special problems and techniques are discussed. And The Federation publishes an educational periodical which deals with practical and theoretical aspects of child care and development. The articles in this periodical are written by both professional educators of The Federation (psychiatrists, lay analysts, psychologists, and others) and nurses and teachers in the various kibbutzim belonging to The Federation.[3]

Although nurses may begin their work without training, all nursery teachers receive formal training before assuming their duties. A nursery teacher may begin as a nurse and, if she reveals exceptional skills and abilities, she and the kibbutz may agree that she be sent for formal training as a teacher. She receives specialized training for a period of two years in the teacher's college sponsored by the inter-kibbutz movement. The chief difference between the nursery teacher and the nurse, therefore, consists in the former's greater degree of formal training in child psychology, children's behavior problems, and techniques of child care and

---

[3] The table of contents from one issue of this journal illustrates, not only the various types of problems with which the kibbutz educators are concerned, but also the level of their educational sophistication.

1. Modern Pedagogy: Attainments and Failures
2. The Functions of the Home Room Teacher in the High School
3. Marxist Criticisms of Intelligence Tests
4. Boys and Girls at Puberty
5. On Educational Techniques with Difficult Children
6. Some Problems of Education for Social Living
7. Purposes of Education in the Younger Ages
8. On the Story for Children
9. Discussions, Comments, Book Reviews.

development. The nursery teacher, consequently, is a more sophisticated worker than the nurse, but she shares the general cultural and psychological characteristics of the nurse. Both receive their training, moreover, from the professional educators of The Federation and the kibbutz movement in general, so that their educational attitudes and values, as well as their techniques of socialization, are similar.

That the nursery teacher's specialized training is important for the best development of children, once the latter reach the age of three years, is recognized by everyone who has worked in the kibbutz educational system. Nurses working with younger children would frequently point out that they would not be able to continue with their groups much longer since they did not feel qualified to do so, or that they would be able to continue only if teachers were assigned to work with them. The nurse in one kevutza, whose members were already three years old, attributed much of the difficulties she was experiencing to her lack of specialized training, and insisted that if she did not receive a nursery teacher she would resign from her post. In a still older kevutza, whose children were five years old, the nurse had to play the role of teacher because of the latter's prolonged illness. Although a warm and friendly person, she was totally untrained, and had genuine difficulties in handling the children. She, too, was very much aware of her deficiencies and admitted to the observer that at times she was at a loss to know what to do.

In addition to formal courses, one source of training which some nurses have employed is self-study. One nurse, with much formal training, managed to keep up with much of the literature in child development in other countries. Prior to World War II, she had taught herself German in order to read the professional literature published in that country; during the war she taught herself English in order to read the literature from England and the United States. She is also able to follow professional developments in the Soviet Union, for she reads Russian as well.

In general, it may be said that the nurses with the most formal training are the most secure professionally, while the professional insecurity of some nurses may be attributed to lack of formal training. Such professional insecurity is reflected, for example, in the frequency with which nurses asked us for our opinions of the children. Were they behaving "properly"? Was this or that behavioral manifestation "normal"? Was this problem typical of children of this age? Was the nurse handling this problem in the proper manner? Often, nurses would apologize for the behavior of the children, as, for example, one nurse always explained during mealtime that her two-year-olds were not well-mannered because "when there is a visitor, they don't eat properly. They want to look at the visitor." In many instances the behavior in question appeared "normal," and some knowledge of children's developmental norms would have alleviated the nurse's doubts. In most instances, moreover, the nurse's approach to the behavior problem with which she was concerned was competent, and, again, greater theoretical acquaintance with the nature of children's problems and with techniques for coping with them would have served to allay anxiety.

The professional insecurity so often found among the nurses is heightened by another type of insecurity they display — "ideological" insecurity. Many nurses, even after years of experience and training, are not wholeheartedly committed to the system of collective education, either in its entirety or in specific details. This attitude of doubt was rarely stated directly, but it was often implied in the many questions directed to the observers — questions that seemed to request reassurance that their work was important; that collective education was superior to, or at least as good as, the more conventional types of child-rearing; that it did not produce the harmful effects that its critics claim or that even they sometimes suspect. To what extent the doubts and insecurities of the nurses are communicated to, and influence the development of the children is difficult to assess, as we have no data that bear on this subject.

CHARACTERISTICS AND DIFFERENCES

With some few exceptions, it may be stated that the nurses are warm and loving toward the children for whom they care, and they appear to be genuinely devoted both to their work and to their charges. Most nurses possess the patience required for their work, and there are only rare instances in which a nurse was observed to lose her temper. This patience is maintained regardless of how trying the children may become, the difficult circumstances under which some of them work, and the long hours they work.

Statements about the nurses are based, of course, on our impressions. Their reliability, if not validity, may be judged by the high degree to which the impressions of both researchers agreed; by the consistency with which impressions recorded at the beginning of a period of observation were in accord with those recorded at its end; and by the high degree of agreement between our impressions and the evaluations made of individual nurses by parents and other kibbutz nurses.

In attempting to evaluate twenty permanent nurses and nursery teachers who work with the younger children, we employed a rating scale based on two sets of criteria: the standards employed by the kibbutz in selecting nurses — love for the children, patience, insight, skill in handling children, and devotion to their work — and the children's observable reactions to their nurses. On the basis of these criteria, nurses were ranked on a five-point scale. Of the twenty so ranked, five who were considered to be as good with children as normal human beings could be received a Superior rating; three were rated as Excellent, six as Good, five as Questionable, and one was considered a tragic error. The average nurse, then, turned out to be better than Good, but not quite Excellent. Of the fifteen nurses who were rated as less than Superior, six were felt to be handicapped by lack of training, seven were considered to lack certain basic personality requirements, one was deficient in both areas, and in one case the researchers felt unable to judge the basis for the nurse's deficiencies. Of the eight nurses who rated as Superior or Excellent, five were among the most highly trained nurses in the kibbutz; the other three had all had some formal training, but their performance appeared to be a function of natural skill and insight rather than of training. That ability as a nurse is not based on training alone is further emphasized by the fact that others who were highly trained did not receive top ratings — indeed, one such nurse was rated as Questionable.

That six of the twenty nurses failed to meet the standards of both the kibbutz and the researchers (by falling into the two lowest ratings) indicates, of course, that the kibbutz is often unsuccessful in its attempts to obtain the best educators for its children.[4] This failure may be the result of several factors. One is that the kibbutz (as represented by its Education Committee) may feel that these nurses, whatever their handicaps, are still the most suitable women for their jobs. In a small community, there simply

[4] Thirty per cent seems a high percentage for a community in which education is of such great concern. That these six nurses fail to meet kibbutz standards is attested to by the fact that they were the most frequently criticized by their colleagues in the educational system. (Some nurses are more than ready to criticize others, which may be another manifestation of professional insecurity. On the other hand, those nurses who appeared to be the most secure in their work were as quick to praise nurses whom they considered to be good, as they were to condemn those who did not conform to their high standards.)

may not be a sufficient number of women who are suitable for this work; alternatively, some women who are suitable and/or even have training in child care do not, for various reasons, wish to work with children (there are such cases in the kibbutz). In addition, there is the ever-present economic pressure that prevents the kibbutz from permitting a trained worker in a productive branch of the economy to become an "unproductive" nurse, however qualified she may be.[5]

In any event, and whatever the reasons, it is apparent that not all nurses are cut from the same cloth. Some take a deeper interest in their charges than do others. Some are dedicated women who view their work as a calling, while others consider it merely a job. In short, not all the nurses are the warm, patient, and skillful persons referred to above. Still others, although warm and affectionate, display qualitative differences that are often difficult to spell out. In describing one nurse, for example, one of the researchers recorded in his diary:

It's impossible to state how Tamar differs from the other nurses — I can only say that she is different. She is very "sweet," never raises her voice, and is very quiet. She doesn't talk very much to the babies, except when she is trying to comfort one of them. Neither is she given to much physical affection. . . . She appears to be very easy going, never bothered by anything, and does not seem to be worn down by the babies. Sometimes, though, Tamar's face wears an expression of "pain," as though she is silently suffering from or being disgusted with the children. . . . Or is it merely a natural expression of hers? . . . It seems to me that one of the reasons she is not bothered by anything is because she often appears to be "not here" — that is, she often seems to me to be withdrawn from the reality situation.

Another reason for qualifying the picture of warm, loving, and kindly nurses is necessitated by the so-called "part-time" nurses. These are relief nurses who may be assigned to work in a kevutza only one day a week, when a permanent nurse has her day off, or for a few weeks when a permanent nurse is ill or on vacation. The behavior of some of these part-time nurses is in marked contrast with the behavior of the typical permanent nurse, for some are highly rigid, shrill of voice, and authoritarian. One part-time nurse worked in one kevutza for almost a month, and

[5] We have frequently noted that the exigencies of the kibbutz economy often take precedence over the needs of the children's community. While this appears to belie the statement that the kibbutz is a child-centered society par excellence, the kibbutz argues that, were the economy to fail, its entire system of child care and education would also fail.

the children's adverse reaction to her extreme irritability and authoritarianism was revealed by the notable increase in disobedience and intra-group aggression when she was on duty. The kibbutz is well aware of the deleterious influence of such women on the children, but, again, the economic pressures are such that it feels unable to rectify the situation. The nurses complain bitterly about such unacceptable substitutes or assistants, but they too admit the helplessness of the situation. When one child in her kevutza was quarantined and, hence, placed in the charge of a part-time nurse, the regular nurse complained to the observer, "Today, RENA is taking care of him, and she is excellent . . . But tomorrow? You will see what they (the work assignment chairmen) will send me!"

Nurses not only reveal personality differences, but they also reveal differences, and even inconsistencies, in their training methods. In one kevutza, for example, the head nurse does not permit the children to take food outside. If they want bread and butter or some other snack, they must eat it in the house. (Her rationale for this stricture is simple: two-year-olds are too likely to drop the food in the dirt and then eat it.) The other nurse in the same kevutza is either unaware of, or disagrees with, this attitude, for she permits the children to take food outside. There are a few occasions when inconsistencies between nurses break into open conflict in the presence of the child. While such open conflicts among nurses are generally rare, there is one kevutza in which two nurses were in frequent disagreement, and this disagreement was occasionally manifested in the presence of the children. The following excerpt is an obvious illustration.[6]

SARA brings cups of pudding to the table. Mirav (two years) wants none, so RACHEL puts her to bed. SARA says she should sit on the chamber pot. RACHEL says she "sits all day and doesn't do anything." SARA goes into the bedroom, takes Mirav from bed, and puts her on the pot. . . . (In a little while) Mirav says "dai" (enough), hasn't made anything. RACHEL gloats and shows the empty pot to SARA. SARA says she is just being trained and should sit on the pot whether she does anything or not.

Differences are found not only between nurses within one kevutza, but among the different nurses who administer to the children at various periods in their development. Hence if a kevutza should receive a new nurse as a replacement for a former

[6] For descriptions of adult-child interaction, we have printed names of adults in capital letters and names of children in lower case.

one, the children may be exposed to inconsistencies, and they may have to unlearn certain things which they have already learned. One nurse may insist, for example, that a child eat his food, and another nurse may tell him, "It's not necessary." Some nurses insist that a child use only his own bib and spoon at mealtime; others are more permissive about these matters and allow the children to use each other's bibs and spoons. Again, while some nurses are insistent that a child sit on his chamber pot at regular intervals when being trained, others are considerably more permissive about this.

Such inconsistencies, admittedly, are trivial. But there are cases in which the inconsistency may involve basic educational patterns or even kibbutz values. When, as sometimes happens, the part-time nurse is not a member of the kibbutz, she may, because of unfamiliarity with certain patterns of collective education, introduce values that are in sharp contradiction to its values. The following example, in which such a part-time nurse employs a competitive socialization technique, is a case in point.[7]

YAFFA (the nurse's assistant) is feeding Esther (one year, four months). CHAYA (nurse) feeds Aryeh. YAFFA says to Esther, "Let's see who will finish first, Aryeh or Esthy" . . . Esther expresses no interest in this proposal, so YAFFA says, "Oh, Aryeh will finish first."

FUNCTIONS

Quantitatively, at least, the nurse is the most important socializer for the young children of Kiryat Yedidim. Among the manifold duties that she performs as *the* socializer, four distinct but closely related functions may be discerned. The nurse, first of all, is a caretaker — she is responsible for the physical care and well-being of the children in her charge. Her second function is that of nurturer — she gives love, affection, warmth, and comfort. Third, it is she who transmits the kibbutz values to the children. And, finally, she trains them in the basic disciplines — such as feeding, toilet training, and independence training.

In short, the nurse assumes virtually all the functions and duties of the parent in Western society. This parental role becomes even more inclusive on those occasions when a child's parents are away from the kibbutz — on vacation, for example.

[7] This is not to say that nurses never utilize the technique of competition. On rare occasion, they do. The distinction to be noted here is that among the kibbutz nurses such a technique is rare; among the "outsiders" who work with children it is frequently employed.

At such times, the nurse will take the child to her own room in the evening and play with him as she plays with her own children; and if he is still at the age where his parents normally put him to bed, she will also perform this task. Thus she is occasionally called upon to play not only her own role as nurse, but the role of parent as well.

Caretaking functions. A nurse who works with any group of children at the age levels under discussion — that is, from birth through grammar school — must serve all four functions, but the amount of time and energy she expends in any one is dependent both upon the specific age level of, and the number of children in, her group. It is obvious that nurses who work with infants and toddlers spend a greater part of their time as caretakers — changing diapers, feeding children, bathing them, and so on — than they do as trainers; and that this ratio is reversed in the case of nurses and nursery teachers who work with four- and five-year-olds. In all groups, however, the nurse is responsible for those other caretaker functions that we may label "housekeeping duties," and there is no great diminution of these duties as the children mature — for beds must still be made, floors must still be mopped every day, food must be fetched from the children's communal kitchen (where it is prepared by the cooks rather than the nurses), dishes must be washed, laundry must be collected and taken to the kibbutz laundry, hand-laundry and some ironing remain to be done. (Children in the kindergartens, however, assume responsibility for some of these chores, such as bringing the food and emptying the garbage.)

This preoccupation with housekeeping duties often interferes with the nurse's execution of her other responsibilities. In the Nursery, for example, where there may be as many as sixteen babies at any one time, there are never more than three nurses on duty simultaneously; and during certain hours of the day, there is only one nurse to care for all the babies. Thus, a nurse is constantly busy performing her many duties, and the care she is able to give the babies must always be evaluated in terms of her busy and exhausting schedule. Like all chaverim, nurses work approximately fifty-four hours a week, but a nurse may often work many more hours if, for example, a child is ill or disturbed, or if, devoted to her work, she feels that her charges need her presence at other than her scheduled hours of work. Many of her caretaking functions, furthermore, may become monotonous and thus affect her performance as a nurse. Even the dedicated head nurse of the

Nursery once remarked as she was undressing a baby, "Every day it's the same thing. Sometimes it gets so monotonous, so boring." Thus, the quantity and dullness of her caretaking chores serve to limit the time and energy that a nurse can devote to the other aspects of her role.

When the children move from the Nursery into their Toddlers' House, their kevutza, composed of eight children, is in the charge of two nurses who, theoretically, have specialized functions. One assumes the housekeeping and other caretaker functions, while the other nurse assumes the primary role of training the children. Both, of course, are expected to give love and affection, but it is assumed that the nurse who trains the children will preponderantly serve these nurturant functions, since the children have greater contact with her than with the other nurse. In practice, this division of labor is not so distinct. It is always true that one nurse is the chief socializer, but because the housekeeping duties are so numerous and the demands of eight children so great, both nurses must serve all four functions — especially during the afternoon hours when only one nurse is on duty with the children. Thus it is that the nurses often have little time for guiding the children in their play and other activities.

The consequence of this preoccupation with the details of the daily routine is that the children often interact with no adult supervision. This means, for one thing, that some of the children's physical needs remain unsatisfied. Children, for example, often wear wet or soiled pants (before they are toilet trained) for a long period before a nurse can change their clothes. It means, for another thing, that certain acts — such as aggression — may go unsocialized because a nurse is not present to observe the act. It means that exceptional children — the superior and the retarded — receive no special guidance and must fend for themselves as best they can. And, finally, it means that a child who cries for comfort and/or protection because he has had an accident or has been the victim of aggression may find that there is no one to care for or console him. This is particularly true for the young toddlers, who are always confined to some play area. If they are in the yard, for example, they are confined by a fence; if they are in the playpen, they are confined by its high rails. It is therefore impossible for them to physically seek out the nurse if she is in the house; and there are times when she simply fails to hear their crying. This is the most frequent consequence of the nurse's necessary preoccupation with what are often mere janitorial chores, and it hàs, perhaps, a most important effect on the child's development.[8]

These manifold duties of the nurse have still another effect on the children. Some nurses are so harassed by the constant demands made upon them, that often their voices betray a shrill quality that can only be the result of tension. The average nurse is almost always patient, but often the effort to control her temper is great, and the children must surely be aware of both this tension and the effort to control it. The shrillness of the nurse's voice merely adds to the noise and confusion necessarily found in a house inhabited by eight toddlers.

These unfortunate effects of the nurse's routine are considerably ameliorated once the children begin to work with a nursery teacher. By then, they have reached the age at which training in many basic skills has been completed, and less time need therefore be devoted to the purely physical aspects of the nurse's work. There is at this age a sharper division of labor between the nurse and the teacher, but they still continue to serve all four functions. The nursery teacher, free of many caretaking duties, is with her charges much more than are the nurses in the younger groups. She is not only present more frequently, but her presence is more creative; that is, she not only supervises the children's behavior, but she is able to lead them and to direct their behavior into productive channels such as painting, modeling with clay, storytelling, and hiking.

Nurturance. Although the innumerable duties of the nurse often prevent her from expressing affection for the children, it must be stressed that she frequently, albeit briefly, expresses her affection for them. These examples of such affection and comfort, taken at random from the Nursery and Toddlers' Houses, illustrate both the occasion for and the quality of the nurse's love.

Uzi (ten months) begins to cry . . . MALKA walks by, hugs him, puts her forehead to his, kisses his forehead, puts him on his back.

SHULAMIT combs Yitzhak's (seven months) hair . . . She holds him, coos, hugs him, returns him to bed.

[8] The Federation strongly recommends that a kevutza be composed of six children and two nurses. Kiryat Yedidim has organized its kevutzot into groups of eight because of its manpower shortage. It may be remarked, however, that some kibbutzim which are much younger and, therefore, not in such good economic condition as Kiryat Yedidim, have found it possible to organize the children into smaller groups. On the other hand, the youth of these kibbutzim means that their children's populations are much smaller, and that they must therefore sacrifice proportionately fewer "productive" workers to the educational system.

Shlomit (three months) is quiet while being dressed . . . RIVKA holds her, coos, squeezes her, jabbers to her . . .

CHANA comes into the room, and Iris runs to her. CHANA picks her up. Iris hugs her, laughs, clings to her . . . CHANA tells her that she is "yefefiya" (beautiful) and says to me that Iris is "niflaa" (a marvel) — in front of all the children . . . CHANA lifts Iris by her hands, and Iris climbs up her stomach . . .

ETTA comes into the room, and says, "Come, Amiki" . . . He comes to her, she picks him up, tells him that, "We are going to see the nurse" . . . ETTA asks him for a kiss, and he kisses her on the mouth . . .

Pnina tries to climb on SHLOMIT's lap . . . SHLOMIT hugs her, lifts her onto her lap . . .

ROSA dresses Omri, talks to him. She picks him up and hugs him, saying, "Where can I buy a good boy?"

Omri is crying . . . ROSA comes in and sits on the table. She puts his head in her lap and strokes him. He quiets . . .

The nurse's affection for the children in her kevutza is best symbolized by the following incident, in which the nurse is so attached to her charges that she can accept certain kinds of behavior in them which she would find offensive in other children. This affection is found over and over again among the nurses.

CHANA brings in Mirav, undresses her . . . Mirav has soiled her pants, and she smells. CHANA says that when the children "make eh-eh," she doesn't mind the smell because she is accustomed to it. But one day, she worked in CHAYA's kevutza, and she almost "went crazy" from the odor of soiled pants. When queried about her different reactions, she said that in the other group, she did not know the children and did not love them as she loves the children in her own kevutza. "*This*," she said emphatically, "is the *best* kevutza!"

In some instances the attachment of nurse or teacher to the children reveals intense ego-involvement that betrays anxious overtones. The comments expressed by a grade school teacher at her class's graduation party are of this nature, as our field notes indicate.

She emphasized how attached she was to the children, how much they had become a part of her, and how difficult — almost impossible — it would be to part with them. (It was obvious that her entire life was involved with theirs, and that she needed their love desperately.) She told about her deep devotion to the children, and about their deep devotion to her. She still has so much to offer them, she claimed, that it was very sad that she could not continue with them in the high school, where she could give them even more than she had in the past.

Another indication of the teacher's extreme involvement with the children may be seen in the following incident. During the summer, when the nurse was on vacation, this teacher substituted for her for one week. Since the nurse eats supper with the children, she is supposed to be in the school by 6:00. But by 5:00 this teacher could no longer stay in her room, and insisted on going to the school because "there must be something that I can do for the children."

The nurse's attachment to her charges is probably based on at least two factors. The first is her genuine affection for children with whom she has constant contact and for whose well-being and development she is directly responsible. The second is her desire to be loved by the children and her consequent anxiety about obtaining and retaining this love. Not all nurses are anxious about the children's love, but so many of them are that one cannot escape the conclusion that this anxiety is a characteristic feature of the nurses' behavior. This personal insecurity is, of course, related to the professional and ideological insecurity noted above. The nurse who has doubts about her professional abilities or about the desirability of collective education is likely to require the children's love in order to prove to herself that she is a good nurse and that the system itself is a good one.

That the nurses need to be loved by the children was indicated in several ways. Nurses would insist, for example, that they were indispensable to the children, that they were the best nurse, and that the children adored them. One nurse, while discussing the problems of a child whose mother had been away for several months, said that in order to help the child her main object had to be "to get close to him." While this was surely true, one could not escape the impression that an important unconscious motive in her desire "to get close to him" was to get him to love her in order to satisfy her own needs. We often had the impression during interviews and conversations with the nurses that their (the nurses') emotional adjustment depended, in part, upon the love of the children, and that their success as nurses was measured, in their own eyes, by their ability to obtain this love.

One cannot avoid suggesting that this need to be loved derives from the fact that the nurse's own child has, in a sense, been taken away from her, and that she compensates for her "maternal" frustration by seeking love from the children for whom she cares. This suggestion is based on statements of nurses and other mothers who implied that their educational system frustrates certain of their maternal needs.[9] In at least one instance, moreover, the nurses themselves not only criticized an excessively nurturant nurse for interfering with the well-being of the children, but they perceived her extreme manifestations of love as stemming from her own unsatisfied needs.[10]

To say that the nurses love the children, however, is not to imply that they love all children equally. With one exception, all the nurses interviewed denied having favorites — "All children are treated equally." This is true with respect to such material objects as food, clothing, and toys which are generally distributed equally or on the basis of need; but it is not true with respect to the nurse-child relationship. A nurse will say, in describing a child, that he is "terribly spoiled"; of another child, she will say that she is "adorable." Another nurse will comment that a boy is "so good-tempered"; of another boy she will say, "He is clever — too clever, like his father."

These differences in attitude were quite apparent to us and, it may be assumed, to the children, in the presence of whom many of these expressions of favoritism occur.

Chana (three years) stands by SHULAMIT, who is ironing. Other children are watching. Chana hugs and kisses SHULAMIT, who says, "This is *my* girl."

Chana was the obvious favorite of the nurse, who never tired of telling the ethnographer how "delightful" she was. Again, at a party for the sixth grade, all the children read aloud the essays they had written for the occasion. When Rachel, the teacher's

---

[9] See Chapter 4, pp. 61–62. Compare, Spiro, *Kibbutz*, pp. 232–233.

[10] The emotional involvement of the nurses in the children has at least one observable consequence of methodological importance. In general, the nurses not only love their charges, but exhibit considerable insight into the nature of their behavior. But the need to love and be loved by the children serves to distort, and even to repress, some of the nurse's observations. The nurse in one kevutza, for example, said that the children in her group did not bite in anger, although we observed such biting on a number of occasions. Another nurse characterized one child as her most difficult feeding problem. Observation, however, showed quite clearly that there were at least two other children who presented far greater feeding problems, and to whom the nurse had to devote more of her time at meals. Perceptual distortions of this kind had always to be taken into consideration in evaluating the reliability of interview data. They also, of course, influence the manner in which a nurse handles a child.

favorite, read her essay, the teacher persisted in looking at me to see if I was impressed, and gestured to indicate how superior it was. The other children noted her behavior and they, too, looked to see my reaction.

Despite these obvious indications of favoritism, only one nurse — a worker in the Nursery — admitted its existence. "Of course," she remarked, "I don't love all the babies equally"; and she observed further that the nurses begin to react differently to different children from the latter's earliest infancy. She believed that there are two reasons why nurses respond differently to different babies, and to older children, as well. The first concerns the child's appearance and behavior. An unusually attractive baby elicits more stimulation from the nurses than do other babies. A fussy and irritable baby, on the other hand, may be less favorably treated, however subtly. The second reason for this differential treatment is that it is often difficult for the nurses to dissociate a child from his parents, and the child of parents who are disliked may receive less affection or fondling than one whose parents are liked. This psychological phenomenon, which is all but ignored in the official educational literature of the kibbutz movement, is probably of more than little importance in the nurse-child relationship. For example, one of the boys in the fourth grade is a talented artist, but at the beginning of the school year he refused to draw in class. It seems that he became hostile to his art teacher after it had become apparent to him that the latter disliked him. When I asked why the art teacher did not like the boy, I was informed that she did not like his parents.

In spite of this differential reaction of the nurses, there is not a single case of overt rejection in the record, and there is only one case of overt dislike expressed toward a child. This involves Rivka. Rivka was obviously and intensely disliked by her nurse. To the observer, there appeared to be little objective difference between Rivka and the other children in the kevutza, but the nurse often insisted that it was difficult to train her as she posed many problems. Although this nurse was generally permissive and objective in her socialization techniques, with Rivka she was often critical and caustic. Behavior which she overlooked in others was reacted to with strong criticism when manifested by Rivka. While napping or resting, for example, the children frequently talked with each other, generally with impunity or with only a mild comment from the nurse. But Rivka would often be reprimanded in the following manner:

Rivka, you yell terribly, and can be heard from the outside; it's not at all pleasant.

Rivka, it's very unpleasant for me, very unpleasant. If you wake up before I come back, you are to be quiet.

As was true in the case of the fourth-grade boy discussed above, the nurse's reaction to Rivka probably resulted from her dislike for Rivka's mother. The mother, an uneducated and coarse woman, was almost universally disliked, and her daughter, apparently, was paying the price for her mother's behavior. Thus, after reprimanding Rivka, the nurse remarked: "The children resemble their parents in many ways, and they usually follow their worst characteristics!" [11]

In addition to the subtle discriminations in amount and kind of love based on personal preferences, the nurse may pay special attention to certain children for "professional" reasons. If, for example, a nurse has a child in her group whom she feels to be a problem, she may make every effort to give that child as much attention and affection as is possible. In some cases, this increased attention to the disturbed child may be noted by the children, who may then react with hostility to the apparently favored child. In one such case that was observed during this study, the nurse was very much aware of her dilemma. If, on the one hand, she gave increased attention to the disturbed girl, this child might suffer from the hostility of her peers; the latter, moreover, could also become hostile to the nurse. On the other hand, if she decided to ignore this girl's enormous needs for love and attention, her disturbance would undoubtedly grow worse. The nurse concluded that the girl's need for love was so great that the benefits she might receive from such love outweighed the suffering she might bear as a result of peer hostility, particularly since the symptoms of her disturbance were such as to invite hostility toward her anyway. Thus, the perceptive nurse is often trapped by the needs of many individual children and must always weigh the consequences of her actions in terms of the individual versus the group.

Disciplines and values. In the Nursery, the only behavior system with which the nurse is concerned is eating; she begins the

---

[11] This generalization of dislike from the parent to the child is another indication of individual differences among nurses. Rivka's siblings in other groups were never observed to be the object of dislike or discrimination, although it was clear to us that their various nurses heartily disliked the mother.

process of teaching the child to feed himself shortly before he leaves the Nursery. This training process is continued in the Toddlers' House, where toilet training is also begun. At this time, too, the nurse becomes concerned with training in independence — with helping the children to develop in motor skills such as walking, and learning to dress themselves. This is the period in which training in the extinction of such responses as crying and aggression is begun. The general attitude toward such training is generally permissive, and the nurses do not expect to attain their goals completely with children of this age.

These training processes are continued when the kevutza reaches the age at which it is assigned a nursery teacher. The nursery teacher continues to view food and toilet behavior as the two most important training areas, followed by aggression, conflict, and crying. Even in the Kindergarten, eating, sleeping, and aggression remain the most important behavior systems to be socialized. It should be noted that none of the nurses mentioned sexual training as one of her concerns and observation supports this lack of concern.

Explicit transmission of certain kibbutz values is generally begun only when the nursery teacher begins to work in the kevutza, and the effort to inculcate these values continues through the years. One of the primary values that the nurse attempts to transmit, beginning with the very young children, is sharing, although none of the nurses listed this as one of her goals. (It may be assumed, however, that it is taken so much for granted that it would not occur to the nurse to single it out for special mention.) Other values that nurses attempt to transmit to their young charges include the love of nature, love of nation, and the importance of work, all of which are discussed in a later chapter.

In the Kindergarten the teacher perceives her most important goals to consist in helping her charges to be "human beings" — to help each other, and to have no feeling of "mine and thine" — and to become an "organized" group. (She feels, incidentally, that she has to a great extent attained these goals.) She also initiates the children into elementary intellectual skills — numbers, for example — and into formal work patterns.

The teacher in the Transitional Class (equivalent to our first grade) continues the training in skills and values begun in the early years and, in addition, lays the foundation for formal instruction in reading and writing, so that the children are introduced to formal education even before they enter the grammar school.

RELATIONS BETWEEN NURSES AND PARENTS

The single most important factor that colors the parent-nurse relationship is the elementary fact that it is the nurse, rather than the parent, who is primarily responsible for the well-being of the child. The first important consequence of this fact is the greater authority which is thereby invested in the nurse. If the parent wishes to do something that the nurse regards as detrimental to the child's welfare, or should he treat his child in a manner that the nurse regards as harmful, she may discuss the situation with the parent and she expects the parent to conform to her recommendations. There are, however, great differences in the manner in which the nurses exercise their authority, as well as in the manner in which parents accept or tolerate it.

Of all the nurses, the one who wields the most authority over the parents is the head nurse in the Nursery. This power does not inhere in the position itself, but in the personality of the woman who happened to occupy this position at the time of our study. Almost all aspects of parent-child interaction are patterned after her advice, recommendation, and — if necessary — pressure. The parents regard her — and she regards herself — as the person ultimately responsible for the babies' welfare; hence, the person who may rightfully make the important decisions concerning their care. Rarely will parents disobey this nurse — and then not openly — and if they wish to make a change in their infant's routine, they will do so only after obtaining her permission.[12] This nurse is well aware of her power. For example, after granting permission to a mother to take her very young infant on the lawn, but forbidding her to take him to her room, the nurse remarked to the observer: "When I tell them (the mothers) 'no,' they don't do it. I never follow them to see. I know they will do as I say."

A second consequence of the nurse's greater responsibility for the child is her desire to prove to the parents that she is a good nurse. One nurse informed us that when she first began to work in her kevutza, she was anxious lest the parents not have confidence in her. Her anxiety was exacerbated by the fact that the nurse who had formerly worked with her group had insisted that the children eat even when they were not hungry, for, anxious about her relationship with the parents, she was eager to show them that the children were gaining weight. Hence, though the

---

[12] It should be emphasized that a nurse's decisions are generally not idiosyncratic, but are based on the rules and regulations of the Department of Education of The Federation.

new nurse had been trained to be permissive about eating, she had serious misgivings about this permissiveness for fear the parents would attribute her behavior to lack of concern or disinterest. Since parents do not hesitate to criticize a poor nurse, the nurses' desire to prove their worth is understandable, but it is still another source of anxiety for them.

Another consequence of the nurse's responsibility may be the jealousy and/or conflict which sometimes arise between nurse and parent. Just as a parent may condemn his child's nurse if he feels that she does not show sufficient interest or concern, so he may also be aroused if the nurse shows so much concern for the child that, as occasionally happens, he begins to prefer the nurse to his parents. A nurse confessed that she was jealous of her own child's nurse when, one afternoon, her daughter preferred to remain in the Kindergarten rather than come to her parents' room.[13] Hence, though parents may become jealous of their child's nurse when the child leaves them in order to be with her, the nurses may be proud when this occurs.

This emotional involvement in the child on the part of both nurse and parent sometimes leads them to compete for the child's affection and such competition may give rise to mutual criticism. Nurses complain that certain parents spoil their children, and that this makes the nurse's job much more difficult. "He is the only son, and you know what that means!," says one nurse. "Her mother spoils her so, that I cannot do a thing with her," says another. After struggling with a little girl while trying to bathe her, a nurse turned to the observer and remarked, "Her mother spoils her terribly. She gives her anything she wants, and never makes her do anything she doesn't want to . . . (but) they're all spoiled here."

Among the complaints voiced by nurses are, that a parent does not love his child enough, that a parent loves his child too much, that a parent does not understand the nature of his child's problems, that a parent has no patience in dealing with his child, that a parent has no skill in helping his child to develop "properly." Most of the nurse's complaints about parents, however, concern

[13] This statement, offered spontaneously, is particularly interesting in the light of her later denial, when questioned directly, of the existence of jealousy between parents and nurses. She admitted, however, that though the mother is not jealous of the nurse, she is "humiliated" when the child displays signs of preference for the nurse. But in the same interview, she stated that mothers are actually pleased, rather than jealous, when a child loves his nurse, for this indicates that the nurse has been "successful" with him. It would appear that her acceptance of the official educational philosophy, with its picture of the ideal parent-nurse relationship, does not permit this woman to perceive the nurse-parent relationship as clearly in her role of nurse as she actually perceives it in her role of mother.

their interruption of the child's daily routine — such as taking the child with them during the day, returning them at inconvenient hours, coming into the house while the children are eating, or putting things back in the wrong place. For example,

All (the children) sit at the table to eat, but Chana has not returned. YAFFA says to me, "Oh, her mother must always take her before she eats. It is not good."

As TAMAR was cleaning up (at night) she noticed that a parent had removed his child's pants, which were wet, and had hung them up neatly. TAMAR commented sarcastically that they think they are saving her work! She took the pants and put them in the tub to rinse them out. (The point is that when pants are wet, they must be rinsed immediately, and then put in the laundry hamper. The parent did not want to be bothered, so merely hung them up.)

Mothers complain about the way the nurses handle their children in the children's houses, and nurses complain about what the parent does with his child in the parental room. Sometimes this criticism takes place in the presence of the children.

Mother stands on the walk, holding Elat. Elat cries. Mother demands to know why Elat has been in bed all day; why not outside? The nurse says it is too hot for her to be outside, when she is still not completely well. The mother says it is not too hot, and as the nurse stalks into the house, the mother continues to grumble about Elat's being "all day in the house."

Amir is eating a cookie. The nurse asks where he got it, and his mother says she gave it to him in her room. The nurse, complainingly, "But now he won't eat his dinner." The mother says, "So, instead of carrots, he will eat the cookie. When the meatballs come, he'll still eat two." The nurse retorts, "Who will give him two?"

While such conflicts are infrequent and usually minor in nature, we do not know to what extent they are apparent to the young child or influence his development. It is difficult to believe, however, that the child does not experience some tension as a result of these conflicts, criticisms, and jealousies.

Parent-nurse clashes may sometimes result in the resignation of the nurse. If the parents of a kevutza unite in criticism of a nurse — whether the criticism is of a minor nature or whether it is a major criticism (for example, "the nurse scolds the children too much"; "the nurse does not love the children enough"; "the children don't look healthy — they are not eating"; "the children don't like her") — her position becomes so uncomfortable, and her work may be so adversely affected, that she may resign, even though she may have the support of the Education Committee.

Lest this description of parent-nurse conflict be overdrawn, it should be emphasized that in most kevutzot the relationship between parent and nurse is one of mutual admiration and respect, and in which there is little if any conflict or criticism. The reasons for this difference among kevutzot was suggested by one nurse — and observations tend to confirm her generalization: when the nurse accepts the parent and makes him feel welcome in the kevutza; when she allows, and even encourages, him to disrupt her routine; and when she consults with him about his child as if he is her equal — he then feels that he is her partner in the educational enterprise, and he views her as an ally in the socialization of his child. In such a situation the potentiality for rivalry, jealousy, and conflict are considerably mitigated, if not eliminated. It was apparent to the researchers, on the other hand, that when the nurse manifests a negative attitude toward the presence or interference of the parent, the parent feels that an important part of his child's life has been closed to him by the nurse, and that she is opposed to his emotional involvement in his own child. Those nurses who appear to be most secure in their work almost always welcome the parent as a partner in the task of raising the child and are most effective in obtaining the parent's cooperation. Conversely, it is among the insecure nurses that attempts are made to shut out the parent, and it is they who complain that the presence of the parents is an intrusion which serves to make their work more difficult.

CHAPTER 4 · PARENTS AND OTHERS

INTRODUCTION

Although nurses and teachers are the child's most important socializers and the adults who spend the most time with him, it is nevertheless his parents who have the most important influence on the child's emotional adjustment.

That parents are necessary for the "normal" development of the child is indicated by many statements of the chaverim. When one nurse discussed a child in her kevutza who is an orphan, she characterized him as being a problem child. "But what can I do?," she concluded, "No one, neither nurses nor aunts, can take the place of parents." Another chaver asked us why we had to travel to Israel to study collective education when we could have remained in America and studied the same system in orphanages. "No," objected his wife, "for such children have no parents, and how can a child be normal if he has no parents?" This difference — living in the same village with one's parents and seeing them frequently and regularly — is the important distinction between the situation of the kibbutz child and that of the institutional child in America.

In spite of recognizing the importance of parents, however, few kibbutz parents would agree with our statement that they are the most important influence on their children, although many believe that they ought to be. When, for example, the respondents to the Questionnaire were asked, "Are you the most important influence on your child?" their responses were distributed as follows:

Definitely yes	0
Perhaps yes	1
Perhaps no	2
Definitely no	11
One among others	1
Unanswered	1
	—
Total	16

In other words, none of the fifteen parents who answered the question felt that they were the most important influence on their children. On the contrary, most (eleven) were quite sure that they were not. If, by "influence," they were referring to the development of skills and the acquisition of kibbutz values, they were probably right. But if they were referring to the general emotional adjustment and integration of their children, they were probably wrong, as later chapters will indicate.[1]

KIBBUTZ ATTITUDES TOWARD CHILDREN

The kibbutz is a child-oriented community, par excellence. In observing parental behavior, and from interviews with them, one cannot escape the conclusion that children are prized above all else, and that no sacrifice is too great to make for them. This characteristic of the parents, it must be emphasized, is not inherent in the system of collective education. There is no *necessary* relationship, that is, between this attitude toward children and the system of collective education — other attitudes are equally compatible with it. But since we observed this system as it is now functioning, this attitude of the contemporary parents must be clearly delineated.

Measured merely by the amount of energy and money expended on the children — and the consequent contrast between the children's comforts and those of their parents — the kibbutz is, indeed, child-oriented. If we take into account the quality of the children's dwellings, the number of conveniences and facilities — such as toilets, showers, hot water, modern kitchens — which they have (and which the parental rooms do not have), and the large percentage of total kibbutz manpower which is assigned to work with children, we can gain some idea of the importance which the kibbutz attaches to its children. For these investments in money, time, effort, and manpower represent a genuine "sacrifice" by the parents. Let us take food as an example. At the time of this study, the food shortage in Israel was acute, and few chaverim ever left the dinner table with full stomachs. The children, on the other hand, always had as much food as they wanted, and their meals exhibited greater variety and possessed a higher

---

[1] It is curious, however, that three-fourths of the parents feel that they, with the equal participation of their mates, make the "important decisions" concerning their children. Since this is in obvious contradiction to their almost unanimous feeling that they are not an important influence on their children, we can only conclude that the questions were ambiguous, or that their responses reflect what the parents would like to be, rather than what is, the case.

quality than those of their parents. For the children there were always fresh fruits and sweets at the evening meal; but there were often months when the chaverim had no fruit, and sweets were always a rarity. Similarly, the chaverim rarely had milk, and eggs were served only three times a week; but children received milk twice a day and an egg every day.

One case serves to illustrate the extent to which the kibbutz will provide for the needs of its children. A retarded child was sent for special training to the city, where it cost the kibbutz one thousand pounds a year to maintain him. When he returned to the kibbutz and required special tutoring, a valuable worker was taken from production to teach him.

PARENT-CHILD CONTACT

The parents always see their children in the evening after work, and this is the time of day when the child always *expects* to see his parents. If the child is younger than six months, his parents visit him in the Nursery or take him to sit on the lawn.[3] If he is older than six months, his parents take him to their room. In either case, the child remains with his parents until his bedtime, which means that he is with his parents every evening for approximately two hours. On Saturdays, however, the parent may take his child to his room for the entire day, if he wishes, but the child must return to his house for his meals and nap.

In addition to these "formal" visiting periods, there are many other times when a parent may see his child. Nursing mothers, for example, have an opportunity to see their babies many times a day, and since a new mother has a six-week vacation before she resumes work, she is free to visit her baby as often as she likes. It is not unlikely, therefore, that the nursing infant sees his mother almost as frequently as an infant in a private home.

Even after a child is weaned, his parents are free to visit him at any time during the day. If, for example, a father passes his child's dwelling on his way to work or on an errand, he will stop to visit for a few minutes. If a mother happens to work near her child's house, she may take a few minutes from work and hasten to the kevutza for a brief visit; and if she is free for a few hours during the day, she may take her child to her room. There are

---

[3] Infants are generally not permitted to go to the parental room until they are six months old because of the supposed danger of infection. If an infant has no older siblings, however, his parents may be permitted to take him to their room at an earlier age, about four months.

also many "chance" meetings during the day — when the children take their daily walks around the kibbutz or into the fields.

Although all parents visit with their children in the evening, there is much variation in the frequency with which parents see their children during the day. Some parents visit their children at every opportunity; others come only in the evening to fetch their children. In general this difference is a function of kibbutz ecology, for those parents who work in or near the living area of the kibbutz have a greater opportunity to be with their children than do those whose work takes them into the fields. For this reason, mothers are generally more frequent visitors than fathers, most of whom work in the fields.

In general, and after the weaning period, the kibbutz mother sees her young child less frequently than does the mother in a private home. The kibbutz father, on the other hand, may often see more of his young child than does a father who lives in the city. For where a city father may not arrive home from work until his baby or toddler is almost ready for bed, the work schedule of the kibbutz is deliberately arranged to permit the parent a maximum of visiting time in the evening. While a child in the city, moreover, rarely has an opportunity to see his father during work hours, a kibbutz child may sometimes see his father during the working day.

Despite the frequency and regularity with which the kibbutz child sees his parents, it is important to qualify this picture by underscoring one important fact about the parent-child relationship. Almost every parent has at one time or another been absent from the kibbutz (and his child) for at least a short time. Some few fathers, for example, work outside the kibbutz and are able to return home only for weekends. Almost every father is away periodically for a few weeks or a few months for army service, although in most cases he is able to come home for weekends. Both mothers and fathers — but especially mothers — may be sent to the city to take courses or to receive training for their jobs in the kibbutz. In some cases, teacher-training, for example, the mother may be away for as long as a year, although she returns home for weekends. In addition to these frequent reasons for absence, some parents have been separated from their children for several months while traveling or studying abroad. And, finally, parents may be separated from their children for two weeks when they take their annual vacation. For a number of different reasons, then, almost every child has been separated for a varying period of time from one or both parents. In general, one parent remains in the kibbutz while the other is away, but on occasion circumstances may lead to both parents being absent at the same time.

The functions of the parent, like those of the nurse, may be divided into four categories and, indeed, into the same four categories — caretaking, nurturance, training, and values. But whereas the nurse is officially responsible for all four functions, the parent is "officially" responsible for nurturance and caretaking only. Indeed, after the child is two years old, the sole responsibility of the kibbutz parent is, according to the philosophy of collective education, "to love" his child. It is true that the parent is expected to transmit the important values of the kibbutz to his child — but he is expected to do this merely by being a good chaver rather than by employing specific pedagogic techniques. If the parent performs other than nurturance functions in his role of parent, he does so voluntarily and with less regularity and frequency than do the nurses.

Caretaking. The most important caretaking function of the mother is the nursing of her infant. Once her child is weaned, she and the father are expected to perform only one other caretaking function — that of putting the child to bed at night (*hashkava*). Until about six years prior to this study, parents were in charge of putting their children to bed until they entered grammar school. At that time the age was lowered to (approximately) the age of two — and the nurses were put in charge — because it was claimed that the children often became so stimulated by parental hashkava that they did not sleep well. Many parents, however, have been most reluctant to give up hashkava, and some — despite the official ruling — continue to put their older children to bed.[4] Others, moreover, visit their child's house at night to see

[4] That parents in many kibbutzim desire to put their children to bed at night is indicated in a published article by an educator of The Federation. He criticizes those parents who insist on performing hashkava, suggesting that this insistence implies that they are not reconciled to accepting the services of another chaver. Hashkava by the nurse is "basic to the structure of collective education," he argues, and the abolition of the former entails the abolition of the latter. Hashkava by the parent "is not economical, it is not worthwhile, it is not educational, and it is not the kibbutz way. It undermines not only the principal foundations of kibbutz education, but also the principles of kibbutz society."

if he is asleep and comfortable, despite the fact that there is a night watch to check on the children and who, if something is wrong in the kevutza, will call either the nurse or the parents.

Parents care for their children in other ways which they are not expected to. Should a mother visit her child at mealtime, and if he is too young to feed himself, the nurse may permit the mother to feed him. Or, if a mother visits her young child at his bath time, she will bathe him. This is also true of some fathers. If, for example, a mother is away from the kibbutz, the father may come to the Nursery to give his baby a bottle or, if a father returns from work earlier than the mother, he may go to the Toddlers' House and feed his child.

This desire of the parent, especially of the mother, to care for her child is apparent when the mother visits the child for a few minutes during the day. Some mothers bring food, such as a cookie or a carrot, for their children. Other mothers may say, "Come have a drink of water," although the child has not indicated that he is thirsty. If a mother observes that her child has wet or soiled his pants, she may change him herself instead of giving him to the nurse. It seems that many mothers need *to do* something for their children.

Training and values. Since kibbutz parents have ambitions for their children, it is of some interest to know how they view their role as inculcators of those values and goals which they want their children to acquire. The Questionnaire reveals that parents are not in complete agreement about how much responsibility they ought to assume for this area of socialization. Nevertheless, more parents feel that they should socialize — punish or reward — at least some of the time, than do those who felt that they should not interfere at all. And, although the specific rewards and punishments that the parents utilize will be discussed later, it may be noted here that when the relative frequencies of parental rewards and punishments listed on the Questionnaire were weighted, and an average computed, the average values for rewards and punishments were the same. In other words, parents reward and punish their children with equal frequency, or so they report.

In view of the fact that many parents feel that they should socialize their children, it is of interest to know which types of behavior they actually do socialize. The following lists were compiled on the basis of parental responses to the Questionnaire. The behavior for which parents punish their children, in descending order of frequency, are:

1. Selfishness
2. {Poor manners
   {Destruction of property
3. Failure to cooperate
4. Lack of parental respect
5. Obscene language
6. Uncleanliness
7. Poor scholarship
8. Aggression
9. Failure in competitive task
10. Masturbation

The behavior for which parents reward their children, in descending order of frequency, are:

1. Generosity
2. Cooperation
3. Private initiative
4. Excellence in work
5. Excellence in studies
6. Obedience
7. Talent or ability
8. Victory in competition[6]

Although the foregoing discussion indicates that parents do include the socialization of disciplines and values in their parental role, it is our observation that the part they contribute to the child's over-all training in these areas is a relatively minor one. This observation is consistent with the children's perception of their parents, as measured by the Moral Ideology Test. For the youngest children in the sample (ages six through eleven),

[6] Those behaviors that are most frequently punished or rewarded correspond generally to those values rated by the parents as the most important, with some few exceptions. Good manners and respect for parents, for example, were ranked as the least important of values by the parents (see above, pp. 20–21); yet poor manners is second only to selfishness as behavior to be punished, and lack of parental respect ranks as fourth in order of frequency. Similarly, of the eight kinds of rewarded behavior, private initiative was ranked third in frequency, although the parents ranked private initiative as only the eleventh of the thirteen values.

parents represent only 18 per cent of the persons whom the children identify as socializers (those who praise or criticize their actions). This figure is not only small compared to that for the other important socializers — 32 per cent, each, for the educators and the group — but it is remarkably small when compared with other societies. In their cross-cultural study, Havighurst and Neugarten discovered that for white children in a Midwest American community, parents represent 45 per cent of all persons whom the children identify as socializers, while for seven American Indian tribes, the percentages range from 39 to 78.[7] In short, parents are seen to play a comparatively minor part in the socialization of disciplines and values, whether the comparison be made with parents in other societies or with other socialization agents in the kibbutz society.

Nurturance. The kibbutz parent is intensely attached to his children whom he views as the "center of the universe." However, since he does not as a rule perform those caretaking and training responsibilities that are generally considered to be expressions of love, how does he communicate this love to his offspring? The nature of parent-child interaction depends upon the ages of the children, but even in infancy — and this is the first way in which a parent demonstrates his love — the parent assumes the role of playmate. The following excerpt illustrates the nature of such interaction when a mother visits her baby in the Nursery during the day. She brings her older son with her.

PNINA comes with Ahuv (four years) . . . PNINA takes Tsvi (ten months) from bed, sits on the floor, her legs stretched out . . . Tsvi laughs to see her, waves arms, lies across her legs . . . Ahuv brings toys for Tsvi . . . PNINA gets up, gets toys . . . Tsvi lies on floor now, looks around . . . PNINA watches him . . . Ahuv is roaming around, returns, sits with PNINA, picks up a toy, talks to her about the toy . . .

[7] Robert J. Havighurst and Bernice L. Neugarten, *American Indian and White Children* (Chicago: University of Chicago, 1955), pp. 117–118. The percentage difference between the kibbutz and the other cultures is even greater than it appears if one considers that the age range for the White sample was from ten to eighteen, and for the Indian samples, eight to eighteen. That is, the range begins at an age which is from two to four years older than the kibbutz sample, when one would expect the role of the parents to be less important. It is reasonable to assume, therefore, that the difference between the kibbutz and the Havighurst-Neugarten samples would have been even greater had the latter included children of a younger age. The logic of this argument is borne out if the kibbutz sample be enlarged to include subjects as old as eighteen (the upper age-range of the Havighurst-Neugarten sample). When this is done, the percentage for the kibbutz subjects is not eighteen, but fourteen.

She hands him another one, he plays with it . . . Ahuv then sits on a stool . . . Tsvi still lies on the floor, looks around . . . he tries to crawl, scoots a little . . . PNINA asks Tsvi, "Where is Ahuv?" . . . Tsvi pays no attention . . . PNINA tells him to come to her, but he does not . . . She picks him up, holds him for a second on Ahuv's lap, then sits him on her knees . . . then holds him again on Ahuv's lap . . . Tsvi laughs, waves his arms . . . Ahuv asks PNINA to do it again, but she doesn't . . . Tsvi lies on mother's stomach and legs, waves his legs and arms . . . YONAH (mother) comes, but her baby is asleep, so she sits and talks to PNINA . . . Tsvi lies on stomach on floor, plays with teething ring . . . PNINA watches him, listens to Ahuv talking . . . PNINA strokes Tsvi, pats him . . . Ahuv is standing on the stool, looking at truck outside . . . Tsvi tries to scoot around . . . YONAH leaves . . . Tsvi scoots a little, comes to me, touches my foot. I call his name, put my pencil in front of him . . . He looks at it, touches it . . . PNINA says, "No, Tsvi, it is forbidden" . . . Tsvi scoots around . . . Mother gets a toy, shows it to him, calls him . . . he turns, comes to toy, takes it, plays . . . Ahuv sees Tamar (baby), asks who she is . . . PNINA tells him, then moves Tamar's crib away from the plant in the corner, talks to her a second. Tamar laughs to PNINA . . . PNINA sits on stool, gets up, walks off porch . . . Ahuv looks out the screen . . . Tsvi plays with toy, scoots under Tamar's crib . . . He plays there, rolling the toy on the floor . . . scoots occasionally . . . Ahuv calls PNINA, walks away . . . Tsvi plays on . . . PNINA returns, Tsvi sees her, stretches arms and chest, smiles and smiles . . . He turns away, lies down, pulls the toy to and fro . . . He watches Mother, then scoots around . . . Mother suggests to Ahuv that they put Tsvi to bed . . . Ahuv jumps gleefully, says yes . . . Ahuv kneels, clasps Tsvi's wrists, stands up, says, "He doesn't want to." Tsvi scoots around . . . PNINA has arms around Ahuv's waist; Ahuv talks to me . . . Mother lifts Tsvi, puts him in bed, hugs him, says goodbye . . . Tsvi cries and cries . . . PNINA and Ahuv walk off . . . Tsvi stops crying . . . Ahuv runs back a second, calls Tsvi . . . Tsvi looks, then turns to look at baby in bed behind him, who is trying to reach him . . . Ahuv goes . . . Tsvi lies quietly . . .

When the child is older and goes to his parents' room in the evening, the time may be spent in various ways. A few toys are always kept in the parental room with which the child may play when he visits. At times, the parents may actually participate in this play with toys; at other times, they may merely observe while their child plays with them alone. Many parents read aloud to their children, and, when the weather is pleasant, almost all families take walks around the kibbutz. They visit the animals, go into the fields, or visit other families. This is also the hour when the teakettle is brought out, and while the parents drink their tea, the child eats his cookie, cake, or a piece of fruit.[8]

It must be emphasized that this evening visit of the child with his parents is the Children's Hour. These (approximately) two hours are set aside by the parent to be devoted exclusively to his child and to whatever his child wishes to do. One of the impressions gained from observing the Children's Hour is that the exclusive attention to the child for two hours places a burden upon the parent that he is not always able to sustain, for he frequently does not know what to do with his child for two whole hours. This is particularly true in the case of very young children whose verbal achievement is still low and whose attention span is always brief. A few parents, indeed, intimate that there are even times when they are bored by their children. In the following illustrations the parents are visiting their children in the Toddlers' House, for the children have been ill and may not yet be taken to their parental rooms.

Ami is sick and his father comes to see him. He reads to Ami, showing him each picture in the book, and asking, "What is this?" If Ami does not know, his father tells him . . . He carries him to the window. They look outside . . . He sings to him, sits with him on his lap. *I have the feeling that he is at a loss to know what to do with Ami, how to amuse him.*

In the yard, the parents sit with their children, holding them. The parents talk to each other and to the children. *Again I have the impression that the parents really don't know what to do with their children.* Avi's parents are the only ones who do not hold him, but who let him play in the yard, while they sit and watch him, and at times talk to him.

[8] When the respondents to the Questionnaire were asked, "What do your young (under twelve) children do when they visit you?," they ranked the six items on the list in the following order of importance:

1. Walk around kibbutz
2. Read aloud
3. Play
4. Converse
5. Study
6. Listen to radio

I was both amused and amazed to discover that not only had I omitted eating from the list, but that not one parent had added it. One can account for this omission only by suggesting that we all took this activity so much for granted that we failed to single it out.

One of the important ways, then, in which the kibbutz parent communicates his love for his child is by creating a feeling of fellowship between the child and himself. A second way in which the parents demonstrate love for their children is by their personal devotion. The early hours of the evening are set aside by the parents for their children. For many parents this represents a sacrifice, since these hours are often the only ones they might otherwise employ in pursuing their own interests, such as reading, studying, or conversing. But no parent would think of making other plans for the Children's Hour. Thus, the visitor who arrives at the kibbutz at this hour will gain some odd impressions. In the winter he may walk through the entire village without encountering a single person, and may think the village deserted. Everyone, of course, is with his children.

It is not only that the parent sets aside these hours to be devoted to his child, but that he spends these hours as the child wishes. If the child wishes to take a walk, the parents take a walk; if the child wishes to visit a friend, they visit a friend; if the child wishes to hear a story, they tell him a story. In short the child controls the situation. Parents not only allow their children to control the visiting situation, but they rarely scold them at these times, and they deliberately refrain from arguing or disagreeing between themselves.[9]

This devotion is seen in most graphic form in hashkava. Whether the nurse or the parent puts the child to bed, the routine is the same (see pp. 211–212) but the atmosphere is quite different. When the parent puts his child to bed the process may take as long as an hour, in contrast to the nurse's half-hour. The parent requires twice as much time to put his one child to bed as the nurse requires to put all the children to bed.

This time difference between nurse- and parent-supervised hashkava is a function, primarily, of the child's insistence that the parent remain, and of the parent's willingness to accept the many ruses he employs to obtain this end. He may ask for a drink of water, say he wants to sit on the pot, ask for another kiss, and so on — all with the goal of keeping the parent in the room. And our observations indicate clearly that these young children have learned that they can delay their parents' departure by crying; for the parents will not leave so long as the child cries.

[9] Some parents claim that they are wrong in never permitting their children to witness normal disagreements between them, for the children consequently gain a distorted view of adult life.

After his mother put him into bed, Moshe began to whine. Mother says, "No, I won't go yet."

Mother puts him into bed, and Tsvi begins to whine — he doesn't want her to leave. He lies down, and she talks to him, plays with him — patting him, etc. Every time she suggests that she leave, he whines. Finally, his sister gets bored, says, "Mother, let's go." But mother says, "What can I do, he doesn't want to go to sleep."

Father puts Amnon into bed, says "shalom." Amnon whines and whines. Father talks to him, *pleads* with him — "bedtime, have to go, you're a big boy."

No matter how trivial a child's request, the parent complies if possible.

At dinner, CHAVIVA sits and slices olive after olive to spread on bread. I ask her, "How do you have the patience to do this?," and she answers that it is not for her, but for her children, who had asked for an olive sandwich. LEAH, also sitting there, says, "For the children, there's always patience; for yourself, never." [10]

A third way in which parents demonstrate love to their children is by affection, both physical and verbal. Verbal affection is seen most clearly in the use of terms of endearment and pet names. Pet names for children are common, the most frequently heard being "Chamudi" (my charming one, my lovely one) and "Boobeleh" (little grandmother).[11]

Physical affection takes the form of hugging, patting, caressing, stroking, and kissing. Babies and toddlers are kissed on any part of the body — chest, belly, arms, legs, forehead, cheek, head — except the mouth, buttocks, and genitals. Older children are generally kissed only on the cheek or forehead. Parents always

---

[10] But when these mothers were asked if this would be reciprocal — would their children do the same for them when they grew up? — one mother said no, "but they in turn will do it for their children. It will be passed on." And a father said that when the parents get old, the children will build an "old-folks home" for them up on the mountain to get rid of them. We shall discuss some possible reasons for the parents' devotion to their children, and their willingness to do anything for them, but one of the reasons is surely not because the parents expect their children to reciprocate.

[11] Almost all names are both Yiddish-ized and diminutized after the Yiddish. Chana, for example, becomes Chaneleh; Yitzhak becomes Itzik; Yaakov becomes Yankeleh. Some children are also given nicknames by their parents and/or nurses. One baby, for example, was called Pushkin, because he closely resembled an infant photograph of the poet. Another baby was called "Nylon Balon" (nylon balloon) because she was round and fat like a balloon!

kiss and/or hug their children when they greet them; they may display physical affection many times during their visit with them; and when they leave they always kiss or hug their children in farewell. In general, when a parent greets his child he is almost always effusive in his affection and, in some instances, the physical affection displayed by the parent reveals clear erotic overtones.

A fourth way, unwitting to be sure, in which parental love for their children is demonstrated to them consists in their emotional involvement. Some parents are so involved with their children that they become dejected should the child not respond with equal fervor. For example:

A mother brings her son to his house at bedtime, and asks him for a kiss at the door. The boy refuses. Mother trembles, turns pale, says, "All right," and walks away. She returns in a few minutes, again asks him for a kiss, and he agrees. She kisses him desperately before leaving.

A mother passes the yard where the children are playing and asks her son for a kiss. He refuses, whereupon she says that she will not leave until he kisses her. He refuses again, and she seizes him and kisses him against his will.

Still other parents indicate jealousy of their children's other attachments.

Father asks Anat (three years) to leave with him, but she insists on remaining in the kevutza. Nurse tells her to go with father, but she says she wants to stay, and goes to sit next to the nurse. Father is manifestly distressed, attempts to induce her to go with him with offers of goodies and the promise of a visitor. He gives the appearance of a man who has been deeply threatened.

Chana (three years) is sitting on my lap, and her parents come in. Her mother, taken aback, says, "What's this?" Her father says (with every appearance of seriousness), "We are terribly jealous of you."

As in other cases, hashkava provides the best clue to this involvement. We have already noted that the child attempts to prolong the parent's departure. But the parent's desire is no less intense than the child's. At times the effusiveness with which parents take their farewell is so extreme that, as we frequently recorded, "It is as if they are never going to see their children again, or at the least, as if they are preparing to leave on a long journey in which they will not see their children for months, instead of the next day." [12]

Kibbutz parents, we conclude, are greatly devoted to their children, expressing their love in various ways. We may assume that parental love in the kibbutz stems from the same motives as such love in any other community, and hence requires no special explanation. But the intensity of parental love in the kibbutz — one of its characteristic features — does require explanation, for it is not unlikely that its various possible motives can have somewhat different effects on the emotional development of the children. Why, for example, does the parent await his evening visit with his child with eager anticipation, regarding it as the high point of his day? Why do so many parents give the impression of anxiously serving their children, lest the child cry and the parent lose his love? Why do so many parents pitch their evening visits at such a high level of emotion — devoting each moment to the needs and attention of their children? Questions like these cannot be answered by reference to universal motives for parental love.

One possible explanation for the intensity of parental love in the kibbutz — an explanation suggested by some parents — is that the parent regards the separation from his child as a severe frustration, and uses his relatively brief visits with his child to obtain as much gratification as possible. This is particularly true for the mother. Even some mothers who believe that collective education is wonderful for the children are less than enthusiastic about its effects on the parents. "Life in the kibbutz is best for the children," said one mother, "but very difficult for the parents." She explained that she and many other parents feel that they are not with their children enough. A few mothers state directly that the system frustrates their maternal needs, and some explain that the woman's function ". . . as a mother has been removed and nothing else has been put in its place."

It is not only the parent-child separation that is frustrating for many parents, but also their lack of opportunity to perform many of the caretaking chores. We have already discussed the insistence of many parents on performing those caretaking chores of which the system was designed to relieve them. This insistence seems to

[12] It is of interest to note that the parents (at least those who responded to the Questionnaire) are opposed to having the children sleep in their rooms. Of fifteen respondents, twelve checked "definitely no," one checked, "perhaps no," and only two checked, "perhaps yes."

represent an attempt to satisfy frustrated parental needs. As one mother, protesting the policy of having the nurses put the older children to bed, expressed it:

> Life in the kibbutz is difficult. The showers and toilets we are forced to use are enough to warrant such a statement. But to that must be added the noisy and hurried dining room, the hard work day, the lack of real recreation. We really don't have much . . . All we have left is our children, and we don't even have them, for they are in the children's house. And now they even took hashkava away from us. Why? because the "experts" say that the parents spoil them when they put them to bed. This may be true, but you have to think of the parents sometimes, too, and not always of the children.

Thus, deprived of those "normal" means of expressing love and of obtaining gratification, and limited to a brief visit each day, the parent exploits to the fullest his two hours in order to gain, as it were, enough satisfaction from his child to suffice till the next visit.

Another possible explanation for the parent's deep involvement with his child — one again suggested by some parents — is the fear of losing the child. One of the radical differences between the kibbutz and the more conventional system of child-rearing is that the child in the kibbutz literally does not need his parents in order to satisfy his physical needs. Unlike the family-reared child, the kibbutz child is not dependent upon his parents for food, clothing, or shelter. Hence, if the kibbutz child does not like his parents, he does not have to maintain relations with them — he does not have to go "home." Indeed, there are times when some children do not. In any event, since the child is independent of his parents, they may be motivated to be as loving to him as possible for fear that they might lose him. This fear, we believe, is one of the reasons why the parent rarely disciplines his child and makes every effort to please him.

Fear of losing the child has still another dimension. One of the basic reasons for which these parents established the system of collective education, it will be recalled, was to preclude a repetition in their children of their own rebellion against their parents. And this motive still operates today. It is as if the parents wish to prevent parental rebellion in their children by lavishing love. Many are quick to speak of the sacrifices they make for their children, and at times one gets the impression that they are implying, "You see how much we love our children?" But it is not so much the researchers, as it is their children, whom the parents wish to convince of this fact. At a grammar-school commencement, for example, three mothers gave short speeches, all stressing the same theme: The school is wonderful for the children, and the teacher is excellent because she is so good to the children. Here the children are happy; here they know no bitterness or difficulty — may this situation prevail in the high school as well! But more important than the words spoken were their overtones, for, as recorded at the time:

> The children must have the impression that they are the most important objects in the world. Nothing matters but that these almost priceless jewels should always "have it Good" and that they should experience nothing but happiness.

The following statement of a chavera reveals the motives for parental devotion and sacrifice more directly.

> In the early days, we did not have many children because conditions were too difficult, but we soon realized that without children we had nothing to do here . . . What is our goal? That our children should follow in our way. That is the only thing we have . . . Here the children receive everything prepared for them — there is no reason for them to rebel.

The future of the kibbutz — and, indeed, of the kibbutz movement — depends upon the children, and the parents want to make sure that their children find it a satisfactory life.

A final explanation for the intensity of parental love — and the one most frequently stated or implied by parents themselves — is the guilt of the parent. A few parents state explicitly that the reason kibbutz children are "spoiled" is that they (the parents) have not really accepted collective education; that they feel that they are depriving their children of a home, of a family, of a private room, and that, as a result, "They bend over backwards to give their children love and affection." It is true that some parents state flatly that their system is the "only way" to raise children and that if the children were ever to live with the parents they would leave the kibbutz. It is also true that of the fifteen respondents to the Questionnaire item, "Do you approve of collective education?," nine checked, "definitely yes." On the other hand, 40 per cent of the parents were willing to concede, even on a paper and pencil test in which defenses are operating at optimum strength, that they had some doubts about the system. Moreover, to the question, "Are the nurses and nursery teachers well qualified?," only five checked "definitely yes." In other words even those parents who approve of collective education in theory have some doubts about its personnel — that is, about its actual practice. On the other hand, two of the parents who expressed some doubts about collective education replied that the nurses were "definitely" well qualified — indicating that their doubts, at least, concern the system as a system.

It should be noted, finally, in refutation of our final hypothesis, that ten of the fifteen respondents checked "definitely no" to the question, "Could you have assured your children of a better life had you reared them privately?," and the remaining five checked "perhaps no." It is our impression, however, that the parents interpreted this question in terms of material benefits. Often in the course of discussions parents, some of whom we know to have doubted the psychological benefits of the system, would point out that they would not have been able to provide their children with as high a standard of living and education had they raised them privately.

Despite the questions raised by the Questionnaire results, we would defend our interpretation on the basis of personal interviews with mothers, most of whom were not so confident about the desirability of collective education as the former results suggest. One mother states, for example, that, while the system is on the whole a good one for the children, it is very hard on the younger children — "for they are lonely for their parents." A mother who has been a nurse for many years says that she is still not entirely convinced about collective education — she doubts that the system, both in theory and practice, is good for the children. Still another mother says that the system is not good for the child because he does not receive real warmth. "This (warmth) can come only from the mother," she explained. "The child here never gets the feeling that his mother cares for him from all the little things — the cooking, mending, and so on that mothers elsewhere do."

On the basis of personal interviews, we are confident about one fact. Many parents view their relegation of their children to the nurseries and the delegation of parental responsibility to nurses as a rejection of their children — as indeed it is, in a physical, if not an emotional, sense. But after "rejecting" the child, by placing him in the children's nurseries, the parent feels guilty, and one may observe in his behavior a typical rejection-guilt pattern:

the parent rejects his child by placing him in the children's house; but he waits eagerly for the child to emerge and dawdles over him before returning him.

If, then, the educational system represents a structural "rejection" of the child, there are other, subjective and personally experienced, bases for rejection. These include the facts that in the earliest days of the kibbutz the physical and social conditions were such that children were not desired, that even today a woman who works in a productive branch and who enjoys her work is forced to leave her work for approximately a year if she has a baby, and that every child born in the kibbutz represents another deprivation for the parent and for the kibbutz as a whole. Thus, the parent who does not really want his child for these realistic reasons reacts to his negative emotion with guilt, and must prove to himself that he really loves his child by lavishing him with affection.

DETHRONEMENT

Although the kibbutz parent is intensely devoted to his children, the expression of his devotion is not the same for all his children. The kibbutz, to be sure, is child-centered, but its focus is almost always on the youngest child. Hence when a new baby is born the older child is almost always "dethroned," and the love and attention originally lavished upon him by his parents are transferred to the new baby.[13] This is not to suggest that all kibbutz children are rejected to the same extent or in the same way when a sibling is born; indeed, many parents are sensitive to the problem of sibling rivalry and attempt to mitigate the effects of the new arrival as much as possible. Such parents, for example, will visit the older child frequently in his nursery; they stay at home so that he may visit them in their room; and in general they show him that the advent of the new sibling has not affected their love for him. Nevertheless, the evidence overwhelmingly indicates that the youngest child is in general the object of greatest parental attention and even preference.

When, on the Questionnaire, the respondents were asked, "Which child do you love the most?," they answered as follows:

[13] Some nurses believe that if the oldest child is a male, this dethronement is not too severe, for such a child — the *bechor* — is still viewed with some of the overtones of traditional Jewish culture, in which he is granted a position of primacy in the family. Theoretically, it is he who carries on the family name and tradition; and he is, moreover, the waited-for *kaddish*, the one who will recite the memorial prayer for his parents when they die. Again, we note the perpetuation of tradition in this anti-traditional society.

Oldest	0
Second	0
Third	0
Youngest	4
All equally	3
Only one child	3
Unanswered	6
Total	16

It must be noted that only the first four entries were listed on the Questionnaire, and of these four, only the *youngest* was checked by any of the respondents. Of even greater interest are those six parents who failed to answer the question at all, but one can but speculate about their reasons for omitting the question.

Far more revealing than the Questionnaire is the evidence based on observation. Observing a family group, one immediately notes that it is the youngest child, often a baby, who receives the most attention. Parents and older siblings alike devote their time to the baby — talking and cooing to him, holding him on their laps, encouraging him to crawl or walk. Any performance on the baby's part is greeted by all with excitement and praise. When we wanted to photograph family groups, both the parents and the older children would help in posing the baby; while our interest was in photographing the entire family, the parents always behaved as if only the baby were to be photographed. It was he who was encouraged to smile and to look at the camera while the older children were disregarded.

Two typical examples of a parent's ignoring an older child or of showing a preference for the younger are:

Father walks into the dining room carrying Tamar (three years), and Yehudit (seven years) is walking by his side. Mother is working in the kitchen. She sees them, runs over, seizes Tamar in her arms, kisses her, hugs her, etc. Yehudit stands there; mother ignores her. Yehudit looks hurt and walks away.

Mother comes in, tries to feed Elat (four years), who has thus far not eaten supper. She refuses to eat and begins to cry. Mother says, "Why are you the last one every day? We'll go home with the baby and wait for you." Father comes in with the baby and gives the baby some of the food and milk. Elat watches with a look of apprehension. Suddenly, as if she can bear it no longer, she screams, "Mother!"

However, despite this dethronement, the older children continue to be important objects of parental pride, conversation, and emotional involvement (except in the presence of their younger siblings). Some, indeed, continue to be overprotected by their parents who continue to bring children of school-age to the dormitory at night, help them to undress, and put them to bed.[14]

OTHERS

Although the children live in separate houses, it would be a mistake to assume that this isolation results in contacts with only parents and nurses. On the contrary, their wide and varied contacts, with both adults and other children, provide an extensive knowledge of the kibbutz world and a high degree of security within it.

In the first place, the children of any one kevutza have contact with their neighbors — children who occupy adjacent or nearby dwellings and who are in the same general age range. Children in neighboring groups may play together, occasionally aggress against each other, and sometimes socialize each other. But such interaction with neighbors is not frequent, and there are instances in which two groups of children may play on the same porch or in the same yard without any interaction between them. When interaction does occur, it always takes the form of one or two children from each group playing together, rather than entire groups. There is no tendency for group cohesiveness to break down or for new alignments to be formed. The integrity of each group always remains intact — a trait that continues throughout the childhood and adolescence of each kevutza. Even in the Grammar School where several groups live, eat together, and share some formal activities, each group remains a distinct unit.

Second, and more important, the children have frequent

[14] Nurturant attitudes on the part of parents are expressed not only toward their pre-adolescent children, but to their adolescents as well. For while, on the one hand, the kibbutz (that is, the parents) imposes adult responsibilities on its adolescents — expecting them to work in the kibbutz economy, for example — it views them, on the other hand, as defenseless children who must be protected from the cruel outside world. This attitude emerged clearly in a debate concerning the proper time for admitting the high school seniors to membership in the kibbutz. The teachers argued that the seniors should not be admitted to membership until their return from army service, lest they think that membership was a status they could gain automatically. And, they contended, the graduates had to prove themselves worthy. The parents, however, were unanimously opposed to this point of view. Life in the army, they argued, is difficult, and their children were about to enter the cruel world for the first time. They should be elected to membership immediately, so that they might have the security of the knowledge that they had a home to which they could return. The parental view prevailed.

contacts with unrelated adults and with older children. For the younger children, such contacts come primarily with visitors to the kevutza — with adults and children who come to the house for a few minutes during the day. Such visiting is extensive, as is illustrated by the frequency of visitors to one kevutza of two-year-olds: over a period of twelve half-days, there were 57 visitors to the kevutza. These visitors may be broken down into the following categories:

Mothers	8
Fathers	7
Grandmothers	3
Siblings	12
Nurse's children	3
Unrelated adults	10
Other unrelated children	14
Total	57

The children thus see many people, both relatives and non-relatives, during the day. As they grow older their contacts increase as they observe other groups of children, as well as adults at work. For the older children — those in the Grammar School — such contacts with other individuals result primarily from their own increasing mobility, rather than from adult visits; for chaverim visit primarily the younger children, and there are few visitors to the school.

The adults who visit any one kevutza may include not only its parents and grandparents, but others as well. Of these three categories, however, the strongest relationship established by the children is with the parents of other children in the kevutza. When a mother visits her child during the day, for example, all the children in the group run to her, sit on her lap, cluster around her. When she kisses her own child goodbye, the others often ask to be kissed too. Such an attachment derives from the fact that parents are attentive to all the children in their child's group. In the Nursery, for example, a mother may care for another baby by changing his diaper, by comforting him if he cries, by talking to him or hugging him if she passes his crib. Her concern for the welfare of the other children continues as they grow older, and she distributes her affection and solicitude among all the children of the group. In similar fashion such a parent may train the children as well. If a child aggresses, he will tell him to stop; if a toddler soils his pants, he may point out that the child should have asked for a chamber pot.

Grandparents[15] — more specifically, grandmothers — adopt similar attitudes toward all the children of the kevutza. If the grandmother brings some goodies with her when she visits her grandchild, she brings enough for all the children. While she is present she exercises her authority over all the children, reprimanding them and comforting them.

Parents and grandparents are constant visitors to any one kevutza; thus all the children form continuing relationships with them. But the children's more casual contacts with other adults also have an influence on them. In view of the extreme child-centeredness of the kibbutz, it is not surprising to find that adults make frequent, if casual, visits to the children's houses, especially to those of the very young children. When a baby is born, for example, friends of the parents go to the Nursery to see the new infant. When an adult passes a yard in which young children are playing, he usually stops for a few minutes to talk to the children or even to sing them a song. If a child is crying, the passerby attempts to console him, hugging and caressing him. If a child aggresses, the passerby may scold him and tell him that "it is not nice."

The children interact with adults in other areas of the kibbutz as well. When the young children go on their daily hike, they may be stopped by an adult who talks to them, praises them, or displays affection. The children have an opportunity to observe adult occupational roles in their walks through the kibbutz. And workers may not only stop work to play with the children but also demonstrate their work, even allowing the children to help them for a few minutes. Such adults also discipline the children if necessary — ordering them "not to touch," occasionally threatening punishment if the children misbehave.

Older children who visit younger ones — whether they be siblings, children of the nurse, or unrelated to anyone in the kevutza — display the same nurturant and disciplinary behavior toward them as do adults. Visits from older children, especially those in the Grammar School, are frequent, and are made more often by girls than by boys. Girls from the Grammar School are important socializing influences on the very young children, the

---

[15] There are as yet too few grandparents in Kiryat Yedidim for them to become important influences in the socialization of the kibbutz children. At this time, grandparents bear no official responsibility, but adopt a role similar to that of the parents — they love and indulge their grandchildren.

toddlers. Indeed, their visits are encouraged by the nurses, for when they visit, they act as nurse-surrogates, performing most of the patterns within the nurse's role. They initiate and supervise play, they discipline and prevent the children from hurting themselves, and they are nurturant toward them — dressing them, combing their hair, hugging and kissing them. Such behavior is not only modeled on the nurse's behavior, but it is also performed with the precise language that the nurse uses and often with the same vocal intonation. The adult attitudes are further perpetuated by such older children when they meet younger ones anywhere in the kibbutz — the younger child is always stopped, hugged, disciplined if necessary. As one might predict, the younger children in their turn are devoted to their older visitors, and almost always greet them with joy and affection. The older child thus gains much maternal gratification from the situation.

Thus it is that young children in the kibbutz have frequent contacts with individuals outside their immediate group. And all these people assume obligations toward the children — for in the eyes of the kibbutz members each child belongs to all. This feeling of belonging to the entire group surely gives young children a strong sense of security in their little world, and the frequency of visitors accustoms them to the presence of strangers — for the young children accept strangers readily, greeting them with interest, curiosity, and often with immediate affection.

But such personalized contact with many people has another important influence. The individuals who interact with children not only give them warmth and affection — a source of security — but they also inculcate kibbutz values by their disciplinary behavior. This is of general theoretical importance, for the children thus become sensitive to the judgments of many people, an experience which conditions them for the adult life in which sensitivity to the entire group is a most important form of social control. Hence, for the children from ages six through eleven, persons other than parents, educators, and peers represent 20 per cent of all socializers — as revealed, at least, by the Moral Ideology Test.[16] If this is a valid measure, the role played by "others" is important indeed, for the percentage is higher than that even of the parents.

There is, finally, one other consequence of these frequent and warm contacts with adults and older children. We have observed

---

[16] This figure is derived from the table (see Appendix C) on Moral Surrogates, in which the values for "kibbutz" (under "group") and for "others" (under "specific person/status") are combined.

that such individuals visit only the younger children, and that their chance contacts with school children, for example, are not characterized by the warmth and interest that describe their relations with younger children. As the children grow older, then, they experience a "rejection" by the entire kibbutz — a rejection that differs only in intensity from that they may have experienced with their parents. Even only children, not displaced by actual siblings, are displaced by their (younger) sociological siblings, so that they too experience rejection by those to whom they "belong." This contrast between expectancy (love and attention) and actuality (rejection) is, according to some nurses, one of the most difficult experiences in the life of the kibbutz child.

NURSES AND NURSERY TEACHERS

Love. If the nurses[1] grow to love the children in their kevutza, the children in turn grow to love and depend upon their nurses. But a child seldom becomes attached to a nurse who is not attached to him. This differential response on the part of the child begins in infancy. The head nurse in the Nursery is of the strong opinion that a baby begins to respond to *her* as an individual only when she begins to respond to *him* as an individual, rather than as a biological organism. Since she responds to each baby differently, each, in turn, responds to her differently. Some babies will go to her immediately when she holds out her arms; others go much more slowly. Similarly, there are nurses to whom some babies refuse to go at all; and some babies refuse to eat if a particular nurse feeds them. The head nurse is emphatic about the reason for these latter responses. "When a nurse picks up a baby and he cries, I know there is nothing wrong with the baby; but something is wrong with the nurse, for babies love to be picked up and played with." Thus a baby responds, even at this young age, to the nurse's covert dislike of or disinterest in him.

Since the typical nurse is nurturer and comforter, it is small wonder that, as one nurse expressed it, "The children are very tied to the people who take care of them." There are times when a child may prefer his nurse to his own mother. Moreover, there is evidence to indicate that some children would like to combine mother and nurse into one person. Children, for example, will unwittingly address the nurse as "Mother," although it is admittedly difficult to know whether they confuse the two women or whether they have a truly synthetic mother *imago* — a fusion of the mother-figure and the nurse-figure. Sometimes children deliberately put the nurse in the place of either parent. One nurse

---

[1] The term, "nurse," will be used for nurse and nursery teacher, alike.

reports that her charges often tell her, "You are my mother." When her parents left on their annual vacation, Dena told SHOSHANNA, "Now that my parents have left, you will be my mother." And when Ziva's father was called into the Army Reserve, she informed ZEHAVA that, "You will be my father."

The children express their attachment to the nurse in innumerable ways. There is, first of all, the fact that they frequently manifest physical signs of affection for her.

CHANA comes in the room, stands. Iris (two years) runs to her . . . hugs her, laughs, clings to her. CHANA lifts Iris by the hands, and Iris climbs up her stomach. Then Rafi tries, and climbs all the way to her chest . . .

As SHLOMIT dresses Yehuda (two years) he laughs, puts his arms around her as she buttons his suspenders, and pats her breasts.

HELKA is ironing. Mimi (three years) stands next to her, watches, thumb in mouth. Suddenly, she hugs and kisses HELKA.

Children not only give physical affection to the nurse, but they persistently seek sheer physical contact with her. If, for example, a nurse sits on the floor to read to the children, or if she sits on the grass to observe their play, children will swarm over her — sitting in her lap and on her legs, lying with their heads in her lap, standing next to her with their arms around her.[2]

The nurse, moreover, is considered by the children as a protector. If a child is attacked by another, he often turns to the nurse for solace and/or protection. If he hurts himself by falling or running into a wall, he runs to the nurse for consolation. If the nurse is available, she is able to pacify him within a few minutes; if she is not, the child's cries may continue for some time. The children not only turn to the nurse for protection; they in turn protect her. On the few occasions, for example, that children in the Kindergarten attempted to aggress against the nurse, other children immediately rushed to her defense.

The child's attachment to the nurse is revealed in his desire for her attention and approval. When children are painting or drawing, they constantly ask the nurse to help them in their work, to get them a crayon, to bring them a clean sheet of paper. A

[2] In general the nurses accept and return this voluntary affection. Sometimes, however, if the acts become too pronounced, a nurse may insist that they cease. Ron (four years), for example, had a tendency to smother his nurses with affection. He would crawl all over the nurses when they were sitting down, and the nurse's response in one instance was typical: "Ron, I don't consent"; "Ron, I don't want it"; "Ron, that's enough."

child eats all his food, and proudly announces this fact to the nurse; another swings on one foot, and demands that the nurse observe this accomplishment; a third rides his tricycle without hands and insists that the nurse come outside to watch him. The following example illustrates not only the children's desire for the attention and approval of the nurse, but their rivalry for this attention and approval.

SHULA and the children (in the Kindergarten) work in the garden that they are making. All have small rakes and hoes, and are working under SHULA's guidance . . . All talk at once and clamor for her attention. "SHULA!" . . . "SHULA!" . . . "SHULA! Come to me!" . . . "SHULA! I will bring fertilizer" . . . "SHULA! I will bring water!" . . . All the children are eager for SHULA's approval and from time to time one will hear, "SHULA, did I work well?" "And I?" "SHULA, did I work terribly hard?" . . . She cannot compliment one without complimenting all . . .

This desire for the nurse's approval undoubtedly accounts for the fact that few acts of disobedience of, or aggression against, the nurses were observed during this study (see pp. 168–170), although this absence may be motivated by fear rather than love. Children, for example, will almost always obey the nurse when they will not obey others. Often we would tell a child to do something, only to have him ignore the request. But if the nurse made the same request, the child would almost always obey her promptly. The children, moreover, generally obey their regular nurses more than they do their substitute nurses. In one kevutza, for example, the toddlers were not permitted to play in the shower room nor were they permitted to play with the dishes. These rules, never violated when their permanent nurses were present, were frequently broken when a substitute was on duty.

The children not only love their nurse, but they are jealous of the love she displays toward other children. One of the few sources of competition within the kevutza is competition over the nurse; for from the earliest ages, the children attempt to monopolize her attention, her affection, or her lap.

RACHEL picks up Aryeh (one year, four months) to feed him, puts him on her lap. He screams . . . and she sets him on the floor . . . takes Moshe and starts to feed him . . . Aryeh then *really* begins to scream and cry, and tries to climb on RACHEL's lap. RACHEL returns Moshe to his mother, picks up Aryeh and feeds him. He eats quietly and very well.

ROSA sits on the floor. Amir (two years) and Mirav pile on her lap. Omri tries to sit too, but there is no room. He tries to force Amir off . . . ROSA helps Omri to sit on her knees.

Amikam (two years) tells SHLOMIT that she belongs to *him*. Pnina says no, SHLOMIT belongs to *her*. SHLOMIT says she belongs to *both* Amikam and Pnina. And Amikam, seeing Avinoam, says, "And to 'Noam too."

ETTA asks Mordechai (three years) to get her an apron from the laundry. He says no, and she asks Miryam, who is delighted; whereupon Mordechai rushes out of the house, pushes Miryam out of the way, insists that he go.

If a nurse comments that one child cleans up very well, another immediately announces, "I can too." If a nurse tells one child that she loves him very much, the others also insist, "Me too." Rivalry for the attention of the nurse is particularly acute when two groups are first combined into one Kindergarten, and the nurse of one group assumes responsibility for the enlarged kevutza. In one such instance the nurse, in order to establish rapport with the children with whom she was not acquainted, decided that she would put this new group to bed at night and have another nurse put the other children to bed. The children in the latter group bitterly demanded that she put them to bed too. The nurse solved the problem by putting both groups to bed at night, but quarrels still existed over whom she was to kiss goodnight first.

The children not only express jealousy of the nurse's attention to their peers, but they may also resent her affection for adults. In one kevutza the children frequently asked the nurse about her husband — where she went with him, what she did with him, and why she loved him so much.

Still another manifestation of attachment to the nurse occurs when she returns to the kevutza, whether she has been away for several days or only several hours. When she arrives, she is always greeted with enthusiasm. One child sees her and exclaims, "GORAH is here!," and the others rush to her with manifest joy, embrace her, tell her what they are doing, etc. Again:

LEAH comes into the house to give the children supper. They had last seen her at noon. All run to her, shouting, "LEAH! LEAH!"

The children are playing in the bedroom . . . ZEHAVA (who has not been here since morning) comes in. One of them shouts, "Look who's here." They run towards her, Ron jumping into her lap first.

Similarly, if a nurse walks past the children's yard on her day off, all the children call and run to her; and if a nurse who has formerly worked with the kevutza returns for a visit, the children run to her, hug her, and in various ways express their continued affection for her.

Still other expressions of attachment occur. The children take great delight in helping the nurse: they set the table, fetch the food, empty the garbage. The nurse may ask one child to fetch the food from the kitchen, and four others volunteer to go with her. The nurse sits on the grass and says that she is going to get up, and two boys immediately rush to help her rise.

A final indication of the children's positive relationship to the nurse consists in the observation that the greatest degree of *esprit de corps* obtains when the nurse is either directing or observing their play. At such times, there is always the most merriment and laughter, and it is then, too, that there is the least aggression and conflict.

Fear and hostility. The above response, of course, may be the result of fear as well as of love, which leads us to record another observation. Children not only love their nurse; they are also fearful of, and sometimes hostile to, her. Fear is expressed in their reluctance to commit any act in her presence of which they have reason to believe she disapproves.

Tsvi (two years) starts to hit Anat. TAMAR looks at him. He stops in the middle.

Avinoam (two years) hits SHLOMIT as she is dressing him. SHLOMIT says no, he is not to hit. Avinoam kisses her, and a moment later, kisses her again and pats her head.

Avraham (two years) pulls a blanket off a bed. I tell him no, but he does so anyway. ROSA comes in, and he drops the blanket immediately, looks sheepish. ROSA picks up the blanket from the floor and asks, "Who took it?" Avraham says, "Noo, noo, noo." ROSA says, "That's right — noo, noo, noo." She looks at Avraham with a pretend-angry look. He stands a second hesitating, then runs to her, throws his arms around her. She picks him up.

Hostility may be expressed in both verbal and physical aggression, as well as in disobedience, although all such acts are very infrequent among these children. If, however, a nurse is disliked by her kevutza, or has difficulty in controlling the children, the incidence of aggression and disobedience increases.

Such a nurse, furthermore, is unable to elicit the cooperation and assistance of the children. One nurse who was disliked by her charges because of the tension and sharp temper she often displayed was often observed to evoke a negative response when she asked for volunteers to help her carry the food from the kitchen.

That the children have hostile, as well as tender, feelings toward their nurses is not at all surprising. Since the nurse is the most important disciplinarian in their lives, it is to be expected that she is the source of much frustration. Among the preschool children the most frequent occasion for crying — other than frustration imposed by peer aggression or conflict — is some action of the nurse which the child perceives as frustrating. A count was made of all crying in two of the children's groups in which the instigation was unequivocally identifiable. Of a sample of ninety-four cases, sixty-seven, or 71 per cent, were seen to be provoked by the nurse. She had prohibited some activity, insisted that the child engage in some activity, refused to accede to a request or desire, threatened to punish a child if he persisted in a tabooed activity or given attention to another child.

This same pattern holds for the older children. According to the Moral Ideology Test, the grammar school children view their nurses (and teachers) as their most punitive socializers. They are not only perceived as playing a critical role twice as frequently as a rewarding role in socialization, but their critical role is as important (quantitatively) as that of all other persons — parents, peers, other kibbutz members — combined. These test results are entirely consistent with ethnographic observations. A fourth-grade child, for example, wrote an essay describing a hike which the children had undertaken during a regularly scheduled class. The trip was fun, she wrote, but the children were most concerned that the teacher not be angry with them. When they returned, she writes, they were "happy to see that the teacher was not angry." Again, when the children of the fourth grade were playing charades, the child enacting the charade attempted to represent the assigned word by feigned scolding and shouting. The other children guessed from his behavior that the word he was trying to act out was "nurse." (They were wrong.)

Insecurity. In general, the attachment of the children for their nurses is much stronger than these negative attitudes; and its positive consequences are of the greatest importance for the children's emotional development. But there are certain maladjustive consequences of this attachment which have an important influence on their development, and which must be examined in detail. These arise from the discontinuity of nurses in the child's life, a discontinuity which characterizes both the daily life of the child and his development over time.

It has been noted that there are two permanent nurses in each kevutza and, in addition, a substitute nurse who works with the children when a permanent nurse is absent. While the kibbutz would like to ensure the continuity of the relief nurse, this is seldom possible in view of its manpower shortage. Thus, the children may be cared for by one relief nurse for a day or two during one week, and on the following week, another may be assigned. This discontinuity exposes the child to different personalities, attitudes, and, in some cases, conflicting socialization techniques (see Chapter 3). What is the reaction of the children to the absence of a permanent nurse to whom they are so deeply attached? That the absence of the latter nurse is frequently disturbing to the child is evidenced by such signs as increased restlessness, whining, and apathy in play when a strange nurse is on duty alone. If, for example, a child awakens from his nap and finds that a substitute nurse is on duty, he often calls for his regular nurse; though he submits to the ministrations of this substitute, often during the day he asks for his regular nurse. Furthermore, if a substitute nurse is working in the house at the same time as a regular nurse, some children will refuse to permit her to perform certain functions, such as dressing or bathing them, demanding that the regular nurse do this. In one group of four-year-olds the typical reaction to a substitute nurse is prolonged sleep and, indeed, one boy simply refuses to get out of bed. In a group of three-year-olds one boy expressed his attitude toward his nurse's weekly absence by announcing that he would not give his "love to the nurse who takes a day off and leaves" him. Hence, children are not only disconcerted by the temporary absence of their nurse, but they may view this absence as a personal rejection.

The most difficult experience of discontinuity, however, is that which characterizes the relations between child and nurse over time. Infants leave the Nursery when they are approximately one year old. In theory, the new nurse or nurses that they acquire at this time should remain with them at least until they enter the Kindergarten, and, preferably, until they enter Grammar School — for the kibbutz believes that the children should know the security of having the same nurse during the entire period of the "tender age." But, as we have observed, this continuity seldom exists and a nurse rarely remains with her kevutza throughout this period. This severance of the deep emotional relationship that exists between child and nurse is a source of great disturbance to the children, and it is all the more intensified if they feel their nurse's departure to be a personal rejection. The readjustment period is made even more difficult by the fact that the techniques of adjustment and interaction developed in response to one nurse must be discarded, and new ones acquired.

Difficult as the departure of a nurse is for the children, its worst consequences can be mitigated if the children get to know and love the new nurse before the old one leaves. Often, however, there is no time for such a transition period. Sometimes it is overlooked from sheer carelessness; sometimes it is precluded by the manpower needs of the kibbutz. In either event, this sudden and abrupt change of nurses only intensifies the difficulties for the children.

Abrupt discontinuity may begin at the earliest age. During the course of this study, for example, the nurse who was assigned to work in a newly created Toddlers' House spent no time at all working with the babies in the Nursery. One morning, she arrived at the Nursery and took the five babies, who had never before seen her or their new dwelling, to their new home. That the infants are disturbed by this abrupt change will be noted later, but it is impossible to decide to what extent their disturbance is a function of change in nurses, and to what extent it is a response to the entirely new world to which they are abruptly introduced.

In the older groups, where the departure of the nurse is not accompanied by consequent changes in the children's physical or social environment (the children remain in the same house and with the same kevutza), the manifest disturbance of the children may be attributed exclusively to their separation from the nurse. When the nurse in one kevutza left to study in Tel Aviv, one two-year-old protested against any nurse who took her place. He cried often and did not want his parents to leave him at night. When at last he accepted the new nurse, he was afraid lest she leave too. One day his mother met him — dirty, crying, and sucking his thumb — on her way to the dining room. The new nurse, whom he had finally accepted, had gone to eat, and he was afraid lest another new nurse come to bathe him. When still another nurse who had left to study in Tel Aviv returned on weekends, she would see the children in her former kevutza. One three-year-old always refused to greet her, and would either look the other way or walk away if she approached him.

These same painful reactions to the departure of the nurse occur even among older children, extending as far as the Grammar School. When the children of the second grade entered the Grammar School, their necessary separation from their previous nursery teacher was almost traumatic. As their new teacher related her initial experiences with these children: "To leave MALKA (the nursery teacher) was a horrible experience for them. They became very aggressive, and my first two months with them were impossible." The children would constantly hit each other, and often became hysterical. They would scream and hit tables, chairs, and doors for no apparent reason. If the new teacher attempted to interfere, they would hit her. Their love for MALKA lasted a long time. They would ask each other, "Who is better — MALKA or CHANA (the new teacher)?," and then agree that to love CHANA was disloyal to MALKA. When they had a class project which they particularly enjoyed, they asked the teacher, "Is it true that MALKA told you to have this project?"

PARENTS

Love. Parents are the children's most important love-objects — a not unexpected finding in the light of the discussion of parental behavior. In spite of the fact that the child may see his parents for only two hours a day, these two hours are the most important of the day for him. In the kevutza, the child is merely one of eight or sixteen children, all of whom must share the love and attention of the nurse. But for two hours every day, he becomes the center of the universe — his slightest whim is immediately gratified, love and affection are lavished upon him, and he has at last the exclusive attention of adults, his parents. Of his nurses the child must always say, "They are *ours*"; but of his parents he may say, "They are *mine*." [3]

The contrast between the child's experience in the kevutza and in his parental room has been noted by Irvine:[4]

It seems likely that the rather unstimulating and frustrating environment of the child under three, and the limited physical and emotional

---

[3] This paragraph applies without qualification to only children. If a child has siblings, he must share his parents. But even then the description is not without validity. Kibbutz children — except for those of sabras — are, for the most part, widely separated in age. Hence, the youngest child, in effect, is an only child, insofar as his opportunities for monopolizing his parents' attentions are concerned.

[4] Irvine, "Observations on the Aims and Methods of Child-Rearing in Communal Settlements in Israel," p. 264.

contact which he often has with his metapeleth, has enhanced for him the intensity of his relations with his parents and the significance of the family room.

In the kevutza, the child from the earliest age is expected to — and must — subordinate his own needs to the needs of the group. Because he cannot have all his needs satisfied immediately, this situation demands a high level of frustration tolerance. But in the parental room, with its extreme indulgence, the child daily receives ego satisfactions in the form of intense love and nurturance. And this indulgence is accentuated by another aspect of the parent-child relationship — the secondary role played by the parents in child training. To the extent that socialization demands require the inhibition of impulse, socialization itself is unpleasant; its unpleasantness is heightened by the use of negative sanctions. The Moral Ideology Test reveals that the children do not perceive their parents as punitive, but, in contrast to their teachers and nurses, as highly indulgent. When asked to name the ones who would praise them for their good deeds, the children (age six through eleven) named their teachers and nurses, on the one hand, and their parents, on the other, with equal frequency. But when they were asked to name the persons who would criticize them for bad deeds, they named their nurses and teachers three times as frequently as their parents. The parental room, in short, is a much more permissive place than the dormitory.

The contrast between these two experiences — the dormitory and the parental room — only serves to intensify the importance of the latter. Thus this overstimulating and highly satisfying two-hour period becomes terribly important for the child, and the parents, who are responsible for it, become strongly cathected. It is the intensity of this relationship that establishes the parent as the most important influence on the child's development.

The importance of the parents in the child's development, as measured at least by the child's deep attachment to his parents, must be seen within the structural context of kibbutz socialization. Parents, unlike his nurses, are relatively stable figures in the child's environment. Attachments to a nurse can be, and indeed frequently are, broken. Because his nurses are transient, permanent attachments to them are necessarily precluded. But however transient his nurses, the child's parents are constant; and the greater the impermanence of his nurses, the more important becomes the constancy of his parents. Thus, his parents become the child's constant and stable points of emotional reference.

But we need not remain content with these speculations concerning the attachment of the child to his parents. On the Emotional Response Test, for example, the role played by the parents is exclusively positive. Parents are *never* mentioned as a source of anger, fear, shame, or sadness. It is only the absence of the parents — due to travel, illness, or death — that is responded to with sadness or is perceived as one of the worst things that can happen.

The child's attachment to his parents is supported, most importantly, by ethnographic observations, from which the following examples are chosen at random. Children often refer spontaneously to their parents during the day. A two-year-old walks around the yard singing, "Come, Daddy"; a three-year-old plays in the sandbox and sings, "Here is Daddy!"; another two-year-old plays outside after supper and sings, "Mommy, come to Elat!" Many children, furthermore, cry for their parents when they have been hurt or when they want something. Often, to be sure, they cry for the nurse, but frequently they cry and scream for "Daddy!" or "Mommy!," or for both. In short, the parent is perceived as protector and comforter.

When a substitute nurse refuses to give Nili (four years) a cookie, Nili says, "My mother says that I'm a sweetie, and she'll give me cookies."

Amos (five years) accidentally bumps into Shula and hurts his head. He wails, "Mother," for a long time.

Yuval (four years) tells Amir (four years) that the children from the next kevutza will come at night and beat him up. Amir looks unhappy . . . Yuval leaves, and Amir says to himself, "My father is stronger than they are, and he won't let them."

Many children visit their mothers at work during the day, if that is possible. A child is praised by his nurse for a drawing he has made, and he says he is going to take it to his mother. A child is reprimanded by the nurse, and he runs to his mother. Or, a child for no immediate reason decides to visit his mother. A four-year-old threatens to kill his nurse, and another child says he should not do it, for the nurse's children would cry.

Children often identify other children by designating their parents. When the daughter of ZEHAVA (the nurse) came into the room, for example, Zeviah said, "Here comes Shula. We too have a Shula, Shula of YAEL. This is Shula of ZEHAVA." At times, a young child will say, "All the parents are mine," and nurses report that a child will occasionally announce that X and Y are his parents although they are in fact the parents of another child.

The importance of the parents for the children may be observed even in peer aggression. Livid with rage, a ten-year-old could think of no more aggressive epithet to hurl at a peer than, "I hope your family dies tomorrow; I hope your family dies today; I hope your family dies right now!"

That the child is deeply attached to his parents is revealed, more systematically, by the joy with which he greets them when they come for him in the evening. The last meal of the day is the meal at which chaos and utter confusion often reign — because the children are excited about the imminent arrival of their parents. This excitement is apparent even among the infants in the Nursery, who become so excited when they see their parents that they refuse to allow the nurse to feed them.[5] The arrival of the parents is always greeted by grins, joyous cries, a great deal of running back and forth, throwing of arms around the parents, and innumerable squeals of "Mommy" and "Daddy."

But the children are not only happy to see their parents when the latter arrive, they are equally unhappy when they do not arrive at the expected time. For example:

> . . . Around 9:00 (A.M.), Esther (sixteen months) begins to cry . . . she cries and cries . . . CHAYA takes her inside, says she doesn't know why she is crying, but thinks it may be because her mother usually comes to see her at this time and has not yet come.

If children are eager to see their parents after the day's separation, they are doubly eager to see them after a more prolonged absence. Children await the return of their parents from a trip with great anticipation. They were frequently heard to tell their nurses or peers, in a tone of great joy, that "in another three days" or "in another two days" or "tomorrow," "my parents will return."

This reaction is found among the very young children, as well. In the example below, Omri's parents have been on vacation for two weeks, and his nurse has told this two-year-old boy that his parents are coming home that very day.

[5] That the babies who are weaned have already begun to perceive their parents as playmates is indicated by the fact that they will often refuse to allow their parents to feed them. When such a baby sees his parents, he is, as the nurses say, "ready to play"; the baby will eat only when the parent gives him to the nurse, who then feeds him.

. . . (In the afternoon, Omri is in his crib) . . . the door opens, and Omri jumps up, yells. CHANA comes in, and Omri looks disappointed, subsides . . . (later) . . . the door opens, and ETTA comes in. Omri hears the door open, jumps up, faces the door, eyes wide — sees ETTA, subsides, looks out the window, jabbers a little . . . (at supper), Omri suddenly begins to cry. CHANA comforts, strokes him. He puts two fingers in his mouth . . . ETTA calls out the window to Omri's mother, tells her she may come in. The mother enters, but Omri does not see her. She calls his name, he turns around, grins, waves his arms to her excitedly.

Similarly,

Naomi (nine years) wrote her mother a letter when the latter went to the city overnight. She gave her the letter upon her return the next day. In the letter she wrote that she loved her and missed her, that she could not wait until she returned, and that she wanted ten kisses in exchange for her absence.

The children are as reluctant to see their parents depart (whether at night or after a brief visit during the day) as they are eager to see them arrive. While most children do not cry when their parents leave, many children do; and some babies, too, will cry for a few minutes after their parents leave. Unfortunately, we have no information on the average duration of such crying, but we recorded instances of a child's clinging to a parent for as long as fifteen minutes, begging him not to go, and then crying "Father" or "Mother" for almost the same length of time after the latter's departure.

The following illustrates the reaction of a child to her mother's departure during the day.

Pua (two years) sees her mother in the distance, yells, "Mommy!," and runs to the fence. Her mother calls, "Shalom!," says that she is working now, and that she does not have time to come — she will come to see her later. Mother stands and repeats this over and over again, not going. When she finally goes, Pua cries — stands at the fence and yells and cries . . . Pua still cries, tries to climb through rails of fence . . .

Another indication of the child's attachment to his parents is revealed by his pride in and identification with them. Children may refer to their parents' work with pride — for example, "My father drives a tractor," or "My mother works in the chicken house." Older children may announce that when they grow up they will do whatever work their fathers or mothers do. In play children often assume the role of their parents: a girl whose mother is a nurse insists on being the nurse when they play "nurse and patient"; a boy whose father is an electrician announces that he will be the electrician when they play with "wires." There are still other ways in which a child expresses identification with his parents. Some children make model objects of sand which they may identify as mother or father. When they look at picture books, adult figures are often identified as mother and father.

The possessive pride which many children reveal toward parents is indicative of strong identification with them. When a group of three-year-olds went for a walk one day, they passed the laundry:

Mimi says to Zevia, "There's your mother's dress hanging on the line" (it was). Zevia becomes excited and runs to the nurse to tell her that she has seen her mother's dress.

The nurse announces that CHAIM (father of Miryam) has to substitute for MOSHE in a kibbutz committee. Miryam begins to shout with glee, "My father! That's my father!"

The nurse says the bicycle is broken and they will have to give it to SHAIKE (the father of Amnon) to be fixed. Amnon asks, "To SHAIKE?" And when the nurse says yes, he says proudly, "To *my* SHAIKE!"

Finally, children refer to their parents as authority figures, or they brag about them both absolutely and competitively.

Chana (four years) says that the birds from Africa like cold weather. When the other children challenge the truth of her statement, she says, "It's true — my father told me."

Nadav (five years) has a pocket knife, and Nili says that her father has a *big* knife. Nadav says his father has a *sharp* knife. Boaz shouts that his father has a *big* knife. Esther says that her father has a sharp pocket knife. Boaz says that his father also has a pocket knife, and that he (his father) will give it to him.

When someone showed a picture of two French beauty queens to Eldad's (twelve years) parents, he commented that "My mother is more beautiful than both of them put together."

Identification with parents is seen also in the children's attitude toward their parental rooms. When asked where they live, for example, some children mention their parental rooms rather than their kevutza. By the same token, the term *cheder sheli* (my room), refers almost exclusively to the child's parental room rather than to his nursery. Among the older children, on the other hand, "my room" becomes "our room," but the reference is the same — the parental room. Thus, when nine-year-old Chana discussed her vacation, she said it would be "after *we* move into our new quarters." It was her parents, of course, who were moving into new quarters, and not her kevutza.[6]

Although the child's relation to his parents is one of deep attachment, it should not be concluded that the children would prefer living with their parents. The children of grammar-school age, at any rate, dislike sleeping in their parents' rooms. When the school dormitory was being replastered, for example, the students had to sleep for two nights in their parents' rooms. When asked if they enjoyed this experience, most of them answered in the negative. So, too, when the seventh-grade students were told that they could not enter the high school dormitory for one week after the beginning of the school term, they insisted upon remaining in the grade school dormitory, rather than moving into their parents' rooms.

Hostility. Despite the preceding discussion, it should be stressed that the relation of the child to his parent is not free from hostility. On the contrary, some children have been observed to express negative and hostile feelings toward their parents. Occasionally a child may refuse to go to the parental rooms in the evening, and may visit his nurse's room instead. One five-year-old girl always refuses to visit her parents, although no one knows the reason for her rejection of them. When her parents come to fetch her, she refuses to leave with them and prefers instead to remain with the nurse. Still another child expresses rather direct hostility toward his mother.

Ephraim (four years), according to the nurses, is deeply attached to his father. One day he was speaking of his parents and said, "I belong to my father and the animals belong to my mother."

[6] By identifying with his parents and with their room, the child is, at the same time, emphasizing a social group whose structural significance in the kibbutz is minimal — the family. For the child there are at least two important groups: one is comprised of those children and adults with whom he interacts in the nursery; the other is comprised of those children and adults with whom he interacts in his parental room. And for the child the latter is both a structural, as well as a functional, unit.

If we are correct in inferring that "animals" equal this boy's siblings, then the statement indicates not only hostility toward the mother, but also hostility towards siblings. The most blatant expression of dislike occurs in the example below.

The teacher of the fourth grade is discussing parent-child relationships with the class, and comments that all children love their parents. Amir, who rarely speaks in class, speaks up to deny this, and says he does not love his parents.

Such expressions of hostility occur infrequently, however, and are negligible compared to the positive attitudes.

Insecurity. Since the child reacts to his parents and apparently perceives them in a manner similar to that with which he reacts to and perceives his nurse — he responds to the presence of both with joy and affection, he seeks comfort and protection from both, he identifies with both, and he may on occasion be hostile to both — what then is the difference between the child's relations with his nurse and with his parents? If emotions such as joy, love, or pride can be described in quantitative terms, we may state that the child responds to his parent with *more* joy, with *more* love, with *more* pride than he does to his nurse. The intensity of the child's attachment is evidenced most strongly by his reactions to the absence of his parents, to the birth of a sibling, and in the behavior of those children whose mothers are also nurses.

There are three types of parental absences to which a kibbutz child may be exposed. These are the daily separation, temporary absences of the parent from the kibbutz, and permanent absence resulting from parental death or resignation from the kibbutz.

The child's feelings about the daily separation from his parents may be inferred from two sets of observations. The first is that most children appear to be content in their groups, which would seem to indicate that they are not disturbed by parental absence. But, as has been noted above, many children seek out their parents — more particularly, their mothers — during the day for no immediate or specific reason; and the frequency and regularity with which many children leave their groups to seek out their mothers is probably an indication either of dissatisfaction with the group situation or of insecurity about the mother, or of both. A few mothers say that all the children under the age of three are insecure because of the mother's absence, and one such mother asked to be assigned to a work-position that would place her near her young son's dwelling. When she first began to work there, her son came every day to make sure she was there. After a few weeks, however, he took her presence for granted, and no longer visited her daily. This mother felt that her nearby presence gave her son a security he had previously lacked. In short, the daily absence of the parents is disturbing for at least some of the children, which in turn may be interpreted as a measure of the latters' attachment to them.

How the child feels about the temporary absence of his parents is quite clear. Parental absence of a few days brings about no observable change in the behavior of the older children, although it may affect the infants. Babies whose parents are away from the kibbutz for only a few days behave no differently, so far as gross observation of behavior can reveal, but one infants' nurse is of the opinion that subtle changes in such babies' behavior always take place — changes which she cannot describe but which she feels are there — and particularly during the afternoon visiting hours. It is this nurse's conclusion, after many years of experience, that babies are always unhappy when their parents go away, even for a short time.

Although apparently unaffected by a brief absence, the absence of one or both parents for a period of more than a few days brings about a number of changes in the older child's behavior. Some reactions of children to such separations are illustrated below.

The most disturbed child in his group is Yitzhak (four years), and he has had the least satisfactory family life. One of his parents has always been absent from the kibbutz — his mother for training in the city, his father for army service. Both were absent together for over two months when he was three years old. He is a constant thumb-sucker and is a social isolate, withdrawn. He occasionally interacts with the other children, but only to irritate them and to elicit their physical aggression. He is afraid of them and never retaliates.

Avram (three and one-half years) is the most aggressive child in his group. His mother was away for six months, returned only a short time ago. After her departure, he became enuretic, although he had been continent before. Prior to her absence, he had been no more aggressive than the other children; indeed, immediately following her departure, he became quite passive and constantly asked the nurse, "Am I a good boy?" The nurse tried to console him for his mother's absence, and would take him to her room after work. When they went on a hike,

Avram would insist on walking next to her and would cry as soon as she left him. He became jealous of the nurse's own child, and even today threatens to kill him or remarks that he is "not sweet."

Shortly after his mother left, he appeared to have forgotten her very existence. One day he told another child that her mother was really his mother. When the nurse pointed out that he had his own mother, he said, "No, I don't have a mother any more."

A few months before his mother returned, he became extremely aggressive, and this has continued up to the present time. That he is still insecure is shown by other symptoms as well. For one thing, he visits his mother at her work at every opportunity. For another, he still demands enormous amounts of love from his nurse, asking her many times a day if she loves him. Often when he awakens in the morning he tells her that, "Today I'll be sweet." The other day, when we all went for a hike, we passed the mail truck. When the nurse asked what the truck was for, Avram answered, "To bring me letters from my mother."

During the course of this study, we were able to observe Amir (twenty months), whose mother was away for six weeks. His father works outside the kibbutz, and comes home only on weekends. The nurse cared for the boy during the week, taking him to her room and putting him to bed at night. During the mother's absence, the father remarked to the observer that his son seemed very sad these days, but that he did not think it had anything to do with the absence of the mother, for Amir never mentioned her! The nurse, however, noted that the boy was now "afraid of all new people," and that since his mother went away, "it has been terrible for him." Amir exhibited two signs of disturbance during his mother's absence — he became the most aggressive child in the kevutza, and he spent a great deal of his time sleeping. His aggression continued after his mother's return; his need to sleep diminished considerably. When his mother returned, Amir either did not or would not recognize her. By the second day, however, he greeted her joyfully when she came to visit him.

The following excerpt from the diary of a kibbutz mother also reveals how painfully a child can be affected by prolonged parental absence. In this case, both parents were away for several weeks. The boy was approximately two years old at the time of the incident. His highly perceptive mother writes:

We have just returned to Kiryat Yedidim. Our absence was very painful for Yaakov. The nurse tells me that many evenings he did not sleep. One night the watchman found him standing in front of our door, with his thumb in his mouth. When SHLOMO (the father, who returned a week before the mother) came home, Yaakov would not let him leave the house in the evening, and cried when he did leave. When I returned, Yaakov did not recognize me, and he ran to SHLOMO. Now when I leave him in the evening, he always asks me: "You'll never leave me again, never?" He has deep fears about being left alone again. He has begun to suck his thumb . . . I have to stay with him at night until he falls asleep.

The same boy reacted with anger when his father went on a trip at a later date. The child, now a few months older, says to his mother:

Father went to Tel Aviv. All the children will be very angry with my father, and father is *fooia* . . . (His mother asks if *he* is angry with his father, and he says) . . . All the children will be angry with Father.

These examples reveal that any temporary separation from either one or both parents may be highly disturbing to the child, who may express his disturbance in a number of ways — with fear, guilt, aggression, withdrawal, enuresis, thumb-sucking. Many of these symptoms, furthermore, continue long after the parent has returned. This disturbance, again, is a measure of the intensity of the child's attachment to his parents.

There are a few children in this age range who have experienced a permanent separation from one parent, the father, either through death or divorce (followed by departure from the kibbutz). From the behavior of such children, we may infer that the presence of *both* parents is important for the child in the kibbutz. For example, Tamar (two and one-half years), whose father died before her birth, is the only child in her kevutza who did not establish a relationship with the observer. That Tamar, even at this young age, realizes that she has no father and suffers in this knowledge is illustrated by the fantasy she once expressed to the nurse. "You know," she told the nurse, "I have no father now. But once my father and I went for a walk, and we went into the fields." (The nurse did not know what to say to the girl, and finally answered that that was right — that *once* her father was alive and with her.) Tamar later repeated her fantasy to the other children.

It might be noted that the other children express confusion and curiosity about a child whose parent is dead, and their questions indicate at least some anxiety on their part. Two-year-old Chava one day asked her mother, "Where is Tamar's Daddy? He is not good!" The five-year-olds in another group frequently spoke about the fact that Shaul had no father. They would ask him why this is so, and finally Shaul asked the nurse, who explained it to him.

The absence of a parent because of divorce can be as disturbing as absence through death:

The parents of Amnon (five years) have been divorced since his infancy, and his father does not live in the kibbutz. Until quite recently, Amnon wet his bed every night, except when his father came to visit him. Recently, this pattern has been reversed. Amnon is now continent and wets his bed only during his father's visits (aggression against father?).

From the great disturbance that the absence of the parent causes the child, it seems quite clear that the latter's relationship to his parent is an intensely emotional one and that the parent is the child's most important love object. Another measure of the intensity of the child's attachment to his parents is provided by the behavior of those children whose mothers are also nurses. Such children visit their mothers every day, often several times a day, and their behavior during these visits indicates that they view their mother's charges as a threat to their own relationship with her. The kevutza of one two-year-old, for example, occupied a house immediately next to the house in which his mother worked as a nurse. He thus saw her caring for children younger than he all through the day. He became so upset by this, and cried so whenever he saw his mother, that she demanded that her son's kevutza be moved to another dwelling where he would not be able to observe her so frequently.

That a child should become highly disturbed by the daily observation of his mother's persistent devotion to eight other children, rather than to himself, is understandable. But it is understandable *only* if he is deeply attached to her and desires her love. For only then is her devotion to the other children perceived by him as a threat to himself; and the more threatening he perceives her devotion to the other children, the more intense, we may infer, is his attachment to her.

The behavior of the child in such a situation not only reveals the intensity of the child's attachment to his parents, but, as in the case of parental absence, it also points to an important source of emotional disturbance in kibbutz children — the child's perception of his mother's maternal behavior toward other children. And this disturbance is increased by the behavior of the mothers. Many mothers who are nurses discourage their children from visiting them at work: first, because many realize that it is disturbing for their children, and, second, because such children — especially when they are very young — interfere with their work. Occasionally such a nurse will become so irritated by her child's behavior — nagging, whining, interfering, or often aggressing — that she will scold her child, telling him to leave and not to come again. Thus, such a child may easily come to feel that his mother's charges are preferred to him. Such a situation is, in a sense, an extended-sibling relationship.

It has already been noted that, as a general rule, parents lavish their attention on the younger sibling, who is almost always the favorite child. Hence the reaction of the older child to what we have termed his "dethronement" is an excellent measure of his attachment to his parents. If he is deeply attached to his parents, he will be greatly disturbed by the new sibling, who is obviously a threat to the continuation of his parents' love. If he is not greatly attached to his parents, the new sibling will not be perceived as a threat and, hence, the child should show few signs of disturbance.

All evidence points to the same conclusion: sibling rivalry (and its concomitant symptoms) is not only found in the kibbutz, but it is very intense. As might be predicted from the parents' preference for the younger child, however, sibling rivalry is typically asymmetrical — in general the older siblings are hostile toward the younger.

That parents are aware of sibling rivalry in their children is revealed by the Questionnaire. In answering the question, "Do you observe sibling rivalry in your children?," the majority indicated that they did: ten of the thirteen parents with two or more children checked "definitely yes" or "perhaps yes." And when these same respondents were asked, "Did your child experience a crisis at the birth of a younger sibling?," their responses were similar: eight of the thirteen checked "definitely yes" or "perhaps yes."

It is comparatively simple to document these figures with both observations and interview data. Hostility toward a younger sibling often begins at the birth of the new baby. Amir (three years) refused to enter his parents' room when the baby was there; his parents could not even mention the baby's name without his becoming upset. Rachel (four years) wanted very much for her mother to have another baby. But after its birth, she begged her father not to go to the Nursery, but to remain with her. Ziva (four years) reacted with great anxiety when a sibling was born. She stopped all creative work (drawing, coloring, and so on), could not perform physical exercises, and required help for every task. She was so hostile toward the baby that her parents were unable to leave the two alone together and feared that Ziva might literally kill the baby. If she learned that the baby was in her parents' room, she would refuse to go there. Shula (ten years), whose troubles began when her baby sister was born two years ago, has become neurasthenic. Her ambivalence to the baby may be seen in almost all their interactions, of which the following example is typical.

Shula's mother is walking with the baby. Shula sees them, runs to them, and kisses the baby many times, accompanied by exaggerated statements of love. The baby hits her in the face with a piece of bread, and she jumps up, complaining to her mother about how badly the baby treats her.

These examples are typical of the reaction of a young kibbutz child to a new sibling, and typify the anxiety that is aroused by this experience. There are instances, however, of much greater and persistent disturbance which are presented in the following case histories. These cases are atypical in their extremity — but by their very extremity they indicate how deeply attached some children are to their parents, and how greatly disturbed they become when they believe they have lost the love of their parents.

Ephraim (five years) is jealous of his baby brother, and has developed hostile feelings toward his mother — for she has transferred her affection from him to the baby. He once told his nurse, "Mother is so irritable; she is always yelling at me." He loves his father intensely, and when the latter went on vacation, he refused to visit his mother and went to his nurse's room instead. When she asked him why he did not go to his parents' room, he replied that his father was away. The nurse remarked that his mother was at home, and Ephraim replied, "She's with the baby, and that does not interest me at all." When the baby is in the same room with him, he becomes unhappy and withdrawn, and returns to his normal self only after she has left. His problem has become intensified now that the baby is older and has begun to receive more attention from the father. Thus Ephraim has lost his mother and is in the process of losing his father. When the baby was born, Erphraim became enuretic. This has improved recently, and he wets his bed only when his nurse is away from the kevutza for more than a day. His mother says that she knows Ephraim's incontinence is a result of her neglect, but she claims that her work and her baby consume all her energies and time so that none are left for Ephraim.

Amir and Yehuda (seven years) are twins. When they were babies, Amir was beautiful, Yehuda unattractive and physically weak. Everyone — parents and relatives — preferred Amir to Yehuda. Their older sister, for example, would go to the children's house and, ignoring Yehuda, return with only Amir. An aunt made a beautiful jacket for Amir, but nothing for Yehuda. As the twins grew older, however, the situation changed. Yehuda was discovered to be quite bright and Amir somewhat retarded. The parental attitudes reversed themselves completely, and Yehuda became the favorite. The parents would often brag about Yehuda in the presence of Amir.

For obvious reasons, the twins did not relate well to each other, and their nurse tried to separate them as much as possible — putting them to sleep in different rooms, seating them at different tables, etc. But when the nurse left the kevutza for a short period, the substitute nurse decided to put the twins together — an act which the twins' nurse describes as "the beginning of the end." For Amir would do nothing without first assuring himself that Yehuda was also doing it, and he insisted on imitating all Yehuda's behavior.

When the kevutza began its first formal education, Yehuda learned rapidly — Amir not at all. He became absorbed in his own fantasy world and was oblivious to external stimuli. He had, moreover, a low level of frustration tolerance, crying frequently. It was decided to transfer Amir from the first grade to the Kindergarten, where he became the oldest child in the group.

Since the transfer, Amir has become much better adjusted. The nurse has tried to give him responsibilities to make him feel important, and he has accepted these responsibilities with pride. For the first time since infancy, Amir is beginning to feel loved and accepted. Originally, when he was transferred, he complained to the nurse that the other children did not love him. The nurse finally succeeded in convincing him that they did, although this was difficult to do, not only because in actuality the other children are ambivalent to Amir, but because his need and demands for love are so great. At the same time, Amir has ambivalent feelings toward the other children, and spends much time scolding them and "tattling" on them to the nurse.

One day, during the course of this study, the children all wrote letters for their game of "post-office." Amir wrote a one-line letter: "RUTHI (the nurse) loves me." Thus Amir has at last found one person who can help him, but his desire for parental love is still frustrated, and it is still intense. One day, for example, the nurse and Amir were walking down the path when they met Yehuda. Amir asked where their father was, and Yehuda replied that he was at home. Amir asked, and repeated the same question over and over again, "Did he ask about me? Did he ask where I was?"

Chaviva (seven years) is the second of three children, and since the birth of her two-year-old brother, she has been completely ignored by her parents. She is always seen hanging in the background while her parents lavish their attention on the younger child. In spite of this rejection, she visits her brother every day in his kevutza, and spends

more time with his group than she does in her own group. When she
visits, she assumes the role of a parent-nurse towards her brother —
dressing him, teaching him to draw, playing with him, and watching
over him when the nurse is not present. She also assists the other
toddlers, and cares for them as she does for her brother. Since she
spends so much time with her brother, Chaviva does not have to interact with the members of her own kevutza. Thus, in one sense, her
behavior represents a retreat from her age-peers, and an opportunity to
regress to her brother's age and still be superior to him.

Yaffa (eight years), the most disturbed child in the school, is probably schizophrenic. Her parents never gave her much love or
affection, and when her brother was born (when Yaffa was three), they
withdrew the little they had given her previously. Her mother claims
that she does not have time to devote to her, and her father does not
even plead this excuse — he is simply not interested. When her teacher
attempted to speak to the parents about Yaffa's problems, her father
refused to listen. As her nurse expresses it, "Yaffa is like an abandoned
child." The extent to which she feels abandoned may be gauged by her
request that her nurse become her mother. According to the nurse,
this is the first time that a child has made such a request.[7]

There are, then, a number of symptoms that seem to occur as
a result of sibling rivalry and of real or imagined rejection by the
parent. These symptoms — hostility, withdrawal, regression, anxiety — are in general the same symptoms that children manifest
when they are separated from their parents. We would suggest
that both situations are perceived by the child as parental deprivation, and that this deprivation is as intensely painful as the former
parental gratification was pleasurable. Indeed, the latter gratification is responsible for the child's ultimate perception of his situation as a depriving one.

It should be noted that the effects of sibling rivalry are, if
anything, stronger among the school children than among those
of preschool age. Because the births of children in the average
kibbutz family are often widely spaced, many children in the
younger grades have only recently acquired a new sibling. And
since the period of indulgence and high nurturance has been relatively long, the "rejection" attendant upon the birth of a sibling,
and the consequent frustration, is concomitantly severe. Almost
all emotional problems in this group can be traced to the arrival

---

[7] Some time after the completion of this study, this child was placed under
psychiatric care with a diagnosis of schizophrenia.

of a sibling and the attendant rejection of the older sibling. The others are associated with rejecting parents in general.

In conclusion, the child's attachment to his parents is a strong one, and any threat to it may lead to emotional disturbance. We know of no instance in which an "emotionally adjusted" child has impaired relations with his parents, or in which an emotionally disturbed child has unimpaired relations with his parents.

PART III · THE FIRST YEAR

CHAPTER 6 · INFANCY

In Kiryat Yedidim the decision to have a baby is an individual matter. Critics of the movement often charge that, at least in the early days, parents had to obtain permission from the kibbutz to have a child. The chaverim deny this, saying that such a decision was always the individual's rather than the group's. In those days, however, many couples had a tacit agreement not to have children too soon or, at least, to limit themselves to one or two children. These decisions were based on a number of considerations. First, there were a few settlers who came to Palestine with the "emancipated" idea of not having any children at all. This was a reaction to the large families they had known in Europe and to the impossibility of providing a good education for so many children. Second, and more important, were the difficult conditions under which the pioneers lived in the early days of the kibbutz. The food shortage, the lack of adequate housing, and the difficult climate convinced many chaverim that it would be unfair to have children under such conditions. The general instability of the kibbutz, furthermore, created an atmosphere of uncertainty, and chaverim were reluctant to have children until their future on their own land seemed assured. A third important factor was family instability. Many of the original "marriages" were so unstable — "There was really no such thing as a family," commented one chaver — that many chaverim felt that it would be unfair to have children. For all these reasons, the birth rate during the early days of Kiryat Yedidim was low.[1]

[1] It is not unlikely, however, that in those first days it was at least suggested that the kibbutz regulate the birth rate, for it was felt that even individual acts should be discussed and approved by the entire group. Members recall with great amusement the town meeting that was held when the first baby was born in Kiryat Yedidim, for the purpose of selecting a name for "their" child. Similarly, when a certain couple wished to leave the kibbutz in those early days, the town meeting debated whether it should permit their child to leave with them, for many chaverim argued that he was not only a child of his parents, but a child of the kibbutz as well. The child was permitted to leave, of course, but even today any child who leaves the kibbutz because of the resignation of his parents still retains the rights of a kibbutz child. Should he wish to return to study in the high school, for example, he may do so as his birthright.

Today, when physical conditions have improved and family and kibbutz stability seem assured, the birth rate is on the increase. Whereas most of the older families limited themselves to two children, it is predicted that the new generation of sabras will have as many as four or five. For today, as a nurse expressed it, "They don't wait — they get married and settle down to their main job of having children!"

Babies are generally planned in Kiryat Yedidim, and modern contraceptive devices are known and easily available. The authors were informed that some kibbutz women, too embarrassed to request contraceptive devices from the dispensary, do not utilize them, but there is no way to determine the reliability of this report. It is known, however, that unplanned pregnancies do occur and that in the past there was a high incidence of abortion because of all the conditions that inhibited the desire for children.

Abortions are infrequent today for two reasons. The original motives for restricting the population of the kibbutz no longer obtain; and Israeli physicians, we were informed, have an informal agreement among themselves to perform abortions only when absolutely necessary, in order to compensate slightly for the mass slaughter of Jews under Naziism. It should be noted, however, that abortion is legal in Israel, so that it is still possible for a kibbutz woman to obtain an abortion, and she sometimes does. Such abortions, however, are not broadcast and one learns of them only through general gossip. According to such gossip, at least two abortions occurred during our stay in Kiryat Yedidim. In both instances, the women had borne children only a short time before again conceiving, and it was assumed that they did not wish to have their work schedules disrupted so soon again. The fear of illegitimacy is not a motive for abortion, for the kibbutz does not recognize the concept of illegitimacy.[2] There have been a few cases of unknown paternity in the history of Kiryat Yedidim, but the chaverim say — and observation confirms their statements — that there is no prejudice or ill-will felt toward either the mother or the child. Both are treated precisely as are other mothers and children.

As has already been indicated [3] neither the husband nor his wife have any economic anxieties, nor must they make any plans concerning their child's future life. These and other problems that

[2] The State, however, does stigmatize a child born out of wedlock, for, according to Orthodox Jewish law, an illegitimate child has no civil rights.
[3] Spiro, *Kibbutz*, pp. 86–87.

confront prospective parents in our society are unknown in Kiryat Yedidim.

The majority of women in the kibbutz enjoy healthy pregnancies, with few difficulties and little complaint. Some of the older women, however, have had difficulty both in conceiving and in carrying, and this the kibbutz physician attributes to the high incidence of abortion in the past. The regimen followed by a pregnant woman is an individual one, but there are always some general changes in her routine. Until her eighth month of pregnancy there are no changes in her activities. Beginning with the eighth month, her workday is reduced to five hours, although she may continue to work in her regular work assignment. This schedule is highly flexible, however, and depends upon the woman's individual needs and condition.

There is generally no change in the woman's diet until her sixth or seventh month, at which time it is supplemented with an extra egg each day, milk at each meal, and fruit at least once a day. It is of interest to note that this supplement is ostensibly provided for the health of the baby, rather than for the health of the mother. Since there are both a full-time physician and nurse in the kibbutz clinic, the woman can receive medical attention and advice as frequently as she chooses, the frequency of medical attention and examination depending upon the individual.

The casualness of the pregnant woman's regimen is a clue to the kibbutz attitude regarding pregnancy. Although this attitude is highly favorable — for "a child of the kibbutz" will soon be born — pregnancy is regarded as a "normal" condition, and it is assumed that the woman will continue with most of her daily activities. It is further assumed that she has sufficient intelligence to take care of herself and to give up those activities which she finds too taxing. There is thus no air of anxiety or overprotection, and little tendering of advice.

The mother does not enter the hospital, which is about twenty minutes distant from Kiryat Yedidim, until she is certain that she is in labor. She is accompanied either by the kibbutz nurse or by a member of the Health Committee, and she goes either by car or truck. Her husband, however, "goes back to sleep," in the words of one informant, as "the woman does not want him to wait so long in the hospital." Only after the delivery does the father visit the hospital.

Prior to the construction of this hospital — that is, for the first thirteen years of kibbutz existence — babies were born in a neighboring kibbutz under less than optimum conditions. The hospital consisted of a wooden shack which had neither electricity nor running water. There was no resident physician, and the physician from the closest town arrived on horseback.

Except in the case of an unnatural delivery, no anesthetic is used during childbirth. So far as kibbutz women are concerned, this is not important, and they have a tradition of evincing no external signs of pain. There are neither cries nor shouting — behavior which the kibbutz claims to be characteristic of non-kibbutz women — for a chavera would be ashamed to cry. "You can easily distinguish a city woman from a kibbutz woman," commented one informant, "by the degree of self-control displayed." Among kibbutz women, those from Kiryat Yedidim have a reputation for being the most stoic. "If you are from Kiryat Yedidim, you don't cry," is the way it is put, and the women from Kiryat Yedidim are careful to maintain this reputation. One of the mothers told the researchers that her labor pains were so great that she did cry, and as a result she was ashamed "for a long time after."

Following delivery, the mother and child remain in the hospital for five days, although they formerly stayed eight days when the hospital shortage was not so acute. There is no rooming-in system, and the infant remains in the nursery, which no one, except doctors and nurses, may enter.

While still in the hospital, the baby is named by his parents. In the past, names were usually chosen from the Bible or from nature. During the Nazi persecutions, however, infants were named for friends or relatives who were killed in Europe. Now that the sabras are having their own children, there has been a return to the Bible and to nature as sources for names.

Upon returning to the kibbutz, the infant is immediately placed in the Nursery where, if he is a male, he is circumcised whenever the kibbutz doctor "has the time." The mother returns to her room where she is confined for one week. Since her meals are brought to her from the communal kitchen, she leaves her room only to nurse her baby in the Nursery. In the past, a woman received a month's vacation from work following her return from the hospital, but this has since been extended to six weeks. She is given a special diet during this period (not only to help her regain her strength, but, again, to ensure nourishing milk for the baby), and she may have as much food as she wishes. When she returns to work, she works only four or five hours a day, for she nurses her child five times a day. As the mother begins the process of weaning, which is begun usually during the third month and ends at the beginning of the ninth month, she adds one hour to her work schedule for every nursing she eliminates. By the time she has given up all but two nursings, the ones in the morning and evening, she has resumed her regular work schedule, as well as her normal existence in other respects.

Physical setting. We may now look at the Nursery where the baby spends the first year of his life. It should be noted that this is a new building and that its conveniences were not found in the old Nursery which was abandoned only a few years ago. The old one was primitive in many respects. It did not, for example, have running water, so that the nurses had to carry water from the kitchen, a distance of about one city block.

The present Nursery is a long, modern building consisting of six rooms. The first room contains six baby cribs and a chair by each crib for the nursing mother; a waist-high bathtub built into the wall; and a dressing table with drawers for diapers, clothing, and medicine. The second room contains a sink where the dishes are washed; a built-in table for food, liquids, teakettle, and so on; an electric hotplate; and cabinets containing clothing, equipment, and white coats for the nursing mothers. The third room is used as a small playroom, although in times of illness or overcrowding it too may be used to hold one or two beds. It contains a case with a few toys, a low table and four tiny chairs, and a collapsible fence. The fourth room is the bedroom for the older babies, most of whom are in the later stages of weaning. It contains cribs for all the babies this age — seven at the time of the study — a round table where the nurse sits when she feeds the babies, and a bathtub and dressing table. Room five is the bedroom for the oldest babies, already weaned, and it is furnished like the other bedrooms but is smaller. The sixth room is a cloakroom and storage room which, in time of illness or overcrowding, can accommodate a crib or two.

Surrounding the entire Nursery on all four sides is a porch, which is divided into three sections. One section, containing seventeen cribs, is screened and the babies are put here during the day to be in the sun. The second section is not screened and is used as a kind of play-pen or terrace for the older babies. Those who are learning to crawl and to stand are put here in the morning, and here too many parents sit with their babies in the evening. The section of the porch in the rear of the house is used for hanging out hand-laundry and for storing extra furniture.

The physical structure of the Nursery, it is apparent, affords a maximum opportunity for interaction among the babies, for observation and exploration of their world in both its physical and social aspects, and for the development of motor skills. They are not confined within individual cubicles, nor are they separated from each other by partitions of any sort; and the bars of their cribs are spaced widely enough apart so that their view is not obstructed.

These optimum conditions characterize the purely physical aspects of the house as well. The rooms are kept spotlessly clean — for example, the floors are washed twice a day. The large windows permit sunlight and fresh air to enter, and if this is not sufficient, the babies can be placed in the sun on the porch. Food, which is prepared in the children's communal kitchen, is fresh, nutritious, and abundant.

Clothing and toys. Since they are not toilet trained until after they leave the Nursery, the babies wear diapers throughout their entire stay. Rompers are always worn to hold the diaper in place. According to a nurse, pins are not used because they do not wish to give the baby any feeling of restraint, and from experience they have discovered that the babies object to the restraint which the pinned diaper imposes upon them. (A young American immigrant pointed out that the Israeli pins were unreliable, so that it would be dangerous to use them on the babies.)

Although babies are swaddled until the age of three months, the swaddling technique exerts little physical restraint. The swaddling is loose and is tantamount to covering the baby with a "receiving blanket," except that the ends are tucked in at the baby's waist — but loosely, so that it is easily and frequently kicked off. Since the days are generally hot, the babies are usually swaddled only at night. According to one nurse swaddling is practiced for two reasons. It keeps the babies warm, and "they seem to want it," so that after the swaddle is removed the babies begin to wear rompers immediately to take its place.

During the day the babies wear unironed shirts and rompers — their "old" clothes. In the afternoon, however, they are dressed in ironed clothes which are both newer and nicer than the ones they had worn in the morning. As in the case of their parents, the former clothes are called "work clothes" and the latter, "sabbath clothes," a distinction which will be made the rest of their lives. All clothing is communal, except for a few exceptions which have been permitted in the Nursery, as they have in the kibbutz at large. If, for example, a baby receives a sweater as a gift from friends or relatives outside the kibbutz, or if he receives a dress or pair of rompers as a gift from America, that garment may be kept for him alone to wear until he outgrows it. Except for these instances all babies are dressed alike, and there are no sex differences other than those introduced because of gifts. A baby girl, that is, may wear a dress if she receives it as a gift, instead of the usual shirt and rompers. Some mothers, moreover, may tie a ribbon in a baby girl's hair which then distinguishes her from the male infants.

Toys, too, belong to the Nursery, and are played with by all the children. But should a baby receive a gift of say, a cradle gym or a rattle, these will be attached to his crib and will be used by him until he leaves the Nursery. For the most part, toys consist of plastic animals and dolls, with an occasional roller toy, such as a chicken on wheels. Every baby six months or older has at least a cradle gym, wooden beads, or plastic teething discs tied to his bed. Rattles and teething rings are also attached to all the cribs. In general, there are few toys, and there are none of the so-called "educational" toys so popular in the United States today. The nurses complain of this, and say that even the few dolls available are poorly made and difficult to keep clean.

Daily routine. The following schedule is by no means inflexible, but it does, within a small variation, describe the typical day of the Nursery.

5:30–6:00 A.M. — The babies awaken and their pajamas are changed.

6:00–8:30 A.M. — The nursing mothers come to nurse their babies, and the weaned babies are fed by the nurses. After this morning feeding the babies are put in their beds — on the porch in the summer, in their bedrooms in the winter. Those babies who can crawl are put out on the terrace to play. The house is cleaned, the beds changed, and the nurses eat breakfast.

8:30–9:30 A.M. — The babies are bathed by the nurses and their clothes are changed.

9:30–10:30 A.M. — The mothers come to nurse their babies, while non-nursing babies are fed by the nurses.

10:30–1:00 P.M. — The babies are put to sleep either on the porch or in their rooms.

1:00–3:00 P.M. — The babies are fed. After eating, the babies are changed and put back to bed.

3:00–5:30 P.M. — The babies are dressed by the nurses. The younger babies are put back to bed; the older ones are put on the terrace if the weather permits.

5:30–7:00 P.M. — Another feeding. After eating, the babies are taken by their parents, who either play with them in and around the Nursery or take them to their rooms.

7:00 P.M. — Bedtime.

10:00 P.M. — Feeding for the younger babies who still have a night nursing.

INTERACTION

There are various categories of persons with whom the infants interact and from whom, presumably, they learn. Their most frequent contact is with the nurses.

Nurses. Aside from their mothers, the infants are in the care of two full-time, trained nurses, one trained nurse who works only a half-day, and one untrained nurse. The latter serves as a replacement for any regular nurse who may be absent. The nurses' schedules are staggered (so that not all are present all the time) to ensure the presence of at least one nurse from the time the babies awaken in the morning until their parents visit them in the evening. There are three nurses on duty in the early morning, one in the late morning and early afternoon, and two in the late afternoon. The nurses' workday ends shortly after the parents arrive to visit their babies. There is no nurse on duty in any children's house at night. There is, however, a night watch (*shomeret lailah*) who goes from house to house to check on all the children. Each round requires approximately one hour. Babies (with the exception of nursing infants) awaken infrequently at night, but when they do, the watch attempts to pacify them. She also covers those whose blankets have slipped off, and in general sees that their needs are met. Should a nursing infant cry from hunger long before his mother is scheduled to feed him, she will call the mother.

The primary duties of the nurse are, necessarily, of a caretaking nature. Almost her entire day is devoted to caring for the physical needs of seventeen babies and to cleaning the house. The affection she is able to bestow on her charges must therefore always come in the course of these caretaking duties. Most nurses perform their duties with a maximum of warmth and affection, but occasionally a nurse cares for a baby in a perfunctory manner, with a minimum of stimulation for the baby. The following illustrates this perfunctory behavior.

SHULAMIT comes on the terrace, lifts Rachel (eleven months) who grins, laughs eagerly . . . Inside SHULAMIT undresses her, puts her in the tub . . . Rachel laughs when SHULAMIT soaps her . . . SHULAMIT says to me that Rachel is ticklish — otherwise she doesn't say much . . . Rachel splashes a little, laughs when soaped and rinsed . . . While drying her, SHULAMIT gives Rachel a comb to play with. She puts it in her mouth . . . SHULAMIT hums while dressing Rachel, does not talk or play with her.

It should be remembered that all the babies are bathed at the same hour, so that the nurse cannot devote much time to each baby. Nevertheless, the absence of conversation, play, and cuddling is conspicuous in this case as compared with the more typical behavior of the nurses. The bath period, including the dressing of the baby after his bath, is the time of day when, theoretically, the nurses deliberately play with the babies. Because most of the nurse's interaction with the babies involves the satisfaction of a physical need, play is a byproduct of this contact. The bath period, however (as well as the dressing period in the afternoon), is recognized as a play period and, according to the head nurse, some nurses actually make a game of the bath itself. This latter statement is true in the sense that the nurse will frequently talk and sing to the baby, as well as coo and caress him, while she bathes him. As a result most babies enjoy their baths, as their smiles and laughter indicate.

Perfunctory care may be found in feeding as well as in bathing:

Rachel (eleven months) is asleep at 10:00. Nurse comes to feed her, wakes her — she was not in a deep sleep. Rachel is crabby, whines. Nurse tells her to come and eat, takes her to other room; Rachel sits on her lap. She drinks greedily from cup, stops for breath only twice . . . Nurse gives last few mouthfuls with a spoon. Rachel eats it well, then gets mashed potatoes and a little meatball . . . Rachel takes, then spits out a little meat, then some potatoes . . . (I am not sure that nurse allows her enough time to swallow each mouthful) . . . In approximately ten minutes from time she began to eat, Rachel is back in bed.

Again the reality of having to feed all the children within a limited time period prevents the nurse from lingering long with each one. Still, the feeding described is unusually rapid and characterized by little interaction between nurse and baby.

Compare these two perfunctory cases of bathing and feeding with two more warm and affectionate examples. It should be noted that in all these illustrations the duties are performed rapidly, but they are quite different qualitatively.

MALKA undresses Danny (six months) . . . He laughs. She says, "He feels that I love him" . . . She pats him, kisses his body . . . In tub he is afraid. MALKA reassures him, tells him it is not hot . . . in a second he laughs and splashes . . . while drying him MALKA talks to him. She coos, he smiles back . . . MALKA gives him nosedrops while she talks . . . He takes it quietly . . . grins . . . Back to bed with a kiss.

MALKA feeds Giora (ten months) on her lap . . . She hugs him, talks to him . . . He laughs, giggles excitedly . . . MALKA says Giora does not want to eat fast, just slow . . . She sings to him, sings his name . . . MALKA tells him to "finish already" . . . then jabbers to him, sings, hugs him, pats him . . . He laughs and laughs.

In general, then, nurses are warm and affectionate with the babies; and it may be assumed that the attitudes of love and permissiveness that pervade the Nursery ensure a high level of gratification for the babies, despite the fact that their opportunities to interact with the nurses are usually limited to those which arise in the process of caretaking. If a baby experiences frustration, therefore, it is primarily because his individual needs cannot always be satisfied in a system based on routine. Differences in need are often great, not only because each infant has his own rhythms, but because there is an age difference of one year separating the youngest from the oldest; and yet they are all expected to conform to the same schedule.

The most frequent occasion for frustration as a result of institutional routine is prolonged crying without attention. Ideally, say the nurses, a baby is not allowed to cry, and when he does a nurse always goes to see what is wrong. This statement is only partially true, however, and often depends upon the particular nurse and the particular baby. An experienced nurse, such as the head nurse, can identify every baby by, and knows the meaning of, his cry. Hence she can distinguish between serious and other kinds of crying and can regulate her response accordingly. Others not so experienced may allow serious cries to go unheeded for some time. The nurses' statement is true, moreover, if a nurse happens to be in the room where the baby is crying. If, however, she is busy elsewhere and the cry does not sound too serious to her, she may wait five or ten minutes — or even longer — before she goes to see what is wrong. For example,

Ron (five months) cries loudly for ten minutes before nurse comes. She puts him on his stomach, and he stops crying . . . In a few minutes, he cries again . . . No one comes . . . In five minutes he cries himself to sleep . . . Awakens in a few minutes, cries again . . . Face is red from crying . . . Nurse comes in four minutes, puts him on his back . . . He stops crying, and falls asleep.

Yaakov (nine months) is in isolation, sick . . . cries and cries . . . no one goes to him . . . RACHEL explains that he is spoiled . . . Fifteen minutes later she takes him a cup of cereal . . . stops crying.

It should be noted in these examples that the nurse not only waits for some time before she attends to the baby's needs, but that her attention consists in a mechanical manipulation of the baby rather than of the giving of warmth and affection. Although this is entirely understandable in terms of the nurse's busy routine, the baby's emotional needs may still remain unsatisfied.

On the other hand, nurses attempt to recognize individual differences and to deal with them to the extent that their schedule permits them to do so. If a baby cries from hunger much before his scheduled feeding, the nurse may bring him his food early. So, too, if an infant finds it difficult to sleep when other babies are present, an attempt is made to give him some privacy. When she finished feeding Shula, for example, LEAH was about to put her in her room when she noticed that Shimon, sleeping in the same room, was rocking in his sleep.

She cannot, says LEAH, put Shula in there now, for Shimon will wake up. She says that Shimon cannot sleep when others are around — he must be alone, for he is a "prince." That is, he is "spoiled somehow" and refuses to sleep when others are in the room. So LEAH takes Shula back to her crib on the porch.

The parents. We have noted that the mother of a young infant has considerably more contact with him at this age than she will when he is older, for she comes to the Nursery several times a day to nurse. She may, furthermore, visit her baby at other times of the day as well, if she happens to be free. But although the mother's primary contacts with her infant occur during the feeding period, the interaction between mother and child is not confined solely to nursing. For at these times, she also changes her baby's diaper, plays with him, bathes him if necessary, and puts him back to sleep. The average mother spends from forty-five minutes to one hour with her baby when she comes to nurse him. Thus the infant has frequent and intimate contact with his mother, and it is not surprising therefore that she is the first individual for whom he shows recognition.

In the past, this characterization of the mother-infant relationship would not have applied. Until about fifteen years ago, the Nursery was viewed as a hospital, in which order and cleanliness reigned supreme. The mother was allowed to visit her baby only at the scheduled feeding periods, and when she arrived the nurse had prepared everything for her — the baby was already bathed and his diaper had been changed. The present head nurse, upon assuming her position, insisted that the Nursery be a "house" and not a "hospital," and that the mothers be allowed to care for their infants in other ways as well. At first, some nurses resisted these changes, for the order that had formerly prevailed was destroyed. Even a few mothers objected, for they had been accustomed to the nurses' doing everything for them. It is apparent, however, that today almost every mother enjoys the opportunity to care for her baby when she visits him. While she does not attempt to prolong the feeding time unduly, neither does she attempt to shorten it by encouraging the baby to "hurry up" or by failing to "play" with him, change his diaper, and stay with him a few minutes after returning him to his crib.

Today, too, fathers are encouraged to visit their infants whenever they please, although permission to enter the room during nursing depends upon the attitudes of the mothers who are nursing at that time.[4] Aside from those infrequent occasions when a father, arriving early in the evening, may undertake to feed his baby, his sole role from the very beginning is that of playmate to his child. In general, it may be said that most fathers display an interest in their infants immediately, holding them, bouncing them, discussing with their wives and the other mothers their baby's particular characteristics, and proudly heralding the appearance of each new accomplishment. This interest in and interaction with the baby increases as the infant develops new skills.

Peers. A source of constant stimulation for the baby is his peer-group. The babies are together the entire day. They sleep in the same rooms, eat at the same time, and play on the floor together. They stimulate each other. Babies were observed to recognize and to be aware of individual babies by the age of five months. By this age they look at other babies and show definite signs of awareness such as laughing, babbling, waving of arms and legs, and touching. This awareness, of course, increases with age.[5] The following excerpts from the process records are typical of the interaction among the babies. The first excerpt occurs on the terrace. These babies are not in their cribs.

[4] The group of nursing mothers observed during this study did not object to the presence of a father of a nursing infant. They did object, however, to the suggestion that I — not a member of "the family" — be present.

[5] The recognition of adults is earlier. According to the head nurse, an infant can recognize his mother during the second month and the head nurse by the end of that month.

Uzi (ten months) and Yaakov (nine months) are on the porch, looking at each other . . . Uzi touches Yaakov with his hand, they touch each other's hands and jabber . . . Giora (ten months) lies on his stomach, Amir (twelve months) crawls to him, lies on stomach next to him . . . Giora touches him, both wave their arms . . . Rachel (eleven months) crawls to Giora, sits by him, rocks, stares at him, pokes his nose with her finger . . . She puts her head on the floor, Giora touches it . . . Rachel stares and stares at him . . . he sucks . . . Rachel puts her fingers in her mouth . . . Rachel sits up, Giora reaches for her hand, shakes it . . . Giora rolls over, touches her head and arm . . . Rachel crawls away from Giora . . . crawls to Avshalom (eleven months) and Amir, "hugs" him . . . Yaakov is almost crawling, gets to Giora, touches him, holds his hand . . . Giora jabbers, touches Yaakov's foot . . . Yaakov crawls away . . . Uzi tadpoles to Yaakov, they sit on each other, touch each other, feel each other . . .

The following incident occurs while the babies are in their beds on the porch. When the cribs are on the porch they are close enough to each other so that the babies can touch each other. (The babies' rocking brings the cribs into contact with each other.)

Amir (twelve months) and Avshalom (eleven months) stand facing each other . . . Amir laughs, hits Avshalom's face. Avshalom laughs . . . Yitzhak (eight months) and Ron (six months) look at each other, babble . . . Ron gets excited, laughs . . . Avshalom and Amir sit . . . Amir puts hands through rails of bed, tries to reach Avshalom . . . Yaakov laughs . . . Giora (ten months) lies on back, waves his limbs, talks to himself . . . Tamar (eight months) begins to cry . . . Naomi (eight months) watches Giora . . . Yitzhak waves, laughs, kicks his leg . . . Avshalom and Amir stand facing each other, Avshalom pokes Amir's eye, hits his head. Amir hits Avshalom . . . They touch each others' faces and hands, laugh, sit down . . . Stand again, "hug" each other . . . Amir jabbers, laughs to Avshalom . . . Avshalom sits and rocks . . . Amir lies down . . . They stand, make "raspberries" at each other . . . Amir lies down . . . Avshalom still stands . . .

There is much evidence to indicate that after the babies become adjusted to the group, they feel secure within it and object to being separated from it. The babies seldom cry in the evening when the adults leave the Nursery, for example, and it is not an unlikely hypothesis that the presence of their group is at least partially responsible for this behavior.

That the babies feel most secure when in the presence of their peers may be inferred from other evidence as well. The babies object to being separated from the group, for example, whether the separation takes the form of isolation in a separate room within the Nursery or in their parental rooms. One baby became so upset when her bed was moved to another room that she refused to nurse. Another baby, when compelled to stay in his parents' room for a short time because the other babies in his group were ill, cried most of the time and would not permit his parents to leave the room. This behavior disappeared as soon as he returned to the Nursery. Babies show signs of disturbance, moreover, even when their cribs are rearranged so that they are no longer near the babies with whom they had previously interacted.

This attachment to the group is most perceptible in the case of the older babies, those ten months and older, who have already begun to form their own selective in-group. They play most frequently with each other, and generally play within an area which makes them visibly a social group.[6] Indeed, a baby no more than a month younger than they has difficulty in becoming part of the group. They interact with him much less frequently than with each other, and it may take several days before he is completely accepted.

SOME BEHAVIOR SYSTEMS AND THEIR SOCIALIZATION

Motor behavior. At the time of observation, there were seventeen babies in the Nursery — twelve males and five females, who ranged in age from four days to twelve months. All were considered to be normal and healthy babies, both in terms of nurses' reports and of the researchers' observations based on American norms.

There appears to be little difference between the motor development of American infants and the oldest kibbutz infants. According to the norms established by Gesell,[7] American infants sit alone and creep by forty weeks. By twelve months, the American infant stands and cruises. At the time of our observations in the Nursery, three children, ages ten months, ten and one-half months, and eleven and one-half months, respectively, were already standing and cruising. They also sat alone and crawled. A fourth infant stood at nine months and began to creep at that age. He could

[6] Their contacts with each other are more frequent than their contacts with the younger babies, for these older babies sleep in a separate room, their cribs are placed together on the porch, and they are more often placed on the terrace to play.

[7] A. Gesell and C. S. Amatruda, *Developmental Diagnosis* (New York: Hoeber, 1941). A. Gesell et al. *The First Five Years of Life* (New York: Harper, 1940).

also sit alone. A fifth baby was able to crawl at eight months, and at nine months was making definite attempts to stand. He was already able to sit without support. One nine-month-old baby began to raise his head and chest at that age, and at ten months began to scoot. This case of retardation was not viewed by the nurses as cause for alarm, as it was felt that his retardation was due to his unusually large head — merely too large for him to support as yet.[8] Of the three other babies in the last quarter of their first year, one was trying to sit alone at eight months, and it was obvious that she would soon be successful in her attempts; the other two, aged nine months, did not yet sit alone, crawl, or stand. They could, however, roll over, raise their heads and chests, and showed definite signs of alertness and interest in their surroundings.

Some kibbutz mothers claim that living in a group accelerates the maturation processes of the babies, for they stimulate each other to talk, stand, and walk, so that kibbutz babies are precocious by comparison with city children in the development of these behaviors. Our observations did not substantiate these claims. For if the infants who were in the Nursery at the time of our study may be said to have constituted a representative sample of kibbutz infants, then the above summary of motor development would seem to disconfirm the hypothesis that communal living accelerates the process of motor development.[9] Nor is there any evidence for the converse hypothesis — that lack of adult encouragement retards such development. Although babies are permitted to develop motor skills at their own pace without special urging or stimulation from the nurses, the observations indicate that their rate of development conforms to American norms. (It is our impression, however, that although the nurses do not encourage the development of motor skills, the parents do.)

As for language development, no words were actually used by any infant, although many parents claimed that their babies could say "a-ba" ("Daddy"), and so the older ones could — but

[8] Although the infant's mother expressed some concern, she was reminded by the nurse that her older child had also had this difficulty as an infant, but had later been able to catch up with his age group.

[9] There does seem to be some indication in the older groups of acceleration in both motor and social development as a result of group living. However, the influence is from the older children in the group to the younger; the younger attempt to emulate the older children. This matching behavior is particularly pronounced when two groups of slightly different ages are combined into one; the nurses report that there is almost always a rapid spurt in the development of the younger children as a result.

there is no evidence that they actually used it in reference to their fathers. Babbling and jabbering appeared to be normal, however.[10]

Feeding. All kibbutz mothers, according to a nurse, are eager to nurse their children (although there was one exception to this rule in the recent past) and they do "anything they can" in order to have milk. Mothers, furthermore, wish to defer complete weaning as long as possible. The mothers have a "myth," says one nurse, that mother's milk is the best food for babies, so that even after the babies are eating solids, some mothers insist on nursing their babies before giving them the solids. For some mothers, moreover, nursing is a source of personal gratification, and they are reluctant to give it up even though their babies may receive little nourishment from the milk.

Today, the entire process of nursing, weaning, and self-feeding is relaxed and permissive. But this was not true in the past. Until approximately ten years prior to this study, babies were forced to eat even if they were not hungry, and many feeding problems resulted from this policy. The policy of forcing an infant to nurse was based on the physician's insistence that every baby should weigh at least eleven kilos at the age of one year.[11]

In the past, moreover, the kibbutz ideal of equality was applied as strictly to infants as it was to adults. Since it was believed, for example, that all babies should weigh the same number of

---

[10] Since, lacking data, motor and verbal development are not discussed in later chapters dealing with the older children, a few observations about the role of the nurse may be made here. Again, as in the Nursery, little attempt is made by the nurses to hasten their development. Each child is permitted to develop such skills at his own pace, and, indeed, one occasionally has the impression that the nurse's behavior tends to discourage, rather than to encourage, achievement. The nurse does not always have the time to wait for a new toddler to slowly walk from one room to another, and in her haste to get on with her work she will often carry such a child, thus preventing him from learning to walk as quickly as he might. On the other hand, should a child be unusually slow in learning to walk, the nurse, insofar as her time permits, will often encourage him to walk — helping him to do so by holding his hands and walking with him, or holding out her arms and asking him to walk to her. Such a child may also receive special exercises from the physical therapist to hasten his development.

While the nurses make no specific attempts to hasten the children's acquisition of language skills, they are concerned with it and quick to praise such development. "Oh," says one nurse, "Chanele is speaking Hebrew so nicely now — you have no idea!" "Iris," says another, "that's not right. Don't say, *chultza-ah*, say, *chultz-a*." "Amir, it's *pee-pee*, not *pee-pee-ee-ee*." "Oy," groans the nurse. "All the children talk like that, it's terrible."

[11] Interestingly enough, many of the babies who were compelled to eat did not attain the prescribed weight — a situation that induced anxieties in both nurses and mothers.

kilos, it was agreed that they should all receive the same quantities of food. Individual differences among infants were not recognized.[12] This rigidity applied to weaning as well. Eating from a cup or spoon, for example, was introduced abruptly, and babies who wished to continue nursing from either the breast or bottle were not permitted to do so.

Within the past ten years, however, this rigidity has been almost entirely replaced by an emphasis on individualization. The ideal of equality is no longer felt to apply to infant development. Hence, infants are not compelled to eat if they do not wish to; no arbitrary optimal weights are established, and the entire weaning process is a gradual one. When cereal, for example, is added to the evening meal, it may be fed to the baby in a bottle, and those who do not eat well from a cup also receive their vegetables in a bottle. As one nurse remarked, they no longer believe in "arguing with the baby," so that the bottle is not eliminated until the baby no longer wants it.

The mother nurses the infant for the first time twelve hours after birth, so that his sucking may stimulate her flow of milk. For the same reason the baby is not given any food except tea (which he receives in a bottle according to a fixed schedule of five or six times a day), for it is believed that by keeping the baby hungry he will want to suck. Being hungry, the babies not only cry frequently during the first few days but lose weight as well.

Upon returning to Kiryat Yedidim the new mother nurses her baby six times a day for six weeks. This is the period, it will be remembered, in which she enjoys a complete vacation from her work, so that the midnight feeding which this schedule imposes upon her is not unduly burdensome. This latter feeding is gradually omitted during this six-week period by progressively deferring the time of the feeding from 12:00 to 1:00, to 2:00, to 3:00, etc.,

[12] This emphasis on equality was applied not only to the gaining of weight and the intake of grams, but to all other matters as well. Parents, for example, were enjoined not to show more affection to their own babies than to others in the Nursery, and all babies were quite literally to be regarded as one's own. The anxieties engendered by the effort to scatter one's love and affection without discrimination soon brought the state of affairs to "absurdity," and a more relaxed and natural approach came to be accepted. Today it is apparent that parents, while primarily absorbed in their own children, have a definite affection for the other babies in the Nursery and especially for those other babies who share their infant's room. It is also apparent, however, that a mother's primary love and attention goes to her own baby. When, for example, a mother works as a nurse in the Nursery, she goes immediately to her own baby if he cries or needs attention. If it is another baby in need of attention, however, she takes her time about helping him. This preference seems to be unconscious, and is denied when another nurse points it out.

until the baby sleeps the entire night without waking for a feeding. Should the baby cry at night much before the mother is scheduled to nurse him, the night watch will call her. In the past, however, the mother was not called and the watch tried to appease the baby. The present system of calling the mother was instituted about fifteen years ago by the new head nurse over the objections of the mothers, who complained that it was an unwelcome burden, particularly in the winter months. Many women still object to the night feeding and, according to one informant, "they wait for the day when the nurses tell them they need not come any more."

Before describing the nursing situation, mention should be made of those few mothers who have no milk. Today a baby is put on a formula as soon as it is discovered that his mother is unable to nurse. In the past, however (until about fifteen years ago), the baby was nursed by other nursing mothers, a procedure consistent with the original notions of collectivism and equality that were rigidly enforced in Kiryat Yedidim. One of the nurses characterized this practice as "a mess," as it created tensions for everyone concerned. The baby, however hungry, was forced to wait for his feeding until his wet nurse had nursed her own baby. The wet nurse, moreover, did not always have sufficient milk for two babies, so that the infant was often nursed by more than one woman. But this practice was hard on the other babies as well. Since it was thought that the principle of equality demanded that all infants weigh the same, it was agreed that all babies be given the same amount of milk at each feeding. Thus even if a woman's own baby wanted one hundred and fifty grams, the feeding stopped at one hundred grams — the prescribed amount — so that she would have enough milk for the other baby. For the mother herself the use of a wet nurse had unhappy consequences. Although the other mothers did not derogate her for her "deficiency," she nevertheless felt inferior to them.[13] Moreover, since she was unable to nurse her infant, it was ruled that she should return to her work immediately — for she was not needed in the Nursery. Hence, such a mother was able to see her baby only after she had completed her day's work.

Eventually the protests of the mothers resulted in the abolition of wet or communal nursing, and infants whose mothers had no milk were instead given a formula by the nurses. This still meant

[13] According to the nurses, the attitude of nursing mothers toward mothers with no milk is "neutral." But, given the prevailing belief that mother's milk is the "best" for the baby, it is not surprising that some mothers who are unable to nurse develop strong feelings of inadequacy.

that such mothers had little contact with their babies. This final inequity was officially recognized by The Federation a few years ago when it ruled that mothers who were unable to nurse should be permitted to give the formula until their babies were four months old.

Although collective nursing of a baby whose mother has no milk has long been abolished, all nursing takes place within a communal framework. All the nursing babies sleep in the same room, and it is there that they are nursed by their mothers. And since all the mothers adhere to the same feeding schedule, they nurse their babies at the same time as well as in the same place. Hence, from infancy, eating for the sabras is a shared experience, and even the intimacy of mother-love is not private. For the mother, nursing becomes a social occasion in which gossip and conversation can be shared with other mothers while she shares her milk with her baby.

In general, nursing today proceeds at a relaxed pace, and often in the process records the relaxed attitudes of the mothers are noted. The following typical excerpt suggests something of the atmosphere that characterizes the nursing situation.

5:45 A.M. . . . In room #1, SHULA, the only nursing mother here, is nursing Yair (two months) now . . . 5:48, RACHEL comes in, wearing a mask and gown,[14] gently awakens Shlomit (three months) to nurse her . . . sits down, holds Shlomit on her lap, offers the breast . . . SHULA puts Yair on his bed, is talking gently to him . . . 5:52, VARDA comes in, wipes off breast — sees Danny laughing and babbling, goes to him, laughs, straightens him out on the bed, asks him what he did (he slid over to one side) . . . then, she wakes Neir (five months) by touching him, gently lifting . . . puts him on her lap, gives him the breast . . . RACHEL is quiet, stares out the window . . . looks at Shlomit to see how she is doing . . . Shlomit puts her hand on the breast, moves her hand around . . . RACHEL holds Shlomit down in front of her, talks to her, calls her pet names, clucks, gets up, carrying her over her shoulder . . . 6:02, VARDA presents breast to Neir, who touches, but does not nurse . . . VARDA smiles at him, looks at him, rocks him, talks to him, holds him up, hugs him, talks, makes noises to him . . . DINA comes in with *daisa* for Danny, says, "good morning" to him . . . Danny grins and waves . . . mother dresses him, he kicks and jabbers . . . Shlomit is dressed, waves and babbles happily. Mother asks her why she is so happy, goes to the tub, pumps out remaining milk (Shlomit is on bed) . . . RACHEL picks up Shlomit,

[14] All nursing mothers wear white gowns for nursing, and they change from their work clothes to these gowns when they arrive at the Nursery. Masks are worn only when the mother has a cold.

who begins to cry . . . mother asks, "What happened, darling, what happened?", sits down, gives her the breast — Shlomit sucks . . . 6:24, VARDA comes back, lifts Neir, talks to him, laughs, kisses him on cheek, hugs him.[15]

The weaning process begins about the age of three months, at which time a cup of fruit puree, consisting generally of mashed banana and/or apple and orange juice, is given to the baby at his 1:30 P.M. feeding. The mother first offers the baby the "solids," either with a spoon or directly from the cup.[16] In most instances the cup presents no problem because of the gradualness with which it is introduced. If the baby rejects the cup when it is first presented, the mother is instructed by the nurse to remove it immediately. They try again on succeeding days until the baby accepts it, a process which rarely takes more than a week. If the baby continues to reject the cup or spoon, the food is offered to him in a bottle.[17] After the baby either accepts or rejects the solid, the mother nurses him. She continues this process, gradually increasing the amount of fruit, until the nursing is completely eliminated. By the sixth month the babies generally double their weight, which may be taken as a clue to the adequacy of the feeding routine.[18]

[15] The mothers in this illustration are considerably more passive at this early morning feeding — that is, they "play" less with their infants and converse less with each other — than they are at later feedings. Having only just arisen, they are not yet fully alert and active. In all cases where the record states that the mother "talks" to the baby, it refers to baby talk and terms of endearment.

[16] The cups used are large china cups which are sterilized prior to each feeding by being filled with boiling water.

[17] At the time of observation, however, only two babies — one nine months old, the other eight months — were taking bottles, and this occurred only at the 5:30 P.M. feeding.

[18] The following represents a detailed summary of the weaning process. In the fourth month, the 9:30 A.M nursing is supplemented with a vegetable puree, consisting generally of tomatoes, carrots, potatoes, and, later, ground liver. If the mother has sufficient milk to continue nursing, this diet will continue until the sixth month. If, however, she begins to lose her milk, other feedings will be supplemented as well. At the 5:30 P.M. feeding, for example, the baby is introduced to *daisa*, a combination of very rich milk, cereal (corn starch), and much sugar. Once the weaning is completed, this is the form in which the baby receives all his milk.

At the age of six months, the infant's 10:00 P.M. feeding is eliminated, so that the baby is then fed four times a day. If the mother has sufficient milk, all feedings will include nursing. There is, however, considerable individualization in this routine. If the baby is feeding well and appears to want to continue the night feeding, the mother may continue to nurse him at night beyond his sixth month. If he is not eating well, however, this night nursing may be eliminated even before the sixth month. The procedure adopted depends upon the individual baby's needs.

Weaning is generally completed by the end of the eighth month for it is rare that the mother has enough milk to nurse beyond the beginning of the ninth month. Many babies, moreover, do not wish to nurse beyond that time and become angry if they are offered the breast. Others want either the mother's milk or the solids, but not both. Hence the general policy is to eliminate the mother's breast entirely by no later than the beginning of the ninth month, and the morning meal then consists of daisa.

Although weaning is not completed until the end of the eighth month, the nurses begin to feed the babies before that time. In general this occurs at the sixth month, when the mother gives up the 10:00 A.M. feeding. If a mother wishes to feed her baby herself, however, and if she can leave work at that time, she may do so. Most mothers do wish to feed their babies, so that the shift from mother to nurse as the giver of food is generally a gradual one. If the baby is not taking solids well, however, the nurse will not permit the mother to feed her baby, as he will want to nurse — and the point is to eliminate the nursing at this time.

Once the babies are old enough to be fed by the nurses, they are fed in the following manner. The food is wheeled on a little table into one of the bedrooms (or onto the porch) where the babies are usually fed. The nurses sit in chairs beside the table and feed the babies, who sit on their laps.

The behavior of the nurse while feeding the babies varies. Sometimes she sings to the baby as she feeds him; sometimes she talks to him or coos at him. At other times, when the baby is first learning to eat at the table or when he appears apathetic, the nurse may pretend to drink from the cup (although she does not put her mouth on the cup) and smack her lips, hoping to stimulate

---

Since most mothers are eager to give up the night nursing, the mother's attitude, as well as the infant's needs, plays its part in this flexibility.

At six months, also, the 10:00 A.M. nursing is eliminated, and egg yolk and butterfat are added to the vegetable puree. By the age of approximately seven months, the 1:30 P.M. nursing is eliminated. By this time, the mother is usually beginning to lose her milk, and she is almost fully reintegrated into her work routine, so that it is difficult for her to come to the Nursery. At this time, a raw egg may be added to the infant's fruit.

At the eighth month, the 5:30 nursing is eliminated, for by this time most mothers have little milk left. If a mother has sufficient milk, however, and wishes to do so, she may continue this nursing until the ninth month. Since the mother does not have to leave her work for this nursing, but comes after she has finished for the day, economic factors do not play a part in determining the conclusion of this nursing period. For most babies, however, this nursing is eliminated by the eighth month, and they receive only daisa.

The early morning nursing, at 6:00 A.M., is the last to be eliminated. The reason for this is that the mothers are rested from their night's sleep, and it is assumed that their milk will be both nourishing and sufficient.

the baby to drink. Frequently, however, the nurses converse with each other while they feed the babies. In any event, feeding is a rapid process, seldom lasting more than twelve or fifteen minutes. The babies are usually hungry and eat rapidly and well, and the nurses do not encourage leisurely eating or playing after the meal.

This rapid feeding by the nurse may be contrasted with the more leisurely feeding by the mother, who spends at least forty-five minutes nursing and/or feeding her infant. Even in the last days of weaning, when she gives her baby only solids, she prolongs the feeding. This sudden shift to a rapid feeding constitutes a discontinuity in the feeding experience of the baby.[19]

The babies are first trained to feed themselves at about the age of nine months, which is also the age at which weaning comes to an end. As is true of many aspects of collective education, there is a wide age range within which this training occurs. Since the nurses do not have the time to devote to the training of one child, they wait until a group of children has attained the maturity necessary for the training. Hence, although no baby is trained to feed himself before the age of nine months, some do not receive such training until they are twelve months old, at which time a number of babies are trained at the same time. In general, the principle concerning such matters is a simple one: in those training areas which demand a certain stage of maturation, the younger child is not accelerated beyond his maturation stage in order to accommodate to the group; rather, the older child is retarded until the younger ones reach the required stage.

When this training begins, the four or five babies who are ready for training are seated at a miniature table — exactly like the ones they will use for the next few years. The nurse places a bowl of food before each child, and permits him to hold a spoon. She feeds each child in turn. If a baby attempts to feed himself, she encourages him by guiding his hand from the bowl to his mouth; if, however, the baby does not take the initiative in feeding himself, the nurse makes no attempt to encourage him. At the time of observation, none of the five babies who had begun to sit at the table made any attempts to feed themselves. The goal in the Nursery, however, is not actually to train the child in self-feeding, but merely to accustom him to sitting at a table with

[19] One may speculate on the relationship between this rapid feeding in infancy and the hurried eating that characterizes the sabra at his meal. The adolescent and adult sabras eat rapidly, and the former leave the table only a few minutes after they sit down.

his own bowl of food and his own spoon, so that when he moves to the Toddlers' House, this arrangement will not be new to him and genuine training can begin.[20]

Because of the generally permissive nature of the nursing and feeding situation, there are seldom any feeding problems in the Nursery. Minor feeding problems do occur, however, when some babies begin to teethe, and they must then be fed with great care. When feeding problems do arise in the Nursery, they are, according to the nurses, almost always the result of a mother's forcing her child to eat. If the mother persists in this behavior, the nurse will intervene and insist that the mother adopt a more permissive attitude. In those rare instances when a mother fails to conform to the nurse's dictum, and the child continues to refuse to eat, the nurse may even refuse to permit the mother to feed her baby.

Two elements of the feeding process in the Nursery — its routinization and its communal nature — result in certain negative consequences for the child. Because the babies are all fed on the same schedule, a baby may cry from hunger for a long time before he is fed. If a nursing baby cries for food when his mother is at work, nothing can be done about it.[21] Some babies were observed to awaken as much as thirty minutes before the scheduled arrival of their nursing mothers and cry the entire time or else cry themselves to sleep again. In the case of at least one infant, the mother invariably arrived late — as much as half an hour — for her feeding (much to the nurses' indignation), and the baby cried with hunger the entire time. A nurse tried, unsuccessfully, to pacify him. Babies who are already weaned may also cry from hunger and often they too are allowed to cry until their scheduled mealtime. In some instances, however, when a baby cries long before mealtime, and cannot be pacified, the nurse may go to the kitchen to bring him his food early.

Again, since all babies are fed on schedule, it is sometimes necessary to awaken them for a feeding. When this occurs, the baby often cries and becomes irritable. Notations such as the following appear often in the process records.

[20] Soon after the weaning is completed, other foods in addition to those already mentioned are added to the babies' diet. At the 10:00 A.M feeding a meatball and mashed potatoes are added to the meal and, at twelve months, biscuit or bread is added. At the 5:30 P.M. feeding, cottage cheese, in a semi-liquid form, and a cookie or piece of bread are added to the meal.

[21] Pacifiers are not used in the Nursery. The nurses know that pacifiers are now commonly used in the United States, but they point out that the problem of accounting for and keeping clean seventeen pacifiers makes their use in the Nursery impractical.

GORAH awakens Uzi (six months) to feed him . . . He cries and cries . . .

A second potentially disturbing element in nursing inheres in its communal nature. We have already observed that both nurses and mothers spend much of their feeding periods in conversation with each other. At times these discussions become heated and may cause the infant to stop nursing or to be ignored by the adult who is feeding him. In the illustrations below, the first is of nursing mothers, the second of nurses, mothers, and visitors. The latter is an extreme example, but serves to indicate the commotion that can arise from communal feeding and its effects on the babies.

RACHEL and POLA are talking (while nursing) . . . RACHEL is heated in argument . . . Neir stops nursing . . . VARDA holds him, kisses him, laughs at him . . . he does not nurse . . . VARDA says, "Phooey on RACHEL." She holds him up, rests his head on her shoulder . . . he still does not nurse.

Three of the oldest babies are sitting at their table, being fed. Baby's mother feeds Uri (ten months); at the same time, she is yelling at a chavera who has come to tell SARA (nurse) something about the work in the communal kitchen . . . Mother listens and talks while feeding Uri . . . Avshalom (twelve months) is balking, not drinking, so SARA takes him from his chair, puts him on her lap . . . He refuses to drink that way, so she puts him back in his chair . . . He still refuses, so she removes the cup . . . Uri finishes eating; mother is still arguing with chavera and SARA, loudly, vehemently . . . mother gets up, holds Uri, goes to the corner of the porch, stands and argues with SARA, while Uri looks around . . . mother walks with Uri, still arguing with SARA, who feeds Tamar (nine months) on her lap . . . Mother listens to SARA while hugging and kissing Uri, then she argues some more . . . Mother is practically crying, her voice is choking, breaking . . . argument continues, with everybody yelling . . . everybody is arguing at once, shouting at each other.

Thus, in this one section of the porch, there were eleven babies (those who were not mentioned in the process record were in their beds), three nurses, two mothers, and three other women of the kibbutz. The presence of eight adults, all arguing vehemently, may have confused the babies as much as the record surely confuses the reader. They were not interested in their food and for the most part, sat quietly watching the proceedings. This example is also typical of evening feedings, where — although arguments are not taking place — great confusion is created by the arrival of mothers, fathers, and siblings. There are many instances of babies' refusing to eat after their parents arrive and/or ignoring their food to watch the people troop in.

Toilet and sexual behavior. Training in eating and self-feeding is the only formal training that babies receive in the Nursery. In the past, however, when babies remained in the Nursery until the age of eighteen months, it was there that they received their first toilet training. Now that they leave the Nursery at the age of one year, such training does not begin until after they enter the Toddlers' House. "Training" in this context refers to formal training, for even in the Nursery nurses and parents communicate their attitudes about excretion to the babies; and in some cases, this communication is so effective that the babies modify their behavior as a result. One nurse, for example, explained that she does not like the babies to defecate on her and that, moreover, they don't. At first she was puzzled by this, for she observed that these babies did defecate on their parents and other nurses. Then she remembered that whenever she holds a baby and he seems about to urinate or defecate, she holds him away from her. Thus the babies learn not to excrete on her, for, "They know I don't like it."

Attitudes toward soiling are communicated verbally as well. Hence:

LEAH changes Avshalom (eleven months), who has soiled his diaper . . . She says, "Phooey, pisher!"

Uzi (ten months) has soiled all over himself and his bed — even has it in his hair . . . later, SARA comes to bathe him, sees the mess, says, "Phooey, phooey," makes signs of mild disgust, undresses him, carries him off to be bathed.

In these ways, negative attitudes toward excretion are communicated to the babies long before formal training is instituted. In general, however, the attitude is permissive. In the past, for example, when babies frequently played in the nude, they had many opportunities to play with their faeces — which they were allowed to do with impunity. Since they are rarely nude today, they have much less opportunity for such play, but if they do, the response of the nurse is permissive.

This permissive attitude prevails also in the changing of diapers. The nurse's routine obviously prevents her from changing a baby's diaper immediately after he has wet or soiled. The youngest babies seem to find a wet diaper uncomfortable, for they cry until their diapers are changed. As they grow older, however, they apparently become adjusted to what had formerly been an uncomfortable sensation, for they no longer cry.

The same permissive attitude applies to sexual manifestations. Masturbation at this age was rarely observed in the course of this study. The nurses say that it now happens infrequently, but that in the past, when the babies were kept nude for long periods, masturbation was not infrequent. In her fifteen years in the Nursery, the head nurse recalls only one case of a persistent masturbator.

PHYSICAL AND EMOTIONAL HEALTH

In general, it may be said that infants lead relatively secure lives in the Nursery, and that attempts are made by those who care for them to provide them with a high degree of physical and emotional gratification. So far as physical health is concerned the kibbutz provides optimum facilities, prophylactic and therapeutic alike.

In addition to the medical care provided by the kibbutz physician and nurse, the babies' health is supervised by a pediatrician, who comes once a month to examine all of them. Infant mortality is low and, while no statistics were obtained, we were told of only two infant deaths in the recent past, both of which occurred while the infants were still in the hospital. Epidemics are relatively unknown, and the incidence of disease does not appear to be greater in the kibbutz than among infants elsewhere. Immediate quarantine (in separate rooms, separate buildings, or in the hospital) is one factor in the absence of epidemics. Shots and vaccinations for smallpox, typhoid, diphtheria, and tetanus are administered during this first year by the kibbutz nurse.[22]

The babies seem to be emotionally healthy, as well, and one's general impression from observing them is of a group of happy, contented babies. At times, however, they display forms of behavior which are generally regarded as symptoms of disturbance. Thumbsucking, for example, is manifest, and occurs

[22] During the period of observation in the Nursery, four infants were ill. One who developed "swollen glands" was hospitalized for a short time; the others who displayed symptoms of fever, excessive crying, and occasional vomiting, were immediately quarantined, and the illnesses lasted only a few days. The nurses reported instances of occasional high temperature, but with one exception there were no serious illnesses.

both when the babies are in bed and at play on the floor. Jouncing occurs frequently, particularly at bedtime. Babies jounce when asleep as well as when awake. Some few babies bump their heads against their beds or against the wall, and the nurses claim they do this when they are frustrated. Although every instance of these symptoms was not recorded, they are noted many times in the record, and babies are characterized as being thumbsuckers, jouncers, and so on. Of the eleven babies who were six months or older at the time of observations, ten were noted as being thumbsuckers. The one exception, a male, was the baby who was nursed for a longer period (through the ninth month) than any other baby in the Nursery at that time. Of the ten babies who sucked their thumbs, four also manifested jouncing behavior, and three were observed to bump their heads against cribs or walls. In sum, three of eleven babies manifested all three symptoms of disturbance, one manifested two symptoms (thumbsucking and jouncing), and six displayed only thumbsucking behavior. One baby manifested no such symptoms. Of the six babies in the Nursery who were less than six months of age, two were characterized by the observer as thumbsuckers.

TRANSITION TO TODDLERS' HOUSE

Since such frustrations as are experienced by infants result primarily from the routinization that must inhere in any collective framework, rather than from lack of interest, understanding, or warmth, it would appear that the first important trauma in the lives of these infants probably does not occur until after they leave the Nursery and enter the Toddlers' House at the age of approximately one year. As a rule, babies do not make this move individually; rather, four or five of the oldest infants who have attained the age of one year are moved as a group, and later, whenever other infants in the Nursery have matured sufficiently, they are added to the group to form the new kevutza of eight toddlers. When they move, they acquire a new nurse; they move into an entirely new physical environment (a new house); and, for some of them, there is a change in their peer-group as well, for they may be placed in a group with several children whom they either do not know or do not remember.

The education authorities are not unaware of the emotional disturbance that such a configuration of abrupt changes may create for the children, and an attempt is made to mitigate some of the more disturbing consequences by ensuring some continuity in nurses. This the kibbutz hopes to achieve by assigning the new nurse to work in the Nursery for several weeks prior to the babies' departure — thus providing an opportunity for them to form an attachment to her in a familiar and secure setting. There are, nevertheless, occasions when this palliative is not applied, and when the babies have no contact with their new nurse prior to moving to their new dwelling. During the course of this study, for example, the nurse assigned to the new kevutza arrived at the Nursery one morning and abruptly moved the five oldest babies — with no previous preparation for them — to the Toddlers' House.

This abrupt transition from familiar faces, house, and schedule — it can be assumed — is highly disturbing for these babies (it will be recalled that the mere shifting of cribs in the same room is sufficient to upset them). Unfortunately, however, we were unable to observe these five babies at the time of their transition. Some months later, however, one baby was moved from the Nursery to this new kevutza, and he was observed at this time.

Ron (thirteen months) is in the crib in the front yard; the others are in the back. He was moved without any previous preparation and without any previous acquaintance with the nurse. He has just awakened, and looks groggy and crabby. But his face also indicates past crying, and I (A.G.S.) [23] have the feeling that this was a period of suffering for him. He recognizes me, and I pick him up. The nurse comes out, and I remark that he does not seem happy. She replies that, of course he isn't — everything is still so new for him, and he is not yet adjusted. I take him into the backyard and set him in the pen with the other babies. He looks "at home" immediately, busies himself with the toys there, crawls around, stands, smiles at me, and seems to accept the other babies casually — as they seem to accept him.

Five days after this observation, the first interaction between Ron and any other child in the group was noted. Three days later, he was observed to laugh for the first time. During this initial period, he ate little, slept frequently, and — when the observer was present — rarely left her side. For Ron, she was the only point of continuity, for he had known her in the Nursery.

Some months following this addition to the group, two more babies were added to complete the kevutza of eight, but their move was made with a nurse who had been working with them

---

[23] Since the children's response to the observer may be a function of his sex and general personality characteristics, and since I observed some of the groups and my wife observed others, it is desirable that the reader be aware of the identity of the observer. The initials, A.G.S., refer to my wife; the initials, M.E.S., are mine.

for several weeks in the Nursery and who then became the assistant nurse in the new kevutza. These two babies had previously been observed in the Nursery, so that their behavior in the Toddlers' House could be compared with their previous behavior. In the Nursery, both babies had been characterized as "active, alert, and outgoing" (although not in equal degree). Immediately after their move, both appeared quiet, passive, and withdrawn (in equal degree). Their initial reactions were in sharp contrast to their previous behavior, as the following excerpt — recorded about one week after they had been moved — indicates.

Naomi (fifteen months) and Chaim (fifteen months) are together in the *lul* (play-pen). They stay together, and seem apathetic. There is no crawling to-and-fro, no jabbering, no happy gurgling — as both babies were wont to do in the Nursery. They are completely silent, just staring. They do not smile, and refuse to respond when I (A.G.S.) call their names (something they had always done). Their faces are alternately sad and serious. SHULA tells me, "All is not well with them." Their first day here, Chaim cried all day, and Naomi refused to look at anyone. They do not even respond to YAFFA, whom they know well.

After observing these babies on later occasions in which they displayed similar behavior, the observer wrote:

I cannot help but feel that this sudden move — to a new house, new physical conditions, new children — is a painfully frightening experience for these babies . . .

Regrettably, this study came to an end shortly after these two babies were moved, so that we were unable to follow their behavior and to discover how much time elapsed before they became adjusted to their new situation. From the recorded observations, however, it is clear that the passivity and withdrawal with which these babies responded to their move continued for at least two weeks, although toward the end of that period they began to display some interest in the other children and in their surroundings.

PART IV · "THE TENDER AGE"

CHAPTER 7 · FORMAL AND INFORMAL STRUCTURE

THE SAMPLE

At the approximate age of twelve months babies move from, the Nursery to a new house — the *Beth Peutot* or Toddlers' House. They remain in this same house until the Kindergarten age of four, at which time they merge with the children of another kevutza of similar age to form a Kindergarten (*Gan*).

Even prior to entering the Kindergarten, however, there is one important change in the formal structure of the kevutza — the acquisition of a nursery teacher in addition to the permanent nurse. This change generally occurs at the age of approximately three years. Toddlers' Houses are composed of eight children and two nurses, and these two nurses remain with the children until they receive a nursery teacher. When two groups are merged into a Kindergarten, only one of the two nursery teachers and one of the two nurses assume responsibility for the new group. The number of adults in charge of any group, therefore, is always two, no matter how many children may be in the group.

In Kiryat Yedidim at the time of this study, there were three Toddlers' groups that had not yet acquired nursery teachers; two Nursery Schools (those that were in the charge of nursery teachers); two Kindergartens; and one Transitional Class (the kevutza that has not yet entered grade school, although its formal educational instruction has begun). Although we observed all three Toddlers' groups, the two older have been combined (for purposes of analysis) into one group (Group II), for they were of approximately the same age and, moreover, few differences in interaction and socialization emerged from an analysis of the data. Of the two Nursery Schools only one was observed; of the two Kindergartens, the older one was observed for such a brief period that it is not included in the analysis, although illustrations from it may occasionally be presented. The Transitional Class was also observed for only a brief period and it too has been omitted

Table 1. Age, sex, and siblings of children of the preschool kevutzot.

Group	Mean age		Age		Sex	Younger siblings	Older siblings
	Years	Months	Years	Months			
I	1	3	1	1	M	0	0
			1	2	M	0	2
			1	3	M	0	2
			1	3	M	0	2
			1	4	F	0	0
			1	4	M	0	0
			KEVUTZA A				
II	2		1	7	M	0	0
			1	8	F	0	3
			1	8	F	0	1
			1	10	M	0	2
			1	10	M	0	1
			1	10	F	0	2
			2	3	F	0	1
			2	3	M	0	2
			KEVUTZA B				
			1	9	M	0	1
			1	11	M	0	0
			1	11	M	0	2
			2	2	M	0	0
			2	2	F	0	1
			2	3	F	0	0
			2	5	F	0	0
			2	5	F	0	2
III	3		2	9	F	1	2
			2	10	M	1	0
			2	10	F	1	1
			2	11	F	0	2
			2	11	F	0	2
			2	11	M	0	1
			3	1	M	0	0
			3	4	F	1	1
			3	7	M	0	0
			3	8	M	1	2
IV	4	4	3	10	M	1	0
			3	10	F	0	2
			3	11	F	0	2
			4	3	F	1	0
			4	3	M	1	0
			4	3	F	0	1
			4	4	M	0	0
			4	4	M	0	0
			4	5	M	0	1
			4	5	F	1	2
			4	11	F	0	1
			4	11	F	1	0
			5	0	M	1	0
			5	0	F	0	2
			5	0	F	0	1

from the analysis. Although three of the eight groups either were not observed or were observed for only a short time, the nurses in all groups were interviewed, both formally and informally. The succeeding analysis and discussion is based on observations of five groups and on interviews with the nurses of all eight groups. The age and sex breakdown, as well as the number of siblings, for the five kevutzot observed is presented in Table 1.

It may be noted that only in Group II is there a balanced sex ratio. Group I presents the most highly unbalanced ratio — five boys to one girl. In Groups III and IV, girls outnumbered boys. The kibbutz attempts insofar as possible to maintain a balanced sex ratio in every kevutza, but since it is considered more important to form a kevutza of age-peers, it is not always possible to maintain this ratio.

While the age spread between the youngest and the oldest children in Group I was at the time of observation small (three months), the age spread increases in the older groups. In Group II the age spread in each sub-group is eight months; in Group III it is seven months; and in Group IV the youngest child is fifteen months younger than the oldest. This range of several months in age makes for important differences in motor and verbal achievements, particularly among the younger kevutzot (Groups I and II) — so that nurses do not interact with eight children of the same age or development. Nor do the eight or sixteen children of a kevutza interact with each other as physical or intellectual peers. In Group I, for example, the two youngest children could not yet walk unassisted, so that they were almost always confined when in the yard to the playpen or to a crib. All but the youngest child in this group were able to form a few nouns, although only one — the single girl in the group — was really capable of expressing her wants verbally, and she had not begun to form sentences yet.

In Group II, all the children could walk unassisted with the exception of one child, a twenty-month-old girl.[1] Verbally, those children who were two years or older could form simple sentences,

---

[1] This child was considered to be physically retarded by the nurses, and her retardation was attributed to her premature birth (at eight months). While her mother expressed concern over the child's inability to keep up with her kevutza, the nurses expressed no concern, although there was some feeling that she should be placed in Group I, where she could become better integrated into the group. She was not considered to be in need of special care or treatment, but she was receiving exercises from the kibbutz's physical therapist. She was able to feed herself to some extent, although she generally received more help from the nurses than did the other children. Verbally, she could form a few words, primarily proper nouns.

and the very oldest children occasionally spoke in paragraphs. Even the younger children in the group, however, were able to communicate in phrases. Only one child in this group — a twenty-one-month-old male — referred to himself in the first person. The range of vocabulary varied considerably, but in every case, the verbal achievement of females was higher than that of males of the same age.

In Groups III and IV, where the difference of a few months no longer necessarily means important differences in maturity, and where motor and verbal achievement appeared to be similar for all the children, the older children nevertheless maintained an advantage over the younger. Although this advantage may have been due in part to increased motor and verbal skill, it was primarily due to the greater size and strength of these older children.

THE PHYSICAL SETTING

The children's community in which these young children live is, as has been noted, a relatively definable section of the living area of the kibbutz, and all the dwellings are relatively close to each other. The houses are not geographically grouped by age, so that, for example, a Toddlers' House may be only a few yards away from the Kindergarten or the Grammar School but a block away from another Toddlers' House.

The dwellings for all these age-groups are modeled on the same general plan, following the recommendations of The Federation. There are, nevertheless, many differences in such characteristics as the size and number of bedrooms, the facilities, and the conveniences to be found among the buildings. The description which follows is a synthetic one, and no single house corresponds to it in every detail.

A dwelling is comprised of several rooms, varying in size. One room is a dressing room and is equipped with a bathtub, shower, and washbasin. Unlike the adult living quarters, hot water is available at all times. In this room are stored the children's clothes, eating utensils, chamber pots, etc. Older groups have bathrooms and toilets, as well. Each child has a towel rack with his name on it, as well as his own shelf in the clothes closet. A small electric hot plate is also kept in this room for the boiling of water, but since all food is prepared in the communal children's kitchen, no other kitchen facilities are provided. Where space permits, one room of the house — furnished with miniature tables and chairs — will be used solely as a dining and playroom, but in the older quarters these activities take place in one of the bedrooms. Bedrooms, of which there are two or three, contain metal cribs or beds (children sleep in cribs until they enter the Kindergarten), the number depending upon the size of the room, and shelves or chests for toys. Newer houses are light and airy, with many windows and light colored painted walls. Decorations of a nursery nature are sparse: plain curtains, a few scatter rugs, and only a few pictures of children, animals, or fairytale folk are found in them.

None of the objects in the children's houses — and this applies with few qualifications to the grade and high schools, as well — are the private property of individual children. Clothes, shoes, and personal effects such as towels and toothbrushes are labeled with each child's name, but these serve as identification tags rather than as designations of personal property. In short the usufruct in these objects is enjoyed exclusively by one person, but their ownership resides in the group. The children's clothes are kept in the warehouse (*machsan begadim*). At the beginning of each season the manageress (*machsanait*) of the warehouse meets with the nurses to determine the kind, quantity, and size of clothes that will be needed for each child. The name of the child is then put on these clothes which he will use for the duration of the season. At the end of the season the clothes are returned to the warehouse, and the labels removed.

Each house has a fenced-in yard that varies from a large grassy plot to a small rocky area. In the yards of the toddlers there are one or two cribs for children who must be isolated, who cannot yet walk, or who simply want to play in them. These yards also contain an enormous playpen (*lul*), in which all eight children frequently play at the same time, and a table with benches. These cribs and playpens are not used among the older children.

All houses are kept scrupulously clean, and floors are mopped after every meal. "The history of the Children's Houses," lamented one nurse, "begins with Lysol." In an effort to have everything as sanitary as possible, she explained, houses were originally flooded with disinfectant, and the smell was so strong as to be often unbearable. Now, however, nurses have discovered that cleanliness can prevail with the use of ordinary soap and water, and disinfectant is used only in times of illness.

The most frequent complaint of nurses concerns the dearth of toys, and they are unanimous in recounting frequently fruitless efforts to wangle equipment for the children. Generally speaking, the oldest kevutzot have the most toys and play equipment, and as each group outgrows various toys, the next age-group inherits them.

A composite list of toys found in the various houses is presented below. It should be emphasized that not all the toys are found in all these groups, but generally speaking, the children will eventually have an opportunity to play with most of the toys on the list.

Rattles
Plastic and cloth dolls, in both male and female dress
Toy racing cars, jeeps, autos, wagons, airplanes, etc.
Picture books — with English, French, and Russian texts
Clay
Crayons and paper
Fingerpaints
Tape spools, lids, etc.
Balls of all sizes
Stuffed animals — dogs, teddy bears, elephants
Small wagons containing wooden blocks of varying shapes
Hammer-and-peg sets
Roller toys
Beads and string
Cans for sand and water
Wheelbarrows
Small buckets
Rocking animals — ducks and horses
Sandbox
Tricycles
Large wagons
Large wooden auto with eight steering wheels
Pedal car
Swing
Slide
See-saw
Slate and chalk
Doll furniture — tables, chairs, dishes, buggies, cribs, etc.

No attempt is made to have *eight* of any one toy (so that each child may have one) and, indeed, such an abundance almost never exists. On the contrary, a house usually contains only one or two of any particular toy. All are the property of the group and not of any one child. If a father wishes to make a toy for his child, he either makes *eight* of one toy (witness the auto, in one of the houses, with eight steering wheels) or *one,* which he will then present to the group rather than to his own child. Children, however, do have some toys of their own which remain in their parents' rooms and with which they play when they visit in the evenings.

THE DAILY ROUTINE

Although the ages of the children under discussion range from thirteen months to seven years, the daily routine that they follow is generally the same. The day begins in every kevutza at 6:00 A.M. in the winter and at 7:00 A.M. in the summer (when the kibbutz observes daylight saving time). The children wash and dress and then usually have a short period of "free play" before breakfast. This meal is served about an hour after the children arise. Following breakfast, the children have another free-play period for about an hour — if the weather is pleasant, they play outside in their yard; if it is raining, they play in the house. By this time, the nurse or teacher has completed a number of her housekeeping chores, and she then begins to supervise the children's activities. The one exception is the youngest kevutza, where there is no supervision of play at any time. In the youngest groups, several of the children may take morning naps, as well. About 10:00 the children have their mid-morning snack, and those in the younger groups are then bathed. After their baths, the children play in the house, and the nurse often supervises their play. In the older groups directed play, which is begun in the early morning, continues until dinner. Dinner is served in the younger groups at 11:00 or 11:30, in the older groups at noon. After dinner, the children in the older groups bathe or shower, and the children in all groups then nap for approximately two hours. When they awaken, they dress in their good clothes, have another snack, and play by themselves in the yard. Supper is served at an early hour, between 4:30 and 5:30, so that parents may fetch their children as soon as they return from work. The children then visit in their parental rooms until bedtime, which comes at approximately 7:00 for the youngest, and at 8:00 for the oldest, children.

It will be noted from this brief description of the formal structure of the kevutza that the child in the kibbutz has a minimum of privacy — a condition that characterizes his existence from infancy through high school. His life, as one article in The Federation's educational journal complained, is "always within the framework of society. . . . (From his earliest years) the child learns that he is a social creation, that he is one of six or twelve or twenty."

Because of group living and the routine that is a necessary result of group living, the child seldom has an opportunity either to be alone or to do what he wants when he wants to. Instead, his life is almost always organized according to the demands of a group schedule rather than according to his own internal rhythms, and his activities are almost always supervised by an adult and/or occur in the presence of other children.

This group living, moreover, compels him to share not only his experiences, but almost everything else in his life. Since there are never enough toys for every child in the group, he must share his toys with the other members of the group; and since there are only two nurses in the group, he must share their love and affection with all the other children. This constant presence of, and pressure from, the group must be borne in mind as a constant factor in the children's behavior.

PLAY

One of the basic assumptions of this study is that the kinds of behavior that are developed in these formative years are of crucial importance for the understanding of adult behavior and personality. Since most interaction among children consists of play or occurs during so-called play periods, the following discussion of play is intended primarily as background.

The children's play may be roughly divided into "organized" and "free" play. Organized play refers to all activity that is organized and directed by the nurse or nursery teacher; free play refers to any activity initiated by the children themselves and in which the nurse plays no role of any kind — generally because she is working inside the house while the children are outside, or because she is in another room from that in which they are playing.

Organized play. The frequency with which the nurse directs the play of the children is much higher in the older groups, III and IV, than it is in Groups I and II. In these two younger kevutzot the nurse's caretaking chores leave her with little time for directing the children's play activities. In the older groups, on the other hand, the division of labor between nurse and nursery teacher relieves the latter of many housekeeping duties, freeing her for such activities as organizing play. The nurses in the older groups, moreover, are able to spend more time with their charges because the latter have achieved a greater degree of independence. Hence they need not spend the greater portion of their time supervising toilet training, feeding, dressing, and the other purely physical activities that consume so much of the time and energies of nurses in younger groups.

The absence of play-supervision in the younger groups results not only in conflict and aggression among the children (as we shall observe), but also in a certain degree of apathetic and aimless activity which is one of the initial impressions. That this seeming apathy is a function, among other things, of the lack of supervised or organized activity may be inferred from the change in the children's behavior on those rare occasions when the nurse directs their play. On such occasions the researchers noted that the children were much more alert and animated.

There is no instance of organized play in Group I (the youngest) nor would one expect much, if any, organized play for children of this age. The only direction of play occurs when the nurse offers a child a specific toy with which to play. (Since most toys are stored in cabinets and are therefore not available to the children, the nurse must distribute them.)

In Groups II, III, and IV, the nurse's supervisory role in play may take several different forms. She may participate with the children in a game in which she is merely one of the several players; she may initiate play — in the sense of motivating the children — although she herself does not participate; she may perform for the children, who become participant spectators. The nurse may also participate in a game in which her participation is restricted exclusively to a leadership role. Finally, the nurse may determine and initiate a specific activity, but permit the children to set their own pace and to decide what they want to do within the framework of the activity.

These different forms of participation are manifested with varying degrees of frequency, but at least two occur almost every day. Every day, weather permitting, the nurse takes the children for a hike after breakfast. Following their return, and sometimes before lunch, she either supervises them in some activity (such as painting or modeling with clay), directs them in some game, or reads to them. Thus there are two times during the day in which the nurse devotes herself exclusively to the play of the children. At other times during the day the children generally play spontaneously at their own games, although the nurse may — if she is free — become involved at their request.

The particular play activities organized by the nurses vary with the ages of the children in each group. There are, nevertheless, numerous games and types of play that occur in all three groups under discussion, but as the children develop in skills, they appear in increasingly complex forms.

Play in which the nurse participates with the children as an equal includes such activities as constructing with blocks, performing simple gymnastic feats, and playing simple imitative games such as train or auto. The nurse may suggest that they all play train, and the children form a single file, each child with his hand on the shoulder of the child preceding him, with one of them — usually the nurse — being the "engine."

Initiation of play by the nurse may be either formal or informal. While the children are playing, the nurse may suggest some activity — dancing or gymnastics, for example — in an informal way, and they generally respond to her suggestion. In Group II, working with crayons or clay is also initiated informally by the nurse, who distributes the materials among the children, but who is rarely able to stay with them to direct these activities. Working with clay at this age, then, takes the form of merely handling or rolling it; drawing consists of scribblings.

In Groups III and IV, however, the nurses may initiate play in a much more formal manner. Every morning the nurses in these two groups announce the daily "work" schedule — an organized play period devoted to some creative or artistic play. This includes finger painting, drawing with crayons, working with clay, drawing with chalk on a blackboard,[2] and playing with such educational toys as building blocks, jigsaw puzzles, board-and-pegs, or stringing beads. Although the children enjoy this kind of play immensely, they do not initiate it by themselves because the materials are stored away by the nurse, who allows the children — indeed instructs them — to play with them only at certain

---

[2] Two of the favorite activities of the children — cleaning and smearing — are involved in this play; indeed observations indicate that the sheer glee displayed and pleasure derived from these activities by children in Groups I, II, and III exceed that which they receive from any other. When, for example, they are given finger paint or water colors by the nurse, few of the children are especially interested in the painting itself. Most of them much prefer to smear the paint or the colors on the paper, on their hands, and on the table. Smearing their hands in the paint can is in itself one of their greatest sources of pleasure.

On the other hand, one of the children's greatest delights is washing off the blackboard after they are finished with the chalk. It is our impression that the actual drawing with the chalk is perceived by the children as a prelude to the real "fun" of wiping off the slate with a rag that has been dipped in a bucket of water. It is not at all unlikely that the pleasure derived from this activity is not from the cleaning of the slates, but from the smearing and dripping of the water.

times. (The reason for this rigid schedule is apparent: if the children were allowed ready access to these precious materials they would not be preserved.) These activities are arbitrarily termed, "work," in order to impress upon the children from the earliest age the value of work. While "working," the children sit at tables, four or five at one table. Generally, each child works by himself, often humming or singing, and seldom interfering with the activities of the others. At times, the children display their handiwork to each other, or ask the nurse to come and see what they have made. This organized play period is one that the children appear to enjoy immensely, and it is only infrequently punctuated by conflict or aggression.

Other types of artistic activities are initiated by the nurse as well. In Group II, the nurse begins to teach the children simple songs, and in Groups III and IV, the nurses introduce group dancing. Many of the songs that the children learn may be classified under three dominant kibbutz values: Zionism, labor, and nature. Thus, the songs have an ideological, as well as an artistic, meaning.

The most important activity in which the nurse performs for the children while they remain primarily participant-spectators is group reading or storytelling. The nurse reads or tells a story to the children as they sit at her feet. In Group II, the nurse does not read the story to the children, but merely shows them the pictures in the book and asks them to identify or to locate the various objects portrayed. She teaches them the various sounds made by the animals in the pictures, and the children imitate the sounds. If the children see a picture of chickens, the nurse may comment, "Pnina's mother works in the chicken house"; if they see a picture of an airplane, she remarks, "Avner's father flies the airplane."

In Groups III and IV, play with books becomes a bit more sophisticated. The nurse actually reads or tells a story and embellishes her account by showing the children appropriate pictures. If the children are shown pictures of animals, for example, they identify the animals, sing simple songs describing their characteristics, and then listen to the nurse's story about one of the animals. This is known as "traveling to the zoo." In contrast to the younger children in Group II, these older children almost always listen with serious attentiveness, interrupting only to ask questions or to have a statement repeated.

The most exciting play activity for the children includes the playing of games that the nurse initiates and directs. In Group II, only two such games were observed, and their simplicity may be contrasted with the increasing complexity of the games in the older groups. In one game, the nurse sings a song while the children walk in a circle to the rhythm of the song. In the second game, the children stand in a row opposite the nurse, who rolls a ball to each child in turn.

Of all the games directed by the nurse in Group III, the favorite is one in which the children are successively transformed into a number of different creatures. The following excerpt describes the game and reveals some of the enthusiasm with which the children participate.

SHULA begins to beat on a toy drum, says to the children, "What do we do? We go to sit on the rug." . . . They all assemble in the bedroom, sit on the rug facing SHULA. They clap hands to the rhythm of the beat and laugh uproariously as the tempo is increased . . . She signals to them to beat time with their feet, and again great laughter . . . She tells them to close their eyes, and at a sign from the drum they are to shout, "good morning!" This is done with real glee . . . To the rhythm of the drum each child walks in a circle about the entire group. When each child has had his turn, they all walk in a circle together, after which they walk on tip-toe because they are giants, and then bent over because they are dwarfs . . . Now they are puppies, down on all fours, and — at the signal from the drum — say *ow* (our *bow-wow*). . . . Now they are rabbits. They place their hands on their heads, fingers in the air (they have the big ears of the rabbit). They jump. They sing a song about the rabbit, doing a dance at the same time . . . SHULA tells the children to crawl under the beds. They are now birds, and they are in their nests. Now the birds are sleeping. SHULA says that HELKA will not know where they are, as they have flown away. (At this they laugh.) "Now it is morning, and the birds get up and fly away," says SHULA. And the children crawl out, run around the room, wave their hands, as she sings them a song about the birds.

Since Group IV has no favorite game, a number of their games may be described. Unlike her more active role in Group III, however, the nurse's role is that of initiator and supervisor.

A game, called "Silence," consists in the children's sitting on chairs in a circle, while one child sits in the center. When the latter points to one of the children in the circle he (the one pointed to) runs to him and touches his hand; whereupon they exchange chairs. And so each child, successively, becomes "It." The distinctive feature of the game is that it must be played in complete silence.

Another game initiated by the nurse is a verbal one, consisting of question and stereotyped answer. One child says, for example,

"A fox is here." The nurse says, "Whom will the fox attack?" The children answer, "the chickens." The nurse asks, "Who will guard the chickens?" The children answer, "the watchmen." After this dialogue is recited, it is then sung.

Another game initiated by the nurse is the game of "It." All the children except the one who is "It" sit in a circle and designate one child as their leader. The leader, whose identity is unknown to the child who is "It," then initiates some movement of the hand — stroking one's leg, pulling one's hair, clapping hands, etc. — and the others imitate his behavior. The child who is "It" must guess the identity of the leader; if he is successful, he joins the circle and the leader becomes "It."

A final type of game activity for Group IV is gymnastics, which, however, is initiated not by the nurse but by a gym teacher who meets periodically with each older kevutza. Although termed "games" by the teacher, these activities are designed by her for their orthopedic value. The children perform many exercises, among which are the following. Each child is instructed to take a dumbbell from the cabinet and to set it on the floor without making any noise while setting it down. Walking in Indian-file, they are then instructed to walk through the dumbbells without knocking any down. Or, the teacher swings a rope, one end of which is attached to the wall, and the children jump through the rope. Or, they climb on the horse, and walk across it while holding the hand of the teacher. Finally, they climb ladders or ropes. Most of the children are eager to perform these exercises, and run to the gym with delight. Some few are uninterested and/or afraid, and the teacher does not compel them to participate.

A most important play activity for all the children is the daily hike. This activity is regarded by the nurses as of primary educational importance, and they employ it to inculcate the love of nature. Even the nurses in Group II, who seldom have an opportunity to direct the daily play activities of their charges, begin to take the children for short, daily walks around the kibbutz as soon as the latter begin to walk well.

The love of nature that the nurses attempt to transmit at these ages includes not only a feeling for nature in general, but a love for the physical and geographic environment in which the children have their existence — Kiryat Yedidim, and its surrounding flora and fauna. A positive attitude toward this environment is not induced through formal instruction or admonition, but through experience in walking through the kibbutz, hiking into the fields and orchards, and observing the various barnyard animals. By teaching the children the names of the flora and fauna, telling them something of their habits, stimulating their interest in their behavior, and making them feel their beauty, the nurses hope to stimulate their love of nature in those manifestations that can be observed and appreciated by young children.[3]

The daily hike is an important experience in the children's lives, one to which they look forward with great eagerness. The hike is taken sometime in the morning before the sun's rays become too hot and is omitted only because of inclement weather or some social emergency. The nurse may inform the children of the route the hike will take or she may ask them where they prefer to go. The hike is confined, of course, to some area within the kibbutz, and its destination may include such diverse locations as other dwellings, the communal dining room, the nurse's own room, the dairy, the horse barn, the olive grove, the garage. The children in the Kindergarten take even more extensive excursions into the vineyards, the orchards, and to the mountain, where they may collect and discuss the stones and flowers to be found there.

These hikes are not only important for teaching the children to know and love nature, but they serve important socialization functions as we have already indicated. As part of their hike, for example, the children get to see many of the economic activities of the kibbutz and to have them explained either by their nurse or by one of the kibbutz members who works in the branch. The knowledge of the kibbutz which is thereby obtained by the children is fairly extensive. In the machine shop they watch the men repair trucks, and they may be permitted to hold a torch or a welding iron. In the dairy they watch the cows being fed and are permitted to help in the feeding by sweeping the feed into the troughs. They see the newborn calves and lambs. They are given a ride by a kibbutz produce truck and are driven to the olive grove where they see the olives being picked, crated, and loaded onto the truck. They stop into the children's kitchen and watch the food being prepared or the pots being scoured. And at

[3] The inculcation of a love of nature at times involves the use of negative sanctions, although such sanctions are mild. One day, for example, some three-year-olds picked grass from an area in which the gardener was trying to grow new grass. The nurse, upon seeing this, came out immediately and told the children to stop this, explaining seriously to them that they should not do this because it was nice to have grass, and that if they picked the young grass now, it would not grow.

every place they are stopped by adults, talked to, joked with, praised, and — when met by parents — kissed. By this device of the daily hike, then, the child's knowledge of the kibbutz as a community is increased, and his identification with the kibbutz as a community of workers is encouraged.

Holidays. Another type of activity which the nurses, even in the younger groups, organize and which at these ages the children view as play, is the celebration of holidays. The inculcation of national values is an important function of the nurse's role, and she can best achieve this aim through ritual and symbolism. The various national holidays are therefore utilized for this purpose, but there is no attempt to teach patriotism on an abstract level. Moreover, since many of the national holidays celebrated by the kibbutz emphasize natural — and particularly agricultural — values, it is almost impossible to inculcate patriotism without also emphasizing love of nature. At the "tender age," the holidays which are most impressive for the children, and which are emphasized in each kevutza, are Chanuka (Festival of Lights), Pesach (Passover), Tu Bishvat (Arbor Day), and Purim (Feast of Esther).[4] Since the kibbutz is antireligious, the religious aspects of these holidays are ignored.

Of these holidays, Chanuka is purely national in spirit, emphasizing the value of national independence. The children in each age-group light the traditional candles, sing appropriate songs, have special food and dress, and receive presents.

Passover, the most important holiday in the kibbutz, is both national and agricultural in its symbolism, and the children are made aware of these values by being taught the appropriate songs, eating special food, and by observing the festive decorations in each dwelling. When Passover was celebrated in the kibbutz at the time of this study a special concert was given for all the children by a well known Israeli singer — a guest at the kibbutz celebration — who sang various folk and patriotic songs.

Tu Bishvat, Arbor Day, is an all-kibbutz celebration, and all the children go into the fields with their parents to participate in the annual tree planting.

The younger children observe Purim by wearing costumes and paper crowns and eating special food. Children in the Kindergarten not only have their own party, but they also provide their own entertainment. Parents, siblings, and even the children in

---

[4] For a detailed account of these holidays as celebrated in the kibbutz, see Spiro, *Kibbutz*, pp. 144–160.

younger groups are invited to attend the party, where they are entertained with songs, dances, and simple skits (only some of which pertain to the Story of Esther).

That these celebrations leave an emotional, if not cognitive, impression on the children is indicated by their references to them at other times and by their spontaneous singing of songs learned during the various holiday seasons. This influence, moreover, is a lasting one. In writing their autobiographies a sample of thirteen-year-olds would uniformly date an important event — birth, a trip, some calamity — in their childhood by its juxtaposition to a holiday. The event is said to have occurred, for example, during Chanuka, just before Passover, or a few days after Purim.

Free play. In all four groups most activity of either an interactional or a non-interactional nature consists of free play or takes place during the free-play periods. Before examining the content of play, we should remark further on one point. Play among the two younger groups is marked by an aimlessness and passivity that are two of its most characteristic features. "Play with toys," often consists in the mere holding or handling of a toy. "Locomotor play" frequently consists of an aimless walking or crawling which only questionably may be termed "play," and it was decided to call it by this term primarily because it occurs during the so-called free-play periods.

In the youngest group (I), this aimless crawling or walking may not necessarily indicate passivity; rather, it undoubtedly reflects the immature motor development of this group — for these are children who are either learning to walk or who have only recently begun to walk. When, however, this same behavior is observed in Group II, whose mean age is two years and whose motor development is advanced, one cannot escape the conclusion that the aimless walking, crawling, and rocking are indices of passivity. This conclusion is strengthened by the frequency of mere "standing around," as it were, in this group. That is, children were often observed to just stand and look — either at other children or into space. This latter type of behavior has not been tabulated, however, because of the difficulty of employing comparable uniform measures. If we note, however, that most thumb-sucking occurs during these periods of aimless activity, and, furthermore, that passivity is a typical response to aggression and conflict in Groups I and II (see below, pp. 174–175), then it can only be concluded that a high degree of general passivity is an important characteristic of these young children.

There are numerous ways of classifying play, and the classification decided upon here makes no claim to special merit. It was adopted because it brings to focus some of the socio-psychological variables with which this study is concerned. The more than fifty types of play found in our sample have been classified into six categories. These categories, in their order of frequency, are shown in Table 2. They include play with children's toys, fantasy play, verbal and visual play, locomotor play, and play in dirt and sand. Play with children's toys is subdivided into microscopic and macroscopic play — the former consisting of play with small toys and other play objects (clothes, for example) which the children can hold in their hands, the latter consisting of play with large toys and play objects which the child may use only by riding in them, climbing on them, and so on.

In all groups play with toys is by far the most frequent kind of play, and within this category microscopic toys play the majority role (with the exception of Group III which will be discussed below). The quality of the play varies greatly among the groups, of course. In Group I, "play with a toy" usually involves a mere holding, turning, or twisting. In Groups III and IV, on the other hand, a child may roll a toy truck on the floor "pretending" he is a truck-driver hauling boxes of grapefruit to the market. Moreover, while the toys in Group I consist of a tin can, ball, spoon, auto, rattle, or cup, those for Group II already include such additional items as blocks, wagon, clay, crayon, and stringing beads. Groups III and IV have advanced to such items as peg-in-hole, finger painting, slate and chalk, jigsaw puzzles, and clay modeling.

For all groups except Group III macroscopic play is relatively infrequent. In Group I it is confined to one object, a rubber tire; in Group II, it includes riding a rocking horse, pushing a wheelbarrow, wagon, and a large cylinder; in Group III it includes playing on a tricycle, rocking horse, pedal car, swing, baby buggy, rocking chair, auto model, and slide. In Group IV the frequency is much smaller and includes play with a rocking horse, chair, table, auto hood, and slide.

Tabulations indicate that the unusually high percentage of macroscopic play in Group III is accounted for by the two tricycles and one pedal car that are found in that nursery and in none of the others. But it is difficult to interpret this difference between Group III and the other groups since we do not know whether the children acquired these toys because of a prior interest in them or whether their interest developed only after they

Table 2. Classification of types of play by percentages.

Types of play	Group I (Σ acts = 85)	Group II (Σ acts = 153)	Group III (Σ acts = 153)	Group IV (Σ acts = 201)
Toys	34	35	52	32
Microscopic	26	28	24	29
Macroscopic	8	7	28	3
Fantasy	3	5	25	15
Verbal and Visual	12	20	10	15
Locomotor	27	23	7	11
Sand and Dirt[a]	20	15	3	23
Miscellaneous	4	2	3	4

[a] Including excreta.

acquired them. Moreover, we do not know if the other groups would play with these as frequently as Group III if they had such toys. It is the author's feeling, however, that play with macroscopic toys is for Group III what "locomotor play" is for Groups I and II, and that when these groups acquire tricycles and autos their present locomotor activities will take the form of macroscopic play.

The second category of play, termed "fantasy play," does not imply that other types of play do not involve fantasy. Rather, the play-acts in this category involve a greater degree of imagination or creative fantasy than the others, since they are invented without the presence or assistance of a material object. The researchers, in short, assumed that it requires less imagination to play "riding to Haifa" if one is riding a toy auto, than it does to play "train" and, in the absence of a toy train, to become a train oneself. Almost invariably fantasy play involves imitation and/or identification (with another person, animal, or object).

It will be noted that there is almost no fantasy play in the two younger groups, but that it is the second most frequent activity in Group III and third in frequency in Group IV. The discrepancy between the younger and older children seems to be a function of maturation. This is patently not the case with respect to the difference between Groups III and IV. Fantasy play is probably more frequent in Group IV than in III, but it is disguised under "sand play." This group, it will be noted, spends much of its time in the sandpile, and much of this play is of a fantasy nature. With one or two exceptions, however, the author neglected to tabulate the fantasy acts involved in this play, so that no figures are available.

In Group I fantasy play includes but one entry, imaginary eating. In Group II it includes playing dog and horse, cleaning house, and feeding and cleaning a child; in Groups III and IV it includes pretending to be dogs, frogs, snakes, calves, baby, nurse, barber, doctor, and so on. In these latter two groups, where there are a sufficient number of cases to be examined and compared, it may be observed that the depth of the identification with either adults, animals, or inanimate objects varies considerably. In some cases a child may perform some adult activity, such as putting a child to bed, without stating, for example, that he is a nurse. In other cases a child may say, "I'll be the mother and you'll be the nurse." In other instances, although the child may not identify the adult role he is playing, it is apparent from the context that he is identifying not only with a specific adult role, but with a specific person as well. In the following incident, for example, the child employs the gestures and intonations of her own nurse.

Shula (three years) "irons" (with a block of wood) her "scarf" (handkerchief). She tells the nurse that she is ironing. Then she tells the children, "Children, I will finish my ironing one, two, and then we will go on the grass."

In instances of identification with animals the children state explicitly that they are dogs or snakes or frogs, and then proceed to act like them. They walk on all-fours and bark like dogs. They also attempt to bite like dogs or to eat like dogs. Like frogs they jump, and like snakes they crawl on their bellies. They run into the barn, and, like calves, eat hay.[5]

The category, "verbal and visual play" is a combined category, including verbal and visual activities. In Group I there are no "visual" activities, and the verbal entries include only jabbering and singing. In Group II, as well, the overwhelming number of entries are either jabbering or singing, although there are a few actual conversations and some looking at picture books in this group. The comparatively smaller percentages in Groups III and IV are easily explained. These two older groups no longer jabber, as do the younger children, but they are not yet old enough to engage in many genuine conversations — except when they relate

[5] In general the children have no fears of animals, only three examples being observed during the entire study. In Group II one girl, who once saw a worm in her toy and perceived it as a snake, since then has been afraid of worms. In the same group, all the children were on a hike when a dog came running toward them; they became frightened and ran away. In Group IV the children were playing in a sandpile when a goat came walking toward them. Some of them started to run away when they saw it.

to some activity in which they are engaged. The absence of jabbering is therefore not yet compensated for by the presence of conversation. Almost all the entries in these two groups involve looking at picture books (and telling a story about, or identifying, the pictures), and the frequency of this activity not only increases sharply in the older two groups, but it increases from Group III to IV as well.

The fourth play category, termed "locomotor," is not intended to imply that other forms of play are not active or that they do not involve the use of limbs in a strenuous way. Most of the play with macroscopic toys, for example, manifests just these characteristics. This category, however, consists of those activities whose locomotor qualities are not dependent upon some object, but involve the use of the body alone.

It will be noted that the incidence of this play is much less frequent in the two older than in the two younger groups. One reason for the difference between one of the older groups (Group III) and the two younger groups has already been suggested: the locomotor activities of the former group are expressed in its high frequency of play with macroscopic toys involving the same locomotor qualities that are found in the younger two groups. The decline in Group IV, however, may reflect a maturational variable or it may be a function of the biweekly gym period which satisfies their locomotor needs.

There is still another reason for the greater incidence of locomotor play in the younger groups, which a closer examination of this type of play reveals. This concerns the important qualitative differences found among the groups. Locomotor play in Group I consists of crawling or walking, "gymnastics" (such as jumping or trying to stand on head), rocking, chasing and running. In Group II it includes crawling or walking, "gymnastics," rocking, chasing or running, clapping or banging, dancing, playing peek-a-boo. In Group III it includes "gymnastics," hide-and-seek, marching, and climbing a tree. In Group IV it includes climbing, chasing, rolling on the ground, jumping rope, hide-and-seek, dancing, playing tag, "gymnastics," and riding "horseback." In short, the locomotor play in the two younger groups is often an aimless passive type of activity which scarcely deserves to be labeled, "play" — in contrast at least with the activities performed by the older groups. If the activities of the latter were to be used as the criteria for this type of play, the two younger groups would have few entries indeed.

The final category of play includes play in "sand and dirt." The differences in the relative frequencies of this category are to be explained both in terms of the physical situation of the groups and of their different levels of maturation. Group III, whose percentage is very low, has no sandpile and, therefore, has few opportunities to play in sand. Unlike the younger children, moreover, many of whose entries in this category consist of playing with dirt, these children do not play in dirt. The other groups, on the other hand, all have sand piles, and the high percentage of sand play in these groups is a function, among other things at least, of this situational factor. Finally, this category includes (for obvious theoretical reasons) play with excreta, an activity which serves to increase the total percentage for this category in the two younger groups (7 per cent of *all* play in Group I consists of play with excreta.) No play with excreta is recorded for the two older groups.

Although Groups I, II, and IV play frequently in sand, the qualitative differences in their play are considerable. In the younger groups it is generally aimless and nonconstructive. At most the children fill buckets with sand; generally they dig in the ground, poke their fingers in the sand, smear mud on the sidewalk, and so forth. In Group IV, however, sand play is both goal-directed and constructive — the children model figures and objects, and construct houses, castles, and trees.

CHAPTER 8 · INTEGRATION AND DISINTEGRATION

INTRODUCTION

The primary characteristic of kibbutz culture is its cooperative nature. One of the primary aims of this study, therefore, is to discover the ways in which those individuals born into the kibbutz learn to inhibit aggressive impulses and to develop cooperative ones. For purposes of analysis all interaction observed among the children has been classified into one of two categories which have been termed "integrative" and "disintegrative," respectively; and each of these is further divided into subclasses which were established inductively in the process of analyzing the entire interactional sample.

Acts in which a child revealed overt, positive affect[1] in interaction with another were labeled, "integrative," while those in which a child revealed overt, negative affect in interaction with another were labeled, "disintegrative." Table 3 summarizes, by per-

[1] It is immediately apparent to the careful reader that we are in this chapter concerned primarily with two systems of behavior — aggression and cooperation — and he may wonder why we have not employed these terms instead of the more ponderous terms which we have chosen. The reason for our choice will become apparent below when it will be observed that we are concerned with a wider range of responses than are conventionally termed "aggressive" or "cooperative." If a "behavior system" (such as aggression or cooperation) be defined as "a class of responses which share a common motive," it is clear that the subclasses listed in Table 3 do not share a common motive. The motives for "aggression" and for "conflict," for example, as we have defined these terms, are not necessarily the same; and yet we choose to view them as subclasses of the same functional class, for though their motives are different they share a common disruptive social consequence. The latter expression, as defined operationally, is an important variable in this study. They are disruptive, first, because they are both (in general) frustration-producing responses and, secondly, because they both (in general) evoke hostile and/or fear reactions from another child. The socializing agents, too, view them as functionally equivalent responses which they attempt to extinguish. The same logic holds for the three "integrative" subclasses. Aiding a peer in distress, which may be altruistic in motive, and playing with another child, which may be exploitative in motive, have integrative or "affiliative" consequences (for both persons). One could, of course, view the two responses in the above example as sharing a common motive — the affiliative motive — but since the "ultimate" grounds for the affiliation are dissimilar it seemed wiser to differentiate them in the analysis.

centages, the interactional frequencies for each of the four kevutzot discussed in this section.

INTEGRATION

Introduction. Although Table 3 reveals that in all four groups there is more "disintegrative" than "integrative" behavior, it must be emphasized that the percentages in the table, if considered by themselves, constitute spurious measures of integration and disintegration. They are heavily weighted in favor of disintegration for a number of reasons. In the first place, and with the single exception of the oldest group, IV, the behavior of the children is preponderantly of a noninteractive nature. Each child, that is, spends much of his time in activities which do not demand the presence of other children. And where others are required, they are not required in large numbers, so that effective interactional groups usually consist of two or three children. Hence, although the children are almost always together, they comprise a group primarily in an ecological, rather than in a socio-psychological or interactional sense. Even in the oldest group, in which the frequency of interaction is much higher than that in the younger groups, genuine interactional play is less frequent than individualistic play. For the most part, therefore, their behavior is best characterized by the term, "action," rather than by, "interaction." In short, since the frequency of interaction is less than the frequency of action, it would be fallacious to assume from the integration-disintegration ratios that the children spend most of their time in acts of aggression and conflict.

Table 3. Classification of interactions by percentages.

Types of interaction	Group I (Σ acts = 97)		Group II (Σ = 391)		Group III (Σ = 254)		Group IV (Σ = 315)	
Integrative[a]		17		41		29		37
Aid, sharing, affection	6		21		9		13	
Physical affection	2		3		5		5	
Cooperative play	9		17		15		19	
Disintegrative		83		59		71		63
Aggression	45		39		57		52	
Conflict	38		18		11		8	
Refusal to share	0		2		2		3	

[a] A chi square test for difference between "integrative" and "disintegrative" behavior, yields:

$$\chi^2 = 11.99 \qquad \text{d.f.} = 3 \qquad P = < .01$$

(Chi squares in this, and in all tables, needless to say, are based on frequencies, not on percentages.)

Limiting the discussion to interaction, however, we must still note that, without important qualifications, the figures in Table 3 give a distorted picture of the nature of group behavior. This distortion results from the fact that the unit of measurement is the act, not the number of children participating nor the duration of the act. Hence, an act of aggression by one child lasting only sixty seconds is accorded as much weight as an act of cooperative play in which two youngsters interact harmoniously for twenty minutes. Similarly, an act of conflict in which two children are involved is accorded as much weight as an act of cooperative play in which three, four, or even more children participate. In the oldest kevutza, for example, there are sixty instances of cooperative play, comprising 19 per cent of all interactions. But these sixty acts include a total of 135 children, which almost equals the total number of children involved in all acts of aggression (see Table 4). If the individual rather than the act had been the unit of measurement, the percentage of integrative acts would have risen considerably; if the duration of the act had been taken into account, the increase would have been even greater.

But the percentages in Table 3 not only tend to exaggerate the preponderance of disintegrative acts in the integrative-disintegrative ratio, they also shed little light on the amount of group solidarity that exists in these kevutzot. Being qualitative in character, this latter characteristic is notoriously resistant to quantification — yet it contributes significantly to an understanding of the degree of integration to be found in these groups.

Group solidarity. One index of solidarity is the child's verbal identification with the kevutza, an identification which does not begin earlier than Group III, so far as the data reveal. The following examples, taken from Groups III and IV, reflect this type of identification.

The children see the mail truck on the way back from their hike and all identify it. When HELKA asks what the truck is for, Micah says it is to bring letters from his mother, but the others retort that "the mail is for all of us."

This is the first day I attempt to take pictures in the kevutza. The children all ask why I am taking pictures, and Mimi retorts, "Because *we* are so adorable." (*chamudim*).

Nili brought some flowers into the house, and when I asked what she was going to do with them she said: "They are for *our* table."

Identification with the group is found at an even more "primitive" level, in both conscious and unconscious imitative behavior. Conscious imitation is found as early as Group II and continues through Group IV. In Group II, for example, if one child rides a horse, the others decide to ride horses. Should one child begin to bang on the table or a chair, the others will accompany him — making an overwhelming din — and once begun there is no stopping. Sometimes a child leaves the table, in the midst of a meal, to run around the room, and the others leave the table and follow him.

Examples from Groups III and IV reveal that these older children persist in this same kind of imitative behavior.

(We are at the dinner table.) Zeviah tells HELKA that she wants an omelette instead of her soft-boiled egg. The others insist that they too want omelettes.

ZEHAVA has gone to get the clay, and the children are sitting at the table. Hamutal bumps Mimi in the head. All insist that they bump her in the head. Miri begins to shout, and all join in the shouting. Now Mimi begins to sway back and forth, singing a song, and the others do the same.

That much of this imitative behavior is motivated by a desire for group identification is borne out by interviews with the nurses. One nurse noted that when she gives a child milk, he first wants to know if the other children have had their milk; or when she wishes to cover a child with a blanket at night, he first asks if the other children are covered with blankets. In short, the children wish to share in the attributes of the group, which is another way of saying that they wish to be identified with it.

Imitation exists on an unconscious level as well, the most impressive example being that of the patterned whining behavior which is found in Groups III and IV.[2]

A second index of solidarity is the great joy with which the children first greet each other upon awakening in the morning or upon returning to the nursery after their daily visit with their parents. Moreover, if they do not find the other children in the dwelling, they insist on knowing where they are so they can go

---

[2] All the children in these groups exhibit two types of whining each with its characteristic inflections. One type, *uh-nuh,* consists of an abrupt rise at the beginning of the *nuh,* followed by a gradual decline. The other, *ah-yah, ah-yah,* is more complex. The first *ah* is high and the first *yah* is low, while the second *ah* is somewhat higher than the first *yah,* and the second *yah* is higher still than the second *ah.*

to them. This desire to be with the group is strong even in Moshe, the most aggressive of the children in Group III. And despite his extraordinarily strong attachment to his mother, he will generally not go to see her if he knows that the kevutza is to engage in some group activity. One day, after Moshe had gone to see his grandmother, his kevutza went on a hike. When he returned to the house, he looked for the children and complained bitterly because he could not find them. For many months after this incident he reprimanded the nurse for having permitted him to go to his grandmother that day.

Desire to be with the children reflects, among other things, the *esprit de corps* that is found in the kevutza, particularly in the two older kevutzot. In these two groups much of the daily interaction is characterized by laughter, "fun," and warmth which surely represent a high degree of *esprit de corps*. Such comments as, "All this is done with a great deal of fun," or, "All through the play period they seem very happy, talking, singing, enjoying themselves," are scattered liberally throughout our records. The following protocol from Group IV reveals the joy derived from group interaction.

The younger children run to the door of the older children's bedroom. It is locked. They look through the window, scream, and run back laughing and shouting with glee. This is repeated a number of times.

Universally the nurses report that though the children ask to sleep in their parental rooms, they are overjoyed, after enjoying that experience,[3] to return to the children's house.

The desire of the children to return to their kevutza after a prolonged absence from the kibbutz is reported by almost all parents. And during their absence their behavior is characterized almost universally by constant references to their kevutza. Throughout the day the children will ask, "And what are the children in Kiryat Yedidim doing now?" Sometimes they themselves volunteer this information — "Now they are sleeping" or "Now they are taking a walk" or "Now they are playing." One mother, when abroad with her son, took full advantage of this fact by using it as a technique of control. When the child resisted her suggestion that he come to eat, or go to sleep, or take a bath, she would say that the children in Kiryat Yedidim were engaged in these activities, and this invariably achieved compliance.

[3] There are certain occasions, such as illness in the nursery or arrival of visiting children, which require the children to sleep in their parental rooms.

But children are "significant others" for their peers in still another sense — they want their approval. In Group IV, where this trait is most frequently found, the attempt to obtain the approval of the others is seen most clearly during their creative work (painting, drawing, sand-modeling, and so forth) in which the child's first response to the completion of a picture or a model is to call the other children to observe what he has made. Sometimes it is not the entire group but only specific children whose approval is desired. There is one child whose favorable opinion the children most frequently seek. (He is the oldest, strongest, and most frequent child socializer of aggression.) And often they will not continue with an activity until he has looked at what they are doing.

If the children refuse to look at another's handiworks, he is often quite dejected. Boaz, for example, caught a live butterfly, and announced this fact, with much bravado, to the other children. They, however, ignored him, whereupon Boaz, sorely disappointed, left the group. On the other hand, should a child's action or aspiration receive the approval of a peer he is very pleased, as the following example from Group III reveals.

Zeviah tells Israel that she wishes to be a tractorist. Israel says that (so far as he is concerned) she may. She beams . . .

Still another aspect of group solidarity is the socialization of children by their peers. This socialization behavior is termed "integrative" because it consists, for the most part, in praise of the child who conforms or who reveals progressive achievements in a given task (see pp. 204–205); or because, as in the case of aggression, it is essentially nurturant — the socializer attacks the aggressor or protects the victim.

This latter type of socialization — nurturance — is found in other areas, as well.

Nadav is playing in the sandbox with other children. Esther says, "Nadav, you are not supposed to be playing in the sand. You have a cut on your leg."

This, then, is the qualitative frame of reference within which Table 3 must be viewed. If it be remembered that the percentages in the table represent gross measures of *quantifiable* interactions, then the interpretation of a greater degree of disintegration may be viewed in proper perspective. With these qualifications in mind, we may now examine the subclasses of the larger "integrative" class, with the exception of "Physical affection," which will be discussed later.

Aid, share, affection. In Groups I and II the kinds of behavior that are characterized as "aid" or "share" include such acts as offering a toy or food to another child, either spontaneously or at the instigation of the nurse; inviting another child to come with the initiator; bringing a chair for an adult or for another child.

The development of the repertory of sharing and aiding behavior may be measured by a comparison of these acts with those found in Groups III and IV. In Group III the following types of acts are to be found: helping a child to get out of bed by placing a chair at the side of his bed, helping a child to dress, volunteering to help feed another child, going to the communal kitchen when asked by another child, combing another child's hair, helping another child to pick up his blocks, sharing food with another child, and ordering a child to desist from hitting another.

In Group IV the development is even more pronounced. Here the acts include offering to help another child to dress, sharing candy with the other children, pulling a child out of the mud into which he has fallen, calling the children to eat the bread and jam which the nurse had put on the table, ordering a child to desist from hitting another.

Although there are examples of spontaneous sharing among the children, particularly in Group IV, most acts of sharing are initiated at the request of the nurse. Moreover, since this sharing is not spontaneous, a child may regret his original decision to share and insist that the shared object be returned to him. Thus in Group II,

Yuval asks for more milk. Nurse asks Dena if Yuval may have some of her milk, and Dena says yes. Nurse gives the cup to Yuval, and Dena immediately begins to cry.

This reluctance to share will be discussed in detail in the discussion of "disintegration." It should be emphasized, however, that almost all aspects of the children's lives represent some form of sharing on their part, if only implicitly. An almost ubiquitous feature of their experience, for example, is the *tor*, or "turn." The children must frequently wait in line in order to receive something, such as clothes from the laundry, or in order to do something, such as play with the swing. In general they take their turns without interfering with each other. Moreover, they may spontaneously form a line in order to do or receive something. One day, for example, the children wanted to use my eraser. When given permission, they formed a line so that each could have his turn. When other children wished to participate, they were told to take their place in the line.

This implicit sharing, as manifested in the tor, is vigorously insisted upon by the children. The boys and girls in Group IV, for example, after making a swing by themselves, had agreed upon the order in which they were to take their turn when a mother entered the yard and said that her daughter would be the next one to try the swing. All the children shouted, "*lo nachon,*" (not correct) — they had arranged a tor, and the daughter would have to wait her turn.

Turning now to affection and solicitude, it will again be observed that there is a development in these responses from Groups I and II through Groups III and IV. In the former two groups the following examples are found: consoling another child who is crying, warning a child of danger or of the fact that some activity in which he is engaging is forbidden, praising another for some accomplishment:

Avner urinates in the playpen, and Iris says, "Marvelous, he is making pee-pee!"

In Group III the following acts are to be found: consoling a child who falls, asking an adult to intervene when a child is being attacked by another, consoling a child who has been hit by another, covering a child with a blanket and singing him to sleep.

In Group IV the following are typical of acts of affection and solicitude: referring to a child by an endearing term such as *chamudi* (my adorable one), consoling a child who has been hit by another, offering a toy to a child who has fallen, consoling a child for some deprivation.

The children are looking at a picture book, and identify certain children in the pictures as "themselves." Moshe is unhappy because he does not see a picture of "himself." Chana says, "Don't be sad, we'll find one of you."

Several intragroup generalizations emerge from an analysis of these data. The first generalization that may be drawn is that the number of integrative acts performed by any one child varies considerably. The range for Groups I–IV, respectively, is 0–4, 1–28, 0–8, 0–7. The second generalization — one consistent with the intergroup comparisons already made — is that in all four groups the older children in each group tend to initiate integrative acts more frequently than do the younger children. Third, the younger children in each group are more often the recipients or objects of integrative acts than are the older children. In some cases this inverse relationship between "initiating" and "receiving" is almost perfect, so that in Group I, for example, the oldest child is the most frequent initiator of integrative acts, but he is never the recipient, while in Group III the youngest child is the most frequent recipient of integrative acts, but never the initiator of such acts. In other words, those who initiate integrative acts least frequently tend to be the objects of integrative acts most frequently. This inverse relationship between initiation and receipt appears to be a function not only of age but of passivity as well. In all four groups, for example, we, although infrequent (and in some groups, null) initiators of integrative acts are among the most frequent recipients of such acts.

Table 4. Cooperative play by percentage of total play acts, number of children, and types of play.

Group	Cooperative play acts[a]		Children participating[b]		Types of cooperative play[c]	
	Σ	Percentage	Σ	Percentage	Σ	Percentage
I	9	11	18	19	7	20
II	66	15	140	27	20	28
III	38	25	96	45	25	43
IV	60	30	135	49	28	43

[a] At the 0.99 confidence level, the upper confidence limit for cooperative play is less than 50 per cent for all groups. The finding — cooperative play < individualistic play — may be accepted with high confidence.

[b] At the 0.99 confidence level, the upper confidence limit for cooperative play is less than 50 per cent for Groups I and II only. The finding — cooperative play < individualistic play — is not significant for Groups III and IV.

[c] At the 0.99 confidence level, the upper confidence limit for cooperative play is less than 50 per cent for Groups I and II only. The finding — cooperative play < individualistic play — is not significant for Groups III and IV.

Cooperative play. Table 4 attempts to reveal in a rough way some quantitative characteristics of cooperative play for all four groups. It will be noted first that if the total number of play acts in the sample be taken as the base, the percentage of cooperative play acts — as distinct from individualistic acts — comprises a minority of all play. (It is never higher than 30 per cent.)

This is not an entirely valid measure, however, of the extent to which cooperation is to be found among these children. As we have observed, using the act as the unit of measurement does not reveal the differences in the number of participants that may importantly characterize the activities being compared. Therefore, when the number of participants is taken as the unit of measurement — as is shown in the second column of Table 4 — cooperative play is seen to play a greater role. This table also reveals that cooperative play, as measured by either of these criteria, increases with age. The increase, indeed, is so sharp that for the two older groups the difference between cooperative and individualistic play is not significant, statistically. But even this latter observation does not adequately characterize the magnitude of this development, however, for it omits two important dimensions: the first of which is "richness." By richness we refer in the first place to the extensiveness of the play repertory, so that richness of interaction may be said to increase as a function of the different types of play in which children cooperate. If types of play are used as the unit of measurement, as the third column of the table reveals, interaction in the oldest group, IV, is more than twice as rich as interaction in Group I. Hence the older children cooperate in a much greater variety of activities than do the younger.

But by richness we refer also to certain qualitative aspects of interaction which also differ with age. In the youngest group, for example, cooperative play is of a simple imitative variety: one child hands a ball to another, who hands it back to the first child; one child rocks in the playpen, another gets down on all fours and rocks with him, and both laugh. Although labeled as "cooperative play," these are not genuine acts of cooperation; they are, rather, imitative acts, that encourage interaction.

If the cooperative acts in Group II are compared with those in Group I, the qualitative differences become immediately apparent. For example,

Amir holds a sand pail, and Rafi puts colored plaster balls into it, while Omri watches. When the bucket is full, Amir empties it. Then Omri fills the pail with the balls, Rafi and Amir watching him. Rafi empties it.

Chana and Anat play together with a strip of wire grilling. They walk with it, each holding an end, Chana in front. Later Pnina takes one end, Yehuda takes the other, and they walk with it,

In Groups III and IV cooperative or interactive play is much more complex and often takes the form of genuine games — such as train, doctor and nurse, work, or tea party. In short there is an increase in the richness of interaction.

But Table 4 omits a dimension whose importance has already been indicated for making comparisons *between* behavioral variables — duration. Duration is equally important for measuring development in one variable. The children in the two younger groups play together for a very few minutes and then return to their individualistic activities. In the two older groups, and particularly in Group IV, the time span is much longer and children may play together an entire morning. If time, as well as frequency of acts and number of children, had been measured, it is our strong impression that cooperation in Group IV would not only have been much greater than in the other groups, but that cooperative rather than individualistic play would have predominated in this group.

Despite the frequency of cooperative play, it should be noted in conclusion that there are almost no instances in any of the groups in which the entire group interacts as a unit. The children in the two younger groups generally interact in groups of two, occasionally three, and, on rare occasions, four. These diadic and triadic interactions are, moreover, never structured into anything resembling a permanent social relationship. On the contrary, these groups are fluid and constantly changing. Children A and B, for example, interact for a brief time, often no more than a few minutes, after which A may go off by himself and B joins C. The interacting individuals change throughout the day. It may be observed that neither personal friendships nor enmities are to be found among the children of this age.

In the two older groups, particularly in Group IV, the number of simultaneously interacting children is sometimes much greater, but the participants change frequently during the day, as in the younger groups. On the other hand, the oldest group has begun to show signs of relatively permanent in-group formation, of cliques, of special if not intimate friendships (and of enmities — at least in the form of scapegoating).

DISINTEGRATION

The category of disintegration includes three distinct subclasses of behavior: aggression, conflict, and refusal to share. Refusal to share, the least frequent behavior, is self-explanatory. Acts of aggression are distinguished from acts of conflict in that the former include those situations in which a child, as far as could be ascertained, was motivated by a desire to hurt or harm another; conflict, on the other hand, includes those situations in which a child seized an object possessed by a peer without intending harm or injury to the possessor. However, acts of conflict may — and often do — lead to acts of aggression, and such acts or succession of acts are classified both as conflict and aggression.

Table 5. Types of aggression by percentages.

Aggression	Group I (Σ acts = 44)	Group II ($\Sigma = 152$)	Group III ($\Sigma = 145$)	Group IV ($\Sigma = 164$)
Tattling	0	0	7	2
Verbal	0	3	9	31
Disobedience	0	10	4	2
Physical	100	87	80	65

Aggression. Table 3 reveals that for all four groups acts of aggression constitute approximately 50 per cent of all interaction (the percentage for Group II, the apparent exception, would rise approximately 10 per cent if the atypical child discussed below (p. 178) were eliminated from the sample). Actually, there is more aggression observed in these groups than is indicated by the Table. When, for example, a child manifests both verbal and physical aggression it would have been recorded as two acts had each expression been employed against different children or against the same child at different times. There are, furthermore, some instances in which either the entire group or a large segment of it is the aggressor, but such acts have not been included in the table because the names of participating individuals were not always recorded.

Four types of aggression were observed in these groups. As recorded in Table 5, they include tattling, verbal aggression, disobedience, and physical aggression. Tattling, or informing on another child to the nurse, is (with the exception of Group III) the least frequent form of aggression and, indeed, is not found at all in the two younger, relatively nonverbal, groups. In Group III, only three of the eight children are responsible for all tattling. Behavior reported to the nurse includes another child's rolling a toy on the wall, taking a cover of a jar, aggressing, and throwing food on the floor. In Group IV, only three of the seventeen children are responsible for the three acts of tattling that concerned another child's being frightened by a goat and two instances of enuresis.

Verbal aggression does not occur in Group I, which has not yet acquired language, is infrequent in Groups II and III, but is relatively frequent in Group IV. In Group II, only two acts of verbal aggression are found in the sample, and both were exhibited by the same child. In one instance she addressed a child as *tipesh* (fool) and in the other she responded to an act of aggression by telling the aggressor that "You are a baby!" Although verbal aggression is infrequent in Group III, it is expressed by all but one of the eight children. The content of this aggression will be discussed together with that of Group IV. In the latter group verbal aggression comprises almost one-third of all acts of aggression. Since most verbal aggression consists of "name-calling" it may be concluded that the greater incidence of this type of aggression in this oldest group is a function of greater linguistic facility and, specifically, of a growing vocabulary. Although only three of the seventeen children in this group exhibit no verbal aggression, there is great variability, ranging from zero to ten responses.

Name-calling, followed by threats to harm or injure, constitutes the bulk of verbal aggression in both Groups III and IV. The absolute frequency with which name-calling is employed is higher in the older of the two groups, however, as is its repertory of opprobrious terms. In Group III, for example, only three such terms are employed: baby, *fooia* (phooey), and lo chamud (not nice). In Group IV, on the other hand, the vocabulary of aggression includes such other terms as *kaker* (defecator), pig, food, *pee-pee* (urine), monkey, donkey, filthy *toosi* (anus), *drek* (dirt).[4]

Peers instigate verbal aggression much more frequently than do nurses. In Group IV 22 per cent of all acts of verbal aggression are instigated by peers, whereas only 2 per cent are instigated by the nurse. But although the nurse — the socializer and presumably important frustrator — almost never instigates a response of verbal aggression, the anthropologist (M.E.S.) — the neutral observer — instigates most of the acts of verbal aggression in Group III. Sixty-nine per cent are instigated by the anthropologist, as compared with 1 per cent instigated by the nurse. (In Group IV,

[4] It is of more than passing interest to consider the terms italicized above for Group IV. These responses, all of an excretory nature, are Yiddish rather than Hebrew. It would appear that some of the explicit elements of the shtetl culture that are still found in the kibbutz, and that enter the child's consciousness quite early in his development, consist of an aggressive, and primarily anal, vocabulary.

however, the anthropologist (M.E.S.) instigates only 4 per cent of the aggressive acts.) Of perhaps greatest interest is the apparent absence of instigation in 64 per cent of the acts in Group IV. This absence of instigation in such a large percentage of cases is particularly interesting when it is observed that the anthropologist is the object of 60 per cent of all the acts of verbal aggression in this group (and of 35 per cent of all acts in Group III). Since these aggressive responses are directed against a neutral object (that is, I am not a frustrator), it might be suggested that these responses constitute displaced, rather than uninstigated, aggression. We shall have reason to return to this question of displaced aggression again (see pp. 167–171).

As Table 5 indicates, disobedience among these groups is rare. The relatively high incidence of disobedience (10 per cent) found in Group II is explained by the role of the observer (A.G.S.) which was different from the observer's role in the other groups.[5]

Physical aggression is overwhelmingly the most frequent type of aggression in all four groups, although its percentage decreases, as verbal aggression increases, with age. With the exception of three children in the youngest group, every child in the sample is responsible for at least one act of physical aggression. The range, however, is wider than that for any other single category — 0–38, 2–22, 1–33, 2–14 for Groups I–IV, respectively.

The repertory of physical aggression is extensive and includes such acts as hitting, hitting with an object, kicking, biting, pushing, throwing an object at the victim, destroying another's property, scratching, gouging, hair-pulling, pushing, smearing, choking, interfering with activity, hair-cutting, penis-pulling. In all groups hitting is the most frequent type of aggression, representing 31, 66, 44, and 47 per cent of all acts of physical aggression in Groups I–IV, respectively. There is no consistency, however, in the second most frequent type, either in technique or frequency. For Group I it is hair-pulling (22 per cent); for Group II, biting (6 per cent); for Groups III and IV, hitting with an object (16 and 14 per cent). It should be noted, too, that acts of physical aggression occur overwhelmingly in the context of play. For Groups I–IV, respectively, play is the context for 100, 69, 86, and 93 per cent of all acts of physical aggression.

[5] As is explained in Appendix A, my wife frequently played the role of socializer in Group II, and she is the object of most of the acts of disobedience in the group. If the acts of disobedience directed toward her are excluded from the sample, the percentage drops to 1 per cent.

Table 6. Instigation to physical aggression by percentages.

Instigation	Group I (Σ acts = 44)	Group II (Σ = 140)	Group III (Σ = 118)	Group IV (Σ = 107)
None or unknown[a]	64	57	64	67
Instigated by peer[b]	16	29	29	27
Conflict	14	14	12	9
Physical aggression	0	13	14	13
Other	2	2	3	5
Instigated by adult	20	14	7	1
Reprimand by nurse	0	4	3	1
Deprivation of object by nurse	0	2	2	0
Deprivation of nurse's attention	11	3	0	0
Anthropologist	9	4	2	0
Other	0	1	0	0
Other	0	0	0	5

[a] At the 0.99 confidence level the upper confidence limit for non-instigated aggression is less than 50 per cent for Groups III and IV only. The finding — uninstigated aggression > instigated aggression — is not significant for Groups I and II.

[b] A chi square test for difference between peer- and adult-instigation to aggression yields:

$$\chi^2 = 14.90 \qquad d.f. = 3 \qquad P = <.01$$

Instigations to physical aggression are summarized in Table 6. Before citing examples of the various categories of instigation it must be emphasized that the instigator of aggression is not necessarily the victim of aggression. The nurse, for example, is infrequently the victim of aggression in Groups I and II and never the victim in Groups III and IV, even though she is occasionally the obvious instigator of such aggression. In the examples of nurse-instigation cited below, therefore, the aggression is uniformly displaced.

This example illustrates aggression instigated by a nurse's reprimand.

Nurse (Group II) comes out . . . sees Shula's shoe and sock on the floor, says, "Shula, I can't keep dressing you," takes shoe and sock in the house. Shula screams, cries and cries. Avner stands and watches her, and Shula hits him, continues to cry. Finally, nurse comes out, puts on her shoe and sock, saying, "Shula, I don't have time to keep doing this, I am working, I will not do it any more, do you hear?" She goes in the house, and Shula stands quietly. Then she begins to throw toys out of the playpen onto the ground.

Deprivation of an object by the nurse refers to aggression that follows an insistence by the nurse that a child share a toy or other object with a peer.

Deprivation of the nurse refers to the latter's absence or departure or to her refusal or inability to give exclusive attention to one child, as in the examples below.

Amnon (Group II) wants to be in the house with ETTA, but she tells the children they must play outside. She leads them into the yard and returns to the house. Amnon runs to the steps and screams and screams, "ETTA." Rafel comes, tries to stroke Amnon. Amnon hits him . . .

Nurse (Group I) holding Eldad, comes in . . . Boaz rushes over, grabs at Eldad, but Nurse prevents him from touching Eldad by shaking his outstretched hand and saying, "Hello, chaver" . . . Boaz turns immediately, dashes over to David, pulls his hair, drags him down . . . (Nurse isolates Boaz) . . .

It will be noted in Table 6 that the anthropologist is the second most frequent adult-instigator of aggression. In all cases, he instigated the aggression either by depriving a child of his attention or (as in the first two groups where he functioned as a socializer) by reprimanding a child for some misdeed.

Adult-instigated aggression is quite definitely secondary to that instigated by peers, as Table 6 reveals. Of all acts that were perceived to be instigated, the most important instigating condition in three of the four groups is some frustration imposed by peers. (The apparent exception to this generalization — Group I — is not statistically significant.) Before examining some of the implications of this quantitative difference between adult- and peer-instigation, it should be observed that the latter assumes three characteristic forms. Either a child aggresses against his fellow and the latter retaliates; or a child attempts to take a toy or other object from his fellow, and the latter resists and is therefore attacked; or the latter attacks in order to retain the object.

Perhaps the most interesting characteristic of physical aggression (a characteristic noted in verbal aggression as well), is its apparently uninstigated nature. As Table 6 indicates, approximately two-thirds of all the acts of physical aggression are uninstigated — that is, no apparent stimulus in the immediate social field of the child was perceived by the observer to have induced an aggression response. It is our hypothesis, based on general behavior theory (all behavior is motivated) and on our own data (to be presented below) that these apparently uninstigated acts actually represent instances of displaced aggression. In some instances, at least, we were able to observe such displacement directly — a child attacks his fellow, and the latter, in turn, attacks a third child. A tabulation of such responses in Groups III and IV reveals that 10 per cent of all acts of physical aggression were observed to be displaced in this manner. Even in those instances in which we were not able to observe the process of displacement, however, there is reason to believe that these apparently uninstigated acts of aggression are, in fact, displacements. And this brings us, again, to the discrepancy between peer- and adult-instigated aggression.

Even in Group I, in which frustration imposed by adults (nurses) is more frequent than that imposed by peers, the incidence of adult-instigated aggression is only 20 per cent of the total. Since the nurse is perceived by the children as one of the most important frustraters in their lives, it might have been assumed that she would have provoked more aggression in the children as a function of the frustrations attendant upon training. The relative infrequency of nurse-instigation to aggression, therefore, demands explanation.[6]

One explanation is that the nurse, though an important socializer, is rarely present during the children's play periods (in which most aggression occurs) so that she had little occasion to frustrate

[6] An examination of Table 6 not only reveals the relative infrequency of nurse-instigation to aggression, but it shows a progressive decrease (statistically significant) from the youngest to the oldest kevutza in her importance as an instigator. This progressive decline in the role of the nurse demands some explanation. The greater frequency of nurse-instigation in Group I may probably be attributed to a structural difference between it and the other groups. Whereas the three older groups were generally in the charge of two nurses (except for a few hours in the afternoon), the youngest group was in the charge of one nurse exclusively. This means that a child who desired the care or attention of the nurse could not easily obtain it, since she was either preoccupied with her manifold duties in the house, or already involved with caring for another child. In the older groups, on the other hand, since two nurses were present, the child could more easily obtain attention. This hypothesis is consistent with the figures in Table 6 which reveal that while all the aggression instigated by the nurse (11 per cent) in the youngest group is a function of deprivation of the nurse's attention, it accounts for a much smaller percentage in Group II (3 per cent) and is nonexistent in Groups III and IV.

There is yet another factor that may account for the progressive decline in the role of the nurse as an instigator of aggression. As the children grow older and acquire greater motor facility, they have more opportunity to frustrate each other by acts of conflict and aggression. Since the percentages in Table 6 are functions of each other, much of the difference among the groups therefore may be explained as an increase in peer instigation (as a function of age) rather than as a decrease in nurse instigation.

the children during our observational sessions. This explanation is not sufficient, however, for, even in those instances in which her frustrating behavior was perceived to be the direct instigation to aggression, she was almost never its victim; the resulting aggression was almost always displaced onto a neutral party. In short, although the nurse is the instigator of aggression, she is *never* the victim of physical aggression and only once is she the object of verbal aggression.[7] It is difficult to escape the conclusion, therefore, that at least some of the uninstigated aggression found in the sample is only apparent, and actually represents displacement of generalized hostility from frustrating acts of the nurse which we did not observe, but which are inherent in the socialization process. And the reason that the children inhibit their direct aggression may be attributed to fear of punishment, either in the form of discipline or in the form of loss of love.

But not all, and perhaps not even most, of the apparently uninstigated aggression represents displacement from the nurse. As we have observed, parents and siblings are also important sources of frustration for the child; yet direct aggression against them is rare. It is probably rare, not only because parents and siblings are not with the child during the day, but (as in the case of the nurse) because of the unfortunate consequences of aggression — punishment in the form of loss of love. Finally, some peer-frustration undoubtedly results in displaced aggression. For although there is no perfect pecking order in these groups, there is a sufficiently strong trend in that direction so that those who are aggressed against by their superiors may displace their consequent aggression against weaker victims.

If children inhibit their aggression against those whose retaliation they fear or whose love they wish to retain, this inhibition should generalize to others who fall into either or both of these categories. There is evidence to support this expectation. In Group II (as in Groups III and IV) the nurse is the least frequent victim of aggression; and the anthropologist — contrary to his high frequency as a victim in Groups III and IV — is the second least frequent victim. This discrepancy between the incidence of aggression directed against the observer in Group II, on the one hand, and in Groups III and IV, on the other, is predictable on the basis of our hypothesis. For while the observer in Groups III and IV (M.E.S.) was always the neutral observer, the observer in Group II (A.G.S.) did not play such a passive role. Hence, it is argued, since she played the role of nurse she was perceived by

[7] See p. 208 for the use of incontinence as a technique of aggression.

the children, and responded to, as a nurse. For the same reasons that the nurse is seldom aggressed against, the observer, too, was infrequently the object of aggression.[8]

For the same reasons, one boy in Group IV is almost never the victim of aggression (he is the victim of aggression [verbal] only once). This child bears a remarkable functional resemblance to the nurse. He is the most popular child in the kevutza and all the children want him to like them. He is also the strongest child in the group, hence, all fear him. He is, moreover, a socializer — indeed, one of the most important socializing agents for aggression in his group. Thus, this child who is the functional equivalent of the nurse is responded to as a nurse.

We suggest that frustration by nurses, parents and siblings, and peers results in displaced aggression, and that this process is reflected in the high percentage of uninstigated aggression in Table 6. This interpretation is indirectly supported by one further finding. In Groups III and IV the frequency with which I was the victim of aggression is extraordinarily high. I was the most frequent victim of *all* types of aggression, accounting for one-fifth of all aggressive acts in Group III and for one-third of such acts in Group IV. Yet in all but two instances, the aggression is apparently uninstigated. This finding, somewhat startling when one realizes that my role in these groups was one of neutral observer, is difficult to explain except as a displacement of aggression against a harmless victim, harmless because he does not punish and because the loss of his love does not constitute a psychological threat. Functionally, then, I was similar to the weak children in these groups who are the most frequent peer-victims of aggression, but who seldom punish their aggressors: such children are not only weak and therefore nonpunitive, but their love is not desired by the other children. In spite of adult status, therefore, I believe that I was perceived as the functional equivalent of these children.[9] That this is so is demonstrated strikingly by

[8] There is no necessary contradiction between this interpretation and the finding that the observer is disobeyed more frequently than the nurse in these same groups. The gradient of generalization principle (from nurse to observer) would lead us to expect a greater generalization to physical aggression than to disobedience. That is, if the observer, in this instance, is perceived as similar to (but not identical with) the nurse, one might expect the children to disobey, but not to aggress against, her.

[9] That the aggression directed toward me could be as severe as that directed toward peers may be seen in the following excerpt from Group IV.

(I am sitting on a chair in the bedroom. The children are just getting up from their afternoon nap.) Yosi pulls at my penis and says, "Michael (my name in

the additional finding that the most frequent aggressors against me were those children who are at the bottom of the pecking order.

The existence of this "scapegoating" phenomenon is recognized by the educational authorities of The Federation. Writing in a kibbutz educational journal, the Education Director observes that

> . . . one incident, which is widespread, demonstrates very well the tensions, and their consequent aggressions, that are found in the kevutza — the scapegoat. In almost every kevutza there is some child against whom all aggression is turned.

When this happens, the aggression becomes intense indeed, as the following excerpt from Group IV reveals.

> Tsvi hits Giora and threatens to cut him with a knife he is holding. Nili and Tsvi hold Giora while Avner threatens to cut him . . . Tsvi and Giora fight, and Giora calls him a donkey. Nili jumps on Giora; Tsvi hits him, Giora cries and cries, calls Tsvi a donkey. Chaim jumps on Giora, chokes him, gouges him in the eye. He seems to be really hurt and screams . . . In a few minutes, Nili pushes him down, Chaim jumps on him and hits him, and Tsvi cuts his hair with a scissors.

This example is, of course, extreme, but there are similar instances to be found in the records. They indicate that once the children's aggression drives are liberated, they may attack another recklessly and mercilessly, knowing neither justice nor sympathy. Giora is the smallest and youngest of the children, yet all attacked him, and no one came to his assistance.

Hebrew) *kaker*" a number of times, and then laughs heartily. The other children repeat this behavior after him. Yosi then says he wants to see what I am "drawing." He looks, and says, "It is not pretty." He tells Yonah to look and she too says it is not pretty. Yonah calls Yosi and whispers something to him. He comes to me and says, "You are a kaker." Yonah tells him to say it again. She now encourages him to hit me. She pushes his hand on me, and when he hits me she runs away. He hits me a few times with his hand, and now begins to hit with his shirt. All the time, Yonah tells him to hit me, but won't do it herself. She picks up a doll, and Yosi tells her to hit me with it. But she says that *he* should hit me. He hits me; I get up, and he runs away, screaming. He comes back and hits me again, now he hits my chest with his fist. The other children are standing around us, egging him on. I get up, and they all run away.

This excerpt also reveals the great importance of peer-influence in behavior. Many acts, instigated by one's peers, are motivated by a desire to conform to peer expectations, rather than by the satisfaction of one's own aggressive needs or the attainment of one's own goals.

Table 7. Responses to physical aggression by percentages.

Response	Group I (Σ acts = 50)	Group II (Σ = 126)	Group III (Σ = 129)	Group IV (Σ = 104)
Cry, scream, whine	56	37	48	29
No manifest response	28	30	23	19
Retaliate (physical or verbal)	2	21	16	29
Retreat	10	4	9	10
Seek help	2	4	1	13
Suck thumb	2	2	2	0
Laugh or talk	0	2	1	0

Testing for differences among three categories—Cry, scream, whine; Retaliate; and the combined category of all others, yields:

$$\chi^2 = 44.06 \qquad \text{d.f.} = 6 \qquad P = <.001$$

Since so much peer interaction consists of physical aggression, it is interesting to consider how the victims respond. These responses are summarized in Table 7. It will be noted that the entry, "No manifest response," occurs with relatively high frequency. In fact, however, the children do respond to actual aggression somewhat more frequently than the percentages for this entry indicate. For, in attempting to measure the frequency of aggression in these groups, all acts of *attempted* aggression were tabulated, whether or not the aggressor was actually successful in completing his intent. In some such instances, the intended victim perceived the imminency of attack and moved away; this was classified as a "Retreat" response. But in a few instances the intended victim, unaware of the attacker's intent, coincidentally happened to move out of range before the attempted aggression was completed, and these acts were classified as "No manifest response," together with those acts in which a child was actually attacked but failed to respond in any overt way.

For all groups, crying is the most frequent reaction to aggression, although, with one exception (Group III) to be discussed below, there is a progressive diminution in this response with age. The crying response, as qualitative analysis reveals, is (except when it is a genuine expression of pain and/or an index of low frustration-tolerance), an instrumental act having a dual aim — to compel the aggressor to desist, and to call upon the nurse for assistance and/or nurturance. Such crying diminishes with age for two reasons. First, the children, as they mature, learn that there are more effective techniques for discouraging the aggressor.

Instead of discouraging him from continuing, crying most frequently encourages the aggressor to persist; once their aggressive energies are liberated, the children show little mercy, and indication of pain only stimulates them to greater efforts.

Crying diminishes with age also because the children discover that protection by the nurse — a second motive for crying — cannot be relied upon. Because of her many duties and responsibilities, the nurse is infrequently present when aggression occurs (on those rare occasions when she is present, she does give aid and comfort to the victim), and the children soon learn that, except for intense and prolonged crying, she will not appear. This interpretation is consistent with, and related to, another finding of Table 7 — the infrequency with which the children seek help from the nurse. The children in the youngest kevutza are generally confined to playpens and cribs, so that they are physically unable to seek help. This is not true for the older children, however, but the percentage of those who seek out the nurse remains small. In Group IV, for example, of the eleven children who sought aid or comfort from someone, only two solicited the help of the nurse — the nine others turned to peers or to the anthropologist.

Retaliation, either physical or verbal, replaces crying as the technique for discouraging the aggressor. The frequencies of these two responses are functionally related — with one exception (Group III) crying diminishes, while retaliation increases, with age. This exception is interesting because it demonstrates in sharp relief one important (maladaptive) consequence of collective education.

In all five kevutzot (five kevutzot are actually included in the sample, it will be remembered, although two have been combined to make one group) there are individual differences both in the frequency of aggression and in the frequency with which the children are the victims of aggression. It has already been stated that, although our analysis reveals no perfect pecking order, there is a tendency in all groups for the most aggressive children to be the least frequent victims, and for the least aggressive children to be the most frequent victims of aggression. Nevertheless, in Groups II and IV the spread in both the initiation and the victimization of aggression is not very great, so that, despite the inequality of the children, no one child is in a greatly advantageous or disadvantageous position.

In Groups I and III, however, the picture is quite different. In the youngest kevutza one child — Amnon — is responsible for 86 per cent of all acts of aggression. Since he is extremely aggressive and, moreover, the biggest and strongest child in the group, the others are terrified of him and never retaliate against him. Their only possible response, therefore, is crying. Hence the extreme ratio of crying to retaliation in this group (56:2).

In Group III, on the other hand, the problem is not so much that of an extraordinarily aggressive child but rather of an extraordinarily passive one. The latter — Zev — is consistently the most victimized child in the group (almost three times as frequently as the least victimized); being the weakest child in the group, he has no technique for coping with this aggression other than crying. Hence in this group crying and retaliation reverse the general trend.[10]

This analysis is of crucial importance for our understanding of interaction in the kevutza. One of the theoretical premises upon which the system of peer-group dwellings is based is the presumed security that the child derives from interacting with equals, rather than with those who are his physical superiors (parents and older siblings). As the official educational philosophy of The Federation expresses it,

> The children's society, with its groups according to age, gives the child a sense of security. Otherwise, in conventional-type societies he feels like "Gulliver among the Giants."

These data reveal that collective education can sometimes intensify, rather than diminish, the "Gulliver among the Giants" phenomenon. In Group I the children are not only terrified of Amnon's aggression, but they are terrified by *him*. Hence his presence in the group is highly disturbing to the other children, and his mere appearance in the play-yard is sufficient cause for crying, whimpering, and retreat behavior on the part of the others. One of the marked characteristics of this group is its marked passivity.[11]

[10] Zev's nurse has commented on his behavior. Zev has never been able to fight back and his sole defense against aggression has been to cry. He seems to have ample justification for his crying:

Micah pinches Zev very hard in the arm. Zev screams. Micah pinches harder, then pushes his hand into his face and gouges his eye. All the time, Zev is screaming from pain, and Micah has a sadistic gleam in his eye . . . The other children, sitting on the porch, ignore the fight.

Pnina comes up to Zev and squeezes him hard. He cries. She hits him with a cloth, then in a deliberate manner beats and bites him. He screams and screams.

[11] A glance at one or two examples of Amnon's aggression will serve to indicate that his so-called peers have good reason to fear him.

Amnon comes over, tries to grab the stick from Pua. She screams loudly, and

The small and weak child in Group III does not disrupt the group, but he suffers from his own defenselessness, not only physically but socially as well. Zev almost always plays by himself and, indeed, is a social isolate. His isolation is self- rather than group-imposed as he prefers to play alone and seldom attempts to enter into the play of others. It is our strong impression that his self-imposed isolation results from his fear of attack, and is his only, if ineffective, defense.

This phenomenon is found in the other groups, as well.[12] One of the most perceptive teachers in Kiryat Yedidim observed that the smallest (usually the youngest) child suffers greatly because he is constantly attacked by the older children, so that if he desires to interact with them he must constantly struggle. This she feels is so important that when her own child was born, she experienced considerable anxiety lest the child be placed in a kevutza in which she would be the youngest.

There are many formal similarities to be found between integration and aggression. In both forms of interaction there is much intragroup variability; in both, the older children are the more frequent initiators; and in both, the younger children are the more frequent recipients. In short, the younger children are more frequently the victims of aggression, but they are more frequently the objects of integration, as well. On the other hand, the older children are the more aggressive, but they are also the more integrative. Despite these formal similarities with respect to age, there are important differences with respect to sex (see pp. 247–248) which show that the inverse relationship between initiation and recipience of interaction does not hold with respect to all variables.

---

he desists. Then Pua bangs the stick on the bench and both laugh. In a minute, Eldad comes and pulls the stick from Pua, who screams and· cries. Amnon pulls on Pua's suspenders, hits her once on the head. Then he goes to Eldad, grabs the stick and hits Eldad on the back with it several times. Eldad looks dazed . . . Amnon hits Pua on the head with the stick several times. Pua is silent at first, then cries. Amnon repeats, whacks her on the head and neck. Pua screams. He starts to hit her again, but I (A.G.S.) call him to come to me . . .

Amnon and Yaakov sit in the playpen, ignoring each other. Suddenly, Amnon pulls Yaakov's hair, crawls on his back, starts to bite him. I (A.G.S.) tell Amnon no. He turns, bites Eldad on the back . . .

[12] That the smaller and weaker children are at the mercy of the larger and stronger is apparently a generic characteristic of collective education and is not restricted to Kiryat Yedidim. In his excellent novel of kibbutz life, Young Hearts (New York: Schocken, 1950), David Maletz (a member of a kibbutz) is at pains to point out how the weaker children have no protection against the stronger and must constantly defend themselves against aggression.

Conflict and refusal to share. Conflict refers to those situations in which it is the desire of a child to take an object from another but not necessarily to harm the possessor. Except for Group I, this behavior, as Table 3 indicates, accounts for a relatively small percentage of total group interaction, and its percentage decreases progressively from Groups I to IV. In all but a few instances the object of conflict is a toy which one child attempts to take away from another.

The responses of the victims of such behavior are summarized in Table 8. With one exception (Group I), the most frequent response to acts of conflict is, as was true in the responses to aggression, crying. The process records reveal that the conflictor, unlike the aggressor, is often influenced to desist from conflict by the crying of the victim; hence the persistence of this response may be explained by the fact that it is rewarded. That this is not the case in Group I is again the function primarily of the one highly aggressive child, previously discussed, who is the most frequent conflictor and who is not dissuaded by the crying of his victim. Fear of him undoubtedly accounts for the greater incidence of mere submission in this group and it may account for the greater incidence of active resistance (or aggression) as well. Since active resistance is never expressed toward this conflictor, but rather toward other children in the group who attempt to appropriate toys, this retaliatory behavior may represent, in part, aggression displaced from that child who is the greatest conflictor but whom the others dare not resist.

Table 8. Responses to initiation of conflict by percentages.

Response	Group I (Σ acts $= 61$)	Group II ($\Sigma = 100$)	Group III ($\Sigma = 37$)	Group IV ($\Sigma = 29$)
Cry, scream, whine	33	50	55	39
Active resistance (aggression)	39	35	21	29
Passive resistance	3	1	14	14
Submission	25	12	10	7
Seek help	0	0	0	11
Other	0	2	0	0

"Passive resistance" refers to the attempt of the victim to retain his toy by holding on to it while the conflictor attempts to seize it from him. "Submission," which tends to decrease with age, refers to his relinquishing of the toy without a struggle. Again, as in the case of aggression, the nurse is conspicuous for her absence on such occasions. In only one of the four groups do the children seek aid in combating the conflictor and, in this group, only once is the nurse's aid sought; in the other instances assistance is sought from a peer. In all groups, however, and regardless of the techniques employed, more than 50 per cent of all acts of conflict result in defeat for the victim — he loses possession of the toy.

The latter conclusion is of importance. Since the weaker children are those who lose possession of their toys, either because they offer no resistance or because they are defeated in the ensuing battle, we are confronted again with the maladaptive consequence of collective education to which we have already pointed — the competitive disadvantage it imposes on the weak. From their earliest years, the children in any one group must compete with each other for toys, and the stronger almost always win.

"Refusal to share" differs from "Conflict" in that it refers to specific requests to share that are rejected. A child or adult asks the possessor to share his toy or food, instead of trying to take it from him, and he refuses. In all groups the incidence of refusal to share is considerably less than that for agreeing to share. This discrepancy does not indicate that children at these ages accede to requests to share more often than they refuse; on the contrary, the incidence of refusal to share is low because the children seldom ask their peers to share. Indeed, the children are often loath to share even when they are requested to do so by the nurse.

The nurses regard sharing as one of the most difficult of socialization goals to achieve. "It is almost impossible," comments the nurse for Group III, "to get children of this age to share." This nurse's son, for example, has a box of old, broken toys in his parental room with which he almost never plays. Should another child come to play with him, however, her son refuses to permit him to play with the toys in the box. It is not surprising, then, that almost all instances of conflict have their origin in the refusal of one child to share a toy or some other object with a fellow.

As we shall later observe, these children have developed fairly strong feelings for private property. Their reluctance to share may be determined, not only by their annoyance at being deprived temporarily of some object, but also by their feeling that the object actually belongs to them.

CONCLUSIONS

In concluding this discussion of integration and disintegration it would be of great importance to be able to point to developmental trends in their incidence. This is difficult to do in any precise way. Though we have relatively precise quantitative data for each group, intergroup comparisons are hazardous since we are not sure that each group was observed for equal periods. Moreover, the number of children in each group was not the same. (For these reasons most of our tables are presented in percentage, rather than in absolute, values.) Despite these difficulties, however, there are consistent trends in all four groups which may be tested statistically. We may note, first of all, that total interaction increases with age, and that this increase reflects an increase in integrative and disintegrative behavior alike. The proportion of integrative behavior that each group contributes to the total sample of integrative behavior is 0.06, 0.28, 0.26, 0.40, for Groups I through IV, respectively. Similarly the proportion of disintegrative behavior contributed by each group to total disintegrative behavior in the sample is 0.14, 0.20, 0.31, 0.35, respectively. In short, both types of behavior increase with age.

The second conclusion to be drawn from these data is that though both types of behavior increase with age, integrative behavior increases more rapidly than disintegrative behavior. There is, as Table 3 reveals and statistical tests confirm,[13] a relative increase in integration, associated with a relative decrease in disintegration, proceeding from the youngest to the oldest group. The magnitude of these changes may be better discerned when it be indicated that while the ratio of integrative to disintegrative acts in Group I is 1:5, in Group IV it is 1:1.4; and while Group IV is seven times as integrative as Group I, it is only twice as disintegrative.[14] In short, there is a marked relative increase in the part played by integrative behavior within the total range of the children's behavioral repertory, together with a relative decrease in the part played by disintegrative behavior. It may be concluded

---

[13] It has already been noted that for all four groups the preponderance of disintegrative over integrative behavior is highly significant. Nevertheless, chi square reveals quite clearly that this preponderance decreases with age (the indices for Groups I through IV, respectively, are 0.17, 0.41, 0.29, 0.37). The apparent reversal in trend, shown by Group II, is caused by the behavior of one highly precocious girl who is responsible for an extraordinarily high percentage of all types of integrative acts within her kevutza. In the subclass of "Aid, share, and affection," for example, she alone is responsible for one-third of the acts. If this clearly atypical child were to be removed from the sample, the total number of integrative acts in Group II would sharply decline, becoming slightly less than that of Group III.

[14] These differences are significant at the .001 level ($\chi^2 = 14.42$ d.f. = 1.).

that the children acquire stronger integrative motives as they grow older.[15]

SOCIALIZATION

Incidence. Since a primary socialization goal of the kibbutz is the raising of individuals motivated to perform integrative rather than disintegrative acts, it is important to learn what techniques are employed to reinforce the former and to extinguish the latter.

The first and most significant fact about the socialization of these young children is that the vast majority of responses — both integrative and disintegrative — are unsocialized. So few integrative acts, for example, were observed to be socialized that no table of socialization techniques for them could be constructed. Although a sufficient number of disintegrative acts were socialized to permit the construction of such a table, the greatest number of disintegrative acts socialized by the nurse — the most important socializing agent — in any one group is only one-fourth of the total number of disintegrative acts. To phrase it more concretely, in Groups I through IV, the nurses socialize only 26, 24, 13, and 13 per cent, respectively, of all disintegrative responses for each

[15] According to their teachers there seems to be a marked decrease in conflict in the Kindergarten and Transitional Class, while aggression continues unabated. Aggression, it is true, had begun to diminish somewhat in the Transitional Class at the time of this study, but it had until then been a serious problem. Any frustration at the hands of another child had led to attacks and beatings. There were, moreover, frequent attacks by the entire group against any one child whom they happened to dislike or whom they perceived as a frustrater. At the time of this study their teacher felt that there had been one recent and important change in their aggressive behavior — the object of their aggression had become restricted to those individuals who disturbed their activities or who interfered with them. On the other hand, they were still prone to take advantage of smaller and weaker children, particularly if the latter were strangers who, presumably, could be attacked with impunity. When, for example, a slightly younger group from a neighboring kibbutz visited them, the children in the Transitional Class became almost savage in their aggressive behavior — beating their guests, biting them, pulling their hair, stimulating chickens to attack them. This behavior occurred in the absence of the teacher. When she learned of their behavior, she compelled them to go to the neighboring kibbutz and apologize to their former guests. The children not only apologized, but they voluntarily invited their neighbors to visit them again the following week. While they did not renew their physical attacks during this second visit, they still continued to call their guests by opprobrious terms.

There are still other instances of organized aggression in this class. When the children were kept awake by the frequent nocturnal crying of one child, for example, they warned her that they would "beat her up" the next morning if her crying continued. When she again cried the following night, they kept their word and the following morning attacked her as a group. These children, moreover, not only attack their peers but — unlike the younger children — they are not reluctant to attack their teacher should she frustrate them.

group. These percentages reveal not only infrequency, but also a progressive diminution in the incidence of socialization — the younger children are more often socialized than are the older ones in the sample.

Both these latter conclusions must be qualified, however, by observing that, although the nurse is the most important socializer, she is not the sole socializing agent. Other individuals also exercise socialization functions among these children, and their responses serve to increase the number of acts — primarily disintegrative — that are socialized. Specifically, these others include peers, older children, siblings, parents, and other adult members of the kibbutz.[16]

In two groups peers assume socialization functions and, in the oldest group, their role is almost as important as that of the nurse. Moreover, parents, older siblings, and older children play socialization roles when they visit the children, as do any adult members of the kibbutz who, when passing a nursery, observe a child in some (generally) disintegrative act. The percentage of disintegrative acts socialized by these latter individuals, however, is small, varying from 2 to 5 per cent. Hence, if the acts of all socializers are included, the percentage of acts socialized is raised slightly, but

---

[16] It has been noted that my wife (A.G.S.) too, played a socializing role in two of the groups, and particularly in the youngest group. Indeed, her interference in the activities of the latter group was of such a magnitude that she played as important a role in the socialization of disintegration as did the nurse — the nurse socialized 26 per cent of all disintegrative acts, but my wife socialized 27 per cent. Thus, during the period in which this group was observed, 53 per cent of its disintegrative acts were socialized.

But this raises the important question of what percentage, if any, of the acts socialized by the anthropologist would have been socialized by the nurse had the former been absent? Can her relatively minor role be attributed to the fact that she was relying upon the anthropologist to assume part of her responsibilities? Or are we to assume that in the absence of the anthropologist these acts would have gone unsocialized? Unfortunately, it is all but impossible to answer this question, but we can hazard a guess. Since the other groups, in which the anthropologist played either a minor role (in Group II he is responsible for only 3 per cent of the acts) or no role at all (Groups III and IV), reveal an even smaller incidence of socialization, it might be assumed, on the one hand, that the nurse's behavior in Group I would have been little changed by the absence of the anthropologist. On the other hand, since this nurse did attempt to socialize more frequently than the nurses in the older groups, it might be assumed that in the absence of the anthropologist she would have attempted to socialize at least some of those acts socialized by the latter. Balancing the two conflicting assumptions, we may hazard that, in the absence of the anthropologist, the nurse in this youngest group would have socialized a few more disintegrative acts than she actually did (26 per cent), perhaps as many as one-third the total number of disintegrative acts. Such a guess implies, of course, that the progressive diminution of the nurse's interference in acts of disintegration is even greater than was first observed to be the case.

in none of the groups does it constitute more than one-third the total number of disintegrative acts. Since the vast majority of these acts remain unsocialized, their persistence is not surprising — they are reinforced (by success) in a preponderant number of instances.

The nurse as socializer. The infrequency with which the nurse socializes the children's disintegrative behavior is attributable primarily to her absence when it occurs. Most disintegrative acts take place, it will be recalled, during the so-called free-play period. Depending on their ages, anywhere from six to seventeen children may be playing in a dwelling, and, moreover, they may be scattered among the several rooms. Since there are never more than two nurses working at the same time (in the youngest group, only one nurse), they obviously cannot be with all the children at once. Furthermore, if the children are playing outside, the nurse or nurses are generally in the house, performing the many necessary household tasks. Thus, they do not observe much of the behavior for whose socialization they are responsible.

This absence of the nurse not only creates a socialization vacuum, but it occasionally leads to incidents of real injustice on her part, as in the following example from Group II.

Rafel sees Chaim with the rope and begins to cry. He runs to Chaim, who just looks at him. Rafel snatches the rope, and Chaim pulls his hair. Sara, who is standing there, pulls Chaim's hair . . . (The nurse comes outside and) calls her, "Sara!"

Thus the child who is attempting to punish for aggression (albeit in an unacceptable manner) is the only child reprimanded because she is the only one observed by the nurse. The following excerpt also reveals how the nurse's failure to observe a situation may lead her to place a false construction on the event. Two-year-old Rachel is standing in the sandbox with several other children . . .

She trips over the side of the sandbox and cries. Iris says, "Oy." Nurse comes outside, picks up Rachel, and asks, "Who did it? . . . You shouldn't do that, children. Stop it."

Although most of the unsocialized acts are attributable to the nurse's absence, a small number are deliberately left unsocialized, for not all acts of aggression are prohibited by the nurse and some are even sanctioned. Retaliation, for example, is never prohibited

— indeed, it is sometimes praised. If one child hits another and the victim hits him back with sufficient force to evoke a cry, the nurse almost invariably points out that the former deserves it, for he initiated the aggression. This not only means that the aggression of the victim is sanctioned, but that the aggression of the initiator is being punished, albeit by a peer.

The sanctioning of aggression in self-defense is an important aspect of its socialization in the kibbutz, and this is the beginning of its cultural canalization. A nursery teacher, when asked about this, said that she has always encouraged the children to hit back when they are hit; for although they are trying to raise the children to live in a cooperative society, "We are not raising Christlike personalities who will always lower their heads."

If a child is usually passive in his reaction to aggression, the nurse is particularly pleased when he defends himself or retaliates, and she manifests her pleasure with praise. Ron was never known to retaliate, and the first day that he did — much to everyone else's surprise — the nurse praised him highly for defending himself, told him how well he had done, and pointed out to the others that "Ron has strong muscles." Now that they are physical peers, she went on to say, he and Amir, the aggressor, can be good friends.

Table 9. Nurse's techniques for socialization of disintegrative acts by percentages.

Technique	Group I (Σ acts $= 21$)	Group II ($\Sigma = 57$)	Group III ($\Sigma = 23$)	Group IV ($\Sigma = 26$)	Total ($\Sigma = 127$)
Neutral	100	89	60	54	79
Statement or demonstration of proper behavior and/or of disapproval	10	42	30	23	31
Order to desist	29	28	17	12	23
Separation	52	5	4	11	14
Order to apologize	0	5	9	4	5
Other	9	9	0	4	6
Punishing	0	9	31	46	19
Physical punishment	0	0	9	4	2
Withdrawal of privilege	0	4	9	38	11
Shame	0	5	13	4	6
Rewarding	0	2	9	0	2
Praise for control	0	2	9	0	2

Testing for differences among the three techniques of socialization yields:

$$\chi^2 = 8.30 \quad \text{d.f.} = 2 \quad P = <.02$$

Various techniques of socialization are employed by the nurses, as Table 9 reveals. Before discussing them it should be noted that this table shows that, despite the discrepancy in the absolute frequencies with which any technique is employed, there is a high consistency in the rank order of the various techniques. Thus, with one exception ("Withdrawal of privilege") all groups share the three most frequent techniques although their rank order may be inverted; and analysis reveals that the exception is a function, not of differences among the nurses, but of the ages of the children being socialized. "Withdrawal of privilege" shows a progressive increase in frequency from the youngest to the oldest group.

The classification of the individual techniques of socialization was arrived at inductively, and examples of each will be given in the text. The first technique in Table 9, Statement or demonstration of proper behavior and/or of disapproval, is not merely a prolix synonym for "reprimand." Unlike the latter term, the former implies neither personal criticism nor scolding. To the extent that it includes a statement rather than a demonstration, it is more "that is not nice" (*ze lo yafe*), than "you are not nice." Included in this category are varying types of acts, however, ranging from implicit to explicit disapproval, from verbal statements to the physical act of removing the weapon of aggression. Examples of this technique, which ranks first in frequency in two of the four groups (Groups II & III) and never below third, are quoted below.

Omri (Group II) pushes Rafel, and the nurse says, "Rafel didn't do anything."

Shula (Group III) knocks over a tower built by Amnon, and the nurse says to her, "It is not nice to break nice things."

Pnina (Group III) hits me (M.E.S.), and the nurse says, "Pnina, is that the way we receive visitors?"

Yosi (Group IV) asks Tsvi for a pail with which to bring water, but Tsvi will not give it to him. The nurse takes the pail from Tsvi and gives it to Yosi.

Naama (Group IV) takes a doll from Chana. The latter cries, and the nurse gives her another doll.

A second and frequent technique is to order a child to stop his aggressive or conflicting activity. Sometimes the order is categorical; sometimes it is stated explicitly as the desire of the nurse.

Shula (Group III) hits Amnon over the head with a stick. The nurse says sharply, "I don't want you to do that again."

Amos (Group IV) attempts to throw stones at Avner. The nurse tells him to drop the stones.

Separation of the aggressor or conflictor from his victim is the most frequently employed technique in the youngest group and ranks third in the other three groups, but with a considerably diminished frequency. In the three older groups it takes the simple form of telling the child to go to another part of the room or yard, or of stepping between the children and separating them from each other. In this form it is highly similar to an order to desist and could have logically been included in that category. In the youngest group, however, in which the technique is most frequently used, its meaning for the child may often be somewhat different. For in this group a mere verbal command on the part of the nurse is rarely effective; and physical separation is effective only momentarily, after which the aggressor reverts to his original activity. In order to preclude this eventuality the nurse must frequently isolate the child by putting him in a crib or placing him in another room. Her intent is nonpunitive: she wishes only to separate the two children. It is possible, however, that the child interprets it as punitive action.

An infrequent technique of socialization in all groups is one in which the aggressor or conflictor is asked to apologize to his victim. In employing this technique the nurse indicates her disapproval of the activity and, at the same time, insists on symbolic restitution. The following three examples are taken from Groups II, III, and IV, respectively.

Iris hits Sara. Nurse tells Iris to "make good to Sara." Iris pats Sara's head. Nurse says, "Kiss her too." Iris goes to Sara and Sara kisses her on the mouth. Both look pleased.

Micah bites Miri. Nurse tells him to say, "Forgive me"; and to promise that he will not do it again.

Ruthi hits Naomi with a strap. Nurse stops her and tells her to say, "Forgive me" to Naomi.

All the techniques discussed above may be considered as nonpunitive interference. That is, the nurse's chief concern is to end the aggression or conflict rather than to punish the aggressor. Hence, affectively viewed (with the possible exception of Separation in Group I), these techniques may be classed as neutral on a reward-punishment continuum. For the entire sample these neutral techniques comprise 79 per cent of the total, but, as Table 9 indicates, they show a progressive decrease in frequency from the youngest (100 per cent) to the oldest group (54 per cent).

Punishing techniques of socialization therefore comprise only a small percentage of the entire sample, 19 per cent.[17] There is, however, a progressive increase in the use of punishment as a technique for extinguishing disintegrative acts as a direct function of the decrease in neutral techniques. That punishment constitutes only an insignificant percentage of the nurses' socialization techniques among the younger children is understandable. The philosophy of collective education is opposed to punishment in general and to physical punishment in particular, because of possible emotional maladjustment for the child. There is also a strong feeling that young children are not responsible for their behavior and that they especially should not be punished. In the course of their training nurses are taught to eschew physical punishment, and no nurse in the kibbutz was ever observed to spank, hit, or slap a child.

We may now examine the punitive techniques found in Table 9. Physical punishment, which is rare, does not refer to spanking. This category refers, rather, to those instances in which the nurse attempts to make the child aware of the painful consequences of his behavior by aggressing against him in the same manner in which he had aggressed against his victim. As the following examples reveal, this may take the form of either actual or threatened punishment.

Pnina (Group III) pinches Miri. The nurse pinches Pnina. Nurse asks Pnina if it hurts, and she says yes. "Then don't pinch *her*," says the nurse.

Dan (Group IV) hits Amos, knocks him over, and jumps on him. Nurse says, "If you do that again, I'll hit you like you hit Amos."

A second technique of punishment, rare in all groups except Group IV (in which it is the most frequently employed of all techniques), consists in either actual or threatened withdrawal of privilege. In almost all instances of actual withdrawal or deprivation the punishment is not imposed until the nurse has asked the child to desist or has warned him of the consequences of his

---

[17] We shall observe in Chapter 16, however, that even the neutral techniques may be perceived by the children as punitive (shaming) insofar as they all occur in the presence of peers.

behavior. In the following typical examples it will be noted that in almost all cases the deprivation consists in removal from the group, which even at this age is viewed by the child as a serious punishment. It will be observed, further, that in some instances the threatened deprivation consists of a predicted retaliation by the child's peers rather than of a withdrawal of privilege by the nurse.

Shula (Group III) persistently attempts to break up the clay model molded by Varda by hitting it with a string of beads. Nurse comes in and asks, "Why do you want to do that?," and threatens to take her beads away. Shula persists, and the nurse takes away her beads, saying that she cannot work with them any more. Shula falls to the ground, screaming, and the nurse lifts her onto the rug and says, "Cry all you want, and when you're done with your crying, you can come back."

Amir (Group III) wipes paint on Miri. Nurse says, "If Amir can't work properly, he must leave." He cries, and she says, "If you think you can work properly, you may stay."

Amos (Group IV) hits Yael with a branch as she plays in the sandbox. Nurse tells him, "Go upstairs and stay in bed, because you don't know how to play with the children."

Moshe (Group IV) takes two apples (instead of one) from the bowl. Nurse tells him to return it. He is reluctant, and she says, "Tomorrow someone will take your apple, just as today you took someone else's."

A final punitive technique, Shaming, is also infrequently employed, except in Group III. The following examples reveal that there is no uniform shaming response.

(I arrive in Group II and sit on the step outside) . . . Iris, Avner, and Omri immediately run, gather round me . . . handle my pencil, notebook, etc. Omri and Iris push each other to see, and Omri falls backward down the steps. Iris cries. Both cry. Nurse comes out of the house — tells Iris to stop, tells her that she is spoiled.

Micah (Group III) destroys the building blocks of Amnon. Nurse sees what happened, and says, "Micah is not well today." He yells that he is well, but she says, no, he is not.

Miri (Group III) persists in taking the nurse's notebook despite many warnings not to do so. Nurse says with disdain, "Why do other children leave the notebook alone, and only you have to take it?"

Avner (Group IV) bites Boaz. Nurse says, "Only dogs bite."

The use of reward in the socialization of disintegration acts is extremely rare and consists of praise for the control of aggression. An unusually aggressive child may, for example, be rewarded with praise if he abstains from aggression for some time. Or, the nurse may praise a child when he accedes to her request to desist from aggressing.

Amos (Group III) bumps his tricycle into Rachel's tricycle. She in turn bumps hers into his, and he falls and cries. The nurse tells them that each should travel to another place, and that "I don't want to hear any more noise. It is not at all nice to make noise." They do what she says, and she praises them, "That's nice."

The children in Group III are playing. For some time there has been no act of conflict or aggression. The nurse calls out to Eldad, "Why have you been such a good boy today? You didn't beat even one child today. I like that. That's good."

In conclusion, Table 9 reveals that, although punitive techniques are employed infrequently, they are used much more frequently than are rewarding techniques. Thus the ratio of reward to punishment is heavily weighted on the punishment side, particularly among the older children in the sample. This same unbalanced picture emerges when the responses of the nurses to integrative acts are examined. Such an examination reveals that, with very few exceptions, almost all socialization responses of the nurses are to disintegrative rather than to integrative acts. In Group IV, for example, the nurse socialized more than 50 per cent of the acts in which children refused to share, but only 5 per cent of those in which the children agreed to share. Indeed, as we noted, there are so few socialization responses in the sample to integrative acts that they are not amenable to quantitative analysis. In Group II, for example, only 4 of the 160 acts of integration are socialized (praised) by the nurses. Hence the socialization ratio is highly unbalanced in the direction of disintegration.

The infrequency with which integrative acts are socialized may be attributed not only to the relative infrequency with which they occur, but also to the absence of the nurse when they do occur. The few responses that appear in the sample all involve public praise.

The children in Group II are playing in the sandbox . . . (Yaakov and Boaz both begin to cry) . . . The nurse comes outside and asks what the problem is. Yaakov is holding two cans in his hand, but Boaz has none. Nurse asks Yaakov to give one can to Boaz. Yaakov debates with himself a moment, then gives one can to Boaz. The nurse praises him: "That's fine. Children, do you all see what a wonderful boy Yaakov is?"

The infrequency with which integration is socialized is qualified, however, by a number of other considerations. First, in almost all those cases of conflict or of refusal to share that are socialized the technique employed by the nurse is that of "statement or demonstration of proper behavior." Hence, when a child refuses to share with another, the nurse responds by telling him that he *ought* to share or by dividing the object under question between them.

Second, although there are very few instances in which the nurse reinforces an act of sharing, many situations arise in the context of the daily routine which enable the nurse to stress the value of sharing or the subordination of personal desire to the desire of others. Since this method of instruction is verbal, it is found almost exclusively in the two older groups, whose verbal achievement is high. In the following typical examples, the first two are from Group III, the last two from Group IV.

Pnina sees the moon through the window, and says, "Look at the big moon in *my* sky." The nurse corrects her, "In *our* sky."

The nurse dries Micah after his shower, and asks him where he had been in the afternoon. He says that he had been in the vineyards with his mother. She asks if he had eaten grapes, and he says, yes. She asks why he had not brought some grapes for all the children, and tells him to tell his mother that the next time they go to the vineyard they must bring grapes for all the children.

Amos begins to cry because the children ask the nurse to sing them another song before they go to bed, and she has consented, although Amos objects. The nurse tells him (with the others listening), "I cannot do what only one child wants, but what the group wants." (She then explains the process of group-decision to him.)

The children decide to play a certain game, but Yuval wants to play another. He is adamant. The nurse says, "You do not know how to play with the children, so you can go play by yourself."

Third, the children not only hear their nurse stress the importance of sharing, but they witness sharing behavior on the part of the nurse throughout the day. The nurse brings goodies to the house and distributes them among all the children; she prepares an afternoon snack and calls all the children to share it; the children go for a hike and meet another kevutza whose nurse had brought carrots for them to eat. Seeing the other kevutza, she divides the carrots in half so that they may all have one.[18]

But it is not only the nurse who inculcates, by both word and deed, the importance of sharing. The child is raised and lives in a cooperative system whose very structure constantly informs him, as it were, of the necessity and desirability — nay, inevitability and naturalness — of sharing. From the earliest age the children perceive that almost everything they have, from their toys and clothes to their nurse, is not their own, but belongs to all the children.

It is therefore not accurate to say that sharing (or kindness, or thoughtfulness, and so on) is not socialized in the kibbutz, but, rather, that the sharing response is rarely reinforced. To the extent that this response is learned by the children, therefore, it is acquired primarily through cognitive and perceptual learning.

What is the role of the nurse in the socialization of integrative and disintegrative acts? First, the great majority of acts, whether integrative or disintegrative in nature, remain unsocialized. Second, of the techniques employed in the socialization of disintegrative acts, the majority are neutral in that they involve neither reward nor punishment; but of those techniques that involve reinforcement, the vast majority consist of negative rather than positive reinforcement. Thirdly, there is little reinforcement of integrative acts, so that the acquisition of integrative responses is a function primarily of perceptual and cognitive learning.

Peers and parents as socializers. The role of child socializers varies from group to group. Although children almost never socialize in Groups I and III, they frequently do so in Groups II and IV. Since the prevalence of peer socialization in Group II is primarily a function of one precocious child, and since peer socialization does not appear in Group III (the next-oldest group), it may be assumed that the prevalence of peer socialization in Group II is an atypical phenomenon and does not indicate that peer socialization begins at this age. We conclude, therefore, that peer socialization really begins in Group IV where, in our sample, peers socialize each other 18 times (as compared with the 26

[18] The most unusual example of sharing, from an American point of view, is that of a birthday celebration. After the usual games and goodies, the birthday presents are all displayed. But these presents, which are brought by the parents of the child whose birthday is being celebrated, are not for the celebrant. They are distributed equally among all the members of the kevutza including, of course, the child whose birthday it is.

socialization acts of the nurse). But only five of the seventeen children in this oldest group functioned as socializers, and all five are among the oldest children in the group. We may therefore suggest that peer socialization appears in the kibbutz at the approximate age of five years, and that at this age, moreover, the role of children as socializers becomes almost as important as that of the nurse.

In Group IV, the child who socializes most frequently is the oldest male.[19] That this one child, Gidon, looms so importantly in his group is no accident. In every kevutza, there is often one child whom the nurses call the *melech* or king. He is the leader in most activities, and it is to him that the others look for guidance and protection. Gidon is the melech in his kevutza. He is the strongest child in the group, and is viewed as a protector of the weak (although at times he attacks the weak himself). It will be remembered, for example, that one of the responses to aggression in this group is to call upon a peer for help. That peer was invariably Gidon. He did not always respond to this plea because he was not always present. But if he were available when help was asked, he would consistently assist the underdog, even if the aggressor were a special friend of his. At least once, on the other hand, he praised the aggressor — although the victim was his friend — because the former was usually a coward. Hence, the kibbutz morality concerning aggression has already been learned by this five-year-old boy.

All the socialization techniques employed by nurses — physical punishment, withdrawal of privilege, order to desist, and shame — are employed by the children as well (although they also utilize some techniques that the nurses do not). The frequency with which these common techniques are utilized by children and nurses differs, however. Nurses, for example, rarely employ physical punishment of any kind, but this is the most frequent socialization technique of the children (seven of the eighteen acts of child socialization involve physical punishment). Thus, peer socialization is primarily punitive, while that of the nurse is primarily neutral.

We may now examine these techniques of the child socializers in greater detail. Physical punishment, as the following examples reveal, may involve either actual or threatened punishment.

Esther takes a chair from Tamar, who tells Gidon. He hits Esther.

[19] It is interesting to observe that the precocious child who assumes such a paramount socialization role in Group II is this boy's sister.

Moshe twists Ron's leg. Ron cries, and shouts for Gidon. Gidon comes to his help and hits Moshe. As Gidon starts to walk away, Moshe hits Ron again. Gidon sees this and hits Moshe, who falls to the ground crying.

Pua attempts to hit Naama with a chair. Shaul says that he'll hit Pua if she continues.

Withdrawal of a privilege, or deprivation (usually in the form of ostracism), is employed by the children almost as frequently as physical punishment.

(Moshe and Tsvi both claim to be the "driver" of the "auto," and Tsvi chases Moshe out of the yard. Later) . . . Tsvi goes to play with Chana and Elat. Chana says, "Tsvi, you can't play with us because you chased Moshe away." Tsvi says, "Do you know why? Only because he wanted to be the driver." Chana replies, "But he had the auto first, and you should not have taken it."

Children occasionally attempt to socialize by merely telling the aggressor or conflictor to desist. If Gidon, the "king" in Group IV, is the socializer, his command is invariably obeyed. If, however, another child is the socializer, a mere command may not be effective, in which case the would-be socializer must either retreat from the scene or use physical means to enforce his will.

The final socialization technique employed by the children in Group IV is shame, and consists in calling the aggressor by some epithet. When, for example, some girls slammed a door in the face of the observer, Boaz told them, "You are bad girls." When Chaim bit Amir, the other children decided to call him, *ha-yeled ha-nashchon* — the boy who bites.

The role of parents in the socialization of integrative and disintegrative acts was, for the most part, not observed directly. Instances of parental socialization, to be sure, were observed in the children's houses, in parental rooms, and in public places. But these observations were not based on systematic observation procedures, as were those of nurses and peers. Instead of describing observed behavior, therefore, we shall rather present the parental attitudes as they were expressed in the Questionnaire. It might be noted, however, that that parental socialization which was observed emphasized almost exclusively statements of disapproval and/or of proper behavior, which is entirely consistent with parental responses to the Questionnaire. It might also be noted, as a general impression, that when a parent visits his child in the kevutza, he is more likely to socialize the other children who engage in disintegrative behavior than he is his own child. Parents, it would seem, tend not to perceive — or perhaps tend to justify — disintegrative behavior in their own children when it occurs in their presence.

That parents are concerned with both the integrative and disintegrative behavior of their children is, however, clearly revealed in the Questionnaire (see Chapter 4). Generosity and cooperation, for example, are the behaviors for which they say they most frequently reward their children, while selfishness and failure to cooperate are, respectively, first and third among the behaviors they most frequently punish. Surprisingly, however, aggression ranks only eighth among the ten responses for which they punish.

Although the Questionnaire reveals that parents are highly concerned with integrative and disintegrative behavior, it also indicates that they infrequently punish their children for the latter type of behavior. Of the sixteen respondents, only two say that they sometimes punish their children, eight say that they do so infrequently, four claim that they never punish, and two failed to answer the question. On those occasions when parents do punish their children, criticism, threatened withdrawal of privilege, and scolding (in that order) are the only socialization techniques regularly and uniformly employed by the respondents. On those occasions when parents socialize their children for integrative behavior, praise is the only frequent and uniform technique employed, although some parents say that they occasionally promise something as a reward.

ORAL TRAINING AND BEHAVIOR

Behavior. The children in these groups eat three meals a day: breakfast, which is served shortly after rising; dinner, which is served between eleven o'clock and noon; and supper, which is served around five o'clock. In addition, there are always a mid-morning snack of fresh fruit or vegetables and a mid-afternoon snack of fruit or bread and jam. There are, furthermore, a number of unscheduled snacks for appeasing between-meal hunger. Visitors, for example, frequently bring food — a mother or grandmother who works in the kitchen will arrive with carrots or tomatoes for all the children; a mother will come with two pieces of candy which she carefully divides among all the children. If a child is hungry and cries for food shortly before the regular dinner or supper hour, the nurse may fetch the food for all the children in order to appease the one child. Or, if a child is hungry in the middle of the afternoon, the nurse may search the house and discover one cookie left from the preceding day. Despite the fact, therefore, that food is stored and prepared in the communal kitchen and not in the kevutza, no child is actually forced to wait for a scheduled feeding to appease his hunger.

Menus are in general the same for all groups of children, although the variety of food at each meal increases with age. The average breakfast consists of porridge, milk or cocoa, cottage cheese, and raw vegetables in season. The older children (Groups III and IV) may also have sour cream and/or herring. For dinner, the children have meat (generally meatballs) or fish, cooked vegetables, potatoes, soup (served after the meat course), and a simple dessert such as pudding. Supper consists of an egg, porridge or milk, fresh fruit, bread and butter, and cookies or a piece of cake.

The children in Group I had not yet begun to sit at a table for their meals, nor had they begun to feed themselves, when they were first observed. Rather, each child was fed by the nurse as he sat on her lap.[1] During the course of observations, however, the children began to sit at a table, and, although the nurse continued to feed them, she encouraged them to feed themselves with their spoons and fingers. All the children in Group II were able to feed themselves, although the younger ones required frequent assistance. In general, therefore, it may be stated that the children feed themselves by the age of seventeen months.

Tables, chairs, and eating utensils are all miniature in size, and the children are always seated in the same positions at the table for every meal.[2] In Groups I and II, the nurses do not sit with the children at mealtime because the tables are too small (in length and width). This is a source of bitter complaint by the nurses, who insist that the children eat better (both in terms of quantity and etiquette) when they are able to join them at the table. (The carpenters had promised longer tables, but were always "too busy" to fulfill their promise.) The nurses in Groups III and IV, however, do sit at the tables with the children, although they generally do not eat. Whether the nurses sit with the children or not, they are always in the room when the children eat, serving the food, feeding those who do not feed themselves, and performing other socialization functions.

In general, meals are occasions of great noise and confusion, and it is the rare meal that is eaten in peace and relaxation. This commotion is an indication of both pleasure and tension. At almost every meal, for example, there is much laughter, talking, and singing; there is also much whining, particularly in the younger groups. The nurses are usually permissive about this commotion and do not interfere unless the children violate one of their socialization goals. The following examples from Group

[1] This is in marked contrast to the oldest children in the Nursery, who were already learning to sit at a table and to acquire skills in self-feeding. The situation observed in Group I, we were informed, is neither normative nor typical for children of this age, and may be attributed to their atypical nurse, who, more than any other nurse in the system, deviated from the educational norms of the kibbutz. Other nurses expressed great concern about her deviance.

[2] This rigidity is primarily a function of the desire of the children rather than of any imposition by the nurse, and is part of the general pattern of compulsivity, which is found especially among the two- and three-year-olds in the sample, and which is expressed in an opposition to almost any change in their normal routine. When Omri, for example, sat in Avner's chair at lunch, all the children became visibly angry and refused to eat until Omri sat in his "proper" place. When the nurse moved Avi's bed into the playroom in order to isolate him from the children who were ill, he refused to sleep there. He cried and screamed, and finally fell asleep from exhaustion. When the nurse put Rafi's chamber pot on the floor for him to sit on, he began to cry — she had not put it in the usual place. When she asked him where he wanted it, he pointed to his "old" place on the floor.

II give some picture of the emotional climate that characterizes the average meal.

The nurse calls the children to come and eat. All yell, "Food," and run into the room . . . They are very excited and sit at the table immediately. Amir calls for his bib . . . The nurse brings the meat and potatoes. All yell, "Meatballs, meatballs," and immediately begin to eat . . . David asks for soup, and the nurse tells him, "Not now — we first finish with this." He begins to cry, and she asks him if he wants to eat. He says no, so the nurse says, "Alright, goodbye," and lifts him out of his chair. David cries and cries. Nurse asks him if he wants to eat, and he says yes. She helps him to sit at the table, and he begins to eat quickly . . . Pua asks for more potatoes. Nurse says she has no more, then gives her some of Amir's . . . Avner eats potatoes with his hands, smears them on his face and bib . . . Rafel is still eating his meat. Nurse tells him to finish and she will give him soup. She helps him eat his potatoes, shoveling spoonfuls down him quickly. Finally, he coughs, chokes a little — his mouth is stuffed full . . . Chana has two spoons in her bowl and she eats with both. She pours soup from one spoon into the other, and most of it spills on the table . . .

(The children have just sat down to breakfast) . . . Elat sings. All begin to jabber. Rafi yells. Elat claps her hands, and Sarah follows suit. Iris climbs under the table. All yell and laugh . . .

The confusion and commotion that characterize meals in general is often intensified in Group I by the presence of parents, particularly at the evening meal. In the three older groups parents are not permitted to enter the house while the children are eating, and they either arrive after the meal or they wait outside for the children. In the youngest group, however, where children must still be helped to eat, parents are encouraged to feed their children. The following example gives some indication of what happens when parents are present, and four adults — not to mention an older sibling — attempt to feed five children. We observe the same commotion that characterizes feeding in the Nursery.

Nurse seats all four children at the table . . . Esther gets up, walks around . . . Nurse feeds Gidon his puree; Nurse's daughter feeds Eldad . . . Moshe cries when he is seated at the table, cries and cries . . . Nurse puts soup on the table. Moshe's mother tries to feed some to him, but he cries . . . Nurse's daughter feeds soup to Eldad; Nurse brings Esther back to table and feeds her and Ofer . . . Moshe is still whining, so his mother puts him into bed. He cries . . . Ofer grabs a spoon and puts it in a cup of puree. The nurse helps him guide the spoon, and he eats some . . . Eldad takes a spoon, dips it into Moshe's puree, splashes the spoon in the air. Moshe's mother removes the cup . . . Nurse puts a spoonful of soup to Esther's mouth; Ofer (seated next to Esther) leans over and sucks from the spoon. Both children are eating from the same spoon at once. Every time nurse offers soup to Esther, Ofer leans over and sucks too . . . Miri's mother returns to the house with her . . . Moshe's mother is holding him; he is quiet. His sister kisses his foot, tries to kiss it again, but he cries. Miri sits at the table, and her mother holds the cup for her. She doesn't want it — turns her head away. Esther eats. Ofer bangs a spoon on the table . . .

In view of the fact that the nurses seldom have difficulty in persuading the children, even those who are not hungry, to come to the table, it may be assumed that the children enjoy their meals. But the atmosphere of the eating situation is hardly a relaxing one.

Most children are hungry at mealtime and require little urging from the nurses to eat. There are some exceptions in Groups III and IV, but not, interestingly enough, in Groups I and II. In the latter groups every child occasionally refuses to eat, but there are no children who consistently refuse to do so. In the former groups, however, there are a few children who consistently leave most of their food or eat only after repeated urgings from their nurses. According to the nursery teacher in Group III, all the children in her kevutza were feeding problems from an early age — at least three children began to refuse food while still in the Nursery. Although they were, as she put it, difficult eaters when she first became their nurse (one year prior to our observations), she feels that they are no longer problems. That the other nurse in this kevutza does not entirely agree with the latter part of this statement is indicated by her persistent urging of the children to eat, and by her frequent insistence upon feeding those children who are not always motivated to eat.

Socialization. If the frequency of socialization acts is a fair measure of the concern that socializers have with respect to any particular behavior system, then the socialization of eating behavior may be characterized as second in importance only to the socialization of disintegrative behavior.[3]

[3] It is possible, however, that the frequency of socialization in this area is a function of the frequency of eating as well as of the presence of the nurses at these occasions. For, although the nurse is seldom with the children in other situations, she is always with them during their meals and has therefore a greater opportunity to intervene.

In general, food socialization has five distinct goals, as revealed by our sample of socialization acts. These include: eating, eating with etiquette, feeding oneself, sharing food, and eating with moderation. In Group I, the most important (most frequent) goal of the nurse is feeding oneself, followed by the goal of eating. In the three older groups, where this goal of independence has, for the most part, already been attained, the nurses are concerned almost exclusively with the two goals of eating and eating with etiquette. Of the 145 socialization acts in these older groups, for example, 46 per cent were concerned with encouraging a child to eat, and 48 per cent were concerned with encouraging a child to eat with etiquette.

This concern of the nurses with eating — with the mere intake of food — is perhaps understandable with respect to those children who are feeding problems. But when we note that in all groups the nurses are frequently observed to tell all the children to eat, to assist them in eating, and, in some instances, to compel them to eat, one is forced to conclude that the concern with eating is not entirely motivated by reality factors. This becomes even more apparent when we recall that such expressions of concern violate the official educational attitude of complete permissiveness in regard to eating.

The author suggests two possible reasons for this concern with food. One factor is the perpetuation of shtetl attitudes — for in the shtetls of Eastern Europe, from which many of the nurses came, food is a symbol of maternal love. As Zborowski and Herzog observe, ". . . (in the shtetl) . . . food is the symbol of the mother's devotion . . . The rejection of food means rejection of the loved ones and of life itself. It is intolerable and excites acute anxiety." [4] Like many shtetl patterns, this one may be very much alive in the kibbutz today, and the nurse's concern that the children eat may reflect this continuity.

There may be an additional factor in her concern. Often when a nurse tells a child to eat or to eat nicely, it is the writer's impression that she is really urging him to hurry up. The nurse cannot leave the kevutza to eat her own meal in the adult dining room until all the children have finished eating. Hence, she is often impatient with the dawdling of the children and encourages them to eat. This impatience cannot be the sole reason for her persistent encouragements, however, for if she were concerned only with appeasing her own hunger, she could remove the plate of a dawdling child. But she does not do this, and her consequent

---

[4] Zborowski and Herzog, *Life Is with People*, p. 303.

urging or even compelling a child to eat lends greater credence to the first hypothesis.

The frequency with which eating with etiquette is a socialization goal does not mean that the nurses expect the children to use adult manners. But they do discourage a number of unmannerly responses such as spitting food, sitting on the table, retaining food in the mouth and playing with it instead of swallowing, taking food from another child's plate, and smearing food.

The socialization techniques employed by the nurse to achieve their goals are summarized in Table 10. One is immediately struck with the absence of consistency among the various nurses and of any trends as the children grow older. This lack of pattern strengthens our suggestion that food is an affectively focal value for the nurses, so that their own personal feelings, as well as official norms, govern their responses to the children's eating.

Table 10. Techniques of food socialization in percentages.

Technique	Group I (Σ acts = 18)	Group II (Σ = 94)	Group III (Σ = 22)	Group IV (Σ = 16)
Neutral	100	75	46	73
Command, prohibition, or forcing to eat	33	49	23	25
Encouragement	44	9	14	38
Statement of disapproval or of natural consequence	6	11	5	6
Competitive motivation	11	0	4	6
Sharing	6	6	0	0
Punishing	0	20	50	25
Shaming	0	1	27	0
Withdrawal of privilege	0	16	5	25
Scolding	0	3	18	0
Rewarding	0	5	4	0
Praise	0	5	4	0

Testing for differences among the three categories of socialization, yields:

$$\chi^2 = 8.30 \qquad \text{d.f.} = 2 \qquad P = <.02$$

Neutral or nonpunitive techniques of socialization are the most frequently employed in three of the four groups. Ranking as either first or second in all groups is the use of some form of compulsion — ordering the child to eat, telling him to eat nicely or to desist from antisocial behavior, feeding him, and so on. The various kinds of acts included in this broad category are illustrated in the following examples, taken from Groups I–III, respectively.

When the nurse feeds Aryeh, he doesn't want his puree, and screams and screams. But she pours some into his mouth with a spoon — his mouth is open, so she just pours it down . . . Aryeh kicks and yells the entire time, and the nurse talks to him soothingly about the birds outside the window . . . In this way, she manages to get almost the entire cupful down him.

(Aliza is sitting at the table, dawdling) . . . She looks at me, says, "Enough" . . . The nurse says, "Aliza, with two hands and eat nicely." Aliza begins to drink slowly — continues to dawdle. The nurse tells her that if she doesn't want to eat, she doesn't have to, but "It's not good that you don't eat nicely."

Shula sits with her back to the table. The nurse says, "Eat properly. Face the table."

A second neutral technique occurring with relative frequency is encouragement. In Group I encouragement is primarily of a physical nature. The nurse is most concerned with teaching the children to feed themselves and attempts to achieve this goal by placing solid food in their hands, giving them spoons and permitting them to splash and mess, and by guiding their hands from bowl to mouth. In the older groups, the encouragement assumes a verbal form, as the following examples indicate.

The nurse (Group III) tells the children she is giving them softboiled eggs for dinner — "Just like the adults get."

Nurse (Group III) says to Micah, who has eaten all his food, "If you eat like that every day, you will grow, and your hair will grow, and you will have strong muscles."

Ruthi (Group IV) does not drink her milk. The nurse says, "I'll count three, and see how much you can finish by then."

Competitive motivation is, of course, a type of encouragement and, properly, should be so classified. It is classified separately, however, to indicate that nurses in this theoretically noncompetitive community employ competitive techniques; and it is to be presumed that the children acquire competitive motivations as a result. The first example below is taken from Group I, the second from Group III.

The nurse picks up Tamar to feed her, puts her on her lap . . . Tamar screams as the nurse starts to feed her, so the nurse says all right and sets her on the floor . . . Amnon's mother, who is feeding him, hands him to the nurse, who begins to feed him . . . Tamar then *really* begins to cry and yell, tries to climb on the nurse's lap. Everybody laughs, and the nurse returns Amnon to his mother. She picks up Tamar and feeds her. Tamar now eats quietly and well.

The children have been sitting at the table for some time. The nurse says, "Pnina, Anat, and Shula will race to see who will finish first."

Another neutral technique is a statement of disapproval by the nurse, or a statement of the undesirable natural consequences that follow from a child's behavior. In the former the nurse does not reprimand the child; she merely indicates that his behavior is improper. In the latter she does not punish him, but explains to him what sequence of events are set into motion by his behavior. Examples are given from Group III and Group IV.

Mimi goes to the porch without drinking her cocoa, and the nurse says, "You have not finished your cocoa." Mimi says, "I don't want to." Nurse says: "All right, but then, children, Mimi will be thirsty all day." Mimi asks why, and the nurse replies, "Because if you don't drink in the morning, you're thirsty all day."

Roni sings while she eats. The nurse says, "Ronile, we sing after meals, not during meals."

A final neutral technique, employed only when a child asks for more food, is to ask some child to share with him. This is rare, as Table 10 indicates.

We may turn now to the punitive techniques employed by the nurses. Although no such techniques occur in Group I, they are not infrequent in the three older groups, and they comprise the largest class of socialization techniques in Group III. Of the three punitive techniques employed, two — scolding and shaming — are found almost exclusively in Group III.[5] The high frequency with which punitive techniques are employed in this latter group does not, obviously, derive from any kibbutz policy governing socialization. It is, rather, a function of the personality of one nurse and of her attitude toward a small number of children whom she dislikes. Again we note that the personality of the nurse and her differential perception of the children may lead to a discrepancy between normative and actual behavior. The following examples of scolding and shaming are taken from her behavior.

Pnina dawdles with her food, and the nurse says, "Pnina, do you want me to get angry? You know I can become very angry."

[5] Eating is one of the very few activities that provokes scolding.

Ahuv takes food from Sarah's plate. The nurse says, "Ahuv, you are like a dog. If you want food, take it from the center plate."

"Do you see how that girl drinks? She doesn't know how to drink at all."

Pnina asks repeatedly for more custard, and the nurse says, "Oh, how that girl bores me."

A final punitive technique is that of deprivation or withdrawal of privilege — the privilege to be lost being that of eating or of remaining at the table.

Yuval (Group IV) shouts for more honey. The nurse tells him, "I will not give any honey to a boy who shouts."

David (Group IV) is shouting. The nurse asks him to stop, then asks, "David, do you want me to take your plate away from you?"

As with the socialization of interaction, we note that the use of rewarding techniques for eating is infrequent and that praise is the sole type of reward. Praise such as "Very nice" (*yafeh m'od*) is occasionally accorded a child who eats all his food or who eats in an unusually polite manner, or the nurse may praise all the children when they eat unusually well or quietly. Occasionally, the praise may be more personal:

(Elat is eating — a rare occurrence) . . . The nurse says, "Elat, today you are really sweet, and today it is pleasant for me."

In general, the nurses are permissive about eating, but their permissiveness is by no means synonymous with indifference. On the contrary, they are deeply concerned with encouraging the children to eat and to eat, moreover, with good manners.

TOILET TRAINING AND BEHAVIOR

Socialization. Toilet training is not begun in Kiryat Yedidim until the ages of fifteen to eighteen months. In Group I, therefore, no child is trained; in Group II, toilet training has begun and, while some of the older children are frequently continent during the day, no child in the group is completely trained; in Groups III and IV, training has been completed, although some nocturnal incontinence persists.

In the past (until approximately eight years prior to this study), toilet training was rigid and began at the age of eight or ten months — that is, as soon as the baby was old enough to sit — and the children were forced to sit on chamber pots against their desires. Today, however, the entire process is gradual and permissive. In Group I, where formal training has not yet begun, the nurse occasionally encourages the older children in the group to sit on chamber pots. She shows the child the pot and suggests that he sit on it and make "pee-pee." If the child whines or indicates his refusal in any way, the nurse removes the pot and comments that "It's not necessary." If a child does sit on the pot, he is free to get off when he wishes. The children in this group urinate and defecate on the floor, in bed, in their pants, and on the ground. Since they do not wear diapers, their incontinence only increases the burden of the nurse, but they were never observed to be reprimanded for their behavior. On only one occasion was the nurse observed to even suggest that the child should have used the chamber pot.

In Group II, where training has begun in earnest, the children are placed on chamber pots as soon as they awaken in the morning or after a nap, after each meal, before their morning showers, and before they go to bed. Although they are not compelled to remain on the pots if they do not wish to, they are encouraged to do so. "Amir, come back and make pee-pee," says the nurse. Amir may come, but if he does not, the nurse does not force him. No nurse, moreover, was ever observed to scold a child for not sitting on the chamber pot or for wetting or soiling during the training period. On the contrary, nurses were occasionally observed to put a child to bed without putting him on the pot, because he was too tired.

Within this generally permissive atmosphere, the nurse is still able to convey her attitudes about excretory behavior to the children in a number of ways. The children are not only placed on pots at regular and frequent intervals, but they are often told to remain on the pot or to return to it after they have left it. Moreover, if a nurse thinks that a child is about to excrete, she will ask him if he wants to sit on the pot and will encourage him to do so; but she will not force him if he refuses. She will, furthermore, always praise a child who excretes in the pot. The most frequent praise is the ever-heard "Yofi!" or "That's wonderful — see what a big boy (girl) we have here!" Often, a child will bring the pot to the nurse to show her what he has accomplished, and always he will be praised. "You see," comments the nurse, "he brings me a gift!" And finally, although she is nonpunitive in her training, she makes it quite clear that she disapproves of a child's excreting any place except on the pot. In general, she indicates this attitude by the favorite "fooia" when she sees a child urinating or defecating on the floor (although she is more likely to make this comment about faeces than urine). She also communicates this attitude when she changes a child's soiled or wet pants by merely commenting that "Amir made pee-pee" or "Mirav made eh-eh," the term (in Yiddish baby-talk) for faeces, and thus calls his attention to this fact. But there is no instance of a nurse's scolding or reprimanding a child for such behavior. Indeed, of all the socialization techniques employed in Group II, 55 per cent were classified as neutral or nonpunitive and consisted of merely telling a child to sit on or return to the pot, or of a statement of disapproval such as "fooia"; but 45 per cent were rewarding techniques, consisting primarily of praise. Thus, rewarding techniques of socialization are considerably more frequent for toilet training than for any other behavior system, and punitive techniques are not employed at all. These techniques are summarized in Table 11.

Table 11. Socialization techniques for toilet training in percentages

Technique	Group II (Σ acts = 45)	
Neutral		55
Order child to sit	35	
Statement of disapproval	16	
Other	4	
Rewarding		45
Praise	27	
Acquiesce in child's refusal (reward for not learning)	18	
Punishing		0

At the .99 confidence level the upper confidence limit for "rewarding" techniques is 64.12. The finding — neutral techniques > rewarding techniques — is not significant.

Since most of the children in Groups III and IV are continent, toilet training is not a crucial concern of the nurses. There are, nevertheless, instances in which the nurses intervene in the children's excretory behavior — but in the same permissive manner that characterizes their behavior in the younger groups. They remind the children, for example, to go to the toilet (to which these older children have graduated) before going to bed or after awakening. They do not punish a child for incontinence, and they disapprove if his peers tease or criticize him for such behavior. When, for example, the nurse in Group IV entered the house one morning,

Naama tells her, "Aryeh made pee-pee in bed." The nurse says, "It's not so terrible to make pee-pee — it can happen to anyone."

In spite of this permissive attitude toward incontinence, however, the nurses do attempt to extinguish it. At least four techniques are employed to do this, but they are used so infrequently that no generalizations may be drawn, except to note that none is punitive. One technique is to bring the matter to the attention of the child, thus reminding him that the nurse would prefer him to be continent.

Amir (Group III) wets his pants. The nurse says, "How did that happen? Couldn't you lower your pants?"

The nurse (Group III) brings Dena's wet sheets into the bathroom to dry. The other nurse says, "How come, Dena? Didn't you go to the toilet last night?"

Another technique, employed in Group IV, is to awaken children who are often incontinent at night and take them to the toilet. In one such case the nurse decided on this measure to save the child from constant teasing by her peers. In another case, the child himself asked the nurse to awaken him. Both children became continent shortly thereafter.

Another device is to promise a reward for continence. Naomi, for example, was the only child in the group who wet her bed in the afternoon. The nurse promised to give her a new dress if she would stop, and within a short time she did. A final technique used by the nurses in these groups is to describe the objective, but undesirable, consequences of such behavior. The children, for example, prefer pajamas with sleeves to sleeveless ones. The nurse points out to the incontinent children that when they wet their pajamas, she will have no other pajamas with sleeves to give them.

Nurses are not the only agents of socialization. As in other behavior systems, toilet behavior, too, is socialized by peers. In Group II, for example, if a child gets off the pot and wanders around, another child may say to him, "Amir, come back and make pee-pee." A child defecates in his pants, and other children comment, "Mirav, eh-eh." Avner, sitting on the pot, urinates on the floor. Iris asks, "What are you doing, Avner? Not on your shoes. What are you making — pee-pee?" A boy defecates in the pot, and Iris says, "Rafi, lovely!"

In Group III, too, the children are not only proud of their own continence, but of their peer's continence as well. Their praise of a peer's accomplishment mirrors the socialization techniques of the nurse. When Tsvi, who was sick in bed, defecated in the chamber pot, Aryeh ran to tell the nurse of this accomplishment. When the other children heard his report, they all ran to the bedroom to see for themselves, and Miri excitedly put her arms around Tsvi and kissed him. Again, while talking to Dena (a bed-wetter) one morning, Anat noticed that her bed was dry. She felt the sheets and said happily, "Dena, you did not wet your bed at all!"

The children in Group IV, however, do not adopt the permissive attitudes of their nurses toward an incontinent child. On the contrary, they often poke fun at those children who wet their beds, and call them "kaker" and "pisher." This sometimes evokes prolonged discussions among the children, as the following reveals.

Nira asks Avner to climb up on her bed. Naama tells Nira not to let Avner on her bed, for he "made pee-pee" the night before. Avner says he wet his bed because the nurse had not put a chamber pot on the floor in his room. Nili says that is no excuse, for he could have gone to the toilet. Chana says it was not his fault, but that he wet his bed because he had eaten candy the night before.

Behavior. The children generally do not object to sitting on the chamber pots once toilet training has begun in earnest. This may well be due to the social nature of the training — for all the children are seated on the pots at the same time. They can, and do, convert this situation into a social event — talking and playing (as well as aggressing against each other).[6] This social nature of excretion is perpetuated even after training has been completed, for the children continue to go to the toilet in a group, rather than individually. In Group III, for example, there are three toilets, and all are generally used simultaneously. The laughter, singing, and talking that emanate from the bathroom indicate clearly that the children enjoy this situation, and they are reluctant to leave voluntarily. If the nurse did not intervene and order them out, they would, she claims, sit on the toilet "for hours."

[6] This group experience is deeply impressed on their memories; the older sabras refer to it when asked about their sexual feelings toward each other — "How can you have sexual feelings for girls whom you sat on the pot with?"

That the children are aware of the nurse's desire to train them, in spite of her permissiveness, is indicated not only by their increasing continence, but by their use of the chamber pot as an attention-getting device. They quickly learn that as soon as they announce that they have to make "pee-pee" or "eh-eh" they can immediately gain the nurse's attention and her praise. In Group II, for example,

Tamar says she has to make pee-pee. I (A.G.S.) take her into the house . . . but the nurse says, no, she doesn't really have to make pee-pee. "Her parents are away, and she wants attention."

Chana made pee-pee in the yard. The nurse dresses her, and, minutes later, Chana says to me, "More pee-pee." I (A.G.S.) undress her, she goes to the corner of the yard, does nothing. Nurse comments, "I thought so, she enjoys the game." When Chana came back, I dressed her, and it was obvious that she enjoyed this very much — prolonging it as long as possible.

In Group III, where training has been completed, the children are proud of having achieved continence, and they too display a desire for praise.

Mimi comes to tell the nurse that she has "made pee-pee," and that she had first removed her pants. (She is carrying her pants.)

Miri runs to me to tell me (M.E.S.) that she has "made eh-eh."

Pnina goes into the toilet and says to the nurse, "I'm going to make eh-eh."

Another factor encouraging continence in the children is the fact that they are permitted to use the device of sitting on the pot as an excuse for avoiding or postponing some other activity — going to bed, for example, or taking a shower. Although the nurse always recognizes the child's motivation, she generally acquiesces in his desire and thus encourages him to repeat his behavior.

It is interesting to note the change in the children's attitudes toward excreta as their training continues. In Groups I and II the children were observed to play with and smear excreta in a matter-of-fact way, often making a group affair of such sport.[7]

---

[7] It should be noted that the nurses disapprove of such behavior, and manifest their disapproval by immediately mopping up the excreta and referring to it as "fooia."

If a child, for example, urinates on the floor, the others may all get down on the floor and drink the urine. In Group I,

David urinates in the playpen . . . He rolls his auto in it, sits, splashes puddle with his hand . . . puts his mouth to puddle, drinks a little. Crawls all through puddle, has it all over him — face, arms, legs. Amir sits by the puddle (what remains of it) and splashes his hand in it. David comes over, lies down by the puddle, drinks, splashes hand in it, continues to drink . . .

In the following example from Group II, we may note, too, the joy a young child takes in excreting.

Rena makes pee-pee in the pot. She jumps up, shouts, "Pee-pee!," dances around joyfully, sings, sucks her thumb, sits back on pot.

In Group III, where the children only infrequently eliminate on the ground, we note a modification in this positive attitude of younger children toward excreta. In the following example, we observe the more gingerly and anxious approach of these older children to excreta.

Miri defecates on the ground, stands and laughs. Tsvi, Pua, and Micah watch her and laugh too. Micah tries to pick up the faeces with a piece of rope, and it falls off. Tsvi picks up the faeces with his hands, and they all laugh uproariously . . . Tsvi picks up some of the faeces with a stone and brings it to me, shouting, "eh-eh!"

Finally, in Group IV, we observe actual disgust for excreta. Amnon, for example, saw some faeces next to him when he sat on the ground. He became visibly upset and threw it away, saying "eh-eh" in a tone of disgust. In this age-group, moreover, faeces may be used as a weapon of aggression, as when a boy became angry and threw his faeces at me.

On the other hand, almost no modesty has developed in the children, even in the older groups, with respect to excretory functions. This is not surprising in view of the absence of modesty training in these preschool years. Thus, urination and defecation alike are performed in the presence of either children or adults of both sexes with no traces of self-consciousness or shame.

Despite the attempts of both nurses and peers to toilet train the children, nocturnal incontinence persists even in those groups in which training is completed. In each of the two older groups there are four children who continue to wet their beds at night. In the Kindergarten nine of the sixteen children regularly wet their beds, and in the Transitional Class three of the sixteen children continue to do so.

That incontinence is difficult to extinguish results from the complex motives that may lie behind it. In many instances incontinence is associated with sibling rivalry and parental "rejection" — a subject discussed in Chapter 6 — although the meaning of this relationship is obscure. Some of the motives for incontinence, however, are more transparent. Incontinence is sometimes a deliberately aggressive act on the part of a child. Whenever Ziva, for example, who is generally continent, has an argument with the nurse, she tells her that she will awaken wet the next morning — and she does. Still another child wets her bed when she is angry, and warns her nurse in advance. One girl is unhappy when a substitute nurse is on duty; should she see this strange nurse when she awakens, either in the morning or in the afternoon, she wets her bed. One boy always wets his bed when, says the nurse, he is in a "bad mood." But another boy says that he wants to wake up "wet" because it is pleasant to lie on the wet sheets. A more explicit act of regression was observed in the case of Yaffa, who, although one of the first to become continent at night, wet her bed every night during a period of illness, saying that she wanted to be a baby.

Continence may be as deliberate as incontinence. Elat, for example, soiled her pants until she was almost four. One day she told the nurse that she would no longer soil "because it will make you happy," and she has not soiled since.

INDEPENDENCE TRAINING AND BEHAVIOR

Independence training is training for the acquisition of motives of self-reliance and responsibility. As the child grows older he is expected to relinquish much of his succorant behavior, both emotional and instrumental. His need for nurturance and for assistance from parents and parent-surrogates is to be replaced by greater self-sufficiency in both of these areas.

Independence. The nurses begin to encourage the development of responsibility as early as Group II. In this group the nurses occasionally ask the children to put their toys away. It is in this group, too, that the children show signs of having acquired responsibility motives. The oldest children always give their empty plates to the nurses or take them to the sink after meals, and a few return their chairs to their regular places. Others help the nurse of their own volition: if she shakes out a rug, a child will help her; if she sweeps the floor, a child will take a broom and "sweep" too; or children will help the nurse pick up stones lying in the yard. Some of these children put their clothes on the proper shelf or fetch their own towels for their baths. Moreover, though no child in this group can dress himself completely, the older ones make many attempts to do so.

In Groups III and IV the children are generally eager to assume as many adult responsibilities as they are capable of — or as the nurses permit. Some of the more obvious activities manifested by the children in Group III include washing themselves in the morning, attempting to dress and undress themselves, drying dishes after meals, fetching the materials for their "work," cleaning up after play, going to the communal kitchen to bring back food for light snacks. The children of Group IV have made even greater strides. All attempt to dress and undress themselves, although some of the younger ones require the nurse's assistance (none of the younger children in the group can tie their shoelaces). The older children fold their pajamas in the morning and put them at the foot of the bed. Some of the children can shower themselves, although the nurse always dries them. In most cases the nurse shampoos the children's hair, but some children insist on doing this themselves.

The children — sometimes voluntarily, sometimes at the suggestion of the nurse — clean the floor after play periods. Usually they work in pairs, one sweeping while the other holds the dustpan. Other responsibilities include buttering bread for all the children, cleaning the table after meals, and helping the nurse to wash, dry, and put away the dishes.

Nurses rarely exert pressure on the children to perform these responsibilities and it is most unusual for a nurse to reprimand or punish a child for *not* dressing himself, for *not* washing himself (there is only one instance in the entire sample). On the contrary, the initiative is generally taken by the child; the nurse usually begins to dress or wash him and he asks to perform this task by himself. Such requests and attempts are always permitted by the nurse. Moreover, though little inducement is required for the performance of these various responses, they are almost always reinforced by the nurse's praising a child as she sees him performing them. Such praise ranges from the favorite "Yofi!" or "You see how they help me!" in Group II to the following, similar responses of the nurses in Groups III and IV.

We are sitting outside . . . Nurse asks Shula to fetch a piece of string, and she does. When she returns, the nurse says, "See children, what a big girl Shula is; see how she can do things all alone!"

Amos brings a jar of honey to the nurse, at her request. The nurse says, "Excellent — now I see that I can send Amos to get things."

Work. Although training in work is training for responsibility, a separate section is devoted to it because of its paramount importance in the kibbutz value system. Many of the activities discussed in the section above as "responsibility" could indeed be labeled "work," for they consist of chores which, though geared to the ages of the children, are performed by kibbutz adults as part of their daily work assignments. In this sense, one is justified in stating that the children begin to perform chores no later than the age of three.

Since, however, these chores are performed voluntarily rather than as a responsibility which the nurse either imposes on or expects of the children, they may properly be excluded from training in work. Moreover, the nurses do not view these chores as "work," reserving this label for activities of an entirely different nature. These, it will be remembered, consist of various types of art work — finger painting, clay modeling, drawing, stringing beads, pasting. At the scheduled time for these artistic activities, the nurse will announce, "It's time for our work," or, "What kind of work shall we do today?" This is a deliberate socialization device. For although these younger children are not expected to assume regular work assignments, the kibbutz attempts to impress its workers' ideology upon them at as early an age as possible by arbitrarily referring to certain play activities as work.

Work, in the sense of a regularly assigned responsibility, may be said to commence in the Kindergarten. Here, in addition to their artistic "work," the children for the first time are assigned agricultural chores; and the service chores, which they had formerly assumed voluntarily, now become regular assignments. Service chores at this age include fetching food from the kitchen, clearing tables, and emptying garbage. Agricultural chores consist of tending their own vegetable garden, small poultry run, and the few goats and sheep for which they are solely responsible. The produce, the children consume at their own table; and the income from their poultry and flocks belongs to them and is used to buy whatever they want for their kevutza.

The children both enjoy and take pride in their agricultural work, and they encourage visitors to admire their garden or their animals. Hence, though these chores are now expected of them, no inducement, other than intrinsic satisfaction, is required for their performance. As in the case of other responsibilities, however, the nurses reinforce successful performances with praise.

Sleep. Since the children sleep in their dwellings without adult attendance, rather than in their parents' rooms, their behavior in this situation constitutes a genuine measure of emotional self-sufficiency. During the course of this study, the three older groups were put to bed by the nurses, while in Group I the parents were responsible for hashkava. Moreover, since the nurse in Group II had begun to put the children to bed only two weeks prior to the beginning of observations in her group, three types of comparisons can be made.

Whether the nurse or the parent is responsible for hashkava, the procedure is the same, however different the atmosphere and dynamics. The following description, therefore, applies to both. In the older groups the children are usually showered before going to bed. Usually the nurse showers two children at a time, and they seem to enjoy the experience immensely, as is indicated by their laughter, shouting, and general good spirits.[8] While showering the children, the nurse talks to them, sings a song, asks them what they did with their parents, and so on. There is little question but that this is one of the children's most enjoyable experiences, marred only by those who may be crying because of the departure of their parents.

After she has dried all the children and put on their pajamas, the nurse puts each to bed. When she turns out the lights, she goes from bed to bed, says "Good night and golden dreams" to each child as she kisses him, and then sings a lullaby to the group before leaving. Her handling of the situation is efficient and, to an observer, most impressive. She is warm, loving, and kindly; but she is also firm. In general the entire procedure, from the time the first child arrives until the nurse leaves, requires about twenty-five minutes. When she leaves she does not turn back or answer when the children call her.[9]

[8] Not all groups enjoy the shower experience. The children of Group II cry in the shower because they are afraid — mostly of the water and soap that frequently trickle down into their faces and eyes.

[9] This description applies, in general, to all groups. There is one qualification to this general pattern, however, found in Group IV. When these children first arrive, it is difficult to control them, and they run about the dormitory singing, shouting, and talking with abandon. The nurses do not attempt to restrain them, and they soon settle down.

When the last goodnight is said and the last child is kissed, the nurse or parents leave, and the children remain without adult attendance until the following morning. The night watch, to be sure, makes periodic checks, and she attempts to pacify the children should they cry, or assist those who want a drink or wish to go to the toilet. Nevertheless since the children are alone for most of the night, one would wish to know whether the crying which is found among the younger children (Group I) — and which serves to delay the departure of the parents — stems from a desire for attention or, rather, reflects their anxiety about being left alone (due, perhaps, to a fear of abandonment).

The latter hypothesis is supported by the reports of the adults who live in proximity to this children's house. They complain that the children "cry and whine all night." It is also supported by the nurses of Groups III and IV who report that at least some of their charges, when of the age as the children in Group I, were afraid of being left alone. In Group IV, for example, at least four children would awaken at night and cry. The nurses decided to keep a light burning all night, and this seemed to reduce their fears — at least it eliminated their crying. In this same group, one girl insisted that her head be covered with a blanket because she was afraid of the shadows.[10]

If sleeping without fear can be said to constitute emotional self-reliance, the nurse's refusal to indulge the children's desire to prolong the leavetaking constitutes one form of independence training. The next question, then, concerns the effectiveness of this training. Do the children in Groups II through IV continue to display the fear reactions observed in Group I? Unfortunately we have no direct evidence on this point. We do know that older children do not attempt to prolong the leavetaking, that they don't cry when the nurse leaves, and that they converse with one another before falling asleep. To that extent it may be concluded that, except for some isolated cases,[11] independence in this area has been achieved.

There are other signs, however, which seem to suggest that, though the children have learned to inhibit such gross fear responses as crying and whining, they continue to experience

---

[10] It is of interest to observe, however, that her fears and night-crying continued only so long as her parents put her to bed. When the nurse began to put the children to bed, her crying and fears lessened considerably.

[11] There is a four-year-old girl who insists on having the blanket pulled over her head before she will fall asleep. A five-year-old boy spontaneously informed me that, "I'm not afraid at night," but insisted that Amos and David were. And there is a girl whose extreme fear responses are "pathological."

anxiety at being left alone at night; and that, in short, they retain their need for dependence. Almost all the children in all four groups, for example, suck their thumbs in bed. And this response, together with the rocking found in the youngest group, suggests that the children are not altogether secure about sleeping at night without the presence of an adult. There is some suggestion, moreover, that the insecurity induced by this condition has a pervasive influence on personality development. On the Emotional Response Test, for example, darkness ranks second and third, respectively, among the things most feared by the high school and grammar school students. It is difficult to explain this fear — given the conditions of kibbutz life — except as a conditioned response to the fear of abandonment at night during these early years.

Dependence. From their reactions to hashkava we may conclude that these children have unsatisfied dependency needs. Other forms of behavior — crying, a need for physical contact, thumbsucking, and regressive play — support this conclusion, as well; and we may now turn to a description of these patterns and of their socialization.

Crying: The type of independence training with which the nurses are most concerned — as measured by the frequency of socialization responses — is the extinction of crying. Crying is not only the most frequent response to aggression and conflict, but the children frequently cry and whine for many other apparent, and often not so apparent, reasons. Yael, for example, cannot put on her skirt and runs, crying, to the nurse; Chana offers to help Ruthi put on her blouse, and the latter throws a temper tantrum; Yosi wants shorts with elastic, and cries when told that there are none; Avner puts his foot on Amir's chair, and Amir begins to scream; Iris touches Mirav's doll, and Mirav screams with rage.

Given the readiness with which the children cry — to peer frustration, nurse frustration, and to unapparent frustration — the children's houses are often in a state of utter confusion. This frequency of crying, however, must be viewed within certain reality contexts. In Groups I and II, for example, crying is often the only technique available to relatively nonverbal children for the expression of a demand or need. But crying is as prevalent in Group III, whose children are verbal; according to their nursery teacher, these children "never stopped crying" when she first assumed responsibility for them a year prior to this study. She thought she would "go mad," and remained with the group only because she was ashamed to resign. This nurse regarded such crying as a symptom of emotional disturbance, and she felt that it was a function, not of low frustration-tolerance, but of three reality conditions — conditions which are all but universal in the experience of the kibbutz children, which may account for much of the crying in all groups, and which, as we have suggested elsewhere, are partially responsible for many of the behavior problems found among these children.

In the first place, the children in Group III had experienced a threefold change in nurses in the brief space of one year, and their present nurse regards this experience as most important in the development of their disturbed behavior. Second, the present nurse, after taking over the group, was the only nurse in the house for almost a year. The pressure of many duties and chores, therefore, left her with little time to devote to the children. Finally, the physical conditions in the house were poor. The house was too small for their needs, there was no play-yard, and there were few toys. This lack of space and facilities led to an increase in aggression which, among other things, contributed to the frequency of crying. The nurse demanded, and eventually received, a larger house, a play area, more toys, and a nurse to assist her. When these demands were met, the children's behavior improved and the indiscriminate crying, she claims, disappeared. The latter claim is not accurate, according to our observations, although crying is undoubtedly less frequent than it had been before the new conditions were introduced. Moreover, from the frequency of crying in this, as in all other groups, one cannot help but conclude that the frustration-tolerance of young kibbutz children is very low.

Crying is handled by the nurses in a number of ways, according to its motivation. If the nurse is convinced that the child's crying is the result of some unsatisfied need, she will almost always attempt to satisfy his demand if she is free. But often, as has been emphasized, the nurse is unable to attend to the child because of other responsibilities. When this happens, the child's crying may continue until he is exhausted. In spite of instances of unrequited crying, however, the crying response elicits the nurse's attention with sufficient frequency that its persistence may be explained as a function of this reinforcement.

There are, furthermore, many instances in which the nurse responds to a child's crying, not to satisfy his need, but to stop his nagging. In Group II, for example, the children frequently ask for chamber pots, not because they have to go to the toilet, but because they wish to play with them. Aware of their real motives, the nurse frequently refuses the requests. If a child begins to cry, however, and persists in crying for a pot, the nurse almost always acquiesces in his demand.

When crying is provoked by aggression or conflict, the nurse — if she is present and/or available — always attempts to discover the root of the crying and to pacify the child. She comforts him with physical affection and soothing terms of endearment. In this sense, she encourages crying, for the child learns that by crying he will, at least occasionally, gain attention and affection.

But the nurses are not always so indulgent toward other types of crying. Except in Group I, where the nurse's sole response to crying (when she responds at all) is comfort and appeasement, the nurses employ a number of techniques — wittingly and un- wittingly — to extinguish crying. The unwitting, and most fre- quent, response of the nurse is to ignore the crying. This is referred to as "unwitting" because she does not deliberately employ it as a training technique — although it may well serve that function — but rather because she is busy elsewhere and with other matters.

Table 12. Technique for socialization of crying in percentages.

Technique	Groups II, III, IV (Σ acts = 36)
Neutral	53
Order to stop	42
Miscellaneous	11
Punishing	41
Shame	22
Deprivation	19
Rewarding	6
Praise for ceasing or	
for not crying	6

At the .99 confidence level the upper confidence limit for "punishing" techniques is 62.13. The finding — neutral techniques > punishing techniques — is not signifi- cant. By the same test, the findings — neutral techniques > rewarding techniques, and punishing techniques > rewarding tech- niques — are significant.

Of the techniques wittingly employed by the nurses in Groups II, III, and IV, and which are summarized in Table 12, the most frequent is a neutral technique — ordering the child to stop his crying. In some instances the order is impersonal — "Stop crying, children" or "Don't cry, children." But in many cases the nurse orders a child to stop because *she* does not want them to cry or because *she* disapproves of this behavior — "I want you to be quiet," "Stop crying because I don't like it when you cry," or "It is not pleasant for me to hear so much noise."

Punishing techniques consist of shaming and deprivation. The former may consist in the use of an epithet or in calling the attention of other people to the child's behavior.

Mirav is in the shower and she cries. Nurse tells her to stand still and "stop acting like a spoiled girl."

(Micah has finally stopped crying after an extended period, and is now sitting all alone.) The nurse comes in, sits down beside him, and asks, "What will be with you?" She repeats the question many times, and he does not respond. She says, "Everyone who passes here asks: Who is making so much noise in SARA's kevutza? It is Micah, Micah the big one."

(The children are drinking lemonade.) Shula lies on the floor and whines. The nurse says, "Look children, Shula just woke up and instead of drinking, she's crying."

A third important technique for the extinction of crying is deprivation, and in this instance all of the instances in our sample are of threatened, rather than actual, deprivation. That is, the nurse threatens to deprive a child of something if he continues to cry, rather than depriving him for having cried. For example:

Elat is crying and the nurse says she will put her to bed if she continues to cry.

Micah begins to shout and cry when the nurse takes him from the shower. Nurse says, "If you continue to shout, I'll send you out of the house."

Shula is crying in the bedroom. The nurse says, "If you don't stop crying, I'll close the door on you."

The socialization of crying during the day is quite different from its socialization at night — when it is simply ignored — and is almost the antithesis of other types of independence training.

In the latter, reward in the form of praise is the exclusive socialization technique; for crying neutral and punitive techniques predominate. Of thirty-six acts of socialization for crying, 53 per cent may be classified as neutral, 41 per cent as punitive, and only six per cent as rewarding (that is, a child is praised for not crying or for ceasing to cry).

Physical contact: The children are attached to their nurse and frequently demonstate this by physical affection and by their desire for prolonged physical contact with her. When a nurse sits down to read to the children or to play with them, they will often swarm over her — sitting on her lap, climbing on her back, standing next to her with their arms on her shoulders.

ROSA sits on the floor. Amir and Mirav pile onto her lap . . . Omri tries to force Amir out, and ROSA says, "Amir also wants to sit next to ROSA," and she helps Omri to sit on her knees. Avner tries to sit on her feet, sits on her ankles. Rafi sits next to Mirav, who has her thumb in her mouth . . .

But the children seek physical contact with other adults as well. Those in the three youngest groups constantly wished to sit on our laps — it was often the only available lap in the house — and in some instances even fought over this privilege. One has the impression that they are seeking love and protection. (It is difficult to decide, however, to what extent such behavior is sexual, rather than succorant.) One example illustrates this point.

Ofer . . . throws his arms around me (A.G.S.) and clings tightly. When I try to let go or write, he clings tighter. He puts his head on my breast and sucks his thumb.

In general the nurses indulge these succorant demands, though a nurse may order a child to desist if his demands become too persistent or annoying. There is a marked decrease in this succorant behavior in Group IV.

Thumbsucking: If we follow Erikson in interpreting thumbsucking (and its various substitutes) as regression to the security of the oral stage by children whose later experiences are less satisfying,[12] then the high frequency of thumbsucking in these children is another sign of their dependency needs.

[12] Erik Homburger Erikson, "Growth and Crises of the 'Healthy Personality,'" in Clyde Kluckhohn, Henry A. Murray, and David M. Schneider, *Personality in Nature, Society, and Culture* (New York, Knopf, 1953), pp. 185–225, 199.

Thumbsucking is usually uninstigated by any stimulus in the child's immediate social field and must be viewed, therefore, as a generalized, rather than a specific, dependency response. Only in Group I does it appear as a frequent (24 per cent) response to some identifiable frustrating situation. In general, and including Group I, sucking occurs most frequently during play or while sleeping (including the period immediately prior to, or following, sleep).

There is considerable individual variability, both in the frequency and nature of sucking. Although most of the children suck their thumbs, if they suck at all, some suck their middle or forefingers, and at least one sucks these two fingers simultaneously. One child has substituted for thumbsucking a compulsive ritual of wetting her fingers, then wetting and pulling her hair with her wet fingers.

Although the frequency of thumbsucking varies greatly *within* each group, there appears to be little difference *among* the groups, with the possible exception of the youngest group which shows the least amount of sucking behavior.[13] In this group only half the children are thumbsuckers, with a range of from 4 to 24 acts in the sample; in Group II, three-fourths of the children suck with a range of from 1 to 25; in Group III all the children suck with a frequency ranging from 6 to 20; and in Group IV all the children are thumbsuckers, with a range of from 1 to 13. In the latter group some children have been thumbsuckers for a long time; others have only recently begun to suck. In almost all cases of recent onset of sucking, the behavior is associated with the temporary absence of parents or the birth of a sibling. In all groups but one, moreover, girls are greater thumbsuckers than boys.

Thumbsucking is not viewed with alarm by the nurses, so that the children may suck with impunity. Not one child was observed to be punished or reprimanded for thumbsucking; indeed, the nurses ignore its manifestation. There are only three instances in the sample of hundreds of instances of sucking in which the nurse was observed even to take cognizance of it. In one instance the nurse told a child, who almost literally never removed his fingers from his mouth, "Stop sucking for one minute." The other two instances are typical of the generally nonpunitive character of kibbutz socialization and may be quoted here.

---

[13] On the other hand, this group exhibits a considerable amount of "rocking" at night, according to those adults whose rooms adjoin this nursery and who complain, in the words of one, that the children "rock their cribs all night long."

Esther is looking out the window towards the Grammar School. She calls to SARAH: "SARAH, I see that Giora sucks his thumb." SARAH says, "Does it look nice?" (implying that it doesn't). Esther says, "No."

Micah comes out to ride his auto, thumb in mouth. ZEHAVA sees him, tells him that he should drive with both hands lest the auto go off the road. She asks him with how many hands his grandfather drives, and he says with two.

Regressive play: Unsatisfied dependency needs are to be found in the play of these children, as well. In fantasy play in which the children identify the roles which they are playing, 8 per cent of the boys' and 15 per cent of the girls' identifications are with babies or children younger than themselves (see Table 17, p. 240). The essentially regressive quality of these identifications is emphasized by the content of the play — "sleeping" in a doll's crib, being sick and having to be cared for, being fed, and curling up within some enclosure. The latter play is of particular interest. It usually includes making a pool or pond of building-blocks and then lying within the enclosure. At times a child may lie on his back, at other times he curls up in foetus-like fashion, usually sucking his thumb. A second enclosure is the doll's crib. The child lies in the doll's bed, either holding a doll in her arms or sucking her thumb. A third enclosure, one which children in Group III, in particular, prefer, is a corner underneath a bed. Few instances were observed in which a child chose to lie in such a corner alone; always at least two — and sometimes more — would decide to do so, each choosing a different bed under which to lie.

This regressive play occurs only in the two older, but not in the two younger groups. It is perhaps not irrelevant to observe that the children in the older two groups already have younger siblings, while those in the younger two groups do not.

Need for approval: A final indication of dependency among these children is their deep-seated need for approval and attention from both peers and adults, which is discussed in Chapters 5 and 8.

SEXUAL TRAINING AND BEHAVIOR

Socialization. According to the sexual ideology of the kibbutz, sexual manifestations in young children are to be viewed as normal and no attempt should be made to interfere with sexual behavior; for any interference with childhood sexuality, it is believed, may be more harmful to the child than the harm which might follow from its expression. Hence the children are to be free to engage in sexual behavior without interference or punishment.

This official viewpoint is, in general, carried into practice by the nurses. We never observed a nurse to prohibit any sexual act on the part of a child, much less punish the child. There is not one instance in the entire sample of a nurse's interference in the sexual activity of the children. Indeed, since sex training (like thumbsucking) is probably the most permissive training of all the behavior systems, it is most curious — or, would be if it were not for other data to be presented below — that the children do not manifest a greater degree of sexuality. It is probable, too, that a great deal of sexual behavior of which we are unaware occurs at night.

The nurses not only permit sexual manifestations in children, they encourage physical expressions of love and warmth among them. A nurse, for example, may ask an aggressor to "make nice" to his victim, by embracing or kissing him. Or, with no prior provocation, she may request a child to embrace or kiss another child. And, of course, the nurses often request the children to embrace or kiss them.

The nurses not only permit the children to express their sexual impulses, but they attempt to answer their sexual questions when they arise. When they ask about the origin of babies, for example, the typical answer given to the younger children is that the mother goes to the hospital, and then brings back the baby. Beginning in the Kindergarten, however, the nurse answers such questions as candidly as the comprehension of the children will permit. Usually the most effective technique for explaining the birth of a baby to these older children is by making comparisons with the sheep and goats, which the children tend, and whose sexual behavior they have observed.

Parents, too, claim to answer the sexual questions of their children in a candid fashion. Twelve of the sixteen parents who answered the Questionnaire checked, "definitely yes" to the question, "Do you answer the sexual questions of your younger children truthfully?"; four checked "perhaps yes."

This characterization of the nurses' *behavior* as being generally permissive does not mean that the children are reared in an entirely permissive sexual environment. The nurses, to be sure, have been trained to respond in a permissive fashion to the sexual behavior of their charges, but some of them retain the sexual attitudes in which they themselves had been reared (in Europe), and it is by no means unlikely that regardless of their behavior, these attitudes are transmitted to the children. One nurse, for example, when reporting that boys and girls in her kevutza had formerly slept together in the same bed, said: "They felt no shame or guilt when I discovered them . . . They didn't even know that it's immoral." [14]

But parents, as well as nurses, influence the children, and parental sexual attitudes and behavior are not entirely permissive. While the great majority of parents who responded to the Questionnaire indicated that they never punish their children for masturbation, almost half the respondents did not answer the question; and it is our belief that their failure to respond resulted from a conflict between private, more conventional, feelings and the official, "progressive" attitude. The former attitude is expressed in the one instance in which a parent was observed to witness a child's masturbation. While sitting on a chamber pot at bedtime, Yehuda (three years) fingered his penis. His father became angry, and shouted at him, *B'li yadaim, b'li yadaim* ("without hands, without hands").

But it is not only toward masturbation that parental attitudes are not entirely permissive. To questions dealing with sexual behavior among older children, a large number of parents indicated a conventional attitude toward chastity (see p. 329), one at variance with the official kibbutz attitude. It is not unlikely that the conventional attitudes of the parents toward sexual behavior in their older children holds for their younger children as well. We may conclude that the children are exposed to conflicting adult attitudes toward their own (the children's) sexual behavior, although the dominant attitude of the nurses, as well as their behavior, is permissive.

The "progressive" sexual ideology of the kibbutz is reflected, not only in the behavior of the nurses, but in an important structural characteristic of the kevutza — its bisexual nature. This feature of group living is an important influence on the sexual attitudes of the children, for it provides them with almost unlimited opportunities for observing differences in sexual anatomy.[15] Boys and girls sleep in the same rooms, shower together, sit on the toilet together, and often run around nude before getting dressed in the morning or after being undressed in the evening.

[14] That a trained nursery teacher — trained in the educational philosophy and ideology of the kibbutz — can still employ the value judgments of Western middle-class culture, indicates to what a superficial level some of the revolutionary changes in the kibbutz have penetrated. It also indicates one of the many inconsistencies in values to which the children are exposed.

[15] But their infrequent opportunities for observing adult nudity should also be noted.

Sexual curiosity and shame. It is not surprising that few indications of sexual shame are to be found in any of the four groups. Only in the oldest group, IV, did the nurse report that some of the children were beginning to reveal signs of sexual shame, becoming reluctant, for example, to remove their underpants in the presence of children of the opposite sex.

Signs of sexual shame are reported by the teachers in the Kindergarten and the Transitional Class. These children have no feeling of shame about exposing their nudity before children of the opposite sex, providing that they know each other, but are reluctant to do so in the presence of strangers. For example, Israel had only recently joined the Kindergarten, and when he first arrived he was reluctant to take a shower with the other children. Later, three other children joined the group, and they too were ashamed to expose their nudity; for the first month they would wrap towels around themselves when leaving the showers.

Curiosity concerning adult sexuality is not found among any children younger than Group III — at least none is expressed. Even in Group III, according to the nursery teacher, the children have never asked any questions concerning sex; and, she claims, they are ignorant of such sexual matters as physiological paternity. Tsvia's father, for example, was killed in the War, but Tsvia believes that her uncle in Haifa is her father; at least, she maintains that he is her father, and the other children — with the exception of Micah — accept this interpretation. I can confirm this; when Tsvia asked me to write the name of her father, I asked what his name was, and she said, "Avigdor," the name of her uncle. Micah denied that Avigdor was her father, maintaining that he was her uncle. But neither he nor anyone else could explain the difference between uncle and father.

The children in Group IV, however, show indications of sexual curiosity, particularly about the origin of babies, and they often question the nurse about this matter. This same sexual curiosity probably motivates the frequent practice of opening up their dolls to examine their insides. And this same interest is expressed in a song which the children were heard to sing and which meant, according to one child informant, "You are pregnant."

Pregnancy and childbirth evoke the curiosity of kindergarten and first-grade children, too. The latter's interest was first aroused while witnessing the copulation of a bull and cow. They were obviously ambivalent toward the scene they had witnessed. On the one hand, many were visibly frightened; on the other, they made joking remarks about it, and some even imitated the copulatory behavior of the animals. And some broached the question of the sexual relationship between their parents to the nurse.

These children refer few of their sexual questions, however, to their parents. To the question, "Do your young children ask you about sex?" none of the sixteen parents who answered the Questionnaire checked, "Frequently." Six checked, "sometimes"; nine checked, "infrequently"; and one checked, "never."

Sexual behavior. It should first be remarked that the definition of "sexual behavior" in children is not an easy matter. When, for example, a child pulls at his genitals is he masturbating or is he engaging in nonsexual motor behavior? Or, is an act which, when manifested by adults, is labeled "sexual," to be so labeled when manifested by children? Is the embrace of two children a sexual act, or is it a mark of affection, or both? For example, one nursery teacher, a person of fine insight, told me that although she had observed masturbation in her kevutza, she had never observed either homosexual or heterosexual behavior. On the other hand, I *did* observe such behavior in her kevutza. Apparently some of the acts which I consider sexual were perceived differently by her.

Since it is all but impossible in many instances to distinguish sexual from nonsexual acts, it was decided to cut this Gordian knot by arbitrarily labeling as sexual all acts which appeared to have some sexual form or content, without intending to imply that these acts do not have other, nonsexual, meanings as well. This method of tabulation has unquestionably had the result of increasing the total number of sexual acts in the sample. On the other hand, since we made no observations on the children after they went to bed, and since it is not unreasonable to assume that at least some sexual activity occurs at night, the figures given in Table 13 are probably inadequate indices of sexual behavior in these children.

Table 13. Classification of sexual behavior by percentages.

Behavior	Group I (Σ acts = 9)	Group II (Σ = 48)	Group III (Σ = 32)	Group IV (Σ = 43)
Autosexual	100	50	69	48
Heterosexual	0	29	19	19
Homosexual	0	21	12	33

Testing for differences among the three types of sexuality yields:

$$\chi^2 = 15.2 \quad \text{d.f.} = 3 \quad P = < .01$$

Although comparisons among the four groups are not entirely reliable (since there is some question about the equivalence of the time-samples taken from each group), a frequency count indicates that sexual behavior increases with age. Groups I–IV committed 9, 24,[16] 32, and 43 sexual acts, respectively (exclusive of those acts, to be analyzed separately, in which an adult is the object). Despite this age trend, however, there is no consistent pattern in development, as the following discussion indicates.

As Table 13 reveals, autosexual activity[17] is the most frequent form of sexual behavior in all four groups. Its incidence is highest in Group I, however, accounting for all the sexual behavior in the group.

Masturbation, the most frequent form of autosexuality, refers to any act of hand-genital contact, and it is not always clear, as has already been noted, that all such acts are genuinely masturbatory, since they are sometimes quite brief in duration. Thus all the examples below (the first example is from Group I, the others from Group III) were labeled as masturbation, although there are important quantitative and qualitative differences among them.

Eldad is in the bed outside, fingering his penis, which is exposed . . . he is masturbating . . . he turns around, with his back to me . . . finishes masturbating . . . sits down . . . Eldad stands, fingers, pulls penis . . . whines, calls, jabbers . . . tries to pull his pants over his penis . . .

Amnon sits nude on floor, fingering his penis. Nurse asks him to get dressed, and while she dresses him he continues to finger his penis.

Nurse reads story to the children . . . Shula sits with one hand in mouth and with other hand is masturbating.

Masturbation occurs in any number of situations. Among the most frequent are play periods, in the shower, in bed in the morning, while being dried by the nurse, on the toilet, while listening to a story, following some frustration. In the two older groups most masturbation, by far, occurs during play, while in the younger groups it occurs most frequently while the children are on the

[16] Since Group II is a composite of two separate kevutzot, the total of 48 sexual acts represents an average of 24 acts for each kevutza.

[17] In the main, autosexual activity consists in masturbation, but there are other autosexual activities as well. In Group II, for example, a girl covered her vulva with a handkerchief. In Group III a boy put a can on his penis, and another put a button on his penis. In Group IV a boy put some clay on his penis. These acts have an element of exhibitionism, as well, since the boys invited the other children to see what they had done.

toilet. In both cases it may be said that masturbation occurs most frequently when the child is more or less inactive. Even in the two older groups a child was rarely observed to masturbate while he himself was playing; he masturbated, rather, while observing the play of other children.

Heterosexual behavior is the second most frequent sexual expression in Groups II and III, but it is preceded by homosexuality in Group IV. Heterosexual behavior includes a number of quite different kinds of activities, both within any one group as well as among groups. In Group II, for example, its most frequent expression consists in a simple embrace of one child by another, followed in frequency by stroking or caressing, kissing, and touching of genitals. Examples of each are found in the following entries.

Ofer (male) and Pnina (female) sit side by side on chamber pots . . . Ofer puts his foot on Pnina's foot, she then does the same — this happens several times . . . finally, Pnina shifts her pot away, then moves back, then away . . . they laugh . . . Pnina stands up, lies on the table on her stomach, says "ADINA." Ofer pats her buttocks. Nurse comes in, and Pnina stands up, sits on the table . . . Ofer puts his foot on her leg. She offers him a piece of bread, and he eats it . . . this is repeated twice . . . Ofer kicks Pnina gently, and they laugh . . . Pnina touches and caresses Ofer's leg with her foot . . . says "more, more" . . . Ofer stands, then Pnina stands, both bounce up and down . . . both children are excited, bounce, laugh together . . . Pnina grabs Ofer's penis, and he pushes her away . . . she repeats, he pushes her away, and turns around . . . Pnina touches his buttocks.

Anat (female) is put on the table with Ofer (male) to be dressed . . . the nurse goes to the other room . . . Anat hugs Ofer, later hits him . . . he cries, and she caresses him, says "dai" ("enough") . . . She repeats the same act — hitting and then caressing, and Ofer smiles . . . later, Ofer puts his hand on Anat's nipple — she cringes, moves away . . . he repeats, and she turns away, with her back to him. He puts his hands on her back; she says "dai" . . . Ofer and Anat sit on their pots, she puts her arm around his neck, they sit that way . . . (later) . . . Ofer puts his hands on his penis . . . has an erection, sits with hands covering erect penis (masturbates) . . .

Heterosexual behavior in Group III includes the same manifestations found in the younger group, but it also includes two acts of voyeurism and one instance of a boy kissing a girl's panties. In the latter case Mimi was sitting on the toilet when Amnon walked in; she put her panties in his mouth, and he kissed them. Both acts of voyeurism include a girl's "looking" at the nudity of a boy. One of the examples may be quoted here.

Mimi's father comes in, kisses her, wants to take her home. She ignores him, insisting on watching Lula who is lying on the bed nude while the nurse takes his temperature with a rectal thermometer. When it is over, she leaves.

Voyeurism is found in Group IV as well — the one group in which homosexual behavior is more frequent than heterosexual. In one instance the girl not only looked intently at the genitals of the boy but, pointing to his penis, she exclaimed, "Pipi." This is the only group, moreover, in which a boy and girl were found to display special, if not exclusive, interest in each other: Nadav and Naama were frequently observed to play together and, moreover, much of their interaction was sexually tinged. That is, while playing together they would hold hands, touch each other's faces, and laugh or giggle while doing so. This relationship was not confined to daytime play. A few months before the beginning of our study, Nadav had the habit of climbing into Naama's bed at night and sleeping with her. When the nurse asked him why he did this, he replied that he was afraid of sleeping alone. She said she would give him a teddy bear to take to bed with him; but even after she gave him the bear he would not sleep by himself, and would take the bear with him into Naama's bed.[18]

Homosexual behavior includes the same activities found in heterosexual play. These acts are often quite simple, as the two following excerpts from Group II and the succeeding two from Group III reveal.

Mirav (female) hugs Sara (female) and both grin . . .

Avinoam (male) and Amikam (male) sit side by side on chamber pots. Avinoam clutches Amikam's chest and nipples, and they both laugh.

Tsvia and Pnina lie on floor with arms about each other.

Shula walks over to Tsvia and kisses her on the chest.

[18] Although this is the only example of a special attachment between a boy and girl that occurred during our study, another such example, which was reported to us by their nurse, occurred in Group III some months after we had completed our observations in that group. It seems that a new girl had been introduced into the group and one of the boys' "fell in love" with her. He would not let her out of his sight, and instead of visiting his mother every day as he had during our observational period, he stayed with her. Moreover when she would hit him, he — the most aggressive boy in the group when we observed it — would never hit her back. Finally, he insisted that the nurses move her bed into his bedroom, or he would refuse to sleep.

Homosexuality is most prevalent in Group IV. The following two examples, albeit atypical, indicate the greater intensity and complexity of such acts in this oldest group.

> Moshe stands by side of Yosi's bed, caresses his head, kisses him on chest, and says "chamudi" . . . Moshe kisses Yosi flush on lips, then kisses his fingers, back of neck, ears. Yosi laughs with glee and tells him to do it again and again.

> Yuval is stroking his penis . . . Amaziah shouts to Nadav to look at Yuval's penis, and Yuval covers it with his hand. Amaziah and Yosi walk over to him and pull his penis. He says it hurts, but he does not attempt to move as they continue to stroke and wiggle his penis, alternately. Yosi bends down and sucks it for a few seconds. By this time Yuval's penis is red and large. He runs into the other room, stops, they follow him, and begin all over again.

In addition to sexual embraces of various kinds, the children engage in behavior which is at least a disguised expression of sexual interest. In Groups III and IV the children sometimes play "doctor and nurse" — a game in which a "patient" comes to the doctor or nurse to be treated for some ailment. In both groups the doctor or nurse almost always proceed to take the patient's temperature *in ano,* with a stick or twig.[19]

Peers are not the only objects of sexual advances. Adults, too, are sexual objects for the children, but since child-adult sexual interaction will be discussed in Chapter 10, we shall merely observe that children make many more sexual advances to peers than to adults. The ratio of child-to-adult sexuality is 9:1, 48:23, 32:10, 43:7 for Groups I–IV, respectively.

Sexual activity continues into the lower limits of that age range which, in our culture, is conventionally regarded as "latency." As is true, however, for other kinds of behavior in these older children, description of their sexual behavior must be based exclusively on interviews with nurses. Using our tripartite classification of sexual behavior, it may be reported that all three types are found in the Kindergarten and Transitional Class, though the children's mean age is 6.2 and 7.2, respectively. Masturbation, moreover, not only occurs, but some children masturbate openly

---

[19] Sexual references in conversation are infrequent. The following excerpt is one of the few examples in the sample.

Boaz says to Nadav, "Do you know why you are five (years old)? Because you have a watch. On your *pipi* there is a watch and it ticks." (Repeats a few times.) Nadav replies, "On your *pipi* is five, and shut up." Naama who is listening laughs.

and constantly. There is also a great deal of symbolic masturbation in these groups — at least this is the nurses' interpretation of the children's frequent hitting of the head against the back of the bed, or swaying of the head while in bed.

Heterosexual behavior, too, is found in these older children. In the Kindergarten, one boy attempts to caress any woman with whom he has contact. He is particularly interested in feeling their breasts. Another boy, who has never seen a nude woman, and who is greatly curious about the adult female body, has frequently attempted to see the nursery teacher in the nude — while she is changing clothes or putting on a swimming suit. These children are interested in each others' bodies, as well, but their teacher has not observed genuine heterosexual behavior in the group. There are other indications of heterosexuality, however. A girl, for example, is greatly interested in "taking the children's temperature," *in ano* (using a stick), and one of the boys has attempted to insert his finger in the girls' vaginas.

Although the Kindergarten children are not known by their teacher to engage in genuine heterosexual behavior, the children of the Transitional Class did exhibit genuine heterosexual behavior when they were of Kindergarten age. Boys and girls would often sleep in the same bed, for example, after the nurses left at night. There is, moreover, at least one case of seductive exhibitionism in the older groups — one girl frequently walks nude through the dormitory, calling to the boys to watch her or to embrace her.

Even in the present Kindergarten, however, there is at least one case of a deep-seated attachment between a boy and a girl. Chava and Amir are always together; they play together during the day, leave the dormitory together in the afternoon, and return together at night. And although Amir frequently beats Chava, this has not seemed to diminish their love for each other. They have, moreover, worked out their own division of labor. When the group is supposed to draw or knit, she does it for him; when they are supposed to work in their poultry-run, he does it for her.

SUMMARY OF TRAINING TECHNIQUES

We may summarize our findings concerning techniques of training employed in the "tender age" in a series of propositions. First, most acts in all behavior systems remained unsocialized. Second, the most permissive behavior systems are dependency (with the exception of crying) and sex; that is, almost any type of sexual or dependent activity displayed by the children is deliberately ignored by the nurses. Third, there are significant differences

among the various behavior systems that are socialized with respect to the techniques of training that are employed. Thus,
though neutral techniques of training are most frequently employed for all behavior systems, punitive techniques are employed
more frequently for crying than for any other activity, while they
are employed least frequently in toilet training. Moreover, rewarding techniques are used very frequently in toilet training, while
they are rarely employed for other types of training (see Table
14). Fourth, for all acts in all behavior systems which are trained,
neutral techniques are used most frequently, followed by punitive
and rewarding techniques. Of a total sample of 360 acts of training, 71 per cent were neutral, 20 per cent were punitive, and only
9 per cent were rewarding. Fifth, there are significant age differences with respect to techniques of training. A greater proportion
of neutral techniques are employed with the younger children
(Groups I and II) than with the older (Groups III and IV). Moreover, the proportion of punitive techniques among the younger
children is only one-fourth that of the older children, while the
proportion of rewarding techniques among them is twice that of
the older children (see Table 15).

Table 14. Techniques of training for the various behavior systems
in the entire sample in percentages.

Behavior System	Neutral	Punitive	Rewarding
Eating	79	19	2
Disintegration	73	23	4
Toilet	55	0	45
Crying	53	42	5

$\chi^2 = 93.95$ d.f. $= 6$ P $= <.001$

Table 15. Comparison of techniques of training in older and
younger children in percentages.

Age	Neutral	Punitive	Rewarding
Younger	79	10	11
Older	57	39	6

$\chi^2 = 39.06$ d.f. $= 2$ P $= <.001$

OEDIPUS COMPLEX

The education theorists of The Federation maintain that the Oedipus Complex is precluded in the kibbutz by several of the characteristics of collective education. Although we have little data bearing upon this problem, we shall present what direct and indirect evidence we were able to collect.

It is true that parents lavish their children with physical affection — the frequency of kisses and embraces is great. In some instances this affection is so intense that one can only suspect an element of "seduction" in parental behavior. Indeed, we often recorded, as a "shorthand" note, that "X (a parent) comes in, goes through his usual seductive routine." But what is most important for our purposes here is that almost always the seduction is between parent and child of opposite sex, as the following excerpts demonstrate.

Father of Pua (two years) comes, lifts her, kisses her and kisses her. Her face, neck, cheek, are filled with kisses. He puts her down, talks to her, and goes . . . Pua sucks her thumb.

Ahuv (four years) and his mother are playing on the grass. He lies between her thighs, and she caresses his hair, kisses his face, embraces him tightly.

Ephraim (four years) and his mother are lying on the grass. He lies on top of her, his feet straddling her, makes thrusting movements on her.

Father of Pnina (two-and-one-half years) plays with her while waiting for the nurse to undress her . . . He kisses her many times on the body — the chest and stomach, which evokes much laughter from Pnina. She is very excited, giggles and laughs, asks her father many times to repeat this.

Since parents are seductive toward children of opposite sex, we would wish to know whether children manifest sexual behavior toward parents of opposite sex. Unfortunately we have no direct data which bear upon this question. We do have data, however, concerning the sexual advances of children toward other adults (nurses and anthropologists); and if we can assume that the latter are perceived by the children as parental figures, it might be possible to draw certain conclusions about their sexual, Oedipal feelings from their sexual advances toward them.[1]

Miri (three years) comes over to me (M.E.S.) sits on my lap, puts arms around my neck, feels my chest and thighs with her hands, kisses me . . . Miri "smothers" me, and I have to send her away.

Ofer (male, two years) climbs on my (A.G.S.) lap . . . Ofer throws his arms around me and clings tightly. When I try to let go or write, he clings tighter . . . He puts his head on my breast, and sucks his thumb. He kneels on my knees, opens my mouth, closes it . . . he kisses me on the mouth several times, hard, then opens my mouth to examine it . . . Ofer again kisses me many times on the mouth, holding to me tightly . . . (Later) . . . Ofer climbs on my lap, puts his head on my neck, sucks his thumb. He seems to want to feel my bare skin. He opens my mouth, looks, closes it, repeats several times, kisses me on the mouth.

Table 16. Sexuality toward adults (exclusive of parents) in percentages.

Sex of child	Group I (Σ acts = 2)			Group II (Σ = 23)			Group III (Σ = 10)			Group IV (Σ = 7)		
	Nurse	F. ob-server	T	Nurse	F. ob-server	T	Nurse	M. ob-server	T	Nurse	M. ob-server	T
Male	0	100	100	35	26	61	10	0	10	43	14	57
Female	0	0	0	26	13	39	40	50	90	43	0	43
Total	0	100	100	61	39	100	50	50	100	86	14	100

Table 16 reveals that there are no consistent trends in adult sex preferences among the children. In Group II, where all adults were female, the boys exhibited greater sexuality than the girls, from which it might be concluded that children tend to seek sexual contact with adults of opposite sex. In Group III, however, where girls exhibit greater sexuality than boys, girls preponderate both with respect to the female nurse and the male anthropologist. Again, in Group IV, though boys and girls exhibit the same degree

[1] As in the case of peer sexuality, "sexual" refers to any activity which would be so labeled if manifested by an adult.

of sexual contact with the nurses, boys exhibit greater sexual contact with the male anthropologist than do the girls. In short, if child-adult sexual interaction be taken as a measure of sexual preference for parent of opposite sex the conclusion to be drawn from our data is negative.[2]

Another criterion for assessing the existence of the Oedipus Complex is the degree to which children show nonsexual preference for parents of opposite sex. The Kindergarten teacher, to be sure, notes that when children speak of their parents — which they frequently do — the girls refer most frequently to their fathers, and the boys talk most about their mothers. On the other hand, references to parents in conversation may be an unimportant measure of attachment to them, and if other measures are used, the father emerges as the more important figure for both sexes. It is our impression, for example, that when the younger children cry for their parents during the day, they more frequently cry for their fathers than for their mothers. Some nurses report that when the children awaken at night, they almost always call for their fathers rather than their mothers. The conclusion of an educational leader of The Federation supports these impressions: "The children are so attached to their fathers," he writes, "as to give the impression that they are tied to them more than to their mothers." Although our own evidence is hardly sufficient to support such an extreme conclusion, it is nevertheless true that almost always, when a nurse discusses a particular child in terms of the important persons in his life, the father emerges as the dominant figure.[3]

Despite the negative evidence, however, there is other evidence that points to the existence of Oedipal feelings in these children. There is, first of all, the children's relationship to the ethnographer, a relationship which will be examined for Group IV only.[4] Because I was in frequent interaction with the children

[2] These conclusions are consistent with the evidence, presented above, concerning the children's lack of awareness of physiological paternity. Since they seem to be ignorant of the sexual basis of reproduction, and since they have no opportunity to witness parental sexual intercourse, one of the important bases for the Oedipus Complex — postulated by classical psychoanalytic theory — is absent in the kibbutz.

[3] This is not surprising, at least in retrospect. Among all adult socializers, the adult male stands out as an exclusively permissive and nurturant figure. Since some females (the nurses) are punitive at times, the child's perception of the nurse is probably an ambivalent one. Hence, whereas all adult females — as a result of stimulus generalization — may be responded to with ambivalence, the father, who is not perceived ambivalently, remains the nurturant figure, par excellence.

[4] Group IV was selected for this test because only in this group were there sufficient controls. In Groups I and II, for example, my wife had to play the role

for more than one month, I became a significant figure in their behavioral environment, my significance being heightened by the fact that I was the only adult male with whom they had continuous contact during the day. If to this is added my nonpunitive role, it is not entirely capricious to assume that I was perceived as a quasi father-surrogate. It is suggested, therefore, that reactions to me may well represent a sample of behavioral responses to fathers. Hence, if the boys show greater aggression toward me than the girls, and if the girls show greater affection than the boys, this sexual difference in response would be in the direction predicted by the Oedipal hypothesis.

An examination of the relationship of these children to the anthropologist reveals that the results are in the predicted direction. Although boys and girls alike display both affection and aggression toward me (the expected ambivalence), boys are responsible for 60 per cent of the aggressive acts, while girls are responsible for 64 per cent of the affectionate and solicitous acts. This is, admittedly, a highly indirect, and by no means conclusive measure, but since it is in the predicted direction, neither can it be dismissed.[5]

A second source of positive evidence for an Oedipus Complex comes from a mother's diary.[6] In the first two excerpts Amir is two-and-one half years old; in the third, he is three.

---

of socializer as well as observer, so that she could not so readily be perceived as a mother-surrogate. In Groups I, II, and III, moreover, the children are not old enough, in terms of classical Oedipal theory, to display Oedipal feelings; nor are their sexual identities, as measured by identification in play, sufficiently strong. Only in Group IV are all the conditions met: a nonpunitive adult, children whose age (four-five) is most propitious for the discovery of Oedipal feelings, and who have already developed some fair degree of sexual identity.

[5] It is consistent, moreover, with some of the responses to the Questionnaire. When asked, "Which parent do your sons love more?," two parents said the preference was for the father, while five said the preference was for the mother. It must be noted, however, that when asked which parent the daughter loved more, no preference was indicated. Of the eight respondents, four said the mother was preferred, and four said the father.

[6] This diary, to be sure, describes only one boy, but the meagerness of the sample does not, in my opinion, minimize its importance. Since social attributes within any society are always characterized by a skewed distribution (if they were randomly distributed, culture, by definition, would not exist), even one instance, if selected from a relatively homogeneous universe whose attributes are well known, is presumptive evidence for a generalization. Since the boy described in the diary was reared as all other children in the kibbutz are reared — in the system of collective education — and since this boy, who is now in his late teens, has many of the personality characteristics of his peers, we are confident that his was a typical childhood. The one difference between him and other children is in his possession of unusually insightful parents.

DAVID (father) is going on a trip. Amir asks him to bring him back a tower for a present. David asks me what I would like as a present, and I say, "Only father." Amir protests, "No, you need only Amir."

Amir is beginning to talk like a girl; that is, using feminine forms. (He is, his mother thinks, trying to identify with her.) He lifts my blouse, and asks, "Do you have a tummy?" I say, "Yes, just like you." He repeats many times that "My mummy has a tummy." Then he says, "Mummy, you must change your trousers, you're cold and wet, aren't you mummy?"

He now asks where children come from. When BATYA came back from the hospital with her baby, he saw her nursing the baby. He wanted to know if the baby sucked at the stomach. I said, no, he sucks at the breast. He asked, "Did I suck, too?" I said, yes. He asked, "Did the baby come from BATYA's stomach?" I said, yes. He continued, "Was I in your stomach?" I said, yes. He asked, "Where was I when you were a little girl?" I said, "You did not exist then." He persisted. "No, mummy, where did I eat, where did I sleep, then? . . . When you are a child again, I'll be your father and take care of you" . . . He often talks now about his having been inside his mother. He often plays like a baby, in both voice and gestures, and uses baby talk . . . He often asks, "Who sleeps in that bed?" and answers his own question, "Father." Then, "Who sleeps in that bed?" and answers "Mother." He then insists that each remain in his own bed . . . He saw Father nude and commented on what a large penis he had. He then asked me if I too had a large penis.

Three-year-old girls, as well as three-year-old boys, may display Oedipal feelings. Sara permits her parents to put her to bed only after she is first permitted to sleep in her father's bed. Her attitude toward her parents is graphically expressed in her response to her mother when the latter is especially good to her — "You are like an *aba-le*" (a little father).

At a still older age, the play of a four-year-old boy provides us with additional insight. It must be noted, however, that this boy — Yehuda — is *not* a typical child. He is a frequent masturbator, a constant thumbsucker, and the most passive child in his group — he never initiates aggression, nor does he retaliate when aggressed against. The following excerpt from our field notes, like those from the diary, speaks for itself.

Yehuda makes a castle of sand, and says it is a father. I (M.E.S.) ask where the mother is, and he says, "Here, by the side of the father," and then proceeds to make a pile about one-fourth the size of the father. He then makes a "baby," about the size of the mother, and a "brother," who is smaller yet. He then destroys the "father," and says immediately, "Here is Father again; he is in the army. Mother is in Tel Aviv. All the family traveled to Tel Aviv with the mother; only father remained alone." . . . He makes a big "father" again and, saying that the mother has returned, he places her next to the father, and says that the baby has returned with the mother . . . He then throws sand out of the sandbox and says, "Father dies." He repeats this statement, throwing more sand out of the sandbox . . . He then makes another pile, says, "Here is father" and asks me to look at the father.

A final source of evidence for the existence of the Oedipus Complex is, like the first, indirect. If the Oedipus Complex exists, then, *ex hypothesi*, castration anxiety should exist. And there is some reason to believe that the latter anxiety is found among some at least of these children. In Group III, for example, Israel was observed to point to Zeviah's genitals and repeat a number of times that she has no penis. In still another case Zeviah looks at a bowl whose handle has been partially severed and says it is broken, that it has no "tussi." Mimi says, no, it has a *tussi* but that it sways. The girls would not tell the observer what they meant by tussi, but it was his strong impression that they meant penis (although tussi is a corruption of the Yiddish word for buttocks).

Mention must be made, too, of the great fear of barbers which characterizes almost all the younger children. Those in Group IV, for example, would refuse to permit their hair to be cut and would cry bitterly when the barber came. One boy is still afraid and, during the period in which this group was observed, he locked himself in the toilet when he heard the barber was coming.[7]

Since our data regarding the Oedipus Complex and related matters are meager, I suggest a speculative hypothesis. In the light of kibbutz socialization I would think that the psychosexual development of kibbutz children — a development that is intimately related to the development of the Oedipus Complex — would be quite different in the kibbutz than it is in Western society, as the latter is conventionally described. In the West the father is both nurturant and punitive, while the mother is conventionally described as primarily nurturant. In the kibbutz, too, this sexual division of labor exists, but the roles are reversed. In the kibbutz it is the adult female who is both nurturant and punitive (although the mother is exclusively nurturant, the nurse is

---

[7] In Groups III and IV, it should be observed, genitalia are used both as agents and victims of aggression. Children have been noted, for example, to pull or kick at another's penis, and at least one boy threatens to urinate on any child with whom he is angry.

both nurturant and punitive so that both attributes would be ascribed to the synthetic female imago), while the adult male is exclusively nurturant. The consequences for psychosexual development which may be deduced from this structural feature of kibbutz family interaction are of considerable speculative interest.

So far as the girl is concerned we would suppose that she has merely to remain attached to the nonpunitive (and seductive) male figure throughout the course of her psychosexual development, while, at the same time, she gives up her attachment to the female figure. The latter renunciation should not be difficult in view of the ambivalence which all children — males and females alike — have for the adult female as a consequence of her dual socialization role. The boy, on the other hand, must renounce his attachment to the exclusively nurturant male and channel all his sexual feelings toward a female, with respect to whom he has ambivalent feelings and of whom, therefore, he is frightened as well as enamored.

We would expect, then, that it would be more difficult for the boys than for the girls to achieve an adequate sexual adjustment, and that there would be a greater tendency among boys than among girls to remain fixated at a homosexual level. This tendency should be strengthened by the fact that in identifying with his father the boy is identifying with a "feminine" figure (so far as the father's relationship to the child is concerned) which, too, should tend to produce passive males with latent homosexual tendencies.

If sabra development corresponds to this postulated outline, we would not expect to find the same constellation of factors which, in the West, is termed the Oedipus Complex. It is hoped that the projective tests will shed light on these speculations.

SEXUAL IDENTITY

Related to the problem of the Oedipus Complex is the question of the development of sexual identity in these children. For if they do not identify themselves clearly as either male or female, then they cannot establish differential relationships to adults of same and opposite sex. But our interest in the development of sexual identity transcends the problem of the Oedipus Complex. From a cultural point of view proper sexual identification is among the most important tasks of childhood. The reasons are not hard to discover. Proper sexual identification is necessary for cultural survival. Since most social roles are sex-linked, the playing of those roles, and the acquisition of the sex-linked personality traits that are necessary for their successful performance, demand that one's sexual identity be clearly perceived. But to the extent that self-identity consists in an identification with one's social roles, sexual identity becomes a necessary condition for self-identity.

Bases for sexual discrimination. Since sex-linked personality traits are, for the most part, learned rather than inherited, it is important to discover to what extent kibbutz socialization encourages or impedes the development of same-sex identifications. It will be recalled from previous discussion that boys and girls are exposed to almost identical experiences in the various children's houses, and that there is a deliberate attempt on the part of the nurses to minimize differences in behavior based on sex. Boys and girls eat, sleep, shower, excrete, and play together; they are taught the same games and are socialized according to the same techniques.

What bases, then, do the children have for making sexual discriminations, and for identifying with a particular sex? The first such basis is the perception of differential sexual anatomy. Since kibbutz socialization does not taboo bodily exposure, and since the children have frequent opportunities for observing the nudity of both sexes, they become acquainted early with the more obvious anatomical characteristics that differentiate the sexes.

In addition to anatomy, however, the children have at least two other objective bases for making sexual discrimination — clothing and language. Although play-clothes are almost identical for both sexes — shirts and overalls in the winter, and shirts and shorts (or merely shorts) in the summer — there are important sex differences in the clothing worn in the late afternoon. These sabbath clothes continue to be shirts and shorts for the boys; but the girls' good clothes are often dresses. Moreover, the boys wear cotton undershorts while the girls wear rayon panties. Finally, by the age of five boys and girls wear different types of shorts — those of the girls have elastic bottoms so that they fit the thigh snugly; the boys' have no elastic.

In addition to these differences in clothing, there are other sexual differences in dress. Boys and girls have different hair styles, similar to those generally found in Western society. Moreover, the nurses show a much greater concern for the girls' than for the boys' hair; they are at great pains to comb the girls' hair attractively and carefully, and they devote more time to combing the girls' than the boys' hair. Finally, the girls are almost always given hair ribbons in the afternoon, whether they request them or not, while the boys are not given ribbons.

Language also serves as a basis for sexual distinctions. The Hebrew speaker must, of necessity, make sexual discriminations in his speech, since Hebrew grammar strongly emphasizes sex gender in both nouns and verbs. All nouns are either masculine or feminine — there is no neuter — and the declination of a noun, as well as its modifying adjective, differs markedly as a function of gender. Hebrew verbs, too, are conjugated differently as a function of the subject (noun or pronoun) to which they refer. In learning to speak, therefore, the children must learn to identify themselves very early as males or as females. And once these distinctions are understood, the children insist upon them. When Ruth, for example, informed me that Naomi was *ben chamesh* — five years old — Naomi corrected her use of the masculine, *ben,* saying that it should be *bat chamesh,* using the correct feminine form.

Another linguistic phenomenon that aids in the acquisition of sexual identity consists in sex-linked personal names. Since the cultural inventory of names is smaller than the population of the kibbutz, and since all names are sex-linked, the same name is frequently used for a number of people (including fictional characters) — all of the same sex. Naming, then, serves to divide all persons into two separate classes — male and female.

If factors such as these tend to encourage the perception of sexual differences and, hence, of the making of same-sex identifications, other factors which can contribute to the development of sexual identity, and which are normally found in other societies, are absent in Kiryat Yedidim. These factors have to do with sexual differences in parental roles. In most societies, allegedly, the child's acquisition of sexual identity is a function of identification with the parent of the same sex, an identification fostered by the marked differences that ordinarily obtain between the roles of father and mother. In Kiryat Yedidim, however — after the infant is weaned, at any rate — there are few differences between father and mother in their parental functions. Both parents play a common parental role. In general the children seldom witness adult male roles; and the adult males with whom they are in most frequent contact — their fathers — interact with them in approximately the same ways as do their mothers. This structural aspect of kibbutz socialization is reflected in the children's perceptions of their parents. In the Moral Ideology Test, for example,

few differences emerged in the children's perceptions of the socialization roles of their two parents.

To this structural aspect of kibbutz socialization there must be
added still another. There is at least one adult role whose nature
is clearly defined, and which is clearly sex-linked — the role of the
nurse. Beginning with infancy the nurses — the most important
socializers in the kibbutz — are exclusively female. Indeed, it is
not until high school that the children encounter male teachers.
Hence, none of the important models encountered by the child,
whom he can imitate and with whom he can identify, can provide
him with distinctive sexual differentiations. Maternal and paternal
roles tend to blend into one parental role, and the distinctive role
of the nurse is played exclusively by females.

Identification with adult roles. Since sexual identity develops
primarily through imitation of and identification with adult
models, an analysis of the identifications found in children's play
can shed considerable light on our problem. We may begin with
identifications found in fantasy play, in which the children
explicitly label the adult roles they are playing. These identifications are summarized in Table 17.

Probably the most significant finding in this table, so far as
identification with adult models is concerned, is the discrepancy
between boys and girls in identification with adults of the same
sex. Boys identify with adult males in only 16 per cent of their
identifications, whereas girls identify with adult females in 47
per cent of their identifications. Furthermore, although both boys
and girls identify with adults of the opposite sex, boys identify
with females twice as frequently as girls identify with males (see
Table 18). In short, girls identify with adult female models more
readily than boys identify with adult male models. It would appear that the boys find it difficult to identify with male social roles,
a not unexpected finding in view of the structural aspects of socialization discussed above. This is not all. The boys not only
have difficulty in identifying with adult male models, but they
actually identify with female models more than they do with
male models. Indeed, identification with the nurse's role is — for
theoretically obvious reasons — the most important adult identification for both boys and girls.[8] Thus the earliest identifications of

[8] On the other hand, though many girls (in Groups III and IV) help the
nurse in her daily activities — do the dishes, set and clear the table, and so on —
not one boy was observed to perform these tasks. Nor are they interested in watching the nurse perform her tasks. When the clothes are ironed, for example, girls
frequently stand around the nurse to observe the process. Boys show no such
interest.

children of both sexes, as measured by fantasy play, are preponderantly with females.[9]

These findings are of the utmost importance. If the imitation of and/or identification with adult roles in fantasy play is a valid measure of sexual identification, we must conclude that the children of neither sex are *entirely* sure of their sexual identity — both identify with adults of opposite sex — but that the girls are much

Table 17. Identification in the fantasy play of children in Groups II–IV,[a] by percentages.

Model	Boys (Σ acts = 49)	Girls (Σ = 81)
Animal	48	23
Adult female	26	47
Adult male	16	13
Baby or young child	8	15
Inanimate object	2	2

[a] Because it contains only one girl, Group I is omitted from the sample.

clearer about their sexual identity than are the boys. It must be noted, however, that there is increasing awareness by the boys of their sexual identity as they become older. In Group II all the

Table 18. Comparison of same-sex and opposite-sex identifications of boys and girls.

	Same sex	Opposite sex
Boys	8	13
Girls	38	11

$\chi^2 = 10.16$ d.f. = 1   P = < .001

boys' adult identifications are with females; in Group III they are divided equally between males and females; and in Group IV the balance has shifted in favor of males. But in none of the groups do the boys' identifications with males even begin to approximate the magnitude of the girls' identifications with females.

The sexual identity of the boys may be less ambiguous, how-

[9] This finding is statistically significant. Thus, $\sigma_p = 5.31$, C.R. = 4.33, P = <.002.

ever, than is suggested by these data when still another finding is considered. The preponderance of boys' identifications — almost 50 per cent — are with animals. The corresponding per cent for the girls, on the other hand, is only 23 (see Table 19). Since the animals with whom the boys identify are almost exclusively "masculine" — dogs, horses, frogs, snakes, and wolves — one cannot help but speculate on the possibility that animal identifications represent male identifications. And if this be so, then the boys' infrequent identifications with adult males may be compensated by their overwhelming identification with animals. This hypothesis is consistent with the finding that while the percentage of animal identification in boys decreases with age, the percentage of explicit identification with adult males increases.

If this hypothesis is valid, then the boys' identifications, like those of the girls, may be said to be primarily same-sex identifications. Still there remains one important difference. Girls' same-sex identifications are with a well-defined, socially sanctioned social role — that of nurse — whereas boys' same-sex identifications are with a vague, inchoate masculinity which is not translated into any identifiable social role. This finding assumes even greater significance if we examine the roles with which boys identify when they explicitly imitate adult male behavior. The male roles imitated include those of barber, doctor, driver, baker, electrician. Two of these roles (barber and doctor) are, in the adult society, played by non-kibbutz members; and not even one, it will be noted, refers to that role which the kibbutz deems most important — that of farmer.

Table 19. Comparison of animal and non-animal identifications in boys and girls.

	Animal	Non-animal
Boys	24	25
Girls	19	61

$\chi^2 = 8.98$ d.f. $= 1$ P $= <.01$

It would seem from this analysis that, though neither sex has achieved complete sexual identity (for the girls, too, make cross-sex identifications), boys have a more difficult problem than girls in acquiring sexual identity. This finding is supported, moreover, by an analysis of parental identifications in fantasy play. In the two older groups — III and IV — approximately one-third of the adult male identifications of the boys is with the father. Since the father, in fact, plays the same role as the mother in the child's life it again appears that the male role is not a sharply defined one, and that there are few cues the male child can use for purposes of identification. In any event, the same conclusion emerges — girls identify more readily than boys with the social roles of adults of same-sex.

The boys not only have difficulty in identifying with male roles, but some boys prefer to reverse their sex. In all four groups, for example, there are at least a few boys who sometimes insist on wearing ribbons and/or dresses, and the nurses always acquiesce in these demands. In Group IV at least one boy told the nurse he wanted to be a girl, and there is another who usually urinates by sitting on a toilet like a girl.

There is one girl (in Group IV) who displays similar behavior. She insists on urinating by standing like the boys. This girl cannot understand why it is that girls don't stand up, like the boys, when they urinate. For a time she was obsessed with this problem, and insisted on knowing how her nurses, their husbands, her parents, and other adult members of the kibbutz urinated. So, too, we recorded one instance of a girl's (in Group III) expressing a desire to be a boy — "Tomorrow I'll be a boy," she said (to which one of the boys responded indignantly with, "Tomorrow you'll be a *girl*").

But fantasy play is not the only kind of play which entails identification and/or imitation. Play with toys, too, often involves identification with various adult persons or adult roles. This assertion, so far as our sample is concerned, is not entirely conjectural. In riding a bicycle or a toy auto, for example, the children frequently simulate the noise of an engine — indicating that they are driving "real" cars. But since our records do not distinguish between play which is deliberate imitation of adult activities (simulating the noise of an engine, for example, while riding a bicycle) and other types of play, we decided to designate certain activities as "male," and others as "female," on the basis of our knowledge of kibbutz culture. Thus all acts of driving — autos, wagons, planes, horses, wheelbarrows, trains, and bicycles — were designated as "male," since all drivers in Kiryat Yedidim are males. Similarly all play with dolls and buggies was designated as "female," since most caretaking of children is performed by the nurses. The conclusions are to be found in Table 20. According to these figures, boys do not have greater difficulty than girls in

Table 20. Identifications in children's play of all types, for Groups II–IV, by percentages.

Model	Boys ($\Sigma = 125$)	Girls ($\Sigma = 139$)
Adult male	61	31
Animal	18	13
Adult female	16	46
Young child or baby	3	9
Inanimate object	2	1

identifying with same-sex roles. If anything, the frequency with which girls identify with male roles would seem to suggest that it is they who experience the greater difficulty, as Table 21 reveals.

Table 21. Comparison of same-sex and opposite-sex models in boys and girls.

	Same sex	Opposite sex
Boys	76	20
Girls	64	43

$\chi^2 = 8.86$ d.f. $= 1$ P $= <.01$

This lack of clarity about sexual identity is suggested by the sexual behavior of the children, as well. Boys and girls alike engage in a fair amount of homosexual behavior, the percentage ratio of heterosexual to homosexual behavior in Groups II–IV[10] respectively being 29:21, 19:12, 17:34. At the same time a comparison of the relative incidence of homosexuality among boys and girls tends to support the hypothesis that boys are more confused than girls with respect to sexual identity. For in two of the three groups for which there is evidence, boys are seen to be more homosexual than girls.

Sex-linked play. Lack of clarity about sexual identity in both boys and girls is consistent with other findings which emerge from an analysis of children's play. These findings, which are summarized in Table 22, reveal that there is little sex-linked play in children of this age.

[10] Neither homosexual nor heterosexual behavior is found in Group I.

Whether play be analyzed into types of play, separate play-acts, or number of children engaging in any play-act, the conclusion is overwhelmingly the same — boys and girls alike engage in the same kinds of activities. The notion that certain kinds of activity are exclusively female and others exclusively male is but slightly developed in these children. In short, boys and girls are primarily children rather than male children or female children.

It should be noted, however, that sex-linked play, though infrequent, increases as the children grow older. Thus, while in Group II, 85 per cent of all types of play were engaged in by both sexes, the percentage drops to 62 in Group III, and to 59 in Group

Table 22. Classification of all play by sex,[a] by percentages.[b]

	Types of play			No. of play acts			No. of children		
Sex	II $\Sigma = 52$	III 50	IV 56	II $\Sigma = 446$	III 153	IV 201	II $\Sigma = 520$	III 211	IV 276
Only males	10	10	21	3	9	7	2	4	6
Only females	5	28	25	1	18	9	1	15	8
Both	85	62	54	96	73	84	97	81	86

[a] Because it contains only one girl, Group I is omitted from the sample.

[b] Differences between unisexual and bisexual play for all three categories of the table are highly significant.

Types of play: $\chi^2 = 6.46$ d.f. $= 1$ P $= <.02$

Number of acts: $\chi^2 = 53.6$ d.f. $= 1$ P $= <.001$

Number of children: $\chi^2 = 50.4$ d.f. $= 1$ P $= <.001$

IV. Despite this trend the conclusion remains unambiguous: preponderantly, boys and girls engage in the same kinds of play — a conclusion which is consistent with the previous finding that neither boys nor girls have yet acquired distinctive sexual identities.

Regardless of the extent to which they have or have not achieved sexual identity, neither boys nor girls exhibit any great tendency to differential sexual association. On the contrary, they not only engage in the same kinds of play but, in the case of group play, they tend to play together, rather than separately. For although much group play is unisexual in nature, children's play groups are generally bisexual in composition.

Sex-linked differences. Although these children have not yet acquired exclusive sexual identities, there are important personality differences between boys and girls which emerge in their play. For though there are few sex differences in types of play, Table 23 reveals that there are important sexual differences in the frequency with which certain types are chosen.[11]

In the first place, boys engage in more strenuous activities than girls. In all groups and for both sexes play with toys is the most frequent play activity. But in all groups boys play with toys more frequently than girls, and, moreover, this difference is most pronounced in the case of macroscopic toys — which demand strenuous activity.[12] This sexual difference can be interpreted in at least two ways. One might say that, in general, macroscopic play demands a greater use of muscle — alternatively, it involves greater "locomotor interest" or "phallic qualities" — characteristics which are generally conceived of as more masculine than feminine. Hence, in view of the minimal stress on sexual differences in kibbutz socialization, and in the absence of a culturally explicit sexual classification of toys, this difference in frequency would tend to suggest an innate, biological basis for certain types of differential sexual behavior.

Table 23. Analysis of play[a] by sex, by percentages.

	Group II		Group III		Group IV	
	Males	Females	Males	Females	Males	Females
Play	(Σ Acts = 251)	(Σ = 269)	(Σ = 94)	(Σ = 115)	(Σ = 119)	(Σ = 149)
Toys	37	25	54	40	33	26
Microscopic	23	18	24	21	26	23
Macroscopic	14	7	30	19	7	3
Fantasy	8	8	22	30	11	21
Verbal and visual	17	23	6	14	18	21
Locomotor	21	21	14	10	14	7
Sand, natural objects	11	13	4	2	23	25
Clothing	2	6	0	0	0	0
Excreta	2	2	0	0	0	0
Miscellaneous	2	2	0	4	1	0

[a] Because it contains only one girl, Group I is omitted from the sample. Chi square test for sexual differences in total sample:

$$\chi^2 = 20.04 \quad \text{d.f.} = 5 \quad P = <.01$$

An alternative interpretation suggests itself, however, which stresses a cultural basis for the difference. Most of the macroscopic toys are models of objects used by adults, and specifically by males. Cars, horses, trucks, and tractors are driven exclusively by males in the kibbutz. To the extent, therefore, that play on tricycles, horses, autos, and so on involves identification with adults or imitation of adult activities — already suggested as a valid

[11] For a description of these categories, see pp. 147–151.
[12] This difference is highly significant. $\sigma_{Dp} = .022$, C.R. $= 3.18$, P $= <.001$.

assumption — and to the extent that these adult activities are sex-linked, it would be expected that more boys than girls would exhibit this kind of play. That this interpretation is at least partially correct is indicated by two findings that do not emerge from the table. In the first place, boys often simulate the noise of an engine when they ride the tricycle or the auto, and girls never do. Secondly, in those instances in which the boys and girls of Group III "travel" together in their toy auto, the boys are always the drivers and the girls the passengers.

Despite these cultural considerations, however, the biological hypothesis receives additional support from still another category of play — locomotor. The latter, it will be recalled, includes gross physical activity — such as gymnastics, climbing, running — that does not involve the use of a toy. Now, with one exception (Group II, in which the percentage for boys and girls is the same) the percentage for the boys is higher than that for the girls. And since these locomotor activities do not involve the imitation of adult roles, it is hard to account for these sexual differences except in terms of biological determinants.

A second difference between girls and boys, as revealed by their play, is the greater artistic, verbal, and fantasy facility of the girls. This is demonstrated by a number of play variables. If microscopic play is grouped into the two subclasses of "mechanical" (play with autos, planes, building blocks, tin-can, repairing, and so on) and "artistic" (clay modeling, finger painting, drawing, and so on) play, the boys are consistently more mechanical than the girls, while the latter are more artistic. Again one is tempted to speculate on the basis for these sex differences in a culture whose socialization system minimizes sexual differences. This temptation is increased when it be further noted that in all groups girls exhibit more "verbal and visual," as well as more "fantasy," play than boys. Indeed, the quantitative difference between boys and girls in toy play seems to be made up by the girls' preponderance in these latter two types of play. Again, it is difficult to account for these sex differences merely in terms of culture; for artistic and verbal and visual activities are performed in the kibbutz by both males and females. It might be suggested, however, in lieu of a biological interpretation, that these activities are identified by the children as part of the nurse's role, and to that extent the greater preponderance of girls suggests an imitation of this feminine role by them. But this interpretation does not account for the sexual difference in fantasy play (see Table 24).

Table 24. Comparison of "masculine" and "feminine" activities in boys and girls.

	Macroscopic and locomotor play	Fantasy and verbal/visual play
Boys	159	133
Girls	124	198

$\chi^2 = 15.66$ d.f. $= 1$ P $= <.001$

A final sexual difference in play is to be found in greater "maternal" behavior among the girls. This conclusion derives from doll play. Girls play with dolls much more frequently — even in that group (II) which exhibits the smallest sex difference, the ratio is 2:1 in favor of the girls — than do boys, and since fathers play with children as frequently as mothers, it cannot be argued that the girls are imitating a socially prescribed maternal role. In this case, however, one need not postulate a maternal instinct which supersedes any cultural arrangement. Doll play may well represent an imitation of the role of nurse, and there is indirect evidence, at least, to support the latter hypothesis. Nurses, we have already seen, are the most important adult identifications for all children in fantasy play; and the girls imitate the nurse's role in non-play activity as well. While it is true that children of both sexes may exercise socialization functions, those of the boys are restricted to the socialization of aggression. The girls, on the other hand, manifest such "maternal" behavior as helping younger children to dress and eat, or consoling a victim of aggression. The maternal behavior of the girls is revealed, finally, in their integrative behavior. In all groups girls exhibit more integrative behavior (aid, assist, share, cooperate) than the boys, and in some groups, as Table 25 reveals, the discrepancy between the sexes is very great indeed.

If all the major categories of interaction — integration, conflict, aggression — are analyzed by sex, other important sexual differences are revealed, as well. In the eighteen comparisons summarized in Table 25, there are consistent sexual differences in all but two. In all groups girls are more integrative than boys and boys more disintegrative. (In all groups boys engage in more acts of conflict than girls, and in all but one group the boys engage in more acts of aggression than the girls.) Boys, moreover, are the recipients of the girls' excess integration (boys are integrated more than girls), but girls are the recipients of only part of the boys' excess disintegration. For though girls are the more frequent victims of conflict, boys are the more frequent victims of aggression.

Table 25. Comparative sex differences[a] in integration, conflict, and aggression.[b]

Group	Integrator	Integrated	Conflictor	Conflicted	Aggressor	Aggressed
II	boys < girls	boys > girls	boys > girls	boys < girls	boys < girls	boys > girls
III	boys < girls	boys > girls	boys > girls	boys < girls	boys > girls	boys > girls
IV	boys < girls	boys > girls	boys > girls	boys > girls	boys > girls	boys > girls

[a] Because it contains only one girl, Group I has been omitted from the sample.
[b] Sex differences in behavior were discovered by comparing intragroup means.

Though more integrative than the boys, girls also display more frequent symptoms of regression than the boys. In all groups but one, for example, girls have a higher incidence of thumbsucking. And in the two groups for which there are data, girls exhibit more regressive play than do boys. In fantasy play girls are almost twice as regressive as boys (Table 17), and in all play they are three times as regressive (Table 20).

Finally there are important differences between boys and girls in sexual behavior. Exclusive of sexual interaction with adults, boys are more sexual than girls — if frequency of all sexual acts be taken as a measure of "sexuality." The author can suggest no reasons for this observed sexual difference except to point out that it is easier to observe masturbation in boys than in girls, and, in the two older groups at least, it is precisely in autosexual behavior that the boys preponderate.

That boys are more sexual than girls is found to hold in the children's sexual interaction with adults, as well. Boys initiate sexual interaction with adults more frequently than girls in three of the four groups studied.[13]

[13] Many of these differences are not statistically significant. Nevertheless, the fact that the direction of the difference is consistent among all the groups tends to indicate that the differences are real.

PART V · SCHOOL YEARS

Until they enter school, the children live in dwellings comprised of only one kevutza each, and for most purposes the kevutza is their effective social group. At the beginning of their formal schooling there is no change in this picture, for the first grade, or Transitional Class, is neither a physical nor a social part of the grammar school. Hence, when the kindergarten children attain first-grade age (at approximately six years) their formal education begins, but they still remain in their kindergarten dwelling. It is believed that the changes attendant upon their new educational experiences should not be added to those which would derive from moving the children to a new building and exposing them to a larger group.

After completing first grade, however, the children not only pass into the second grade, but they move into the Grammar School (*bet-sefer*). Here their interactional group is expanded to include not only their own kevutza, but the entire student body. It is this group of children, from the ages of seven through twelve, that we shall now examine.

FORMAL STRUCTURE

Physical. The Grammar School is a white stucco, two-story building surrounded by a wide lawn and a playground. On both floors there are three bedrooms, a classroom, a shower, and a toilet. There is, in addition, an isolation room on the second floor, and a third classroom in the basement. Although the school is a combined classroom-dormitory building, it has no eating facilities; the dining room is a wooden building about fifty yards from the school. Attached to the school are a small vegetable garden and a poultry-run which are tended by the children.

There are three kevutzot in the school, each with approximately sixteen members, and each occupies its own bedrooms. The typical bedroom contains eight beds. Next to each bed there are a small stool and a night-stand. In the wide halls between the north and south rooms, there are toilets with doors. Across the hall from the toilets is a shower room containing shower-stalls, a bathtub, and benches which line the walls. Wall hooks for the toothbrush and towel of each child circle the room. On the walls of the staircase are hooks for the children's jackets, and a shoe-rack is on the hallway landing.

Although most objects are collectively owned, the children possess some private property, which they may acquire in one of three ways. First of all, each child (like his parents) receives an annual cash allowance of one and one-half Israeli pounds (about one-and-a-half dollars) to spend as he wishes. Second, parents may buy presents for a child from their (the parents') annual cash allowance. Third, the child may receive presents from relatives who live outside the kibbutz. Hence all the children own such inexpensive objects as marbles, pencils, and books, and such moderately expensive articles as rollerskates. A few children own watches, an "expensive" object in the kibbutz, possessed only by those with relatives outside the kibbutz. Watches constitute the only form of wealth which is unequally distributed.[1]

Schedule. The daily schedule for the Grammar School is standardized for the entire year, except for the summer vacation months and for special occasions, such as holidays. The children rise at 6:30 and are ready for their day's activities at 6:45. From 6:45 until 7:30, two of the kevutzot work while one starts its first class of the day. Breakfast is eaten from 7:30 to 8:00. All three classes meet from 8:00 to 9:30, followed by a recess from 9:30 to 10:00, at which time they also have a snack (*aruchat eser*). The two younger groups have classes until 12:00, the older group until 11:45, for the latter group may have additional work responsibilities from 11:45 until 12:00. Dinner is eaten from 12:00 until 12:45. From 12:45 to 1:00 the children take their showers, and some go to the library (one of the classrooms also serves as a library) to exchange books. From 1:00 to 2:30 the children rest or nap. At 2:30 they have an afternoon snack (*aruchat arba*), after which the youngest kevutza is free for the afternoon, while the two older kevutzot have classes until 4:00. After 4:00 all the children are free until supper, which is served at 6:00. After supper the chil-

---

[1] The existence of private property in luxuries, and its unequal distribution, is an innovation that has accompanied the introduction of private property into the adult kibbutz. It would have been unthinkable in the past.

dren usually visit their parents, returning to the school at 8:15 to sleep.[2]

Staff. Since there are a total of six nurses and teachers for the forty-five children in the school, the supervisor-child ratio is 1:7. Both nurses and teachers are female, and both work with a particular kevutza throughout the latter's stay in the grade school. As the children pass from a lower to a higher grade, they do not change teachers or nurses (unless the latter retire from their positions) but remain with the same adults from their seventh through their twelfth year. The nurses in the grade school often have less professional training than those who work with younger children, since they are not responsible for the intellectual development of the children. They are primarily mother-surrogates as well as housekeepers, doing all the heavy work in the dwelling, including the cleaning, ironing, and mending.

Unlike the nurses, teachers receive specialized training, generally in a teacher's college which is affiliated wtih the kibbutz movement. In this way the kibbutz is assured that its teachers will have been trained in kibbutz ideology. This is very important, since their function is not only to impart knowledge to the children, but also to train them in kibbutz values. Hence the teacher of each kevutza is known as its *mechanech,* or "educator," rather than merely as "teacher."

In addition to the mechanech, each class has teachers for instruction in specialized subjects. These teachers — of music, art, and English — may or may not have specialized training, and may or may not be members of the kibbutz. The children are exposed to them infrequently, however, since these subjects are taught only twice a week. These teachers are not viewed as members of the faculty, and they have no decision in the determination of general policy. They are known as *morim chelkiim,* parttime teachers.

The teachers keep the parents informed of the progress of their children. Should a child have special difficulty in school, either of an emotional or intellectual nature, the teacher arranges

[2] The summer schedule is, of course, different from the winter, since the children have vacation from classes during the months of July and August. If they remain in the kibbutz, the only schedule to which they must conform is restricted to the times of rising, eating, rest, and bedtime. Otherwise their behavior is unsupervised. Usually, a student from the high school is appointed to work with them as a "play director" during the summer, and he may take them swimming or hiking during the day, or arrange for various group activities in the evening.

a meeting with his parents in order to discuss the problem with them. In addition, the teacher arranges a meeting with all the parents at the end of the academic year for a progress report on the class as a whole. She tells them what material was studied that year, the proficiency with which the students performed, and her plans for the coming year.

Children's society. The children, it will be remembered, are members, not of the kibbutz, but of the *chevrat yeladim,* the "children's society." The latter, according to The Federation's educational philosophy, represents an attempt to use the educational system explicitly to create the kind of personality and future society that the kibbutz deems desirable. The kevutza is viewed as the "core" of the children's society, and every attempt is made to strengthen the child's identification with it. Upon entering the school, each kevutza adopts a name by which it is henceforth known. Rarely is a kevutza referred to by its grade — first, second, third, for example. Children, teachers, and the entire kibbutz almost always use the kevutza name when referring to it or to its individual members. This name, adopted from nature, history, or ideology, is retained by the kevutza from its entry into the grade school until its graduation from high school. By then this name has been so intimately identified with the members of the kevutza that when they become members of the kibbutz itself, they continue to be designated, in conversation or at meetings, by the name of their erstwhile kevutza.

The various kevutzot comprise the *chevra,* or society; and the children's society, like that of the adults, is characterized by self-government. They have their own general assembly (*sichat chevra*) during which their common problems and goals are discussed. The meeting is presided over by an elected officer, usually a student in the sixth grade, and decisions are made by open vote — although the teacher who is advisor to the chevra may attempt to influence the vote.

FORMAL EDUCATION

Goals. "The purpose of our (grade school) education," states an educational pamphlet of The Federation,

. . . is to assure to each child a happy life, so as to bring the maximal good to his society; that is, education that is meant to foster a healthy child — psychologically, physically, and spiritually. (Therefore, he should be characterized by) joy, love of society, optimism and humor, trust in men, and tolerance for the other person and his opinion.

It therefore follows, according to this same pamphlet, that it is more important to develop critical thinking and independence of thought than to transmit mere facts. Hence the minimal goals to be attained by the student are: (1) an understanding of, and a desire to be active in, his society; (2) an ability to express his thoughts and feelings; (3) an ability to meet life's crises; (4) the three R's; (5) an ability to use cultural artifacts; (6) the value of artistic and intellectual experiences.

Curriculum. The curriculum and teaching methods to be described have, for the most part, been taken from the standards set by the Department of Education of The Federation. Almost all subjects are taught according to the "project method."

For the first and second grades it is recommended that the project be taken from the immediate surroundings of the child; that each project be one or two weeks in length, so that there are about twelve a year; and that the important sources be the children's own experiences and observations, while doing and making things.

For the third and fourth grades it is recommended that the project be taken from the immediate, but a broader and more complex, environment; that it be about four weeks in length; and that the important sources, in addition to those noted above, include books.

For the fifth and sixth grades it is recommended that the project be broad, including many lands and peoples, both past and present, and embracing the entire world; that it be six weeks in length, including about five projects in all; and that the following subjects be covered during the year: agriculture, literature, zoology, botany, biology, geography, cultural history, and art.

The following projects are suggested for each of the two-year periods. For the first two years:

1. Animals: a list of about twenty, "from the dog to the ant."
2. A list of approximately ten flowers in the immediate environment.
3. Seasons of the year, including such natural phenomena as wind and rain.
4. Agricultural seasons: planting, harvesting, etc.
5. Hikes, to forests, mountains, wadis, etc.
6. The man in the kibbutz economy — shepherd, gardener, carpenter, etc.

7. Our chevra: our house, our kibbutz, etc.
8. Holidays: Chanuka, Passover, May Day, etc.
9. Activities: all adult activities of the kibbutz.
10. Times: day, afternoon, night, etc.
11. Machines: various machines used in the kibbutz.
12. Stories: *Pinocchio*, Eskimos, Indians, etc.

For the third and fourth grades, the projects include:

1. The animal world: chicken coops, birds, bird nests, ants, etc.
2. The botanical world: orchard, woods, garden, etc.
3. Homeland: its conquest, our kibbutz and the city, Jewish National Fund, etc.
4. Cultural history: architecture, fire, money, clothes, early man, etc.
5. Ourselves: our chevra, camping, etc.
6. Holidays: stressing the agricultural and political holidays.
7. Bible: our shepherd fathers; Joseph and his brothers, etc.

For the fifth and sixth grades, the projects include:

1. Animate world: migrations of birds, orchards, fields, etc.
2. Cultural history: our food, fire, mail, books, etc.
3. Homeland: water resources, the Emek, Mt. Carmel, etc.
4. Activities: photography, health, musical instruments, etc.
5. Bible and literature: from slavery to freedom, from tribe to nation, the child in literature, Bialik, Shalom Aleichem, etc.

Ideological emphasis. Before describing the actual classroom situation, one aspect of kibbutz education (more heavily stressed in the high school than in the Grammar School) which cannot be inferred from merely reading the curriculum must be described. This is the ideological nature of kibbutz education. The kibbutz schools are more than academic institutions. Courses are taught not only for their academic interest, but for the truth which they contain. Hence one of the primary functions of the kibbutz schools is to transmit the sacred values of the kibbutz to the younger generation. As the educational journal of The Federation puts it, the aim, even of the grade school, is the "planting of a deep emotional attitude to the basic political values (Zionism, Socialism, Kibbutziut), of The Movement." Hence,

The aims which express our *weltanschauung* should be expressed in every study-project, in every discussion, and in every socio-cultural activity. In every subject — nature, the Homeland, Bible, economics — one should uncover the political causes that are concealed in these subjects: criticism of society, social injustice, existence of social classes, national oppression, Exile and suffering of Jews, wars, positive attitude to science and the progress of science, faith in man and in his ability, emphasis on progressive ideas in history, literature, and the Bible.

Thus, all courses in the humanities and the social sciences are taught "in the light of Marxism." For though scholarship, it is believed, will succeed in discovering new facts about the nature of the universe, society, and man, the method by which these facts can be best understood has already been discovered — this is the Marxist method. Since the kibbutz affirms unqualifiedly that Marxism is true, there is little point in presenting alternative views, except to point out their errors. Many classroom discussions, therefore, are not merely discussions; they are ideological indoctrinations which are labeled, however, as scientific truth rather than as ideology.

It is inevitable that this ideology should be most frequently expressed in terms of contemporary political events. In the grade school, for example, when interpreting the story of the Biblical Samuel, a boy in the sixth grade compared the modesty of Hanna with that of The Party, and the arrogance of Pnina with that of an opposition party. When studying the social organization of ants, their teacher asked the students of the fourth grade to what in the human world slave-holding ants could be compared. Two answers were given — the Americans and the bourgeoisie. When, in the same lesson, they learned about big ants who attack smaller ants, the analogy to the big Arab states attacking the small state of Israel was volunteered.[3]

[3] But it is not only in the classroom that the teacher attempts to transmit political truths. When, for example, asked by the children if I were "for America" or "for Korea" in the then-raging Korean War, I said that I could not answer the question as it was phrased, and that, in order to answer it, I would have to discuss the whole Korean situation. The following day the fourth-grade teacher came to my table in the children's dining room and, saying that I had been asked an "interesting" question on the previous day, requested that I answer it. Immediately the other teachers and nurses came to the table to hear the answer. When I replied that I could not answer the question with a simple yes or no response, the teacher said, with all the children listening, that kibbutz children do not need long "explanations." They know, when a strong bully attacks a weak person, that they instinctively go to the latter's defense. She then turned to the problem of the Negro in America, saying that "all" Americans have a blind spot with respect to the Negroes, and that they always end a

Teaching methods. The discussion method, rather than the formal lecture, is the customary classroom procedure. The teacher generally attempts to make the subject matter meaningful in terms of the child's own experiences and his immediate (physical or temporal) environment. In a fourth-grade art lesson, for example, the objects cast in plaster-of-Paris were animals and flowers with which the children were immediately familiar; in seeking for a subject for a drawing class shortly before the advent of Passover, the teacher suggested that the children draw a Passover scene.

This emphasis on the experience of the child is generalized to include an emphasis on experimentation as one type of personal experience. In the second grade, for example, the teacher completed the project on flowers by discussing the differences between flowers and men. After other children had suggested the more superficial differences, one said that men, but not flowers, breathe. Others pointed out, however, that flowers breathe, too. The teacher asked them how they knew this to be the case, and they replied that it was written in their books. The teacher said that such an answer was unsatisfactory; it was not enough to know what the book knows, but also how the book knows. She then described an experiment in which a flower was put in a vacuum. This account interested them greatly, and they were unusually attentive. Similarly, a cocoon was kept on the front desk in the sixth-grade room so that the children could observe what they were being taught — the development of the mature animal from the larval stage. In the midst of a grammar lesson, one day, the cocoon started to open, and the butterfly began to emerge. The children, although absorbed in their lesson, ran to the desk to observe this event. Again, the fourth grade, which was studying about ants, systematically observed an ant hill every day.

But the teacher attempts to relate the materials not only to the child's immediate experiences, but to his deepest interests as well. In a second-grade lesson in arithmetic, for example, the exercises in addition and subtraction were concerned with the winning and losing of marbles — an activity in which almost all the children were temporarily absorbed.

Another characteristic of grade-school teaching is the extraordinary amount of classroom time which is devoted to writing. After the discussion of a subject has been completed, the students

---

discussion of the Negroes with, "Would you like your daughter to marry a Negro?" And the same is true of Korea.

This, then, is one, among many instances, in which children receive their political education in a non-formal manner.

summarize in their notebooks what they have learned. The disproportionate emphasis on writing is necessary, according to the teachers, because of the poor textbook situation — textbooks are either lacking or deficient. Hence much of the material must be presented by the teacher, and by putting this information in their notebooks, the children acquire permanent records of the material.

Discussions are not the only subjects for notebook entries. Almost all intellectual or group experiences are recorded. After spending the morning observing ants, the children return to the classroom to record what they have observed. Upon returning from a hike, they write an essay recounting their experiences. In addition to writing up each lesson or experience, each project is recorded upon completion. Everything must be written in ink, and the notebooks are then bound. The children, moreover, are requested to write many essays and themes. Almost any group experience becomes a subject for an essay. So, too, they are frequently requested to copy passages from a book, a chapter from the Bible, and so on. Indeed, there seems considerably more writing and talking in the kibbutz school than there is reading. One cannot help but get the feeling that the children spend a disproportionate amount of time in the sheer mechanics of lessons and projects, to the detriment of the subject matter itself.

The teachers place great emphasis on creativity and imagination. Indeed, this is a primary justification for the writing of essays. The teachers claim that the practical and realistic environment in which the children live has a tendency to mute their creative and fantasy lives, and that the writing of essays enables them to transcend this practical world. When the children read their essays in class, the points which the teachers particularly single out for praise are the imaginative elements. Such characterizes the comments of the art teacher as well. It is not so much technique that she praises, since, as she tells the children, technique is to a considerable extent a matter of talent; it is rather, the level of imagination revealed by the drawings which evokes her commendation. This emphasis on fantasy emerges in other subjects, as well. For example, when a child reads a Biblical passage aloud, the teacher digresses from the discussion of content to point out such stylistic points as a nice phrase, a choice word, a beautiful image.

Despite the emphasis on discussion and writing, the teachers employ visual techniques to a considerable extent. The blackboard is in constant use. When the teacher asks for suggestions for an essay or a picture, or for the site of a hike, the suggestions invariably are listed on the board. When a teacher discusses the

Ten Plagues with a second-grade class, the plagues are written on the board, each in a different color.

A final characteristic of kibbutz teaching methods — one which is found in the high school as well as the Grammar School — is the absence of competitive rating systems as a motivational technique. All students are promoted at the end of the school year, regardless of their performance. The system of passing and failing, it is held, places a stigma on the dull student and, moreover, it violates the kibbutz ideals of equality and of equal opportunity. Consistent with this educational philosophy is the absence of examinations or grades which, until recently, characterized this system. The latter were viewed either as unnecessary — intellectual curiosity being a sufficient motive for study — or as undesirable — they would induce competitive feelings and insecurity among the students. Recently, however, examinations in the guise of "questionnaires" have been introduced; and grades have found their way into the system in the form of teacher-evaluation of written work.

There are two types of questionnaires. At the end of a block of work, the teacher may give the students a list of questions, to which they write answers and read them aloud when called upon. The second, and more elaborate type covers and entire project. The answers, which are submitted on completion of the project, are graded. But the grades are used to indicate how well a student is performing, and not to determine whether he should pass or fail. In general, the students are eager to know their own grades as well as the grades of their fellows. They are not embarrassed to have their grades made public, the teachers claim, since everyone already knows the level of their performances. This argument may not be entirely cogent. It is true, however, that since grades are not used for purposes of promotion or retardation, and since the students are not under the psychological pressure that examinations often induce (they answer the questionnaires outside of class, and have the entire quarter in which to complete the work) the competitive element that usually characterizes our own school system is less intense in the kibbutz.[4] Hence the punitive aspect

[4] There are certain elements of competition in the high school, however. Athletic events are usually competitive, and there is competition among the kevutzot for excellence in various kinds of extracurricular activity. These are all group activities, however, so that there is little opportunity for feelings of personal glory or personal failure.

One of the very few personal competitive events in the high school is the literary competition sponsored by the student newspaper. Prizes (books) are awarded to the winners. The year of this study, thirty-one students entered the

of our own system with its competitive grading, and its attendant potential meaning of loss of love, insecurity, lack of success, and so on, is generally less intense as well.

Despite our remarks about its permissive, nonpunitive structure, there are certain aspects of the classroom situation, potentially anxiety-provoking, which must be mentioned. The first concerns primarily the behavior of the teacher. The teachers, it will be remembered, employ the discussion method almost exclusively; and to the extent that a child is ego-involved in his studies, he is ashamed, if he is ignorant of the subject, by his inability to participate in the discussion. Secondly, the teachers tend to prefer the "brighter" students, and the child who desires the love of the teacher perceives those children who are brighter or more verbal than he, as competitors. Finally, the emphasis on group criticism can potentially engender competitive, if not hostile feelings among the children. Frequently, for example, the children read their essays aloud, and the others are then asked to comment. Only infrequently could we detect any hostility in the criticisms of the students, and often the evaluations were filled with praise. Nevertheless, the possibility of a child's developing hostile or envious feelings toward those whose work is more highly praised by either students or teacher, is real. In short, the environment is not always supportive.

A second source of potential anxiety stems from the absence of a structural separation between classroom and dormitory, an absence which permits personal difficulties in the one to "spill over" into the other. Irvine has drawn explicit attention to the possible consequences of this situation:

> The child who fails in school work cannot localize his difficulties into a dislike of school, since the school is an indistinguishable part of the home, nor can he as a rule project them comfortably on to the teacher, who is not at a convenient distance, being something between a big brother and a father . . . It is more difficult for him to split it off from the rest of his life than it is for a child for whom home and school are separate entities; it therefore tends to have a more pervasive effect in undermining his self-respect and group status.[5]

Intellectual interest. Despite these potential sources of anxiety, the pedagogic techniques of the teachers appear to be very

competition. First prize was awarded to a senior who argued, in an essay entitled, "Should There Be Prizes in Our Life," that prizes should not be awarded in the high school.

[5] Irvine, "Observations on the aims and Methods of Child Rearing," p. 252.

effective, as judged, at least, by the generally high level of interest maintained in most subjects. Frequently our notes record such observations as, "They appear very interested," "They seem to be highly motivated." The general level of interest is reflected also in the children's eagerness to participate in class discussion and to express their opinions. The motivation for such participation is, of course, a matter of conjecture. In addition to their interest in the materials, it may be motivated by a desire to impress their teacher — for they almost always address themselves to her, rather than to the other children — or by a desire to express themselves as individuals when the opportunity arises, instead of always being a part of a group.

In general, however, the children seem to be sincerely interested in their school work and are motivated to study without external inducements. And their interest in books and in reading extends beyond the classroom. For many of the children reading is a favorite pastime. When they awaken in the morning, they read until it is time to get up. In the afternoon almost all the children read before taking their naps, and some read during the entire rest period. This reading, which consists for the most part of novels, biography, and history, is entirely spontaneous — neither the nurses nor the teachers exert pressure on them to read.[6]

Classroom behavior. The kibbutz classroom, in both the grammar and high schools, is marked by the greatest degree of informality. The discussion method and the absence of techniques of competitive and punitive motivation contribute to this in-

---

[6] Related to this interest in books and in study is the general curiosity of the children. Since their world is small, there are few new stimuli within it to elicit their curiosity, but a strange person or object immediately arouses their interest, and they are quick to ask questions. A few minutes after I first began to take notes on the behavior of the children, for example, two second-grade girls approached to inquire about what I was writing, and why had I come to the kibbutz anyway? When I replied that I had come in order to observe their lives, one asked, "Why? Don't they eat and sleep in America too?" For several weeks after his observations began, children continued to sit by him and ask what he was writing.

The children not only wanted to know what we were doing, but what America was like. Frequently, before they went to sleep at night, they would ask me to tell them about America, and were eager to hear as many details as possible. Curiosity about the psychological tests was very high. Like many other interests, this curiosity did not last long, but while it lasted, it was intense. Each child would insist that he be tested first or that he be the next to be tested. Curiosity about new gadgets is another indication of this general trait. The children had never seen a tape recorder, and when I brought mine to the school, the children swarmed about it, observing it from every angle. On the other hand, few, if any, wanted to know how it worked, or what the nature of the mechanism was.

formality. But there are at least two other aspects of the kibbutz school which are the major determinants of informality.

There is, first of all, a structural (in a literal sense) basis for this informality. In both the grammar and high schools the dormitory and classroom building are one, so that there is no transition from the building in which one sleeps and plays to the one in which one studies. And, it soon becomes apparent that this lack of physical transition is accompanied by an absence of psychological transition as well. The same informality that characterizes the interaction of the students in their dormitory rooms characterizes their interaction in the classrooms. The students' dress, which reflects this lack of transition, contributes to the spirit of informality. In both winter and summer, shorts constitute the standard clothing for both males and females, whether in dormitory or classroom; in the summer, shoes are rarely worn in either place.

A second basis for classroom informality is inherent in the student-teacher relationship, part of whose characteristics are structural and part of which derive from kibbutz educational philosophy. Structurally, it should be emphasized, the teacher in the kibbutz occupies a status different from his status in most other societies. The teacher is a member of the community — a chaver kibbutz — in which the child lives. The students generally know him before they enter his class, and they continue to see him outside the classroom in his various roles of parent, spouse, chaver, and so on. Furthermore, the teacher is a friend — and sometimes an antagonist — of their parents, and the children hear his name mentioned at home with the same frequency and affect as the name of any other chaver. Hence, the teacher is not a person from a different world, who is seen only in the classroom, and who can maintain the authority and formality that is so frequently a function of social distance. As one teacher put it,

. . . the teacher's life is an open book to the students; the latter know all the intimate details of his life. Furthermore, they can always hold up his faults to him, if he criticizes them, for they know them all. He might, for example, tell them to work better; and then a work draft comes along, and he works with them in the garden and they see what a poor worker he is.

But the student-teacher relationship is influenced, too, by the kibbutz educational philosophy, in accordance with which the teachers attempt to structure the classroom situation as a "democratic" environment. Students, for example, address their teachers by their first names, and the latter address their students as chaverim, "comrades," which effectively destroys that psychological distance which can be symbolically created by the use of formal names.[7] The teacher, furthermore, generally consults with his students, rather than informing them of decisions he has made independently. Even in the Grammar School, for example, the teacher chooses a project only after consultation with the class. It is true that she presents them with the suggestions from which a project is to be chosen, but the final choice rests on the decision of the class. An even more "democratic" procedure is adopted with respect to the writing of essays for which the children themselves suggest the topics.

Most important, however, is the lack of restraint or discipline in the classroom. For the most part, formal discipline is abjured, because, in the words of The Federation's educational journal, "The psychological foundation on which we build discipline in our education is the love of the child for the adult."

If these are some of the bases for classroom informality, we may now examine some of its expressions. Classroom informality is expressed, first of all, by the freedom and spontaneity that characterize student behavior. Students leave the classroom at will — to get a drink, to go to the toilet, or for any other reason which they deem important. Similarly, they may leave their desks without permission — to get supplies from the cabinet, to sharpen a pencil, and so on. They may talk among themselves both during oral lessons and while working privately at their desks; some hum or sing to themselves while writing or studying.

A second expression of classroom informality is the readiness of the children to criticize the teacher when they feel he is wrong. A final expression of classroom informality is the poor discipline that frequently characterizes student behavior — particularly in the second through fourth grades in the primary school, and the eighth through tenth grades in the high school — and which often results in utter chaos.[8]

---

[7] In the past, when "democracy" was carried to an extreme, all symbolic status differences were eliminated. For example, students and teachers alike sat around one round table so that another basis for social distance could be eliminated.

[8] The nature of the students' criticism will be examined later, as will discipline. Poor discipline seems to be a general characteristic of kibbutz schools. A chapter in The Federation's educational textbook is devoted to refuting the "many" complaints expressed on this score.

SOCIAL ACTIVITIES

In addition to general assemblies, there are other occasions when the entire student body, or parts of it, assemble formally. These include birthday parties, kevutza parties, and holiday celebrations. In general the children of this age join their elders in the celebration of major holidays. On Passover, for example, the children participate in the Seder, together with their parents, in the communal dining room. Similarly, children and parents celebrate Shevuot together on the wide lawn in front of the dining room. Indeed, these holidays are oriented to the children's interests, and the children play a large role in their celebration. Sometimes, however, holidays are celebrated independently by the different age groups in the kibbutz. Thus those holidays which have political or ideological significance — such as May Day or the Russian Revolution — are celebrated separately by adults and by children. Other holidays (such as Purim), which entail a maximum of gaiety and abandonment, are celebrated separately by adults and by children because of obvious age differences in what is considered to be amusing.[9]

Birthdays are always celebrated in the kevutza. Sometimes the party is given by the child's parents and is held in their room; sometimes it is held in the school and is sponsored by the kevutza. In either event the typical party includes group singing and games, a performance (recitation, vocal, instrumental, etc.) by the person whose birthday is being celebrated, and some activity which the latter requests.

A third type of formal group activity is the *mesiba*, get-together, which is held frequently. At the end of the school year each kevutza has a mesiba to which the parents are invited. The program includes a display of their year's work and a reading by each child of an essay, poem, or story he has written during the year. Often the children present a dramatic sketch, as well, dealing with one of their projects for the year. The fourth grade, which had as a project "The Biblical Patriarchs and their Times,"

[9] The year of our study the primary school presented a most elaborate Purim pageant, witnessed by the entire kibbutz. Presented at night, out of doors, it consisted of a series of sketches — song, dance, recitation — representing different peoples: Arabs, Spaniards, Chinese, Russians. The children were elaborately dressed in the folk-costume of these countries. Each sketch emphasized the political or social aspects of the people portrayed, and ended with the hope that all men would become brothers. The children performed with much verve, and the audience was most enthusiastic.

presented a series of tableaux representing various incidents in the lives of the Patriarchs. In addition to the mesiba of the kevutza there is a mesiba of the entire school, to which the kibbutz is invited. The formal program includes a play (we saw an excellent production of "The Emperor's Clothes") songs, dances, and instrumental music.

In addition to the annual mesiba at the end of the year, there is a mesiba every three weeks during the school year. These are less formal than the ones previously discussed, since they do not include adults or other persons outside the school. In general the programs at these parties include reading aloud from the school paper, listening to a musical program on the radio, and folk dancing, and they almost always induce a spirit of great fun, laughter, and even hilarity. The favorite games played at these parties are "It" (see p. 143) and charades. All these parties and celebrations, it should be stressed, are pervaded by an unusual sense of warmth, fellowship, and goodwill. Parents and children interact with spontaneity and informality, and one has the feeling that there are genuine bonds of love and affection between them. Parents beam with pride when their own children recite; and some are the typically anxious and overprotective parents whose attempts to assist the children during the performance serve only to confuse them. Nor can the importance of these celebrations in the children's lives be underestimated. Celebrations and recreation are, for example, by far the preponderant causes of happiness in the Emotional Response Test.

WORK

Induction into work begins in the "tender age," but, for the younger children, "work" consists either of creative play or of token work. The work activities in the school are not token; they have genuine economic value. In some instances this work yields a cash income; in others it serves, however slightly, to relieve the pressure of the continuous manpower shortage in the kibbutz. The youngest class works half an hour a day; the middle class, three-quarters of an hour; and the oldest group, an hour; but an attempt is made to include children from all three kevutzot in each work group. Work assignments are changed periodically, so that no one child works continuously at the same job for more than one week.

There are certain tasks for which the children are either wholly or partially responsible. In the dining room they set the tables, put the food on the tables, remove the food and dishes after the meals, dry the tableware, and remove the chairs from the floor so that it can be mopped. The children also have the responsibility of bringing the afternoon snack from the kitchen and of returning the dishes.

With the exception of mopping the floor, children perform all janitorial services in the classrooms; they clean, straighten, and tidy-up. They perform the janitorial services in the bedrooms, as well, making beds, straightening the rooms, and sweeping and mopping floors.

In addition to these domestic chores, the children are in charge of their own "farm." First they assist in caring for the school's grounds. This includes watering the grass, pruning the shrubs, removing litter, etc. Secondly they are in charge of a poultry-run. Three times each day the poultry yard is cleaned, and the fowl are provided with feed and water. The children sell the eggs (to the kibbutz) and their profit is kept in their treasury. (The year in which the study was conducted they voted to buy records with their annual profit.)

The children are also in charge of their own vegetable garden. The produce is kept in the school and is used for their own meals.

SOCIAL CONTROL

Educators. In general the nurses and teachers employ three techniques of social control: punishment, group meeting, and nonpunitive admonitions (what, in previous sections on socialization, has been termed "statement of proper behavior"). We shall begin with the latter technique. Throughout the day individual children may be spoken to by the nurse or teacher concerning the impropriety of some act they have committed. These criticisms are usually spoken in a matter-of-fact tone and, in a sense, serve to emphasize a rule or norm which the child already knows. For example:

At breakfast, Asnat (sixth grade) leaves her table in order to get some cinnamon from the next table. She brings the bowl of cinnamon to her table and does not return it. The teacher tells her that she may have all the cinnamon she wants but that she should return the bowl so that other children may have some cinnamon too.

Such admonitions are employed when a child fails to comply with a cultural norm. But should he actively violate a cultural norm (by aggression or conflict, for example) the nurse may not only state the norm, but she may punish him as well. The punishments we observed included withdrawal by the nurse, expulsion of the child, and withdrawal of some privilege. Examples illustrate these techniques.

(Threatened withdrawal of nurse.) Giora and Esther are quarreling over the newspaper, and the entire group joins in the argument and shouting. Finally, the nurse intervenes and says that neither of them may have the paper. Giora says that if he does not get the paper, he will continue to make noise for the entire rest period. The nurse says that if he or anyone else continues to make noise, she will leave the dormitory and will not return. At this, everyone, including Giora, becomes quiet . . . and remains so for the duration of the rest period.

(Expulsion.) During the singing lesson, Shlomo constantly interrupts by pounding on the floor, shouting, pinching the others around him. After repeated warnings by the nurse, he is finally told to leave the classroom.

(Withdrawal of privilege.) Shlomo refused to get his slippers (he is in his stocking feet, since his shoes were muddy), after the teacher had requested a number of times that he do so. The teacher says that they will continue the lesson without him, and that he may not participate. Moreover, all the children are to ignore him.

There is bedlam in the room, and it is impossible to continue with the lesson. The teacher finally quiets the class, and announces that, since they have behaved so badly, she will stop the recitation period, and will not give them homework again. At this they all protest, and some begin to cry. The teacher says she will give them another chance, and they are quiet for the remainder of the period.

When there is a gross violation of the kibbutz code, such as stealing, the nurse is not content to punish the child in one of the ways described above. The case is referred to the entire kevutza for public discussion, and often for adjudication. Meeting with the kevutza, the nurse and teacher discuss the nature of the violation, allowing the violator as well as any other member of the group an opportunity to speak. Generally, a final decision is made by the nurse and teacher with the cooperation or agreement of the children. Since this technique most probably has an important bearing on superego development, one such meeting — of the members of the second grade — is described in detail.

When we first began our study of the school, marble-playing was at the height of its popularity. Yehuda, a poor player, soon lost all his marbles, while Giora, an excellent player, had won a great many. Yehuda took some marbles from Giora's desk without his permission. Giora claimed that Yehuda had stolen his marbles, and cried to his teacher about this. Since, moreover, all the other children were talking about the "robbery," RACHEL and DEVORA (teacher and nurse) decided that this was a serious matter, and called a meeting of the kevutza.

RACHEL opened the meeting by recalling that at a previous meeting it had been agreed that no one would take another's marbles without his permission, and that "whatever is agreed upon at a meeting is binding." Despite this agreement, some children — "the names are unimportant" — had taken marbles belonging to others. (The children immediately shouted, "Yehuda, Yehuda," but RACHEL repeated that names were unimportant at this time.) Taking another person's property is a very bad thing. How could the kibbutz survive if people took what belonged to others?

She then asked Giora to explain what had happened. The latter said that he had left his marbles in his desk, as had been agreed upon, and that Yehuda had taken them. After Giora spoke, RACHEL asked if others had anything to say. At least half the kevutza wanted to say something, and the teacher permitted each child to speak. They all said that Yehuda had taken the marbles.

RACHEL then said that Yehuda could now have a chance to explain what had happened, for perhaps he had done nothing wrong. Yehuda refused to talk. He sat, without moving, eyes straight ahead. When RACHEL questioned him, he admitted that he had taken the marbles, but he refused to say anything else.

After waiting a few minutes for Yehuda to talk, the nurse began to speak. She said that Yehuda had become "impossible," (she then proceeded to enumerate the many "wrong" things he had done that week), and that every day he was becoming worse. She had tried in a hundred ways to be his friend, but he would not permit her to become one. She then turned to him directly, saying that in the cities there were police and jails to take care of thieves, but that in the kibbutz there were neither, because in the kibbutz everyone can trust everyone else. Imagine what would happen if the chaverim began to take the property of others. No one would trust anyone else, and life would break down. No one in the kibbutz ever locks his door because he knows that when he comes back to his room everything will be there, just as he left it. Yehuda, too, can be taught to be good without a jail or police because he has two tendencies (*yetzer*) within him — the good and the bad — and the school has tried to bring out his good tendency, and she is sure that the school will succeed. (At this Yehuda laughed.) DEVORA then asked Yehuda if he would continue to steal, or if he would stop — but Yehuda would not reply. While waiting for his reply RACHEL decided to speak. In the future, she said, the children would leave all their belongings in their desks, and no one would take them; no one! David suggested that the children lock their desks, but DEVORA and RACHEL said that under no circumstances would they allow that to happen.

The nurse then spoke again. Games are generally played for en-

joyment. They have become a serious business. Recently she went to
town, and saw a mother of one of the children going from store to
store trying to buy marbles, because her son owed them to Giora.
This must stop. She suggested that since Giora has many marbles, and
Yehuda has none, that the former give some to the latter. Giora at
first refused, and then finally consented to give five, although DEVORA
and RACHEL had asked him to give ten. It was then discovered that four
other children had no marbles, and DEVORA and RACHEL suggested that
all the children who had some should share with those who had none.
When that was decided, the meeting was adjourned by RACHEL.

  Peers and others. The role played by peers as agents of
socialization extends beyond such formal meetings. Peers comprise 22 per cent of all agents of socialization, according to the
results of the Moral Ideology Test. This is less than the percentage
for nurses and teachers, but larger than the corresponding percentage for parents. Of equal importance, however, is the additional finding that whereas the educators (nurse and teacher)
play a more prominent socialization role than peers, their greater
prominence is a function of their frequent use of negative sanctions. Both peers and educators employ positive sanctions with
approximately the same frequency, but educators employ negative
sanctions three times as often as peers. This positive role (praise)
of peers may partially account for the *esprit de corps* which is an
important characteristic of social interaction.

  But peers are not the only sources of "diffuse" control. The
importance of this latter control appears in sharp relief when the
roles of all socialization figures mentioned on the Moral Ideology
Test are examined. If all socializers referred to by the children as
"others," "everyone," and "the kibbutz" are added to "peers,"
then a category of socializers which may be termed, "the group,"
can be constructed. It is then seen that "the group" is mentioned
as frequently as the educators as an agent of socialization. It is
apparent, therefore, that the children are sensitized to a large
number of socializing agents rather than to a small number of
authority figures.

SOCIAL INTERACTION

  Disintegration. Quantitative data, upon which so many of the
generalizations concerning the preschool children were based,
are lacking for the children in the primary school. Generalizations
here are based on my observations combined with the reports of
nurses and teachers.

Much of the overt aggression found in the preschool children no longer appears in the behavior of these older children. This difference probably reflects the effect of prior socialization on the internalization of the kibbutz value of nonaggression. On the Moral Ideology Test, for example, aggression is by far the most frequently mentioned tabooed activity. There is, nevertheless, still a great deal of overt aggression among these children, as is made abundantly clear by both observational and test data. On the Emotional Response Test, for example, being aggressed against by peers is the most frequent cause of anger among these children, and it is the second most frequent cause of sadness.

Aggression among these children assumes a number of characteristic forms. One form, which appears infrequently, is physical aggression against a peer. Characteristically, this consists of an apparently unprovoked attack.

(At a party) Chanan walks over to Yehuda, twists his arm with considerable force; Yehuda cries out.

(The entire class is walking together to the swimming hole.) A group of children pushes Ruthi from the rear.

A second, and by far the most frequent form of aggression is symbolic or verbal aggression against a peer. Unlike physical aggression, this is generally provoked. The children — particularly the younger ones — frequently call each other names which make them furious. David (second grade) is often called "Leale" (a diminutive, feminine, proper noun) by children whom he angers, and his response is often sheer rage. In this same group, "elephant" is frequently used as an opprobrious term. Ruthi is called a "red tomato" by the other children, a term which makes her furious.

Verbal aggression, including shouting, is the most frequent response to peer frustration or conflict, although at times the affect aroused during the dispute leads to physical aggression as well.[10]

---

[10] It is of interest to observe in this connection that an argument between two children often spreads throughout the entire group, so that they all "take sides" and participate in the quarrel, although they have no personal stake in it. (Sometimes, too, according to the nurses, all the children of a kevutza become "wild," call each other names, and remain enemies for many days.) The following example is typical of verbal aggression that spreads beyond the original disputants.

(It is the afternoon rest period, and both Esther and Giora wish to read the newspaper. There is usually a schedule, but the schedule is lost, and each claims

But peers are not the only objects of aggression, for children also aggress against nurses and teachers. One expression of this aggression is the readiness of the children to criticize their teacher when they feel she is wrong. At the beginning of their spring vacation, for example, the teacher of the fourth grade informed the children of certain plans she had made for them. They immediately protested with their favorite complaint, *ze lo beseder* — "it is not proper." They accused her of poor planning, saying that she should have informed them the previous week, for now it was too late for them to change their plans. (She conceded that she was wrong, and dropped the plans.) Again, the sixth-grade teacher announced, after a show of hands from the class, the results of their vote on a certain issue. Some of the children disagreed with her count, saying, *lo nachon*, "that is not right," and insisted on a recount. (The teacher is almost always required to explain her statements or to justify her decisions, for the children are unwilling to accept them merely on her authority.)

A second expression of aggression against nurses and teachers may be seen in the poor discipline which characterizes the classroom. By "poor discipline" we do not refer to that informality which has already been described, but rather to those situations in which the children are so unruly or inattentive that all instruction ceases. The children are frequently restless, they talk among themselves, and, at times, move about the room at random, refusing to stay in their seats even when asked to do so by their teacher. The following examples — from second- and fourth-grade protocols — give something of the flavor of the kind of behavior to which we refer.

RIVKA called on the children to recite (their math lesson). They were constantly interrupted by the others, and all of them were shouting for RIVKA. One girl kept walking around the room, ruler in hand . . . The class became so noisy that complete chaos broke out, and it was literally impossible to hear the children reciting.

The teacher asked for suggestions from the children for the story or poem that each was to write, putting each suggestion on the blackboard. They became very boisterous, talking and shouting. One of the girls modeled a hand out of paper, tore it into bits, and threw the

that it is his turn.) Esther takes the paper from Giora, who takes it back. Each is now shouting at the other that it is his turn. The others have awakened, and gradually they are joining in the shouting. Now everyone is shouting, and it is impossible to quiet them. It seems that the majority favor Esther . . . (The nurse finally quieted them. She tells me that if the disputants had been two boys there would definitely have been a fist fight.)

pieces on the head of the boy in front of her. Then the class broke into bedlam, everyone crying, "ESTHER," simultaneously.

(The children are reading their essays aloud.) They are not entirely attentive, and at times they become so clamorous that it is impossible to hear the speaker.

Insolence, or *chutzpa,* is still another expression of children's aggression against nurses and teachers. Adults, as has been pointed out, are quite informal with the children. They play the role of an older sibling rather than a strict authority figure. Nevertheless, the children are willing to accept their authority so long as the adults are their superordinates rather than their peers. The children are quick to detect weakness on the part of the adults, however, and should the line that separates permissiveness from weakness be blurred, they are quick to take advantage of the situation and to exploit it to its fullest. As a nurse put it, "If you let them have their own way, they will walk all over you." The validity of this generalization may be seen in the children's relationship to one teacher who, according to the nurses, came to be perceived by the children as a peer because of her extreme informality. She not only had difficulty controlling the children in her class — the other teachers had little difficulty in this regard — but they became openly insolent toward her.

Displacement of aggression may be observed among these children, too. Animals, particularly cats, are sometimes attacked mercilessly by them. Even the nurses comment on the cruelty that the children sometimes exhibit in their attacks on cats. Cats have been killed by stoning and pounding, and one kevutza buried a cat alive. Yosef, a boy in the second grade, killed a cat by himself, but, for obscure reasons, the others condemned him for this and would not forgive him. They buried the cat in front of the school and placed a sign over it, reading: "Here lies the cat that Yosef killed."

Integration. Antisocial behavior in these children is less frequent than are expressions of goodwill and fellowship and affection. That the children are generally fond of each other may be inferred, in the first place, from their almost constant group interaction. Even when they have the opportunity to leave, they often prefer to stay in the dormitory, reading or playing. With one or two exceptions, they are happy to return to the school at night after visiting in their parents' rooms. Moreover, though they are permitted to roam throughout the kibbutz, and to play wherever they wish, the locus of play is the school playground. Almost always they are to be found playing there, rather than in other places.[11] Hence it is not surprising to discover that the school is the children's constant frame of reference even when they are far from it. Parents report that these children, like the very young children, become lonely for the kibbutz and their peers after they have been away for only a short time, and that they constantly talk about what the children are doing in the school — now they are sleeping, now they are eating breakfast, now they are going swimming, and so on.[12] The children not only remain within their groups when there is no necessity to do so, but their group behavior seems to be characterized by genuine fellowship and *esprit de corps*. This is particularly true of the play groups.

The children rarely seize upon situations of potential aggression as opportunities for vindictiveness. It will be recalled, for example, that the teachers frequently ask the children to read their essays aloud, to be evaluated by the others. The children almost never abused this opportunity. They were almost always fair in their criticisms, and only rarely were aggressive feelings detected. On the contrary, they would invariably praise in glowing terms those essays which were particularly good.

Still another index of peer solidarity is the alacrity with which the children respond to another's need for help or assistance. This, incidentally, is one of the reasons why the adults have few qualms about leaving these children alone at night. If a child becomes ill or frightened, the others take care of him, change his sheets if necessary, bring him water, and so forth. This concern for, and willingness to help, their peers is, of course, a major socialization aim of the kibbutz, so that the children's behavior, in this regard, is an expression of their training. That this is so is seen from the Moral Ideology Test. Overwhelmingly, the activity which is most

[11] This attachment to their current living quarters leads to a certain regressive behavior on the part of the children: a return to the previous dwelling after having moved to another. It was frequently noticed that some children who had recently entered the high school would return to the primary school to play, while the youngest children in the grade school would, at times, return to the Kindergarten to play.

[12] The children's attachment to their own peer-group results in a provincial attitude with respect to the outside world, even to other kibbutzim. The school is but a few hundred feet from the school of a neighboring kibbutz. Nevertheless, there is little interaction between the children of these two kibbutzim; they almost never play together or engage in any joint enterprise. These two kibbutzim could as well be hundreds of miles apart.

frequently cited as evocative of praise is generosity (of effort, help, or goods).

An excellent indication of this solidarity of the group is seen in its rallying to the defense of a member who is in trouble with the "authorities." When Ahuv, a sixth-grade boy, left the kibbutz without permission, and was found by a search party later that night, the teachers and nurses decided that he must be punished. But at the student meeting which was called to discuss the case, the children consistently voted against punishment. It was finally decided by the teachers, however, that he be confined to his bedroom for one day. The children opposed this decision, and throughout the day they brought food to Ahuv, and spelled each other in staying with him, so that, in effect, he was never alone.

A final indication of the solidarity of the group is the security which the children feel in it. No child in the school wakes up, afraid, in the middle of the night, although there are no adults with them. That they feel secure with the other children is the interpretation of the nurses. This interpretation receives support from the observation that when the children are placed in isolation (due to illness) they frequently are afraid, and ask that the light be kept on all night.

This security is seen, as well, in group performances, such as skits and plays, in which the children consistently manifest a genuine stage presence, performing their parts with no visible signs of fear or of embarrassment. Our field notes are filled with comments concerning public performances of which the following extract is typical.

Again we were impressed with the freedom of the children, their spontaneity, lack of shyness, and naturalness.

SEX

Socialization. These children, like those of preschool age, live in bisexual dormitories and thus continue to have ample opportunity to witness the nudity or semi-nudity of other children. This structural aspect of dormitory life, which contributes to a permissive sexual environment, is reinforced by the nurses' perpetuation of the enlightened attitudes found among the nurses for the preschool children.

Nurses and teachers do not respond to the children's sexual behavior, neither encouraging nor discouraging its manifestations. At the same time, they do not, with the exception of menstruation, instruct the children in sexual matters, unless the latter themselves ask questions. The nurse explains the nature of menstruation to the six-grade girls, although she almost always discovers that they have already been enlightened by their friends in the high school. Still, she feels that her instruction is valuable because, though they know about menstruation, "they really do not believe that it will happen to them."

When the children do ask sexual questions — and, according to the nurse, the girls, but not the boys, ask — the nurse answers them candidly. They are taught none of the sexual folklore. Typical questions concern menstruation, the reason for and the nature of sexual intercourse, and the reason for marriage. In general, children are more likely to discuss sexual matters with their nurses than with their parents, although parents report that children do ask them questions concerning sex. In response to such a question on the Questionnaire, only one parent indicated that his children ask no sexual questions. On the other hand, none felt that such questions were frequent.

Although parents report that their replies to children's questions about sex are candid, there is reason to believe that their sexual attitudes are frequently quite conventional. When, for example, a mother came to the school late at night and discovered the children running nude through the halls, she was shocked. Claiming that their behavior was "immoral," she demanded an immediate public airing of the whole affair, despite the nurse's protest that the children's behavior was a technique of satisfying their sexual curiosity and reducing their sexual tensions.[13]

Sexual behavior. Because of the wide age range in the school, it is impossible to generalize about the entire group. Hence we shall discuss the two younger groups (grades two and four) and the older group (grade six) separately.

There is a great deal of bodily contact, in the form of wrestling, sham-fighting, "horseback" riding, and various gymnastic exercises among all the children. In the two younger groups contact between members of opposite sex is as frequent as contact between members of same sex. This is not true in the older group. Here, heterosexual bodily contact is infrequent; only in the case of the

[13] This incident serves to remind us that not all members of the kibbutz have accepted its "liberal" sexual morality, and that these members, willy-nilly, transmit their own conventional morality to their children. Much of sexual shame found in the children must, with good reason, be attributed to the attitudes of their more conventional parents.

tomboy, Ahuva, does heterosexual contact occur as frequently as it does in the younger children.

Aside from such diffuse bodily contact, nurses and teachers report activities which they perceive to be consciously sexual in intent and in sensation. The boys in the second and fourth grades, for example, like to wrestle in bed, either in the nude or in their undershorts, covered with a sheet. They especially like to do this with one particular boy who is big and fat. The nurses report similar "homosexual" behavior among the girls of the second grade. Miri and Shula, for example, like to roll on the floor together and to lie on top of each other. This they do with considerable laughing and giggling. Two other girls, moreover, have been seen sleeping together by the nurse when she entered the school in the morning.

Heterosexual behavior has been observed by the nurse and teacher of the second grade, although they have never observed either attempted or actual intercourse. The nurse is confident that boys and girls often get into bed with each other at night, but she does not know how frequently this occurs, nor does she know what they do. These children frequently play "clinic," a game in which the boys "examine" the girls, who are nude. Moreover, boys and girls often lie on top of each other, and hug and kiss each other in public, even in the classroom and in the presence of the teacher, "with no sense of shame." At least one boy would "kiss like a man of twenty."

"Couples" are found at this age more frequently than in the "tender age." Couples consist of boys and girls who are constantly together, who do their homework together, play together, and stay with each other in the afternoons. They are found among the fourth-grade children as well. Whether these friendships are entirely platonic or whether they include sexual interaction as well is unknown.

A final form of both homo- and heterosexual behavior among the second-grade children is found in their relationship to their teacher. The former reports that she was amazed by the great sexual interest expressed by the children toward her when she first became their teacher — a year before this study began. Both boys and girls would kiss and caress her, although this behavior was particularly marked among the girls. It seems that their nursery teacher, from whom they had just parted, had stimulated them sexually by encouraging them to seek physical contact with her. As one of the girls put it, "We loved Rachel (the nursery teacher)

so much; we loved to touch her skin; she had such smooth skin."
After moving to the school, they transferred this physical affection
to their new teacher. One of the girls was so extreme, both in the
frequency and intensity of her kisses, that the teacher had to tell
her that there were other ways in which she could display her
affection. They finally came to an agreement that the girl would
kiss her only twice a day — when the teacher came in the morning
and when she left in the afternoon.

Among the boys, Hillel, who "hates" all women and who idol-
izes his father and all things masculine, is the most extreme in
his "sexual" attitude toward the teacher. One day when she was
leading the class in physical exercises, Hillel blurted out, "Look
how DEVORA's breasts shake up and down." The other children
rebuked him for this, saying that one doesn't say such things.
Another time, after DEVORA had been away for a few days, she
went to the school to kiss the children goodnight. Hillel would
not permit her to kiss him but the next day he said that since it
was her twenty-eighth birthday — which it was — he would give
her twenty-eight spankings. The teacher reported that the spankings were more like caresses.

Masturbation among the second-grade children is reported by
the nurses and teacher, and was observed by us. At least six children — three boys and three girls — are regular masturbators.
Few attempt to conceal their masturbation, and some even masturbate in class. At least one boy becomes so absorbed when he
masturbates that he is oblivious to the presence of others or to
the fact that they are watching him. At least one girl masturbated so intensely that she developed severe vaginal inflamma-
tion. Some of the children suck their fingers and masturbate
simultaneously.

Sexual shame and curiosity. In the sixth grade sexuality is
more complex, and includes both greater sexual curiosity and
greater sexual shame. Sexual shame increases quite conspicuously
with age. In both the second and fourth grades boys and girls
shower together, seemingly enjoying the activity as they run
around, laugh, and joke. The children of the second grade ignored
my presence when they showered, and showed no signs of embarrassment; but in the fourth grade, the girls became shy when
I appeared, running behind the door to conceal their nudity. The
nurse explained that the girls had no feelings about appearing
nude before their peers, but were shy in the presence of strangers.

In the sixth grade the children — at least the girls — are ashamed to be seen nude by their own peers of the opposite sex, and boys and girls shower separately. When queried about this, the nurse said the girls are either prepubescent or already in puberty, so that it is only "natural" that they feel shy in the presence of the boys. It was later discovered, however, that another factor, in addition to the nurse's hypothesis of its being "natural," entered into their feeling of shame. It seems that until one year prior to this study, the boys and girls of the sixth grade had showered together without shame. Then a refugee girl from Poland was admitted to their kevutza. She not only refused herself to shower with the boys, but she prevailed upon the other girls to imitate her behavior, and soon all of them refused to shower with the boys. Their shame became so extreme that the girls soon refused to shower with other girls; if one came to the door of the shower room while another was showering, the latter would scream. They even decided to keep a guard at the door, to prevent this from happening. One of the girls would not even undress in the presence of the other children; she would return to the dormitory in the evening before the other children arrived, so that she could be undressed and in bed when the latter returned.

This situation lasted about a year, but at the time of our study the situation had altered. Some of the girls were again showering with the boys, and even those who refused to do so were calm and dignified about it. They took their showers separately without the turmoil and tension that had characterized their behavior of the previous year. The nurse does not know the precise cause of this change in behavior, but it is surely not unrelated to the following fact. The boys decided that something had to be done about the irrational behavior of the girls and they devised some scheme to destroy their unexpected sense of shame. The nurse does not know the nature of the scheme but whatever its nature, it apparently worked.

Extrapolating from our high school data (see p. 329) it is not improbable that the sense of shame felt by the girls was due yet to another factor — their precocious maturation relative to that of the boys. Although only one of the girls had begun to menstruate, others were beginning to manifest secondary sexual characteristics, such as development of the breasts and pubic hair. This change in their bodies may well have caused them to feel shame in the presence of the boys, particularly since the boys had not yet undergone their pubertal changes. The plausibility of this interpretation is strengthened by the fact that the one boy who refused to shower with the girls was himself beginning to develop pubic hair. Interestingly enough, the girls ignored this development, whereas the other boys poked fun at him.

The children of the sixth grade, according to their nurse, are both curious and naïve about sexual matters. When their teacher got married, they teased her about her husband, and sometimes peeked through her window in order to see him. Two of the boys were curious about the nature of intercourse, and, to satisfy their curiosity, hid under the bed of two immigrant workers to observe the couple having intercourse. Some of the children, on the other hand, are more sophisticated than some of their parents believe them to be about sexual matters. When the children learned about the existence of houses of prostitution, one girl, who knew that her father was shy about sexual matters, would frequently ask him what a house of prostitution was.

Interaction between the sexes. In general, group interaction, including games, is bisexual; boys and girls not only play the same games but tend to play them together. On the other hand, small, intimate, play-groups are usually unisexual, and close friends, too, are generally members of the same sex. The latter generalization does not hold for the second grade, some of whom, as we have already observed, have "boy friends" or "girl friends." Indeed, as a generalized statement it may be said that bisexual intimacy decreases with age. Boys and girls in the second grade are frequently very intimate with one another; in the fourth grade they have ceased these intimate friendships and are neutral; in the sixth grade they have developed hostility for each other. The sense of shame developed by the sixth-grade girls, for example, was not merely a shame phenomenon. It also involved great hostility toward the boys, and their attempt to create unisexual showers was, among other things, an expression of this hostility. As their nurse pointed out, the relationship between the sexes at that time was "terrible." They practically "hated" each other, would not talk to each other, and were constantly involved in petty altercations. This mutual hostility decreased considerably subsequent to the boys' intervention in the shower incident, but much of it still remained.

Sex-linked personality differences. Grammar school, like preschool, education draws few sharp distinctions between boys and girls. Indeed, the only distinctions are those which have already been discussed in the chapters dealing with the younger children. Nevertheless, there continue to be important sexual differences in behavior among these children as there are among the younger children.

For one thing, girls seem to be more spontaneous and out-going in group situations — particularly in the presence of strangers or adults — than are the boys. It was observed that at birthday parties, at which parents were present, or at parties with children of other kibbutzim, the girls spontaneously sang, danced, played games and, in general, were eager for activity and ex-pression. The boys, on the other hand, sat on the sidelines, watch-ing the girls and joking among themselves; they participated in group activities only reluctantly. The girls also display less physi-cal aggression than the boys. One seldom, if ever, observes physi-cal aggression among the older girls. If frustrated or angry they may resort to name-calling or to shouting, but not to physical fighting.[14]

There are a number of sex differences that reflect identification with adult roles of same sex. At the end of a party or a meeting, when the children are requested by the teachers to help put tables and chairs back in place, boys always volunteer, girls al-most never. There seems little doubt but that the boys are more interested in agriculture than the girls, and at least one of the boys actively assists in the adult stable and machine shop. Some of the girls, on the other hand, spend much time in the dwellings of the younger children, assisting the nurses in their work and supervising the children's play. Consistent with this "maternal" behavior on the part of the girls is their choice of subjects in drawing. When the fourth-grade children were asked by their art teacher to draw a picture portraying some event in the life of Moses, almost all the girls drew pictures portraying his infancy — Moses lying in the bulrushes, or Moses being discovered by Pharaoh's daughter — while the boys portrayed events taken from his manhood.

Although some of the older boys seem to be more alert politi-cally than the girls, it is among the older girls that the greatest devotion to the values of the kevutza and the strongest sense of group responsibility is to be discovered. A small group of sixth-grade girls (which may also include one or two boys) comprises

---

[14] It is of interest to observe, too, that, in the sixth grade, at least, when a boy is provoked by a girl, he does not attack her physically, as he well might had she been a boy. On the other hand, the boys do not hesitate to fight Ahuva, who is a tomboy, as efficient as the boys in sports and fighting.

the moral leadership of the entire student body. It assumes most of the responsibilities of the group, and it spurs the others on to activity.[15] Finally, according to interviews with nurses and teachers, the boys tend to be more egotistical than the girls, while the girls show greater sensitivity to ego-threat than the boys.

INDEPENDENCE

If independence, as a behavior system, be divided into the subclasses of self-reliance and responsibility, these children would score high on the latter, and relatively low on the former. The basis for the responsibility score is their behavior at work.

Work. The children not only perform their work assignments efficiently but they carry them out responsibly and without adult supervision. Thus the sixth-grade children require no adult supervision in executing such relatively complex assignments as cleaning out the chicken coops and providing the chickens with food and water. Even the younger children fulfill their duties responsibly, even when they are disliked. For example, a boy in the fourth grade was mopping the dormitory floor one morning and when I asked him if he liked to mop the floor, he said he did not. When asked why he performed a task he did not like, he said that he had to; it was his job. This attitude is reflected in the Moral Ideology Test, which reveals that the need to work well is experienced by these children as second only to generosity and the inhibition of aggression as the most important socialization demand.

The older children not only carry out their assignments without adult supervision, but they also voluntarily supervise the behavior of the younger children.

Naomi and Chana (second grade) are cleaning the classroom. Ofra (fourth grade), who is cleaning the bedroom, comes in to see if they are doing their work properly. She corrects them, criticizes them, tells them how to hold the broom and the pan. When she finishes cleaning the bedroom, she returns and helps them to clean the classroom.[16]

---

[15] This core group phenomenon appears so frequently in other kibbutzim, as well, that the educational director of The Federation, in an article in the official kibbutz educational journal, characterizes it as "almost a law."

One of the effects of this female moral leadership, according to this article, is that it serves to cast the boys into an opposition group which violates the group norms, because the girls insist so urgently on upholding them. This process may well explain the boy-girl conflict we observed in the sixth grade.

[16] On the other hand, there is at least one example of blatant irresponsibility. One evening during their summer vacation before the children went to bed, the

Dependence. Many of the dependency needs that characterize the preschool children are to be found among the second-grade children, as well, but they are much less prevalent among the older school children. Unlike the latter who do their class assignments independently, both of each other and of the teacher, the younger children are greatly dependent upon the teacher. They constantly call upon her to look at what they have done, to help them draw something, to assist them in their arithmetic lesson. To the classroom visitor it seems as if the name of the teacher is repeated a thousand times during each lesson. The children not only insist on obtaining the teacher's attention, but they demand her exclusive attention. Thus it frequently happens that, after the teacher explains something to the class, each child insists that she then explain it to him individually.

This reliance upon the teacher is accompanied by a low threshold of frustration tolerance — a marked characteristic of almost all the second-grade children (as well as of some of the children in the higher grades). Should these children undertake some task — an arithmetic problem, a drawing, a theme — and be unsuccessful at their first attempt, or should the task be difficult and demand some effort, their first response is to cry and to call upon the teacher for help. If she does not respond immediately, they wail, scream and stamp their feet. Even for such simple matters as an answer to a question, they cannot tolerate delay. If the teacher is busy, or is talking with someone else, they continue to repeat the question until she answers it. If she does not answer, they break into cries.

This same behavior characterizes their initial response to a new task. Their teacher reported that it is exceedingly difficult for them to adjust to a new situation or a new task, and that they become very confused until it has become routine. This reaction was observed when I attempted to administer the P-F Test. After carefully and slowly explaining the nature of the test to them, giving careful and explicit instructions, the children required at least fifteen minutes of additional explanation. They did not, they said, understand what they were to do, it was too difficult, they could never do it, would the teacher explain it again,

---

head of the kibbutz vineyards came to the school and said that twenty workers were required for the next day — Would any of the children volunteer? Almost all the children said they would work, with Avner — the oldest boy in the sixth grade — taking command. The next day, however, not one child, including Avner, appeared to work in the vineyard. When Avner was asked what had happened, he said that only five children had appeared for work that morning, so he canceled the entire plan.

would the anthropologist explain it to them individually. Even after all these problems were settled, one child immediately handed in his test without attempting to answer it; one kept it at her desk, but did not answer it; one would not continue to a succeeding picture unless he could answer the previous one; and all of them cried or whined whenever they felt they could not "answer" a particular picture. The teacher was constantly called upon for help.

Their nurse speaks, not of frustration tolerance, but of ego-centrism in characterizing similar behavior among the sixth-grade children. When they do not or cannot get what they think is rightfully theirs, they complain or cry. She explains this behavior as a function of the easy life which the children lead. They have everything, she says, and they think that everything is theirs by right.

Other indications of dependency needs are thumbsucking and enuresis. And both are found in some measure among these children. In the fourth and sixth grades there is only one thumb-sucker each. But in the second grade, there are at least four thumbsuckers, two of whom are constant suckers; that is, they almost never have their fingers or thumbs out of their mouths, unless they must use their hands for some other purpose.

Unlike thumbsucking, enuresis is more prevalent in the sixth than in the second grade. In the latter grade there are two bed-wetters, in the fourth grade there are none, but in the sixth grade there are four (three girls and a boy).[17]

A final index of dependence may possibly be provided by the tendency of the children to visit the younger children's houses. This return to the scene of one's own younger years is particularly characteristic of the girls, who not only play with the children but who also supervise them. One of the motives for this return, we may speculate, is to reinstate previous dependency satisfactions. For observe: these children are no longer visited by adults, and their contacts with them are not characterized by the warmth and interest that characterize the adult relationship with younger children. The same adult, for example, who will almost always stop a nursery child if he passes him on the sidewalk, will pass by a school child with a simple hello. Thus, when a school child

[17] The policy of the nurses is to say nothing to the bed-wetters, although this policy is not always carried out. In the not-too-remote past it was believed that the children could be shamed out of their enuresis. Hence, although the enuretics were not scolded by the nurses, they were required to take their wet sheets to the laundry by themselves; thus announcing to all observers that they had wet their beds. Unlike enuresis, thumbsucking is consistently ignored by the nurses.

visits a younger kevutza, he is, in a sense, returning to a situation that he once enjoyed; but he maintains his superiority over the younger children by adopting the same adult behavior that was once displayed toward him — he is affectionate toward the younger ones, he plays with them, and he socializes them. In this way, he perpetuates his own experiences. This interpretation is strengthened by the further observation that when these younger children grow older, he will no longer visit them, but will visit the new toddlers, instead.

INTRODUCTION

When, at the age of twelve, they graduate from the sixth grade, the children leave the primary school and its dormitory and enter the combined junior-senior high school (*Mosad*). In its early years there was no Mosad in Kiryat Yedidim, and its children were sent to a kibbutz regional high school about forty miles away. There they remained during the week, returning home on Saturdays, holidays, and for summer vacations. From casual comments of older sabras it may be inferred that they did not adjust too well to this new experience, and (perhaps as a result of their maladjustment) they did not — so they claim — learn very much or study too hard. With the increase in its student population, Kiryat Yedidim in cooperation with two other kibbutzim erected its own Mosad. All sabras under twenty-five have graduated from this high school.

The student population of the Mosad numbers 163 children — 83 boys and 80 girls. Since the Mosad is a cooperative inter-kibbutz enterprise, and since it also accepts a limited number of children from the cities, only 86, or 53 per cent, of the students are from Kiryat Yedidim (and 15 of these 86 are not children of the kibbutz, but rather refugee children who were taken into the kibbutz upon their arrival in Israel).

Since we are concerned with the children of Kiryat Yedidim, all descriptions of student behavior, unless otherwise indicated, refer only to them. It should be stressed, however, that the 47 per cent of the student body which does not come from Kiryat Yedidim has important effects on the nature of social interaction within the Mosad. Three-fourths of these outside children are from other kibbutzim, so it may be assumed that their personalities are similar to those from Kiryat Yedidim. And even the non-kibbutz students are not entirely different from the kibbutz children in their value orientations, since they have been raised in families whose parents were members of The Party, and they themselves had been members of The Movement before coming to the Mosad. Nevertheless, the over-all influence of these students is probably a negative one. Most of them come from broken homes and/or had been behavior problems before being sent to the Mosad. In the main, therefore, they are disturbed children, and much of the interaction in the Mosad is undoubtedly influenced by this fact, though this influence is hard to assess.

FORMAL STRUCTURE

Physical. Although the new Mosad was built on land owned by Kiryat Yedidim, it is physically separated from the kibbutz by a wide expanse of land and by a public highway. Objectively the distance separating the Mosad from the living quarters of the kibbutz is not great — about three hundred yards. Subjectively, however, they comprise different worlds. The adults speak of "going down" to the Mosad (the Mosad campus is on lower land than the kibbutz proper) as if such a walk constituted a trip to another village, and the same feeling-tone is conveyed by the children when they speak of "going up" to the kibbutz.[1]

The Mosad occupies a beautiful campus of approximately ten acres. It is carefully landscaped, with a pond, trees, shrubs, and flowers. The buildings are, in general, constructed of red brick and white stucco, which, with their tiled roofs, creates a Spanish bungalow effect. The main buildings are arranged around a large quadrangle, forming a mall.

There are seven buildings which serve as both living quarters and classrooms. Each kevutza occupies such a building. One wing of these L- or T-shaped buildings serves as a dormitory, consisting of four or five rooms, with four or five beds in a room. All of these buildings include toilets, some include a shower room as well. The bisexual dormitory system that obtains in the grade school is continued into the Mosad — the typical room contains two boys and two girls — and, until two years prior to this study, the showers were bisexual as well.

Although the children are seldom in their dormitory rooms, the existence of four or five children in one room is considered excessive by the parents and teachers. The early ideology of the

[1] This separation frequently leads to lack of communication between the Mosad and the kibbutz. More than a month after our arrival in the kibbutz a high school student with whom I was working in the fields did not know who I was, and had not even heard that two Americans had come to do research in the kibbutz. This came as a great surprise in view of the fact that the kibbutz is a small village in which, presumably, every novel event is known to all inhabitants within a very brief time.

kibbutz favored such a large number of children in one room, but experience has shown that this places too great a burden on the individual child. For one thing, he must constantly adapt his behavior to the needs and demands of his roommates, which deprives him of autonomy and which is often a source of irritation. For another, he has little opportunity for privacy. He can never be alone. As some recent graduates of the Mosad expressed it in an interview in the student magazine:

. . . there is a tendency to enter into the private life of the individual.

The individual does not have much freedom. . . . There is little attention paid to the individual who finds it difficult to live in the group. . . .

The main objection is that the student has no corner where he can work quietly.

The other wing of the T or L is the classroom, with the usual classroom appurtenances and paraphernalia. Each kevutza, then, both sleeps and studies in the same building. With the exception of music and gym lessons, the teachers, rather than the students, move from one classroom to another for different lessons.

Since the children take their meals in the Mosad, it has a large combined kitchen and dining room. Unlike the kibbutz dining room, it is new, spacious, bright, and airy, with small, instead of long, tables, at which no more than eight can sit. Its kitchen is entirely modern, and its working conditions are much superior to those found in the kibbutz kitchen.

In addition, the campus has a workshop consisting of a carpentry shop and a bookbinding room; a large building which contains a library and a nature laboratory (the latter is an amateur natural history museum); a small bungalow, half of which serves as living quarters for a bachelor teacher, and the other half as an isolation ward; a music building in which musical instruments are stored, and in which choral and orchestral rehearsals are held; and a combined clothing-sewing room. The Mosad campus also includes a large vegetable garden and poultry-run, which are the responsibility of the students, and whose products are consumed in their dining room; and an athletic field with a basketball court.

The Mosad, like the rest of the kibbutz, is characterized by the almost complete absence of private property. Only in those instances in which equality can be maintained is private property allowed to exist. Wrist watches, for example, are owned privately because every student owns one. Although some girls have more clothes than others (they receive them as presents from relatives outside the kibbutz), they generally share their clothes, so that this creates no problem of inequality.

One serious problem concerning private property arose the year before our study. Some of the students had acquired bicycles which, they insisted, were their private property. This inequality (between those who owned bicycles and those who did not) precipitated many tensions, and the students finally decided at an assembly to "collectivize" all the bicycles. They were put in a pool to be used on a rotation basis or according to special need.

Schedule. It is apparent even to the casual observer that the lives of the students are, as they put it, "full." Classes begin at 6:45 A.M. and continue until 12:30, with time out for breakfast. All students work in the afternoon following their noon rest. The older students barely have time to shower, after returning from work, before eating dinner. Then follows a busy round of activities such as meetings, clubs, Movement, and committees, in addition to school work. By 11:00 all lights are out.

Staff. The Mosad has a staff of twenty-eight, including teachers, nurses, a gardener, cook, and seamstress. The activities of this staff, and the general administration of the Mosad, are coordinated by various administrative bodies and personnel, of whom the most important for our purposes is the principal.

The principal is elected by the entire high school staff, including its nonacademic personnel. He usually holds office for two years. Theoretically, his is an educational and policy-making position, but since he himself is one of the staff and enjoys but a temporary superordinate position within it, he is loathe to exercise authority concerning other than perfunctory matters. The principal, as head of the instructional program, is also responsible for supervising the work of the teachers. He may sit in on their classes and give them the benefit of his criticisms and suggestions. This is never done, however, because — as the principal at the time of this study put it — "Who will criticize the work of his colleagues?"

Although the entire Mosad staff interacts with the students, the important authority figures in the Mosad include the "educators," teachers, and nurses. The student body in the Mosad is divided into kevutzot of approximately fifteen to twenty children, each kevutza with its own dormitory-classroom building, and its own educator and nurse, both of whom remain (ideally) with the kevutza from the time they enter the Mosad until they graduate.

The educator (*mechanech*) is a teacher who, in addition to his usual instructional responsibilities, is in charge of a kevutza. Administratively, he is similar to the American homeroom teacher. Psychologically, he is (ideally) a combined parent-surrogate, socializer, intellectual mentor, ideological guide, father confessor, and social model. He teaches most of their courses and, therefore, may spend as many as sixteen to twenty hours a week with his students in the classroom. He supervises the academic progress of each of the students, providing them with private instruction, if necessary; and it is he whom a teacher contacts if a student is doing poor work in other courses. He introduces the children to literature, encouraging them to read certain novels, poetry, and so on; the kevutza may meet with the educator for an informal discussion of a book or to read aloud. He brings important political problems to the attention of the kevutza, refers them to important political articles, and holds political discussions with them.

In addition to these intellectual and political functions, the mechanech serves as a psychological counselor. Students with personal problems turn to him for advice and guidance; or, if he recognizes a "problem" child, he may call him in for consultation. He is usually responsible for the sexual education of the kevutza, conducting informal discussions with the group, or serving as a sex counselor to individuals. Since, however, the educator is almost always a male, many girls are diffident about bringing their sexual questions to him, and they are more likely to bring them (if they bring them to anyone) to the nurse.

The nurse (*metapelet*) does not officially play an important role in the kevutza. Officially, she is responsible for the physical well-being of the children: she cleans the buildings, the toilets, and shower rooms; she is in charge of the clothing, its repair and distribution; and she is concerned with the children's health, and nurses them when they are ill. The nurses complain about their relatively minor role, and there have been discussions within both the Mosad and the kibbutz concerning their complaints. Since the nurses are seldom trained or specialized persons, it would be necessary to provide them with some type of professional training before they could be assigned more responsible duties; this has been suggested.

The unofficial role of the nurse may be different from her official role. Almost the entire instructional staff of the Mosad is comprised of males, so that the nurses are, for the most part, the sole adult females on the campus. For children whose entire previous educational experience has been exclusively with females, she may serve as an important transitional buffer from an all-female to an all-male adult environment. For those children who desire such a female figure, or for girls who may wish to discuss sexual matters with a female, her potential psychological role may be great. In the main, however, these untrained nurses are not equipped to handle these interpersonal needs.

The teacher (*moreh*) is the third adult authority figure in the Mosad. His role as teacher, as distinct from his role as educator — and not all teachers are educators — consists almost entirely of classroom instruction. Teachers are trained, either at the Hebrew University or at the Teacher's College sponsored by the kibbutz movement, or at both. In general, they are members of the three kibbutzim which sponsor the Mosad, and, in general, they were regular workers in one of the economic branches of their kibbutz before being elected-drafted-requested to become teachers. Having been chosen to serve as teachers, they are sent by their kibbutzim to study for two years at the Teacher's College. Since at least some of the teachers prefer to do physical labor, it is usually understood that they need not remain in their teaching posts permanently. On the other hand it is uneconomic to train a teacher for two years, only to have him leave his teaching post after a few years. In general, therefore, it is agreed that a teacher will remain in his post for at least six years before he asks to be relieved.

Not all the teachers, however, are kibbutz members. Parttime teachers (*morim chelkiim*) — those who teach special courses such as English, Arabic, or physical education — may be brought into the Mosad from outside the kibbutz movement. Moreover, in the event that a teacher from a kibbutz is not immediately available, it is sometimes even necessary to hire a fulltime teacher from the outside. Although this recourse may be had for those subjects which are labeled *realistika* (roughly, the physical and biological subjects) the Mosad would never hire a teacher for *humanistika* (the humanities and the social sciences), because, it will be remembered, these are taught from a Marxist point of view, and only a member of The Party would be permitted to teach them. Moreover, since the average teacher is with a class as much as eleven hours a week, and the educator as much as twenty hours, the Mosad feels that it must be careful in the selection of its teachers.

The Children's Society. A leader in The Federation's educational system has observed that the Mosad is built on three principles: "synthetic culture" (nonspecialized education), a children's economy, and the "Children's Society" (*chevrat yeladim*). Even more than in the grade school, it is the kevutza which is — in the words of kibbutz educational authorities — the foundation stone of the Children's Society in the Mosad. The official rationale for the Mosad kevutza is stated by the educational director of The Federation. It had been hoped, he writes in the educational journal, that most of the personality characteristics which the kibbutz hopes to develop in its children — cooperation, altruism, and so on — would arise through the influence of the chevra. But this has not been the case, for, he says, the educational theorists had not taken into account the play of the instincts — aggression, laziness, and others. These often remained unaffected by life in the chevra since the latter does not reach each individual, who can, if he tries, become anonymous within it.

It is the kevutza, he continues, which, theoretically, assumes the role previously assigned to the chevra. The kevutza is led by a mechanech whom the children love, and through their common love for him, they learn to love each other.[2] This theory, he admits, has not always worked out in practice for at least three reasons: there are too many children in a kevutza; there is no psychological selection of children, so that the Mosad kevutza may begin with children who had learned to dislike each other in grade school; the children are thrown into such frequent contact with each other that they often have no desire to interact beyond the occasions when such interaction is demanded.

The kevutza has considerable authority over its own members. It functions by means of six institutions. First, and most important, is the Meeting (*sichat kevutza*) which convenes once a week. It is the ultimate authority within the kevutza, and is its governing body. In addition to the Meeting the kevutza has five standing committees. The Kevutza Committee (*vaadat kevutza*), with the assistance of the educator, handles most of the social and technical problems that arise within the kevutza between Meetings; it prepares the agenda for the Meetings; and it acts as an advisory committee to the educator who usually consults with it before presenting some new plan to the kevutza.

Other committees include the Decoration Committee (*vaadat kishut*); the House Committee (*vaadat bayit*); the Athletic Com-

---

[2] Note the similarity to Freud's theory of leadership and group psychology. The similarity is probably not coincidental.

mittee (*vaadat sport*); and the Library Committee (*vaadat sfarim*).

The various kevutzot of the Mosad comprise its chevra. The latter, too, includes a Meeting as its highest authority. Meetings are held approximately every three weeks. Their agendas are first presented to the kevutza, where their important points are discussed.[3]

The various activities of the Children's Society are administered by committees. The Chevra Committee (*vaadat chevra*) is comprised of elected representatives of each kevutza and a teacher elected by the faculty. It has jurisdiction over all matters, other than those purely academic, that may arise in the Mosad. This committee, moreover, serves as an important agent of social control. If a student violates some Mosad norm, the Committee has the power — with the consent of the student's educator — to call him before its members for a *beirur*, a "clarification," and possible punishment.

Heading the Chevra Committee is a representative of the senior class. The "Coordinator," as he is called, is similar to the Secretary in the kibbutz. He presides at the Meetings of the chevra, and he is usually consulted by the Mosad authorities when they wish to bring some matter before the students.

In addition to this important executive body there are standing Cultural, Athletic, Music, Library, and Work committees. The respective activities of these committees, whose members are elected by the various kevutzot, are implicit in their names. In addition, there is a student editorial board in charge of publishing the student newspaper.

FORMAL EDUCATION

Curriculum. The high school curriculum, as has already been noted, is divided into humanistika and realistika, a division which corresponds roughly to the humanities and social sciences, on the one hand, and the physical and biological sciences, on the other. Humanistika has always dominated the Mosad curriculum for at

---

[3] One of the difficulties in the effective operation of these Meetings is the great age difference among the children. The youngest children, some only twelve years old, are extremely diffident about expressing their opinions in a public meeting which includes seniors who are eighteen years old. This problem was sufficiently serious to be discussed in the monthly magazine of the Mosad, and the younger children were criticized by the editorial writers for their lack of participation. In an attempt to cope with this problem it was decided to hold two Meetings — one for grades seven through nine, and another for grades ten through twelve. This experiment was highly successful, for the younger children were willing to speak under these conditions.

least three reasons. The kibbutz has been most interested in these subjects, not only because its *weltanschauung* is intimately related to them, but because it is based on an explicit interpretation of them. Furthermore, there has never been an adequate supply of teachers in realistika, so that a balance between these two types of courses has been difficult to achieve. And finally, there has been a shortage of laboratories, which has made instruction in certain subjects difficult if not futile. Nevertheless, such realistika subjects as physics, chemistry, biology, botany, astronomy, as well as one course in agronomy, are a standard part of the curriculum.

As in the grade school, the project method is used in the Mosad. In a ninth-grade physics class, for example, three months are devoted to the study of light. The project by means of which the physics of light is taught is the movies. Hence, the course includes such topics as the physics of light, optics, eyeglasses, the microscope, the camera, and the projector — all of which are followed by an examination of films as art and as social documents.

The same class, in its study of chemistry, has a special project devoted to water. This includes a study of the oceans, rivers, islands, rain, human geography relevant to water, the human and social uses of water (with special emphasis on the uses and problems of water in Israel), and, finally, the economic uses of water in Kiryat Yedidim.

Since the humanistika curriculum is the core of the Mosad education, and since this education is aimed at creating not only well-educated men, but men who are imbued with the kibbutz *weltanschauung*, it is of importance to examine it in some detail. The curriculum outline, found in Appendix B, is taken from a syllabus issued by the Teacher's College of the kibbutz movement, and is followed not only in Kiryat Yedidim but in all the kibbutzim of The Federation.

The project method, it will be noted from an examination of this curriculum, stresses culture history: Topics for the various grades are as follows: Grade 7 — The Ancient East, and First Period of (Jewish) National Independence; Grade 8 — Ancient Greece, and The (Period of the Jewish) Second Temple; Grade 9 — Feudalism, and From Independence to Dispersion (in Jewish History); Grade 10 — From Feudalism to Capitalism, and Beginnings of (Jewish) Redemption; Grade 11 — The Victory of the Bourgeoisie, the Beginnings of Proletarian War, and The Jewish Problem and its Solution; Grade 12 — The Period Between the

Two Wars, and The History of the Jewish Workers' Movement. In short, instead of offering separate courses in literature or history or geography, a broad historical period is chosen for study, and the various aspects of that period — its economics, politics, social structure, literature, philosophy, science — are related to each other. Moreover, instead of reading from secondary sources, the students read, in their appropriate periods, selections from such writers as Plato, Goethe, Marx, and Pushkin. In my opinion the breadth of this humanistika curriculum and the level at which the courses are taught are much higher than what is found in the average American high school, although it probably does not approach the level of the European gymnasium.

Although not included under the humanistika rubric, art education occupies an important part of the Mosad curriculum. Drawing, painting, history of the graphic and plastic arts, music history, comparative musicology, choir, and orchestra are all part of the curriculum from the seventh through the twelfth grades. The arts are popular among the students. Though a knowledge of an instrument is not compulsory, 110 of the 163 students at the time of our research were studying at least one musical instrument, the more proficient among them playing in the band and in the string orchestra.

The curriculum includes the study of two foreign languages — Arabic and English — but the Mosad has not been successful in carrying out this prescription. Since the War of Independence, many students have resisted the learning of Arabic, we were informed, because of their antagonism to the Arabs. During the year of our study, the Mosad was unable to acquire a teacher of Arabic so that we were unable to observe the forms which this resistance assumed. Nor does the Mosad fare much better with English. The latter is taught, beginning in the sixth grade of the primary school, but the children are not strongly motivated and do not learn very much. In a system in which discipline is a generally serious problem, the English classes present an even greater problem.

A final aspect of this curriculum should be noted. Despite the "progressive education" orientation of the Mosad, and despite the fact that the students will eventually become farmers, there is little if any vocational or home-economics emphasis in this curriculum. Almost without exception it is exclusively academic and could well constitute the curriculum of a private school in the United States. This emphasis, of course, is the result of deliberate planning and is consistent with the kibbutz self-image as a community of worker intellectuals.[4]

Classroom behavior. Since we have already described the informality of the kibbutz school, little need be added but that the problem of maintaining order in the classroom, so that the teacher or children who are reciting may be heard, is ubiquitous. In some grades and with some teachers the situation is less acute than in others; some lessons, too, evoke less intense disciplinary problems than others; and certain hours — mid-morning — are less difficult than others. But the generalization holds: the attempt to maintain discipline in the classroom is a constant pedagogic problem. Talking, interrupting, fighting, shouting, walking about — these patterns characterize much of the student behavior in the classroom.

Intellectual interest. In a system of this type intellectual interest becomes almost the sole impetus to study and learning. One measure of intellectual interest is classroom motivation. Here the data are equivocal. To the extent that there is so much disturbance it could be inferred that the students are not interested in their studies, for if they were they would be more attentive than they are. Yet poor discipline may reflect a deficiency in abstract ability and an inability to concentrate, rather than the absence of intellectual interest.

[4] The ideological emphasis of kibbutz education must not be forgotten. Instruction in the light of Marxism is even more pronounced in the high school. A typical example from a tenth-grade course on "The Rise of the Proletariat" may be instructive. The *Communist Manifesto* is used as the textbook, not only for an analysis of the past, but for the analysis of contemporary social life as well. While discussing the differences between slaves, serfs, and proletarians, the instructor pointed out that technological change has always been opposed by the ruling classes, for they have large investments in the current technology and would, therefore, encounter financial loss by any change in the *status quo*. Hence, the American rulers would necessarily oppose the industrial use of atomic energy, for they do not wish to lose their profits from coal and oil. The Russian rulers, on the other hand, would welcome such an innovation since, in their case, it would benefit the entire society.

Repeatedly in this course the thesis is stressed that all capitalists are villains who spend most of their time plotting against the workers. Thus, for example, they deliberately create a situation of permanent unemployment so that, having a backlog of workers to fall back on, they will not be dependent on their own workers whom, consequently, they are able to fire with impunity.

Just as the capitalists are always villains, so the workers are always heroes. Since all wealth is created by the workers, the property of the capitalists is obtained by "stealing" from the workers. In capitalist society, therefore, production is for the benefit of the capitalists; in socialist society it is for the benefit of the entire society.

There are other ways of measuring intellectual motivation. Taking a random sample of twenty-four observational protocols, we rated the students' apparent interest on a simple interested-disinterested dichotomy. Lively group participation, careful attention, intelligent questions, and so on, were taken as indications of interest; while such statements in the protocols as: "The children look bored and sleepy"; "They daydream, doodle, play with objects in their desks . . ."; "The children are apathetic and listless; they do not participate in the discussion. They look bored. At least three heads are on the desks"; "The children are bored, some are sleeping, others catching flies. . . . Few participate in the discussion the teacher is attempting to arouse"; these were taken as indications of disinterest. On the basis of these simple criteria, fifteen of the twenty-four sessions were judged to elicit the students' interest, and nine were rated as sessions in which they were disinterested or bored.

It is difficult to evaluate the intensity of interest from this procedure, but there is some indication that the sabra's intellectual interest stops when great effort is required to master the material. The teachers, too, complain that students are unwilling to expend great effort in order to understand, so that they often make no attempt to master some difficult point.[5] When the ninth grade was given a series of algebra problems to solve in class, only three, of a class of eighteen students, even attempted to solve them. The others waited for the teacher to explain the solutions. The general reluctance of these students to undertake problems that involve great effort is consistent, it is to be observed, with their reluctance to engage in individual activity. They much prefer to work at group projects.[6]

But an important structural variable must be taken into account in evaluating this characteristic — the absence of selective promotion. Throughout the entire school system there are no failures — everyone passes. Assuming that intelligence is normally distributed in the Mosad population, then a certain percentage of these students are not of high intelligence and, consequently, find the work much too difficult for them. In another system they either would have left school or would have been assigned to

[5] The Educational Director of The Federation, in an article in its education journal, writes that some people say that "the children are inclined to do the minimum of work, not to put in effort, to give up very soon in any activity that requires effort." Apparently in this too Kiryat Yedidim is not unique.

[6] This same characteristic — dependence on the teacher when confronted with difficulties — has been noted for the grade school children, as well. See, pp. 283–284.

special classes with other students of similar ability. In the kibbutz, however, even the dull students are expected to complete high school, and the Mosad does not place them in special classes. According to the principal at least 15 per cent of the students (this figure refers to the entire student body, including those from the cities) fall into this category. In a group-centered culture such as the kibbutz, these students have a great influence on the others. If they display little interest, assume no initiative, refuse to solve difficult problems, and so on, many of the others will follow suit. It is they, moreover, who soon become bored and often initiate the disturbances described above.[7]

A third basis for evaluating student intellectual interest is provided by the opinions of kibbutz members. In general, many parents, recent graduates of the Mosad, and some teachers feel that the intellectual interests of the students are not very strong. "The fact is," commented a recent graduate, "for many students studies are not the central activity of the Mosad." "It is no secret in the kibbutz," said a mother of a high school student, "that our children have no great desire to study." Some of the teachers agree with these statements, though they may interpret this situation differently than do the parents.

At least two reasons have been offered for the sabras' alleged lack of intellectual interest. One teacher believes that it is a function of biological maturation — at this age, he argues, adolescents are interested in matters other than intellectual. He and his comrades in Europe experienced this same loss of intellectual interest at this age, and it was at this period that the Youth Movement entered their lives and captured their interests. This interpretation is probably the least cogent of all. There is no evidence to show that adolescence, in general, brings in its wake a loss of intellectual curiosity. If anything, the evidence points in the reverse direction — this is a period in which curiosity about the world is intense. Why should kibbutz adolescents be an exception?

A second reason offered for the alleged lack of intellectual interest among the students is the absence of more formal in-

[7] The Mosad has recently attempted to cope with these children by offering private instruction by a special teacher. This is a stopgap method, however, rather than a solution. At a kibbutz meeting, the question of the advisability of continuing the system of compulsory high school graduation was raised. Since these children were learning little, and since their education was very expensive, perhaps some alternative could be devised. Three suggestions were discussed, but no decisions were made at that time. The suggestions included organizing special classes, sending such adolescents to study in a trade school, or permitting them to quit school and to work in the kibbutz.

centives (such as grades, exams, and merit promotions) for
academic performance. The lack of such incentives, say many
chaverim, is particularly bad for the better students; in the
absence of the stimulation afforded by grades they are content
not to work, for even without working they can remain at the
same level as the mediocre students.

This latter charge is probably a valid one. In the course of
interviewing teachers about individual students, the author was
struck by the frequency with which a teacher would say: "This
is an intelligent child, but he does not do well in his studies"; or,
"He is a brilliant boy, but he is lazy." [8]

Some of the students, too, complain about the absence of a
genuine grading system. Those from the city want grades because,
they say, they want to see where they stand in comparison with
other students. The kibbutz children, in the main, do not understand this reasoning. "Who wants to know?" is their feeling about
the matter. They too are in favor of grades, but for another
reason: there should be, they believe, some penalty for the shirker,
so that he who does not work should not graduate at the same
time, nor with the same academic degree, as those who do.

But if the students will study only because of external incentives, does this not indicate that intellectual activity has little
intrinsic value for them? The answer would seem to be that these
students in the main are little different from students in general:
their classroom motivation is not intense; on the other hand, it is
not entirely absent. It is probably accurate to state that it is
normally distributed here as in any other community.

But classroom behavior is not the only index of intellectual
interest. Despite their intensive schedule, many students find time
and are motivated to read books extraneous to their formal studies.
In a survey made of the twelfth grade (exclusive of children
from outside Kiryat Yedidim) it was discovered that the students
read an average of 3.5 books a month outside of their classroom
assignments. These include fiction, history, science, and essays.
More important, these books are not confined to Israeli authors
or subjects; on the contrary, most are translations of foreign
literature from the Mosad library. During their two-month
summer vacation, moreover, these same students read an average
of 9.4 books within these same general categories. This would

---

[8] That this problem is universal in The Federation may be seen in an article by
its Educational Director who cites the common complaint (with which he is in
partial agreement): ". . . the children do not actualize to the full their intellectual
or moral powers, and the level of their attainments falls short of their real abilities."

indicate that these students have a not inconsiderable degree of intellectual interest, however disinterested they may be in some of their classes.

There are, moreover, a small number of highly motivated intellectuals in the high school — despite the absence of those competitive motivations which are found in our own culture, and despite the fact that education is not a means to professional and social mobility.

Intellectual attainments. Many parents complain that the intellectual attainments of the students are low, and that it is the urgent responsibility of the Mosad to remedy what they consider to be a deplorable situation. Indeed, the parents are so deeply concerned with this "problem" that four consecutive town meetings were devoted to it during the course of this study.

The Mosad teachers do not agree with the parents, and they counter with a number of arguments. In the first place, they contend, though the students know less Bible than urban high school students, they know more modern history, labor movement history, and Marxism. And in terms of kibbutz educational goals these latter subjects are more important than the Bible. Second, though the students are not experts in Jewish literature, they probably know more about world literature than the urban students. Third, though the linguistic level of the students — especially their knowledge of spelling and grammar — is not good, this is a characteristic of students throughout the country. And, finally, the students' intellectual level cannot be so high as that desired by the parents, for they have a heavy work program, which takes up most of their afternoons and leaves them physically fatigued, and they are engaged in an intensive social life which takes up most of their evenings. Hence, the teachers can assign only the barest minimum of homework. But since the work performed by the students is economically important to the kibbutz, and since "you can't expect the children to give up their childhood," this situation cannot be changed. Moreover, since both work and activities are necessary for the development of the normative kibbutz personality type, no one has seriously suggested that they be abandoned. The consequence, however, is a lowering of the students' intellectual attainments.[9]

[9] Apparently pressure of extracurricular activities is cited by many kibbutzim as a primary reason for the poor intellectual progress of their students, because this question was raised at a seminar conducted for The Federation's high school teachers. Statistical findings were presented, however, which refuted this notion, and which indicated that only a small number of students participate actively in

It is my opinion that the intellectual attainments of the Mosad students are higher than those of the average American high school students but are lower than the European gymnasium standard which their parents hold up as the norm.

WORK

Student work is viewed by the Mosad and by the kibbutz as serving two purposes: it makes an important contribution to the kibbutz economy, and it prepares the students for their adult economic roles. Hence, the principle underlying the distribution of work is that one-third be in the productive branches (*meshek*) of the kibbutz, one-third in the productive branches of the Mosad, and one-third in service branches (*sheirut*) of both the kibbutz and the Mosad. In addition, the students are responsible for making their beds and cleaning their rooms. (Each makes his own bed, but the cleaning of the room is delegated to a different student each week.)

The assignment of students to the three types of work enumerated is determined by the student Work Committee, headed by a work coordinator. As is the case with the adult Work Committee, it posts on the bulletin board outside the Mosad dining room a daily work list on which the assignment of each student is listed. Not all students work the same amount of time, however, for the hours are graded according to age. The seventh grade works one and one-half hours; the eighth grade, two hours; the ninth grade, two and one-half hours; the tenth grade, two and one-half to three hours; and the eleventh and twelfth grades, three hours. During the summer, except when they leave on vacation, each of these kevutzot works an additional hour.

The service jobs performed by the students include janitorial work (in the classrooms, the dining room, the toilets and shower rooms); work in the Mosad kitchen, as well as in the clothing room, sewing room, and laundry of both the Mosad and the kibbutz; gardening and landscaping in the Mosad; and assisting in the various children's dormitories. The productive work in the Mosad includes tending the poultry-run and the vegetable garden. Productive work in the kibbutz includes working in all its agricultural branches.

Since one of the objects of student labor is to prepare the students for their eventual adult economic roles, no student is permitted to specialize in any one branch; hence his work assign-

---

extracurricular activities; most do not. And the inactive students — those, presumably, who have time to study — do as poorly as those who are active.

ment is changed each academic quarter. An attempt is also made to discourage the development of a sexual division of labor; both sexes work in service and productive branches. This generalization must be qualified, however. The Mosad has always been opposed to girls working on tractors, or in those agricultural branches, such as field crops, which demand strenuous physical labor; and no girl has ever volunteered to work in these branches. On the other hand, none of the boys works in the clothing or sewing rooms, although the Mosad has favored such work for them. Since the boys performed this work so poorly, and impeded the smooth operation of the work in these "service" jobs, it was decided that it would be best not to assign them to these branches.

In general the students are reported by their work supervisors to be good workers, a not unexpected finding in view of sabra desire for recognition and their realization that efficient work is a means to that end. That this is so is revealed in their responses to the Moral Ideology Test. Among all the activities which are said to elicit the praise or criticism of one's fellows, work is the activity most frequently cited by the students.

SOCIAL ACTIVITIES

The Movement. The Movement with which the students are affiliated is the youth movement which the founders of Kiryat Yedidim had organized while still in Europe.[10] Today it retains its original scouting and Zionist orientations, and has added a strong political orientation, as well. For both city and kibbutz children the political aspects of The Movement include the entire political program of The Party, with its emphasis on labor, a socialist state, and a pro-Eastern, international orientation. Indeed, The Movement, in its political aspects, may be viewed as The Young Party.

Structurally, each kevutza of the Mosad constitutes a kevutza in The Movement, and all the kevutzot constitute a "nest" (*ken*). Each kevutza has an appointed Leader (*madrich*), who is chosen either from among the older students in the Mosad or from the young Mosad graduates. Their immediate superior is the ken Organizer, who is both a member of the National Executive, as well as a member of the kibbutz. In the ken, unlike the Mosad, decisions are made for the students, not by them.

The activities of the kevutza — aside from such political activities as marching in political parades and obtaining signatures for the peace movement — are of an intellectual and a scouting

[10] See Spiro, *Kibbutz*, pp. 43–48.

nature. The former are arranged by the Leader, who, in consultation with the Educator, chooses a subject for discussion and investigation. One kevutza, for example, was studying anthropology at the time of our research; another was studying the "history of the 'group,' from the ancient family to the modern state."

The scouting aspect of The Movement includes hiking, camping, and forestry. Camping trips may be arranged by the kevutza or by the entire nest. Every three years The (National) Movement sponsors a national jamboree which includes, among other things, competition in various types of scouting activities.

In general, The Movement in the Mosad is not successful. The students seem to be apathetic to its program and display only a perfunctory interest in its meetings. The ken Organizer attributes its lack of success to the absence in the Mosad of the usual motivations for participation in youth movements — camaraderie, group belongingness, social activities, the opportunity to meet members of the opposite sex — since these needs are already filled by other aspects of Mosad life. It has been his experience, moreover, that a successful youth movement rests on rebellion against parents and the latter's way of life; and in the kibbutz The Movement is supported by the parents. The kibbutz nest, to be sure, attempts to encourage rebellion against certain aspects of contemporary kibbutz life — especially in those areas in which it has departed from its original ideals — but this does not increase the interest of the students; it may even have a reverse effect. When criticism is leveled against the kibbutz — for violations of its collectivistic ideals, for example — the students will often retort with, "So, are you saying that my father is not a good man?," or, "Why should the Mosad do things differently from the way they are done in the kibbutz?," or, "If the kibbutz has faults, they can be corrected when we become members, but not while we are still students."

Despite their lack of great interest in its program, initiation into The Movement seems to be an important event for the students, as we ourselves perceived while witnessing the annual installation ceremony.[11] Although not enthusiastic about the

[11] On the day of Lag Beomer, a spring nature festival, The Movement sponsors its annual scouting competition, and on the following night the installation is held, at which time members are formally initiated by being presented with their emblems, and awards and promotions are announced. The installation is a quasi-military event. It is held at night, in the light of giant torches and flares. Each kevutza is lined up in military fashion facing the ken Coordinator. As its name is called, the kevutza marches forward and salutes the Coordinator.

ceremony, the students were moved in some way since, as a chaver pointed out, they were quiet and orderly during the entire proceedings! That the initiates were impressed is revealed also by the fact that for more than a week after the ceremony they talked about their emblems with great pride. Moreover, in an article in the student magazine describing their first year in the Mosad, the members of the seventh grade referred to this initiation as "one of the profoundest experiences of the year."

Other activities. In addition to The Movement, whose five meetings a month are compulsory, there are numerous other activities which occupy the time and energies of the students. These activities, for the most part, are centered about a number of *chugim*, or clubs (literally, "circles"). Sponsored by the Cultural Committee, clubs meet once a week under the supervision of a faculty advisor. In addition to the choir and orchestra there are clubs devoted to literature, politics, science, chess, folk dancing, dramatics, and art. During our study it was decided that no student could participate in more than two clubs.

There are at least five other activities besides clubs which must be mentioned: the biweekly mesiba or convocation, athletics, the "literary trial," the student newspaper, and the Mosad annual. Unlike the clubs, the mesiba is an all-Mosad activity. Each mesiba is devoted to a different theme, such as politics, literature, dancing, or art. One mesiba which we observed was devoted, for example, to the folk songs and myths of different peoples. Each kevutza represented a different country, so that ranging from the seventh to the twelfth grade, respectively, the program included: Legends from the Bible, The Birth of the Hero, Chinese songs and legends, Russian songs and a Russian skit, American folk songs, Hindu dances. Holidays and their values may also constitute the theme of a mesiba.

In addition to the biweekly mesibot, a concluding mesiba at the end of the school year is presented for the entire kibbutz. This is an elaborate event, which requires many weeks of preparation on the part of both students and teachers. The program begins with an exhibit of the year's work, displayed in a number of rooms, and including the following features: paintings, handicrafts, scientific collections and exhibits, and the summary of the various projects conducted by each class during the year. Following the exhibit a program is presented consisting of modern dances, orchestral and band music, and a play.

Many of the students, particularly the males, are very much

interested in athletics, basketball being their favorite sport. When the weather permits, the outdoor basketball court is in constant use between classes and before meals, as well as at regular recreational periods. The Mosad, moreover, has a basketball team which competes with other teams, and great interest is displayed in its fortunes by the students.

Another activity, the Literary Trial (*mishpat sifruti*) is held annually. During the year all the students read a novel selected by the faculty (Steinbeck's, *The Pearl*, was the novel selected for the trial we observed) which forms the basis for the "trial." In the trial, which is conducted like a court proceeding — with judge, jury, witnesses, and prosecuting and defense attorneys — the main character in the novel is indicted and judged. Much time is devoted to the preparation of the trial, which usually lasts two successive nights.

Mention should be made of the student magazine which appears monthly during the academic year. It is edited by a staff which is headed by an editor-in-chief, and which enjoys the counsel of a faculty advisor. This magazine covers a variety of subjects, and includes many literary forms. A typical issue includes one or two editorials, essays —both humorous and serious — on diverse subjects, one or two short stories, a poem or two, some cartoons, and reports on the activities of various branches of the school. Almost all the contributions are by students, with an occasional report by a member of the faculty. The general level of the magazine, both substantively and editorially, is high.

This magazine, read in its entirety by almost all the students, is an important index of student opinion on a variety of subjects. A numerical listing of its articles from five issues published during the year of our study follows:

Problems and aspects of Mosad life	23
Problems and aspects of kibbutz life	8
Politics	6
Zionism	2
Problems of editorial staff	2
Short stories	2[12]
Movies	1

The articles on Mosad life included an essay on its gardens and landscaping; two complaining about the turmoil in the dining

[12] This is a spurious figure, for it refers not to two stories, but to two separate issues in which a series of short stories were published as part of a short story contest.

room; three on The Movement; two reports of the Cultural
Committee; one article criticizing the lack of interest in student
government; one giving the results of a poll on student self-
government; a humorous report of the Literary Trial; a report by
the Committee on Athletics; a survey of the year's work, written
by the principal; humorous cartoons of daily events; a series of
articles by a representative of each kevutza, surveying its year's
activity; and a report by all standing committees. They also
included a criticism of students who accept "bourgeois values"
when they visit in the cities; criticism of the poor spirit with
which the Mosad celebrates holidays and other events; criticism
of younger students for their lack of participation in group discussions; three articles criticizing the possession of money in the
Mosad; and a humorous essay on a student draft to exterminate
rats.

Articles on kibbutz life included such topics as the reasons for
the success of the kibbutz, in contrast to former utopian com-
munes; a poetic eulogy to Kiryat Yedidim; a humorous essay on
students who work in agricultural branches; opposition to hired
labor in the kibbutz; reaction of students to a meeting of the
executive committee of The Federation; the necessity to perpetuate kibbutz culture; a symposium on the desirability of
kibbutz industrialization; opposition to the introduction of private
property into the kibbutz.

The political articles included a criticism of the Army for
alleged maltreatment of the Arabs; a discussion of the lack of
ideological interest among the students; a criticism of the students
for their exclusive interest in Russian art and literature; a criticism
of the Scouts for being apolitical; a translation of an article by
Stalin; a symposium on the desirability of awarding prizes in a
socialist society.

The Zionist contributions included a poem by a professional
poet, and a defense of displaying the pictures of Herzl and Weiz-
mann in the dormitories.

Attitudes toward participation. Though the students are group-
oriented, many complain about the heavy round of activities that
is their daily routine. In the first place, some complain, it leaves
them physically fatigued, and it is true that, when they awaken
in the morning, the students are often visibly tired. Two recent
graduates of the Mosad, now working in the kibbutz, said that
they no longer feel tired (as they had in the Mosad) although

they were now working a full day. At 6:00 P.M., they pointed out, their work is done, and they can do what they please. In the Mosad, on the other hand, a whole new schedule of activities is just beginning at that hour.

Others complain, not because of the drain on their energies, but because of the lack of privacy which these activities, together with other aspects of group living, impose on them. The fact is, that the high school youth, like all children in the kibbutz, have almost no opportunity for privacy. The group is ubiquitous.[13]

One sometimes has the feeling, however, that some of the student complaints are an excuse for not giving more time to their studies. The students themselves place great value on the importance of group activity. Next to the *shvitzer* (see Chapter 15), the most disliked student in the Mosad is the one who refuses to accept group responsibilities, and who participates in few of its activities. When the senior class, for example, was interviewed, almost all the students referred spontaneously to one student who kept to himself, and who was seldom active in group activities, as an example of the wrong kind of student. And for the entire high school our interview data reveal that the active student is accorded the greatest prestige.

The Mosad authorities are aware of the full schedule of the students but they justify this schedule on social and intellectual grounds. The Children's Society, with its full program of activities, they maintain, is a framework which provides a "strong moral and social force" for the Mosad. If there were no formal structure of group activities, they argue, the students would have to invent their own activities. Of what would these consist? — spending time in their parental rooms, sleeping, or various forms of isolated activities (some of which might be undesirable) such as smoking, drinking, sex, or "just wasting time." They point to a neighboring kibbutz where, in the absence of a structured program of activities, this is exactly what is happening. In a Children's Society, however, this cannot occur. The existence of these activities, they argue, compels the students to participate almost every night in worthwhile intellectual and social experiences — experiences

[13] This constant round of activities not only places a premium on privacy, but it establishes an extreme routinization of the daily schedule. No wonder the students seek as many novel and nonroutinized experiences as possible. Hence there are numerous fads which come and go in the Mosad, such as dancing fads, the development of private newspapers, playing of records, competition in some work activity, worm-eating contests, and a contest to see who would eat the eye of a recently slaughtered cow.

"which are good for them and which they probably would not have had otherwise." [14]

SOCIAL CONTROL

Peers. Peers exercise informal, semiformal, and formal control. There are at least two types of informal peer control. Older children exercise a degree of social control over the younger both through imitation on the part of the younger as well as by instruction and reprimand on the part of the older. Instances of the latter are frequent: a group of children are eating in the dining room, for example, and an older girl criticizes the younger students for their poor table manners; or, the students are working in the fields and an older student criticizes a younger child for indolence or inefficiency. This is essentially an informal technique in which one student or a group of students acting informally exercise control over a fellow student by verbal criticism.

Another informal peer technique, one quite different from that mentioned above, consists in criticizing an offender by an appeal to the group values. This technique combines both peer and superego techniques, for one is exhorted by a peer to conform to group values on the assumption that one will feel bad (guilty or ashamed) if the violation is brought to one's attention.

Dan (ninth grade) had an argument with one of the refugee boys, and in anger called him "black and filthy." The latter retorted that such a statement on Dan's part was "in contradiction to all your values, and how can you claim to be a good kibbutznick if you do that?" Dan immediately apologized, saying that he did not mean anything by it, that it was "just a way of talking."

There are two types of semiformal peer control, as well. One type consists of criticizing an offender in the student magazine. Individuals are rarely criticized by the magazine, but many articles and editorials are devoted to deploring or criticizing some wrong in the Mosad and, in general, the criticism rests on an implicit or explicit appeal to the group values. It is difficult to assess the effectiveness of such criticism, but it is my guess that it is relatively ineffectual. The following types of behavior were

---

[14] On the other hand, the director of The Federation's Education Committee has himself expressed some doubts concerning the desirability of this intensive extracurricular program. He writes that the organized activities in the Mosad system train the child in such a way that he does not know what to do with his free time when he has any, for he has become accustomed to having all his activities planned for him.

the objects of criticism in editorials or articles in the sample of issues analyzed.

1. Students who complain, but who never have positive suggestions.
2. Lack of interest in Meetings.
3. Lack of classroom discipline.
4. Poor relations between boys and girls.
5. Swearing.
6. Acceptance of "bourgeois values" by students vacationing in cities.
7. Apathetic celebration of holidays and festivals.
8. Apathy to The Movement.
9. Lack of group participation of younger students.
10. Students who possess private money (it should be turned in to the Mosad treasury).

In rare instances, however, the magazine may become personal and, as the high school principal pointed out, since the respect of the group is a primary motivation for social conformity, such personal criticism is highly effective. For example:

A tenth-grade boy from the city was a braggart. Bragging is despised in the Mosad, so that he was the object of constant teasing. When the latter technique did not show any results, a cartoon appeared in the student magazine caricaturing his behavior. He resigned from the Mosad.

The latter example illustrates, as well, the use of aggression as a technique of social control. And this brings us to a second semi-formal technique of peer control. Students who violate important Mosad or kibbutz values frequently find themselves the objects of group derision and, if that is not effective, of physical attack. The instances to be cited below are important for two reasons: they show the extent to which this aggression may be carried, and they incidentally reveal some important student values. It should be noted that both verbal and direct physical aggression are employed.

Chanan (a seventh-grade boy) is interested in painting. Whenever the art teacher comes to the Mosad, he tries to be with her, and to obtain her help with his painting. The children have teased him about this, calling him a "shvitzer." Yesterday their taunts became so severe that he burst out crying and could not be consoled until much later, when the teacher spoke to him.

David, an eighth-grader from the city, was heartily disliked because of his lying and teasing, which the others found very annoying. They responded by hitting and even throwing things at him, but he persisted in his irritating behavior. One day when David was sick in the isolation ward, a group of boys whom he had particularly annoyed descended on him, stripped him of his clothing, and forced him outside. The high school authorities decided that the only effective method of preventing any more violence was to ask David to resign from the school.

The most extreme case occurred in the twelfth grade. Tamar was the most brilliant girl in the class, but she violated all the Mosad values. She would brag about her abilities, tease and taunt the others, show off her new dresses. Her peers responded with verbal aggression until her provocations became unbearable and, one day, they hung her by her hands to a tree.

Formal peer control, by either the kevutza or chevra, includes the use of such techniques as calling the student to a *beirur* or "clarification," ordering him to conform, and, finally, imposing some sanction. A most painful experience for the average student is the beirur. Should a student do something of which the group disapproves, it may demand that he "clarify" his conduct before the group. Since he dreads this more than almost any other experience, he usually behaves in such a manner as not to be called.

Should the beirur prove ineffective the kevutza may simply order a student to conform. To cite but one example: a committee had been appointed to plan for a large celebration, and one of the appointees refused to serve. The kevutza was called into session, and it voted that he must serve. The student acquiesced.

Should such a command be ineffective, the group then resorts to the more drastic technique of group sanction. It may give the student a difficult assignment in the kevutza or the Mosad as punishment for his behavior, or it may punish him by withdrawal of some privilege. When two students violated a polio quarantine, their kevutza voted to deprive them of all privileges for two weeks; and when a male student described, in coarse language, how a female student gets dressed in the morning, his kevutza voted that he not be given his emblem at the initiation ceremony of The Movement.

As a last resort, the group has the power of expulsion, a power which only one kevutza has ever exercised. This power is absolute. The teachers and other adults may attempt to change the students' minds, but they may not reverse the group decision.

The extraordinary importance of the peer group as an agent of social control is revealed by the Moral Ideology Test. Although peers play an important socialization role among the younger children, they are less important than the educators. In the high school, however, the positions are reversed. Peers are mentioned by students more than twice as frequently as educators (and more than three times as frequently as parents) as agents of socialization. It should be added that peers are mentioned in connection with positive and negative sanctions with almost equal frequency, whilst among the grade school children they are mentioned much more frequently in connection with positive than with negative sanctions.

If all others — named on the Moral Ideology Test as "others," "everyone," "the kibbutz" — be combined with members of the peer-group, "the group" becomes the overwhelmingly most important socialization agent for these students — almost three times as important as educators and almost four times as important as parents.

Adults. Adult techniques of social control are numerous. In the first place there is a simple appeal to reason. This may take a number of forms, two of which are revealed in the following examples.

In a seventh-grade geography class the teacher is asking questions, which the students are to answer aloud. They all attempt to answer simultaneously, and the resulting din precludes any discussion. The teacher responds a number of times with, "I can't listen to a choir."

A boy in the tenth grade was eating sunflower seeds in class. The teacher said it was unwise to do so, since this habit was "unhealthy."

A second technique is to deprive (or threaten to deprive) the students of some privilege. It is my impression, in the absence of quantitative data, that this technique is rarely employed by the teacher (though it is frequently employed by the kevutza).

The teacher was explaining to the students at a regular meeting of the kevutza the reasons for a particular decision which had been made by the Mosad authorities. They were indignant and constantly interrupted him. He said that if they continued to interrupt him he would adjourn the meeting. Later, as they continued in their obstreperous behavior, he pronounced the meeting adjourned.

For more serious breaches of Mosad norms, the deprivation is much greater.

On a hike of all the branches of The Movement in the Mosad, the senior class refused to participate in the night watch; instead, it left early in the evening to watch the movie in the kibbutz. The authorities decided that this was a serious matter, and punished the entire group by not permitting them to participate in the final ceremonies of the year, and by withholding their emblems which they were to have received at this time.

A third technique employed by the teacher, particularly with respect to classroom discipline, is to order or to request the student to comply with his demand. This is in general an ineffective technique — at best it is of temporary relief. Often, if neither the request nor the command is effective, the teacher may shout at the students to be quiet, and if this does not work, he may say that he will not continue until the students are quiet, and then wait until they become quiet. Generally they come to order after a short time.

A fourth method employed by the teacher is shame.

In the tenth grade, the teacher asks a girl to define a verb, but she pleads ignorance. Yair says that a noun is a bird, and laughs. Teacher tells him not to display his boorishness.

The teacher attempted to interest the eleventh grade in grammar. He said that they did not really know Hebrew grammar, although they spoke the language, that they did not even know the difference between a noun and a verb. He did not want them to be like "the farmer" who spoke prose for forty years without knowing it.

But most of the techniques employed by the teacher do not include the exercise of his own authority. Instead, he manipulates the situation so that the responsibility for ensuring conformity devolves on the group or the individual. We have already seen that almost all antisocial or nonconformist behavior which involves peer-interaction is handled by the group itself; but often it acts at the instigation of a teacher or teachers. If, for example, a difficulty or a problem arises and the teacher feels it ought to be met, he calls a meeting of the class, poses the problem, and asks them to suggest a solution. Hence, though it is the teacher who usually initiates the process, it is the group which imposes the sanction, so that instead of exercising authority himself, he delegates it to the peer-group.

The teacher not only asks the students to assume ultimate responsibility for the conduct of its members, but he also utilizes group decisions for the manipulation of the students' superego — a technique which we have already encountered in the grade school. Thus, since group edicts and decisions are, in general, accepted by the students as inviolate, teachers frequently appeal to such decisions in order to obtain compliance with their own demands. When the students wish to do something of which the teacher disapproves, he may say, "But you yourselves voted not to do it" (or, to do it), in order to obtain compliance.

A variant of this technique of appealing to the students' superego — probably the most frequent — is to remind the students of their great responsibilities to the kibbutz, of their noble future calling, of the hopes which The Movement and The Federation have reposed in them.

The reluctance of the teachers to exercise authority themselves, which ideologically[15] stems from the emphasis on a permissive and democratic social climate has two consequences: it gives great freedom to the students and, at the same time, it places great superego demands on them. For both reasons many persons — parents, students, and some teachers — have criticized the teacher for what they consider to be an abdication of his proper disciplinary role.

With respect to the first criticism a recent graduate of the Mosad expressed it this way. The students do not have enough discipline imposed by a superordinate authority and would welcome such authority. He characterized the present situation as similar to one in which a child has done something wrong, and waits to be punished, but the punishment does not come.

He is not unique in his sentiments. In a poll of upper classmen and recent graduates of the Mosad, conducted by the high school magazine, it was revealed that all the respondents, without exception, demanded greater discipline and authority from the teachers. Some of the responses to the question, "What is your opinion concerning the system of studies in the Mosad?" are quoted.

[15] We are not concerned with the personality characteristics of the teachers which make them reluctant to assume authority.

Male, senior, sabra (paraphrased): The system is "perfectly adapted to the need of kibbutz living," but the teachers and educators are not sufficiently strict with the students . . .

Male, graduate, sabra: There is too much freedom for the individual . . . The role of the "fearful teacher" of the old system must be played by the "criticizing chevra" in our system. If this cannot be guaranteed there is no basis for the success of our system.

Male, graduate, non-sabra: There is too much freedom . . . It is not necessary to appeal constantly to the conscience; it is desirable to use threats, even the threat of expulsion.

Male, graduate, sabra: When we first came to the Mosad I said: "This system will not work. The freedom will be turned into anarchy. A child is a child, and he'll exceed the limits . . ." The extreme freedom we have is not good . . .

By refusing to exercise greater personal authority, the teacher not only gives the students too much freedom, but, it is claimed, places too many demands on them. To ask the students to discipline their own erring members, said one Mosad official who is strongly opposed to this system, "is to impose too great a responsibility on them." A parent, discussing the technique of appeal to student conscience, complained that this is too great a burden for them to bear. It should be borne instead, he complained, by the teachers "through their proper exercise of authority and discipline."

Students feel the same. Responding to the poll referred to above, a senior wrote:

In general the system is not good. Each of us is given an overabundant use of our conscience. Our system appeared excellent at first in contrast to the older system which created tensions and fears in the child. But this system doesn't work; there must be external demands . . . and not leave everything to conscience.

Discussing this situation, a graduate of the Mosad made the same point. The students are always made to feel, he said, that they must work hard, study hard, and so on, because of the great responsibility that is theirs. When they participate in an inter-kibbutz contest of any kind, they feel they must do well since their performance reflects not only on them as individuals, but on the entire kibbutz. His was the first class to be graduated from the Mosad, and they were constantly reminded of their consequent responsibilities — since they were the first, they must do well so as to set an example for the others. This, he protested, imposes on the students a constant burden of conscience.

That the students chafe under this burden of conscience is indicated by another incident. In discussing an emotionally disturbed student, a senior noted that the student was not treated kindly by the others. He then turned on me, asking, "What do you think? We're different from anyone else?"

The burden of conscience is exacerbated, according to one parent, when the students begin to work in the kibbutz economy. For then, he said, the students are reminded in many implicit ways (and sometimes explicit, too) that the time has come for them "to repay their debt" to the kibbutz for "everything it has done for them."

Many teachers agree that this appeal to conscience is not a desirable technique. But, complained one teacher, "What other technique is available?" The use of greater discipline on the part of the teacher, he claimed, would be ineffective since the student always has a refuge. Whenever he is criticized, he goes to his parents, who always side with him. In short, this teacher went on to say, "there is always a piece of sugar waiting for him at home."

TURMOIL

It is difficult to decide whether the now familiar *Sturm und Drang* experience of Western adolescence is found among kibbutz adolescents. Both teachers and parents attest to the fact that many students experience some type of adolescent emotional disturbance. Even parents, whose defenses were usually mobilized in answering the Questionnaire, were quite prepared to concede this point. Of the nine adults with adolescent children who answered the question, "Did your child undergo a 'crisis' during adolescence?," three answered, "definitely yes," three answered, "perhaps yes," and one did not respond; the remaining two answered, "no."

Teachers too report the existence of adolescent personality problems. In analyzing our teacher interviews the following conclusions emerged: at least 16 or 21 per cent of the students from Kiryat Yedidim were sufficiently disturbed to elicit the attention of their teachers and/or students. These included a girl who suffers from nightmares; two highly neurotic boys, who are characterized by extreme insecurity and lack of self-confidence; a neurotic girl who is a passive, dependent type without self-confidence, and with little ability to concentrate; a highly withdrawn girl who interacts with a minimum of affect; three enuretics — two boys and a girl — one of whom is also a thumb-sucker; an aggressive, "cold" girl who is described by her teacher as having "no soul"; a boy with a serious emotional block to studying; five highly aggressive boys; and a boy who is probably schizophrenic.

Despite this incidence of disturbance — it is impossible to assess the significance of these figures, since there are no comparative data available — the question of adolescent *Sturm und Drang* remains an open one. We feel confident, however, that kibbutz adolescence — whatever the eventual evaluation of adolescent adjustment may be — is qualitatively different from the typical adolescent pattern described in professional journals and monographs.[1] This statement is based on an analysis of three areas which usually occasion or undergo some stress in our own culture during adolescence — aggression, sex, and relationship to parents.

AGGRESSION

Introduction. That the students in the Mosad are highly aggressive will be noted shortly. But it should be emphasized that there are no manifestations that correspond, even roughly, to what we term "juvenile delinquency." Nor is this surprising. Those kinds of juvenile delinquency that are motivated by such needs as social prestige, desire for material things, conspicuous consumption, the desire to belong (as well as to hurt those who prevent one from belonging), or by such cultural characteristics as invidious social class differences or poverty, are unlikely to be found in the kibbutz. None of these motives operates in the Mosad. They are effectively muted by the social structure of the kibbutz. All the students wear the same kind of clothes, which none of them own. All of them enjoy the same, relatively high, standard of living. The absence of social classes, in either an economic or social sense, means the absence of invidious comparisons and competitive prestige as a function of family background. No one, in other words, is excluded or made to feel inferior because of family or class affiliation. No one is left out because he lives "on the other side of the tracks," and no one feels inferior because his family is poor or dirty or immigrant or speaks with an accent. In short, there are few objective conditions that can give rise to feelings of deprivation, whether of material goods or of social prestige, and, hence, to that kind of juvenile delinquency which is motivated by desire for revenge or by the desire to bolster one's feelings of low self-esteem.

But self-esteem, though frequently a function of group-acceptance, is not always a function of social structure. Persons may be rejected by the group because of personal characteristics, and the

---

[1] One thing is evident — whatever its intensity or form, kibbutz adolescent turmoil is not somaticized. We did not observe a single instance of acne among the Mosad sabras. On the contrary, one is immediately struck, on meeting the students, by their clear complexions.

unpopular adolescent, who feels that he does not belong and is not wanted, is generally miserable. This source of misery, too, is absent from the Mosad. Some students, to be sure, are unpopular; and they know it. But no student is ever left out and therefore made to feel rejected, because of his unpopularity. And this is not because kibbutz adolescents are kinder than adolescents elsewhere, but because of the social structure of the Mosad. All activities encompass the entire group, so that everyone has an equal opportunity to participate in the group activities. There are no private parties from which certain students are excluded, nor are there other forms of exclusion. In short, there is no differential group participation. Students may, of course, form personal friendships, but such friendships are never the basis for exclusive group activities. These always comprise the entire kevutza, or the entire Mosad, or the entire branch of the Youth Movement.

Although aggression does not assume delinquent forms in the Mosad, it does exist, and it is expressed in many ways. Like most of our other categories, however, it is all but impossible to evaluate its significance for lack of comparative data. Although the opinions of the teachers are of little weight (for they too have no basis for comparisons) it should be noted that they were sufficiently disturbed by what they felt was an unusually high degree of aggression in the Mosad, to have devoted a number of faculty meetings to this problem. They were particularly disturbed, according to the report of one of the teachers, by the cruelty found among some of the students.

Despite the teachers' concern, I am confident that interpersonal aggression — at least in its physical form — is much less frequent in the Mosad than it is among the younger children. Whereas physical aggression is the most important cause for anger among the grammar school children — as revealed by the Emotional Response Test, at any rate — it is among the least important for the high school students. And, of the two possible hypotheses which could account for this downward shift — accommodation to aggression, or a diminution in aggression — our observations would support the latter.[3]

Interpersonal aggression is found in a number of forms other than physical attack — gossip, teasing, laughter, name-calling,

[3] The evidence from the Emotional Response Test with respect to verbal aggression, however, is ambiguous. Though there is a diminution in the frequency of anger responses caused by aggression, there is an increase in the frequency of sadness responses.

and so on; and it is expressed against a number of persons — teachers and other adults, kevutza peers, students who fall into certain socially disliked categories, younger students, outside students, and refugees and other immigrants.

Racism. In general, students are aggressive toward strangers, that is, persons from outside the kibbutz. Hence, it is difficult to decide whether aggression against some of the teachers is a function of their status as teacher or as outsider;[4] or whether aggression against some of the city children is really instigated by their aggression, or is merely a function of their status as outsiders. On the other hand, there is no question but that the following incident is to be attributed to simple out-group aggression. When a group of students from a neighboring kibbutz first entered the Mosad, the students from Kiryat Yedidim were hostile toward them, particularly toward the girls. They teased them whenever they recited in class, so that to this day they are reluctant to speak up. There were several instances, moreover, in which the boys of Kiryat Yedidim physically beat the girls from this neighboring kibbutz.

The immigrant children bear the brunt of this out-group aggression. Many students, ideologically in favor of immigration, are hostile to the immigrants from the Middle East, whom they view as inferiors — they call them *shchorim,* "black ones." They are the constant butts of verbal aggression, taunting, and teasing. European immigrants may also be the objects of hostility. The Mosad authorities decided that, instead of remaining as a group apart, the Polish immigrant students should be integrated with the other children. But these refused to live with the kibbutz children (because of their aggression) and threatened to leave the Mosad if the proposed integration were pushed through.[5]

---

[4] In general the students are better disciplined in classes taught by kibbutz, than by non-kibbutz, teachers.

[5] The racist attitude of the Mosad youth is shared by the adult sabras — as indeed it is shared by the older adults. "Things were good in the country," remarked a sabra, "until the shchorim came." A female sabra, referring to my previous research among "shchorim" (in Micronesia), said, sneeringly, that I approached the kibbutz as if it were a tribe of shchorim.

This attitude may be seen in work activities as well. The sabra who supervises the work of the youth in the gardens is consistently more demanding of the oriental youth than of the Mosad students. When it was decided that the former could have an extra day for their vacation, the sabra supervisor became furious at their "indolence," although this extended their vacation to only ten days, whereas the Mosad students had three weeks.

The immigrant children feel like pariahs as a result of this treatment. Describing their year's experience in an article in the student Annual, the members of this group wrote:

> We do not feel part of the Mosad. The other children laugh at us and do not accept us as friends and comrades . . . We feel lonely and lost.

This prejudice against immigrants extends beyond the immigrant students, for it includes the adult immigrants as well. A group of new immigrant workers was employed by the Mosad in its construction program and, of course, they were invited to eat their meals in the Mosad dining room. This created a serious problem, however, for some of the students refused to eat at the same tables with them. A girl in the seventh grade stood up and walked away when one of these workers sat at her table. It made her ill, she said, to sit at the same table with "them" — they didn't know any Hebrew, and besides they were "the new immigration."

Aggression against adults. Teachers are the primary adult victims of aggression. One expression of this type of aggression is to be found in the poor classroom discipline commented on previously. The following examples give some notion of the magnitude of the disorder. That such disorder is, among other things, an expression of aggression (disobedience) is indubitable. The students know that the teacher desires order, yet they refuse to comply with his request.

> The teacher (female) of the eighth grade and I enter the class, and she explains that I have come to observe. The children begin to shout and scream, and she cannot get their attention. When the geography lesson finally begins, each child talks at will, insisting that he be heard above the shouting of the others. She cannot discipline them . . . After the intermission, the children enter the classroom with great shouting. They cannot be calmed. Teacher asks questions, and they all answer at once. She refuses to continue until there is quiet, but there is no quiet. The children blurt out whatever idea they have as soon as it arises. . . . One boy becomes angry because the teacher calls on another when he — so he insists — had his hand up first. . . . Teacher reprimands boy for disturbing, and he laughs. Another boy beats a rhythm on the desk. Teacher shouts at children but cannot control them. (At least half of her time is spent trying to obtain order.)

The ninth grade is discussing the Jewish community in ancient Alexandria. The class is in constant turmoil, and at times it is impossible to hear what is being said. The children walk in and out of the class, and move about the room to get books or paper. Some, instead of walking, slide across the desks to get what they want. To add to the confusion, children shout, *"sheket!"* (quiet!), to others.

After writing their answers to a history questionnaire, the ninth-grade students are called upon by the teacher (male) to read their answers aloud. They say whatever comes to mind without waiting for teacher to call on them, interrupting another speaker if necessary . . . A boy does not want to answer a question and walks out of class, only to be called back by teacher . . . a boy is reading a paper, another is drawing a map, a girl is eating sunflower seeds. . . . A discussion ensues on plans for a program. The suggestion of the executive committee is presented. This creates such a furor that the class cannot be quieted for at least five minutes: all shout at one another, insisting that the suggestion is either good or bad; and teacher is helpless.

(Early morning class in biology — male teacher, non-kibbutz member.) Only half the eleventh grade is present, but it is difficult to get order. Teacher begins lecture, but girls are looking at pictures, and will not listen. . . . They discuss the possibility of starting a project on "the Dead Sea." This leads to the mention of a hike they had taken to the Dead Sea the previous year. Teacher cannot get order. For twenty minutes there is talk and argument about this hike; emotions are high, voices strained, and all ignore teacher's plea to return to the subject at hand. . . . Near the end of the lesson, two boys begin to wrestle in class, hitting and pinching one another. Girl shouts at them to stop. They ignore both her and teacher.

Class begins with two boys looking at ancient coins and talking together as teacher (male) of eleventh grade tries to begin. Teacher asks them a number of times to stop, but they continue to talk while he lectures. . . . Kibbutz electrician walks by classroom with wire for the new dormitory. Girl jumps up and down with joy. Other students ask her what she sees. Noise becomes terrific, and teacher cannot continue . . .

(Early morning class in Marxism — male teacher.) Twenty minutes after class begins, two boys of the twelfth grade walk in, talking, laughing, stopping to talk to other students as they make their way to their desks . . . Some students are sleeping, some bored, some are talking, two are reading newspaper, some are catching flies, others are fighting, or laughing . . . Suddenly they all decide to participate in discussion. The result is bedlam, everyone shouting at once.

It should be noted that these disciplinary problems tend to diminish in grades eleven and twelve of the Mosad. It is not the youngest students, however, but those in the middle range —

ninth- and tenth-graders — who present the greatest problems.

Students are not only disobedient; they are also insolent. A universal characteristic of the sabras, according to almost all observers of the kibbutz movement, is their *chutzpah* or insolence, a characteristic which we found in the grade school students as well. The sabras have little respect for authority, per se, and they have few compunctions about criticizing authority figures. It might be argued that there is a difference between a student who feels completely secure in his relationship with the teacher, and who, as a consequence, acts "fresh" in class, and a student who is insolent; I accept this distinction. Thus one might argue that it is the secure, not the insolent student, who retorts with *"lo nachon"* — that is incorrect — to some statement of the teacher. This student feels that the teacher is wrong, and says so without fear of punishment. Or, it might be claimed, it is the fresh, not the insolent student who, when the class suggests that they meet outside and the teacher insists that they meet in the classroom, retorts with, *"maichpat lecha?,"* What difference does it make to you? The cases below, however, have an altogether different ring. They do not reflect a merely "brash" or "fresh" attitude. It is insolence, rather, which is their outstanding characteristic.

Girl is not listening, and teacher (male kibbutz member) of the ninth grade tells her to do what rest of class is doing. She says that she *is* doing what the rest of the class is doing — wasting time!

Some ninth-grade students come in late to class, singing. Teacher (non-kibbutz male) tells them to leave the room. They become hostile and argue with him, finally leave by jumping over the desks. . . . Later they pass the room, say something derisive to teacher, and pass on.

Girl is disturbing ninth-grade class in English, and teacher tells her to be still. Girl says, "What for? You haven't taught us a thing all year anyway."

Teacher (non-kibbutz male) asks how long Israel is. The tenth-grade students do not know, and become angry at him for asking such a question. "We never memorized it," says one boy in disdain.

Teacher (non-kibbutz male) of the tenth grade asks children to be quiet, to no avail. He calls on girl to read; she says, no. He says, "I told you, not asked you." She replies, "I told you, not asked you that I did not want to." . . . Class is in state of disorder . . . Teacher stops lesson, saying there is no point in continuing as no one is listening.

They agree, saying it is very boring. He tries to discuss it with them, and they shout at him as if he were a fellow student.[6]

It is to be noted, in conclusion, that the students not only behave disrespectfully toward authority figures, but that respect for authority is an unimportant value for them. This conclusion may be inferred from the results of the Moral Ideology Test. Obedience to, or disobedience of, authority for the children of a Midwest American community, comprises 20 per cent of their responses to this test.[7] The corresponding figure for the kibbutz subjects is 4 per cent. Indeed proper respect for authority is the least important of all the values mentioned in the test.

Peer aggression. There is some evidence to suggest that much of the hostility feelings that give rise to interpersonal aggression are evoked by peers. In the Emotional Response Test, to be specific, 70 per cent of all provocations to anger mentioned by the students are caused, whether wittingly or unwittingly, by peers. How much of this hostility is then expressed directly against them, and how much is expressed in some other way, we do not know.

Peer aggression may be classified into six categories. First, there is aggression against violators of group values (see pp. 309–310). The second category consists of generalized group gossip, which, according to the high school principal, is a favorite student pastime.

Derision is a third form of peer aggression. Typical examples follow.

Teacher returns a questionnaire to the members of his eighth-grade class, reading the names and the answers of those who did well and those who did poorly. When he reads the latter answers, the rest of the class laugh scornfully.

Teacher in ninth grade explains a grammatical construction for the fifth time, for the benefit of Ron, who does not understand it. Tamar calls Ron a "fool." Rivka laughs at him. Ron becomes angry, says, "What are you laughing at? You don't understand it either."

[6] Some teachers find it impossible to teach under such difficult psychological conditions and, if they are not members of the kibbutz, they resign. Just prior to our arrival, an English teacher resigned because of the continuous chutzpah to which he was exposed. The students consistently came to class late, laughed at his Hebrew, and criticized his teaching methods. Finally he quit — which was the original aim of the students.

[7] Havighurst and Neugarten, *American Indian and White Children,* p. 106.

Teacher in tenth grade calls on Yael; she says she does not know the answer. Yehuda, sarcastically, says she "never listens to anything." She says angrily, "Do you know that I was ill?" He says with disdain, "So why didn't you tell him that?"

Derision often turns into simple name-calling, such as: *Nilavok*, Your father should die (this is not a Hebrew term); *mamzer*, bastard; *chamor*, ass; *tipesh*, fool; *menuval*, abomination.

While the above-mentioned names are reserved for special situations, the following phrases seem to punctuate any conversation, whether with peers or with adults.

Al tevalbel et ha-rosh (don't confuse the head): This is the invariable reply of the person whose statement has been contradicted or disagreed with, or who thinks that the other has raised an irrelevant matter.

Al tedaber shtuyot (don't speak foolish things): This is the response to a statement with which one disagrees. Instead of refuting the statement with evidence, the student insults the person who makes it.

Hishtagata? (have you gone mad?): The ubiquitous retort to any idea, statement, proposal, with which one disagrees. This is probably the most frequently heard phrase in the Mosad.

Ma ichpat lecha? (what concern is it of yours?): This, incidentally, is the favorite form of chutzpah that the students use against adults; and (because?) the latter become infuriated by it. It is also employed, of course, in conversation with peers. A teacher may tell a student to be quiet or not to interfere with someone else; he may ask him why he was late to class or why he did not go to work: and the response is "ma ichpat lecha?", that is, I don't see why this should concern you. Or, what difference does it make to you? Or, why should you butt into this?

A fourth form of peer-aggression consists of generalized rudeness and ill-manners toward one's fellows. Sabras seldom observe such simple amenities as greeting a fellow student with a "hello," or saying "thank you" when some courtesy has been extended them. More important is their disruptive behavior during public performances. Often they are so obstreperous during a mesiba, that it is all but impossible to hear what is being said from the platform. The following excerpt is typical.

The chairman calls for order, but he cannot obtain it. Finally RUTH (the faculty advisor) tries to quiet them, and she is successful — for a few minutes. This lack of order and of silence continues throughout the program. At times the noise is so great that it is impossible to hear the students who are performing on the stage.[8]

This disrespect for peers finds other expressions as well. The student magazine complained editorially, for example, that most articles submitted for publication are written in pencil, and on dirty scraps of paper, without punctuation.

A fifth form of aggression consists of mild forms of hazing, bullying, and practical jokes. The favorite objects of such behavior are the younger students. That the older children bully the younger is well known; they dominate them and subject them to a kind of hazing. I was unable to discover the exact nature of this behavior. The students in the grade school are aware of this hazing, and express genuine anxiety about entering the Mosad. At the sixth-grade graduation party, for example, almost all the students said they were afraid to enter the Mosad. Although none articulated the reasons for this fear, one of the teachers feels that at least one of them was this fear of hazing. He also suggested that one of the causes of the perceptible change in the children once they enter the Mosad — from outgoing and poised, to shy and withdrawn children — is this hazing experience.

But the younger children are not the only victims of this type of behavior. The infinitive, *le-sader,* is a ubiquitous term in the Mosad. This term, which literally means "to fix," or "to put in order," has undergone a shift in connotation to one similar to the American slang expression, "to fix him good." If one says that he intends to *le-sader* someone, he means that he intends to play some practical joke on him, such as causing him to miss a bus, obtain the wrong book, attend the wrong class, and so on. Such behavior is practiced with sufficient frequency that the students frequently suspect their fellows of trying to "fix" them.

A final form of aggression is physical attack, which we have already indicated to be infrequent; and it is used almost exclusively as a technique of social control. There is one instance of fantasied physical aggression, however, which we feel merits mention here because of the social attitude, as well as the intensity

[8] This expression of hostility toward peers is identical, of course, with their undisciplined behavior in the classroom, which we have interpreted as hostility toward the teachers. Such behavior characterizes attendance at kibbutz affairs as well. The following excerpt, recorded at a kibbutz mesiba attended by Mosad students, is representative.

The students from the Mosad, and particularly the girls, made so much noise that it was difficult to hear the speakers on the stage. Their giggling and whispering in loud tones persisted during the speeches as well as the dramatic presentation.

of hostility, which it expresses. This case involves Avraham, the eleventh-grade boy who, we feel, is schizophrenic.

When it became known that Avraham was to return to the kibbutz after having been away for a year, his kevutza had a long discussion, led by their mechanech, about how this might affect them. At least two of the students argued that he should not be readmitted to the group. In the biological world, they argued, an organism dies if it cannot adapt. Analogously, Avraham should be rejected. (They finally agreed to accept him.)

It should be noted that many students do not participate in these various forms of aggression, and some oppose them. Avraham, for example, had a protector — a fellow student (female) who would go out of her way to help him and to draw him into the group activities whenever possible. So, too, despite their use of derision, only rarely do students exploit the disabilities of their peers for aggressive ends. Avner, for example, is a sixteen-year-old enuretic. The entire kevutza knows of his difficulty, because every morning he hangs out his wet sheets and pajamas to dry. But no one has ever teased him about it.

It should be noted finally that though the students aggress against each other, they maintain their solidarity in the face of outside interference. They may punish or taunt a fellow student, but they resent someone else who does it. Even in the case of Tamar — the most hated of all — this solidarity is maintained. When an English teacher (non-kibbutz member) chastised her in class, the students not only demanded that he "explain and clarify" his behavior, but they insisted that he be fired.

SEX

Sexual conflict. The sexual conflicts that are frequently at the core of adolescent turmoil in our own society do not seem to be strong in the Mosad. When sexual problems occur, they do not seem to form the basis for morbid or obsessive thoughts or fantasies; nor are sex, sexual exploits, and sexual attractiveness the basis for much of social behavior. These findings are not unexpected in view of the culture of the kibbutz and the social structure of the Mosad.

To the extent that the sexual problem of adolescence involves more than glandular development, and is concerned, rather, with curiosity about the body and the "mystery" of sexuality, the formal structure of the Mosad, as well as the students' past experiences, would tend to preclude the development of sexual problems. From infancy through adolescence boys and girls are exposed to both the bodies and sexual anatomy of the opposite sex. They have, as youngsters, slept and bathed together, gone to the toilet together; and even now they sleep in the same rooms together. The obsession to *see* is probably absent. In addition, their sex education, which began at an early age, has been open, frank, and intelligent.[9] Hence, anxiety about anatomical and physiological changes is undoubtedly minimized, if not eliminated, and obsession with sex, which often results from viewing it as a great mystery or (as among certain groups in our own society) as sinful or dirty, does not occur among these students. They are taught that the sex drive is normal and natural, that it is neither sinful on the one hand, nor of overwhelming importance on the other.

Moreover, the host of sexual stimuli that evoke sexual fantasies in adolescents in our society — pictures, billboards, magazines, movies — are not found in the kibbutz; so too such artificial techniques as cosmetics and perfume for arousing sexual desire are taboo. The normal sex drives of these adolescents are, for the most part, effectively sublimated in their busy and exhausting round of classes, work, and extracurricular activities.

Finally, "dating," and all its attendant problems, is absent from the Mosad. All social activities are group- rather than couple-oriented; so that the student attends any social affair as a member of his kevutza (a group which includes both boys and girls) or as an individual. But he never attends as the partner of a person of the opposite sex. Though the couple phenomenon, in the form of "going steady," exists, the casual date is unheard of. A girl is not invited to a dance by one boy, to a swimming party by another, and to a movie by still another. Indeed, unless she is going steady, she is not invited to any affair by any boy. She (and he) goes alone, with her kevutza, or with certain members of it.

In short, a major sociological determinant of sexual maladjustment in our society is not to be found in the Mosad. For dating, with its values of competitive success, prestige, and the "dating and rating" complex; with its demands for clothes and the concern for style and fashion; with its demand for money (on the part of the male); with its implications of rejection and exclusion for

---

[9] It should be noted, however, that despite their sexual education a recent graduate of the Mosad said that, in her opinion, the girls in the Mosad are sexually naïve and should be given more sex education. A teacher, on the other hand, informed me that she was amazed to discover, when lecturing on sex to her seventh-grade class — she lectured separately to the boys and to the girls — that they already knew everything; indeed, she claimed, they knew more than she did about certain matters.

those who are not "popular" — all these are absent in the kibbutz.

Moreover, no girl need worry lest she not be invited on a Saturday night date, and no boy need be alarmed because he is unable to obtain a date. No one need be anxious about his poor dancing, his inability to engage in small talk, his lack of a "line," and so forth. Since dating does not exist in the Mosad, a major obsession of American adolescent culture, and the whole host of anxieties and tensions that derive from it, are absent as well.

Adult attitudes. Although sex is viewed by the Mosad (and by the kibbutz) authorities as a natural, rather than as an evil or sinful, appetite, and although the mixed dormitories (and formerly, mixed showers) are vigorously defended, they are (following the philosophy of The Movement) opposed to sexual intercourse among the students. This paradox must be explained.

The Mosad is an educational institution; its task, as it sees it, is to impart knowledge, skills, and values to its students. All three are imparted in the classroom, but many values and skills are also acquired through participation in the many extracurricular activities sponsored by the Mosad. Were sexual intercourse permitted or encouraged, it is felt, students' interests and energies would be withdrawn from their studies and from the many group activities which are such important preparation for their future lives. By discouraging sexual behavior, therefore, the authorities seek to channel adolescent energies in these culturally important activities. Nevertheless, should a couple be genuinely in love, the authorities will not interfere with their sexual activities. Such couples are left to themselves unless their relationship proves to be socially and/or emotionally disruptive. When the latter happens, students, as well as teachers, may take action, as the following example indicates.

The couple in question consisted of a fifteen-year-old girl and an eighteen-year-old boy. The Mosad authorities became concerned about this case because they felt that the girl was too young to be involved in such a relationship. Because she was with her boy friend almost every evening and did not return to her room until the early hours of the morning, she did not participate in Mosad activities, she did not have time to prepare her lessons, and she was too tired to be alert in class. Her kevutza, too, was concerned, because they felt that she had, in effect, broken away from them. The kevutza, probably at the instigation of its mechanech, called her to a beirur in which she was censured for her behavior. She apparently took their criticisms to heart, for she began to change her mode of living, at least to the extent of getting to sleep at an earlier hour, and fulfilling her academic responsibilities.

Unfortunately, we do not have direct data on parental attitudes toward sexual behavior among their adolescent children. The questions on the Questionnaire which were designed to measure parental attitudes toward sex refer to all premarital intercourse, and not merely in the period of adolescence. If we may assume, however, that parental attitudes regarding this age are less permissive than their attitudes toward post-high-school sexuality, we may perhaps draw some not invalid conclusions from the results of the Questionnaire. Dichotomizing their responses — by combining the responses of "definitely yes" and "perhaps yes" into one category, and their responses of "definitely no" and "perhaps no" into another — the results reveal that more than half the parents believe that they should attempt to ensure their children's virginity until marriage.[10]

Student attitudes and interests. Despite their sexually "enlightened" environment, certain aspects of sexual shame found in our own society are found among these students, as well. Its most instructive expression is to be found in the abolition of the mixed showers, an instance of paramount theoretical importance but one which, unfortunately, remains somewhat obscure.

Until a few years before this study, boys and girls showered together, and, according to the Mosad principal, they accepted this system without protest until the Mosad adopted the policy of admitting students from the city. The latter opposed the prevailing practice, and some viewed it as an opportunity for smutty and obscene behavior. These city students, with their typical Western attitude toward sex, were responsible for the abandonment of the mixed showers.

A teacher reports that it was the girls (of the kibbutz) who favored the abolition of the mixed showers, which they viewed as "a form of torture." The girls, he said, matured more rapidly than the boys, and their developed secondary sexual characteristics were the objects of taunts and teasing. It is not clear, however,

---

[10] It is interesting to observe that, despite the sexual egalitarianism of the kibbutz, both male and female respondents show a slight tendency toward a double standard. Of eleven respondents, three believed that a mother should ensure her son's virginity until marriage, but five believed that she should ensure her daughter's virginity. Of sixteen respondents, five believed that a father should ensure his son's virginity, but six believed that he should ensure his daughter's virginity.

whether it was the boys from the cities or from the kibbutz who were responsible for this teasing behavior.[11]

Granting that pressure for the abolition of mixed showers came primarily from the city children, they received no little assistance from many kibbutz parents. Many parents (as well as teachers) opposed the mixed showers from its very inception. Some parents informed us that sexual shame about nudity is "instinctive," and that it was wrong to expose the students to such an experience. Others thought that mixed showers caused sexual fears, and opposed them on this basis. Hence, the student opposition to mixed showers, said one parent, proves that "the children's instincts are superior to the educators' theories."

It is difficult to assess the degree to which student attitudes to mixed showers reflect those of their parents. Since the latter's attitudes, however, generally have considerable influence on their children, the opposition to, and the shame felt in, the mixed showers may well be a result (among other things) of parental influence, however subtly it may have been expressed.

In any event, the great majority of kibbutz students are opposed to the restoration of the mixed showers. In interviews with twenty-two students over the age of fourteen, only three said they favored the restoration of the mixed showers, and one was neutral. The reasons given by the opponents are identical with those suggested by the adults for its abolition. Eight of the eighteen opponents stressed the difficulty of maintaining mixed showers past pre-puberty or puberty, because of the differential rate of sexual maturation and the attendant discomfort for the girls caused by the curiosity and shaming behavior of the boys. Ten discounted this factor and stressed, instead, the embarrassment caused by showering with outsiders — either from the city or from other kibbutzim. Had their original kevutza remained intact, they said, they would have no opposition to the mixed showers.

Much of the sexual shame that led to the abolition of the mixed shower continues to characterize the attitude of some of the girls in their rooms as well. Most of the girls, for example, attempt to conceal their nudity from the boys. Even in the hot summers that are typical for Kiryat Yedidim girls wear night clothes so that, should the sheets fall off the bed, they are not exposed. Boys and girls undress in the dark, with their backs to each other to avoid exposure. At the same time there seems to be an unwritten code among them condemning voyeurism for, with but one exception,

---

[11] Both interpretations are consistent with the sequence of events that precipitated the mixed shower problem in the Grammar School. See pp. 279–280.

there have been no complaints about this. In spite of all these pre-
cautions, however, not one of the student interviewees preferred
to live in unisexual dormitories. On the contrary, all of them
stressed the importance of bisexual living because, they said, it is
less boring; it reduces the sexual curiosity and sexual tensions that
accompany the separation of the sexes; and it contributes to group
solidarity.

Although, as we shall observe, there does not seem to be a
great deal of overt sexual behavior among these students, their
sexual interest and curiosity appear to be strong. Much of their
gossip, for example, centers about boy-girl relationships, and
especially about the couples. Their curiosity about the sexual activities of others is not necessarily confined to gossip. A recent
graduate of the Mosad claimed that the girls, at least, always
know about the sexual behavior of the couples because the girls
tell each other what they do with their boy friends.

Equally strong is their interest in the sex life of the adults,
whose sexual irregularities seem to be well-known to them. The
ninth-grade students, for example, like their parents, were well
aware of the sexual exploits of the father of one of their classmates.
Indeed, when his son criticized a girl in the classroom, she retorted
with "You should be quiet, since your father has a concubine
(*pilegesh*)." The students of another class were intrigued by the
fact that the divorced father of one of them was having an affair
with the divorced mother of another; and, when they were married, the girls in this class stayed up until two o'clock in the
morning excitedly discussing the marriage.

Although the students have a strong interest in sexual matters,
the teachers claim that theirs is a "healthy" interest, in contrast
to the salacious interest of many non-kibbutz children. Kibbutz
students, they claim, seldom, if ever, tell dirty stories, nor do they
employ sexually obscene words. Moreover, though the younger
students may giggle at the sexual passages in the Bible and are
frequently embarrassed by them, this attitude seems to disappear
after a year or two.

An important measure of healthy sexual attitudes is afforded
by sexual fantasies, but, unfortunately, we have almost no data
in this area. None of the students gave sexual responses to the
Rorschach, but it is our impression that they suppressed any
sexual percepts. One student, for example, told his teacher that
one of the Rorschach plates was obviously that of a man and
woman copulating, but that he was embarrassed to tell the ethnographer. Again, when the girls asked what the ethnographer did

with the boys when he took them from class, this same student said that he undressed them in order to take their physical measurements.

The one spontaneous fantasy obtained in the Mosad was developed by the ninth-grade students. Shortly after the disappearance of one of the girls in this class while on a hiking trip near the Syrian border, her fellow students in the ninth grade asked their English teacher if he were going to the circumcision ceremony. When he asked to whose circumcision they were referring, they said, the circumcision of the son of Miryam (the girl who had disappeared) and Pasha (her putative abductor) which will occur in nine months. It seems that their sexual fantasies were stimulated by Miryam's disappearance, and they had visions of the Syrians' raping her.

The teachers also claim that, as a result of the positive attitude of the Mosad and of the instruction which they receive, the students have no sexual fears. In the absence of comparative data it is impossible to evaluate the validity of such claims. However, it should be noted that the nurses can recall only one instance of menstrual difficulties among the girls — and this involved a delay in the onset of menses.

On the other hand, the girls in the ninth grade developed a fear of childbirth, and their nurse discovered that they would frequently talk about the pain involved. When she discussed this matter with them it became apparent that they had acquired this notion from a few girls whose mothers had told them that they loved them very much because of the pain they had suffered in giving birth. The nurse was shocked by this, and devoted much time to explaining the nature of childbirth to the girls, discussions which she believes were effective.

Sexual behavior. It is our impression that these students have less sexual experience than their counterparts in our own society. Homosexuality seems to be entirely nonexistent; the author observed no manifestations of it, nor did any respondent or informant report its existence. Masturbation exists — at least, so the teachers report — but we have no information on its incidence. The Mosad attitude toward masturbation is permissive, unless it is decided the student's behavior constitutes a problem either to himself or to others.

Heterosexual behavior does not begin in the Mosad, apparently, until the ninth grade; at least there are no reports of it, nor are any of the students for whom the author has information concerning heterosexual behavior in grades lower than the ninth. This means that heterosexual activity, if found at all, begins at about fifteen. At this age, an interest in sex, restricted almost exclusively to the girls, may be observed. Not directed toward the boys of their own kevutza whom they view as immature, hence, asexual, this interest is in the older students and the young unmarried males in the kibbutz. These girls, insists a recent graduate of the Mosad, are well aware of the attraction of their developing bodies, and are not unwilling to use them to attract males. In the heat of the day, for example, kibbutz field hands strip to the waist or, at least, to their undershirts. The Mosad girls who work in the fields remove their blouses, and work in undershirts. According to our informant, at least some of the girls remove their blouses with the specific intention of attracting the males.[12]

Although casual dating is nonexistent in the Mosad, "going steady" exists. Couples are known as *zugot* (sing., *zug*), the same term that is used in the kibbutz to refer to married couples. There is little question but that couples engage in the preliminaries of lovemaking, but it is only the rare couple that has a sexual affair. Indeed, according to all reports — from teachers, students, and former students — there seem to be almost no violations of the Mosad taboo on sexual intercourse. Two reasons, other than the simple motive to comply with Mosad norms, have been suggested for the observance of this taboo. A sophisticated graduate of the Mosad said that the girls while in the Mosad are opposed to sexual affairs as a kind of "instinctive self-preservation." Others say that its observance is a consequence of the absence of great sexual tension. As one former student put it, "We simply did not feel a need for it." It is my guess that most students are virgins when they graduate from high school.

The number of couples is small — with this statement everyone seems to agree — but the exact number is difficult to determine since only those that are publicly known came to our attention. These included a ninth-grade girl and a male senior, a male and female senior, a female senior and a recently graduated male, and a female senior and a young kibbutz male. An important characteristic is that the couple is never comprised of individuals who

[12] In general, however, the students would poke fun at girls who attempted to enhance their attractiveness by wearing expensive or "sexy" dresses. A student from the city was the object of much criticism and teasing from her tenth-grade class because of her elaborate wardrobe and her great concern with her appearance. When the class was planning a trip to the Negev, some of the students predicted, jokingly, that this girl would not go because she did not have the proper undergarments for the *wadis*.

have grown up together in the kibbutz. Students who have always been members of the same kevutza have never been known to engage in sexual behavior with each other.

In general, couples are secretive about their relationship; according to some students, they are "ashamed" to have it known. The typical partners give few overt indications of their relationship; they never appear together in public as a couple, nor do they seek each other out informally, between classes or at work. It would be unthinkable to show any physical sign of affection in the presence of other people. As a result, their meetings are clandestine, and this gives rise to gossip and intrigue, and converts a typical case of "puppy love" into a minor *cause célèbre*. If the Mosad culture provided for dating, couples could interact publicly at dances and movies. But in the absence of a formal dating pattern, they must meet at night, a practice which surrounds the relationship with an aura of secrecy and danger and imparts an unhealthy air to a simple boy-girl relationship.

Interaction between the sexes. In general, boys and girls appear to interact as asexual peers rather than as potential sex objects. There seems to be no differential behavior between unisexual and bisexual groups, as there is in other societies. There is no special etiquette which governs specifically the interaction of members of opposite sex. Nor does one observe such typical Western manifestations as flirtatiousness, coquetry, and seductiveness.

Important age differences must be recorded, however. In the seventh and eighth grades male-female interaction is marked by social distance which is expressed in a number of ways. Boys and girls sit separately in the classroom, in the dining room, and at assemblies, and they seldom interact after class. What cliques or friendships exist are almost always unisexual in nature.[13] This social distance seems to be a continuation of a pattern which first develops in the last few years in the Grammar School where, it will be remembered, the children of the sixth grade break up into unisexual groups, in contrast to the younger grades in which the children's play is almost always bisexual. Sometimes, however, simple social distance between the sexes develops into aggression. The girls view the boys as immature, and treat them with disdain. The boys retaliate with aggression. Boys, for example, are highly

[13] Apparently this is a characteristic found in all kibbutzim. An article in the education journal states that in later childhood the kevutza often splits up into factions. "The boys become distant from the girls, they do not permit them to participate in their activities, they will not allow them to sit next to them in the dining room."

critical of the girls in class, and they scoff at them whenever they make a mistake. The girls, though disdainful of the boys, usually remain passive in the face of this criticism. The eighth-grade teacher reports that he must frequently defend the girls against the hostile criticism of the boys, for which the latter accuse him of favoritism for the girls.

At times this hostility takes extreme forms. It has already been noted, for example, that some eighth-grade boys physically attacked some female students who came from outside the kibbutz. During this study another incident — one which shocked even the boys — occurred in the ninth grade. One of the boys disliked a girl in his kevutza and decided to make life difficult for her. He decided that she was to undress before her roommates; and to show her how easy this was he undressed before her, and strutted in the nude about the room.[14] A few days later he awakened just as the girl was getting dressed; he observed her carefully and then told what he had seen, in a coarse way, to the other members of the kevutza.

Hostility between the sexes diminishes with age, and by the ninth or tenth grades it is all but absent. All the students who reported that male-female relations were bad, were under fifteen years of age, as were those who reported that there were still some problems remaining. On the other hand, the seventeen students (out of a sample of twenty-six) who reported a good male-female relationship were over fifteen years of age.

Sex-linked personality differences. A number of sex differences may be noted at this age. First, the girls tend to be cleaner than the boys — at least they clean the rooms better and they complain that the latter leave the rooms dirty. Second, the girls — as measured by their interest in academic work — seem to be less intellectual than the boys. Over and over again our notes on classroom behavior include such statements as "The girls have little interest in the discussion," or "The girls don't participate in the discussion." This apathy is particularly characteristic of the seniors. After they had graduated from high school and were working in the kibbutz, the author asked them to compare the kibbutz with the Mosad. The unanimous response of the girls was that they much preferred the kibbutz because by their senior year they had become bored and disinterested with their studies and were just "marking time."

[14] In stressing the aggressive aspects of this behavior, the exhibitionism and voyeurism should not be overlooked.

In general, the girls are more interested in humanistika than in realistika, for, they claim, the latter is much too difficult for them. In the senior class, for example, physics is an optional course, and at the time of our study, all but one of the girls registered instead for a discussion group in psychology. Even in the latter course, however, their performance was poor. Their teacher complained that the girls have less capacity for logical thought than the boys, and that only rarely can they think abstractly.[15]

Almost all teachers and nurses agree that the girls are much more mature emotionally than the boys. This is one of the reasons, it will be recalled, for the tensions that exist between them — the girls view the boys as infantile — as well as for the disturbances in the classroom. Finally, girls tend to retain closer ties to their parents than boys. They visit them more frequently, and they are more intimate with them.

RELATION TO PARENTS

Rebellion. The Mosad student is not exposed to conflicting values in either of the two senses — longitudinal and horizontal — in which American adolescents may experience such conflict. There are, that is, few conflicts between the values he had learned in childhood and those he must learn in adolescence; and there are few conflicts between the values he has learned in his family and other primary groups, and those which the school is trying to inculcate. The kibbutz is, so far as its values are concerned, a monistic community. The values of one's family are pretty much the same as those of all other families, and the values of these several families are the same as the values of the school. The student is rarely conflicted therefore by the problem of choice of values: my family's or another family's? my family's or the school's? the school's or the community's? These are all of one piece.

Related to this homogeneity in values is the absence in the students of rebellion against parental values — since the student does not have to choose competing values, he willy-nilly retains those of his parents. He could, of course, choose those values of the outside world, which are in conflict with kibbutz and parental values, but such a choice would be tantamount to leaving the kibbutz; and this, few, if any, students are willing to do. The

[15] This sexual difference, for which I can suggest no plausible interpretation, is particularly interesting for it represents a reversal from what is observed among the younger children. Among the preschool children, the girls preponderate in artistic and intellectual activities. So, too, they contribute a greater share than the boys to the intellectual elite of the Grammar School.

kibbutz is their home and in the kibbutz they intend to remain.

Nor would one expect to find typical adolescent rebellion against parents. For all practical purposes the high school student is dependent upon his parents for nothing — except affection. His material, social, and intellectual needs are satisfied by the kibbutz and the Mosad. Unwilling conformity to parental desires or demands is not the price he must pay for either social privileges or economic goods. In short, subjected neither to his parents' control nor their authority, he has no need to rebel against them. And this expectation is confirmed by the all but unanimous reports of the parents. Only nine of the respondents to the Questionnaire had adolescent children, but of the nine only one felt that his children had rebelled against him.

Estrangement. But the parent-child relationship is more complicated than the simple absence of value-conflict and adolescent-rebellion might suggest. For other types of strain are possible, and in the kibbutz this strain seems to be characterized by psychological distance between child and parent. Indeed, a most important characteristic of the adolescent's relation to his parents is his psychological distance. Although the high school is no farther than a five-minute walk from almost any parental room, only nine students, in a representative sample of thirty-one, said they visited their parents daily, and all but two of these were less than fifteen years old.[16] The majority visited their parents less frequently, ranging from five and six times a week to once a week, the median being three or four times a week. If we can assume that the rate of voluntary interaction is an adequate measure of psychological distance, we may then conclude from these data alone that psychological distance is a true description of the student attitude.

Some teachers, however, insist that the frequency with which students visit their parents is not a valid index of their feelings, and that, despite their irregular visits, the students do maintain an intimate relationship with their parents. These claims, however, are generally ideological in nature, for, having made them, the teacher then usually points out that, since the child is not economically dependent upon his parents, he has no reason for not maintaining a good relationship with them. The implications of the latter argument have been discussed elsewhere, and its merits have been noted. No child, it is true, need feel bitter because his parents cannot provide him with the material goods

[16] Eight of the nine were females.

which other parents give to their children; and no student need feel aggression toward his parents because he must acquiesce in their demands in order to retain their material support. But this conclusion is not incompatible with our thesis concerning psychological distance. The kibbutz adolescent does not rebel against his parents. Instead he stops taking them into his confidence. He becomes uncommunicative.

In order to obtain a more direct measure, the students were asked about the quality of their relationship with their parents. Of the ten respondents (the sample is unfortunately small), only three claimed to be intimate with their parents. The others said that they only sometimes took their parents into their confidence, or that they never did.

Parents feel even more strongly that their adolescent children have drifted away from them, and they complain bitterly about this.[17] The students, their parents say, tell them nothing, so that they never know what they are doing, thinking, or feeling. They are, their parents say, "closed" (*segurim*), and if the parents wish to know something about them they must, as one mother put it, "drag it out."

The following report by one mother is typical. Observing her son to be in a bad mood, she asked him what the matter was, and he "almost tore my head off." Since then she "never asked him anything." Another time, when her son was again in a bad mood, she went on a vacation. While she was away, he wrote her a wonderful letter, but he did not "even mention what was troubling him."

One father was particularly bitter. The students visit their parents, he said, only out of a sense of duty, but not out of desire. At best, they visit them because they feel that they still might need them for something. In general, however, "the parents are

---

[17] Our description of parental feeling is based on informal conversations with them. And though their responses to the Questionnaire are at variance with the sentiments expressed during conversations, we are inclined to accept the latter as a more valid expression of their true sentiments. Nine parents with adolescent children responded to the question of the schedule — "Do your older children confide in you?" Four checked "definitely yes," four, "perhaps yes," and one did not answer. Even from the Questionnaire, however, it is possible to deduce an attenuation in the child's overt affection for his parents. To the question, "Do your *younger* children want to visit you?," thirteen of the sixteen respondents checked, "definitely yes," and three checked, "perhaps yes." To the same question concerning their *older* children, only three of the nine respondents checked, "definitely yes." Five checked, "perhaps yes," and one did not answer. It should be noted, finally, that five checked, "definitely yes," and three checked, "perhaps yes," to "Do your older children admire you?" One did not answer.

superfluous in their lives; they feel they can get along without them."

In view of the psychological distance that characterizes the child-parent relationship, it is not surprising that the students — the males at any rate — rarely express physical affection for them. An eighth-grade student will not permit his mother to kiss him for, he claims, it is not manly. An adult sabra responds with the exact words — "it is not manly" — when his mother wants to kiss him, although as a child he told her that she was the most beautiful woman in the world and that when he grew up he would marry her. So, too, a boy who has just entered the Mosad visits his parents infrequently and, when he does, he shows his mother no physical affection, although only two months previously he had spent all his spare time with her, wanted to sleep in the room with her, and had called her his "queen."

The parents not only complain bitterly about their relationship with their children,[18] but they are bewildered by it. "How can you explain it?" asked one of the teachers, herself a parent of two adolescents. "After all, it was necessary for us to conceal things from our parents, for we had to rebel in order to come to Palestine. But what do they have to conceal?"

Another parent said,

I can understand why my generation was estranged from its parents. They had nothing in common. Take my own case. My parents were religious and I was not. My parents wanted me to enter business and I wanted to be a worker. I wanted to go to Israel and they wanted me to remain in Poland. But in the kibbutz what is the reason? Parents and children share the same values . . . I can only conclude that parent-child conflict is biological.

One interesting aspect of this estrangement is that it begins only after the child enters the Mosad, and in general it occurs regardless of the previous relationship between parents and children. Take Yaakov, for example. While in grade school, he was probably the most deeply attached of any of the students to his parents, particularly to his mother. He was, what might be called in our culture, a "mamma's boy." While Yaakov was still in grade school I had occasion to discuss the problem of adolescent estrangement with his mother — an intelligent and sensitive

[18] This bitterness is particularly poignant when it be remembered that an important motive for the establishment of collective education was to preclude parent-child estrangement.

woman. This would never happen between her and Yaakov, she said; their relationship would remain unimpaired. A few months later Yaakov graduated from Grammar School and entered the Mosad. When, a short time later, I asked Yaakov's mother how he was getting along, she said that she could not answer the question, for she never sees him. He is so busy, she continued, that he has no time to visit her; and that very week he even missed the usual Saturday afternoon tea with his parents. The previous night his parents had met him accidentally in front of the dining room, and when they asked him why he had not come to tea, he explained that his kevutza had recently obtained a new book which everyone wanted to read. He was fortunate to get the book on Saturday, and it proved to be so interesting that he had forgotten to visit his parents.

A short time later, the author again asked Yaakov's mother about her son. The answer was the same — she never sees him. She then volunteered an explanation. While in the grade school, he was repressed, he was "like a colt who wanted freedom." Now, suddenly, he has this freedom and he "doesn't know what to do with it." But she says nothing to him, she went on, because, "It is necessary to be a clever mother. He will return, you will see. Other sons, maybe not; but Yaakov will return."

The explanation of Yaakov's mother for his apparent estrangement is but one of many and conflicting parental interpretations of this phenomenon. Some say that their children visit them infrequently because of their very busy schedule. But this interpretation does not explain their psychological distance when they do visit them. Others, responding to this objection, say that, since their children love them very much, they do not wish to tell them their problems lest they hurt them. Still others maintain that the children's reticence springs from their feelings of superiority to their parents. The latter are the "generation of the desert" [19] and remain strangers, as it were, to the Israeli landscape. The children, on the other hand, are native Israelis; they are completely adjusted to the country which is their home. Feeling this difference, they feel superior to their parents, and are therefore "distant."

Another possible explanation may be found in the students' attitudes toward Judaism and the Jews of the Diaspora which is

[19] This is a reference to the ancient Exodus from Egypt. According to the Biblical story, the emancipated slaves wandered in the Sinaitic wilderness for forty years, so that it was the second generation — those who had not experienced slavery — that entered the Promised Land.

highly negative. It is not until the Mosad that the students become estranged from their parents, and it is in the Mosad that they acquire detailed knowledge of that East European Jewish culture (shtetl) to which they react with strong hostility. But, it must be remembered, their own parents originated in this culture; and, just as the sabras refuse even to read about the shtetl lest they be reminded of their own origins, so — it is our hypothesis — they are reluctant to see their parents, the living representatives and reminders of that hated past. In rejecting their Jewish past, the students reject their parents.

But the rejection of their parents may be related to the latter's European background in still another way. Although the sabras reject the shtetl, they do not reject Europe. On the contrary, there is reason to believe that European culture is highly admired by them, and that, by contrast, Israel is perceived as inferior. If their parents had not come to Israel, they might have been living in the superior cultures of Europe or the Soviet Union instead of in "our tiny country," as they refer to Israel.

The fundamental reason for parental estrangement, however, we believe to rest on a long history of insecure interpersonal relationships whose implications will be dealt with in Chapter 16.

Attachment. Despite their psychological distance, the students continue to view their parents, to some extent at least, as sources of authority and nurturance. When a problem arises in the Mosad, the students frequently support or oppose suggested solutions by an example from their home, or by an appeal to their parents' opinion. So, too, they are not loathe to fall back on their parents when they come into conflict with a teacher. Should the latter reprimand them, they may complain to their parents from whom they can expect support.

Moreover, although most sabras maintain a psychological reserve with their parents, there are a few who are deeply attached to them. Amir's parents, for example, are divorced, and fifteen-year-old Amir waits for his mother's bus (she lives outside the kibbutz) for hours before her expected arrival, so eager is he to see her. Rani (fourteen years old) is so attached to his mother, who works near the Mosad, that he follows her about in her various activities during all his free moments. Amnon (fifteen years old) is deeply devoted to his step-father, whom he thought from his earliest childhood to be his biological father; when informed of the truth, he rejected it in favor of his former belief.

In some cases student relationships to parents assume over-

tones that are usually associated with unresolved Oedipal difficulties. Meir (seventeen years old) dislikes his father intensely,
and is deeply concerned lest he act like him; he is somber and
serious unlike his gay and witty father. Moshe (fourteen years
old) is, as his teacher puts it, "abnormally devoted" to his
divorced mother. When she announced her intention of marrying
a man notorious in the kibbutz for his many love affairs, he
screamed at her, calling her a prostitute. Rena's parents are
divorced. Sixteen-year-old Rena is hostile to her mother, whom
she rarely visits; but she adores her father, who lives in another
kibbutz and waits hours for the arrival of his bus. Recently, he
has discontinued his visits to the Mosad, saying that Rena is a
big girl and no longer needs him. She has responded to his
absence by reverting to a habit she had always had difficulty in
overcoming — enuresis.

Emotional disturbance. The last example of enuresis illustrates
another aspect of the parent-child relationship, and one which we
observed among all preadolescent children as well — the crucial
role of parents in the development of emotional disturbance in
their children. Almost invariably the students with problems are
those who have histories of disturbed family lives — that is, they
did not get along with one or both parents and/or the latter did
not get along with each other. It is these students, moreover, who
either encounter intellectual difficulties with their school work
or who become highly intellectual and/or intensely political.

To say that the emotionally disturbed children are products
of a disturbed family relationship is only partially correct. As in
the case of the preadolescent children, disturbed sibling relationships contribute heavily to the emotional disturbance of the child.
Frequently the student who has great prestige needs and who,
consequently, is extremely active in extracurricular activities, is
one who suffers from intense sibling rivalry.

PART VI · SABRAS

TRANSITION FROM MOSAD TO KIBBUTZ

There are eleven sabras, ranging in age from twenty-one through twenty-eight, who are functioning members of Kiryat Yedidim. These are not the only adult sabras of the kibbutz, but the others are temporarily absent — studying, working, or serving in the army — so that generalizations about adult sabras are based on these eleven only.

Kibbutz children are not officially members of the kibbutz, but of the "Children's Society." Membership in the kibbutz is viewed as a "privilege, not as a right," and biological descent from a kibbutz member does not, theoretically, alter this situation. Any person, sabra or stranger, wishing to become a chaver of the kibbutz must apply for membership, and after a year's probationary period his application is voted upon at a town meeting. The sabras are eligible for membership upon graduation from high school. The kibbutz feels, however, that its sabras should be given the opportunity to reject kibbutz life if they so choose, and before the War of Independence (1947) high school graduates were sent to the cities where they worked for one year. At the expiration of the year they could elect to remain in the city, or apply for membership in the kibbutz. This practice is no longer in effect, as high school students are drafted into the army immediately upon graduation. Instead of living in the city, therefore, they now spend two years in the army.

Election to the kibbutz, an important event for both the sabras and the kibbutz, is marked by a ceremony and celebration (mesiba). Upon entering the kibbutz the sabras are treated equally — as they had been throughout their early years — regardless of their family name or of the importance of their parents. They enjoy the same privileges and assume the same responsibilities as any other chaver. The economic branches to which they are assigned are, in most cases, agreed upon before they enter the kibbutz, on the basis of their work experience in high school.

When they first enter the kibbutz, their living quarters are, from the point of view of present kibbutz norms, substandard. As the kibbutz has grown, both numerically and economically, new housing developments have been periodically constructed to keep pace with the growth. Thus there have been a number of stages in kibbutz housing — from tents to wooden cottages to concrete-block houses. The latter have developed from one-room dwellings without porches, to one-room dwellings with porches, to one and one-half room dwellings with porches and indoor plumbing. It should not be concluded, however, that previous housing is discarded as new developments are erected. Indeed, though the first tents may by now have been discarded, the first cottages are still standing, and all are inhabited. With certain qualifications, based on health and age, the allocation of housing is determined by seniority. As better housing units are erected, chaverim move from their current houses to the newer dwellings, so that each housing unit is occupied in turn by those who had been living in less desirable housing.

As far as sabra housing is concerned, this policy has two consequences: each graduating class lives in a common bloc of houses; and the sabras occupy the least desirable dwellings. The older sabras live in the wooden cottages which were the first permanent houses erected by their parents, while the younger sabras live in former pillboxes and shacks, and some tents (with concrete floors). Despite the crude exteriors of these dwellings, almost all are attractively furnished and decorated. In general the most pleasant rooms in the kibbutz are to be found among the married sabras; and, in general, their rooms include fine prints, many records, and good books.

Housing symbolizes a fundamental change which occurs in the lives of the sabras when they enter the kibbutz. Kiryat Yedidim, it has already been observed, is a child-centered community. This means, among other things, that the standard of living enjoyed by the children is higher than that of the adults. While still in high school, for example, the new chaver had lived in a very pleasant, if crowded, dormitory; he ate meals which were far superior to those eaten in the kibbutz dining room. For the sabra, then, entry into the kibbutz means moving from a condition of relative privilege to one of relative deprivation. One wonders if part of the adult sabra insecurity is not traceable to a feeling of rejection deriving from this abrupt transition.

The sabras are as concerned with their own appearance as

they are with the appearance of their rooms. Although their wardrobes are not extensive, the females are not only carefully groomed when they enter the dining room in the evening, but they are attractively dressed in "feminine" clothes. They may wear shorts and go barefoot during the workday, but they are careful to wear attractive skirts or dresses at all other times. This represents a decided change in kibbutz values, and some of the old-timers view this as a sign of retrogression in kibbutz standards. One chavera, indeed, viewed this change as symbolic of all the departures from the original pioneering folkways.

MARRIAGE AND THE FAMILY

Sexual behavior and attitudes. Although sexual intercourse is strongly discouraged in the Mosad, this qualified taboo does not extend beyond high school graduation. Once the sabras leave the Mosad, at approximately eighteen years of age, it is their private concern, and they may do as they please. Although our information concerning the sexual activities of adult sabras is unsatisfactory in the extreme, it is almost certain that most of the sabras have some experience before marriage. According to one informant, all the unmarried females have had affairs, but some of the males have not. It is highly probable, moreover, that none of the married sabras was entirely inexperienced at the time of marriage. Their premarital sexual experiences were limited, however, since with one exception — a twenty-eight-year-old bachelor — all were married in their early twenties, the mean age being 21.5.

It is fair to say, then, that the sexual experiences of the sabras are limited to a few partners. Moreover, they not only marry early, but they tend to remain married — as yet there has been but one divorce. So far as we know, with one possible exception, they remain faithful to their spouses.

There are two aspects of sabra sexuality that require comment. The first concerns the choice of sexual partner — whether for intercourse or for marriage. In not one instance has a sabra from Kiryat Yedidim married a fellow sabra nor, to the best of our knowledge, has a sabra had sexual intercourse with a fellow sabra. If, in the light of additional data the latter part of the generalization be rendered false, I would be highly confident of the validity of its following reformulation: in no instance have sabras from the same kevutza had sexual intercourse with each other.

The reason given by the sabras for their exogamy is interesting: they view each other, they say, as siblings. We have then an instance of a self-imposed primary group exogamy, despite the absence of any prescribed — formal or informal — incest taboo. By stating that they view each other as siblings the sabras do not mean to imply, at least not consciously, that they therefore view any sexual relationship between themselves as incestuous. They mean rather that they, like biological siblings, have no sexual interest in each other.

But if psychoanalysis has taught us anything, it is that siblings *do* have reciprocal sexual interests, albeit (for the most part) unconscious. If this be so, and if the sabra "siblings" perceive one another as ordinary siblings do, it would follow that they, too, have a (repressed) sexual interest in each other. Hence the absence of either sexual intercourse or marriage among them would indicate that they have spontaneously evolved their own incest taboo. They are, that is, attracted to each other but, *ex hypothesi*, they have repressed this attraction, and have, thus, precluded its expression. If this interpretation is correct it would explain why, despite their claim of mutual asexual feelings, they insisted on the abolition of the mixed showers while in the high school.[1]

The only positive evidence for this hypothesis comes from an atypical sabra. Moshe is the most extroverted and uninhibited person in the entire group — and one whose unconscious seems frequently near the surface. He scoffed at the suggestion that he was not attracted by the famale sabras. This, he declared, was nonsense. When a female sabra, immediately after we had discussed this problem, entered his room he confronted her with the same question. She too thought that the sabras had no sexual feelings for each other. "After all," she exclaimed, "You and I went together to Jerusalem the other day, and we made no attempt to arrange for a date or to make advances to each other." On the surface her statement says that they had no sexual interest in each other. By her tone, however, the author had the definite impression that she had wished that they had made "an advance" and that she was sorry that they had not.

But if the sabras *are* sexually attracted to each other, why, I asked Moshe, do they not marry? To this he replied that there were so few sabras that it was seldom that a male and female, who were attracted by each other, fell within the same age range.

[1] The adult sabras agree that mixed showers are acceptable until puberty and/or so long as there are no outsiders in the group. Of the ten adult sabras interviewed, only one favored the continuation of mixed showers through the twelfth grade.

In short, he views sabra exogamy as a function of elementary demographic facts, rather than as a consequence of obscure psychodynamic motives. In the absence of data, we can go no further with this analysis, except to note that voluntary sabra exogamy seems to be a characteristic feature of the kibbutz movement.

A second aspect of sabra sexuality that is of theoretical interest is their conservatism relative, at least, to their permissive sexual training, and to their own parents, particularly when the latter were young. This conservatism is expressed in a number of ways. Despite the sexual freedom permitted them after high school graduation, few take advantage of it; most have few premarital affairs. Second, their marriages are not only stable but they remain faithful to their spouses. (Their own parents engaged in much sexual experimentation; their marriages, while they were still young, were unstable; and the incidence of extramarital relationships and divorce was high.)

The sabras are conservative not only in their behavior, but in their sexual attitudes as well. Not only do they not engage in extramarital relationships, but they are strongly opposed to them. As an indication of, what he called, sabra "puritanism," a chaver pointed sadly to their attitude toward a female chavera who was having an affair with another kibbutz member, both of whom were married. Most of the chaverim ignored the affair, but some of the sabras raised it as an issue at a Town Meeting, arguing that the woman should no longer be allowed to work with the children, since she was an adulteress — the very term was foreign to the vocabulary of the kibbutz founders.

Another indication of their conservatism in sexual matters is the eagerness of the sabras to have a legal (religious) marriage ceremony. Their parents had always opposed such ceremonies, believing that a marriage is formally sanctioned when the kibbutz grants a couple a joint room. But because bastards have no civil rights in Israel, the parents would become legally married sometime after the wife became pregnant. They viewed this ceremony, however, as both a farce and an indignity. Apparently their children have acquired a contrary attitude. They prefer the legal marriage, and are usually legally married about the same time that they become married in the eyes of the kibbutz. Some of them still joke about the religious ceremony and say it is a farce. Nevertheless, in the two cases we observed during our stay in the kibbutz, it was the day of the legal ceremony which they chose as the occasion for their wedding party.

This changed attitude may be interpreted as a possible reaction to their parents' behavior. Marriages of the latter were
unstable, and the sabras suffered from the accompanying insecurity. They may want the security which their own parents did
not have in their marriages, and they may wish to prevent their
own children from suffering the insecurity which they experienced as children. But this is all speculative, for we have no
pertinent data.

It should be noted, finally, in summarizing sexual attitudes,
that the sabras share with their parents a marked reticence about
the discussion of sexual matters or the use of obscene words.
Indeed, the latter do not occur in Hebrew, so that when obscenity
is employed at all, the sabras must have recourse to Arabic.
During an entire year's work in many branches of the kibbutz
economy neither my wife nor I ever heard a dirty story, and
almost never an obscene term. This absence of verbal obscenity,
according to sabra informants, characterizes their private as well
as their group interaction.

"The problem of the woman." Unlike the high school youth,
the adult sabras reveal little unisexual clique behavior; social
interaction among them is almost always bisexual. There is, however, some indication of hostility between the sexes.

A sabra male, for example, speaking of the females in his
group, said that they were worthless; none, he insisted, had any
ability. A sabra female, on the other hand, characterized by a
strong masculine protest, was recounting how difficult it was for
her to perform a certain economic task. When I suggested that
her husband might undertake this task, she replied, "The men
would never do that kind of work. All they do is ride around all
day, and I have to do the hard work . . . If my husband took
my job he wouldn't last for one day."

This above quotation is related to a serious kibbutz problem
— "the problem of the woman." Since we have discussed this
problem in some detail elsewhere[2] we merely indicate that it
refers, among other things, to the difficulty encountered by kibbutz women in achieving full economic, social, and cultural
equality, despite the fact that equality of the sexes has been a
kibbutz value of paramount importance. Many kibbutz women
complain that sexual equality has not been achieved; and the
affect displayed in the above quotation reveals that at least one

[2] See Spiro, *Kibbutz*, 221–236.

female sabra shares this complaint. She is not alone. According to another sabra, should a woman talk at a town meeting she is not listened to. The men "know best." Men can talk nonsense at a meeting, but there is no negative response. Should women speak in a similar vein, the men laugh. If a woman expresses herself on education, "It's not worth anything." Should a man speak on this subject, what he has to say is wonderful. In short, this sabra insisted, there is indeed a "problem of the woman" in Kiryat Yedidim. Unlike the first sabra quoted, however, she believes that the sabra males do not share the attitudes of their elders, so that the situation can be expected to improve.

Another female sabra is not too sure that this problem exists. When she was younger, she said, she believed that women worked under such hard conditions that they were too tired in the evening to develop any broad cultural interests. She no longer believes this to be true. It is now her feeling that women merely have different interests from men. They are (legitimately) concerned with their children and their rooms, both of which consume their time and their energy. Men, on the other hand, are physically stronger than women, and although they work hard during the day, they have a surplus of energy for other interests and activities. This sabra is willing to accept a permanent division of labor based on sex:

> I think that woman should do the work for which she is suited; not on tractors or in the fields. Women, by nature, cannot be active in economic production, particularly if their family life is to be well-integrated. Of course, some do it, and they do it in Russia. Still, I think it's not natural.

But, she hastened to add, the social importance of any person is to be measured not by his productivity — for then men would be superior to women — but by the devotion with which he performs his work. In the last analysis, she concluded, women in Kiryat Yedidim are really the social equals of men; and although some men view women as inferior, still, "it is not as bad as some say."

Finally, there is the sabra who categorically denies the existence of "the problem of the woman." But her response to the question was so rapid, the affect with which she spoke was so intense, and the attitude which she assumed was so dogmatic that one wonders if her oration were not an attempt to convince both the interviewer and herself of something of which she was not convinced at all.

I deny it (the problem of the woman) completely . . . Some say that women work harder, that they are not appreciated, that there is a negative attitude toward them. That is not at all true. I feel the complete equal of all chaverim.

She then went on to "prove" that women do not work harder than men, for though kitchen work is hard, "Is it any harder than harvesting field crops in the hot sun or rain for fifteen hours a stretch?" In contrast, she argued, take the women's work in the children's houses, in which hours are not long, and in which afternoon work is "easy and pleasant." Laundry work, she conceded, is difficult, "but the women always complain. First (they complained that) the machine was too small; so they bought a new one. But now (they complain that) it is too big."

There is a problem, she admitted, with respect to female participation in the economic administration of the kibbutz, in which women play a negligible role. But, she said, it is their own fault. A few years ago a woman was appointed to the executive committee for economic affairs. "She sat for two years and never once opened her mouth, because she had nothing to say." But it is not true, she insisted, that women are less respected or honored than men.

I am as respected as David (the economic manager). Everyone fills his job, and all jobs are equally important. If everyone considered his work as important as any other, there would be no problem.

Despite her verbal statements, however, this sabra reveals — both in her behavior and in other sections of the interview — that the "problem of the woman" does indeed exist for her, as it does for the first female sabra quoted. After working beside them in the fields over a period of months, I can testify that they worked harder and longer than almost all the men with whom I worked, and that they were concerned that those who worked with them did the same. They always gave the impression that they were trying to prove to others (and to themselves) that they were as good as the men. This impression receives additional confirmation from our interview data.

One of them, in response to an interview question, stated that her one ambition was to obtain satisfaction from her work, "That is the main thing." When asked if she derived satisfaction now, she replied in the affirmative, but, she continued, "there are difficulties. It is very hard for a woman with children to work in the fields." Indeed, "sometimes it is so hard that it does not seem worthwhile to continue." She does continue, however, and her motive is to obtain status — not any kind of status, but status as an agricultural worker. Her deepest concern, as expressed in the interview, is that, despite her hard work, she still does not have status. This she must acquire by more study, "and this is very hard to do after work hours." Nevertheless, she studies in the evenings. In short, she insists on obtaining status in "men's work" instead of in "women's work" which would not be so difficult. And it is precisely because she desires status in competition with men that she persists in her difficult path. And though she feels that she does not yet have "enough knowledge" she continues to work. And because she does not have "enough knowledge," she works harder than ever, in order to compensate for this felt defect.

Marriage and children. Of the sabras over twenty-one who were in the kibbutz at the time of this study, four of the five females were married, and one was divorced. Of the six males, three were married; and two of the three who were unmarried were no more than twenty-three years old. Their spouses, for the most part, are city sabras who were trained in The Movement, and whom they met either in high school or as members of the youth group that joined the kibbutz (*hashlama*).

With one exception there have been no divorces among the sabras; and this exception is a girl who had been married "involuntarily." Marriages are not only stable, but for most sabras the marriage relationship is probably the most important and intimate interpersonal relationship they have had (excepting the early child-parent relationship). In general spouses are deeply devoted to each other, and some, in fact, are inseparable.

All the married sabras, the oldest of whom is only twenty-eight, have at least one but no more than two children, with an average of 1.3 children per family. It is probably safe to predict that the number of children in the average sabra family of procreation will exceed those in their family of orientation. None of the parents of the adult sabras, for example, had more than two children, while some of the sabras, although still in their middle twenties, have already had two children.

The sabras seem to be genuinely fond of children, others as well as their own. Many of the high school girls, for example, work in the various nurseries as afternoon relief nurses and, with rare exceptions, they are warm, loving, and intelligent workers. Their interest in children is developed early. Young girls in kindergarten often assist their mothers who are nurses in younger children's houses; and girls in the Grammar School frequently supervise the play of nursery children.

Sabra parents, both male and female, are, with perhaps one exception, warm and affectionate with their children. But they are also, again with one exception, relaxed and unanxious about them. This is in sharp contrast to many of the older chaverim, who display, both in attitude and behavior, considerable anxiety about their children. The exception to the previous generalization is a sabra mother whose child almost died in early infancy, and who consequently is unusually absorbed in her. She visits her in the Nursery more frequently than other mothers visit their babies, and she is particularly concerned about her at night.

The least affectionate of the sabra mothers is a woman characterized by strong masculine protest. The following excerpt from a conversation reveals her attitude.

CHAYA (the sabra mother) was saying that she was kept busy with her work and did not see her child very much. I remarked that kibbutz parents see their children more frequently than some city parents. She sees her child only two hours a day, she replied. I pointed out that the entire two hours were devoted exclusively to the children. She denied this. Her child is in the room, she conceded, but she does not devote herself to him — "It is boring." She wishes he would not stay about the room, or that he would go do something by himself. She is only too happy when he leaves her alone, so she can read.

Although the sabra parents love their children and show them much affection, they have no desire to reinstitute the conventional pattern of private socialization. Here, too, there is a marked difference between the sabras and the older chaverim. The latter, though committed ideologically to collective education, are frequently unhappy with it personally and express misgivings about it. This is not true of the sabras, who view collective education as a highly desirable institution. They betray no anxieties concerning their children's welfare nor do they feel deprived because of the separation from their children. On the contrary, they welcome it. When a baby is sick, for example, he is frequently put in his parents' room so that he can be isolated from the others. The older parents are, as one nurse put it, "thrilled to death." But the sabras have just the opposite reaction — they look forward to the day when the baby can be returned.

The best proof of these differences in attitudes is found in the evening departure. The non-sabra adults, many of whom are reluctant to part from their children at night, spend many minutes kissing, hugging, and fondling their children, often returning many times for another kiss and another hug. The sabra parents, on the other hand, show no such signs of reluctance. They say goodnight, kiss the child affectionately, and depart without a fuss. This matter-of-fact attitude, it is our impression, does not show that the sabras do not love their children, but that they have no insecurities (guilt-feelings) about collective education.

The sabra mothers are aware of the difference between their mothers and themselves in this regard. As one of them put it:

Not one of us (sabras) has any doubts about having the nurses take charge of hashkava. Many of the older women, however, are opposed to it. Our own parents put us to bed.

All such generalizations, of course, require qualification. The interview data reveal that, of the eight sabra parents, six favor collective education, one expressed mild doubts, and another — the mother whose behavior revealed anxiety about her child — expressed serious doubts about it. Since the latter is in all other respects intensely devoted to kibbutz values and institutions, her comments are of more than ordinary interest.

At first (when her baby was born) it was all right. I nursed him and he was in my hands. But the first crisis came at six months, when I gave him to the nurses. I gave him with all confidence, but still it was a crisis. When I stopped nursing, I went to see him often, every night, to see if he were cold or wet, etc. Now I see how good it is for him; but nevertheless there was a period when he would cry when we left in the evening, and I felt as if I were abandoning him. I felt that it was not right for the baby. Everywhere else the baby is with his parents, and here we leave him. Maybe I felt it more than he. Everything is fine, but still it (the departure) is a difficult moment . . . All day he has the nurse with him, and at night he's left alone. When the child is young, this is very difficult for the parents — at least it is for me.

Those who favor this system often give as their reasons personal gratification or comfort, such as the following:

Here I don't have to be a housewife.

Take a woman in the city: no matter how active she is she can't be independent. She still has her children and house to take care of.

I would not like my children to live with me. It's more comfortable that way (living in children's houses).

I want my children to live in the children's houses, primarily for my own enjoyment.

My trust in the nurses is so great that I have no worries or doubts about entrusting him to their care. Once he lived in our room for a few weeks, and I realized that I didn't want it. I simply don't want it . . . In the city the child is always "in its mother's mouth," so the possibility of satisfaction from one's child is ruined. Here the relationships are freer and much better.

That the sabras prefer to delegate the responsibility for the rearing of their own children to kibbutz nurses does not mean that they do not perceive important social and psychological values inherent in the system of collective education. Indeed, their first response to our interview question was to point out these values. First, they agree generally that collective education is the most efficient educational system for training in collective living. Second, they believe that important kibbutz values such as cooperation and responsibility are best developed in this system, although they are not unanimous in their evaluation of the extent to which the products of this system actually display such characteristics.[3]

In addition to personal or ideological reasons for preferring collective education, the sabra parents feel that the children are happiest in such a system. Almost all the sabras, to the extent that they remembered their childhood, believe it to have been a happy one; and on the basis of this experience they feel that their children, too, will be happy in such a system. Those few, moreover, who had any experience in living with their parents much preferred the children's house. One sabra, for example, had wanted very much to live with his parents, and when they took him "for a day or two" he was happy, "because of the novelty." Once, however, he had to live with them for a few months, and "I must admit I suffered from it. I was not free with them. I felt I was in a strange room as a guest."

Another sabra, when asked to compare the relative merits of collective education with the more traditional type, said:

It is difficult to say, for I know no other kind. I can't see myself in any other kind of education. Generally I was happy with it. It was

---

[3] Six of the nine sabras who commented on this question felt that the sabras are responsible, two felt they were not, and one was not sure. Of the seven who commented on cooperation, five agreed that the sabras were cooperative, and two were not sure.

excellent for me as a solution to my difficult family life. . . . We never lacked anything. We liked it, and preferred not to go to parents.

The above two comments are typical for the group. With but one exception, they preferred, in retrospect at least, living in children's houses to living in their parental rooms, and they believe, therefore, that their own children share this preference.

Regardless of their attitudes to collective education, the family of procreation is unquestionably the most important group in the sabras' lives. Indeed, some of the female sabras have been accused of retreating, in *petit bourgeois* fashion, to their rooms and families; and, dismissing the implicit value assumption of this charge, the fact itself, in its psychological implications at least, is easily confirmed. Whereas, according to their responses to the Stewart Emotional Response Test, the preadolescent sabras derive happiness from celebrations, recreation, and so forth, the most important source of happiness for the adult sabras, according to the same test, consists of experience within the family of procreation (or with the spouse, in the case of childless couples). Family interaction, for the adult sabras, has been substituted for the larger group interaction of the younger sabras.

Relations with parents. High school students are not intimate with their parents whom they frequently exclude from their private lives. With perhaps one or two exceptions, this pattern, established in early adolescence, continues after the sabras enter the kibbutz. If she wants to know anything concerning her adult son, said one mother, she must always ask, because he never volunteers any information. Nor can she ask him directly; she must always ask by indirection. Under no circumstances will he discuss his personal problems with her.

Nevertheless, there is reason to believe that the parent-child relationship improves as the sabras become older, and though it is rarely intimate, it is always cordial. In the first place, the adult sabras visit their parents more frequently than do the high school students. Of the nine adult sabras whose parents live in Kiryat Yedidim, two visit them daily, three visit three or four times a week, one visits twice a week, and three visit sporadically. Visiting includes having afternoon or evening tea with their parents and spending part of the sabbath with them.[4] Only rarely,

[4] The cohesive role of grandchildren in promoting parent-sabra interaction must not be overlooked. As sabras who have children indicate, one of the important reasons for their relatively frequent visits to their parents is their desire to see their grandchildren.

however, do parents and their adult children dine together, although it would be no trouble at all to make such an arrangement for the evening meal.

The sabras do not respond to both parents in the same way. Nine of the ten interviewed expressed a preference, either in the present or in the past, for one of the parents; and in all but two the preference was for the father (of the two sabras who preferred the mother, one was male and one was female). Sometimes the preference is expressed intensely, sometimes weakly; but that it is expressed at all is of considerable importance, since their statements were offered voluntarily and not as a response to probing.[5]

Although the preference for the father is expressed by males and females alike, it is found most intensely among two of the females, both of whom show signs of deep emotional involvement with their fathers. One, for example, said her father was like a chaver. She "can ask him anything because he knows everything. He always makes the right decisions." This same sabra was observed by the author to leave the dining room in anger when, after bragging about her father to a visitor, the latter retorted that he had never heard of him.

That the sabras identify with, and are therefore attached to, their parents is indicated, moreover, by their choice of occupation. Four of the five adult males chose the same occupations as one of their parents — two chose the agricultural branch of their fathers, two the agricultural branch of their mothers.

THE SABRAS AND KIBBUTZ VALUES

In an important sense the system of collective education must be judged by the extent to which the sabras, who are functioning members of the kibbutz, have acquired its values, and express them in daily living. These values, as listed by kibbutz parents, include work, devotion to the kibbutz, education, Socialism, Zionism, and collective ownership.[6] Although we are concerned here with the adult sabras and their adjustment to kibbutz culture, the data from which our generalizations are derived are, in some

---

[5] This is consistent with parental preference among the younger children. See p. 232.

[6] When asked to rank a series of values in order of importance, they ranked work, love of humanity, responsibility to kibbutz, good character, education, Socialism, Zionism, in that order. Since "love of humanity" and "good character" are difficult to measure, we shall confine our discussion to the remaining five values. We have added collective ownership because of its crucial importance in the kibbutz and because, from the point of view of the kibbutz, one of the measures of both "love of humanity" and "good character" is the willingness to share property.

instances, taken primarily from the high school sample; in others, from the adult sample; and in still other instances from both. It is our strong conviction, however, that in all these instances the generalizations — if valid at all — are valid for the entire sabra population over the age of sixteen.

Attitude toward the kibbutz. With one possible exception all the sabras view the kibbutz as the best form of societal living — this at least is what they say in personal interviews. There are, moreover, some behavioral indications of such an attitude. Before the War of Independence, when all high school graduates were sent to the cities for a year to enable them to choose between kibbutz and city life, all elected to return. So, too, now that all graduates are drafted for two years into the army, none has chosen to leave the kibbutz following this experience with the outside world. Moreover, although many of the sabras have been abroad, all have returned to the kibbutz where they prefer to live.

The sabras view the kibbutz as best not only for them, but for others as well. Not only have they returned to the kibbutz, but they have brought others back with them. They, like their parents, insisted that my wife and I would and should return to the kibbutz. As one put it, "Life is not always pleasant here, but it is always interesting and there is much to be done."

This does not mean that some sabras have not thought of leaving. One of the ten adult sabras interviewed said he had thought of leaving the kibbutz movement, and two said they had thought of leaving Kiryat Yedidim for another kibbutz. Nevertheless, with one exception[7] they have chosen to remain in the kibbutz, and their ambitions reflect this decision. For the most part, sabra life ambitions are restricted to those goals that are attainable within its context, and that are consistent, moreover, with its values. Their ambitions therefore do not include long-

[7] The exception is a nineteen-year-old girl who, though not born in Kiryat Yedidim, has lived in the kibbutz since childhood. Naomi was a highly aggressive adolescent who, as has been noted in a previous chapter, was expelled from the high school by a vote of her kevutza. The kibbutz sent her to a city high school from which she graduated.

Naomi is atypical in a number of ways. First, she has decided to become a teacher, a vocation which every other sabra has repudiated. Second, she is interested in clothes, and she not only dresses like a city girl, but she uses cosmetics and smokes. (Although their parents smoke, the sabras continue to adhere to the Movement's taboo on smoking and drinking.) Third, she has no interest in manual labor. In short, she is, as one chavera put it, "a typical bourgeois girl" who would be entirely adjusted in the city, but who is miserable in the kibbutz. Apparently Naomi agrees with this analysis, for she has decided to leave the kibbutz for the city.

range mobility aspirations, for example, because their basic status goal — kibbutz membership — has already been attained. Nor do they have competitive economic goals since, as they put it, their individual economic status is contingent upon the economic welfare of the kibbutz as a whole.

The sabras, in short, possess no mobility strivings whose realization entails leaving the kibbutz. To the extent that they are concerned with status goals, their goals are those which confer prestige within the kibbutz, such as proficiency in work or self-improvement through study.

Some sabras not only have no ambitions outside the kibbutz, but they view kibbutz membership in itself as their ambition. Indeed, four of the ten[8] indicated that they possessed no aspirations beyond continuing the kind of life they are now leading in the kibbutz. As one sabra put it:

> My ambition is to be a chaver kibbutz, and that tells the whole story. A chaver kibbutz can't say, for example, that his ambition is to be a painter or a musician. This is impossible. If you want to be a chaver kibbutz, that must be your ambition.

Some sabras, indeed, did not quite understand what I meant when I queried them about their ambitions. One asked me to repeat the question as if the very notion were alien to her. She said, finally, that she had never thought about the subject, so that "I cannot, offhand, talk about it." Another one put it this way:

> For a chaver kibbutz that's difficult to answer. To be a chaver kibbutz was my ambition, but I've already realized it. I really don't know — I can't answer it.

The decision to remain in the kibbutz is based on a variety of motives. Content analysis of the interviews yields the following classification of these motives (the number, in parentheses, following each motive indicates the number of times this motive was given).

"I was born here; it is my home." (7)
"For me it is the best life." (7)
"Because it is just, equal, free, etc." (5)
"For reasons of social conscience." (2)
"My parents live here." (1)

[8] One sabra refused to be interviewed.

"To repay my debt to the kibbutz." (1)

Since this summary scarcely does justice to their true feelings, some of the interview protocols are quoted below.

I think it (the kibbutz) is the most progressive and just of all societies. A person can best develop here, become a "human being," and help society.

I want to be in the kibbutz because I think that's the Way, both personally and socially. I could not be happy any other place . . . This is a life in which a man can give of himself, and no power restrains him from giving of himself.

I did not choose the kibbutz; I was born here. I remain because it is the way of life I like the best, and the one I believe in.

The basic reason is that I was born here, and all my life was lived here; and I am tied to this way of life. I have the feeling that I could not live any place else, for example, in the city; and the thought has never arisen. It (the kibbutz) is in my blood. . . . It is a just form of life, and people are more or less equal . . . People help each other . . . There is no problem of exploitation; as far as possible we try to eliminate it. When I think of other ways of life, particularly in America, where people exploit each other because only through exploitation can they attain success — then I realize how important our way of life is . . .

This is the way of life that is best for me. It is best in terms of my interests and my hobbies.

Many people say we are here out of habit. Maybe. But I also feel a sense of responsibility. If they worked twenty years to rear me, and at a great financial cost, I think that I should repay them.

I feel at home here. It's my house . . . Although I can be alone in my room for many weeks, I feel myself part of the family (the kibbutz).

That the kibbutz is perceived as "home" by the sabras may be inferred from the Emotional Response Test as well. One of the worst things that can happen to them — second only to physical harm (either to self or others) — is separation from their group. That the group is a source of great emotional security for them may be inferred, moreover, from their fear responses to this test: in none of their responses is the kibbutz or its personnel the source of their fears. All fears have as their source extra-kibbutz stimuli or conditions.

Similarly, an analysis of aggression in the same test reveals, if only indirectly, that the sabras feel a sense of security in the kibbutz. Aggression by others against oneself is the most important source of anger, as well as a major source of sadness, for the school children and high school youth. For the adult sabras, however, this same category accounts for only 4 per cent of their sadness responses and zero per cent of their anger responses. This difference between the younger and older sabras could imply that the latter have developed a greater tolerance for the aggression of others; but our observations do not support such a hypothesis. On the contrary, observation reveals a dearth of overt aggression in the kibbutz; and the results of the Emotional Response Test reflect this fact, as well as the emotional security that is attendant upon it.

This positive attitude toward the kibbutz is not a recent acquisition of the adult sabras. It has, on the contrary, a long history going back to the earliest years of their life cycle. The preschool children are not only deeply attached to the kibbutz, but they tend to perceive the world as one large kibbutz. Parents, whose preschool children have accompanied them to the cities, almost universally report that the children make frequent reference to Kiryat Yedidim, or to the social and physical characteristics of kibbutz culture, while in the city. Thus, when five-year-old Yehonatan was taken by his mother to the city, he saw some candy on the shelves of a grocery store and wanted to know when they were going to divide the candy. Again, Tamar, a four-year-old girl, was taken by her parents to Tel Aviv. As they walked through the streets, she kept exclaiming on how strange the city was, for *ein adama*, "there is no soil." Suddenly, between two buildings, she spied land. "Adama," she cried, and bent down to pick up some earth in her hands.

This tendency to perceive the outside world in the same terms in which they perceive the kibbutz holds for those children who have traveled outside the country, as for those who travel within Israel. The following excerpt is reported by a kibbutz mother who took her child to Europe.

He (her four-year-old son) connected everything to his past experience in Kiryat Yedidim. On the ship, for example, he called the dining room, "chadar ha-ochel" (the term for the kibbutz communal dining room); and the waiters he called "toranim" (the term for the waiters in the kibbutz dining room). He watched the ship unloading and said, "Look mother, all nice things are from Kiryat Yedidim."

The overvaluation of the kibbutz contained in the last sentence is not unusual. Many such statements were reported to me, among which the following is surely the most amusing.

Sara (two years old) heard a cow from an adjacent kibbutz mooing at night. She told her parents that the cow was "crying" because, "she wants to live in Kiryat Yedidim."

This belief in the superiority of the kibbutz is found in the grammar and high school students, as well. Tamar, a ten-year-old girl, had spent a year in the United States, where she had gone to school. When asked about her visit, she replied that Kiryat Yedidim was better than New York and that, in particular, the kibbutz school was better than the New York schools. The children in the United States, it was her feeling, read and study only "for the teacher." They are not interested, she said, in studying or reading for its own sake, but in order to please the teacher and to get a good grade. Furthermore, the children were "selfish" and would not share with others. They were particularly bad to the smaller children, whom they would not permit to play with them. Finally, she complained, the teachers are not like kibbutz teachers. They do not permit the children to talk in class, but compel them to sit quietly. If the children disobey, they must sit in a corner or leave the room. To Tamar it was obvious that on these, and other counts, the kibbutz was much superior to America.

This attitude continues to prevail in the high school. In a sample of 31 students, 29 said the kibbutz was superior to the city. (One was doubtful, and one said the kibbutz was superior for children, but not for adults.) The reasons given for this superiority, in order of frequency, follow.

Mutual aid and socialism
Equality
Economic security and prosperity
Interesting life
Group interaction
Freedom
Peaceful life
Contribution to national reconstruction

These same students not only prefer the kibbutz to other forms of social life, but they, like the adult sabras, structure their life ambitions almost exclusively in terms of some aspect of kibbutz life. This is revealed in their responses to the interview-question, "What is your life ambition?" Of a sample of 27 students, 19 stated their ambition to be one of the following: to work in Kiryat Yedidim; to be a member of Kiryat Yedidim; to improve Kiryat Yedidim. Three of the respondents gave as their ambitions: to found a new kibbutz; to fight for a better world; to change the present Israeli government to a revolutionary one. Five either had no ambition or did not know what it might be.

The sabras not only feel at home in the kibbutz, and view kibbutz culture as superior to other cultures, but they have positive attitudes to the members of the kibbutz — both older members and peers. These attitudes find their most intense expression in the willingness of the sabras to come to the assistance of other kibbutz members, and even to make personal sacrifices for them.

A chavera with special nursing skills had been asked by the government authorities to work in the immigrant camps, and the kibbutz had consented to relieve her one day a week for this work. When she requested to be released for two days, the town meeting, at the recommendation of the women's Work Chairman, declined to grant her request because of the shortage of workers in Kiryat Yedidim. The chavera, believing that it was her duty to devote more time to this work, voluntarily sacrificed her sabbath to be able to do so.

When Yona — a sabra who had been absent from the kibbutz when the decision had been made — discovered that the chavera had no day of rest, she became incensed with the Work Chairman. How could she, Yona fumed, permit a chavera not to have a rest day? And particularly when the Chairman herself worked with this chavera and saw how tired she was. The Chairman replied that the kibbutz had so voted. "Yes," said the sabra, "but does this mean that you must follow the letter of the law? They voted that way because you told them to, but you know that there are days in which other workers are available to work in her place." Shortly thereafter, the chavera began to receive her sabbath.

This same attitude is found in other sabras. One of the "coldest" of the sabras, for example, pointed out that though she has no intimate friends among her peers, she is deeply tied to them. Hence when a sabra whose first baby had died became pregnant again, she was intensely concerned that it turn out right.

And when the baby was born alive, "I was very happy. I felt as if she were my own sister, I felt it so deeply."

Again, a sabra in speaking of the kibbutz noted spontaneously and undramatically that, "People here are prepared to give anything for another person (in the kibbutz). If I had to sacrifice my life for Yaakov, Rachel, Dan, et cetera, I would do it freely." Although her rhetoric may be exaggerated — the sabras are given to hyperbole — the sentiment is sincere. For this sentiment — a feeling of belonging to the kibbutz as a home, and a feeling of attachment to, and responsibility for, one's fellows — emerges in many other contexts. The sabras, according to the Emotional Response Test, not only feel ashamed when they themselves are discovered to be inadequate to a task, but when their fellows show incompetence as well. Their own death and injury to themselves is the worst thing that can happen to them; but death and injury to others is second, and separation from the group is third, in importance among the "worst things."

The responsibility which sabras feel for the kibbutz and its members is revealed most clearly in their motives for work. Responsibility for the welfare of the kibbutz is, according to the interview data, their most important work motive. The following comments are typical.

This is my society. I want it to progress, to be on a sounder basis than now, so that people can live together in harmony.

Everyone is here out of *hakkara* (sense of responsibility). This is his way of life. Therefore he lives here, and therefore he works here.

We must work so the kibbutz can exist. It must be that way. When we work it is for the kibbutz as a whole.

That question (motive for work) is very easy. I work in order to maintain and to further our kind of life. . . . The motivation is not the economy itself, but the economic ideal; and not really the economy, but the kibbutz, the way of life.

Although the sabras — adults and youth alike — prefer kibbutz living to other forms of social life, they are prepared to criticize its shortcomings and to recommend necessary changes. These recommended changes are of two types: a return to some of the original institutions of the kibbutz, from which there has been backsliding; and improvements in some of these original institutions. These recommended changes which, in effect, represent criticisms of the kibbutz as it is now constituted, are, in order of frequency:[9]

Return to original ideals of kibbutz

Abolition of private property
Improvement in interpersonal relations
Greater equality (for women, the aged, etc.)
Greater sense of dedication
More social participation
Stronger group authority

Improvements beyond the original ideals of the kibbutz

More material amenities
Cultural improvements
Greater economic efficiency
Improvement in lot of young people
More privacy
Less conservatism

Note that those improvements which entail a return to the original values of the kibbutz preponderate. This is consistent with a finding in the Emotional Response Test, according to which the most frequent single instigation to anger among the sabras consists in the violation, by kibbutz members, of kibbutz norms. In some cases this desire for a return to the past represents nostalgia for a highly romanticized past, as may be seen in the following excerpt taken from the interview with a female sabra.

I see the kibbutz as it used to be. I remember small things that, for me, symbolize the kibbutz. In the past the chaverim would sit for hours in the dining room — talking, singing, drinking coffee. I still remember very plainly how, every night, we used to go to the dining room in our pajamas because we could hear our parents dancing and singing; and later they would carry us on their backs to the children's house, singing all the way. It was beautiful, lovely. Why even my name was chosen by the entire kibbutz. That was when it was nice in the kibbutz. Now it's all changed. Everyone remains in his room. All have radios and teakettles in their rooms. The question is, what will be the future of the kibbutz? A few more years (if it continues in this way).

[9] Since there are no significant differences between responses of adult sabras and the high school students, the results of both sets of interviews have been combined. There are twenty-six student and ten adult sabras in the sample.

In addition to these criticisms of the kibbutz, there is in almost all the interviews a current of hostility toward the kibbutz which, together with their affirmation of kibbutz superiority, indicates a marked ambivalence in sabra attitudes. This hostility is barely repressed in some sabras. But even among them the ambivalence is strong, for, having made a hostile remark about the kibbutz, they immediately follow it with a positive statement which almost entirely negates the negative one.

That the kibbutz is an important source of frustration for the sabras is revealed most graphically on the Emotional Response Test. When all the responses to the question, "What makes you angry?," are classified into those whose source resides in the uniquely kibbutz aspects of kibbutz culture or in some action of other kibbutz members, and those whose source is external to both, it is discovered that the former category comprises 71 per cent of the sabra responses, while the latter comprises only 21 per cent (8 per cent are ambiguous). In short, the kibbutz — as measured by its tendency to elicit sabra anger — is a highly frustrating stimulus for the sabras.

We may now examine some of the sources of this frustration, as they emerge in the course of personal interviews. One sabra has periodically thought of leaving the kibbutz. People "here are always fighting and quarreling and they are very intolerant, until often I despise it all." He went on to say how difficult kibbutz life is, primarily because of the lack of privacy and the necessity for conformity.

In general, a major source of sabra discontent with the kibbutz is the necessity, they feel, for constant interaction and the persistent pressure of public opinion. This discontent is expressed behaviorally in a physical retreat from group activity — a retreat which stands in marked contrast to the intensive social participation of the high school students. Typically, the adult sabras are content to remain in their rooms in the evening — reading, listening to the radio, or talking with a few friends. Indeed, the sabras are frequently criticized for not participating more actively in kibbutz activities. As one such critic, referring specifically to the females, put it, "They have closed their doors to the outside world, and have become typical *balebostes*,[10] interested in their homes and children."

[10] A Yiddish term, used either honorifically or contemptuously depending upon one's values. A baleboste, literally, is a "housewife." Its connotation is much broader, however, referring to a woman who is constantly occupied with

This latter charge does not apply to all the females — I am not prepared to estimate its provenience — but it does apply to some of them. One sabra, when asked to name her ambition, said: "In the past, yes. Now, my life is centered around my family. My child consumes most of my time."

This relative disinterest in group participation is explained by the sabras as a reaction to and a retreat from their past. They have had enough of group life, many complain, and now they wish to be left alone. An extreme reaction is found in the following statement.

From the beginning in the Mosad we had to see the same people and the same faces, from early morning until we went to sleep, until it actually became disgusting. In the Mosad you are a machine, not an individualist. Now everyone wants nothing better than to be left alone.

If the former statement is extreme, the following are typical.

In the younger ages there is no time to be alone, and after many years we begin to feel how much we have lost. For collective education does not give one the opportunity to be alone, think alone, and arrange one's own time. But he (the child) does not realize how much he misses until he gets older. This is a big loss, in my opinion. This has a big influence on later life. For after that there is a reaction. When they leave the Mosad and enter the kibbutz, everyone wants to live alone, and they are prepared to fight for it.

Others know exactly what you do all the time. At times it simply becomes too much, and you feel that you want to run away from everything. In Venice it was wonderful. People lived upstairs, but one never saw them, and one could do exactly what one wanted. But in the kibbutz there is always gossip: "he was seen with her," or "she did not enter the dining room with her husband" . . . It's almost impossible to take this all the time.

Sabra disinterest in social participation can be easily demonstrated by objective indices. For example, four of the ten sabras have never served on any of the many kibbutz committees (although four have served on more than one). Six of the ten, moreover, are definitely opposed to increasing their social participation, and the remaining four say that they would be willing to do

---

domestic chores, and who performs them all with excellence. But, it should be remarked, such devotion to these responsibilities leaves her with little time or interest for anything else. The "baleboste," as the ideal female type of the shtetl culture, was repudiated by the women who founded the kibbutz. Hence the baleboste is a scornful epithet in the kibbutz ethos.

so only under special considerations. Only two of the ten adults always attend town meetings; five, however, attend more than 50 per cent of the time. Of those who do attend, few ever speak or express their opinions; no one speaks more frequently than "sometimes." An examination of their hobbies and of the ways in which they spend their evenings reveals that the sabras prefer private to public activities.

The following activities, in their order of frequency, were named by the sabras in response to the interview question, "How do you spend your evenings?": reading, conversing with friends, studying, playing a musical instrument, sleeping, athletics, knitting. Sabra hobbies, listed in order of frequency, include: reading, art, knitting, photography, athletics, choir, gardening. It is apparent that the sabras do not interact in large groups unless they have to, and that almost all of them prefer to spend their evenings in the privacy of their rooms, or in the company of a small group of friends.

Another basis for dissatisfaction with kibbutz life is the feeling on the part of some sabras that the kibbutz frustrates their personal inclinations and talents. One sabra, for example, said that she had always wanted to paint — not as a profession but,

I liked it. If I had had the opportunity to study what I wanted, I would have studied something like painting, but here you learn only what's in the curriculum . . . In our education a person cannot develop his natural inclinations.

A final basis for sabra hostility to the kibbutz is its alleged monotonous and unrewarding way of life. Completing an interview with the author late at night, the sabra turned to him and remarked bitterly:

This is how our lives go on. You work all day, have a few hours in the evening, and then you go to bed so that you can work again the next day. How nice it would be to live in places like South Africa, where they do nothing all day but gossip.

It will come as no surprise, then, to be informed that this sabra's greatest desire is to travel abroad. He does not want to live abroad, he wishes "merely to travel." But since his desire entails a lifetime of travel, it would nevertheless effectively remove him from the kibbutz.

Travel, it should be noted, is an important goal for the other sabras as well. Indeed, second only to study it is, in the Emotional

Response Test, the "best thing" that can happen to them. The frustration of the desire for travel — and almost all suffer from this frustration — is the most frequently cited instigation of sabra sadness. If it is fair to assume that people who are happy where they are have no great need to travel elsewhere, their strong desire to travel indicates some measure of sabra discontent with the kibbutz.

Labor. The sabras are hard and devoted workers. Even the high school students approach their economic tasks seriously, and few if any adults were heard to complain on this score. As the principal said, "With respect to work, they are 100 per cent." Indeed, one of the reasons that some students have little interest in their studies is that their work is of greater importance to them; and their strong desire is to enter the kibbutz so that they can devote full time to it.

This same positive attitude toward work characterizes the adult sabras. My wife and I, who worked beside most of the sabras for almost a year, can testify to the dedication and devotion they display in their work.[11] The sabra in charge of all the parttime workers — immigrant and high school youth, visitors, and so on — in the garden is a driving, tireless worker who in her zeal spares neither herself nor her charges. She is the first to leave for work and the last to leave for home. When the wagon or truck that took the workers out to the fields was delayed, she would become visibly upset, repeating *chaval al hazman* — "(what) a waste of time."

This characterization of the sabras as hard, responsible workers who have a deep sense of responsibility to the group and who fill their assignments with devotion is attested to by the older members of the kibbutz. They not only praise them for their work, but have elected some of them, despite their youth, to the chairmanship of their respective economic branches. This, more than anything else, reflects the confidence which the kibbutz places in the sabras' efficiency and responsibility in work.

The sabras are not only efficient workers; they are imbued

[11] Having worked in almost all the branches of the kibbutz economy while still in high school, the sabras are fairly well decided on the branch of their choice when they are elected to kibbutz membership. Like any other kibbutz member, they are, with certain qualifications, usually assigned to the branch of their choice. (For a discussion of the various factors in the determination of work assignments, see Spiro, *Kibbutz*, pp. 75–79.) Of the adult sabras who at the time of this study were working full time in the kibbutz economy, three worked in the vegetable gardens, two in field crops, two in preschool education, and one each in fodder and the dairy. One had no permanent assignment.

with the importance which the kibbutz attaches to work. As one sabra put it, "A person can do any bad (thing, and get away with it), but if he's a *batlan* (loafer) he won't feel good." The awareness by the sabras of the importance of work in the kibbutz value system is expressed most dramatically in the Bavelas Moral Ideology Test. For the adult sabras, labor leads all other categories by a wide margin in those activities which the kibbutz deems most praiseworthy; and dereliction in labor takes great precedence over all acts which the kibbutz deems most blameworthy. The importance which sabras attach to work is further revealed in letters which they wrote to a chaver visiting America.[12] Much of these letters was devoted to a description of the agricultural situation in the kibbutz and to the praise of the younger sabras for the excellence with which they were carrying out their economic tasks. This was the highest praise they could proffer.

The sabras not only view work as a paramount value, but, in accordance with kibbutz ideology, they consider physical labor as the most important type of work. Not one sabra, for example, has chosen to be a teacher.[13] When the members of a recent graduating class were asked to become teachers, they refused — despite the shortage of teachers in the kibbutz. They would rather, they said, work in the dairy — the most despised of all agricultural work — rather than become teachers. Similarly, the present head of the fodder branch is a young sabra who the Mosad authorities had hoped — on the basis of his brilliant academic record — would become a teacher. He refused. When I asked about his refusal, he explained that, "young men should work, not teach." When the author asked if teaching were not work, he said, "Yes, but it's not physical work."

Consistent with this attitude is the fact that none of the sabras has expressed an interest in medicine or dentistry, although the kibbutz has difficulty in obtaining practitioners from the outside.[14] When asked for the reason, the kibbutz nurse replied, "They are interested only in tractors." [15]

Although the sabras have internalized the kibbutz value of the

---

[12] Who permitted me to read the nonpersonal parts of these letters.

[13] One member of the high school class that graduated while this study was in process had decided to become a teacher.

[14] A department of dentistry was established a short time ago at the Hebrew university, and it was particularly interested in enrolling kibbutz students. Not one kibbutz sabra from the entire country applied.

[15] It should be noted that this interest in tractors is found among the very young children, as well. Should a tractor pass a children's house, for example, the children abandon every other activity in order to observe the tractor. Much play consists in playing "tractor" or "auto."

importance of work, they have not for the most part imbibed the original motives behind this value. The kibbutz founders were imbued with the notions of work as a "calling," and of agricultural work as a means to self-realization through the discovery of nature.[16] Neither notion, so far as we can tell, is strongly held by the sabras. That they — at least the male sabras — have no special, Tolstoyan attitude toward the soil is seen in their dislike of gardening. They do not, as one chaver put it, wish to "work with a hoe." They want to work *on* the land, but not *in* the land; they want, that is, to "work on wheels." Part of this desire stems, of course, from the sabra involvement in, and admiration for, machinery; as one teacher put it, perhaps extravagantly, they are "machinolators." But another reason is the one hinted at above: although work in field crops is extremely enervating — it requires long hours, sometimes around the clock — the men prefer it to almost any other type of work. It permits them to work on tractors and combines rather than with hoes, working bent over the soil. As a chavera put it, "they have lost the 'feel' for nature."

Similarly, only rarely had I the impression that the sabras viewed labor as a calling, as their parents had originally conceived of it. The following response, taken from a sabra interview, is the only one of fifteen recorded responses that approximates this notion.

There is no reward (for work) in money, but there *is* a great reward. Satisfaction from work is the reward . . . Now I derive great satisfaction from my work. It is very pleasant and interesting . . . There is happiness in it.

For the most part, however, and although they work long and hard, the sabras seldom work for the love of labor, *per se.* Indeed, I was shocked to hear one of the hardest-working sabras in the kibbutz say, "No one likes to work — the best thing is shabbat." She went on to say that "everyone would agree that if there were no work it would be much better." Coming from a person who gives of herself unstintingly, and who laments every "wasted" moment, this statement indicates how strongly motivated she must be in order to work so hard at something she would prefer not to do. What is most interesting, however, is her generalization that "everyone" agrees that it would be better if there were no work. For this is the antithesis of a major premise of

[16] See Spiro, *Kibbutz*, pp. 11–19.

the original ethos of the kibbutz: that it is work, not its absence, which makes life worthwhile.

The results of the Emotional Response Test support the above conclusions. Not one sabra mentioned work as one of the best things that could happen to him; and work accounts for only 4 per cent of sabra responses concerning the sources of happiness. In fact, it plays a negligible role in all the emotions included in the Test.

For the most part, however, work motives include the "consciousness" (*hakkara*) of one's responsibility to the kibbutz, to the kibbutz ideal, and to one's agricultural branch; the desire for prestige; and the power of public opinion. The first motive, mentioned by eight of the ten respondents, is clearly the most important.[17] The sabras have uniformly acquired the kibbutz value of the importance of labor, and they are strongly motivated to conform to it. To the extent that the perpetuation of kibbutz culture demands dedication to its paramount value of physical labor, there is strong reason to believe that this tradition has been successfully transmitted.

Collective ownership. Sabra attitudes toward private property and the accumulation of personal possessions are implicit in their attitudes to the kibbutz. The desire to live in the kibbutz entails the acceptance of its most important and characteristic feature — collective ownership. Even the preschool children know that except for the toys which they keep in their parental rooms, they possess no private property. Food, toys, clothing — all belong to the group. Hence the many instances of conflict, discussed in Chapter 9, in which the children are seen to be reluctant to part with a toy do not necessarily mean that they have some feeling that the objects belong to them. A child's refusal to give up a toy may merely mean that he wishes to play with it at that particular time, and not that he harbors any proprietary feeling for it.

On the other hand, there is abundant evidence, in all but the very youngest children, that the preschool children do perceive certain objects as belonging to them. The following examples are fairly typical for children ranging in age from two to four years.

[17] In addition to the motives of hakkara, intrinsic satisfaction, prestige, and public opinion — the motives which the sabras attribute to themselves — I believe that at least two other powerful work motives exist among the sabras. Some want desperately to prove to themselves and to their elders that they are capable of working hard and of maintaining the kibbutz economy. And the females are eager to prove that they can work as hard and as efficiently as the males.

The nurse passes out water-colors for painting. When Tsvi gets his colors, he sings repeatedly: "This is *mine*, this is *mine*."

The nurse wraps towel around Shula (after bath). Shula looks at towel-rack, and says she has the wrong towel. She says she wants her *own* towel.

The assertion of private possession in property is not unilateral, however, for the children also recognize the proprietary rights of others. The following excerpts are from children of the same age-range as those quoted above.

Avi has a marble which the others say belongs to Anat . . . Nurse asks Avi if he will give it to Anat, and he refuses. But he will give it to Chana for, he says, it is really hers . . .

Miri always brings me "my chair" when she offers me a chair on which to sit. No other chair will do. It belongs only to me.

Pua and Yael are playing in the shower room and they see the towels hanging on the hooks. They go from towel to towel, and identify each by its rightful "owner." [18]

Concern with private property is strong, among at least some of the older children as well. In the Transitional Class, for example, two girls not only esteem material possessions, but they are highly envious of the possessions of others, becoming agitated should another child have a "nicer" dress, blouse, or hair ribbon. One day, for example, one of these girls changed blouses four times because she felt that another's was prettier than hers.

Similar attitudes are to be found in the grade school, especially among the younger children. Their few private possessions — books, marbles, wristwatches — are jealously retained as their own. They are strongly assertive of their property rights, according to their teacher, insisting that an object "is mine," should another child wish to take it. Some are envious of another's possessions, resenting the fact that another has something which they do not have.

These younger students not only indicate desire for private

[18] At least some of the proprietary feelings of the children, it should be remarked, may be reinforced by the nurses, who sometimes permit the children to become aware of the existence, as well as the desirability, of private property.

Yaffa found a handkerchief on the grass that Hagar's mother had given her (Hagar), and laundered it. Hagar claims the handkerchief as her own and demands it from Yaffa. Nurse asks Yaffa where she got it, and she says she found it. "Then it's not *yours*," says the nurse. Hagar says that her mother gave it to her. Yaffa, sulking, gives it up to Hagar.

possession of some objects, but they also place great value on material things in general. The Emotional Response Test reveals, for example, that the acquisition of material things is by far the "best thing" that can happen to them, and that, conversely, the deprivation of material satisfactions is one of the most important causes of sadness.

The importance which these preschool and grammar school children attach to possessions seems to diminish greatly among the adult sabras. When queried about private property and the desire to amass personal possessions, their responses were unanimously negative.

I've never felt any desire for personal property. But if someone offered me a million dollars, I'd take it.

This question really never presented itself to me. Sometimes I would like to dress better, to have a nicer room. But the lack of these things does not ruin my life, and I really feel that I lack nothing. I have satisfactions from living here, and I have never felt that I was not working for myself.

I have never lacked the desire to give away that which was dearest to me, of either a financial or an emotional value. And that is a direct result of collective education. There is an absence in me of any sense of private property.

That their desire for personal possessions is weak is supported by the Emotional Response Test. Although the desire for possessions looms large in the responses of the younger children, it is negligible in the responses of the adult sabras. The acquisition of personal possessions occurs not even once among twenty-five responses as a condition for happiness; and it constitutes only 6 per cent of their responses concerning the "best thing" that could happen to them. Conversely, the lack of possessions constitutes only 4 per cent of their responses concerning the cause of anger, zero per cent concerning the causes of sadness, and zero per cent concerning the worst thing that can happen to them.

As in the case of their attitude toward labor, the sabra attitude toward private property would suggest that the kibbutz value of collective ownership has been successfully transmitted from the founding to the second generation. And this, as our data on early childhood indicate, is no easy task. For these data suggest — with respect to private possessions, at any rate — that the child is no *tabula rasa*, who, depending on his cultural environment, is equally amenable to private or collective property arrangements.

On the contrary, the data suggest that the child's early motivations are strongly directed toward private ownership, an orientation from which he is only gradually weaned by effective cultural techniques.

That the sabras have been successfully weaned from their earlier attitudes is shown by the data from the Emotional Response Test. This test indicates that personal possessions are not an important source of pleasure for the sabras, and that the lack of such possessions is not an important source of frustration. But the sabras are more than indifferent to private property; they view it as an evil. In the same test, for example, the most frequently cited cause of anger was the violation by the kibbutz or by some subgroup within it of its own norms. And, for the most part, such violations had to do with the introduction of private property and the inequities that accompany its introduction. In the light of this consistent and uniform attitude to possessions, it is not surprising that the abolition of what private property has been allowed to enter the kibbutz is the most frequently mentioned sabra suggestion for the improvement of the kibbutz.

Marxism. The kibbutz perceives itself as both an agricultural collective and a cell in a revolutionary political movement. In its socialization endeavors it attempts not only to educate for kibbutz living but for political activity. From the point of view of The Federation, if not of all the parents in Kiryat Yedidim, both goals are of equal importance. The kibbutz has been successful in the first endeavor; it has been less successful in the second.

The first expressions of political interest among the sabras appear among the children of the fourth grade. Political interests are found among only a few children in the primary grades, and the attitudes expressed almost always reflect the dominant ideology.

Except for a few girls, most high school students have some interest in politics and, compared to the average American high school student, their interest is probably high. This interest is expressed in a number of ways. First, pictures of Lenin and Stalin hang in some dormitory rooms. Second, apathy in the classroom can almost always be changed into interest by a political discussion. Third, the students frequently discuss political questions in the dormitory or while working in the fields. Favorite topics of conversation with me, for example, included America and her role in international affairs, and American Jewry and its apparent obstinacy in refusing to migrate to Israel. Fourth, the student magazine sometimes publishes articles and editorials dealing with political subjects.

Although some of the political articles which were published in the Mosad magazine during the period of our study attacked the propensity of the students to accept the "party line" on political matters, this tendency continued to dominate political activity. For example, in a skit prepared for a Purim celebration, the (then) recent assassination of the Premier of Iran was explained in accordance with the explanation given in *Pravda* — he was the victim of an American agent. It is of interest to note, therefore, that when the tenth-grade students were asked to comment on an early Soviet short story which indirectly attacks the Soviet dictatorship, they unanimously agreed that everyone should have the right to make his own decisions and to choose his own way of life, without being dictated to from above.

Acceptance of the party line has at least one interesting consequence for political thought among the students — it frequently leads to political naïveté and, among the younger students at least, to considerable political distortion. This is shown most dramatically in the essays written by members of the seventh grade on the subject, "What is a Socialist?" Many, to be sure, stressed the principle, "from each according to his ability, to each according to his needs." In addition, however, they stressed such values as "equality," "progress," "peace," and "justice" as being unique to socialism — implying that non-socialists were opposed to them. It is difficult to deduce from the essays themselves what some of these abstract terms denote in actual social organization. But when their referents are explicitly stipulated, it comes as a surprise that these terms often refer to goals and institutions which have long existed in many non-socialist societies, such as universal literacy, abolition of child labor, and the seven-hour day.

Our comments on the political interest among these students should be qualified by the observation that this interest is confined to practical politics and seldom embraces theoretical ideology — that is, Marxism. As measured by their interest in the ideological aspects of The Movement, at any rate, and by ideological discussions in the classroom, it would be fair to say that Marxist ideology has little importance in their lives, and that their interest in it is, for the most part, perfunctory. The rhetoric is repeated dutifully, but for the most part the students seem to be bored with it. In attempting to measure intellectual interest in the classroom, for example, I discovered a significant relationship between ideological content and classroom interest. In the ideological courses, for the most part, students were disinterested or bored. Non-ideological courses (such as biology, algebra, art, Biblical archeology) more readily evoked interest.

This same attitude is manifest in the students' relationship to The Movement, in which, except for its scouting program, they manifest almost no interest. My impression from participating in meetings of The Movement — an impression reinforced by interviews with its local leadership — is that its political program evokes little enthusiasm in the students, and that The Movement itself would collapse without pressure from the authorities. This conclusion is supported by a poll taken by the Mosad magazine which revealed that almost none of the respondents saw any function for The Movement in the Mosad. Typical comments were: "It has no function, since we are already living in the kibbutz"; "None"; "Practically none."

In general one has the feeling that the students suffer from a surfeit of ideology. As one senior remarked in conversation with the author, "How much Marxism can you take? There's a limit." Many of the students feel that concern with ideology can be carried to an excess — a feeling that their parents do not share. This attitude, accompanied by overtones of hostility, is graphically expressed in the derogatory expression, *le-hatif Tziyonut*, "to preach Zionism." When someone lectures the students on ethics, emphasizing their many responsibilities to the kibbutz, the workers, and mankind, the speaker is characterized as "preaching Zionism," and their usual response to him is "Don't preach Zionism to us," implying, "Get off your high moral plane; you're not addressing a Zionist (or socialist) convention, so forget about the platitudes."

The adult sabras, like the high school students, have only a mild interest in either the ideology or the political program of The Party. In the course of lengthy interviews, only two adult sabras indicated a relatively strong interest in politics; four indicated an average interest; and four were mildly interested or indifferent. This lack of strong political interest may be inferred from other data as well. Among the various emotions — such as happiness, sadness, and shame — which are presumably tapped by the Stewart Emotional Response Test, only the question concerning "anger" elicited any reference to politics; and its percentage was very low. Since political activity is the *leitmotiv* of their parents' lives, and since continuity and change in the social structure of the kibbutz are, to a large extent, a function of political values, it is highly important to examine the political attitudes of these adult sabras in some detail.

We may begin by quoting from the range of political attitudes expressed in interviews. One politically indifferent sabra, critical of the Mosad curriculum, complained that while the latter precludes the development of one's "natural abilities," it "emphasizes Marxism and Zionism and other such foolishness." Another sabra, whose political interest was rated as "mild," said that though he reads the daily newspaper, he does not read the political literature prepared by The Party. He generally accepts the opinions of The Party, but he has "no deep understanding of politics." For the same reason he "devote(s) little time or interest to the 'Arab Question,' although I do not agree with The Party's stand on this issue." [19] Hence, he concluded, whatever political opinions he has are not "solidly based." In response to another question he acknowledged some feeling of solidarity with other members of The Party, but, he continued, he feels no great solidarity with the city proletariat. Moreover, he views himself as a worker only in the sense that "I want to live from my own work rather than from the work of others." Hence, he has no interest in the class struggle. Although at one time he was interested in reading Marx and Engels, "In recent years I have left this out of my life completely."

Another sabra, whose political interest was rated as "mild," reads The Party's daily newspaper, but is most interested in the travel articles. His neglect of articles and editorials of a political nature stems not from disinterest, but from lack of comprehension — "I just don't grasp it."

The following comments are from sabras whose political interest was rated as "average." One reads the daily newspaper, and "like(s) to talk politics with serious people . . . but it (politics) does not consume my life . . . If I see someone who doesn't read the newspaper, it makes a bad impression on me." The other complained that she and her friends were neither sufficiently interested nor informed about politics. "I think it's not right. I think few of us do much about it."

Even those whose interest is "average" have no deep political feelings or ideological commitments. This leaves the two whose political interests were "strong." The first reads *Soviet Union*, as well as The Party's daily newspaper. His interest in ideological matters dates at least as far back as his early high school years when, he says, he was strongly influenced by the Communists —

[19] The Party favors a more "lenient" attitude toward the Arabs than is practiced by the present government.

even to the extent of opposing immigration to Israel from the Soviet Union. In fact, he is still not sure about his position on this issue. He definitely feels identified with the city proletariat, together with whom he is prepared to join in revolution — indeed, he is the only sabra for whom we felt "The Revolution" to be more than rhetoric. He is prepared to accept the "dictatorship of the proletariat" as a necessary means to the final achievement of its (the revolution's) goals.

The other sabra, who has apparently given more than cursory thought to ideological matters, is, however, not always in agreement with The Party. Moreover, he thinks that its newspaper is "not very good"; it is "extreme and one-sided." Though a Marxist, he strongly feels that his Marxism is, as he put it, "accidental," a product of growing up in a Marxist kibbutz. Had he been reared in a non-Marxist environment, he believes that he would have been a non-Marxist. He favors the "dictatorship of the proletariat" as a means to the communist end, but he is entirely opposed, as he put it, to the "leader-worship" found in the Soviet Union,[20] as well as to other aspects of Soviet life.

The relatively mild interest displayed by most sabras in political matters stands in sharp contrast to the strong interest displayed by many members of the hashlama. The latter frequently engaged us in political discussions — the sabras almost never — and it was from among their ranks that it was suggested that my wife and I were spies for the United States State Department. A compelling example of the political difference between the hashlama and the sabras is afforded by the following conversation between a representative of each. The member of the hashlama had observed that the political situation in Israel was rapidly "deteriorating" — from the point of view of revolutionary socialism — and suggested that The Party should make immediate plans for the Revolution, before it was too late. The sabra was highly amused by this suggestion, as well as disdainful of the person who made it. "You're crazy," he told her; to which she replied that he had "sold out to the enemy."

It should be noted, in conclusion, that however mild their interest in politics, most sabras are in general agreement with The Party on almost all issues; and even when they differ with it, they unanimously support it at the polls. Even the most apathetic would be startled by the suggestion that they support some other party. But in this, as in other aspects of their political behavior,

[20] He was interviewed five years before the Soviet attack on the "cult of personality."

the sabras — adolescent and adult alike — seem similar to those Western church members who continue to adhere to traditional religious beliefs without displaying the emotional involvement or dedication which were once associated with them. To use the felicitous expression of Max Weber, the "routinization of charisma" has set in.

One might speculate on the reasons for this "routinization." It is my thesis — a simple one — that if political beliefs are to become powerful motivational drives, it is necessary for these beliefs to be acquired emotionally rather than cognitively. It is my hypothesis, in short, that any world view, whether secular or religious, becomes truly functional — motivational — in a person's life when it corresponds to those early experiences out of which the child's perceptions of his world first develop. In the process of socialization, the child learns many things about his world, and he is taught many things about his world. When the cognitive beliefs (which he is taught by cultural surrogates) correspond to the perceptual hypotheses (which he learns in early experience) the former are truly motivational, for they then reinforce, and provide cultural sanction and authority for, the latter. If, on the other hand, one learns, for example, from early experience to perceive the world as hostile, then a culturally transmitted belief premised on the notion that the world is benevolent will play but a small role in his motivational system, however much he may give verbal assent to it.

The sabras, we suggest, are taught an ideology whose assumptions are at variance with their personal perceptions of the world. The ideology of the kibbutz (derived from that of The Party) is an ideology which, in its unconscious psychodynamics, rests on rebellion against, and the ultimate banishment of, the father — it is in opposition to the patriarchal aspects of Western culture, and it wishes to abolish the capitalist civilization of its cultural fathers. This, in daily political activity, entails a hatred of those who, like Ben Gurion, are perceived as bad fathers and the love of those who, like Stalin, are perceived as good fathers. All this could have little meaning for the sabras who, having no need to kill or to idealize the father, are not motivated by political slogans or programs resting on such a need.

Again, for reasons of their personal history, the sabras cannot identify with the workers and other "oppressed" groups in society. Experiencing little Oedipal struggle (in the power, not in the sexual, sense) themselves, they are not motivated to identify with other persons and groups who are perceived to be oppressed. In short, there is little correspondence between cultural belief and perceptual hypothesis. This interpretation, albeit speculative, is supported indirectly by the observation that (among the adolescents at least) political interest is related to emotional disturbance. Like the intense intellectuals, it is among those sabras whose family relationships (parent-child, sibling-sibling) are disturbed that the most intense political interest and activity is found.

There is, we believe, another reason for the sabras' relative disinterest in political activity. The Party, through which such activity is expressed, demands strict party discipline — which means acceptance of its authority. But the sabras have little respect for authority; obedience to authority is of little importance in their value system. If our assumption about the relationship between personality and politics is correct, it is hard to see how an authoritarian party could win their enthusiastic allegiance.

To sum up, the sabras support — and probably will continue to support — both The Party and its policies. But this support will increasingly be motivated by loyalty, training, or an impersonal sense of justice — not from that personal emotional involvement that transforms political activity into personal dedication, and that transmutes political belief into world-view.

But, if the sabras are not emotionally committed to a Marxist world-view, neither have they turned to a religious one. The kibbutz has been eminently successful in transmitting its anticlericalism and philosophic naturalism to its children. The latter phrase is of theoretical importance. For naturalism, it is apparent from our observations of kibbutz children — observations which fully support the conclusions of Piaget[21] and others — is not a naïve philosophy of childhood, but one which is developed — if it is developed at all — in later experience and/or as a result of education.

The kibbutz toddlers exhibit many kinds of animistic thinking. There is abundant evidence to indicate that they do not fully distinguish between animate and inanimate objects, and, moreover, that they perceive inanimate objects as animate. The clearest and most interesting evidence consists in their attribution of blame to inanimate objects, and their consequent "punishment" of those objects that have "harmed" either them or their peers. Children were observed, for example, to trip over a box, and then to spank it for "causing" them to trip. They were observed

[21] J. Piaget, *The Child's Conception of the World* (New York: Harcourt Brace, 1929).

to "spank" the door for banging against another child's finger. They were observed to reprimand a bicycle after falling off it. The following excerpts are taken from observations recorded for two- and three-year-olds.

Anat falls down on the walk. She . . . stands up, cries, bites her tin can, hits it.

Avinoam enters the room and the door slams on his fingers. He screams and screams. SHLOMIT picks him up and runs to the basin, letting cold water run on his fingers. All the children run to see . . . Amikam hits the door; then Yehuda, Anat, and Ofer hit the door. SHLOMIT explains that they all want to hit the door because it hurt Avinoam.

Iris falls over a toy. Amir slaps the toy, saying, "noo, noo, noo."

If it be remembered that the kibbutz is a secular community which discourages animistic and supernaturalistic thinking, it can be suggested that animism, if found in kibbutz children, represents a natural way of perceiving the universe at an early stage of ontogenetic development. That the preschool children, according to the nurses, never ask questions about theological matters, lends additional support to this conclusion.

In the primary school children receive an explicitly naturalistic world-view. The curriculum and its philosophy derive from a scientific view of man and the world, and are explicitly opposed to supernaturalism in any form. The opposition to religion is based not only on intellectual conviction but on the belief — as an educational authority of The Federation states — "that a generation educated without God will have its faith in man strengthened."

Since the Bible, however, is a basic literary and historical text-book in the school system, it is necessary that the term, "God," be explained as soon as it is encountered. The teachers explain that belief in supernatural beings arose among early peoples, before they acquired scientific explanations for natural phenomena, and that even today some people, who have not received a scientific education, continue to use this belief for the explanation of matters which they do not understand.

Since this type of instruction is consistent with everything else they are taught, the children have no difficulty in discarding their earlier animism. Indeed, they are as vigorously "antisuperstitious" as their parents and teachers. One of the first questions which the sixth-grade class would ask of strangers was whether or not they believed in God. If the answer were in the affirmative, the latter would be teased for their "superstitious" belief.

Again, on the traditional religious New Year (Rosh Hashana) some of the refugee children who live in the kibbutz attended religious services — as they do on other holy days — which are conducted by the orthodox parents of the chaverim. As they entered the synagogue, two of the second-grade children stood at the door, shouting, "but there is no God."

One night at the behest of the second-grade children, I recounted several experiences from a previous field trip in the South Pacific. One such experience involved the intervention of a supernatural being to prevent the violation of a local taboo. When I explained that those people believe that God will punish them for the violation of certain taboos, the children responded with, "But we don't believe in God here." The children in the sixth grade, to whom the same story was told, complained to their nurse the following day that I had told them a "bluff." That evening they asked if I were going to tell them another "bluff."

There is no diminution in this naturalistic orientation among the adult sabras. All, without exception, are opposed to religion; although the reasons for, and the intensity of, their opposition differ. The following excerpts indicate the range of their attitudes.

I think it is all foolishness.

Religion says nothing to me. Zero. I hate the religious sector. I lived for two months in religious kibbutzim, and was very much impressed with them. But generally I hate it (religion).

I have never thought about it.

I have never had reason to doubt my atheism, and I am bitterly opposed to clericalism. But I value religion for having held the Jewish people together.

(I asked if he did not think it strange that all the world believed, and he did not. He laughed and said): "From my point of view it is just the reverse — it is strange that they believe."

I will not forgive a person, even if he is a good human being, for being religious. Religion is a big bluff. It enables people to deceive others. In these matters I am extreme.

Zionism. The sabras accept one crucial plank in the Zionist platform — the Jewish State. Other planks, however — such as the importance of Jewish culture, the unity of the Jewish People, and *kibbutz galuyot* (the Ingathering of the Exiles) — do not evoke unanimous agreement. Indeed, there is abundant evidence to suggest that the sabras do not share these Zionist values because they view Judaism and Jewishness as inferior and would like to dissociate themselves from them. We shall begin this discussion with their attitudes toward Jewish culture, which, for all its ambiguity, we shall refer to by "Judaism."

Almost any form of Jewish literature is viewed by the sabras as "boring," so that they make no attempt to read it. Since the non-historical portions of the Bible are interpreted by them as a series of fairy tales, they can see no value in them. Only when a Biblical lesson contains material of archeological or historical interest, or when a place name or historical site is personally known to them, or when the lesson is related to some political or scientific interest of theirs, do the high school students reveal any interest in the Bible. An extreme, but not entirely atypical, response to Biblical literature is the following comment of a ninth-grade student. After referring to the Bible as "terribly boring," she said that the book of Psalms was just *zift,* or "no good" (literally, "tar," from the Arabic).

But it is not only Biblical literature that is "boring." Much of modern Jewish literature is characterized by the same term. Bialik, for example, is a "sentimentalist" and mere "publicist." And only under protest do they read Mendele or Shalom Aleichem, both of whose works are included in the Mosad curriculum.[22] Since, however, they are fascinated by accounts of Chinese and Indian village life, the twelfth-grade teacher asked his students to approach Shalom Aleichem's stories of the shtetl in the same attitude with which they would approach the descriptions of the former villages. This they could not do. The latter, they argued, "holds no interest for us."

Jewish music is responded to in a similar fashion. Despite the efforts of the music teacher to stimulate their appreciation, the students "hate" the Jewish music of the Diaspora. He once taught his tenth-grade class a Jewish song which, however, he labeled as Russian. They thought it was marvelous, and when he revealed to them that it was a Jewish song, they refused to believe him. Jewish history fares no better. The eleventh-grade class, in des-

[22] These are three of the dominant figures in modern Jewish literature. Haim Nachman Bialik (1873–1934) is viewed by many critics as the greatest of modern Hebrew poets. Mendele Mocher Seforim (1835–1917) and Shalom Aleichem (1859–1920) are pseudonyms for Shalom Jacob Abramowitch and Solomon Rabinowitch, respectively. They are known for their realistic, but sympathetic (and humorous) sketches and stories of shtetl life.

peration, asked their teacher why they could not skip most of Jewish history and begin, rather, with the history of modern Israel. Although general history is one of their favorite subjects, Jewish history is "boring."

"Boring," it should now be apparent, is their favorite characterization of Jewish culture and the Jewish past. A ninth-grade girl summed it up when she commented, "In general the Jews are a very boring people." It was her opinion, moreover, that "the two thousand years of the Jewish Diaspora were a complete waste. Better they (the Jews) should have been buried there." This latter statement, to be sure, is extreme; but though few sabras would articulate it in precisely that form, many would agree with its general sentiment. The consensus seems to be that Diaspora Jewish history was boring and dull, and that Diaspora Jewish life was confining, oppressive, and — as one put it — "miserable."

The intense affect which any encounter with Judaism, as symbolized by the culture of the shtetl, arouses in the sabras is vividly demonstrated by their reactions to an exhibit of the works of Marc Chagall. In a heated, four-hour discussion of the exhibit, the interest of the eleventh-grade students never flagged. They were visibly and deeply affected by the paintings, and the following comments, recorded during the discussion, serve to give some flavor of their attitudes.

Chagall's *weltanschauung* was destroyed with the creation of the State of Israel. Therefore, he has nothing to say to us.

Chagall's portrayal of Jewish village life says nothing to us.

Chagall is immersed only in his narrow village life.

I am opposed to his *weltanschauung*. People outside of Israel may be able to understand him, but those in Israel simply cannot.

Life in the Jewish village was sick. He should paint modern Israel and the kind of progressive life we want to live.

We should not be educated to understand them (Chagall's pictures). We are educated for something else.

We can understand him, but we don't want him hanging here.

The sabra disdain for Judaism has been generalized to encompass those who were, or are, its "carriers." Thus, traditional, religious, and Oriental (Near Eastern) Jews are the objects of disdain and/or hostility. The attitude of the high school students to the Oriental Jews, frequent victims of their taunting, teasing, and name-calling, has been outlined[23] and the attitude of the adult sabras is best expressed by the following statement. Voicing his antagonism to the new immigrants, a sabra concluded, "They are necessary, but they are not desirable."

Historical European, more particularly Eastern European, Jewry is responded to similarly. Writing on "What is a Jew?," only one of the ten essayists (all seventh-grade students) identified the Jews with something which, from the essayist's point of view, was positive; the Jews, she wrote, had made "important contributions to civilization." All the other students stressed two characteristics: the Jews have always been persecuted, and everywhere they are despised.

To the nations of the world, the word, "Jew," is a word of derision and contempt.

The Jewish people, most persecuted of all peoples, is found in all the countries of the world, and most of them persecute him. The Jew is not a happy man.

A Jew is a person who, when found in other countries, has many troubles. The Jewish nation is a nation of many troubles.

What is most interesting about these characterizations, in context, is the implication that persecution and derision are qualities possessed by Jews, rather than behavior patterns manifested by Gentiles — a point to which we shall have occasion to return. Hence the essayists are quick to dissociate themselves both from these qualities and from the persons to whom they are attached. "Modern" Israelis — but not the Yemenites and other Oriental immigrants — say many of the essayists, are not at all like the "Jews" referred to above who may most often be identified by such characteristics as beards and skullcaps. On the contrary, in Israel, writes one of the essayists,

[23] Pp. 319–320. It may be argued that sabra hostility to the Oriental students is a simple example of out-group aggression, and that the principle of parsimony — if nothing else — should dictate the discarding of our hypothesis — namely, that the Orientals arouse hostility because they symbolize Diaspora Jews and Judaism. It is our strong feeling, however, that, whereas the sabras' hostility toward students from the cities and other kibbutzim does represent mere out-group aggression, the intense affect characterizing the hostility toward the Orientals requires a more complex interpretation.

. . . you will hear singing — songs of farmers, songs of rebuilding.
. . . That is the song of the future, and the rebirth of the Jewish
Nation.

Religious Jews — or more accurately, orthodox Jews whose
Jewish "visibility" is pronounced — are the objects of similar attitudes. A fourth-grade girl, after asking her father if he had ever
prayed, proceeded to describe with much laughter how the "Jews
in Europe" had prayed. Her description, accompanied by gro-
tesque gestures, was in the tradition of anti-Semitic caricature.
And from the other end of the age scale came this comment from
an adult sabra: "I hate them (the orthodox Jews), and when I see
them I can understand why people become anti-Semitic."

It should therefore come as no surprise that many sabras —
like some of their parents — are proud of the fact that many kibbutz children do not look "Jewish." Holding a blond baby for me
to photograph, one sabra remarked proudly, "In America, they will
never guess that these children are Jews — they will think they
are *goyim.*"

In effect, the sabras feel no tie — other than a negative one —
with much of Jewish tradition or with peculiarly Jewish values;
they want little to do with the last 2000 years of the Jewish past;
and they wish to dissociate themselves from those Jews who,
actually or symbolically, represent those values and that past.
Hence, those aspects of Zionist ideology which stress the unity of
the Jewish people, the glory of Jewish culture, and the importance
of Jewish values, they reject out of hand. To them, Zionism means
Israeli patriotism.

Despite their genuine patriotism, there is some suggestion that
the sabras view the State of Israel as they view Judaism and the
Jewish past — as something inferior. Some of the sabras, at least,
are impressed with quantity; in conversation with them one frequently feels that what are really important for them are the
biggest ships, the *most* combines, the *fastest* planes, the *largest*
farms — all of which are lacking in Israel. It is mock rather than
genuine humor that characterizes their frequent references to
Israel as "our tiny country." The high regard in which some sabras
hold the Soviet Union may well stem from their adulation of bigness and quantity, rather than from ideological conviction (their
ideology would preclude a corresponding adulation of the United
States).

For other sabras, however, the inferiority of Israel is a political
one, and those few who are politically oriented draw invidious

comparisons between Israel and the Soviet Union. Nor is this surprising. Socialism, they have been taught, is the only desirable way of life, and only in the Soviet Union — but not in Israel — is socialism the dominant economic system. Moreover, the Soviet Union is in the "vanguard" of man's quest for peace and justice. Israel, tied internationally to the apron-strings of the West and dominated internally by a "reformist" party, is relatively backward. It is little wonder, therefore, that those who are serious in their political interests should have some doubts about their relationship to the State of Israel. If, commented one sabra,

. . . the Government continues as it is, it may be that we will have to leave here. It's true that life in Russia is hard and terrible. But they know for what purpose they're building. And they are progressing. I see no purpose to our building (in Israel). It is possible, if the policy here will not change, that I will not want to build this country.

Still other sabras believe Israel intellectually and artistically inferior to other countries. The books they read, the plays they see, the ideas they discuss — all for the most part are creations of foreign minds; their Israeli counterparts they view as inferior. After a trip abroad one sabra refused to read Hebrew books because they were, "all trash." As for the opera and the theater, after Europe, "everything here was hopeless." Nor did Israeli architecture escape his criticism. Soon after returning from abroad, he had occasion to visit Tel Aviv, but "after Rome it looked so ugly, I refused even to get out of the car."

These comments were made to me in the course of a long evening, during which this sabra obviously felt some need to unburden himself. His usual attitude toward the outside world, one expressed by all sabras who have been abroad, is, rather, one of superiority. "Israel is better," may be said to be the theme of those who return from foreign travel. This superiority is often expressed in moral terms. "Paris was dirty," said the sabra quoted above, so that he was "impatient to return to Israel." True, the food was good, but, he remarked contemptuously, "the French live to eat, while we eat to live." Such remarks, we feel, are defensive maneuvers rather than expressions of true sentiments. An individual who is secure in what he is or has has no need to distort or justify; and the compulsive insistence on the superiority of Israel seems to stem precisely from such a need. This attitude, we believe, is a justification for the Zionist enterprise, a justification that enables the sabras to accept their "tiny country," toward which they are painfully ambivalent.

This interpretation is supported by the remarks of this same sabra who, in the first interview, affirmed the superiority of Israel over all countries and, in the second interview, expressed great despair at having to live in it. It is further supported by the remarkable fact that every adult sabra expressed an intense desire to travel abroad. Their favorite books, moreover, are those depicting life in foreign countries. It does not seem unfair to conclude that people whose desire for travel is so intense are people who are dissatisfied with where they are.[24]

At least two bases for the (largely unconscious) anti-Zionist feelings of the sabras suggest themselves. Their feeling of discontent with the State of Israel is not too difficult to understand. Part of this discontent has already been mentioned: the important values to which various sabras are devoted — bigness, socialism, material amenities, art, culture, and so on — are found in greater abundance in other countries. To the extent that the sabras know, or think they know through reading and travel, that these are more prevalent in other countries, they are discontent with what they find in Israel.

Since their parents, who share many of these values, have not expressed similar negative attitudes toward Israel, there must be an additional factor that serves to differentiate the sabras from their parents. That factor, we believe, is a vision. Dedication to the State of Israel must, in the nature of things, be a dedication to a vision rather than to a reality. Life in Israel is hard. For many reasons — lack of abundant natural resources, necessity for heavy armament expenditures, an influx of a huge and unskilled immigrant population — most Israelis live at a relatively low level of material prosperity. And to maintain even this level requires hard physical labor. The average chaver kibbutz, for example, works a fifty-four-hour week, under a hot Israeli sun, with few of the compensations which air-conditioning, well-prepared and

[24] One might argue (as above, p. 370) that the desire to travel stems from discontent with the kibbutz, rather than with the country. If the desire for travel were phrased in terms of domestic travel this interpretation would be the most cogent. Since, however, it is expressed almost exclusively in terms of foreign, rather than domestic, travel, we can conclude that there is discontent, both with the country and the kibbutz.

Desire for travel (and its consequent implication for their attitude to Israel) probably accounts, too, for the sabras' insistence that it was all but immoral for me to have come to Israel as an observer rather than as a participant. This attitude, I believe, stems from their own guilt about wanting to do the same as well as from envy of those who are able to do what they themselves would like to do.

plentiful food, and such, can offer. In addition, the country is experiencing great tension, induced by its precarious international situation, and by its barely disguised domestic conflict between Oriental and Western immigrants. All these conditions demand great sacrifice, both physical and emotional, from Israeli citizens, and this sacrifice makes life in Israel a constant series of hardships.

Because of these hardships, personal commitment to the State of Israel requires a motive more powerful than immediate personal gratification. This motive must entail the willingness to defer present for future happiness and/or the conviction that personal frustration has meaning in the light of some higher value or some ultimate end. Hence only those who are dedicated to a vision of a Heavenly Jerusalem have the emotional staying power that the present earthly Jerusalem demands. Raised in a community which has demanded little sacrifice from them, socialized in a way that precludes the development of dedication to abstract ideals, and encountering the Zionist vision only after the "routinization of charisma" had set in, it is little wonder that for the sabras the vision is all but dimmed. (Indeed, it has become blurred even for many of their parents, who encountered it at the height of its charismatic appeal.)

Precisely what is the Zionist vision that is supposed to evoke the sabras' loyalty? It is our thesis that the vision that the sabras have been taught to seek is incapable of providing an ideological basis for the willingness to make personal sacrifice. The Zionist theory that the sabras have learned is not based on the notion — promulgated by Achad Haam, Martin Buber, and others — that the perpetuation of historic Jewish values and ideals is a sacred task, and that the *raison d'être* of Zionism is the establishment of a spiritual Homeland where a uniquely Jewish culture might flourish. On the contrary, the important kibbutz and Israeli values are, according to the Zionism of the kibbutz, universal. A teacher, one of the kibbutz intellectuals, reacted with great hostility when I asked him if he believed Jewish culture to be unique. Jewish culture, he insisted, is part of European culture, and in the future there will be but one world culture. Hence, Zionism is concerned, not with Jewish culture, but with Jewish bodies. Then followed the classical analysis of Marxist Zionism with which all sabras have been inculcated: anti-Semitism is inevitable in a non-socialist society; first, because of capitalism's need for a scapegoat, and second, because of the socio-economic structure of Diaspora Jewish society, characterized by what Borochov termed its "inverted" economic pyramid. Hence, until the international socialist society, with its world culture, comes into being, Jews are being killed, and it is the task of Zionism to rescue their bodies.

Is such a theory capable of sustaining a vision of Zion for whose ultimate realization the sabras should be willing to sacrifice present gratifications? Since the important ethical values of Judaism are universal, and since its theology and ritual are, for them, superstitious products of a pre-scientific stage of culture, can the sabras have a vision of perpetuating a "glorious" or "noble" heritage? Rather, the desire to "normalize" a pathological situation — to enable Jews to become economically productive, rather than remaining economic "parasites"; to escape anti-Semitism, rather than to suffer pogroms — this is the stuff of which their Zionist vision is comprised. And such a vision may be incapable of supplying that emotional dynamic which is necessary to compensate for their various dissatisfactions and for the various hardships which they must suffer.

Those aspects of Marxist Zionism which have been discussed above help to explain the sabras' lack of enthusiasm for the State of Israel. Other aspects of this theory — aspects which it shares with classical Zionist theory — explain as well their hostility to Judaism and Diaspora Jews. It is our thesis — one which Kaufman[25] has already explored — that an anti-Semitic bias is inherent in the very logic of classical Zionist theory.

Classical Zionism, it can easily be documented, is based on a profound antagonism, if not hatred, for Diaspora Jews and Judaism. One of the bases of classical Zionist thought is described by Kaufman.

Jews of the Galut . . . really deserve to be hated: their customs, tendencies, businesses, attitude to their environment, etc., are the source of the hatred, the justifiable hatred.[26]

Among the epithets which various nationalist and Zionist writers have used to characterize the Jews of the Diaspora, and which Kaufman quotes, are: cheats, moneylenders, exploiters, separatists, haters of Gentiles, rogues, fools, people who live by crooked deals and usury, who believe in vanities, who wear filthy clothing, who speak a confused language; not a nation, not a people, not human; gypsies, fifthy dogs, inhuman, wounded dogs; a people fundamentally useless.

[25] Yehezkel Kaufman, "Anti-Semitic Stereotypes in Zionism," *Commentary*, 7:239–245 (1949), p. 241.
[26] *Ibid.*

If these attributes characterize Jewish life in the Diaspora, it is little wonder that a basic motive for Zionism was to escape that life — or that the rationale for Zionist immigration was to literally and physically abandon it and to begin anew. The goal of the Zionist enterprise in Israel was the creation of a new and healthy culture out of an old, sick culture. And the fewer connections with the old, the healthier it would be. Hence, the paradox in Zionism: "Come to Israel to build a Jewish state" entails, "Come to Israel to escape the Jewish past."

And this argument is not dead. It is still a vital part of current Zionist thought in Israel. Kaufman cites this banner headline published in the important daily, *Davar*, on the anniversary of the Histadrut: "National Renaissance, the regeneration of a parasitic nation" — and it is one to which the sabras have been exposed from childhood. The following quotation from an Israeli textbook cited by Kaufman could be duplicated by quotations from kibbutz textbooks.

The Jews in the Diaspora are living unhealthy lives, as unsavory tradesmen, and sometimes they have unsavory private lives too . . . They are corrupt . . . The Gentiles around them are living healthy lives.

To this general picture of Diaspora Jewry and Judaism which informs the Jewish thinking of the sabras and which could hardly evoke any great enthusiasm for Judaism, must be added still another variable: the sabra perception of Jewish history as a series of unheroic — "boring" is their term — persecutions.

The sabras admire heroism. But, for them, according to two teachers who know them well, there is only one type of heroism — that of physical struggle as found in war or in the conquest of swamps and deserts. The absence of physical resistance to persecution that has characterized much of Diaspora Jewish history could leave them with only a feeling of revulsion. As one of the teachers put it, they do not understand "the heroism expressed in living in persecution and yet, as Thomas Mann has put it, 'of remaining superior.' All they see is the narrowness of their (the Jews who suffered persecution) lives." [27]

[27] If this interpretation is valid, it is not unlikely that a potent factor in the brilliant successes of the Israeli forces in the War of Independence was the necessity felt by many Israelis to prove that they, unlike their ancestors, were real heroes. It would also account for the sabras' great admiration for the Revolt of the Warsaw Ghetto, and for their exclusion of ancient Jewish, and particularly Biblical, history from the category of "boring."

For the sabras, therefore, the last two thousand years of Jewish history are primarily a series of "boring" persecutions and expulsions, unredeemed by the conviction that the suffering of these Diaspora Jews was dignified by a heroic loyalty to an ancient culture. This is perhaps the reason that even the younger sabras view persecution itself as almost a trait of the Jews rather than as their historic fate. Even if loyalty in itself were to be viewed by the sabras as heroic, the peculiar loyalty of Diaspora Jewry could hardly elicit their admiration, as it was a misguided heroism, consisting of loyalty to certain religious values — theological beliefs and ritual practices — which the sabras have been taught to view as superstitious products of a prescientific stage of culture.[28]

Education. The transmission of intellectual and artistic values is an important manifest function of the kibbutz educational system, and its predominantly "liberal arts" curriculum. Artistic expression — in the form of dancing, drawing, painting, singing, and dramatics — is especially encouraged, beginning with the preschool children. This encouragement continues into grade and high school, where artistic expression may now take the form of participation in band and orchestra, and of private lessons in painting and in music for those who demonstrate unusual talent.

It is not surprising, therefore, that intellectual and artistic values occupy an important position in the sabra value hierarchy. This is indicated by their aspirations and behavior alike. In the Emotional Response Test, intellectual and artistic achievement and experience comprise the sabras' third most important source of personal happiness, and the opportunity for study is the best thing that can happen to them. These test results are consistent with data derived from personal interviews. Almost all the sabras interviewed mentioned additional study as their most important ambition.

The value which sabras place on education may be seen in the ambitions they have for their children. Sabra parents are very much concerned that their children become "cultured" adults and that they have the opportunity both for creative growth and for the expression of intellectual talent. Typical is the comment of a sabra mother when, due to a shortage of workers in the kibbutz, some of the chaverim had suggested drafting the students. She was ve-

---

[28] It is not irrelevant to observe that in recent Knesset debates concerning the raising of hogs in Israel, a Mapai Member supported the religious bloc, arguing that Israeli children would be terribly confused by the premise implicit in the sanctioning of hog-raising — that much of the martyrdom of their ancestors had been in vain.

hemently opposed, concluding that "My child will study even if I must starve."

Still another sabra, when asked what ambition she had for her child, replied:

Many. I want him to have a soul, to be talented. He's already musical, and I'm very happy about it. I want most of all that he should be an intellectual. (She looked at me, and said, perhaps in response to my facial expression), Doesn't everyone want his child to be an intellectual? (When I replied in the negative, she looked surprised.)

The importance which sabras assign to intellectual and artistic activity is reflected in their behavior. Their intellectual interests and attainments are much higher than those of the socio-economic class — the working class — of which they are, in fact, members. Indeed, their intellectual *attainments* in such nontechnical subjects as literature, art, and history are probably as high as many of the author's college students, and their intellectual *interests* are unquestionably more intense. Most of them not only read extensively (primarily literature), but many utilize their precious free time for study. Foreign languages, particularly English and Russian, are favorite subjects. The books they own (which they buy from their small annual cash allowance), the pictures that hang on their walls, the music to which they listen, their interest in and attendance at concerts and plays, all betoken a high intellectual level.

For some sabras, intellectual activity is highly practical in motivation. Interested in acquiring special technical competence in their chosen branch of work, books on plant genetics, dairy, poultry raising, and so on, are to be found in their rooms. Although none of the sabras has evinced desire to enter the learned professions, some of them have expressed a desire to study engineering; and at least two were making serious plans for such study.

Objective social and economic conditions in the kibbutz do not permit the sabras to satisfy their intellectual and artistic interests adequately.[29] Indeed, the one activity in which creative interest and talent can be more easily expressed within the limitations of kibbutz resources and the pressure of its work schedule is the dance. Folk dancing is a frequent and an admired artistic activity

[29] There are always exceptions, of course. Two high school students, for example, became passionately interested in archeology. They read almost all the books on this subject to be found in the library, and voluntarily went to dig at archeological sites near the kibbutz. Their efforts yielded a number of finds which they worked up into a small exhibit.

in the kibbutz; many of the sabras are excellent dancers, and one is a choreographer. Some of them were chosen to participate in the two dance festivals that were held in the Iron Curtain countries shortly before our arrival in Kiryat Yedidim.

In general, however, their work schedule is oppressive, leaving little energy for intellectual endeavor; and the excessive communal demands on their leisure time allow them little opportunity for study. But the inability to satisfy intellectual needs is a function not only of these two factors; it is intimately related to the kibbutz value system. Physical labor is unquestionably the paramount value in the kibbutz value hierarchy and, we have seen, this value has been successfully transmitted to the sabras. As in other aspects of its culture, however, the kibbutz has set up mutually inconsistent goals. On the one hand, it expects its children to emulate and respect the great creative minds in science, art, and scholarship; on the other, it not only expects them to excel in agricultural work, but, in effect, discourages intellectual and artistic activity by rewarding primarily excellence in physical labor. Knowledge, therefore, for all its importance in the kibbutz, has little social-reward value compared to labor.

The consequence of these incompatible goals is twofold. Some sabras have passionately embraced the value of work, desiring from their earliest high school years to work in the kibbutz economy, and viewing the learned professions — as does the kibbutz accounting system — as "unproductive." It is for this reason that many sabras refuse to become teachers.[30] For other sabras the conflict in cultural goals has resulted in personal conflict. Having chosen the path of work, those among them who have artistic and intellectual interests have had to inhibit them — because of guilt feelings or external pressures. Some accept this inhibition stoically; others are bitter about it. In either event, the kibbutz emphasis on physical labor as the most important avenue to prestige has precluded the development of the intellectual or artistic abilities of some of the sabras:

There was even a time, when I was a fool, when I wanted to be a teacher. (When asked why he changed his mind, he said:) To be a

---

[30] This attitude has resulted in a type of anti-intellectualism — even among those sabras whom we know to be deeply interested in learning. While teaching English to one of the latter, I remarked that an older chaver who was engaged in various activities for The Federation spoke English quite well. The sabra replied that after all he had nothing to do but study. When I pointed out that the chaver studied English only after his work, she replied contemptuously, "You call what he does 'work'?"

teacher in the kibbutz is not important. Cultural matters are not important here. The important thing is work. This is the opposite of what is true in The Movement; but in the kibbutz itself only the worker is respected. . . . If you don't work in agriculture, you're looked upon as a batlan.[31]

While still a child, the ambition of another sabra was to be a composer. But,

The kibbutz does not respect extreme persons, particularly in artistic matters. To devote oneself to art is something the kibbutz does not understand; they laugh at it. For example (he named two kibbutz members who devote all their spare time to artistic matters) — these things they do are all right, for they are hobbies, and they (the chaverim) respect those who do them as hobbies. But to want to do them professionally or full time can only bring derision.

Another sabra, surprised by my denial that raising an intellectual is every parent's ambition, said:

I suppose they (her peers) tell you they want their children to be good workers? (I said that many did. She flushed.) I want my children to be good workers, too, but there need not be a contradiction between the two.

That she really does believe that there is a contradiction between these two goals, however, is clear from her later remarks. When she repeated her desire to have her children become intellectuals, she said it was highly doubtful if this end could be achieved in the kibbutz. She pointed to two examples of unusually talented persons in her generation who could not develop their talents because of lack of opportunity in the kibbutz.

This conflict has its roots in the Mosad. In discussing the level of academic studies, a senior commented that, in the absence of a grading system, the students make little effort to study. When I observed that, if the members of the kibbutz could work hard without the need of some external incentive, perhaps the students should be able to study hard without such an incentive, he retorted, "There is a difference. Everyone recognizes the importance of work."

Another senior, a talented artist, said he would be ashamed to study art — which is what he wanted to do — because he

[31] See Spiro, *Kibbutz,* pp. 156–157 for an analysis of the kibbutz attitude to the batlan.

should really be working in the fields; moreover, "it is not pleasant that chaverim, with whom I sat on the toilet (as a child), should be working while I'm painting." Even now, when he is given time off from his regular work schedule to draw for the student magazine, others tease him and poke fun at him. It is bad, he concluded, to be an artist exclusively; one must combine work and art.

A junior wants intensely to paint but predicts bitterly that she will not be permitted to be an artist because the kibbutz "has a negative attitude to art. It views art as a waste of time, and thinks that only agricultural work is important. The students share this feeling." As a result, she claims, one student who formerly wrote poetry no longer does so because of the critical attitude of his fellows. "Those chalutzim," she said, "will never learn."

INTRODUCTION

The adult sabras not only live in the village of Kiryat Yedidim, but they have acquired as their cultural heritage its kibbutz culture. For the most part, they conform to its patterns; they have not only learned the cultural norms, but they practice what they have learned. A characteristic feature of sabra behavior — one which they share with their parents — is a high degree of cultural conformity, together with an almost complete absence of serious deviance. As juvenile delinquency is absent among adolescent sabras, so criminal behavior is absent among adult sabras.

"Cultural conformity" refers to at least two dimensions of behavior — performance and inhibition. One can perform a culturally prescribed response or one can refrain from performing a culturally proscribed response. In the former one conforms to a culture pattern, in the latter to a taboo.

Cultural conformity among adults may be a function of a number of motives. (1) The performance of the culture pattern may be intrinsically rewarding because the goal attained by the response satisfies a personally felt need. When this is the case, no sanction extrinsic to the performance itself is necessary to insure conformity. However, conformity to many culture patterns and most taboos is not intrinsically satisfying. Working nine hours a day under a hot Israeli sun, or sharing one's few luxuries, or refraining from attacking an offensive person may be highly frustrating. When this is the case, other motives extrinsic to the response itself are necessary to insure cultural conformity. These include: (2) esteem from peers, or (3) shame from peers — which may be referred to as *alter-ego* sanctions, viewed from the perspective of social control; (4) esteem from self, or (5) anxiety from self — *super-ego* sanctions, viewed from the perspective of social control; and (6) esteem of authority, or (7) fear of authority (natural or supernatural) — *super-alter* sanctions viewed from the perspective of social control. We assume that all three techniques are found in all societies, but that their relative importance in any society is a function of its complexity and of its culturally prescribed techniques of socialization.

Since, despite their ambivalence, the adult sabras prefer the kibbutz to other forms of social life, we may assume that for the most part they experience life in the kibbutz as rewarding, that the performance of many kibbutz culture patterns is for them intrinsically satisfying. We may also be sure, however, that many of its customs and taboos are not intrinsically satisfying, and that some other techniques of social control (social sanctions) are necessary to motivate conformity. We intend, therefore, to discuss the relative importance of the three social sanctions noted above. Since, however, expulsion is the only super-alter sanction employed by the kibbutz, our discussion will be restricted to alter-ego and super-ego sanctions.[1]

EGO DRIVES

Desire for esteem from others is, we may assume, a universal drive.[2] Although little of a definitive nature can be said about its origin in the child's early experience, it is our hypothesis that its intensity is a positive function of (among others) three socialization variables: the use of competition as a technique of training; the holding up to children of goals whose achievement is competitively structured; and the existence of an early period of high nurturance, followed by a period of relative deprivation of nurturance, and a skewed punishment-reward ratio in childhood training.

The kibbutz, as we have observed, attempts to minimize the two former conditions in the socialization of its children. The formal structure of kibbutz socialization includes few competitive goals and the agents of socialization employ few competitive techniques.

[1] We need only observe in this connection that the absence of super-alter techniques may imply that such extreme measures are unnecessary for one or both of the following reasons: kibbutz culture is so highly satisfying that its members are infrequently tempted to violate its norms, or the sabras have strongly internalized one or both of the other sanctions. Kibbutz members as citizens of the State of Israel are subject to the super-alter sanctions employed by any modern state. It would be desirable to discuss the relationship between these sanctions and sabra conformity, but our data on this point are too meager to be useful.

[2] The identity and extensiveness of the "others" is, of course, highly variable. I may desire esteem from my boss, my family, my community, my entire society. I may desire esteem from the wealthy, the scholarly, from God.

Although parents, according to the Questionnaire, rarely punish their children for failure in "competitive" tasks, they not infrequently reward them for victory. To no small extent, moreover, parents motivate their children by comparing their behavior with that of other children.[3]

Nurses, too, employ competitive techniques of socialization, although these comprise a small minority of total socialization practices[4] — surely less than 5 per cent of all techniques. Nevertheless, if kibbutz education is examined more closely, it would not be inaccurate to conclude that competition is inherent in the very system of collective education. For, to the extent that socialization is public — and almost all socialization, it will be remembered, takes place in the presence of other children — praise meted out to one child stimulates competitive motives in the others. When a nurse says, "Micah, what a good boy you are for . . . ," she is implicitly comparing Micah with the other children, or at least they assume that she is. This is shown by the many cases in which the children respond to the praise of another with, "Me too," or, "I'm a good boy, too."

More important as a determinant of prestige drives among the sabras, however, is the kibbutz child's experience of discontinuity in nurturance. We have been at pains to demonstrate (Chapters 3 and 4) that this discontinuity in nurturance is a function of two conditions. One is the not-infrequent change in nurses, as a result of which a highly nurturant person abruptly disappears from a child's life. A second condition is the relative withdrawal of nurturance by parents from the older children in favor of the younger. This withdrawal, it is our hypothesis, is traumatic for a child who has previously been highly indulged. We would expect, therefore, that it would produce a desire for the renewal of the previously rewarding situation.[5] Such children, then, should have a great need for approval — for approval is a sign of love. And approval *can* be obtained by behaving in accordance with the cultural norms.

---

[3] It should be remembered, however, that the sample is small.

[4] For example:

Amir is in the shower, CHANA washes him; he cries and cries. ROSA says to him, "Amiri, it's not nice to cry." Amir refuses to stand under the water to have his hair rinsed. He cries and cries . . . ROSA bathes Rafi, who is quiet. CHANA says to Amir, "See how good Rafi is? Rafi is not a baby. Rafi is a big boy. Is Amir a big boy?"

ESTHER tells the children that it is time to go upstairs to draw. When they are reluctant to leave, she says, "Let's see who can reach there first."

[5] Another consequence is examined below on pages 431–433.

A final variable which is assumed to be positively related to the intensity of the desire for esteem is the punishment-reward ratio. This hypothesis, as formulated by Henry, is phrased, "Where the possibilities for social rewards are relatively few, while those for social punishments are relatively numerous, then in such a society a psychogenic 'need for recognition' is likely to become an issue."[6] And this is precisely what is found to be the case in kibbutz socialization. Only 9 per cent of the entire sample of training techniques employed by the nurses, we have observed, are rewarding. Only 20 per cent, to be sure, are punishing. But if, as is likely, many of the neutral techniques are perceived by the children to be punishing, it may be concluded that the punishment-reward ratio is highly skewed in favor of punishments.

In addition to these functional characteristics of kibbutz socialization, there are important structural characteristics which, theoretically, should produce competitively structured prestige needs. Kibbutz children must compete with their peers for the love of their nurse; they must compete with their siblings for the love of their parents; and they must compete with their peers for the use of toys and other play objects in the children's house. Hence we would not only expect the sabra desire for esteem to be strong, but we would assume it to entail competitive elements.

Turning to the data, we find that the sabras do in fact have a strong need for approval and esteem, and that it does entail, for some of them at least, strong competitive elements. This need can be traced continuously from the children in the nurseries to the adult sabras in the kibbutz. The former, it will be remembered, frequently ask their nurse if they are nice (*chamud*), and seek her praise, and that of their peers, for the many activities in which they engage. The students in the lower grades of the Grammar School constantly ask their teachers and peers to look at their themes or their drawings to see how well they have done. And almost all the students to whom the projective tests were administered were highly concerned about their performance. They wished to know if others had responded as they did and how their own responses compared with those of their peers. Some wished to know if they finished in less time than others.

Similar reactions were found among the adult sabras. One was intensely pleased when I told him he was doing well on the tests, and repeatedly asked whether he was doing what I wanted. Another became greatly upset when he could "see" nothing in one

[6] Jules Henry, "Toward a System of Socio-Psychiatric Invariants: A Work Paper," *The Journal of Social Psychology*, 37:133–161 (1953), 154.

of the Rorschach cards, despite the non-ego-involved test instructions, but he beamed when told that his responses showed high intelligence.

Sabra desire for esteem is revealed most dramatically in their concern with status or prestige (*emdah*). This concern was expressed in almost all the interviews.

(My only ambition) is to prove myself in agricultural work.

Everyone is interested in status. It's obvious — I don't want others to laugh at me.

I won't say that I am not concerned about what others think, but if I think I am (morally) clear, I don't care what others say. I've never worked hard, in order for others to say that I work hard. To hear someone in the shower praise my work — I don't care for that. On the other hand I am concerned if someone accuses me of work sabotage. Once someone did, and I was so deeply hurt that I remember his words to this day.

This same concern is reflected, in part, in the sabras' desire for knowledge. In some instances this desire derives from intellectual curiosity; in other instances it expresses a feeling of intellectual insecurity. In still other instances, however, the desire for knowledge reflects their desire for status. Since the combination of expertness in work and good character is the most frequent sabra response to the question of what confers the most prestige in the kibbutz,[7] it is no coincidence that many sabras say they want to study in order to achieve greater technical competence in their work. They aspire to greater prestige by augmenting their technical skills.

Data from the Emotional Response Test also support this conclusion. Second only to family experience as a source of happiness is the attainment of status or prestige. Conversely, the second most important source of shame is inadequacy, or discovery in wrongdoing (loss of status).

In some cases the desire for prestige is clearly competitive in motive. In the sixth grade, for example, one boy was most concerned, when taking a Rorschach, with exhausting the alternative responses to each card; and he insisted on knowing how many responses other children had given. Although he was instructed not to reveal anything about the test to the other children, he proceeded to brag to his peers about the great number of re-

[7] Followed by social participation, expressiveness in town meeting, intellectual power, age, political expertese.

sponses he had given. This induced a feeling of competition in the others, so that the three subjects who succeeded him were primarily concerned with equaling or surpassing him in total number of responses.[8]

The high school students, despite their desire for esteem, deny that they are competitively motivated. Only one of the twenty-eight students interviewed said that he was generally competitive (it was his feeling that everyone was competitive). Five admitted that they were competitive in certain restricted activities — athletics, work, studies — but that in general they were not; three said they were competitive sometimes; and two, denying that they were competitive, asserted that other students were. Seventeen of the twenty-eight, however, denied that they were competitive in any sense. For the most part, they asserted that their desire to excel did not imply a desire to excel over others, but that, on the contrary, they desired to be equal, rather than superior, to others. In short, though they strongly desire esteem and approval, they deny that this entails competitive elements. The latter statement is consistent with other student attitudes that are found in both primary and secondary schools. In general the students heartily dislike those who are competitive or who aspire to leadership or to dominance over others. In the Grammar School such students are rarely elected to positions of leadership or responsibility, being passed over in favor of the more modest ones. The hostility toward competition in the high school is so marked, according to one teacher, that the students become ashamed if they are too frequently at the top of their class in any activity. *Al ta-aseh roshem* — "don't try to make an impression" — is the universal reaction to the student who comports himself in the above manner. Indeed, should a student persistently exhibit competitive behavior, he is labeled a *shvitzer* — the most opprobrious term in the children's lexicon. A shvitzer (a Yiddish term whose literal meaning is a person who sweats) is a rate-busting, norm-raising, glory-seeking, apple-polishing, competitive grind.[9]

Personal competition plays an important role, however, among

[8] Sometimes, however, competition may lead to a depression, rather than to a stimulation, of achievement drive. In the fourth grade, Ephraim and Yoav were both interested and proficient in drawing. When Ephraim concluded that Yoav was better than he, he stopped drawing, and the art teacher could not induce him to start again.

[9] Although opposed to personal competition, the students are competitive about group activities. When the Mosad basketball team lost a game, some of the students were visibly shaken. Many of them cried after one such loss, and the next day they could neither concentrate on their studies nor prepare their lessons.

some of the adult sabras in their prestige aspirations. Four of the
ten adults admitted that they were competitive:

Sometimes I feel competitive in my work. I think that others have
this feeling too.

I am competitive in my work. I want to be known as a good worker,
and be given responsibility, and be recognized. But I also want the
reputation of being able to do things better than others.

Yes, it (competition) exists, but not in the brutal way in which it is
found in other societies.

Everyone wants to be better than others. The sense of competition
is strong in me.

Others, however, deny the existence of competition as a personal motive. Their attitudes are to be found in such statements
as:

I have no desire to be better than others. I want everyone to be
better.

In general it is not found here. There is no one I want to compete
with.

I do not want to be better than others. I want to do as much as I
can with my intelligence and will to fulfill my responsibilities.

In work I want to work well, sometimes I want to be better. But not
out of competition with others — more as a game. In some kinds of
work I am better than others; but I don't compete.

Some of the difference between those who assert and those
who deny competitiveness is probably semantic, inherent in the
ambiguity of "competition." The sabras are highly status conscious,
displaying a deep need for prestige. But for many of them it seems
that this need is absolute rather than relative. That is, they wish
to have prestige in the eyes of others (particularly in the eyes of
the adults) without perforce demeaning the prestige of others.
They may be compared, analogically, to a person who wishes to
become wealthy, but not by making others poor.

There seems to be little question but that the sabras have
a strong desire for approval and esteem. This desire, we believe,
functions as an important technique of social control, for it motivates them to conform to those cultural taboos and culture patterns which are not perceived by them to be intrinsically satisfying.

SUPEREGO

Introduction. Social control that is motivated by either alter-ego or super-alter processes does not involve the notion of conscience. Because it is usually assumed that conscience — or super-ego — develops primarily as a function of family interaction, one of the paramount questions raised by this study is whether or not individuals reared collectively, and by persons other than parents, can develop a superego.

Some anthropologists hold that there are societies whose members have no superego, or conscience, at least in our sense of that term. Hence, they would distinguish between, what they term, "shame cultures" and "guilt cultures." As now conceived, the distinction between shame and guilt cultures entails the notion that there are societies — those characterized by shame cultures — whose members have no superego in the Euro-American meaning. In societies with guilt cultures, people have presumably internalized the cultural values and conform to them even when their fellows are not present. In societies with shame cultures, people are deterred from violating the values only if their fellows are present — either physically or in their "mind's eye" — to shame them. They have presumably learned what the cultural values are, but have not internalized them. Because they themselves do not believe their intended violations to be wrong, they are deterred only by the fear that they will be discovered. Should the latter possibility be negligible, they have no hesitation — no "pangs of conscience" — about committing the tabooed act.

Like some other writers,[10] I am not persuaded that shame cultures exist — that there are societies in which people have not internalized the cultural values. Indeed, if the values were not internalized, parents would have none to transmit to their children because, *ex hypothesi*, they would not have internalized any in the course of their own socialization. Further, if no one has internalized the values, who would do the shaming? The existence of agents of shame implies that at least some members of society have internalized the values; if there were no such individuals, the culture would contain no values. And since all cultures do contain values, we must conclude that most individuals have internalized many, if not all, of them.

In short, one may argue that, although in any society there may hypothetically be some individuals who have not internal-

[10] Gerhart Piers and Milton B. Singer, *Shame and Guilt* (Springfield, Ill., Charles C. Thomas, 1953).

ized any values (the so-called psychopaths), and many individuals who have not internalized some of the values, there is no society in which most individuals have only learned about the values of their society; they also accept these values, evaluate their own acts in accordance with them, and experience anxiety ("moral anxiety") should they desire to violate them — which is usually a deterrent to their violation.

How does this moral anxiety develop? What does it represent? To answer the second question first, this anxiety presumably represents the, largely unconscious, expectation of punishment — as distinguished from the rational, conscious fear of being punished.

The individual who has internalized a value, not merely learned about it, perceives his anticipated violation of it as a transgression and hence as deserving of punishment. It is this perception, we assume, that induces his anxiety response (the anticipation of punishment). The mere intention of committing an act which he himself labels as a "transgression," leads him to expect that this act, which is deserving of punishment, will in some way be punished. Where the individual believes that punishment is his due, "expectation of punishment" is but another term for "moral anxiety."

On the other hand, the individual who has merely learned about the value but has not internalized it suffers no moral anxiety as a consequence of his anticipated violation of it. Because he himself has not internalized the value, he does not — though others may — consider his anticipated violation to be deserving of punishment, since he does not consider his act to be "wrong." He experiences no moral anxiety. He may, of course, experience anxiety about the punishment which would be meted out to him were he caught. In moral anxiety, however, it is not the fear that one might be punished if caught, but the belief that one merits punishment — whether or not he is caught — that evokes the anxiety response.

Moral anxiety therefore has both drive and cue properties. It informs the individual that his anticipated act is wrong (worthy of punishment), and that its performance will lead to punishment; and it motivates him to remove the anxiety by refraining from transgression. Hence the anxiety serves as a motive for conformity.

To answer the first question, this process develops, we believe, out of certain universal features of human socialization systems. In all societies, agents of socialization are more than trainers; they are also nurturers, satisfying the child's most important need — the need for love. To the extent that these agents employ rewards and punishments as part of their training methods, and to the extent that such rewards and punishments are, for the child, symbolic of their love (as we believe them to be), the child is motivated to comply with the demands of these "significant others" in order to retain their love or, conversely, to preclude its withdrawal. Through the use of rewards and punishments, the child not only learns what the agents of socialization judge to be good and bad behavior, but he also learns to concur in their judgment; in short, he models his behavior in accordance with their values. He learns to accept their judgment as his own because the acts which these significant others judge to be bad are indeed "bad" for him; they lead to the withdrawal of love (punishment) by those whose love he so strongly desires. Since he agrees that certain acts are bad — and therefore deserving of punishment — his mere intention leads to the anticipation of punishment (moral anxiety). He has developed a superego.

But having denied the validity of one distinction — that between shame and guilt cultures — we shall introduce another. We have defined the superego operationally as the anticipation of punishment, experienced as anxiety, attendant upon the anticipated violation of a cultural taboo. But we have not specified the agent of punishment — the "significant other" whose anticipated withdrawal of love motivates the individual to conform. We suggest that two types of superego, based on the agent of anticipated punishment, can be distinguished. This agent may be outside the individual or within him. It is our hypothesis that societies in which the child is trained by only a few agents of socialization, who themselves administer punishments, produce individuals who not only internalize the values of the socializing agent but who "introject" the agent as well. The introject, then, is the significant other for such individuals; it is withdrawal of the introject's love that constitutes the anticipated punishment. Since this punishment, when it comes — and it comes after the transgression — is experienced as guilt ("pangs of conscience"), we may refer to this type of superego as "guilt-oriented."

We also hypothesize that societies in which the child is trained by a number of socializing agents, or in which the trainers discipline the child by claiming that other agents will punish him, do not produce individuals with "guilt-oriented" superegos. For, though these individuals internalize the values of the socializing agents, they do not introject the agents themselves. Since the significant others continue to remain external, it is withdrawal of the love of others that constitutes the anticipated punishment.

Because this punishment, when it comes, is experienced as shame, we may refer to this type of superego as "shame-oriented."

It must be emphasized that a shame- no less than a guilt-oriented superego constitutes a conscience. By producing anxiety concerning anticipated punishment, both of them inform the individual that his anticipated act is wrong, and motivate him to refrain from transgression. Both serve to deter nonconformity whether others are present or not. Nevertheless, they function differently after a transgression has occurred. A person with a guilt-oriented superego suffers guilt when he transgresses, even if no one perceives his transgression, because the agent of punishment (the introject) is always with him. However, a person with a shame-oriented superego does not suffer shame when he transgresses unless others witness his trangression, for no agent of punishment (the external others) is present. Instead of experiencing *actual* punishment (shame), he continues to experience *anticipated* punishment (anxiety).[11]

Socialization and superego formation. In this discussion we shall focus primarily on the observance of taboos (because it is simpler to study superego processes in this connection) and, specifically, on the aggression taboo. Within this restriction we may now attempt to analyze sabra superego in developmental perspective. The most important trainers for the preschool children are unquestionably the nurses, and their techniques of socialization[12] may be characterized as "nonpunitive, negative reinforcement." For although there is little reward for the correct response, neither is there much punishment for the incorrect response. That is, although socialization consists primarily of negative reinforcement of incorrect responses, most of the negative techniques — both in intent and objectively described — are cognitive, rather than punitive, in nature (see Table 7). The nurse's behavior rests on the assumption that if a generally nurturant environment is

[11] This anxiety may be so painful that persons who live in so-called shame-cultures may be led to commit suicide. This fact, incidentally, is sufficient to cast doubt on the validity of the shame-culture guilt-culture dichotomy. The Japanese, who allegedly have a shame-culture, are driven to suicide when they perceive themselves to have lost face, even in the absence of any other perceiver. In the terms we have been employing, the Japanese would be said to have shame-oriented superegos; they experience anxiety when they anticipate performing a forbidden act or not performing a prescribed act. After committing the transgression, they continue to anticipate punishment, anxiety mounts, and suicide represents the last desperate attempt to remove the anxiety.

[12] We are referring here to their active techniques. It will be remembered that the great majority of aggressive acts remain unsocialized.

created for the child, he will, given other outlets for his instincts, behave in accordance with the norms which his socializers demonstrate to him by word and deed. As the educational journal expresses it, the kibbutz does not try to extirpate the "animal side" of the child, but to direct his energies into "positive social paths."

We do not throw the child into depths of fear for loss of love of his educators when he cannot withstand the pressure of his instincts, but we base our education on the love of the child, and not on his fear, as the principal restraint . . . Our system diminishes in the child the necessity of escaping from the seductions of his instincts by repressing them . . .

Although the nurse's techniques of negative reinforcement are primarily nonpunitive (in intent) she does employ some punitive techniques as well; they constitute 19 per cent of all training techniques for the first five years. That these punitive techniques, which include physical punishment, withdrawal of privilege, and shaming, are indeed painful to the child is a thesis supported by our observations, as well as by the previously noted finding that the nurse is perceived by the children to be the most frustrating figure in their environment.

If, then, these techniques are painful to the child, we would expect the fear of nurse-inflicted pain to become an important motive for conformity. And, indeed, we know that these young children rarely aggress against the nurse or in the presence of the nurse. This analysis sheds no light, however, on the bases for their fear. Are the punitive techniques of the nurse merely intrinsically painful, or are they also instrumentally painful — symbolic of her withdrawal of love? This is a crucial question. For if the punishment by the nurse is perceived only as intrinsically painful, the children will learn to inhibit the prohibited response in her presence in order to escape punishment, but not in order to retain her love.[13] But only if they desire her love would they be motivated to model their behavior after hers, and, thus, to eventually internalize the prohibition. Since the nurse is highly nurturant, and since the children are strongly attached to her, we can only conclude that, in addition to the intrinsic pain, punishment is perceived by them as a withdrawal of love. Since her love is so important to them, we would expect the fear of losing this love to become an important motive for conformity.

[13] If the nurse were highly punitive, which she is not, the children would learn to perceive her as evil, and would therefore be motivated not only to avoid any activity that might evoke her punishment, but to avoid *her* as well.

The nurse's role in socialization may give rise, however, to a second motive for conformity, one which is suggested by an analysis of the context of her socialization — for almost invariably the child is socialized in the presence of many children. And this characteristic feature of kibbutz socialization, we suggest, may serve to convert what are intended as (and what appear to be) nonpunitive — cognitive — techniques into punitive — shaming — ones as far as the child is concerned. If this is so, we would then expect the fear of being shamed by peers to become an important motive for social conformity. And since the children have a strong desire for the approval of their peers, their fear of being shamed means the fear of losing the esteem of their peers.

This brings us to an examination of peers as active agents of training. Preschool peers, it will be recalled, serve important training functions, especially among the older children (Group IV), where the frequency of peer-socialization of aggression almost equals that of the nurse. Unlike their elders, however, these children are primarily punitive in their socialization, employing the techniques of physical attack, ostracism, and name-calling. It would not be remiss, therefore, to suggest that the fear of peer-inflicted pain would be an important motive for conformity. But since peers are also significant others, whose approval the children strongly desire, they should fear not only the intrinsic pain of peer-punishments, but the symbolic pain (withdrawal of approval) as well.

Parents too play a role in socialization. If much nurse-socialization is only apparently nonpunitive, most parental socialization is genuinely so. The most frequent technique of training employed by parents — according to their responses to the Questionnaire — is "criticism," or telling the child that he has done wrong. This essentially cognitive technique is to be distinguished from the punitive technique of scolding which is almost never employed. (And since parental socialization occurs in a private context, there is no reason to believe that this cognitive technique has punitive consequences for the child.)

What is most important about the behavior of the parents, however, is the very limited extent to which they employ *any* disciplinary techniques. The reasons are readily apparent. Preschool children spend most of their time outside the parents' orbit, so that the latter have little opportunity to train them. But even when an opportunity does arise, parents are loath to discipline their children for fear of losing their love. A basic rationale for collective education is the delegation of this responsibility to the nurses, so that the parents can function primarily as nurturers. The un-importance of parents as disciplinarians is attested to by the re-markable results of the Emotional Response Test, wherein parent-child interaction is mentioned not even once as a source of sadness, fear, shame, or anger. Parents must discipline their children in-frequently indeed.

In middle childhood, and consistent with what is found in the preschool period, the disciplinary role of the educator (nurse and teacher) continues to be much more important than that of the parent, with that of the peer group being intermediate. This is reflected in the responses to the Moral Ideology Test, in which educators comprise 32 per cent of all trainers ("praisers" and "blamers"), the peer group comprises 22 per cent, and parents 18 per cent.

As in the younger age group, the educators employ few tech-niques of reward, and although here too their techniques are pri-marily cognitive, there seems to be a higher incidence of punitive techniques. This is also reflected in the Moral Ideology Test, where the children perceive the training role of the educators to be primarily punitive in nature (whereas educators comprise only 21 per cent of the "praisers," they comprise 43 per cent of the "blamers"). Since the important punitive techniques are expulsion, withdrawal of privilege, and withdrawal of educator, we would expect the fears of ostracism by the group and withdrawal of love by the nurse to be important motives for conformity, strengthen-ing these same motives whose basis, we have argued, is first established in the preschool age. Again, the strength of the former motive should be enhanced by the public context within which socialization occurs.

These same motives should be further strengthened by two other techniques employed by the educators. One is an appeal to the child's conscience — "How could the kibbutz continue if you (or others) act in that way?" — a technique with which the edu-cator shames the child into feeling bad. The other technique is to convene a student meeting, so that the child's peers may discuss his violation and suggest some course of action — which again establishes the peer-group as an important disciplinary agent.

But peers also play an autonomous role in training. As we have noted, the peer-group occupies an intermediate position be-tween educators and nurses in its importance as a trainer. But if the adult kibbutz is added to the peer-group in our summary of trainers, the resultant category of "the group" becomes as im-portant as the educators (each category comprises 32 per cent of the total). According to the Moral Ideology Test, however, there is an important difference between these two categories of trainers. Whereas the educators are much more important as blamers than as praisers, the group is much more important as a praiser than as a blamer. Indeed, the importance of the group as a praiser is greater than that of the parents and educators combined. We would expect, then, that desire for group approval would become an important motive for conformity, a conclusion entirely consistent with the findings (discussed in the preceding section) concerning the sabras' strong prestige drives.

As in the previous age group, the parental role is relatively unimportant. Parents comprise only 18 per cent of all trainers in the Moral Ideology Test — as compared with other cultures in which they range from a low of 39 to a high of 78 per cent. More importantly, they are perceived to be relatively nonpunitive — parents comprise 14 per cent of the blamers, compared with 43 per cent for the educators.

The socialization variables in adolescence — at this age more properly termed "techniques of social control" rather than "techniques of socialization" — are little different from those found in middle childhood. The trend in the educator's role from the employment of affectively neutral, or cognitive, techniques to more punitive ones continues. Withdrawal of privilege, shame, and an appeal to conscience are the most frequent techniques of discipline employed by the teacher. As in the Grammar School, moreover, the high school teacher also employs the technique of convening the peer-group to sit in judgment on the transgressing member.

Peers, still very important agents of control, employ such techniques as censure, shame, physical attack, "clarification," and ostracism. Parents, however, remain unimportant agents of control.

Techniques of social control among adolescents are, therefore, consistent with the earlier techniques of training. The public context of punishment administered by educators, together with the active punitive role of peers, results in the group's being the most important agent of control. The fact that the sabras are so sensitive to group censure indicates that the group has become a paramount significant other.

What can be predicted about sabra superego development from this socialization? Since the kibbutz socialization system holds up values to be learned, and since it includes a system of rewards and punishments, administered by love objects (nurses, peers, parents), for the transmission of these values, we would expect the sabras to develop strong superegos. But we would expect that they would develop shame-oriented, rather than guilt-oriented, superegos. This expectation is based on our theoretical analysis of the superego.

The kibbutz child, it is obvious, has three sets of "significant others," three classes of persons whose love and esteem he desires — his parents, his nurses, and his peers. For the development of the conventional superego it is necessary, not only that the values of one of these classes of persons be internalized, but that these persons themselves be introjected. We believe that this introjection is unlikely.

The kibbutz child is seldom presented with models of any kind to emulate. The nurse rarely prohibits or encourages a response by invoking an adult authority figure — as other societies might invoke the authority of priest or god, chief or clan. Only twice in our entire sample did a nurse invoke the sanction of adult models ("grandfather" and "adults" were each invoked once) to ensure conformity. Sometimes, of course, the nurse holds up herself as a model — "I don't like it," or "I don't want you to do it" — but this too is rare. In the great majority of cases an act as prohibited because "this is not the way we act," or "that is not nice," or "that is fooia" — by referring to a general and implicit behavioral norm rather than by holding up a model to be emulated. There is, to be sure, an implicit model — "human being," or "kibbutz members," or "kevutza children" — in the statements of the nurse, but it is seldom made explicit.

Reference to models is not a necessary condition for introjection or identification. Children may, even without verbal stimulation, imitate and/or identify with models. Kibbutz children identify with both nurses and parents, and it might be concluded that one or both of these identifications provide the basis for the formation of the conventional superego. This conclusion, however, does not stand up under analysis. It is our strong impression that though the children imitate the nurse's behavior in their play, it is actually her role, rather than a specific nurse, with which they are identifying. Since the nurses are the child's most important socializers, they, rather than his other significant others, are probably the most strongly associated by the child with the values he is expected to acquire. But since the child does not identify with his nurses as persons — probably because the transiency and plurality of nurses precludes such identification — they cannot become the basis for introjected imagos, however much he may internalize their values.

On the other hand, kibbutz children do identify with parents, both behaviorally and verbally, and their identification is with their specific parent rather than with a generic parental role. But though the child identifies with his parents as persons, it is difficult to see how the latter can form the basis for the superego. Since the role of the parents is not punitive, how can the parental imago be punitive? If the anticipation of parental punishment is not a motive for the conformity of the child, how can the anticipation of guilt (the punishment of the introjected parental imago) be a motive for the conformity of the adult? Whiting and Child observe:

Where an important role in negative discipline is assigned to people outside the family, the parents may be able to maintain a consistently nurturant attitude towards the child. Thus . . . the child will not be motivated to adopt the parental role in evaluation of his own behavior and will instead retain the dependent role of infancy, expecting and presumably receiving love from his parents no matter what he does.[14]

The third class of significant others consists of the child's peers, whose role in training the child is a dual one. Peers not only exercise active punitive functions in the training of the child, but they also serve as highly important passive agents in the training process. The context of socialization by the nurse always includes the presence of peers, and the child thus becomes highly sensitized to their opinions. Nevertheless, it is difficult to see how an entire group can be introjected. An individual can identify with a group in the sense that he becomes a part of it, but how can he identify with a group in the sense that it becomes part of him?[15] Therefore, neither peers nor nurses can be introjected by the child.

[14] John W. M. Whiting and Irvin L. Child, *Child Training and Personality* (New Haven: Yale, 1953), p. 262. Their conclusion about the role of non-relative socializers in the development of the superego does not apply to the kibbutz for obvious reasons.

"An important role in socialization assigned to non-relatives may interfere with the development of guilt feelings because the child is then being disciplined by people with whom he does not have the intimate contact and knowledge out of which a widespread imitation of their evaluation responses could develop."

[15] One critic has questioned this assumption, arguing that it is not as self-evident as I seem to imply. I can only say that it is self-evident to me; I find the contrary assumption counter-intuitive. The scientific — as contrasted with the in-tuitive — justification for this assumption is the apparent confirmation of the above prediction, which is based on this assumption.

Since those with whom the kibbutz child identifies (his parents) do not discipline him, and since he does not (cannot) identify with those (nurses and peers) who do discipline him, it is improbable that the sabras would develop a guilt-oriented superego. Nevertheless, we would expect them to internalize the cultural values, and they should therefore develop a shame-oriented superego.

Behavior and superego. How does sabra behavior, specifically, aggressive behavior, correspond to our predictions? Although the percentage of aggressive responses in the preschool children's total behavioral repertory decreases with age, its absolute frequency continues to increase. The persistence of aggression indicates that the children have not internalized the aggression taboo, but it most definitely does not mean that they have not learned about the taboo. Their awareness of the fact that aggression is considered to be "wrong" is demonstrated by the observation that they rarely aggress against the nurse and that they rarely aggress against children whose retaliation they have reason to expect. From these data it may be concluded that the important motive for conformity to the aggression taboo at this age is fear of punishment, from both nurses and peers. Though the child is aware of the value of the socializer, he has not internalized it.[16] These young children show little evidence of superego formation; the true test will come with older children, adolescents, and adults.

An examination of aggression during middle childhood reveals that physical aggression, presumably as a result of prior training, has decreased, and that verbal aggression has superseded it in importance — although physical aggression is the second most important instigation to anger, according to the Emotional Response Test. Nevertheless, its sharp decrease indicates that the children are well aware of the cultural taboo on aggression — an assumption supported by the Moral Ideology Test, which reveals that aggression is perceived to be the most important cultural taboo.

To what extent their increasing conformity is motivated by moral anxiety rather than fear of punishment (by nurse or peers)

[16] There is some anecdotal evidence, on the other hand, for the internalization of another value — sharing. When his parents offered food to a beggar girl in the city, four-and-one-half-year-old Yaakov was deeply affected. His mother writes in her diary:

"Her joy at receiving the food made a tremendous impression on him, and he continued to talk about her. He said, 'Isn't it true, mother, that we gave her everything with willingness? With willingness?' Or he would say, 'You have no money for chocolate, but to poor people you give willingly. True?'"

exclusively cannot be deduced from these data for we have no information on value internalization. From these data we can conclude that the children know that others consider aggression to be wrong; we do not know if they themselves consider their own aggression to be wrong.

There is evidence for all the components of the superego among the adolescents. That they are aware of the aggression taboo may be concluded, not only from our previous observations that even the preschool children are aware of it, but from the finding that it is, for the adolescents, the most frequently mentioned taboo on the Moral Ideology Test. That they have internalized the taboo — that, in short, they themselves believe physical aggression to be wrong — is indicated by two sets of observations. First, physical aggression is almost completely absent from their behavior; they do not engage in physical aggression, even when they can do so with impunity.[17] Second, they themselves voluntarily label their own nonconforming behavior as wrong. For example, a group of eleventh-grade students contritely informed me that it was wrong for them to have treated the immigrant children in the Mosad so unfairly, and that they hoped that conditions would improve. The seventh- and eighth-grade students wrote in the high school annual that their year's progress had been marred by disturbance and aggression in the classroom.

The best index for the internalization of a cultural value is moral anxiety. Although we have no direct measure of moral anxiety (the experience of inner tension at the anticipation of transgression) among the sabras, there is indirect evidence. If sabras feel "bad" (the ambiguous "bad" is used in preference to "guilty" for theoretical reasons which will be clarified below) subsequent to the violation of taboos of lesser importance than the aggression taboo — a phenomenon for which there *is* evidence — the following conclusions would surely seem to be suggested. First, that sabra conformity *is* motivated by some type of inner control and, second, that, although this inner control is not sufficiently strong to motivate conformity to lesser taboos, it is strong enough to motivate conformity to such important taboos as that on physical aggression. Hence, the absence of physical aggression in their behavior.

[17] The absence of physical aggression is also reflected in the Emotional Response Test, according to which physical aggression comprises only 6 per cent of all instigations to anger. This finding, to me, indicates that aggression is truly infrequent, and not that their tolerance for aggression has increased.

Examples of this evidence would be illuminating. When coming into class a half hour late, for example, the first comment of an eleventh-grade boy was, "It was not my fault . . ." The student knew he was late, he knew his behavior was wrong, and although tardiness is not punished by the teacher, his statement indicates that he felt the need to absolve himself of blame. Here, in short, is a case in which the student not only knows that he has violated a rule, but in which he experiences some inner tension as a consequence.

Again, a tenth-grade student became visibly disturbed when told by an Iraqi immigrant student that his name-calling was racist and violated kibbutz ideals. After apologizing, he promised that he would not taunt him again. The student has accepted the cultural judgment concerning the immorality of racism, and when his behavior is characterized as such he feels "bad," and promises to mend his ways.

Some eleventh-grade students, after recounting the ways in which they had made the life of a former teacher miserable, said that if they had been living in a "real democracy" they would have been "hanged" for their behavior. Here, too, are students who are not only aware of the cultural values but who have also internalized them. And although in this case their moral anxiety was not a sufficient motive for conformity, the transgression, once committed, left them with inner tension — the feeling of deserving punishment.

A final observation indicates even more clearly how painful nonconformity can become. The students, it will be recalled, complain about the "burden of conscience" under which they labor, a complaint compounded of three determinants. It refers to their belief that they are under pressure to repay, by their devotion to its ideals, the debt which they owe the kibbutz. And it refers to the fact that the teacher exercises little authority so that it is their responsibility as individuals to control their own behavior, and as a group to control that of their wayward members.

Now if the students have not internalized kibbutz values, why should they complain about a burden of conscience? Their complaint makes sense only on the assumption that their own violation of group norms is painful to them. For only then would their seeming inability to comply with excessively high standards lead to a feeling of moral "burden." If, however, they experienced no inner pain from the violation of group norms, they could remain indifferent to the, allegedly, excessive demands of the kibbutz — for they would suffer no burden of conscience. Indeed, the sabras sometimes do feign indifference to kibbutz demands, an indifference which is best interpreted as a defense against the anxiety which lack of compliance induces.

Similarly, the preference of the students for greater external restraint, and their seemingly inexplicable resentment against the permissive high school environment, becomes entirely explicable if we assume that the violation of group norms induces inner pain. By exercising greater authority, the teacher would decrease the incidence of violation and thus preclude the inner suffering brought on by such violation.

On the basis of such evidence I believe that sabra conformity to the aggression taboo is motivated by moral anxiety. For if violation of a cultural value causes the sabras great pain, we may conclude that the anticipation of this pain is an important motive for sabra conformity — particularly with respect to values of paramount importance (like the aggression taboo) for which the anticipated pain for violation is especially strong.

But, if the sabras suffer inner pain after transgression, may we not also conclude that their superegos are guilt-oriented — that the agent of anticipated punishment is within the individual (an introject) rather than external to him, as we had predicted? Before arriving at such a conclusion, let us examine additional data that may shed further light upon the inner pain they suffer.

According to the Moral Ideology Test, the sabras perceive "the group" (with the peer-group being overwhelmingly preponderant) to be more than one and one-half times as important an agent of control, as all other agents combined. Moreover, although the group praises more than it blames, it is overwhelmingly the most important of all the "blamers." [18] If, in listing the agents of social control, the students are in effect listing the individuals (or classes of individuals) to whose opinions they are most sensitive, whose anticipated punishment they most fear, then the group rather than an introject clearly emerges as the agent of anticipated punishment. For nowhere in this test is the self — the expected agent of punishment for those with guilt-oriented superegos — mentioned as an agent.

This conclusion is most tellingly supported by the sabra complaint of a burden of conscience, and specifically by their objec-

[18] For the Grammar School children, educators are listed as blamers more than twice as often as is the group; among the adolescents, the group is the blamer twice as often as the educators. Among the school children, parents and the group are about equal as blamers (both playing a minor role); among the adolescents, the parents continue to play a minor role but the group is six times as important.

tion to the teacher's abdication of responsibility. To be weighed down by a burden of conscience is to be in a state of anxiety or tension. But why should this anxiety be experienced as a *constant* burden? What accounts for its persistence? I believe that this question can best be answered by the statement of a high school graduate. The permissive environment in the high school, he said, means that the students are like children who, having done some wrong, wait to be punished; but the punishment does not come. It is for this reason, he continued, that the students complain about the abdication of teacher responsibility.

This is a statement of profound psychological insight whose implications for the sabras led me to the present formulation of guilt and shame processes in general. It seems to imply that the sabra burden of conscience is not the pain of guilt (actual punishment), but rather the pain of anxiety (anticipated punishment). If a person desires to violate a cultural norm which he has internalized, he will experience moral anxiety — the expectation of punishment either from his introject or from the group. If he actually violates the norm, the individual who anticipates punishment from his introject will indeed be punished — he will suffer the pain of guilt. However, his guilt feeling need not be permanent; it can be diminished, if not removed, by proper atonement. If the shame-oriented individual violates the norm, he will suffer the pain of shame only if the group, or some other authority, punishes him. If he is not punished, he remains in his previous emotional state of expecting punishment. In short, shame-oriented individuals may suffer more than guilt-oriented individuals, for in the absence of external punishment, the former have no means of reducing their persistent anxiety about anticipated punishment. If external punishment is not meted out, they remain in a constant state of moral anxiety.

This, we suggest, is the basis for the sabra complaint concerning the teacher's abdication of authority. The students would welcome external punishment because only the pain of actual punishment can serve to reduce, if not eliminate, the pain of moral anxiety.

Turning now to the adult sabras, we find no reason to alter the conclusions at which we have thus far arrived. Having observed the internalization of values among the younger sabras, it is not surprising to find that the inhibition of aggression is, appropriately enough, second only to labor as a moral value; that physical aggression has disappeared from their behavioral repertory; that even verbal aggression is almost entirely absent, as well; and that aggression is the single most important instigation to feelings of shame.

Again, all the evidence points to a shame- rather than a guilt-oriented superego. For it is the group — comprising three-fourths of all agents of control mentioned on the Moral Ideology Test — to whose judgment the adult sabras are most sensitive. If an introjected parental imago were the basis for moral anxiety, we would expect the "self" to be listed as the important source of control. But the findings reveal that, while the self constitutes 22 per cent of all praisers, it constitutes zero per cent of the blamers. This is what was predicted on the basis of our analysis of early socialization in the kibbutz. Parents, the persons with whom the sabras truly identify, are exclusively nuturant and rewarding; their socialization role provides no basis for a punitive superego. The introject praises; it does not blame. The basis for sabra moral anxiety must therefore be an external group imago.

That the group is a powerful force in motivating conformity is revealed by sabra interview data as well. Nine of the ten adult sabras said they were always sensitive to public opinion; and of these nine, five said that they were always influenced, while four said they were generally influenced, by it. Only one said that public opinion was of little consequence to him.[19]

The sabras are not only responsive to public opinion but, when this opinion is officially enunciated as a decision of the town meeting, they are prepared to acquiesce in it, even when it conflicts with their own desires. Natan, for example, wanted to study in Tel Aviv after his graduation from high school. The kibbutz debated his request at its town meetings; and although Natan was strongly motivated to study, he said that he would accept the decision of the kibbutz even if it were negative. So, too, Ahuv longed to have two free evenings a week. But when it was decided at a town meeting that he should become a Youth Leader — an activity which would consume the two desired evenings — he accepted the decision.

This sensitivity to public opinion, it might be argued, indicates that sabra conformity is motivated primarily by fear of external punishment rather than by moral anxiety. But these are not incompatible alternatives. Our argument has not been that sabras

---

[19] Sabra sensitivity to public opinion is manifested even in matters of artistic appreciation. When discussing the movie, "The Red Shoes," a sabra said that she did not feel that it was as good as other sabras believed it to be. But she could not, she emphasized, criticize the movie for she had seen ballets in Europe and she was apprehensive lest her criticism lead her friends to think she was trying to be "superior."

do not fear external punishment. On the contrary, fear of public opinion is a powerful motive for social conformity. Our concern, however, has been to show that the sabras would conform even in the absence of external punishment. Having internalized the cultural values, they believe that transgressions of these values are wrong, therefore deserving of punishment. We conclude, therefore, that another powerful motive in prohibiting the transgression of cultural values is moral anxiety; that, in short, the sabras have developed a superego. We have emphasized the fact of sabra sensitivity to criticism by the group to underscore the thesis that the sabra superego is shame- rather than guilt-oriented; that the anticipated agent of punishment is the external group, rather than an introjected imago.

CHAPTER 16· ASPECTS OF EMOTIONAL ADJUSTMENT

INTRODUCTION

Indices of positive emotional adjustment are notoriously difficult to establish; and, if established, they are hard to apply. In general (with the exception of obvious instances of mental illness), it would be extremely hazardous to rank a series of societies on a scale of emotional adjustment — I at least would not attempt such a task. From a cross-cultural perspective it is probably fair to say that most human societies exhibit signs of both "good" and "poor" emotional adjustment, and that these signs vary (substantively and quantitatively) from society to society.

Since the system of collective education has produced individuals who seem to be rooted in their society, who have accepted its culture, and who are motivated to perpetuate and transmit its institutions; and since, moreover, these individuals show signs of creativity, of curiosity about their world, and of sensitivity to the creations of both nature and art; and since, finally, they show capacity for both work and love (Freud's favorite indices) — it can be concluded that the sabras fall well within the range of normal human emotional adjustment.

This, though important, is not a particularly interesting conclusion. If different societies exhibit somewhat different signs of both good and poor adjustment, and if these signs are a function of (among other things) their systems of socialization, we would like to know what these signs might be for the sabras, and how they are related to the system of collective education. We have attempted to do this in this chapter. If we seem to have stressed certain negative aspects of sabra adjustment, it is because they are somewhat more dramatic, and because they are more easily analyzed in terms of present personality theory. A description of sabra adjustment, stressing the more positive aspects of sabra personality, is a task for future researchers.

"Introversion and insolence," commented a kibbutz mother, "are the two oustanding characteristics of the sabras." Like many other statements of the chaverim, this remark betrays shrewd psychological insight. For though the sabras possess other outstanding characteristics, this particular configuration is diagnostically significant for an assessment of sabra emotional adjustment.

Sabra introversion may be observed in three forms. They are notably shy and embarrassed when interacting with both strangers and kibbutz members who are not their age-peers. They are reserved with almost everyone, seeming to maintain a barrier of psychological distance. Finally, they seldom form emotional attachments or intimate friendships.

Very few sabras have intimate friends. Even in the high school, the "chum" or "buddy" — the inseparable same-sex friend that is so characteristic of American adolescent behavior — is all but nonexistent. Moreover, the ordinary close friendship is also infrequent. Of seventeen Mosad students interviewed, only five said that they have close friends; and all five were in their first year in the high school. (Only one of the five was a male.)

The situation is no different among the adult sabras. Of the ten adult sabras, only one claims to have an intimate friend with whom confidences can be exchanged. Most keep their innermost thoughts and problems to themselves, although two said that they discussed their personal problems with their spouses.

The sabras not only avoid deep emotional relationships with a few, but they maintain an attitude of psychological distance with the many. In almost all their relationships they are, as the kibbutz puts it, segurim, or guarded (literally, "closed"). They seem to be enveloped within a shell, from which their psyches rarely protrude, and which prevents others from penetrating beyond the surface.

This emotional reserve is perceived by their fellow-students, by teachers and youth leaders, and by strangers. The urban students in the Mosad are disturbed by the sabras' avoidance of anything beyond a superficial relationship with them, and they complained about it at a public meeting. This complaint is significant, for it suggests that the roots of sabra emotional reserve are to be found in the uniquely kibbutz, rather than in the broader Israeli, aspects of their culture.

The sabras are reserved not only with their peers but with adults as well. The mechanech, it will be remembered, is theoretically a father-figure to whom the high school students bring their problems. The teachers unanimously report, however, that few sabras turn to them either for advice or consultation. The teacher-student relationship, like the parent-child relationship, seems to be marked (on the student's side) by psychological distance. One teacher, who had at one time been a youth leader in America, said that even after two years he had not achieved rapport with his students. Whereas in the United States he had known his charges intimately after only a brief period, in the Mosad he felt like a stranger to his students.

Again, this lack of close rapport with adults does not seem to characterize other Israeli youth. The leader of the youth movement said that it was not difficult to establish rapport with the Oriental youth groups (one of which was native-born) stationed in Kiryat Yedidim. The sabras, he noted, are "not one-tenth as open" with their leader as are the Oriental youth.

If sabras are reserved in their interaction with peers and other kibbutz members, it is not surprising to learn that they are even more reserved with strangers. Again there is sharp contrast between the sabras and the Oriental youth who are generally friendly and outgoing toward strangers. They immediately welcome a stranger into their midst, both in the fields and in their living quarters. When a visitor works with them in the fields, for example, they display considerable interest, interrogate him about his life and country, and, if he is a novice, explain the work to him. The sabras, on the other hand, remain a group apart, neither initiating interaction with, nor responding to the overtures of, the stranger.

When my wife and I first arrived in the kibbutz, I was warned by the parents that it would be difficult, if not impossible, to get to know the sabras. A city-born sabra living in the kibbutz agreed and suggested that we abandon our efforts. "They do not like strangers," she commented, "and almost never permit a stranger to get to know them." She suggested a study of city-born sabras resident in the kibbutz, for, she said, they are not so "closed." These predictions were confirmed. With but two exceptions, the sabras initially ignored us. Two months after our arrival in Kiryat Yedidim, for example, the son of close friends would ignore our presence in his parents' room and behave as if we were not there. Gidon, a sabra with whom I worked side-by-side in the fields for three months, did not once address me.

A final expression of sabra introversion is their shyness and embarrassment when interacting both in public and in private with almost anyone except their peers. With some few exceptions, Mosad students become psychologically tongue-tied when they must appear before a group. When a dancer was employed by the Mosad to arrange a program for an impending celebration, only six students came to rehearsals; the others complained that they were ashamed to dance in public. At the high school graduation party attended by the entire kibbutz, one of the seniors had been designated to represent the graduating class in the round of speeches that characterizes such events. The embarrassment with which he spoke was so pronounced that it was as painful for the audience as it was for him.[1]

This social embarrassment is revealed very clearly on the Emotional Response Test. The category which includes the highest percentage of shame responses to this test is "Embarrassment in interaction with others." This category includes such behavior as talking to nonpeers in the kibbutz, talking to strangers, being looked at, receiving guests, and calling on relatives — most forms of interaction with persons other than peers or members of one's nuclear family. This category, to be sure, is not so important among the adult sabras as it is among the grammar school children or the high school youth (the percentages, from the youngest to the oldest, respectively, are 79, 59, 30), but even in the latter it is the single most important category.

This embarrassment is of particular interest in view of the fact that its immediate stimulus consists, not of strangers, but of people whom the sabras have known from infancy, and with whom they have played, eaten, worked, and talked from childhood. With strangers they are even more embarrassed. In some cases during an interview the embarrassment of the sabras was so intense that it was painful for me to enter their rooms.

Sabra introversion comprises two related, albeit distinct, characteristics. They refrain from interacting with others, and, when they do interact, they avoid forming intimate emotional relationships with them. Such a pattern might imply that the sabras have no interest in or concern about other people, and that they have no desire either to give affection to or to receive affection from others. But there is good reason to doubt the validity of this obvious explanation. That the sabras are concerned about other people is demonstrated in a number of ways. The deep responsibility for the welfare of others in the kibbutz which they feel is expressed in work, in their positive feelings toward others, and in

---

[1] This is in marked contrast to the grammar-school children, who are remarkably poised and sophisticated in public performances.

their willingness both to fight and to sacrifice for others. Concern for others is expressed on the Emotional Response Test; indeed, it pervades the entire test. The welfare of the group is important among the best things that can happen to the sabras; the death and illness of others, as well as separation from the group, are important among the worst things that can happen to them. From these data alone it would be difficult to conclude that the sabras are not concerned about, or have no feelings for, other people.

But, if the sabras show indications of concern and affection for others, they show even greater indications of wanting affection from others. They have a strong need for approval; indeed, it would not be inaccurate to state that the need for affection and approval is perhaps the dominant need in their need-hierarchy. If sabra introversion is not a function of lack of affection or concern for others, or of the absence of a desire for affection and approval from others, what explanation for it is there?

Introversion may refer either to the withdrawal from, or the avoidance of, others. And if, in general, withdrawal is a response to pain, and avoidance is a response to the anticipation of pain, then sabra introversion may be motivated by pain resulting from past experiences with others, or by pain anticipated from further interaction with others. In short, sabra introversion may be based on the perception of others or of interpersonal relationships as either painful or dangerous; if so, it may be taken as a symptom of insecurity.

HOSTILITY

The second outstanding characteristic of the sabras, according to one mother, is insolence (*chutzpa*). Insolence, however, is but a subclass of aggression. That the mother chose to note their insolence is not, however, an accident. For it is surely the most characteristic expression of the hostility of the sabras in their interaction with kibbutz members. Their insolence is most frequently manifested (and best symbolized) in the expressions, *ma ichpat lecha* — "What concern is it of yours?," and, *ma ichpat li* — "What concern is it of mine?" The first is an almost universal response to criticism, the second an almost universal response to the prediction of some unpleasant consequence to the behavior criticized.

But the sabras are also hostile toward those who are not members of the kibbutz. Since, however, they are rarely overtly aggressive, their hostility — by which we mean a generalized set for the activation of aggression — must be inferred from such indices as facial expression, vocal inflection, and body tonus as well as from various subliminal cues that are not immediately identifiable. Thus, despite my inability to specify all the cues for the inference concerning sabra hostility, I have the strong "clinical" impression that the sabras are hostile in their relationships with strangers. And if their hostility toward kibbutz members takes the form of insolence, their hostility toward strangers takes the form of, what might be termed, antagonistic withdrawal. If it is difficult for a peer or kibbutz member to interact freely with a sabra, it is much more difficult for a stranger to do so. The former encounter withdrawal, the latter, resistance. It is not until the stranger gets to know him that sabra hostility is seen to be a façade.[2]

Hostility like withdrawal may best be interpreted as a symptom of insecurity. If, in general, aggression is a response to frustration, and hostility is a response to the anticipation of frustration, then sabra aggression must be motivated by painful encounters with people in the past, and their hostility must be motivated by the continuous anticipation of such contacts. Sabra hostility, in short, is based on a perception of others or of interpersonal relationships as either painful or dangerous.

Thus, a configuration of withdrawal and hostility, together with a great need for approval, is a syndrome suggestive of marked insecurity. And this, indeed, is my "clinical" impression of the sabras. I believe that they are both capable and desirous of giving and receiving love, and that their hostility and introversion stem from a belief that people are either unfriendly or indifferent to them. They give the impression of wanting to establish interpersonal relationships but, at the same time, of being frightened by such relationships. And, in interacting with them, one receives the impression that their hostility and introversion are defenses against, as well as responses to, whatever it is about people and human relationships that they fear.

My relationship with Gidon is typical. Gidon not only avoided me, but his entire demeanor gave strong indication of hostility. When, after three months of working together, he addressed me for the first time, it was to inquire about my camera. He did not speak again for two weeks, and then it was to ask for advice about the use of certain film. A short time later, I approached Gidon,

[2] Since my impressions of sabra hostility are "clinical," their validity remains in doubt. It should be observed, however, that of all the groups in the kibbutz — adults, parents of members, the various youth groups, and sabras — only the sabras gave that impression.

saying that I would like to interview him. He looked pleased, and an appointment was made. The two interviews that followed left me amazed. Gidon was cooperative, open, and desirous of answering the questions put to him in the best way possible. When the interviews were concluded, he was eager to talk about himself and to display his personal mementos, especially his creative work — sketches, drawings, and paintings. Thus, in a period of four months, Gidon's behavior had undergone a series of changes — from hostility to nonhostile avoidance to shy friendliness and loquaciousness — that were truly dramatic.

Upon reflection, it became apparent that these changes in Gidon's behavior — changes whose pattern was almost identical with that of my interaction with the other sabras — were highly consistent with my perception of the sabras as insecure. Gidon's first response to others is one of hostility and withdrawal because his initial perception of others is threatening; he fears that they will hurt him. When he has reason to believe that they do not or will not hurt him, the hostile façade disappears. If, finally, he is assured of their warm and sympathetic interest, he responds with genuine, if guarded, warmth.

SOCIALIZATION AND INSECURITY

We have concluded that hostility, introversion, and an intense need for affection and approval are symptoms of insecurity. And since this syndrome is a generic sabra characteristic, we may assume that kibbutz culture systematically provides them with experiences that give rise to these characteristics. Since this syndrome is not characteristic of the sabras' parents, we may further assume that such experiences are a function of kibbutz socialization rather than of some other kibbutz institution or set of institutions.

Such assumptions receive strong support from an analysis of kibbutz socialization. On the basis of such an analysis, a series of predictions were made concerning sabra personality; introversion, hostility, and a strong need for love were among the predicted consequences. These predictions, to be sure, are contaminated by the fact that in field work all variables — those that, predictively, comprise the antecedent conditions, as well as those that, predictively, constitute the consequent conditions — are studied simultaneously. Nevertheless, it is of some importance that the theoretically derived predictions coincide with the empirical observations.

If kibbutz socialization be analyzed into its three aspects —

caretaking, training, and nurturance — it soon becomes apparent that the first two aspects can hardly account for sabra insecurity. The physical conditions of the children's lives are excellent, if not ideal. The kibbutz child suffers few, if any, privations of food, shelter, clothing, and so on. Sanitary conditions are optimal, so that the incidence of illness is low. Neither the physical conditions of their existence, the institutional apparatus for the satisfaction of physical needs, nor the personnel involved in the institutional apparatus seriously frustrate the child's physical needs.

The training system which inducts the child into the major childhood disciplines is similarly nonfrustrating. Comparison of kibbutz training with norms derived from the cross-cultural sample studied by Whiting and Child[3] reveals that the former is, in general, permissive, gradual, and nonpunitive. If oral, anal, sexual, aggression, and independence training are analyzed separately into "initial satisfaction" and "socialization anxiety," the following judgments concerning kibbutz socialization emerge.

In oral training initial nursing indulgence is not high because the nursing period is brief (nine months, compared to the two and one-half year average for the Whiting-Child sample), and because of the pattern of scheduled feeding. The severity of weaning, on the other hand, is low, weaning being gradual and nonpunitive. We may summarize by saying that, since oral training is relatively nonfrustrating (for although initial satisfaction is lower than the average, socialization anxiety is also low), we would not expect it to produce serious insecurity feelings.

In anal training initial indulgence is rather high since little punishment is employed, and the age at which training begins is approximately the median age (two years) for the Whiting-Child sample. So, too, the severity of training is low, being both gradual and nonpunitive. Rewards are employed exclusively. Since initial satisfaction is high and socialization anxiety is low, we may conclude that anal training is not productive of insecurity.

For all forms of sex training — masturbation, modesty, homosexuality and heterosexuality — initial satisfaction is high and socialization anxiety is low. The adults are almost completely permissive in their training. Sex training, then, is surely not a source of great frustration.

In aggression training, both initial satisfaction and socialization anxiety are about average, rated against the Whiting-Child criteria. Rewards, to be sure, are few, but so are punishments;

[3] Whiting and Child, *Child Training and Personality*, ch. 4.

and the latter, in addition, are not severe. Aggression training, we feel safe in concluding, is not highly frustrating.

This consistently nonfrustrating pattern characterizes kibbutz independence training as well, if, that is, "independence" refers to self-reliance and responsibility, and "training" refers to those practices which socializing agents consciously employ for the attainment of this end. For the age at which kibbutz training begins approximates the median age for the Whiting-Child sample (three and one-half years), and socialization anxiety — as measured by the severity and frequency of punishment — is low.

It seems that on most counts the kibbutz is considerably better than average with respect to its child training practices. In general it permits gratification for the child's initial impulses, it does not attempt to train the child prematurely, and its training practices are not severe. There is little that might be expected to produce strong insecurity feelings.

Since it is highly improbable that sabra insecurity derives either from physical care or training, we may turn to the third socialization variable — nurturance. "Nurturance" refers to those acts of the socializing agent that satisfy the child's needs for love and protection. If "dependency needs" be used very broadly to refer to the child's need for love and protection, then nurturance may be said to refer to the satisfaction of dependency needs. If so, we should have to alter our previous judgment concerning kibbutz independence training. For though the severity of training in physical self-reliance and responsibility is low, it can be easily demonstrated that the child's emotional dependency needs — needs for protection and love — are seriously frustrated.

In all instances, however, these frustrations are "accidental." None of them is a necessary consequence of the structure of collective education, nor do these frustrations generally follow from nonnurturant attitudes of either parents or nurses. They are, rather, unintended and unanticipated consequences of certain practical aspects of kibbutz socialization which, with minor modifications in the system, could perhaps be obviated.

Since the child's nurturant figures are his parents and nurses, they are primarily responsible for his emotional frustrations. The important insecurity-arousing characteristic to be noted about the child-nurse relationship is the impossibility of the child's retaining the same nurse throughout his childhood — indeed, the high probability that he will experience frequent changes in nurses.

Since, in general, the children are deeply attached to them, a change in nurses is usually a source of intense emotional frustration.

This pattern of discontinuity in nurses begins at an early age — an age at which the consequences for the child are "traumatic." The first change in nurses occurs when the child, who is less than a year old, is moved from the Nursery to the Toddlers' House. Its magnitude is to be measured, of course, by more than a change in nurses; it entails a change in the child's physical environment as well. In any event, the child responds with, what appear to be, symptoms of passivity and fright. If this were the only change in nurses experienced by the child, perhaps it would not contribute importantly to his personality development. Its importance lies in the fact that it is but the first in a series of changes. For, having learned to adjust to the new social and physical environment induced by this change and to establish warm emotional ties with his new nurse, the child must later undergo the experience of still another change in nurses (as well as in physical environment). This departure of a nurse, with whom the child has established a deep emotional tie, constitutes, we suggest, an important emotional frustration. Its traumatic quality is probably accentuated by the fact that the child, regardless of the objective bases for the nurse's departure, frequently perceives her departure as a personal rejection. The pain which the child suffers as a result of the permanent departure of a nurse may be gauged by the emotional disturbance provoked in some children by even the temporary absence of a nurse. Aggression, withdrawal, and enuresis as well as other signs of disturbance are frequently the immediate observable consequences of the nurse's absence.

The child-parent relationship, like the child-nurse relationship, contains within it still another source of sabra insecurity — and for a similar reason. For the parent also permanently "rejects" the child — by "dethroning" him following the birth of a sibling. After an earlier period of overprotection and intense love, the older child is now replaced by his younger sibling as the center of his parents' attention and affection. We should expect this experience — even more than the one with the nurses — to lead to great emotional pain. Since the attachment of the child to his parent and the parent's love for the child are both very intense before the dethronement, the intensity of the reaction should be correspondingly great. This expectation is confirmed by the many insecurity symptoms which are found in these "rejected" children.[4]

[4] See pages 93–95.

But these are not the only "rejection" experiences encountered by the kibbutz child. The change in the child's relationship to his parents, as a function of the acquisition of a younger sibling, is paralleled in his relationship to other kibbutz members, as a function of his growing up — roughly, in the transition from the "tender age" to middle childhood. The kibbutz, as we have stressed, has many of the characteristics of a large extended family. The child receives love and attention as well as training from many adults. And, as his parents eventually reject him in favor of a younger sibling, so the entire kibbutz eventually turns its attention from him to the younger children. Thus, the child who had formerly been fondled and pampered by any adult he encountered now finds himself relatively ignored. This experience, too, should be emotionally disturbing to the child, leaving him with a feeling of rejection.

On the basis of any of these experiences (rejection by nurse, parents, and kibbutz members), one would expect the kibbutz child to develop feelings of insecurity. The combination — and often all three, or two of the three, occur at approximately the same time — should surely produce insecurity. In addition to these rejection experiences, however, kibbutz socialization leads to other frustrations of the child's dependency needs. The children, it will be remembered, are left alone at night. The departure of the parents and/or the nurses at night, we would predict, constitutes *for the very young children* a highly threatening experience. They have literally been abandoned for the night; and if the former experiences, described above, are perceived by the child as "rejection," the latter — we would expect — are perceived by him as "abandonment." It is not surprising to discover, therefore, that among the younger children crying, whining, and jouncing continue late into the night.

There is another "abandonment" experience which is undergone by almost every kibbutz child. The parents are frequently away from the kibbutz, and their absence causes the child much disturbance; indeed, it usually induces the same signs of disturbance that accompany the temporary absence of the nurse. But since parental absence may be more extensive than that of the nurse — the nurse may be absent for a day or two, while the parent may be absent for periods of weeks or months — the emotional consequences are often even more pronounced.

If certain structural and functional features of kibbutz socialization directly frustrate the child's dependency needs, still another structural feature, one which inadvertently results in poor nurturance, produces still another basis for sabra insecurity. The preschool children, we have observed, exhibit much aggression and conflict. Since the nurse is seldom present to prevent such behavior the potential victim, frequently defenseless, always loses out. His only defense against aggression is to withdraw from the situation. Thus the weak child retreats in most situations of conflict or aggression, and the child who is universally the victim of aggression or conflict eventually becomes a social isolate. Others respond to struggle by retaliation — they aggress against the aggressor or conflictor. In either event, poor nurturance — attendant upon the nurse's busy schedule — leaves the child to cope with aggression as best he can.

In all these instances of "rejection," "abandonment," and "aggression" the child responds in such a way as to indicate that these experiences are painful to him. In addition, these children manifest general symptoms of insecurity, or, to be more precise, we observed certain kinds of behavior which are usually interpreted as symptoms of insecurity feelings. Thus, a strong need for approval, frequent crying, thumbsucking, regressive play, withdrawal, the seeking of physical contact, and enuresis seem to be characteristic features of the behavior of many sabra children; not a few children display all of them. These experiences it would seem not only evoke situationally confined responses from the child, but they also contribute to his general personality structure.

In addition to these direct observations, there is also indirect evidence for childhood insecurity among the sabras — evidence furnished by dreams. Of a sample of twenty-eight sabras, ranging in age from thirteen through twenty-eight years, from whom we attempted to collect dreams, six reported that they did not dream, nine said that they did not remember their dreams, and thirteen both recalled and were willing to relate their dreams. All eighteen dreams recounted by these thirteen sabras were either remembered from childhood or, if they were contemporary dreams, the subjects reported that they had persisted since childhood. The content of twelve of the eighteen dreams is anxiety-provoking throughout; two begin as anxiety-provoking, but the anxiety is dissipated before the dream ends; and only four are affectively neutral.[5] It is difficult to escape the conclusion that these subjects

[5] Those dreams which are anxiety laden throughout include: the appearance of devils; the eating of kibbutz children by the adults; being attacked by snakes; being attacked by strangers; being engulfed by snow; being threatened with a gun; having a tiny ball roll over one's body (characterized by the subject as a nightmare); being threatened with death by a giant's sword; being threatened by

perceived certain aspects of their childhood experience as highly threatening. Much of this perception, we would suggest, is determined by their rejection experiences.[6]

These, then, comprise the childhood experiences which we assume to give rise to the sabra insecurity syndrome. It was from these experiences, viewed as the antecedent conditions of our predictions, that hostility, introversion, and a strong need for love were predicted as sabra personality characteristics. These predictions and their derivations are summarized in the first four columns of Chart I (the fifth column consists of the observed behavior that corresponds to the predictions).

These predictions, it should be remarked, are based on a limited number of assumptions derived from an adaptation of psychoanalytic, learning, and perception theories. The child, it is our assumption, not only *responds* (overtly and emotionally) to his various experiences, and he not only *learns how to behave* so as best to cope with these experiences, but he also *learns about* his world from these experiences. That is, he develops perceptions or hypotheses about his world which, in turn, motivate and govern his behavior. These perceptual sets are not necessarily permanent; they can be altered on the basis of other, both simultaneous and subsequent, experiences. If, on the other hand, the experiences which give rise to these perceptions are not countered by other experiences, the initial perception can be expected to persist as a (relatively) permanent personality characteristic.

Turning now to Chart I, it will be seen that two perceptual hypotheses are predicted from the first two experiences, temporary absence of the parent(s) from the kibbutz (for children of preschool age) and the departure of the parent or nurse from the children's house in the evening (hashkava, for children under the age of two). The predictions include the child's perception of the parent and/or nurse as having abandoned him, and, therefore,

the collapse on oneself of a revolving world; being attacked by a bull; being chased by people; being chased by wolves. The dreams whose anxiety is dissipated prior to their conclusion include: mourning the death of loved ones, followed by a return to the normal affective life; being pursued by a wild animal, followed by successful escape.

Since there are only thirteen subjects, and since they produced only eighteen dreams, it would be hazardous in the extreme to draw any definitive conclusions. Nevertheless, since the dreams are consistent with our direct observations of children, their importance is evident.

[6] If we are correct in our analysis of the affective content (anxiety) of these dreams, there is then an obvious conflict between the sabras' conscious memory of their childhood as an exclusively happy period and the picture that emerges from the dreams.

CHART I

CHILDHOOD EXPERIENCE AND ADULT PERSONALITY

Experience →	Predicted perception →	Predicted emotion/drive →	Predicted response =	Observed behavior (corresponding to predicted response)
1. Parental absence, 1,2,3, … n	a series of perceptions of nurse/parent as abandoner	fear of abandonment →	?	
2. Hashkava, 1,2,3, … n	a series of perceptions of self as abandoned			
	perception of nurses, parents, kibbutz as rejectors	pain (= frustration) →	withdrawal from rejector =	infrequent visiting with parents; psychological distance from parents and other chaverim
3. Change in nurses				
4. "Dethronement" by parents	perception of self as unloved	pain (= anxiety) →	aggression = attempts to reduce anxiety by obtaining love =	insolence to chaverim; conformity, study, work, self-love, and so on
5. "Dethronement" by kibbutz	perception of emotional relations as dangerous	anticipation of pain (= fear) →	avoidance of emotional relations =	avoidance of friendships; psychological distance from peers and strangers
6. Peer aggression	perception of others as hostile	anticipation of pain (= fear) →	hostility = avoidance of potential aggression =	hostility to peers and strangers; reluctance to interact with strangers

the perception of self as having been abandoned. Both perceptions cause him pain — respectively, "frustration" and "anxiety" — and both give rise to characteristic responses. Neither perception, however, can be expected to persist. Since, in the case of hashkava, the parent and/or nurse returns the next morning; and since, in the case of parental absence, the parent returns after a few days, weeks, or months, the child does not develop a permanent perception of the nurse and/or parent as an abandoner. And since the nurse remains with the child during parental absence, he is never completely abandoned, even when the absence is extensive.

Although it is unlikely that the child develops a persistent perceptual set either of himself or of others from these experiences, we would expect him to develop a strong and persistent fear — the fear of being permanently abandoned. Instead, that is, of acquiring a permanent *pain* (the perception of abandonment), the child acquires a permanent *dread* of being pained. The response to this fear is not predicted. Avoidance or aggression are typical responses to fear, but they are hardly relevant in this connection, since the fear is not of an external stimulus. One would guess, however, that this fear gives added poignancy to the child's rejection experiences. For the latter are painful, not only in themselves, but they serve to confirm his worst fears; for though he is not abandoned literally, he is abandoned emotionally (rejected) by these experiences.

The three rejection experiences, unlike those of abandonment, are not temporary. The departure of the nurse, the dethronement by parents and by other kibbutz members — these are permanent. Hence, the child not only suffers the pain of these experiences, but he also — it is predicted — develops three important perceptions of his world from them. He perceives his nurses, parents, and other kibbutz members as rejectors; he perceives himself as rejected; and he perceives emotional relationships as dangerous ("Those whom I love eventually reject me").

It should again be emphasized that none of these relationships (with parents, nurses, and other kibbutz members) need in themselves produce a permanent disposition to perceive emotional relationships as necessarily dangerous, or of oneself as entirely rejected. Indeed, if only one of these relationships remains unimpaired, the child need not acquire such a perceptual set. For though he suffers the pain of one rejection, his subsequent hypothesis, that emotional attachments necessarily cause pain, will have been disconfirmed by at least one of the other relationships. Similarly, he need not develop a perception of himself as rejected, for rejection by any one of these groups — painful as it may be — will not lead to a feeling of absolute rejection. Since his experiences in all three relationships, however, are remarkably consistent, he has little disconfirming evidence for the initial perceptions.

In themselves, perceptions have no motivational properties, but they are indirectly motivational, for they may give rise to drives. And the perceptions which are predicted from the sabras' rejection experiences should each, so we would assume, give rise to a pain drive or to the anticipation of pain. The following predictions may therefore be made: The perception of others as rejectors gives rise to the pain of frustration (since the rejectors, in this case, are persons whom the child loves). And frustration should, in turn, give rise to two responses — withdrawal from, and aggression against, the frustrater.

The perception of self as unloved or rejected elicits the pain of anxiety; the latter, we would expect, should motivate attempts to reduce the anxiety (by obtaining love). The perception of emotional relationships as dangerous should give rise, not to pain, but to the anticipation of pain as a consequence of such relationships. And the latter, in turn, should lead to the avoidance of emotional relationships as a means of precluding the anticipated pain.

The final source of sabra insecurity — derived from a deficiency in nurturance — is peer-aggression. Peer aggression should evoke a hostility response from the children. Some children express hostility in overt aggression, while others inhibit their aggression in favor of a withdrawal response. But since hostility and withdrawal are responses to a situational determinant, they would not be expected to persist beyond the situation that evokes them. Since, however, peer-aggression is a recurrent phenomenon, we would expect the children to develop a permanent perception of others as hostile — that is, as potentially aggressive. This perception, in turn, should be expected to give rise to the anticipation of pain ("People may attack me"). And just as actual pain leads to aggression against, and withdrawal from, the source of the pain, so the anticipation of pain is expected to lead to hostility toward, and avoidance of, the source of the anticipated pain (other people).

Withdrawal and avoidance, hostility and aggression, and the pursuit of affection and approval — these are the personality characteristics which are predicted from the sabra experiences of rejection, abandonment, and aggression. These predictions closely correspond to those sabra personality characteristics previously described. But each of these predictions refers to a general class of responses, rather than to specific behavioral or emotional characteristics. We should like, therefore, to compare these predictions with the specific sabra characteristics (as summarized in the fifth column of Chart I), and to assess their psychodynamic functions.

Withdrawal from rejector. This prediction, we believe, is reflected in two sabra characteristics — infrequent visiting with parents, and the psychological distance that characterizes the sabra relationships with parents and other adults. The first may be viewed as physical withdrawal from the source of the painful frustration ("Because you don't love me, it's painful for me to interact with you"); the second may be viewed as a withdrawal of the ego from the source of the painful frustration ("Because you don't love me, it's painful for me to remain emotionally involved with you").

These responses, however, may be viewed not only as responses to the pain of frustration — the interpretation predicted by behavior theory — but they may, in addition, be interpreted as psychological defenses against the pain of frustration — an interpretation corresponding to our "clinical" impression. Thus, an obvious psychological defense against the pain of rejection is to deny — by denying one's love for the frustrater — that the rejection is, in fact, frustrating ("Because I don't love you, I'm not hurt by your rejection of me"). And such a defense mechanism would lead both to infrequent interaction with ("Because I don't love you, I have no desire to interact with you"), and to psychological distance from ("Because I don't love you, I have no desire to seek love from you"), the frustraters.

Shyness and embarrassment in the presence of other kibbutz members are characteristic features of sabra "introversion." Although they are not predicted in Chart I, they are consistent both with the predictions and the data concerning sabra withdrawal. For, if this analysis is correct, shyness and embarrassment are symptoms of the pain felt by the sabras when they interact with kibbutz members.

Aggression. This, we believe, is reflected in sabra insolence to kibbutz members. It is not an attempt to remove the pain; it is, rather, an expression of resentment or anger because of the pain ("Because you pain me, I'll pain you"). But aggression, like withdrawal, may also be a defense against pain. And again it is my "clinical" impression that sabra insolence is (among other things) a defense mechanism. The repeated expression of insolence, "ma ichpat li," to an admonition that their behavior may have unpleasant consequences can only lead the observer to conclude that the sabra does indeed protest too much, and that, despite his denial, it *is* of concern to him. And his denial is related to his other denial that he loves his "rejectors." For, by being insolent toward those whose love he desires, he is in effect saying that he is not pained by their rejection — for he really doesn't want their love anyway.

Attempts to reduce anxiety. Sabra attempts to reduce the anxiety of being unloved may be observed in their strong desire for approval and prestige. One of my first impressions of the sabra (after penetrating the façade of hostility) was of a person who deeply wanted love and affection. This desire is expressed in such attempts to gain approval as conformity, excellence in and dedication to work, and study. Since these means are unsuccessful, some of them attempt to achieve their goal by self-praise or by fantasy satisfaction.

Generally the attitude of the people toward me is one of love and admiration. This is because I'm not stupid and can talk about many things. Also I'm good in work, and rooted in our society. And also I am gay.

He showed me his paintings, commenting after each one, "That's beautiful, isn't it?" When I asked if his work would ever be exhibited, he replied, "No. But after I die people will see my work and say that Kiryat Yedidim had a fine artist."

After saying that initiative was not strongly developed in the kibbutz, he said, "As for myself, I have much initiative."

I don't have great status (for a number of reasons), but my dancing is looked upon as the best in the kibbutz; in music I am good; and in personal discussion I am tops. The young people, particularly, look up to me, as I know how to laugh, crack jokes, and be a "good guy" in the group.

The sabra desire for approval, as an attempt to reduce their anxiety about not being loved, is not confined to seeking approval from kibbutz members only. It was evidenced also in their interaction with me. It could be observed in their anxiety about their test performances (Rorschach and TAT), and in their concern that they do well. It was seen in the eagerness of some of them when interviewed to talk about, and/or to display their creative work. One of them even read aloud his high school themes and poems that had been written some ten years previously.

Avoidance of emotional relations. If the sabras learn from their various rejection experiences that emotional relationships are dangerous, they can be expected to protect themselves against the pain of rejection by avoiding emotional relationships. This predicted avoidance is expressed in two sabra characteristics — the avoidance of intimate friendships and the maintenance of emotional reserve with peers and strangers. The avoidance of intimate friendships is an obvious protection against pain. It is as if they were to say, "If I don't love you, I can't be hurt if you reject me"; and, alternatively, "If you never love me, I can't suffer the pain of your eventual rejection."

On the other hand, emotional reserve may be viewed as a protection against pain by resisting the temptations of friendship. ("If I remain reserved with you, I can avoid entering into a friendship which, I know, will eventually lead to pain.") Having learned that emotional relationships inevitably result in pain, the sabras attempt to avoid this pain by avoiding such relationships.[7]

Hostility. This predicted consequence of peer-aggression cannot — unlike the other predictions — be confirmed by "objective" data. Since hostility is a *disposition* to behave, rather than overt behavior, it is supported only by the author's "clinical" impressions. Among the adolescents, to be sure, hostility frequently breaks out into overt (verbal) aggression, as it sometimes does among the adult sabras. It is in their relationship with strangers that, although aggression is rarely expressed, hostility is *initially* felt.

This hostility, it would seem, is both a response to, and a defense against, the anticipated pain. Just as retaliatory aggression

[7] After writing this chapter, the following quotation from the work of Robertson and Bowlby came to my attention. Referring to the child who has had the experience of becoming attached to a series of people, each of whom in turn leaves him, they write: "He will learn by bitter experience that it is folly to become attached to any one nurse, because nurses move on to other wards; thus, after a series of upsets at losing several nurses . . . he will gradually commit himself less and less to succeeding nurses and in time will stop altogether taking the risk of investing love and dependence in anyone." Robertson and Bowlby, "Observations of the Sequences of Responses of Children Aged 18 to 24 Months During the Course of Separation," *Courier of the International Children's Centre*, 2:132–142 (1952), as quoted in M. F. Ashley Montagu, *The Direction of Human Development* (London: Watts, 1957), pp. 215–216.

is a technique for the removal of the pain of peer-aggression in childhood, so hostility betokens a readiness to employ this technique if the anticipated aggression materializes. But sabra hostility is primarily — this, at least, is our impression — a defense mechanism. Perceiving others to be potentially aggressive — and for the adults "aggression" most probably means rejection — the sabras defend themselves against this threat by rejecting the other before the latter has a chance to reject him. His own hostility, that is, is a rejection of the other.

Avoidance of potential aggressor. This prediction is reflected in the sabra's avoidance of interaction with strangers. Since other people are perceived as potential aggressors, an effective technique for the avoidance of their aggression is to avoid them (as withdrawal was one of two techniques employed for escape from aggression in childhood).

If the above interpretations of sabra introversion and hostility are sound, we are confronted with the following picture of the sabras. They are people who deeply desire love from other people, but who — because of early experiences involving the lack or loss of nurturance — are overtly indifferent and hostile to others. If this is so, then "sabra" is a psychologically appropriate designation for them. For this term is taken from the botanical world, and refers to the fruit of the cactus plant — hard and thorny on the outside, but soft and tender in the center.[8]

We have attempted to demonstrate that the sabras are insecure because they perceive others to be rejecting and hostile; and we have attempted to relate their introversion, hostility, and need for approval — which we view as symptoms of their insecurity — to a small number of childhood experiences. Indeed, these three symptoms of insecurity were predicted on the basis of these childhood experiences. These predictions, it is obvious, are derived

[8] These findings, if valid, have important theoretical implications for the relationship between child-training practices and emotional adjustment in adulthood. They suggest that, with respect to emotional adjustment, the crucial behavior system is dependency. Since the training of other behavior systems in the kibbutz is generally both permissive and indulgent, it may be inferred that *the frustration of dependency needs, however indulgent or permissive the approach to other behavior systems, is a sufficient condition for emotional insecurity.*

In addition to this inference drawn from these data, I would like to suggest another hypothesis, one which goes beyond the data: *techniques* of child training are in themselves irrelevant for explaining (or predicting) emotional adjustment. The crucial determinant of emotional adjustment is the degree of nurturance which the child receives; the various techniques of child training are important only to the extent that they result in either the giving or the withholding of nurturance.

in part from psychoanalytic theory, according to which childhood experiences leave a permanent imprint on the emotional adjustment of the adult. Our predictions, however, were based, not on the notion of the fixation of response but on the acquisition of perceptual sets and hypotheses. The question which remains to be answered concerns the persistence of these perceptions. Why do these perceptual sets not change? Granted that parents and kibbutz members "reject" the sabras after a certain age, why don't the latter eventually alter their perception of these adults, thereby modifying their introversion and hostility?

Two answers — one theoretical, and one empirical — may be suggested. The theoretical answer, following psychoanalytic theory, is that these perceptions are, for the most part, unconscious; and the unconscious is notoriously resistant to change. Indeed, the entire emotional structure we have described is probably unconscious, and for an obvious reason — the perception of self as abandoned and unloved is painful, and the most efficient defense against such a self-perception is repression.

On the other hand, it would be rash to deny that the perception of self or of *alter* cannot change — and I, at least, would surely grant that experiences subsequent to those of abandonment and rejection could conceivably change or modify sabra insecurity feelings. The fact is, however, that their later experiences, if anything, serve to confirm, rather than to alter, the sabras' initial perceptions.

Many sabras consciously hold that kibbutz love is contingent upon their vindicating the time, effort, and money which the kibbutz has invested in them. They believe that they are guinea pigs who must prove by their behavior and personality that the experiment conducted by their parents has been worth while. The proof is to consist in their ability to carry on the kibbutz, and in their being "different" from those who have not been reared in the carefully planned educational system of the kibbutz.

These beliefs may represent a conscious reflection of their unconscious feelings of abandonment and rejection. It is more plausible to interpret them as an only slightly distorted reflection of present reality. When, for example, parents express misgivings about the efforts and sacrifices they have made for collective education, it is almost always because their adult children — so they claim — are no different from those raised by the more conventional techniques of child rearing. The parents wanted the sabras to be different, and by their difference to vindicate the sacrifices which they have made to ensure this outcome. It is little wonder that, when I expressed surprise about something they said or did, the sabras frequently and bitterly countered with, "What do you think — we're different from anyone else?"

But though the sabras are expected to be different from others, they are expected to be similar to some others, their parents, in at least one respect — their ability to carry on the work of the kibbutz. Thus the adult sabras, now that they have entered the kibbutz and are working in its economy, are under constant observation to see whether they can "make the grade." As one parent put it, "Until now it's been like a nice game, but now that they've entered the kibbutz the test has started." It is little wonder that the sabras believe, according to the Moral Ideology Test, that self-reliance or competence is the most important goal that they are expected (by the kibbutz) to achieve. The various types of behavior that comprise this category — intellectual, artistic, economic, and leadership activities — are mentioned most frequently as praiseworthy, and failure to perform them are mentioned most frequently as blameworthy, activities.

But the notion of a test is not only anxiety-provoking in itself, it also serves to reinforce the sabras' perception of the kibbutz as a potential rejector — for failure to pass the test means the withdrawal of love. Indeed, in some cases the feared "rejection" has already occurred. The sabras know, as we shall observe, that many chaverim are already both dubious and critical of their abilities.

This feeling of being unloved was expressed most dramatically by an incident that occurred during our stay in Kiryat Yedidim. When the kibbutz debated the question of electing the high school graduates to membership before or after their army service, the students of the graduating class were bitter in their denunciations of the entire debate. Despite their anticipated election to membership in the kibbutz, they did not feel like chaverim of a kibbutz which, they complained, had displayed little genuine concern for them.

We may summarize, then, by suggesting that the sabras' initial perception of others as rejectors, which derives from their childhood experiences, is reinforced at a later, and equally crucial, period in their development. This reinforcement exacerbates their original feelings of insecurity, and adds additional force to its symptoms — need for approval, introversion, and hostility. And it is the experiences in the latter period which may also account for the otherwise inexplicable discrepancy between the younger and the older sabras.

Until roughly the age of eleven or twelve, sabra children do not correspond to the personality picture which has been sketched for the adolescents and adults in at least one important respect. The need for love and approval, to be sure, seems to be as strong in the children as in the older sabras. Preschool children, moreover, are highly aggressive; but their aggression may reflect those aspects of their social environment which permit the expression of aggression, rather than undue hostility. But in the third important characteristic the children differ greatly from the older sabras. They are not withdrawn. True, the grade school children are shy with strangers and embarrassed when they interact with them, but they do not reveal the avoidance-hostility syndrome that characterizes the older sabras, nor do they display signs of psychological distance with parents. Their relationship with the latter is, on the contrary, an intimate one.

Two *ad hoc* explanations for this discrepancy are available. Conceivably there is a relatively long latency period — its duration still to be tested — between childhood experiences and the formation of those personality sets that are a function of these experiences. This is at least consistent with other situations in which a period of latency intervenes between some stipulated condition and its consequence. Why, in this case, the consequence should first occur in high school is suggested by the experiences — and this is the second suggestion — which we have been examining. Since it is at this time that the sabras consciously perceive the kibbutz to be a potential rejector — its love is contingent — older memories, perceptions, and feelings of rejection are reactivated and, thus, it is in early adolescence that they first find their strong expression. These explanations, however, are both *ad hoc* and speculative; they are offered with no great confidence.

INFERIORITY FEELINGS

Up to now we have attempted to analyze sabra insecurity in terms of their painful perceptions of others. But there is still another basis for this insecurity — a painful perception of self. The sabras may be characterized by feelings of inferiority both with respect to their identity (as Jews) and to their abilities (intellectual accomplishments and self-reliance).

Sabra inferiority feelings were not predicted from knowledge of kibbutz socialization. Nor — except in the case of sabra embarrassment with strangers — did I originally perceive any systematic relationship between their inferiority feelings and their symptoms of insecurity. Although I now believe that childhood experiences are, in part, responsible for the sabra feelings of inferiority, and that these feelings are functionally related to previously discussed symptoms of insecurity, these interpretations are *post hoc*. That is, after discovering indications of inferiority feelings, we attempted to discover the factors which conceivably could have produced them, as well as those forms of behavior which conceivably could serve as defenses against them. This section, therefore, is less systematic and more speculative than the previous section.

Self-reliance. The first measure of their feelings about self-reliance is the degree to which the sabras feel adequate to assume exclusive responsibility for the kibbutz. This is a question with which their elders are deeply concerned and to which the sabras, too, have given much thought.

That many sabras have doubts concerning their ability to carry full responsibility for the functioning of the kibbutz is a proposition which is either supported by, or may be inferred from, their own statements. Of the seven adult sabras who commented on this point during the interviews, three explicitly denied that their fellows are reliant, and two were doubtful. As one of them put it:

> Our way of life is a result of living here; it's natural, so we never think about it . . . We are not educated to solve many problems of life. Our way is already paved for us. If we had been told at the age of eighteen to leave and to build a new kibbutz — I don't say we couldn't do it, but we've never had the opportunity. Everything is served to us on a platter; the menu is known in advance. . . . About this (self-reliance) I have doubts. We are so accustomed to think that everything is done for us.

A frequent refrain in the sabra interviews when the question of their ability to carry on is raised is, "But I know I can prove myself." This comment, I believe, was designed to convince themselves, rather than me, of that which they were not altogether sure.

But sabra doubts about their ability to carry on by themselves is probably best expressed by some of the sabras in the excessive and obsessive preoccupation with work — a preoccupation which may be interpreted as symptomatic of a feeling of inadequacy. That some females are obsessed with work status has already been noted; and although much of this obsession is motivated by a feeling of inadequacy, *qua* females, some of it seems motivated by a feeling of inadequacy, *qua* sabras. For male sabras too are obsessed with work and work status, and in their case the interpretation is not contaminated by the vexing "problem of the woman." One male, for example, is so obsessed with work that he spontaneously referred to it in almost every question of the interview (although only one question was devoted to it). The following quotations are selected at random from various parts of his interview.

I am interested in my work and devoted to it . . . I like it so much, that at times I am sorry the day is over. I already have status in my branch . . . Moshe and I are unique in that we are so young and already have high status in our work.

The main defect in the kibbutz is that a person does his day's work, and that's all. I feel a sense of responsibility, and so I work hard. Sometimes I work during the lunch hour and, if I feel that something has to be done, I work late in the evening.

There is too much freedom and not enough compulsion in the kibbutz. For example, people come late to work and there is no one to compel them to come on time, and there are some who exploit this fact . . . I would like to see the institution of work-lists, to be posted on the bulletin board, and a system of work norms in each branch, to which they must conform.

The children grow up with no understanding of farm work . . . The majority of students in the Mosad have no proper attitude to work. They work with a maximum lack of desire. This continues through the kibbutz . . . I don't mean that they don't work well. It's that they have no great motivation or feeling that "The farm is me." The sabras do not stand out as exceptional workers.

Sabra doubts about their own abilities are exacerbated by a comparison of their achievements with those of their parents. They know, and are frequently reminded, that their fathers are heroic pioneers, and that they have been "spoiled children" — as the Youth Movement leader put it — for whom "everything has been done." Moreover, regardless of what they may be able to achieve, their achievement will be of less moment than that of their parents, who, after all, were the real pioneers. This feeling is frequently articulated by the sabras. As one of them remarked, "We feel that everything has already been done by the older chaverim, and that there is nothing left for us to do."

Sabra doubts about their ability to carry on may be inferred, finally, from certain characteristics which seem to represent defenses against their attendant inferiority feelings. The sabra pose of "unconcern" (*lo ichpatiut*) provides one such clue. Calculated indifference becomes a defense against their feeling that perhaps they cannot carry on. It is as if they say, "Who cares? What difference does it make if I do something or not?" And this pose, combined with their lack of strong goal orientation seems to serve as a psychological defense against their inferiority feelings. If one projects no goals, one cannot be viewed as a failure, for he has made no attempt to achieve them. If, moreover, he is viewed as a slacker for not attempting to achieve them, he is protected by his unconcern — the goals to be attained are not worth striving for anyway.

Sabra feelings of personal inadequacy relate not only to their ability to continue the work of the kibbutz, but also to their ability to adjust to a non-kibbutz environment. The sabras are attached to the kibbutz, and none has left. This is a positive sign as far as the continuation of the kibbutz is concerned; but their attachment to the kibbutz has a negative aspect as well, for the older sabras seem unable to make a positive adjustment to a non-kibbutz environment. As one sabra expressed it, "The general result of collective education over many years is that it restricts initiative. If I had to live in the outside world, I could not adjust to it" (in the sense of being able to care for herself).

This prediction is not entirely conjectural. Those sabras who, prior to the construction of a high school in Kiryat Yedidim, attended school in another kibbutz were extremely unhappy and eager to return to Kiryat Yedidim. They could not face the demands of their new environment. Similarly, the average sabra who visits the city is, as one father disgustedly remarked, "Lost. He becomes confused by having to make decisions for himself. In the kibbutz everything is planned for him, and he is eager to return to the framework within which his life is ordered." When, formerly, the sabras lived in the city for one year following their graduation from high school, they made a point of living together with other kibbutz sabras, with whom they could maintain a regulated kibbutz-like existence. Even those who travel abroad seek out other sabras with whom to live.

This response to new situations is, to be sure, not a necessary index of low self-reliance, nor is it confined to the sabras; it is probably shared by most people in most countries. But, since the sabras themselves take it as such an index, we may conclude that it is one of the factors which contributes to their feeling of inferiority.

It is difficult to evaluate the degree to which the sabras are or are not self-reliant and, specifically, to judge their ability to assume exclusive responsibility for running the kibbutz. So far as the high-school youth are concerned, we believe they are as *responsible* within their own social environment as other youth are within theirs. It is our feeling, however, that they may not be so *self-reliant* as some youths are. In the classroom, for example, the students are more likely to complain about the difficulty of a problem than to attempt to solve it. *Oi, ani lo yodea* — "Oh, I don't know how to do it" — is the typical response to a difficult assignment, following which the student waits for the teacher to help him, or to do it for him.

As for the adult sabras, there is little reason — despite their own gnawing doubts — to question their ability to carry on the economic aspects of the kibbutz. According to all accounts, they are excellent and dedicated workers. What is more, they are sufficiently responsible — as well as personally competent — to have been elected to the foremanships of various economic branches.[9]

On the other hand, as of 1951, none has served in any crucial leadership position in the kibbutz economy, nor in any non-economic leadership position. Indeed, it is in the non-economic aspects of kibbutz life that they are still to be tested. It is my opinion, however, that they will not be found wanting.

Many chaverim, on the other hand, with a poor opinion of sabra ability, take a dim view of the kibbutz future. Kibbutz doubts have been expressed with respect to both high-school and adult sabras. The former, kibbutz opponents of collective education argue, are neither responsible nor reliable. This criticism is sufficiently widespread, both within and without the Federation, for the educational director to have felt it necessary to "refute" these critics in print.[10] But the criticism remains, and it is shared

[9] Their sense of responsibility probably accounts for the fact that, according to an Israeli army officer, sabras are excellent military officers. He argued that, accustomed to being concerned for the welfare of others, the kibbutz sabra reacts responsibly to the troops under his command. It is not enough that he himself have shoes or extra trousers; he makes sure that his men have them also — something which he does naturally and almost automatically.

[10] His most important argument is the valor displayed by the sabras in The War of Independence.

"They are wonderful children. We have raised a generation to be proud of. We ourselves did not realize what we had: children healthy in body and soul, free, dignified, strong, disciplined when necessary, and free when there is no necessity for discipline. A group building and fighting for the future, responsible, loving their kibbutz home with a powerful love, with deep roots in the soil of the Homeland, prepared for any test, comrades devoted to each other."

by some members of Kiryat Yedidim, parents and sabras alike. As one parent put it, few demands are placed on kibbutz children, so that when demands are made of them when they grow older, they cannot meet them. If asked to do something, they can refuse with, "So what can you do to me?" The high-school principal, on the other hand, insisted that many adults expect too much of the youth. They expect them, he said, to be as responsible as adults, and they make demands on them which they, when young, could never have fulfilled. These adults, he noted, exemplify the Russian proverb: "The bull forgets that he was once a calf."

But doubts concerning their self-reliance — specifically, their ability to carry on the work of their fathers — is heard with respect to the adult sabras as well. One parent, for example, asked me point blank if I thought the sabras would be able to continue the kibbutz. I answered in the affirmative, but he said:

From the standpoint of the economy, yes, but from the standpoint of continuing the whole conception of kibbutz living, I doubt it. The kibbutz is a difficult way of life; it's not easy. It requires exceptional people to continue to live it. When one is young, it's not too bad. But when one becomes older, the discipline that's required, the willingness to accept group decisions and to have your life controlled by group decisions, is very hard. Some people can't take it, and that's the main reason for leaving the kibbutz. I am doubtful if the sabras have what it takes. They are mentally "dry"; they have no great imagination, no fertile ideas.

When I pointed out that most people anywhere may be characterized in these terms, and that only the few are exceptional, he said,

Yes, but the kibbutz is not like most places. The people who founded the kibbutz were exceptional. They *did* have ideas and imagination.

A chavera expressed similar sentiments:

I don't think that the kibbutz has a future. . . . The idealism and pioneering spirit that characterized the founders are gone. The sabras do not have it, and without this spirit the kibbutz cannot survive.

Another chaver put it this way:

The government is trying to destroy the kibbutzim. I don't think the sabras have the ability to withstand this pressure.

We have quoted some of these expressions of doubt, not only because they constitute additional data for an assessment of sabra self-reliance, but because they suggest a possible source of sabra feelings of inferiority. We assume that a person's self-conception is to a great extent a function of the conception which others have of him (or, more accurately, of the conception which *he thinks* they have of him). So, if the sabras know that many chaverim are dubious about their ability to carry on — and they cannot help but know this since such sentiments are expressed quite publicly — they too must begin to share these doubts.

Our theoretical assumption must be qualified, however, by another consideration. A person need not inevitably feel inferior if he knows that others consider him to be inferior; only if he shares their values need this consequence follow. Thus, if the sabras do not place a high value on self-reliance (and the consequent ability to carry on the kibbutz), they need not develop feelings of inferiority solely because some chaverim believe them inadequate. The fact is, however, that the sabras do share this value. Not only do they view self-reliance or competence as the most important goal to be achieved (according to the Moral Ideology Test), but the lack of self-reliance (personal inadequacy or failure in a task) is the second most frequent occasion of sadness (according to the Emotional Response Test). One source, then, of sabra inferiority feeling about their self-reliance is to be found in the opinions which others have of them.

I would like to suggest another explanation — also speculative — to account for this self-perception. Since the infant is not self-reliant, it is fair to assume that self-reliance is acquired in childhood. It is well-known that strong dependence on others renders it extremely difficult to become dependent on oneself (self-reliance). It is also plausible, however, that the frustration of dependence needs renders it equally difficult to become self-reliant. The acquisition of self-reliance, in short, must develop from a previous state of reliance on others. Hence, if one learns that he cannot rely on others, it is entirely possible that he will not develop the feeling or the ability of self-reliance.

The sabras are exposed to important experiences from which they learn that they cannot rely on others. In infancy there is often a long delay between the onset of the infant's need and its satisfaction by a nurse or mother. In childhood, when peers attack them, they learn that they cannot rely on their nurses for defense. When they are afraid at night, they learn that they cannot rely on their parents or nurses for protection. A helpless and defenseless child cannot develop that confidence which, in adulthood, is manifested in a feeling of self-reliance.

But one might speculate upon still another childhood basis for sabra feelings of personal incompetence, one related to the frequent change in nurses. If it be granted that one's security is a function, among other things, of successful adaptation to one's environment, then a frequent change in nurses must place a great burden on the security system of the kibbutz child. For, although all nurses are, in the main, similar to each other, they do exhibit individual differences in their interaction with the children. Hence those techniques of adaptation which the child has formerly employed in interacting with a previous nurse may be inappropriate in interacting with the new nurse. Responses which were formerly instrumental for obtaining love or satisfying other needs may now be relatively inefficient. In short, previous adaptive techniques are now unadaptive and, in some cases, even maladaptive. The consequence for the child can only be anxiety, for he does not know which of the responses in his total repertory will elicit from other people those responses which will satisfy his needs.

This anxiety can produce at least two results. Either the child will integrate an ego around those responses which have become adaptive in his interaction with an early nurse, or else — in order to achieve the flexibility which such a situation demands — he will refuse to synthesize these various responses into an integrated ego. In the former case his limited number of instrumental responses (synthesized to form his ego) will, in fact, be maladaptive in interaction with other nurses. Instead of obtaining some goal — love, for example — he may obtain the contrary of what he desires. In the latter case he retains the flexibility which a changing environment demands, and this flexibility enables him to adapt fairly well to each change in nurses. But he pays a price for this adaptation. In order to retain a maximum of flexibility, he is prevented from developing a strong ego (by synthesizing a limited number of instrumental responses). Without a strong ego he cannot cope with the problems of later life. Sabra feelings of inadequacy, we could then argue, reflect a weak ego, which, in turn, is based on their "decision" to retain maximum flexibility in childhood.

Intellectual ability. Another source of sabra feelings of inferiority is their level of intellectual competence. As a group, the adult sabras believe that they are less educated than, and consequently inferior to, Western-trained persons. There are many indications of this feeling. One sabra, whose job takes him outside the kibbutz, said that he felt inferior to his colleagues in the city because they knew more than he. He blames his ignorance on the kibbutz school system, which did not compel him to study when, at sixteen, he lost interest in academic matters. Now, he would "do anything" to study. A younger sabra reported that more than half his class felt ignorant, despite their formal education, and are now eager to study more. Another sabra, engaged in study in the city, said that he felt "ashamed" that he knew so little compared to the city students. When, on one occasion, I referred to the "high intellectual attainments" of the adult sabras, they broke into loud laughter, and one accused me of "typical American salesmanship."

It is hard to understand how the sabras acquired this self-image, for their intellectual interests and attainments are unquestionably higher than those of the average American high-school graduate. In the absence of explicit evidence, I can suggest at least three bases for this self-image. First, it may be a reflection of the perception that others — parents and outsiders — have of them. Their parents make no secret of their belief that the sabras are not well-educated. This "deplorable state" they attribute to the school system which, they claim, maintains a low level of studies.

Although the parents' complaints are not directed toward any specific sabra, the mere fact that the "problem" of the "low level" of studies was the subject of an entire town meeting at which the products of this "low level" were present, must influence the opinion which the sabras have of themselves. That the sabras are aware of, and respond to, the adults' perception of them as inadequately educated is reflected perhaps in the Moral Ideology Test. For second (only to labor) among praiseworthy activities is intellectual and artistic accomplishment.

The sabras are affected by the opinions of non-kibbutz persons, as well. They are members not only of Kiryat Yedidim but also of the larger social category of "kibbutz sabras," and the stereotype depicts them as strong, blond peasants, devoted to their country and attached to its soil, but ignorant — if not contemptuous — of intellectual and spiritual matters.[11] This public image has unquestionably affected the sabra self-image.

A second postulated basis for the sabra feeling of intellectual inferiority is the discrepancy which they perceive to exist between themselves and their intellectual models. It is true that some of their parents (the older settlers) are their intellectual superiors,

[11] See Arthur Koestler, *Thieves in the Night* (New York: Macmillan, 1946).

but such a comparison is neither surprising nor fair. For the most part, the kibbutz founders were trained in European gymnasiums whose intellectual level is very high. Moreover, they were raised in a culture which placed a high premium on intellectuality, whereas their children are expected to excel in work as well as studies.[12]

But parents are not their only models. The persons held up to the sabra students for emulation (aside from the great political emancipators) are scientists, artists, and scholars. That these continue to serve as important figures for the sabras is evidenced by the many references made to them in ordinary conversation, in interviews, and on tests. Compared to them, the sabras, of course, *are* intellectually inferior. Again, the distorted self-image of the sabras is a function of exaggerated adult demands.

Although the sabra perception of themselves as insufficiently educated is to a considerable extent a distorted one, nevertheless, there may be some realistic basis for their feeling of intellectual inferiority. This has to do not so much with their intellectual interests or attainments but with their intellectual functioning. There is some reason to believe that the creative powers of at least the younger sabras are poorly developed. Their TAT stories, for example, are very brief. This may be due to factors other than lack of imagination or repression — boredom with the task, for example, or lack of rapport with the administrator. Both appear unlikely, however, in view of the following incident. Two second-grade students, attached to me, who had originally been excluded from the testing sample, pleaded to be allowed to take the TAT. When I agreed, they were overjoyed. In spite of their eagerness, however, their stories were as brief as those told by the other students.

Even more important is the testimony from kibbutz teachers. When informed of the brevity of the children's TAT stories, a nursery teacher with many years of experience replied that she was not at all surprised, because, in her opinion, the children have

---

[12] Their parents' motivations, moreover, were different from theirs — an observation that suggests a hypothesis concerning intellectual achievement. The parents were not only members of an underprivileged minority group; they were also in rebellion against their parents. It is our hypothesis that motivation for intellectual achievement, particularly when other avenues for achievement are closed, is a function of either of these above two conditions. Where both conditions obtain, such motivation is magnified. Hence, the lower achievement of the sabras may be interpreted as a function of their lack of minority group status and of the absence of parental rebellion. This interpretation is supported by the observation that the most intensely intellectual students in the Mosad are those whose family lives are the most disturbed.

little imagination. Similar opinions were expressed by Mosad teachers about their students. The latter, furthermore, were characterized by some of their teachers as being deficient in abstract ability. They have, it is claimed, no interest in abstract discussions, and it is all but impossible to get them to write essays on abstract subjects. This resistance to the abstract was graphically demonstrated during a grammar lesson. Although the students have no difficulty expressing themselves in correct grammatical usage, the tenth-grade class became utterly confused in discussions of grammatical theory. Although they do not confuse the active and passive forms of the verb in ordinary discourse, the teacher had to explain the theoretical difference repeatedly before the distinction between the two forms was finally grasped.[13]

A final characteristic of sabra intellectual functioning that may contribute to their feeling of intellectual inferiority is their inability to concentrate for long. (This inability is characteristic, at least, of the adolescents. We have no data for the adults.) They cannot, as one teacher put it, "stay at any one thing for any length of time. They scatter their energies over a number of things, or they jump from interest to interest." Another teacher said that the students reminded her of the eight-year-olds she had taught in England, insofar as their ability to concentrate is concerned. Hence, the ninety-minute lesson, she felt, was too long a time span in which to sustain their interest.

Thus, although some of the bases for the sabra feeling of intellectual inferiority are, in my opinion, groundless, there are, nevertheless, some realistic grounds for it. Since the study of intellectual functioning was not an explicit aim of our research, I have little data on this problem, and could only speculate on the causes of the minor deficiency which is tentatively suggested by some of the data. It is to be hoped, however, that the projective tests will yield additional information.

Jewish identity. As discussed above, the sabras harbor few positive feelings for Judaism. They are not merely indifferent to Judaism but actually hostile to it. Their reluctance to read Jewish literature, to study Jewish history, to listen to Jewish music, it must be obvious, is based on more than intellectual disagreement or aesthetic dissatisfaction. For if the music is labeled "Russian," rather than "Jewish," they admire it. And Shalom Aleichem and Mendele are "boring," not because they are inferior writers, but

---

[13] A resistance to the abstract, rather than lack of intellectual interest, may well motivate some of the disturbance so characteristic of the kibbutz classroom.

because they write of the "narrow" and "superstitious" shtetl. But the narrowness and superstitions that characterized the shtetl are surely no less evident in the Indian and Chinese villages about which the sabras delight in reading. Sabra hostility to Judaism must, therefore, be emotionally rather than cognitively grounded. And it is our hypothesis that their hostility is a defense mechanism, a mechanism which serves to protect them from those feelings of shame and inferiority that any encounter with a negatively evaluated identification arouses. In short, the very hostility which the sabras display toward Jews and Judaism leads us to infer that they experience deep feelings of inferiority because of their identification with them.

"Identification" is an ambiguous term, as far as its agent is concerned. One may be identified with a particular group or culture by persons other than oneself, or one may oneself identify with a particular group or culture,[14] or both. It is well-known, and frequently observed, that these two types need not necessarily coincide. Both types, however, are crucially important for one's self-conception. For to the extent that the self is a product of one's various identifications, one's evaluation of them provides an important basis for the evaluation of one's self. Identification, in either sense of that term, with a positively evaluated group or culture, produces feelings of self-regard and self-esteem. Identification with a negatively evaluated group or culture, on the other hand, produces self-feelings of shame and of inferiority.[15]

The sabras are identified, in both senses, with Jews and with Judaism. They are willy-nilly labeled as "Jews" by others — a practice which inevitably establishes their cultural pedigree. And they have unconsciously identified themselves with Jews and with Judaism if only by virtue of the many Jewish models — parents, nurses, and such — who served as objects of imitation or identification in the process of sabra personality development. But their identification with a culture assumed to be inferior produces a self-conception which necessarily entails feelings of shame and inferiority. Since, however, they cannot undo the identification — the defense mechanism of "denial" would, in this instance be to

[14] The latter may be divided into two subclasses — conscious and unconscious — identification.

[15] Although the self-conceptions which derive from either type of identification are similar in valence, it is possible, if one likes, to make phenomenological discriminations between them. Depending on one's personal evaluation of the group or culture, the self-conception which derives from being identified by others with the group or culture in question involves feelings of pride or shame; but the self-conception which derives from identifying oneself with that group or culture involves feelings of superiority or inferiority.

no avail [16] — the only defense against such painful feelings is one of dissociation from their instigation — Jews and Judaism. If one does not interact with the object of one's identification, one is not reminded of it.

If this analysis is valid, then one must label as naïve their teacher's suggestion that the sabras view the shtetl as they view a Chinese or Indian village. Although all three villages may be equally quaint and exotic to the indifferent — that is, the detached — observer, the sabras are not detached from the shtetl. As detached observers, they can find entertainment in descriptions of the Chinese village; as attached observers, they can only be pained by descriptions of the Jewish village. To read Mendele, therefore, becomes a highly threatening experience. For to be reminded of the shtetl is, since they are identified with it, to experience feelings of shame and inferiority. The refusal to read Mendele may thus be interpreted as an ego-defense whose function is to preclude the arousal of these emotions.

This same mechanism probably motivates their reluctance to study Diaspora Jewish history. For the desire of the sabras to be known as heroes is threatened by their identification with those who in their opinion have acted unheroically. By the same token the sabras both hate and fear the Oriental immigration. They fear the immigrants, perhaps, because that ghetto culture, of which they are so ashamed and which they believed to have been destroyed, is in danger of being revived by them. They hate them perhaps because the constant sight of these living representatives of the hated ghetto culture and mentality is a threat to their own self-image. Moreover, the sabras fear that the presence in Israel of these Oriental Jews may result in their (the sabras') being identified by others with them. Hence, even the young students of the seventh grade are at great pains in their essays to distinguish between "modern" Israelis, on the one hand, and Oriental and orthodox Jews, on the other — and to identify themselves exclusively with the former.

This hatred and fear become even more understandable in view of the fact that the realization that the Oriental and the orthodox are, like themselves, Jews frequently comes as a shock to the sabras. For kibbutz children the word "Jew," if used at all, has only one contemporary referent — a *chaver kibbutz*. That this

[16] Some Israelis, of course, have adopted the mechanism of denial. Those who are affiliated with *Alef* explicitly deny any historical connection between (superior) "Israelis" and (inferior) "Jews," viewing the former as the spiritual, if not physical, descendants of the ancient Canaanites.

label applies as well to persons so dissimilar often comes both as a confusing experience and as a rude awakening. This is illustrated by the following story recounted by a kibbutz father. Some years before our arrival in the kibbutz, he took his six-year-old daughter to Safed, the center of Chassidism, where for the first time she encountered bearded, orthodox Jews. She asked her father who these strange people were, and when he said that they were Jews, she became terribly confused. Until then she had encountered only two kinds of people — Jews, by which term she understood the kind of people she saw in the kibbutz, and Arabs. She could not understand, her father recalled, where these other "Jews" fitted in. For her, and her peers, to have to accept, when adult, the fact that the bearded Jews of Safed and the Oriental immigrants are Jews, must be a painful experience.

Thus, a third source of sabra inferiority concerns, not their personal abilities, but their group identity. Being identified with an "inferior culture" and an "inferior people," they feel themselves inferior too.

This explains the functional relationship between sabra inferiority feelings and certain of their symptoms of insecurity — hostility and introversion. Perceiving themselves to be inferior, they are reluctant to interact with strangers lest they also perceive their inferiority. An important motive for the sabra reticence with strangers (including the reluctance of some to be tested and interviewed) is probably their fear of revealing what they think to be their ignorance. Thus, the sabra with the least formal education refused even to talk with us, and the sabra whose conversation and behavior revealed the greatest intellectual insecurity refused to be tested. A third acceded only after much resistance. When the latter first became aware of my desire to test him, he began to avoid me, although he had formerly been friendly. He later told my wife that he did not want to be tested because he did not want to know about himself — and he did not want others to know either. He was, he said, afraid. But when, after postponing the interview a number of times, I chided him by suggesting that he was putting me off, he responded with, "Why should I put you off? What have I got to be afraid of?" And, again, when I chided him for canceling an interview, he said that he had no reason to put me off, for why should he have "anything to be afraid of?"

The sabras' inferiority feelings perhaps also contribute to their acute embarrassment with strangers. Embarrassment is a frequent response to those situations in which one feels subordinate or inferior. It is painful to interact with those who, one believes, perceive one to be inferior. Sabra hostility to strangers may similarly be traced to their feeling of inferiority. Fearing rejection at the hands of those who, they feel, regard them as inferior, the sabras respond to this anticipated rejection with hostility. Hence, their hostility is a defense in which the sabra seems to say, "I'll reject you before you can reject me."

SABRAS AND INSTITUTIONAL CHILDREN

For the reader familiar with the literature on institutionalized children[17] it should now be apparent that there are striking similarities between them and the sabras. But these similarities are frequently more apparent than real. The institutionalized children are characterized by a *flattening* of affect; the sabras by a *repression* of affect. The former cannot establish emotional ties; the latter can, and do, though they are initially wary in the extreme. Their warm relationships with spouse and children, for example, indicate their ability to form emotional ties. Their relationships with others, moreover, though not of an intimate nature, are characterized by affection and concern. Studies of institutionalized children, moreover, show them to be often psychopathic; that is, they have either deficient superegos or none at all. Hence they are frequently characterized by stealing, deceit, evasion, lying, and so on. None of these characteristics applies to the sabras, who have strong superegos. I know of only one instance of stealing among children (see pp. 268–269), and, to the best of my knowledge, there are no instances in adolescence or adulthood. Evasion, deceit, and lying are the antitheses of the sabra personality. If anything, always forthright in behavior, they are guilty of the opposite. Honesty — sometimes austere and painful honesty — is one of the most characteristic of sabra personality traits. "Regardless of what you might think of the sabras," commented one parent, "they are always honest." In this judgment, the kibbutz, to a man, would concur. All of my experiences with the sabras only serve to confirm the truth of this unanimous judgment.

Institutionalized children, finally, reveal serious intellectual deficiency — lack of concentration and of abstract ability. Some sabras reveal a similar deficiency, but the degree of impairment is much less serious among them than among the institutionalized children. If our data are reliable, about 15 per cent of kibbutz high-school students reveal some intellectual deficiency — but

[17] For a detailed summary and analysis of the literature, see John Bowlby, *Maternal Care and Mental Health* (London: World Health Organization, 1951).

there seems to be no reliable basis for assuming a lower percentage among American high-school students. There is reason to believe, moreover, that at least some of these 15 per cent are not permanently impaired. The special teacher who works with these children informed me that many of them had made remarkable progress in the course of a few months' work with her.

The sabras, in sum, are not institutionalized children. They show signs of disturbance, but — for the most part — they are not neurotic, and they most definitely are not psychopathic. For the social and emotional structure of the lives of kibbutz children differ in some crucial respects from those of institutionalized children. The conditions responsible for emotional deprivation in these latter children — from which most of their difficulties allegedly derive — are divided by Bowlby into three broad types: "(a) lack of any opportunity for forming an attachment to a mother-figure during the first three years . . . (b) deprivation for a limited period — at least three months and probably more than six — during the first three or four years . . . (c) changes from one mother-figure to another during the same period." [18] The first condition is not found at all in the kibbutz, and the others are found only with important qualifications. The kibbutz child patently establishes a relationship with a mother-figure — indeed, more than one mother-figure — in the first three years. His relationship to both his biological mother and father is exceptionally strong, as is his relationship to his mother-surrogate, the nurse. His mother may, of course, go away for a limited period each year — sometimes for a few months — and this, as we have shown, is frequently a source of deep disturbance for the child. But the kibbutz socialization system protects the child from absolute deprivation. Though his mother is gone, his nurse — who is a genuine mother-surrogate, and to whom he is deeply attached, prior to his mother's departure — remains. She not only continues to give him the nurturance which he has come to expect from her, but — in the case of perceptive nurses — she tries to compensate for his mother's absence by giving him an abundance of love.

Similarly, though the child experiences a change in mother-figures (nurses), which is painful in the extreme, he nevertheless is protected from the more drastic effects of change by the constancy of his parents. Though his nurses are transient, his parents are permanent. And it is the permanence of the latter figures — emotionally, the more important ones — that deprives the change in nurses of its potentially extreme consequences. However, should

[18] Bowlby, *Maternal Care*, p. 47.

his parents go away at the same time that his nurses are changed, the kibbutz child does suffer extreme deprivation. And we would guess — though we have no data on this point — that the seriously disturbed sabras are those who suffered this double deprivation.

It is for the same reason — the existence of multiple parental figures — that parental "rejection," although severely frustrating, does not lead to pathological consequences. For though the parent may no longer shower the child with love, the nurse continues to play her normal, nurturant role. And, moreover, although nurses are changed, the average nurse is a highly nurturant figure with whom the child — despite his frustration by the departure of a previous nurse — does establish a warm emotional relationship.

Two other conditions which serve to mitigate the painful reaction to the sabra's "deprivation" experiences must be mentioned. The very existence of multiple parent figures protects the child from exclusive cathexes. Since his emotional attachments are diffuse rather than concentrated, the pain attendant upon the severance of one of these cathexes is probably considerably attenuated.

A final mitigating influence in sabra "deprivation" is the peer-group, a source of protection and an object of love for the kibbutz child. Though abandoned at night by his parent figures, he remains together with his peers. Their importance as dispellers of fear may be inferred from the difference between the child's behavior when he is with them at night and when he is isolated from them. But the peers not only serve to protect him from fears, they are also sources and objects of love. Thus, to no small degree, they compensate him for any emotional deprivation he may suffer from parent figures; and they serve to further diffuse his emotional cathexes, thereby mitigating the pain of deprivation by the parent figures.

The socialization system of the kibbutz not only precludes the possibility of severe deprivation, but it contains other characteristics which, according to our present knowledge of personality development, make for positive emotional adjustment. Both nurses and parents are warm and nurturant, and their love is non-contingent. These adults neither give nor withhold love as a function of compliance by the child. They do not offer their love as a bribe to the child. Moreover, they never, objectively viewed, withdraw their love (although the child perceives certain aspects of their behavior as withdrawal of love). Second, members of the entire kibbutz play nurturant roles toward the child. Since he has numerous opportunities to interact with almost every member, he soon achieves a measure of security in the entire kibbutz. Third, training in the various behavior systems — oral, anal, sexual, and aggression — is highly permissive. In the terminology of Whiting and Child, "initial satisfaction" — with the single possible exception of nursing — is high, and "socialization anxiety" is low. Fourth, the great *esprit de corps* in the various kevutzot gives the child a sense of security within his group.

Similar conditions making for security are to be found in later childhood. There are no marks, exams, or passing and failing grades in school to induce feelings of anxiety. And, since the kibbutz is a community of social and economic equals in which, moreover, differences in parental ability or prestige have no influence on the social status of the child, no child need feel insecure because of the social or economic "inferiority" of his family. Invidious standards of worth and unequally distributed symbols of success in childhood, as well as in later life, are additional pathogenic conditions which are absent in the kibbutz.

It is hardly surprising, then, that the sabra — despite certain indications of insecurity — is an efficient, productive, and functioning adult. He is an adult with a sense of values and a conscience that assures the implementation of those values. He is motivated to carry on the basic features of kibbutz culture — its collective ownership, distribution according to need, agricultural work, collective rearing of children, and its devotion to intellectual and aesthetic values. In short, though his interpersonal relationships are somewhat disturbed, and his self-perception contains painful elements, the sabra is not an "institutional child." He is — once the barriers of introversion and hostility are penetrated — a warm, sensitive, and, in some instances, gracious human being.

The last sentence is not meant as a final peroration to what has been, for the most part, a technical discussion. If some observers of the sabra have failed to perceive these qualities, it is because they have not taken the trouble or have not had the time to uncover the façade. For those who, like ourselves, have the time and take the trouble, these qualities eventually emerge in bold relief. Speaking personally, some of our pleasantest memories concern our own experiences with the sabras of Kiryat Yedidim.

LESLIE Y. RABKIN AND AUDREY G. SPIRO

INTRODUCTION

The findings and speculations of the preceding chapters are based on a study of Kiryat Yedidim conducted by Audrey and Melford Spiro in 1950–51. Since that time many changes have occurred in its system of collective education, and the kibbutz children described in those chapters are its contemporary adults. It is now possible, therefore, to assess at least some of the effects of their childhood experience on these adults. To be sure, this was attempted in some of the previous chapters (see Part VI), but that early assessment was limited in two important ways: the oldest kibbutz sabra was only twenty-eight at the time of the study, and the total population of sabra adults—those over twenty-one—was only eleven. Thus, the original sample was not only small, but it comprised "adults" who had only recently made the transition from adolescence.

Although the Preface to the 1965 edition records additional observations made during a visit to Kiryat Yedidim in 1962, more than ten years after the completion of the original study, the visit was brief and the observations cursory. In 1967–68, Leslie Rabkin and Karen R. Seger conducted a follow-up study of Kiryat Yedidim, and both have continued their contacts with the kibbutz to the present day. In addition, Melford Spiro has briefly visited Kiryat Yedidim (and other kibbutzim) on three occasions between 1968 and 1972. The present chapter is based on these recent studies and visits. It does not, it must be emphasized, take into account the serious impact of the October 1973, Arab–Israeli war, an impact which will eventually modify much of what is said here.

Although the questioning reader and serious student will want much more than the selective discussion of this short chapter, its brevity is governed by two considerations. First, many issues that might appropriately have been treated here have already been dealt with in Chapter 9 of Melford Spiro's *Kibbutz: Venture in Utopia* (Harvard University Press, Cambridge, Mass., reissued 1975), and it is unnecessary to recapitulate those data here. Second, Leslie Rabkin and Melford Spiro intend to write a full-length technical monograph on the subject in the near future, and until the data are fully analyzed, it is better that discussion of certain issues, and especially the more technical issues of personality structure and personality formation, be deferred until its publication. Corroborating data for many of the comments in this postscript will be presented in the future monograph.

Essentially, this chapter will attend to three questions. First, to what extent have the sabras—who have replaced their parents as the moving actors and leaders of the kibbutz—perpetuated the cultural values and social system which their parents, the kibbutz founders, brought into being? Second, what changes, if any, have taken place in the system of collective education, and to what extent have they occurred at the initiative of the adult sabras? Third, to what extent are the personality traits of the mature sabras similar to or different from those of the post-adolescent sabras described in Chapter 16?

THE SABRAS AND COLLECTIVE EDUCATION

The basic character of collective education remains the same—children still live in children's houses; they continue to be socialized primarily by professional and semi-professional caretakers (metaplot, teachers, and madrichim); their contacts with their parents remain time-limited. At the same time, many changes have occurred within the system. But both the continuities and the changes in collective education have been responsive to the attitudes and behavior of the sabras, for it is they who now comprise the core of the adult generation. Thus, the very continuity of the system implies its acceptance by the sabras, and they manifest little anxiety about collective education. Unlike their parents, however, they do not view the institution in particularly ideological terms nor seek to justify it on such grounds; rather, they perceive it pragmatically, as something "good" for the children or "good" for the parents. The absence of sabra insecurity or guilt feelings about collective education—noted a generation ago—is even clearer today. Products of a system which has indeed left its influence on them, the sabras are not inclined to be innovators within that system.

The kibbutz as a child-oriented community. For the sabras the kibbutz is still a child-oriented community, although less so than in the past. The notion of sacrifice (in living conditions, working hours, self-comfort) for children no longer prevails. In part this is a result of economic factors—the prosperity of the kibbutz is such that no material sacrifice is needed—but psychological factors are even more telling.

Children are no longer imbued with the mystique of a generation ago. To be sure, they are still considered the most viable means of perpetuating kibbutz life (especially so since natural increase from in-migration is very slight), and as serving a national purpose which stresses a high birth rate. But this is only one part of the story, for children are seen not only—indeed not even primarily— from an ideological perspective as carriers of tradition, but also from that of a family orientation. As such, they are cared for, loved, enjoyed, and accepted, with all the pleasure which attends the presence of children in most societies. As kinship ties and family-centeredness have acquired greater saliency in kibbutz life, children have become important for intra-familial and emotional reasons, as a source for personal satisfaction, narcissistic gratification, enrichment of family life, and as a hedge against loneliness and isolation in the future.

The framework described by Talmon as early as 1956 for understanding kibbutz fertility trends was an accurate portrait of what was to happen over the next two decades. Summing up her study, she wrote: "We found the tendency toward family limitation at two extremes of a continuum—in extreme collectivism at one end and in extreme individualism at the other—whereas the tendency toward family expansion was anchored in moderate collectivism and in familism. The desire for many children is thus rooted in the intent of the family to serve the community or in its wish to consolidate its independent position." [1] Her figures were portents in other ways. Among her second-generation sample, for example, 87 percent favored families with three or more children, a significantly higher figure than among first-generation chaverim.

It is this *family-centeredness* which has come to take precedence more and more over *community-centeredness* in relation to raising children. A child is still a "child of the kibbutz," and everyone is likely to be aware of and interested in a new birth, but (and as important) he is also the child of Moshe and Chana, as well as— and this is a new kibbutz phenomenon—a new member of the X clan. The clan has come into being in the last generation as a result of marriages between children of chaverim. In some cases, especi-

[1] Yonina Talmon, *Family and Community in the Kibbutz* (Cambridge, Mass., Harvard University Press, 1972), 73.

ally when their members are highly respected, these clans represent something of a power bloc within the kibbutz. (In one case, the clan has thirty members.)

As a summary example of the diminution of straight-forward child-centeredness, we may instance an occurrence on the eve of the 1967 Six Day War. The tension which gripped the kibbutz during the prewar days had, of course, affected the children, and there was a rash of psychophysiological symptoms, night fears, and a generally high level of anxiety. In an attempt to alleviate the situation, both men and women were assigned (on a rotational basis) to sleep in the children's houses. Soon, however, there was a falling down on the job; some did not come early enough to calm the children, others resented the imposition.

This state of affairs led to some harsh criticism on the part of a professional kibbutz educator. She noted how "egoistic" parents and nurses had become in relation to the evening situation and to child care in general. They seemed annoyed, she went on to say, that the children were not more "reasonable," that explanations proferred by their nurses did not suffice to allay their anxieties.

Would this have been the situation in previous decades? Would the first generation of nurses and parents have reacted in this way to a dangerous situation? Whatever their deeper feelings regarding spouse and self, it is doubtful that they would have failed to respond to the needs of the children. This is one indication that the kibbutz can no longer be considered a child-oriented community to the excessive degree of a generation ago.

To sum up, it might be said that rather than being a child-centered community, the kibbutz is now moving towards a mixture of family-centeredness and community-centeredness, with children occupying a key role in both circles but not necessarily a central one.

Sentiments regarding collective education. We have suggested that collective education, as an institution, is accepted by the sabras, but for very different reasons from those of their parents. The collectivist orientation of the first generation has been increasingly countered by a new family orientation. At the same time, however, the latter has been tempered by the equally new *self-orientation,* that is, by the acceptance of one's own desires for comfort, self-fulfillment, and creativity as legitimate needs. It is this new self-orientation (combined, of course, with their ideological education and their own socialization experiences) that constitutes the important basis for the sabras' commitment to collective education. Criticism of and dissatisfaction with the system seem to be primarily confined to those females who are frustrated in their extra-maternal roles. Thus, the less satisfied a woman is in her work role, the more likely she is to express a desire for more time with her children. Male sabras almost never express strong reservations about collective education.

Most sabras, therefore, find collective education a congenial means for meeting their needs, which have been progressively moving in the direction of self-enhancement. For the typical sabra, communal upbringing of children is a convenience, and many have abdicated a large part of their role as parents, preferring to leave much of the socialization process to the nurses. The imputed "egoism" of the war anecdote reflects this, as does the manner in which sabra parents (mothers, especially) react to the "demand" made on them to spend a specified amount of time with their children. Unlike many of their parents, they do not complain that this is too short a period nor do they display undue reluctance to part from their children. Indeed, some see this visiting time as an imposition, and the kibbutz has considered easing certain of its "demands," especially with regard to parents of infants.

Thus, it is rare for even the most disenchanted sabra to rationalize his thoughts about possibly leaving the kibbutz by reference to the greater amount of time he would have with his children.

Sabras as nurses/teachers. Currently all the children's houses, from infancy through kindergarten, are staffed mainly by sabra women, all of whom have had specialized training at kibbutz seminars or at The Federation's training school for teachers. Unlike their mothers, however, they do not view their work as a poor alternative to more "productive" agricultural labor, although some see it as less fulfilling than other work—often undefined—they would like to do. For a good proportion, child care is the only relatively suitable or attractive work available. As one woman wryly noted: "Sometimes when the children really get on my nerves and I feel like dropping the whole matter, I just picture myself sitting all day in the clothing room—and I go back to them with a smile!"

On the whole, sabra nurses take their work seriously, although they are not particularly warm and giving. Often they act as if their role were that of a "fireman," who is relatively inactive during times of peace and quiet, and who intervenes only when trouble is brewing. For the latter, their repertoire of socialization techniques ranges from gentle soothing to vindictive shaming. One might say that they like the children, are concerned about them, are interested in their development, but that they do not display deeper feeling of love for them. Some show a great tolerance for all forms of behavior, others lose their tempers rather swiftly. Insight into children's development is, despite their training, somewhat limited. This is true with respect to both developmental norms and emotional needs. The former are rarely referred to, and then only when they have been informed (typically by the kibbutz' head educator) that a certain child is retarded in some way. Attention to emotional needs varies. In some cases needs are satisfied because of the nurse's basic ability, in others they are either not heeded or their frustration is ascribed to some structural defect of the system.

One nurse, for example, lamented about how much better it would be if the children in her charge—all under two years—had toys to play with while confined to their beds: "I feel bad they have to be in bed alone all day, but Yoram throws everything out of the bed." Meanwhile, the other nurse working with her complained: "All the time work. Sometimes I wish I had time to sit down with the children. Sometimes there's a little time in the afternoon at 12:30 or so, but only a little. If you work in the kitchen all the time you look at your watch and say 'Oh, how early it is, so many hours left to work.' Here, all the time you feel, 'It's late, it's late.' " Both these nurses spent an extraordinary amount of time tidying up, some of it clearly to avoid the necessity of interacting with their charges.

The variation in skills in handling children is also great. Some nurses apply a set of formulistic concepts learned in a training course, others (a smaller number) demonstrate genuinely creative skills. For the former, when the routine is smooth, performance is high; but deviancy, trouble, or the need for a new approach are difficult for them to handle.

Finally, an important emotional difference between sabra nurses and their mothers must be noted. Although sabra nurses have affection for the children, they do not have a driving desire to be loved by them. Rarely does a sabra speak of her "indispensability" to her charges—except in cases where it was clear that the child's own mother was inadequate or rejecting—or display insecurity about obtaining their boundless affection.

Sabra nurses thus appear as varied as any group of nursery school teachers elsewhere. Their work is precisely that—a job—and is not imbued with ideological or frustration-drive overtones. They promulgate kibbutz values by stressing cooperation, self-care, and sharing, but their motivation is less ideological than pragmatic:

such behavior makes the job easier. They like children, but do not become overinvolved with them. In general, the familial trend in kibbutz living has led to greater stress on the nurse's *own* family needs.

Although all the nurses are kibbutz sabras, there is only one sabra teacher (out of six) in the Grammar School. The fact is that very few sabra women have expressed any desire to teach, despite their considerable respect for teachers. Many of the sabras, especially those who have gone outside the kibbutz framework to study, have turned instead to nursing, physiotherapy and social work.

SABRAS AND THE FAMILY

One of the most important changes that has occurred in the kibbutz since the 1950 study is the new and ever-increasing importance of the family. Although contemporary sabra attitudes toward love, sex, and marriage have been discussed sufficiently in the *Kibbutz* volume, the recent emergence of the family as the most important group within the kibbutz deserves renewed attention here.

The kibbutz originated with the intention, among others, of destroying the bourgeois family, of eliminating the traditional relationships between husband and wife, and, more importantly, between parent and child. As we have stressed, the child was to be a child of the kibbutz, rather than of his parents alone; all chaverim were to be parents of the children. If there had to be social differentiation of any kind, it was to be based not on family ties, but on other kinds of social relationships, such as friendship. As for the family—the kibbutz itself would be one big family.

But all this has changed dramatically. The family has become the most important social group in the kibbutz, and its present prominence represents an important conceptual change as well. That is to say, the kibbutz now conceptually and psychologically places a strong emphasis on the family and views with favor acts that strengthen its importance.

But "family" can no longer be defined as it was in the original study, when it was defined as the parent-child unit. Today, the family must be defined to include grandparents, their children, and their grandchildren. And, within a very short time, their great-grandchildren. In short, a genuine clan organization is beginning to emerge in which these three generations constitute a social unit. It is within this unit that much social interaction takes place—the sharing of afternoon tea, spending the Shabat together, and so on.

Importantly, this social unit not only meets together privately, but publicly asserts its social indentity and collectivity: as when its members eat together in the dining room and save places for each other at sichot, parties, and meetings.

Moreover, some chaverim suggest that without a family it is now almost impossible to get along in the kibbutz. If a chaver is ill, if he has to be taken to the hospital, for example, it is the members of his family who will attend to his needs. If he has no family, the kibbutz itself will make the necessary arrangements. But that means, as one chaver pointed out, that the individual must rely on the formal institutions of the kibbutz, rather than on informal relationships with family or friends. The kibbutz, in short, is no longer viewed as the appropriate or desirable source of help; which is to say that it is no longer viewed by the chaver as his family.

Thus, as the kibbutz has grown larger and can no longer itself serve as a family, social differentiation and social groupings have returned to their primordial form of family groupings. This is perhaps the most important change that has occurred in the kibbutz. If family and even clan differentiation continues to be an important factor in kibbutz social organization, it is possible that the sabras will no longer view the kibbutz as a kinship group, and that there will be marriages between members of the same kibbutz.

Hence, the adult sabras who are the focus of this brief chapter must inevitably view themselves and their roles as parents in socially complex ways that did not occur to their parents. Their own responsibilities as parents can be shared with grandparents, aunts, and uncles—so that the kibbutz becomes, among other things, the framework and setting for family responsibilities. Whereas in the past it was assumed that the sabras' primary identification would be with the kibbutz as such, we might today suggest that perhaps in the future the sabras' first and strongest identification will be with the family, and his secondary identification with the kibbutz.

Sabras as parents. As for the general behavior of contemporary sabra parents, the description of sabra parents of a generation ago requires little modification. Given the framework within which they function as parents, they are good ones. Compared with their parents, they are observably less anxious, pressured, ambivalent, guilt-ridden and insecure about their relationship to their children. They generally like their children, play adequately with them, and respond (within the constraints of the system) to their needs.

They are not, however, especially intimate with them, nor do they express much discomfort about this.

Sabra fathers are generally less ambivalent about themselves as parents than are mothers. They almost always seem to be having fun with their children, of whatever age; mothers, however, tend to be more restless with their children, somewhat long-suffering and grumbling, and more often at a loss as to how to "entertain" them. This sex-role differentiation is not unlike that of the earlier generation. Both as mothers and nurses, females are more involved with caretaking, which may account for the fact that—on the rare occasions that this is called for or carried out—they tend more often to be the disciplinarians. Fathers take the children out of the home more, and generally present them with kibbutz-oriented rather than family-oriented stimuli. Talmon shrewdly observes that: "In the eyes of the growing child, the father gradually emerges as the representative of the kibbutz and its values within the family while the mother is primarily the representative of the family in the kibbutz." (p. 25.)

This differentiation of parental roles, not surprisingly, affects the children's perceptions of their parents. Thus, the response of third-generation sabra children to a parental role questionnaire indicates that mothers are perceived more ambivalently (on a love-hostility dimension) than fathers. Similarly, children's occupational preferences also reflect this differentiation. Even when the mother holds an important job, it is far rarer for a sabra child to want to follow in mother's footsteps than in father's.

Sabra relationship to their own parents. Adult sabras maintain a friendly but not familiar relationship with their parents. The withdrawal and rebellion syndrome of adolescence gives way in adulthood to greater affective involvement with parents. Prior to marriage, they maintain a relative distance from their parents, preferring to spend time with their peer group, especially when on leave from the army. In this period, visits with parents are primarily confined to the Sabbath and occasional pre-dinner visits.

Marriage and the advent of children change this pattern, and family interaction becomes far more frequent and normative. The typical pattern is for married sabras and their children to spend the Sabbath afternoon visiting in one or both grandparental rooms, and during the week the grandparents occasionally make a visit to their children's rooms. In both cases, the focus of the visits is on the grandchildren. Some intergenerational tensions focus on the children, but these rarely go beyond the normal expression of

differences of opinion. The minimization of the socialization role
of the family mutes much of this source of potential conflict. When
conflict does occur, it is typically confined to such trivial issues as
giving candy, or it involves a displacement from other underlying
tensions between parents and adult children or between mother-in-
law and daughter-in-law. Grandparents often act as parents when
one or both parents are absent from the kibbutz for vacations,
military service, schooling, or work assignments.

The overall attitudes of sabras towards their parents are positive.
What complaints they voice are rather benign, such as too much
pampering and worrying by their mothers and occasional parental
intrusion into their lives. Among the older sabras there is an
undercurrent of worry about their aging parents, mingled with a
barely stifled resentment. In the *Kibbutz* we spoke of the continuing generation gap between sabras and kibbutz veterans, due,
in part, to the elders' disappointment in their offspring. But there
is the other side of the coin which we did not mention—the sabras'
resentment of this disappointment. It is relevant to observe in this
connection that parental absence from the kibbutz is not only a
source of potential insecurity in sabra childhood, but that it has
importantly influenced sabra attitudes towards their parents. Thus,
many sabras of all ages note the fact that their parents were not
always around when they needed them. Sabras sense that behind
the endless pampering they received was an implicit message of
"Don't resent us," but they do. They resent the endless pressures
on them to be special; the high expectations constantly under-
mined by criticism (with the resulting chronic sense of self-doubt
and failure); the paradox of expecting both continuity and innovation from them; the sense of guilt they were made to feel over
displacing their parents from the seats of kibbutz power. All these,
and the myriad other confused messages they have received in the
process of their socialization and development, have made for
hidden and not so hidden tensions between the sabras and the
kibbutz veterans.

There is, however, less generational conflict between sabra
parents and sabra children, due to a lack of neurotic ambivalence
in their relationships. The adolescent children of the sabras are
somewhat aloof from their parents, but this is not generally
countered with anxious concern. Similarly, sabra parents appear
more willing to let the children find their own paths through life.
In part, this is a reaction to their own struggle for *lebensraum*, in
part it is a "living through" their children, permitting them to do
what they could not. In sum, in the area of parent-child relation-

ships, as in so many others, a greater flexibility and openness have replaced rigidity and confinement.

CONTINUITY AND CHANGE IN COLLECTIVE EDUCATION

Although the basic character of collective education remains the same, and although the apparatus of age-graded living, the timing of moves to new houses and the methods of effecting this, and the sequence of habit-training have not fundamentally altered, changes have occurred in several aspects of the system. Some are due to "objective conditions," some to parental pressure; still others are due to long-standing feelings of dissatisfaction with educational methods or to the input of new socialization data by Movement educators. Needless to say, most changes have resulted from a combination of these factors. Let us examine these changes through the various age levels.

Infancy. The most prominent innovation in socialization has been the decision of 1970 to allow parents to keep their newborn infants at home for the first six weeks. This decision met with some criticism in The Movement, where it was portrayed as an anticollectivist move. Subsequently, however, it has been adopted by a small number of kibbutzim in The Movement.

In this new procedure the mother is allowed, indeed encouraged, to keep the newborn infant in her room during the six-week post-partum period, when she does not work. When she returns to work, she may choose to bring the baby to the Nursery at 6:00 A.M. and take him to her room again after working hours, or, if she prefers, she may leave him full-time in the Nursery. In actual practice, few mothers keep their babies at night for more than three months, while some even return them to the Nursery before the end of the initial six-week period. In short, the implementation of the new policy has been strongly dependent on individual maternal and family factors.

The impetus for this innovation was twofold. On the one hand, a sudden spurt of new births taxed the resources of the existing Nursery and presented the kibbutz with the choice of either building a new one or finding another solution. The reluctance to spend money on a new structure played its part, but, in addition, there had long been pressure from young sabra mothers to be allowed to have their infants with them for a period of time. This was expressed in several ways. For example, a primipara (and they are mainly the ones who have fought for this) said, as she was leaving the Nursery after a feeding: "Each time I have to just stop and leave my baby it bothers me. I would like so much to just continue to sit with him, see him asleep—be a full-time mother. Someday, perhaps, we'll be able to have them with us." Others demonstrated their feelings in a certain diffidence towards other mothers and the nurses while tending their baby, finding a quiet corner and avoiding contact. Sometimes a young mother would stretch her time, holding her sleeping baby for an extended period after finishing a feeding. It was not rare for sabra mothers to ask (as their own mothers had asked), "Is this [our child-rearing method] normal?"

The nurses were aware of this trend, but expressed several reservations about it. One nurse said simply, "The young ones want to have their child with them—but they don't know what trouble it is." She went on to point out the advantages of the collective system, primarily the greater freedom a woman has when her child is tended by another. Other nurses alluded to the fact of individual differences among the mothers, some being viewed by them as inadequate for full-time mothering.

There are, indeed, marked individual differences in mothering, as there have always been. Some of these differences are related to previous experience, others to the mother's kibbutz job—a teacher, for example, is more likely to rush through a feeding in order to return to her work; but, more importantly, they are related to personality variables. Thus, for example, while observing an early-morning feeding in a group of six mothers, three were relaxed and apparently enjoying the experience, one was deeply immersed in her baby to the exclusion of all else, one was exhibiting dramatic but ineffective display of her mothering, and one (despite prior experience) was anxious and uncomfortable. Similar individual differences were noted in bathing, diapering, stimulating, verbalizing, and playing. It is not surprising, then, that not all mothers were eager to care for their babies full-time. One commented, "I'd be scared if I lived in the city and had to take care of my child myself: I'd be afraid I'd hurt her. This way, I have someone to help me and guide me."

It is apparent then, that any system the kibbutz might develop as a collective procedure will have its real or potential casualties. The emotional impact of "forcing" a mother to "give up" the care of her infant to a stranger has its counterpart in the stress caused another mother by "forcing" her to take full responsibility for caretaking when she feels unable or unwilling to do so.

Other changes have also occurred within the structure of the

Nursery, but they are mainly the results of greater understanding of infant needs. Thus, there is much more flexibility in the application of feeding schedules and weaning, and greater sensitivity to individual differences. There is more concern for stimulation, so that there is now a variety of toys hung on the cribs to provide environmental complexity and stimulation for the babies.

There is also a heightened concern to minimize frustration. Thus, loudspeakers are used in the Nursery to enable the watchwomen to hear a crying baby at night, and a buzzer system is now linked to each nursing mother's room, allowing for quicker signalling when a baby cries. Pacifiers are still not used, but the reason offered—that the child should discover and use his thumb in order to depend on himself for immediate gratification—differs from the one offered in the past. Mothers can use a pacifier at home, but they have been warned by the dentist that it is not good for the teeth, and very few make use of them.

One of the most important findings in the follow-up study concerns the considerable amount of time that waking babies spend with their mothers and other family members.[2] Thus, in a sample of five infants, ranging in age from nine days to four months, observed for several days each, it was discovered that mothers and other family members spent from 71 percent (the oldest child) to 98 percent (the youngest child) of the baby's *waking* time in his proximity. When these observations are combined with the more specific data of Gewirtz and Gewirtz,[3] which show that during the first eight months of life, the kibbutz infant sees his mother for at least *twice as long* as he sees the nurse, it is apparent that Bettelheim is in error in claiming that "Most of his [the infant's] stimulation comes from the metapelet and the infants he rooms with, since his mother spends at most only a few hours a day with him (and none at night), and these few hours are broken by absences." [4]

The general impression obtained from the follow-up study was that the Nursery experience is *not* a traumatic one for the child. No observations of neglect, mishandling, or excessive frustration were recorded. We observed considerable individual differences

[2] Fathers today appear to spend more time with their infants, now that they are at home, and take a more active role in infant care, even feeding their infants in the Infants' House.

[3] Hava B. Gewirtz and J. L. Gewirtz, "Visiting and Caretaking Patterns for Kibbutz Children: Age and Sex Trends," *American Journal of Orthopsychiatry*, 38:427–443 (1968).

[4] Bruno Bettelheim, *Children of the Dream* (London, Macmillan Ltd., 1969), 71.

in maternal approach to the infants, and some of these might easily have had deleterious effects had the mother been full-time caretaker for her child. The overall atmosphere of the Nursery itself is gentle and warm, and mother-infant separations are handled in such a way as to cause a minimum of anxiety, and with much more flexibility than was the case at the time of the first study.

Toddlers. Although there have been improvements in the quality and outfitting of more recently built toddlers' houses, these are of little importance. In general, the group nature of the child's life, with the consequences described above (pp. 137–138) remain unchanged. The child is almost never alone, he must conform to a group schedule rather than act in accord with his own internal rhythms, and almost everything around him—toys, children, and nurses—must be shared.

In addition to the measures recorded in the first study, there have been further attempts to ease the transition from the Nursery, mostly by the use of overlapping nurses.[5] Nevertheless, the general impression remains that the children experience a brief period of unease before they become accustomed to their new surroundings.

In general, this age group presents the greatest problem for socialization. There is, first of all, far less maternal continuity, and separations after visits or feedings are often quite upsetting. It happens often, as well, that a mother is not available to feed a child, a situation which leaves him alone at a crucial time, for the other mothers are busy tending their own children, and the nurse is busy with her chores and can provide only the most cursory attention. This, of course, becomes less important with advancing age, when the children all begin to eat together at the table. But during the one-to-two-year age period, there is a great deal of frustration, and on all levels, which the child must bear. Importantly, neither the nurses nor the parents seem particularly comfortable with children of this age, certainly not when it comes to "entertaining" them. A mother may look to see what the others are doing, or she may plaintively turn to the nurse to ask, "What does he want?" when her child does not respond to her blandish-

[5] Three mechanisms have been proposed to provide greater continuity for the infant, but none has yet been successfully implemented. These are: (1) the same nurse stays with a group of six infants from the Nursery through the Kindergarten; (2) when the children are about five months old, a new nurse begins to work side by side with this nurse in the Nursery, and she continues with them to the Kindergarten; (3) the same nurse stays with her kevutza from the nursery through the completion of toilet training, when a new metapelet takes over.

ments. It is not easy to "have to be" with a child for half an hour (the morning visiting time), especially when group pressure "demands" that one spend this time in interaction with him. Although, again, there were clear-cut individual differences in their flexibility, creativity, patience, and affection, the sabra mothers as a group do not seem to feel entirely at home with their small children.

In general, kibbutz rules formally allow for parental visits during the day until the age of one and a half. But some parents find it hard not to see their children all day, and come by when they can. In one kevutza of six children under the age of two, for example, there were two mothers who always visited early in the morning. Again, the interaction of parental personality and structural factors plays a part: the two visiting mothers happened to be nursery teachers whose daily work began later than that of other mothers. Nevertheless, all mothers make at least one visit a day.

It continues to be the case that "most acts in all behavior systems remain unsocialized" and that toddlers continue to socialize each other. They may be left to cry for lengthy periods, or they are summarily deposited in their cribs and casually given a toy to play with (which commonly finds its way quickly to the floor, thus creating more frustration), because the nurse is busy carrying out her household chores. These are often excessive and useless, and seem designed more to avoid contact with the children than for purposes of order or hygiene. Additionally, children are left alone when a nurse goes to visit her own child in another children's house. "After all," one nurse lamented when leaving for an unscheduled fifteen-minute visit with her own three-year-old child, "it's hard to go a whole day and not see your child."

All in all, then, this age period still seems one of deprivation for the child. He is tended to less, criticized more, and is treated like an object more than at any other period of childhood. Interestingly, what appears to be the most fulfilling experience for the toddler is that of *hashkava*. The following field notes from one evening give the flavor of this:

The parents begin to arrive at about 6:15 P.M. and continue to drift in for about half an hour. The bedtime situation varies with the parents, from a cursory put-'em-down-and-goodnight to lengthy play. Not always is this a function of personality; it can be 'need' as well, if there are other children in the family to tend to. Orly is obviously tired, and is put to sleep quickly with some playful interaction. Asaf is tired but interested and displays his customary nervousness while being undressed, eating, and clearly so in being put to bed. He is placed in bed and quickly left. He begins to cry quite strongly and painfully. His mother stands uncomfortably for a few moments, returns to him, leaves, and as he continues to cry loud and clear, goes again to him, comforts him, and all is well in a few moments. He obviously found the separation experience painful (as he does being alone during the day). Yochai is put to bed by his father who plays with him a good deal and which he enjoys. He cries briefly when father leaves, but after he returns to him for a moment, he is quiet. Ayelet is brought by her mother, Amnon by his father, and Dror by mother. All get a snack before bed, usually some *daisa* [gruel], some water, maybe a cookie. Other things are also attended to: For example, Ayelet has her nails cut. The children, despite being tired, tend to be in a better mood, happier, more expressive. This evening, this is especially true of Ayelet, but even Asaf seems more satisfied and content. The contrast with the ordinary run of the day is clear—compared to now their day world is relatively empty. There is physical expression through play, a variety of interactions with each other, passers-by, parents, and the metapelet, but at this age they are mainly alone. The care now is personal, even more so than in the morning when mothers are sleepy, and this makes for a clear difference in their behavior. Frustrations can be dealt with at once and in a loving situation, and there is not such a rushed atmosphere as in the morning. The children enjoy the tender care of the metaplot, but there is more than a just-noticeable difference in their reactions to parents. In this situation it is the best of all possible worlds, with parents who have time, can be in a good mood, and tend to the baby completely.

Although in most kibbutzim the system of hashkava has changed so that nurses no longer put the children to bed after the age of two, in Kiryat Yedidim the procedures are as they were in the past. That is, parents put their children to bed until the approximate age of two, after which it is in the hands of the nurses. As in the past, this transition creates some problems, evinced chiefly by greater fussiness on the part of the child. The nurses recognize that the children are old enough to understand what is happening, and they try to be patient and help the children through this transition. After the transitional period, however, the children seem to accept the change, and, if there still seems to be a problem, the difficulties, as the following notes on one evening's hashkava show, lie elsewhere.

The parents come with the children about 7 P.M., bathe them, put them into nightclothes, play with them for varying amounts of time, but generally briefly, clearly not unduly prolonging the time, and leave them in the hands of the nurse. The children usually have a little snack of fruit, a drink of water or juice, and play a game: this evening one in which they must respond to the nurse's signals and put their arms up, down, etc. They do this for a while and then go to bed. There was no problem around the parents leaving or going to bed. At this age, when the parents leave, the children seem almost unconcerned and it's more the parents who ask for a response, wait for a kiss, request a good-bye, and who seem more disappointed if this is not forthcoming. Once the children's attention is drawn to the nurse or an activity, they tend to turn to this with no problem.

Middle childhood. The most important change observed in the middle period is the result of greater recognition of sexual differences in maturation. There are now separate, partitioned toilets and separate shower rooms for the boys and girls in the Grammar School. A second structural change relates to the separation of dormitory and classrooms. Nevertheless, the "informality" of the classroom, which has been discussed above, has not changed.

Except for these, the living conditions, socialization techniques, formal educational methods, and the overall framework of this period are little changed from 1951. However, although the older children of the Grammar School continue to eat breakfast and lunch with their metaplot in their own dining room, their evening meals are taken with their parents in the adult dining room.

In the classroom there is greater emphasis on individual differences in learning and maturation, and, expectedly, there are more facilities and materials available. There is also greater involvement of parents in the educational process: parents give demonstrations of their work, and grandparents relate "living history"; teachers explain the curriculum to parents in greater detail, and encourage the children to tell their parents what they have learned.

High school years. Two important changes have occurred in the structure of the high school. One concerns interpersonal relationships, the other educational objectives.

Over the years, there has been much criticism from female sabras about sharing a room with males. This dissatisfaction, as previously noted, was a consequence of differential sexual development.[6] If, as sometimes happened, separate quarters were provided

---

[6] The heterosexual arrangements are disliked for many reasons, some of them rather surprising. One young Mosad metapelet suggested that the excessive intimacy engendered by such arrangements left her with the feeling that "something is missing from the relationship with boys," what she characterized as a "missing gentlemanliness." She attributed the adolescent male assumption that females should always be able to do whatever needs doing, from lifting heavy loads to undertaking thirty-hour hikes, to the uniformity of their lives—they live together, share everything, and do the same things. Two generations ago, this assumption was exactly what the founders hoped for when they devised their system of socialization; today, a young product of that system deplores it.

for boys and girls, it was typically in the guise of solving a specific problem, and was always portrayed as being a special situation. By the 1960's, a semi-formal decision had been made to offer those who requested it the opportunity for unisexual dormitory rooms, and several girls opted for this. Since then—although still not a formal decision—this has become a quietly accepted pattern not only in Kiryat Yedidim, but in The Movement as a whole. Where the older pattern still prevails, embarrassment leads most girls to sleep in their underclothing or to remove them after lights are out, or, at the very least, to ask the boys to turn around while they are dressing or undressing. It is little wonder that students react with nervous amusement when told of the early days of mixed showers!

With respect to educational objectives, the kibbutz has changed its traditional objective to include higher (formal) education, and as many as 30 percent of the senior class now sit for the matriculation examination. It is worth noting that the main impetus for this change came from a single student (*not* a son of the kibbutz), who defiantly, and with great opposition from the educators, proceeded with his plans to take the exam. As with so many other changes in the kibbutz, the willingness of one person to fight for a goal and to defy the *status quo* in some way opens the floodgates of long-suppressed needs, which culminates in some (major or minor) structural change. In this case, the permission to transgress what was once a most strongly held value has now been formally recognized by The Movement.

Structurally ordered insecurity. Insofar as there were in the past structural conditions conducive to the frustration of dependency needs in childhood, these still exist. Neither the good intentions of the kibbutz nor the professional edicts of The Movement have produced a satisfactory solution to this problem.

The major problem of frequent changes of nurses continues. Despite the schemes devised to ensure continuity, the old problems persist essentially unchanged. Thus, in the course of his movement through the age grades, a child will experience at least four changes of caretakers—from infant to toddler's house, thence to kindergarten, and finally to school. The symptomatic effects of these changes on the children seem to be the same today as in the past. Even the briefest separation from the nurse, for whatever reason, can engender high anxiety among younger children, as the following description of a group of two-year-olds suggests: "Their attachment to the nurse is strong, and when she leaves to get food or other items, they all go to the porch to watch, wait, and cry."

It is interesting to note, therefore, that today, as in the past, there are surprisingly few specific nurse-oriented memories—indeed, there is little mention of them—among the adult sabras. Reminiscences of childhood experience almost never focus on a nurse, nor do nurses appear in the Sentence Completion Test. Thus, in a sample of 31 male and female adult sabras, ranging in age from 18–37, not a single response to the sentence root, "My most vivid childhood memory . . .", concerned an experience with a nurse. Again, the root, "In school, my teachers . . .", produces only four positively toned responses, while the rest consist of varying degrees of negative evaluation of the teachers' abilities or behavior, or of vague characterizations of them as "rather sympathetic."

In short, although direct observations of the children indicate that separation from a nurse is a frustrating, traumatic event, there is no evidence that this experience leaves adult residues. It may contribute, however, to the abundant evidence in the fantasy productions of the adult sabras of a generalized, heightened sensitivity to themes of *separation*.

Yet another possible contributing factor to these themes is the "abandonment" of the children at night, a practice which still persists, and which remains a source of debate and concern. We have noted the technological innovation designed to improve the nightly supervision of all children. This is a loudspeaker system which links all the children's houses with a central station where the nightwatch is posted. This has superseded the tiring and rather ineffective older system of constant rounds, and allows the nightwatch to become aware of a crying child more quickly. The watch still makes rounds, of course, in order to minister to problems of uncovered, restless, and silently frightened children, and to ensure that all children are asleep in their own beds. There are now two watchwomen on duty until 3 A.M., then one until 6:00 A.M.—who, however, is helped in her duties by the nightwatchman until 4:30 A.M. Despite this, the "crying, whining, and jouncing" noted in the past is still found among the children at night.

Another persistent pattern is that of parental absence from the kibbutz. There is hardly a family in which one or both parents have not been absent for a shorter or longer period. To be sure, better means of transportation have reduced the percentage of parents who are *totally* absent, but not infrequently mother or father (more commonly the latter) attend a course or are engaged in some kibbutz-oriented activity which necessitates their being away throughout the week. The extent to which parental absence has a disturbing effect on the children depends on such factors as age, closeness to the absent parent, the character of the ties to the parent, and the availability of substitute caretakers. These are more readily available today than in the past, because of the presence of grandparents, uncles, and aunts. Nevertheless, these substitute parental figures do not completely satisfy the child's need for his own parents, and the symptoms which were observed in the 1950's are evident today as well.

Finally, something must be said about the "dethronement" issue, of which much has been made in previous chapters. Today, as in the past, sibling rivalry is much in evidence among the children; moreover, and in general, younger siblings continue to be preferred. Nevertheless, this seems to be much less of a trauma for at least two reasons. One is the greater number of children the sabras are producing, with far shorter spacing as the rule, thereby diluting the duration (if not intensity) of the smaller child's period of maximal gratification. Related to this is the second important fact that sabra parents generally do not have the same overemotional tie to their children that their parents had towards them. This may or may not reflect the intensity of the child's tie to them, or lessen his *perceived* effect of dethronement, but it does mean that (after infancy, at least) the parental relationship towards *all* children tends to be more balanced. Where one does see a truly heightened and over-determined relationship with the youngest child is in the case of older parents for whom the youngest is also likely to be the last. But even here the discontinuity for the older children is softened by the fact that they are already at least of school age and deeply involved in their group life. On the other hand, the frequency of larger families (and four or more children in a family is no rarity) may possibly lead to even greater competition for available parental attention, with a resulting complex of symptoms; but this is still to be investigated.

Another contributing factor to the dethronement experience is a sex-linked one, characteristic of girls much more than boys. Observations of parent-child interaction consistently indicated that when the mother's attention is focused on the infant, the young boy finds his place with his father; the young girl, however, tends to follow after the mother, and thereby feels the effects of the new sibling more keenly. This is especially evident in the most "vulnerable" of the mother-child pairs, those in which the mother is a nurse. Not only do her children face the prospect of intra-familial "dethronement," but they are forced as well to share the attentions of the mother with an extra-familial group of children, for it is not uncommon for the child of a nurse to wander from her own group to make an unscheduled visit to her mother. The female adjective is used purposely, for the great majority of such visitors are daughters. These visits are often accompanied by tense rivalry on the part of the daughter with her mother's charges, and by conflicting loyalties on the mother's part.

In general, however, "dethronement" seems to be of relatively minor importance as an *anlage* for later insecurity. It exists, but it is best perceived as normal sibling rivalry. As such, it appears to be no more intense in the kibbutz family than in other types of family, and its intensity is related to particular parental personalities, rather than to the socialization structure of the kibbutz. "Dethronement" by the kibbutz as a whole is also much less of a problem today. Perhaps as a function of greater fertility and of general growth, the kibbutz members no longer make a great fuss over every new child and thereby seem to reject the older children. All this, at least, is far less in evidence today than it was in the past.

THE SABRAS AND THE KIBBUTZ

We have seen the changes (and continuities) in the educational and family systems of the kibbutz as it and the sabras have matured. But these are not the only social domains of interest to us. The sabras have been reared to live in and to perpetuate the cultural values and social structure that constitute a kibbutz community, and we must now examine the extent to which they are both committed to and behave in accordance with these values and structures.

Collective ownership. As we have noted in the *Kibbutz*, the sabras have internalized and are entirely committed to the kibbutz value of collective ownership and control of the means of production. Although the political, moral, messianic, and transcendent dimensions of the socialist *ideology* play little part in their *weltanschauung*, collective ownership is perceived by the sabras as sensible, tolerable, and viable. They are well aware of the impressive standard of living which collectivism has provided, even when compared with the general growth of the Israeli economy. The more economically sophisticated sabras point to other advantages of their socialist economy—its flexibility, which can, for example, call upon manpower replacements in the event of illness;

its ability to maintain constraints on inflationary manpower costs; and its higher labor efficiency which derives from the fact that the workers themselves own the means of production.

Social equality. Social equality is still maintained to a greater extent in the kibbutz than anywhere else, although this has been qualified to a certain extent by the dramatic increase in private property and its gradual institutionalization. The latter trend has necessarily led to imbalances and inequalities, but for many reasons this has not become an issue, although objectively there are now obvious discrepancies in individual possessions.

In addition, the kibbutz educational system has come to recognize certain shortcomings in the traditional kibbutz standards of equality. The notion, for example, that not everybody is similarly endowed was not easy for the kibbutz to accept, although the sabras recognized this long ago, and accommodated their perceptions of and dealing with one another—in work assignments and friendship patterns, for example—accordingly. Today, even conservative Kiryat Yedidim has instituted a track system in the high school designed to provide the maximally suitable type of educational experience, academic or vocational, for its students.

On a day-to-day basis, equality is maintained in reasonable fashion. Undesirable service jobs, such as kitchen duty, are still rotated; similar services and kibbutz-provided hard goods and housing are still allocated on an equal basis. No one is excluded from any location or activity because of his social role or status. There are those who are selected for and maintained in certain work activities (sometimes productive, sometimes administrative) because of their special skills or the nature of the job, but this is not viewed as elitism nor is it the subject of complaint.

There are two forms of inequality (if such be the correct word) which should be mentioned, one related to age, the other to sex. The age-related inequality is expressed in the problem of leadership replacement. In any branch of the kibbutz economy there is, inevitably, a skilled and experienced leader, and the possibilities for succession to leadership for younger recruits are clearly limited. The older sabras, who witnessed or participated in the traumatic experience of the displacement of the kibbutz founders from their leadership positions, are sensitive to this problem and have attempted to remedy it. Thus, there is now a leadership rotation system which, to a large extent, obviates the more overt problems of the past. Nevertheless, there is at times (especially during the psychologically difficult post-Army re-entry period) a feeling of relative deprivation and impatience on the part of younger sabras. Thus far, at any rate, it has not been a source of great discontent.

The issue of sexual inequality has also been discussed in our companion volume. Women are dissatisfied to a far greater extent than are men with kibbutz life, and in most areas they have provided the impetus for structural, physical, and psychological changes. Their search for greater fulfilment has taken many sabra females out of the kibbutz into a variety of learning settings and experiments with other styles of life. Some of them are pessimistic about the life which awaits them within the narrow confines of the kibbutz, and feel a need to rebel against the kibbutz equivalent of "Kinder und Küche." They appear to be actively seeking a new identity for themselves, mainly expressed in the work sphere, different from that of their mothers (laborers) and grandmothers (housewives). The intensity with which they seek their new goals of training and life experience is indicative of their discontent with the role models and images which have heretofore been held out to them. The kibbutz is making every effort to deal with this problem by offering more opportunities for women to study and work outside the kibbutz, but these procedures are often mocked and mildly scorned by the girls, who see them as grudging and conditional sops to their private needs.

With these qualifications, then, the kibbutz continues to be a community of equals.

Physical labor and agriculture. We have previously pointed to "demythologizing" of the kibbutz work ethic, which is a continuing and perhaps an irreversible process. A newly developing need for the re-evaluation of physical labor is emerging from national economic realities, to which the kibbutz is finely attuned. Agriculture is declining in economic importance, and, where it is not, advancements in agricultural technology have made manpower less important. Equipment is both expensive and labor saving, and the kibbutz must raise the money for purchase of the equipment as well as utilize the freed time of the dislocated workers. To cope with both problems, the kibbutz has turned to industrialization. The sabras are ready for this. The work ethic is still strong and shirking is certainly minimal, but few of them—unlike the founding fathers—would insist that twelve hours wielding a hoe in the blazing sun makes one a better kibbutznik.

Kiryat Yedidim is actually well behind other kibbutzim (of all Federations) in the extent of its industrialization. Some 80 percent of all kibbutzim are now involved in manufacturing or tourist-based industries, and their overall success is impressive. Although kibbutzim comprise only 3 percent of the Israeli population, they account for over 4 percent of all industrial employees, over 5 percent of industrial sales (excluding diamonds, one of Israel's specialized exports), nearly 7 percent of industrial exports (excluding diamonds), and (for 1973) 15 percent of total industrial investment. Expectably, output per worker in kibbutz industry is about one-quarter above the Israeli average.

Kiryat Yedidim's small factory was not particularly successful as a sheltered workshop for the elderly—the original incentive for establishing it—but economically it has proved to be very successful. With the infusion of new and young sabra leadership, there is no question that Kiryat Yedidim will make a strong move toward increasing industrialization.

But this raises problems for the kibbutz, not the least of which being the effect on its self-image. While private industry can hire more workers in the event of an expanding market, the kibbutz ideology, with its emphasis on *self*-labor opposes such a move. Still, this is what every kibbutz has done, although by self-conscious efforts the number of hired workers in kibbutz industry has dropped from 57 percent in 1969 to 45 percent in 1972.

In spite of the kibbutz's ideological opposition, however, the sabras have no compunction about the use of hired labor. And although the vattikim may rage about it, hired laborers are now employed in the kitchen and in several agricultural branches, especially field crops, where they operate the huge combines and tractors. For the sabras, socialism does not, by definition, exclude the employment of hired labor. To them, socialism means, insofar as it has any meaning to them at all, that the means of production are owned collectively, and that there is more or less economic equality among the members. It is this lack of concern about hired labor that is perhaps the most disturbing of the changes to the older generations and that leads some of them to insist that Kiryat Yedidim is no longer a "kibbutz."

Asceticism. If physical labor as an end in itself, with agriculture as its *sine qua non,* has lost its mythic force among sabras, it is not surprising that the same is true with respect to asceticism. Here the trends we observed in the *Kibbutz* volume continue apace. There is hardly a trace left of the old asceticism, and it is doubtful that it could ever return. There are still a few Jeremiahs, mainly adolescents and veterans, who rail against the new style of life, but the change is probably irreversible. The most recent sign, as well as symbol, of this trend is the luxurious swimming pool-sauna-tennis court complex, which gives an almost country-club aura to that sector of the kibbutz.

Group dynamics. Nearly every change in the structuring of everyday life in the kibbutz can be seen as a move towards enhancing the private sphere of individual existence. This is as the sabras want it, and there is little opposition to this. The sabras show a strong need to locate some private sphere for themselves, both physically and psychologically. They like their rooms, take pride in them, and prefer to spend a great deal of time there. Doors are still not locked and, other than at rest time, people come and go freely across each other's thresholds, but there is a basic territoriality, and it is respected.

Another counter to group-centeredness is the growing resistance of sabras to put personal decisions affecting their lives to a vote of the collective. Today, much of this sort of decision making—leaves of absence, plans for schooling, special needs, and others—is made in consultation with various committees set up as buffers between the individual and the whole community. Only when agreement cannot be reached within this form is the request brought before the assembly.

Still another expression of assertiveness against the group is the "temporary" resignation or "leave of absence" initiated by at least three sabras in recent years. This involves requesting (really, *insisting on*) time off from the kibbutz—a year or two—without financial support, to be used for travel, study, or some other personal goal. The kibbutz is caught in the bind between refusing and thereby risking the angry loss of one of its sons, or relenting and thereby losing at least some manpower, as well as displaying its impotence when faced with strong, unwavering, individual assertiveness. (The typical compromise of delaying the request for a year is a semi-conscious face-saving device.)

Despite this pressure for self-determination in the face of group needs, sabras continue to be highly group-oriented, in the sense of identification with, responsibility for, and interaction with, their peer-groups and (secondarily) the kibbutz as a whole. Both are for them a source of identification and security, and this has not lessened even with advancing age. Such identifications are seen most dramatically when a group of sabras are together in a strange context. Here, where an individualist might seek out new information, explore the surroundings, or attempt some kind of accommodation, the sabra insists on merging with the group and *avoiding* the impact of the new and strange. He can accommodate himself in a physical, surface sense to any situation, but the bulk of his energies is spent in trying to assimilate the new to his prior cognitive and emotional structures.

The sabras are accustomed to a great deal of freedom, but within a framework of togetherness, and it is this togetherness upon which they rely under stress. They prefer to know what everyone knows, and to follow a leader. As one sabra angrily said, when a foreign visitor insisted on exploring on his own during a trip: "Since we've been children, we've been used to having a leader and we do what he says—even in the kindergarten, and even if we don't like where the teachers take us!" In short, from earliest childhood they acquire the habit of subordinating individual desires to group needs and a general framework.

Ideology. For the sabras, the ideology of Revolution and Marxism is dead. One can still find fervor for Marxist rhetoric in some isolated sabras in a few other kibbutzim, but it is doubtful that any sabra of Kiryat Yedidim would leap to the barricades in the name of the class struggle. The old ideology is almost never touched upon outside the classroom, except by an occasional kibbutz lecturer. Marxist revolutionary ideology simply has no relevance for the sabras, and even The Party has joined forces with the reformist labor parties. Just as irrelevant and anachronistic is the ideology of charismatic Zionism. For the sabras, their life is the fruit of this vision; for them the palpable reality of *being there,* not the abstract question of the meaning of this experience, is what is important. They do not have the need of their parents to reduce dissonance through a thunderous, death-defying commitment. They have no ghetto mentality to root out, no tyrannical father to fear or kill or worship. As we observed twenty years ago, Zionism remains for them neither more nor less than Israeli patriotism.

Unlike twenty years ago, however, they no longer view Israel as something inferior. Like other Israelis the sabras have a love-hate relationship with the outside world, but the overt successes of Israel over the years have led to a genuine, if increasingly shaky, pride in national achievement. That which impressed the adolescents of twenty years ago, quantity and bigness, has been achieved to some extent in Israel as well as in the kibbutz.

Although relatively indifferent to the ideology of their parents, the sabras show no inclination to revert to that ideology—traditional religion—which their parents had renounced. In general, sabra attitudes toward traditional Jewish concerns range from indifference through embarrassment to outright contempt.

But if traditional Judaism is dead, and Marxism a hollow shell, what are the sabras to do with their vague, gnawing sense of incompleteness? Work has been demythologized, "kibbutz" has been demystified and normalized, and nationalism has become less vital as external pressures abate. Here and there one feels a search —tentative, embarrassed, groping—for *Something* else. Some of this energy has been channelled into learning or the search for self. But some remains unfulfilled and free-floating. And in this connection one hears isolated reports of games played with a Ouija board, an interest in spiritualism, a toying with Yoga, and even an interest in listening to a non-kibbutznik describe an LSD experience.

These, of course, are isolated events, and none are taken seriously. But they do reflect a general feeling among the sabras that something is wrong or missing, and in their own inarticulate way they are making the first gestures towards searching this out. At present this is mainly expressed as one motivational strain in their attempts to find personal fulfillment.

At the same time, there is no real concern with the metaphysical among the sabras. Life is lived on a concrete basis, and problems of "meaning" arise only as a vague sense of personal discomfort and as a feeling that one ought to do something more with one's life. There was some vague philosophizing about life and death after the Six Day War, but in general this kind of abstract musing seems to be foreign to the sabra mentality.

Careerism. As we have already indicated, there is a strong push among the sabras for higher education and professional training. In the main, they choose from subjects that are relevant to the kibbutz and usefully applicable to its needs, such as physiotherapy, social work, occupational therapy, special education, sociology, technology, psychology. The realm of relevance, moreover, is changing nearly as fast as the demands. The lessening importance of agriculture, and the concomitant rise in importance of manufacturing, technology, and service occupations, make it important for the survival of the kibbutz that such training be undertaken.

Although few sabras today would say that their ambition is to be a painter or a musician, few also would say, as was said twenty years ago, that being a kibbutz member is their sole ambition. On the other hand, it is still true that "For the most part, sabra life and ambitions are restricted to those goals that are attainable within its context, and that are consistent, moreover, with its values." (p. 359) To be sure, the context has changed, broadened, and expanded, but the values are still maintained, even if sometimes it is their paradoxical nature which is expressed.

To the degree that ambition is fired by prestige, it is kibbutz-conferred prestige that is sought. And today such prestige, as derived from work within the kibbutz economy, does not preclude the acquisition of more knowledge or specialized training. Nor is ambition devoid of competitive strivings, and the latter, too, are maintained within the kibbutz framework—by pitting one economic branch against another, or by setting their kibbutz against others.

Resignations, departures, and defections. There have been but a handful of sabra resignations from the kibbutz over the years, probably no more than a dozen. These have not been occasioned by ideological or social issues, but by conflicts between kibbutz policy and personal goals, especially educational and academic goals of a type irrelevant to kibbutz interests or needs.

It is our impression that many of those who have left have been marginal, in the sense that their parents have not been fully accepted by the kibbutz community, or that they themselves have never fully accepted the kibbutz, or that their family life has been broken or less than happy. That is to say, they have been subjected in overt and covert ways to multiple identifications and values which were difficult to integrate. On the one hand, there was the group identification with the concomitant regulatory function of group control and the maintenance of ties; on the other, there was the identification with the discontented parent, whose fantasies of "what might have been" or unexpressed frustration within the community could now be acted out by the child.

It might be noted here that sabra defections paradoxically demonstrate the success of certain aspects of the kibbutz value system. One of the aspirations of the kibbutz founders was the creation of a "new man," who, among other things, would be both intellectual and farmer. Yet, severe limitations were imposed on the development of the intellectual component of this new hybrid, especially the discouragement of higher education outside the kibbutz. And yet it is inevitable that in some cases, at least, once one has begun to learn and invest energy in knowing, there will at some point arise a need to know more, or to test out what one already knows. And this is what has happened. Most sabras who leave the kibbutz are not in search of the fleshpots and pleasures of the world. They seek, rather, an opportunity to flex their intellectual muscles, or at least to exercise their abilities—something they have always been told to do, while being simultaneously told to curb such desires.

It is similarly so with other kinds of actual or would-be leavers. There are, for example, younger sabras who speak of joining or establishing a new kibbutz, where they can feel a sense of personal achievement by building something, rather than having it all "handed to them." Here again we witness a maintenance of kibbutz values, but heightened (to a degree unacceptable to the veteran founders) by personal motivational input.

In short, to some extent the sabra who leaves the kibbutz is saying to his parents: "I am doing what you really always wanted me to do and trained me to do; I am stronger than you think, and more my own man than you give me credit for; I will try to achieve those very goals which I acquired from you and your aspirations."

SABRA PERSONALITY: ADOLESCENTS

The description of adolescent personality and behaviour in previous chapters is more or less accurate for the current generation as well. There is no doubt but that the move from grade school to high school is a difficult one for the children to make. From the "hothouse" of the kibbutz, where their group was the senior at school, the children cross the road to a wider world of expectations, demands, and desires, a world in which they are now the youngest. In addition, the poor work habits they bring with them must now be emended if anything useful is to be learned. As one teacher noted, they have been accustomed to either being praised indiscriminately, or to just doing whatever they like and, when they become bored or frustrated, to dropping it. The new demands for planning and responsibility induce insecurity, which is expressed and defended against through a variety of mechanisms: minimization, unconcern, self-puffery, insolence, and so on.

The youngest children are the hardest hit by the move, as is evidenced, for example, by more frequent visits to their parents in the evening. Although initially they tend to find solace and support in the group, gradually shifting pairs begin to emerge, and, for the first time, their reference group becomes separated and diffused. As the years pass, their discomfort and dependency give way to (what is in part) a defensive "clinging" to independence, including freedom from parental control, and to a self-aggrandizing image of themselves as the envy of the typically confined city adolescent.

It is in the Mosad that, for the first time, sabras are personally "blamed" for displaying the consequences of their socialization experiences. This may have been true a generation ago as well, but it is worth mentioning here as it indicates that the sabras' own experiences in the Mosad have not made them particularly understanding of their children's problems. There is, first, the problematic image of the "spoiled" child. At a kibbutz meeting devoted to the problems of the Mosad, one member complained of the "passivity" of the children, "because of all we do for them"—a complaint often echoed by the educators themselves. Bemoaned one teacher: "All the children have to do is open their mouths and say 'ah' and they get what they want. They get everything, but they never learn to give." In a somewhat different vein is the complaint that the children have imbibed the rigid, nonreflective certitudes of their educators; for just as the official policy is that "our" way in education is the "best" way, so the children have the attitude that "we're best" or "our kibbutz is best" or "I'm the prettiest." In short, the children are criticized for internalizing the very attitudes and values which they are taught and for expressing them in their own behavior.

A few examples serve to illuminate this process. One concerns the expectation that the ideal kibbutz member should be a thoughtful, self-reliant individual, interested in learning for learning's sake. The Mosad system, however, stresses a rote, mechanical approach to learning, in which a series of "facts" are duly set forth—written down with the expectation that they will be memorized. The children are rarely challenged to think for themselves, or to organize and plan. Where this is attempted, as for example in a shop class, the teacher must confront the ingrained attitude that making plans "is a waste of time," as well as the action orientation of the children. Rarely, with respect to formal education, do kibbutz children have to accommodate themselves to environmental demands; rather, every attempt is made to find something to interest *them.* This makes it difficult when they must learn something that *seems* irrelevant to them or does not excite their immediate interest.

The same holds for the feelings of infantile omnipotence of the children, one basis for their insolence towards authority. They have never learned to respect authority, which has either capitulated to their demands or which has been externalized ("This is the time we eat," "This is how things are done"). At the same time they are told that they *should* do the right thing and *should* respect the authorities who, after all, are doing what they're doing for *their* sake. The emphasis in socialization on shaming techniques, and the use of *Ma Hem yagidu*—"What will they say?"—as a method of social control are not very effective in constraining adolescent students when the entire class is in an uproar, to which each student contributes his share. Hence, the consequences of a long history of refusal to set firm limits, especially to insolent behavior, are the same today as they were a generation ago. This is all the more evident from observations of the positive effects of a firm, imperturbable teacher on the students' disruptive behavior.

SABRA PERSONALITY: ADULTS

Cognitive factors. One of the questions raised in the preceding chapter and in Bettelheim's work on kibbutz sabras (see pp. 289–294) is that of sabra intelligence. Attempting to answer this question a generation ago, we referred to a "minor deficiency" in sabra intellectual functioning and Bettelheim (basing his assessment on a "nationwide study of scholastic achievement in Israel") comments on the "leveling impact" of kibbutz education. Both assessments are based on impressionistic evaluations. We are now in a position to add some objective measures of their intellectual functioning based on the Raven Progressive Matrices Test.[7]

Overall, the sample of 90 adult sabras (males and females ranging in age from 18–42) produced a mean Raven score of 68.7 percent (males: 69.4 percent; females: 67.6 percent), which places them as a group well into the "Normal" range of performance. Moreover, 54 percent of the males and 44 percent of the females scored in the highest quartile. Interesting, too, is that there is a clear increment in performance with advancing age, a factor which appears throughout the age spectrum.

Thus, despite the *feelings* of intellectual inferiority expressed by sabras of a generation ago, there is no basis in reality for considering them to be poorly equipped intellectually. Indeed, today there is little expression of these feelings. We have already noted that some complain of having had a rather poor education, but they do not compare themselves unfavorably with the outside world in the intellectual sphere.

As a group, the sabras read a fair amount, but with little depth or perseverance. Outside the kibbutz-Israeli context, their range of information is often neither wide nor deep, tending to the

[7] J. C. Raven, *Progressive Matrices (1947), Sets I and II*, rev. ed. (Dumfries, The Crichton Royal, 1963). The Raven does not provide a standard IQ score but can be considered by quartiles of performance, the distribution of which is based on the norms of the manual.

opinionated and prejudicial. In their own individual spheres of competence (mechanics, specialized farming, etc.) they are, of course, highly knowledgeable, but essentially in a pragmatic way.

Although there are sabras with artistic talents, on the whole they appear to be—like people anywhere—of average originality, and they tend to conformity. They react quickly to crises, and exhibit a flair for ingenuity and improvisation, but much of this is like the do-it-yourself mechanic who manages to improvise a stop-gap measure for a leaky pipe, but who does not follow through to repair the systemic problem. In this sense the adult sabras continue to express, in their pressured self-confidence and action orientation, a problem-solving style which is already clearly evident in the Mosad. Their action orientation is accompanied by a tendency to belittle planning, and to expect that their innate creativity will spontaneously flower in the act of doing. This expectation inevitably leads to frustration and a reactive defensiveness.

In commenting on the cognitive-intellectual functioning of the sabras, it is important to keep in mind the context in which this is embedded. The kibbutz is an egalitarian society in which there is negative regard for the overachiever, and this is particularly true in the intellectual or creative arena. To be sure, there are those sabras who are more esteemed than others for their intelligence, insight, and clear thinking, but if they are to find approval, these qualities must be reined in, not flaunted, and they must be utilized for the community's benefit. Too much intellectual display, especially outside the culturally acceptable framework of problem solving, will meet with criticism and mild stigma—one should not be a shvitzer, after all. This confluence of pressures, which leads to a suppression of intellectuality, also muzzles the abilities of those with above-average talent. What emerges, then, is conformity and a strong process of leveling within the kibbutz, combined with a desire on the part of many for more education and intellectual achievement outside the kibbutz.

But, if the sabras are classified as farmers—and how else *can* they be classified?—their intellectual motivations and attainments are far above the typical cultural level of the class. The sabras, like their parents, do very well with what they have and with what is available. Perhaps they are not the farmer intellectuals that the kibbutz founders had envisioned, but they certainly approximate this synthesis to the degree that is realistically expectable.

Emotional adjustment. The most important questions in the area of emotional adjustment relate to the continuities and discontinuities in adult sabra personality from the primarily adolescent portrait depicted in the earlier chapters.

The constellation of traits which was said to characterize sabra insecurity, for example, included shyness, maintenance of emotional distance, an absence of intimacy, hostility, and a strong need for affection and approval. This constellation, however, was observed in what was primarily an adolescent sample, and much too early in the history of Kiryat Yedidim to warrant the assumption that these traits would continue into maturity.

On the basis of contemporary evidence, the adult sabra remains rather reserved with strangers, but not nearly to the degree as the adolescents; the range of individual differences, moreover, is very wide. For adults, shyness with strangers is partly a function of the degree of exposure. Those who have spent time in the outside world are both more willing to relate to strangers and far more relaxed in doing so. They possess a greater variety of social-coping mechanisms and more common ground to evaluate and share the variety of experiences and viewpoints a stranger brings with him. Nor is it surprising that the average sabra lacks the social skills to cope with a wide variety of people. The kibbutz is, after all, a small and closed community which, until the 1967 War, was visited by few strangers. Since then it has been much more open to outsiders, a situation which has provided an opportunity for far more interaction with others.

More importantly, the sabras, like members of small communities anywhere, clearly differentiate between in- and out-groups, and grant implicit and explicit rights and privileges as a function of this distinction. Hence their reserve with strangers is perhaps no different from that of small communities elsewhere.

In any event, the sabras are not nearly so insecure as adults as they seemed when adolescents. The fact that until adulthood they have had little opportunity to test themselves as individuals *does* leave a residue of uncertainty in their approach to new challenges (especially from the outside world), but in most cases this is quickly dispelled by the discovery that they can successfully meet the challenge. Their response to such self-confirmation, however, suggests underlying tensions of self-doubt, for their response (characteristic of perhaps all Israeli sabras) tends to be self-puffery—but a puffery that emphasizes the others' inadequacy rather than their own superiority.

But the sabras' perceptual reality has changed since the earlier days in almost all ways. They are successful as kibbutzniks, they have proven themselves in peace and war, they have experienced love from their spouses and children, they do not feel abandoned any longer. In short, the adult has had new experiences which make him rather different from what he was as an adolescent.

The guardedness and emotional reserve noted among the adolescents in the previous chapters are *not* characteristic of these same adolescents as adults. They are certainly not gushy, self-expressive people, but they just as certainly form deep emotional attachments and intimate friendships. To be sure, there are constraints on expression of intimacy, just as there are constraints on most overt expressiveness which brings private feelings into the public domain. Observing public behavior, one is struck by an absence of our own culturally-defined indices of intimacy—physical contact, obvious secret-sharing, hovering, proximity behavior—but it is a mistake to confuse social structure with psychological structure, to assume that the form of social interaction is a *direct* expression of underlying *psychological* states. It is our impression that there is a relatively long moratorium on identity formation among the sabras, and that a strong sense of ego identity is achieved only in their mid-twenties. Since, as Erikson has pointed out, ". . . it is only after a reasonable sense of identity has been established that real *intimacy* with the other sex (or, for that matter, with any other person or even with oneself) is possible," [8] it is only then that the sabra begins to experiment with and experience real intimacy— with spouse, peers, and the kibbutz.

The hostility and insolence which were seen as adolescent characteristics twenty years ago, are again best conceived as age-specific, developmental traits. Overt aggression, for example, is almost totally absent among the adult sabras. During the follow-up study only two physical confrontations were witnessed or reported, and both involved a sabra considered to be deviant or disturbed. Adult sabras can be thoughtless and direct, and in some cases they express a great deal of shouting and arguing. But such hostility, if it can be called that, does not result in—nor does it even have the intention of—goal-directed aggression. Rather, it is an affective outlet, a self-expression with little consequence or force. It is more an assertive act, designed to make oneself heard—sabras claim that, as children, they had to learn to shout to be heard by the nurse in a group of many children—and noticed. When frustrated, their anger does not lead to attempts to remove the sources of frustration, which they tend to view as something inevitable,

[8] Erik H. Erikson, "Identity and the Life Cycle," *Psychological Issues*, I (1959), 95.

about which they can rail, but not change. Frustration, for the sabras, has a certain fatalistic quality to it.

In general, it may be said that the adult sabras demonstrate a resiliency, resourcefulness, and plasticity that enable them to make use of later life opportunities (and crisis resolutions) to alleviate and compensate for early deprivations and traumata. The *anlage* of these early experiences are present in certain feelings of insecurity, concern with rejection, search for approval, emotional reserve, etc. More obviously, however, they are, to quote from the preceding chapter, "efficient, productive, and functioning adult[s] . . . with a sense of values and a conscience that assures the implementation of those values."

CONCLUSION

Throughout the years since the first study of Kiryat Yedidim, the original observers have been asked repeatedly, "Is the kibbutz a success?" For this planned, collective society has excited an interest—ideological, sociological, and psychological—far beyond that which its actual number of adherents in the world might warrant.

The question of a society's success is rarely asked of a social scientist: One doesn't recall ever being asked, "Are the Hopi a success?" for example. It might be suggested that the kibbutz and its dream have a personal meaning to outsiders—to some, who seek the vindication of their own dreams in their realization by others; to others, who seek confirmation of their ideological convictions in another's failure.

How shall one measure the success of the kibbutz? Kiryat Yedidim has been in existence only a few generations, and it has undergone many changes, some as a result of internal needs, others due to external pressures. It will continue to change, and this chapter is but an interim report of what is hoped will be an ongoing study of an ongoing society. How, then, shall one speak to the question of success?

When the founders weigh the contemporary reality against their original vision, many of them feel that their struggles were in vain; the very stability and success of the kibbutz excite their contempt. But let us, the outsiders, take the measure of that reality.

Is it to be counted as failure that the sabras have so successfully succeeded to leadership in Kiryat Yedidim? And of this success, there can be no objective doubt. Economically, the kibbutz is flourishing. The quality of life, certainly in its external trappings, has improved beyond the wildest fantasies of the founding generation. With all the stresses and strains, the community persists as a kibbutz.

This *is* the measure of things. And here, if the founders could appreciate it, is the measure of *their* success. The transition to sabra control is not yet fully complete—and non-sabra members who have married into or joined the kibbutz also play a key role—but it is constantly increasing. In 1969, for example (the latest year for which we have complete records), some 40 percent of the Secretariat and Committee members were sabras, and the key positions of Economic Manager and kibbutz Secretary had for several years already been filled by sabras.

Moreover, in all these positions they have had great success. Needless to say, not every sabra wishes or volunteers to serve on a committee, but a number of sabras have already proven to be even more competent and creative farm managers than their parents. In short, the kibbutz is flourishing because of the hard work, foresight, planning, creativity, and flexibility of its offspring.

Surely it is some measure of success that, despite a few defections from Kiryat Yedidim, there can be no doubt about the sabras' commitment to the perpetuation of the kibbutz. As the preceding pages have indicated, there have been, and no doubt there will continue to be, changes in every realm of kibbutz life, but there is nothing to suggest a sabra desire for a major restructuring.

The core values and institutions of the kibbutz—collective production and consumption and collective education—are firmly maintained by the sabras. But the emotional has been replaced by the cognitive, and few values—as they are lived, not simply declared—go unquestioned. Unlike the founders, they have not and will not continue the kibbutz because of its transcendental value, but rather because emotionally it is home, and cognitively it works. This combination of sentiment and pragmatism seems perfectly attuned to the realities of the kibbutz situation. As a basis for the perpetuation of the kibbutz it is far more flexible, if not nearly so romantic, as the adolescent dramaturgy of the first generation.

And, finally, that two generations of observers can characterize the adult sabra as a "warm, sensitive . . . gracious human being" must surely be counted as a measure of success.

To suggest that the Utopian vision of the kibbutz founders has been tempered by the frailties of man is merely to suggest the inevitable. Could Kiryat Yedidim have survived, physically and psychologically, the tensions of a continuous otherworldly com-

mitment? Would not the demands of its charismatic, its revolutionary fervor have left it spent in time, too weak to cope with the
pressures of this world?

> Not in Utopia, subterranean fields,
> Or some secreted island, Heaven knows where!
> But in the very world, which is the world
> Of all of us,—the place where in the end
> We find our happiness, or not at all!
>   *Wordsworth*

APPENDIX A · METHODS OF RESEARCH

Various techniques were employed for the collection of the data which describe the kibbutz socialization system as well as selected aspects of sabra personality and behavior. These techniques included systematic and unsystematic observations, interviews, psychological tests, questionnaires, and written and published documents.

OBSERVATIONS

The vast majority of statements and descriptions concerning kibbutz socialization and personality development for the first six years of life are based on systematic observations of behavior made by my wife and me. These observations were facilitated by the fact that kibbutz children live in small groups of eight to sixteen in special children's houses. Since these children remain together for most of the day (and night), it is possible to obtain a fairly adequate sample of the entire behavioral repertory of a restricted age range without too much difficulty. By the same token, and with the same ease, it is possible to obtain a good sample of the behavior of the child's most important (quantitatively viewed) socializer — the nurse.

At the time of this study there were in Kiryat Yedidim one Nursery or infants' house, three Toddlers' Houses, two Nursery Schools, and two Kindergartens. With the exception of one Kindergarten, which was only briefly observed, and one Nursery School which was not observed at all, each was observed for periods of from four to six weeks by either of us. Since we worked in the kibbutz economy for half a day, we devoted only a half day — as well as the evening — to formal research. So that we could obtain a representative sample of behavior, the kibbutz graciously consented to a weekly alternation of our working hours — one week we worked in the mornings, the next week in the afternoons. This enabled us to alternate our research schedule and to make both morning and afternoon observations in each of the children's houses studied.

Since one-way screens were not available, observations were made in full view of children and nurses. Nevertheless, we attempted, and — with the exception noted below — succeeded in becoming unobtrusive and neutral objects in the environment. The first few days after our arrival we obviously constituted an intrusive element in the children's social field. Almost everything about us was the object of curiosity. Why did we use sun glasses? Did we sleep with our glasses? Why did we wear white shirts? Why was there a spiral ring on the notebook? Why were we writing? Why were we not writing? Why was the string on the camera so short? Why was the pencil so long? What were we doing in their group anyway? Why did we speak "that way?" (with an accent)? Where did we live?

After a few days, however, their curiosity wore off (or was satisfied) and our presence was accepted. According to the nurses, the children's behavior in our presence differed in no observable way from what it was in our absence. Though their behavior was not perceptibly affected, it should be noted that the children's attitude toward us was not neutral. In general, and despite overt aggression toward us, good rapport was unquestionably achieved, and, though taken for granted, we seemed to be welcome.

Although we were generally able to remain in the background and take notes unobtrusively, an important qualification must be made. Because of their busy schedules, the nurses cannot always attend to all the children's needs. Aggression, for example, is frequently unsocialized in the children's houses and the victim unprotected because of the absence of the nurse from the scene. Thus we were frequently confronted with a conflict between our scientific and humane values. The latter demanded that we intervene to protect the victim; the former demanded that we refrain from intervention. For the most part, our scientific interests prevailed. But this procedure was more easily adopted by me than by my wife. It became quite apparent that she, being a female, was expected by the harassed nurse to help when necessary. This expectation created yet another conflict in interests for the observer: on the one hand, she wished to obtrude as little as possible into the group; on the other, it was important to maintain good rapport with the nurses. The result was the compromise solution of interfering only when it was felt to be absolutely necessary, or when the nurse specifically requested it.

In only one house did a nurse's implicit pressure for assistance interfere with my wife's scientific role. In the youngest Toddlers' House only one nurse was on duty for the greatest part of the observational period; she expected my wife to assume a socialization role. Thus, she had little alternative but to intervene actively in the behavior of the children when, for example, the nurse went to breakfast, leaving the house unattended. This active role of the observer unquestionably influenced the children's behavior in this house, and must be weighed in interpreting the data for that group.

Our system of observation and recording was simple: we attempted to record the behavior of the children and nurses in as great detail as possible. This, of course, included verbal behavior. I knew Hebrew before going to Israel, but my wife did not learn the language until after settling in Kiryat Yedidim. Her knowledge was adequate for the comprehension and recording of most conversations — except for the first house in which she worked, when she began to study Hebrew.

Obviously, this ideal was impossible to execute. First, we could not write rapidly enough to record everything; second, we could not observe all the children simultaneously; and third, our theoretical framework and research interests inevitably served as important selective factors both in the perception of behavior and in our recording of it.

In the Nursery, the babies spend most of their day in their cribs. Though older babies are put in playpens with their peers, for the most part there is little interaction among them. At this age the important interaction is between infant and mother, or infant and nurse, rather than between infant and peer. Observations in this house, therefore, were made primarily on individual infants. Sometimes one infant was observed for an entire observational period; sometimes many were observed successively.

In the other children's houses, even where the children play in groups, not all could be observed simultaneously. The children seldom remain together in the same corner of the house or playyard, or seldom play in one large group. Our procedure was to observe behavior and/or interaction in smaller play-groups, without determining, beforehand, an arbitrary time period for each session. (Since these play-groups are transient and their duration is unpredictable, this would have been futile.) If a play-group remained together for a long period, the decision to remain with it or to move to another group or another individual was determined by at least three considerations. If the group under observation persisted in some ongoing activity with little change in behavior or in group structure, we would turn to another group in order to sample as wide a range of behavior as possible. When the nurse was perceived to intervene — to discipline, inform, console, and so on — in the behavior of a group we were not immediately observing, we would almost always turn to this latter group in order to have as large a sample of nurse-child interaction as possible. Finally, when a group was perceived to engage in some theoretically important behavior, we would generally shift our attention to it.

The expression, "theoretically important," points to a second qualification of our stated intention of observing and recording everything. Among the multiplicity of stimuli to which we might conceivably have attended, our perceptions were most sensitive to those responses and activities which were most relevant to our theoretical framework and research interests. Except in the case of infants, we were not, for example, interested in psychophysiology or motor behavior. Only in the Nursery, therefore, were we concerned with observing and recording molecular responses. Among the other children, our unit of interest was molar activity.

Since we were primarily concerned with the social and emotional development of young children as the basis for adult personality structure and cultural behavior, our perceptions were even more narrowly focused. Our interest lay primarily in those personality variables which, presumably, would be most influenced by the uniquely kibbutz aspects of this culture, particularly by its unique socialization system. It was natural, therefore, that we should be interested in the fate of aggression in a noncompetitive society; or in the vagaries of the Oedipus Complex in a society in which children are primarily reared by parent-surrogates; or in the profit motive in a society whose economy is communistic; or in sexual behavior in a society in which boys and girls sleep in the same rooms.

Just as the study focused on a limited number of personality variables, so too it focused on a limited number of socialization variables. The latter were chosen from among those variables which personality theory (particularly psychoanalytic theory) and culture and personality studies have emphasized. We assumed that personality is most importantly influenced in childhood by the ways in which socializing agents structure the oral, excretory, sexual, aggressive (and cooperative), and dependency behavior of children. Hence our most sustained interest was elicited by those activities of children, peers, and nurses, which related to the satisfaction, frustration, or canalization of such drives and these were faithfully recorded. With some additions and qualifications based on interviews with nurses and parents, the description of kibbutz children and nurses rests primarily on the behavioral protocols which emerged from these observations.

Although it was among the preschool children that systematic observation provided the most important data for the analysis of behavior and socialization, it was employed extensively among the older children and adolescents as well. In the latter two age-groups, however, it was confined primarily to the classroom. I spent two months each in the grammar and high schools, observing classroom behavior in the second through the twelfth grades. Since the kibbutz classroom is highly informal, this technique probably yielded richer data on peer-peer and peer-adult interaction, and on children's attitudes to peers and adults, than would have been obtained had this same procedure been employed in a more formal classroom situation. But since the classroom situation is focused on a relatively few dimensions of experience, and since the observational sessions in each class were — because of the large number of classes to be observed — relatively few, it was decided that little could be gained by quantifying the data. A number of generalizations nevertheless emerged from these behavior protocols which, together with conventional ethnographic observations, comprise much of the data on these age groups.

Conventional ethnographic observations differ from those discussed above in that they are less systematic. The behavior observed is frequently not recurrent; if it is recurrent, it is not repetitive; if it is repetitive, the ethnographer — in order to obtain as wide a sample as possible — discovers it by sampling the behavior of a wide variety of individuals (or groups) rather than by taking time samples of the same individual or group. In this study ethnographic observations were made on the following types of interaction characteristic of the children and adolescents: parent-child interaction in the children's houses, parental rooms, and public places; adult-child interaction in the children's houses and in public places (adult other than parent or nurse); sibling-sibling interaction in children's houses, parental rooms, and public places; peer-peer and child-adult interaction in the grammar and high schools — in such variegated activities as play, club-meetings, parties, celebrations, student government, work, meals. Ethnographic observations on the behavior of adult sabras were made during work, in the dining room and showers, at public meetings and celebrations, in their rooms, and in test situations. In some of these situations, student government, for example, we were observers; in others, such as work, participant-observers. In the former, detailed notes were made of ongoing behavior; in the latter, brief summary notes were recorded during the session and later transcribed as fully as possible.

Although we were able to observe much, because we lived and worked in the kibbutz, and because many aspects of living which are generally private in our society are of a public nature in a collective society, the data derived from ethnographic observation are, nevertheless, spotty. For some categories, such as aggression or work, they are abundant and conclusive. For others, such as adult sabra sexual behavior or parent-child interaction, the data are less satisfactory. Since adult sexual behavior is always private, no observations could be made. More serious (and more frustrating) is the almost complete absence of *systematic* observations of child-parent interaction. Only for early infancy and for the daily leave-taking in later childhood do we have systematic observational data. Infants remain in the Nursery the entire day and parents must go there in order to see their babies. The observer was therefore able to make observations of child-parent interaction as systematic as those for child-nurse interaction. Except for early infancy, however, children go (or are taken) to their parents' rooms for the evening visit, and our observations of child-parent interaction — as far as the parental room is concerned — are of an ethnographic, rather than of a systematic nature.

This regretful gap rests on decisions made during field work. Since the parental room is small, we did not request permission to make systematic observations. For this would have meant a two- or three-week intrusion into the privacy of what, in the kibbutz, is a cherished relationship. We may have been overly sensitive on this point, and, in retrospect at least, it seems probable that some of the parents would not have viewed our daily intrusion as unduly burdensome. Nevertheless that was our feeling at the time. Consequently, observations on child-parent interaction in the latter's room were of an ethnographic nature; that is, they were made during those frequent occasions when we happened to be in a parent's room when his children arrived, or when we were invited to the room at the same time that the children were there. And since we lived in the kibbutz for almost a year, we were probably not unsuccessful in observing a fair sample of such interaction. However, since we were in the rooms as friends rather than as scientists, we refrained from making an immediate record of our observations. And since these were not recorded until returning to our own room, statements based on them are necessarily qualitative.

The same characterization may be said to apply to other ethnographic observations of parent-child interaction — in the kibbutz dining room, on the lawns, at celebrations, and at other public places and occasions. The one exception is the parental departure from the children's house in the evening. Here it was possible to make systematic observations. And though these data are a rich source of information, they are hardly representative of the range of behavior patterns encompassed in the parent-child relationship.

Wherever possible we attempted to maximize the possibilities for either systematic or ethnographic observations, and to use the resultant behavior protocols as the primary data for the generalizations found in this monograph. This method has dangerous pitfalls. In systematic observations, the time samples chosen may not yield a representative sample of the various classes of behavior which are being studied. These observations, moreover, may be biased by both the conscious and unconscious selection which guides our perceptions. The quantification of the data is another source of possible error. The frequency of an act is not necessarily a valid measure of its psychological significance. Ethnographic observations raise an even more critical question with respect to their representativeness. And the impossibility of quantification, in their case, raises the perennial problem of the validity of qualitative descriptions and judgments. Despite these problems, like most anthropologists, I am convinced that field work is the indispensable technique for the study of social behavior and of modal personality. Whatever its shortcomings, it seems obvious that if one is interested in generalizing about behavior, behavior itself, rather than statements about behavior, should be sampled. And if one is interested in such hypothetical constructs as drives, emotions, and attitudes it seems equally obvious that these are most cogently inferred from behavior in its natural context rather than from verbal or written statements, screened — as they inevitably are — through the subject's defenses.

Moreover, the difficulties inherent in other techniques, including the increasingly popular schedules and questionnaires, are even more serious than those raised by field work. I do not doubt that questionnaires are both efficient (that is, time-saving) and valid instruments for the acquisition of factual data — where there is no need to trust the respondent's memory, and for those topics concerning which the respondents have little ego-involvement. Yet I have considerable doubt concerning their validity in those instances in which a correct response depends on the recall of past events and on topics, such as behavior, in which the normative and the descriptive need not necessarily correspond. In this study, for example, there are important instances in which the claims of the nurses — that they employ, or that they refrain from employing, certain techniques of child training — are inconsistent with our observations. We do not impugn the integrity of the nurses to explain this. We need merely call attention to the psychological truism that there may be little correspondence between the way a person thinks he would or does behave, when queried in an affectively neutral situation, and the way he actually behaves under the stress of internal need or of environmental press.

Questionnaire responses, in short, are frequently filtered through psychological defenses. And the parent or nurse in the kibbutz may be assumed to erect such defenses, not only to protect their own self-image, but to protect the image of the kibbutz (with which they are identified), which is under attack by its enemies and under the careful scrutiny of its friends. In informal conversation, when the parents perceived the ethnographer as a friend, not as a scientist, bitter complaints were expressed concerning the lack of intimacy between them and their adolescent and adult offspring. These same parents, when responding to a written Questionnaire, said that the latter relationship was excellent. This is not to deny completely the importance of questionnaires. Indeed we used one, but its findings were used as ancillary to, rather than as a substitute for, observational data.

INTERVIEWS

Since observation — even systematic observation — is inadequate to the task of answering the many questions to which we wanted answers, other techniques, including formal and informal interviews, were employed. Most interviews, of course, were conducted in Hebrew. Where observational data were either absent or poor, these techniques provided the primary data. When observational data were good, they were used to supplement those data, to check on their reliability, and to support the generalizations which were derived from them. "Formal interviews" were those situations in which an appointment was arranged with the interviewee, and the interview proceeded according to a schedule. "Informal interviews" are those instances — working in the fields, observing in the children's houses, visiting in rooms — in which questions were asked and answers obtained regarding any facet of our research which came to mind in the situation. Moreover, since, in the latter situation, it was incidental to the activity at hand, the interview was not structured as such, either by the ethnographer or the subject. In all, open-ended questions were employed; but in the formal interview, the responses were recorded immediately; in the informal interview, they were often not recorded until later.

Respondent-type[1] interviews — both formal and informal — were conducted with all nurses, nursery teachers, and teachers in all age groups in which we worked. These were designed to get at three kinds of data: information about the socialization and educational systems, information on the children — individually and collectively — under their supervision, and an expression of their attitudes toward, and an evaluation of, both the children and the system.

Respondent-type, informal interviews were conducted with a large number of parents, and informant-type informal interviews were conducted with many kibbutz members, in order to obtain similar information.

The great bulk of the interview data, however, is derived from the sabras themselves. In addition to informal interviews with a majority of sabras, formal interviews — both respondent- and informant-type — were conducted with approximately half the sabra population from the ages of six through eighteen, and with all but one of the adult sabras — those over twenty-one.

In order to obtain certain types of personality data — particularly, on emotions, attitudes, and values — all sabra subjects were administered the Stewart Emotional Response Test and the Bavelas Moral Ideology Test.[2] Although termed, "tests," I viewed them primarily as interview schedules. Hence the instructions for the latter test were changed from "What could a boy (girl) of your age . . . ?" to "what could *you* . . . ?" The data derived from these interview schedules are employed extensively throughout this book. When used with caution,[3] they provide a rich source of quantifiable data, which are particularly useful for age-grade comparisons, both within the kibbutz and between the kibbutz and other societies. The Emotional Response

---

[1] Respondents are interviewees from whom information is requested concerning themselves. The interviewer is concerned with *their* attitudes, beliefs, opinions, and behavior. Informants are interviewees from whom information is requested concerning their culture. Viewing them as experts on their culture, the interviewer wishes to elicit information on such matters as cultural beliefs and norms.

[2] For a description of these tests, see Havighurst and Neugarten, *American Indian and White Children.*

[3] Caution is required for a number of reasons. First, the responses tell us nothing about *unconscious* motives or about the role which these attitudes, values, and so forth, play in the personality dynamics of the subjects. Second, they provide no information about the intensity of response preference, but only about the frequency with which responses occur. And, conceivably, though certain responses occur less frequently than others, they might be much more important in the motivation of behavior because they represent drives of a greater intensity than those mentioned more frequently. Third, the importance of certain categories may be unduly inflated because some subjects give more responses than others. Finally, since apparently different responses of many subjects, when coded, were assigned to the same category, it was necessary to compute the percentage of each category on the basis of the total number of responses, rather than on the total number of subjects. This, too, might serve to distort the conclusions since the responses of productive subjects might, consequently, have been given undue weight.

and Moral Ideology tests constituted one part of a larger interview schedule used with all subjects over thirteen years of age. The other questions of the schedule concerned such matters as interpersonal relations, sex, relationship to parents, attitudes to the kibbutz, political attitudes, and other aspects of their private and public lives. Data obtained from these interviews form the basis for many generalizations about sabra personality.

Since interviews are vulnerable to the same criticisms directed against questionnaires, some comments on the validity of these interview data are necessary. These comments apply with equal force to our behavioral observations, as well. Neither interview responses nor behavioral observations speak for themselves. Like the answers to a written questionnaire, they must be interpreted. Though it is important that observations be made of behavior in its natural context — in its ecological and socio-cultural setting — it is equally important that it be interpreted in its psychodynamic context — in terms of the needs which the actor hopes to satisfy, and of the system of defenses which mediate his various needs (particularly his drives and values) when, as so often happens, they are in conflict.

This stricture applies to verbal behavior as well. Without an understanding of the interviewee's defenses, the interpretation of many of his statements may frequently fall short of the truth. Our preference for the open-ended interview (which we used extensively) over the closed-ended questionnaire (which we used infrequently) lies in the fact that the former lends itself more readily to the understanding and analysis of defenses. Two subjects, for example, might have identical high scores on an attitude scale designed to measure parental love. In one case, however, the high score may reflect a strong reaction formation against a deep-seated hatred for the child; in the other it may represent genuine love. It would be a grievous error to assume that these identical scores reflect an identical attitude; and it would be compounding the error to assume that they stem from the same antecedent conditions or that they lead to similar behavior.

In an interview, on the other hand, it is often possible to detect a genuine from a defensive attitude by various verbal and motor cues, and by skillful questioning in those areas in which one suspects the operation of defenses. The validity of psychodynamic interpretations of interview data is, of course, no better than the current state of dynamic personality theory available to the researcher, and — perhaps more important — than his clinical skill and insight. Psychodynamic interpretations are hazardous in the extreme. But, if it is the case that behavior is a product of unconscious, as well as of conscious, drives, perceptions, and cognitions, and, if it is the case that much behavior is a product of psychological defenses which function to protect the integrity of the self by resolving conflicts between drives and values, then any interpretation of behavior which does not come to grips with these crucial aspects of behavior is more hazardous than one which

does. For, while the latter interpretation *may* be, the former most
certainly *is*, false.

QUESTIONNAIRE

Since systematic data on parental socialization was lacking, a ten-
page questionnaire was constructed dealing with various aspects of
parental socialization techniques, which all interested parents were
requested to fill out. Only sixteen parents — representing, it is assumed,
sixteen married couples — complied with our request.[4] Because of the
smallness of the sample, and the author's skepticism concerning questionnaire data, this instrument is used with extreme caution indeed.

DOCUMENTS AND PUBLICATIONS

To obtain information on sabra attitudes and values, as well as on
their imaginative and fantasy life, various types of literary products
were analyzed. These included a one-year sample of essays written by
grade- and high-school students, and a two-year sample of the high
school monthly magazine. Moreover, a series of essays on various
political and ideological subjects were obtained from the students in
the seventh grade. The topics, suggested by the author, were assigned
by their teacher to be written in class as their weekly theme.[5]

Data on the history and philosophy of collective education were
obtained, not only from interviews, but also from published materials
of various kinds. These included books, magazines, and newspapers
published by The Federation.

PROJECTIVE TESTS

Since the personality theory which guided our research lays great
stress on unconscious motives in behavior, a battery of projective tests
was employed for at least two purposes: to check on the inferences
concerning personality dynamics derived from our clinical impressions,
and to provide information on those topics for which data were not
(or could not be) obtained by other techniques.

The Rorschach and Thematic Apperception Tests were administered to approximately half the sabra population between the ages of
six and eighteen, and to nine of the eleven adult sabras (the other
two refused to be tested). In addition, free drawings were collected
from all children between the ages of two and six, and the Picture
Frustration Test was administered to all children from six through
twelve.

[4] The Questionnaire was printed in Haifa only after our return to the
United States, and it was only through the cooperation of Professor William
Brinner, who also helped to translate the questions into intelligible Hebrew, that
the cooperation of even sixteen subjects was obtained.

[5] Again I wish to acknowledge my debt to Professor Brinner, whose efforts
made this project possible.

Originally, I had intended to analyze these tests myself, but later I decided against this procedure for technical reasons.[6] This decision served to delay their analysis, so that the present volume is not based on them. A third volume in this series — devoted exclusively to sabra Rorschach and TAT protocols — is therefore planned.

[6] First, I felt that these instruments could yield maximal data when analyzed by a specialist — which I am not. Second, I felt that my own interpretations would reflect personal knowledge of the people — a possibility which would cast doubt on the validity of the interpretations. And, if this were the case, one of the purposes for which they were used — to provide some measure of reliability for clinical interpretations of observations and interviews — would be seriously compromised. I therefore decided to enlist the cooperation of a clinical psychologist who, working independently, would make "blind" interpretations of these tests.

GRADE 7

The Ancient East — 75 hours

1. What is history and what is its function?
2. Prehistoric period. Techniques of Investigation. Culture of Early man. Palestinian finds concerning prehistory.
3. Two discussions on causes of development of human society. The importance of objective conditions (geographic, climatic). Social forms; the spiritual world of man in progressive steps.
4. Development of writing.
5. Egypt — the Nile. Structure of ancient Egypt. Division into sections. Techniques of early agriculture. The place of the large cities. Egypt today.
6. The first periods in history of ancient Egypt. The early and middle kingdoms. Dates in history.
7. Basic expressions of Egyptian culture. Physical and spiritual culture. Life in village and city. Architecture; how technical difficulties were solved. Medicine; art; literature; social classes; religion; archeological sites.
8. Late kingdom; imperialism; exceptional personalities; Egypt and Israel; religious reform; contact with Babylon.
9. Last period, till conquest by Persia.
10. Mesopotamia. Mesopotamia today.
11. Sumer and Akkad.
12. Basic expressions of Babylonian culture. Cities; basic economy; laws; religion; art; literature and myth; classes; Hammurabi.
13. Discussion — differences between Egyptian and Babylonian culture.
14. Assyrian imperialism in rise and decline. Mainstreams in Assyrian society and culture; Babylonian language and alphabet; Assyrians and their international functions; cuneiform.

15. New Babylonian kingdom; Babylonia and Egypt; city of Babylon as cultural center of time.
16. Other peoples in the fertile crescent at that time.
17. Concluding discussions; questionnaires; art, models; etc.

First Period of National Independence — 90 hours

1. Objective and subjective conditions for political crystallization; Bible as historical source; Jewish historians.
2. Questionnaire review of period of David and Saul.
3. Solomon — attainments and difficulties in this period; agriculture; industry; commerce; architecture; classes; relations with neighbors; cultural influence on other peoples; social life; customs; figure of Solomon in legend.
4. The splitting of the kingdom — reasons; reasons for general flowering; Israel and Aram; dynasties; foreign cultural influences.
5. Beginnings of prophesy.
6. From Jehu to the destruction; Assyria and Israel; ten lost tribes.
7. Amos; function and work of prophets; summary discussions on this period.
8. Judah after the split; Judah and Israel; Judah and its neighbors.
9. Hezekia period; economic and political conditions; Isaiah and Micah; Assyrian conquests.
10. Destruction of Judah; internal and external conditions; exile and remnant; Jeremiah and Ezekiel.
11. Babylonian exile.
12. Return; political exchanges; first aliah.
13. Summary, notebooks, etc.

GRADE 8

Ancient Greece — 81 hours

1. Greece and the Eastern Mediterranean; Balkan Peninsula; economy; economic conditions today.
2. Life of ancient tribe; internal structure; transition from nomadic to sedentary life.
3. Age of wandering in Greece; cultures of Aegean.
4. Homeric period; ancient legends; early Greek religion; Troy and Mycenae; legends, Iliad, Odyssey; Homer.
5. *Polis*; geographic causes; class struggle in city-states; spiritual and material culture; personalities; written and unwritten law; Athens and Sparta; cities of Asia Minor.
6. Discussion of city-states in Egypt and other countries.
7. Persian wars; historical writers in Greece; after Persian persecution; economic and social results.

8. Golden age of Greece; art; drama; literature; philosophy; science; daily life; holydays; education; read two plays — Prometheus and Antigone.
9. Athens and Sparta; struggles between them; Peloponnesian War; personalities; Thucydides.
10. The tottering of Athenian democracy; reasons for failure of Athens in war; individual and group; slavery; imperialistic designs.
11. Ancient regime.
12. Conquests of Alexander
13. Culture of Egypt and the East.
14. Summaries, etc.

Second Temple — 78 hours

1. Period of return — Ezra and Nehemiah.
2. Suzerainty of Greeks — contact of cultures; Septuagenta; Hellenizers; Jewish centers in the Fertile Crescent.
3. Seleucid dynasty and "orders of conversion."
4. Maccabean rebellion; social and political backgrounds of rebellion; historical events; Maccabees as historical mission.
5. Judean freedom; political causes that aided the strengthening of Judah; economic organization of country; spiritual and social streams.
6. Review discussions on Mediterranean countries.
7. History of Roman republic.
8. Road to loss of independence; Roman intervention — house of Herod; rule passes to foreigners; economics and material culture; overthrow of high priesthood; struggle for national values; Sanhedrin and Spiritual hegemony; religion of Israel and of the East.
9. Agrippa.
10. Loss of independence; Roman rule; sects; necessary causes of revolt; the revolt; Josephus; destruction and exile; Yavneh.
11. Historiography and falsifications of this period; literature on the period.
12. Literature of period — from *Sefer Ha-aggadah.*
13. Conclusions.

GRADE 9

Feudalism — 122 hours

1. Geographical background.
2. Rome under the Caesars; economics; society and culture in the period of the flowering of Caesars; economic and social exchanges in late empire; decline of empire.
3. Eastern empire; Byzantine rule; Byzantine culture.

4. New kingdoms — wanderings of peoples; development and beginnings of peoples who inherited Roman empire; decline of cities and commerce; beginnings of barter economy; beginnings of natural and autarchic economy; new social hierarchy; new social structures; customs.
5. Development of Church from early Christianity till rule of Papacy; Jesus and disciples; Christianity in Roman Empire; structure and activities of Church; struggle between Papacy and kings.
6. Feudalism — conclusions.
7. Islam; geographic backgrounds of Arabia; beginnings of Islam; spread of Islam; political and cultural centers of Islam; cultural expressions.
8. Crusades and results; development of trade, rise of cities; rise of commercial classes — bourgeoisie.
9. Social movements — peasants' rebellions.
10. Political development in thirteenth through fifteenth centuries.
11. Cultures of middle ages — art — religion — knowledge.
12. Conclusions.

Literature to be read: selections from New Testament, Koran, Omár Kháyyám.

From Independence to Dispersion — 81 hours

1. Autonomy in Israel — oppressive economic and political struggles; new organization; rebellions (Bar Kochbah and the others); Mishna; final breaks between Judaism and Christianity; literature — Mishna and aggadah.
2. Babylonian center; beginnings; autonomy in Golah; economic changes — from agriculture to middle-men; Talmud; hegemony of Babylonian Judaism; social movements (messianic); decline.
3. North African centers.
4. Spanish center — in days of Visigoths; Jews under Islam rule; Jews in cultural and economic life of Spain; revival of Hebrew creativity; secularism in spiritual creations; Ibn Gabirol and poetry; Yehuda Halevi; philosophy and religion — Maimonides, and sections from *Moreh Nevuchim*; development of mysticism.
5. Conclusions.

GRADE 10

From Feudalism to Capitalism — 132 hours

1. Decline of feudal economy and rise of cities — development of international trade; division of labor and begin-

nings of manufacture; decline of feudalism as social and political system.

2. The new man and his world — Renaissance inherits the Gothic; literature — revival of classic values, and contemporary creations; revolution in science — Copernicus, Galileo, Kepler, Bruno; Renaissance in other parts of Europe; Dürer, Holbein; new political concepts — Machiavelli; humanism, utopianism (read T. More).

3. Geographic background.

4. Social background — religious stirrings in central Europe; rise of oppressive and exploitative regime; political splits; economic decline after these revolutions; revolt against Catholic church; Luther; peasant rebellion; revolt of knights and princes; status of the bourgeoisie; commune of Münster; Calvinism; Thirty Years' War; Counter Reformation and war of independence of low countries; Reformation in England.

5. Geographic background.

6. England — rising power — order after War of Roses; rise of power of commercial bourgeoisie; manufacture; England inherits rule of sea.

7. English revolution; class conflicts before revolt; religious sects; Cromwell; Restoration; Bloodless revolution.

8. Period of absolutism; mercantilism; struggle between bourgeoisie and nobility; philosophy in sixteenth through seventeenth centuries; Shakespeare.

9. Slavic countries — freedom and unification of Russia; Peter the Great; rise and decline of Feudal Poland.

10. Conclusions.

Beginning of Redemption

1. Rise of Jewish centers in Europe (France, England, Germany); changes in economic and political conditions; spiritual creations; expulsions and wanderings; Rashi, R. Gershom, etc.

2. Decline of Spanish center and rise of new centers — expulsion from Spain; centers in Near East; Italy — Jews and Renaissance; Holland — Spinoza; Uriel da Costa; Jewish community and its organization; social structure and economic life; participation and influence of Jews in social, economic, and cultural life of general society.

3. Survey of messianic movements from Bar Kochbah — rise of longings for Palestine, immigrations there; the center in Palestine; Karo, Ha-Ari; mysticism in Judaism; Kabbalah; David Reuveni and Shlomo Molcho.

4. Jews in Poland — persecutions of 1648–49; Shabtai Zevi; Shabtaitic movements and development; Frankists.

5. Hasidism — social background of social conflicts; conceptual sources; concept of redemption in Hasidism; weltanschauung of Hasidism; persons and currents in Hasidism; social contributions in Hasidism.
6. Conclusions.

GRADE 11

Victory of Bourgeoisie and Beginnings of Proletarian War — 126 hours

1. Social, economic, and spiritual ferment in eighteenth century; extension of absolutism and remnants of feudalism; sharpening of class conflict; Encyclopedists; Rousseau; development of science and technology.
2. United States; geography of United States; settlement in United States in eighteenth century; Declaration of Independence and causes; war of independence and development of United States; liberation of slaves; civil war and causes; United States as manufacturing power.
3. French Revolution (1) from Rights of Man to Civil War (2) Jacobin Dictatorship (3) Thermidor (4) England and Germany in period of French Revolution.
4. Reaction and progress; geography; Napoleon; conditions in Europe; restoration; reading in neoclassicist literature; *sturm und drang;* art; romanticism.
5. Beginnings of proletariat and its theory; industrial revolution; chartist movement; Utopians; 1848; Marx-Engels; Communist Manifesto; First International.
6. Beginnings of Central European states.
7. Literature and art — late romanticism and realism — Heine, Balzac, Flaubert, Pushkin.
8. Paris Commune.
9. Conclusions.

The Jewish Problem and its Solution — 110 hours

1. The Emancipation period — economic and legal changes of Jews in eighteenth century; Haskalah in Western Europe; science of Judaism; Neo-Orthodoxy; the Jews and industrial capitalism.
2. Jews of Eastern Europe; economic life under Czarism; Haskalah; Hasidism; Jewish community and class structure.
3. Literature — Jewish crisis in mirror of literature; Y. L. Gordon, Mendele.
4. Anti-Semitism.
5. Solutions: assimilation; immigration; autonomy; territorialism.

6. Zionism: Smolenskin; "Auto-emancipation"; Hibath Zion; Mosche Hess; Ahad Haam; political Zionism; socialist Zionism, aliah and settlement; new Yishuv.
7. Conclusions.

GRADE 12

History and culture of the period between the two wars.

History of Jewish Workers' Movement, in Golah and Israel (one hundred years of Jewish history); read Herzl, Borochov, Ahad Haam, Syrkin, etc.

Marxism — reading of sources: Marx, Stalin, Lenin; as well as secondary sources.

STEWART EMOTIONAL RESPONSE TEST (PERCENTAGES)

N = 64

Category	6–11	Age groups 12–17	18+
	HAPPY		
Σ =	39	99	25
Property and possessions	*5*	*12*	*0*
(Food, clothes, presents, etc.)			
Pleasurable group experience	*70*	*36*	*48*
Celebration and recreation	41	19	**4**
Family of orientation	21	12	**4**
Reunited with absent parent	8	8	4
Desire for sibling	13	4	0
Family of procreation	0	1	24
Visit by relatives and friends	8	3	**8**
Social participation	0	1	**8**
Pleasurable private experience	*21*	*19*	*12*
Travel	15	7	**4**
Recovery from illness	3	3	**0**
New experience	0	2	**0**
Intellectual and artistic experience	0	5	**8**
Social privilege	3	2	**0**
Achievement	*3*	*23*	*32*
Group achievement	0	3	**0**
Intellectual	3	7	**4**
Status or prestige	0	10	16
Work	0	3	**4**
Sex	0	0	**8**
Miscellaneous	*0*	*8*	***2***
Reject	*0*	*1*	**7**
	SAD		
Σ =	40	71	21
Illness, injury, death	*25*	*29*	***5***
Illness and injury to self	12	4	**0**
Death to others	15	25	**5**

| | Age groups | | |
Category	6–11	12–17	18+
Aggression	*24*	*27*	*15*
Object of physical aggression	5	3	0
Object of verbal aggression	10	17	5
Physical aggression in group	5	1	5
War	2	0	5
One's own anger	2	6	0
Personal inadequacy	*0*	*17*	*19*
Failure in task	0	17	19
Deprivation	*27*	*17*	*38*
Material	15	7	0
Non-material (play, travel, etc.)	12	10	38
Separation	*12*	*2*	*5*
From parents	10	1	0
From group	2	1	5
Miscellaneous	*2*	*4*	*5*
Reject	*7*	*3*	*14*

ASHAMED

	$\Sigma = 24$	56	23
Embarrassment before others	*79*	*59*	*30*
Interact with strangers	71	43	13
Be looked at	8	16	17
Personal failure or inadequacy	*4*	*7*	*4*
Failure in task	0	7	0
Failure in work	4	0	4
Wrong-doing (aggression)	*4*	*12*	*19*
To be discovered in wrong-doing or inadequacy (error)	*0*	*5*	*26*
Oneself	0	5	17
Another	0	0	9
Sexual behavior or exposure	*0*	*9*	*13*
Object of aggression (verbal)	*4*	*2*	*0*
Motives misunderstood by others	*0*	*2*	*4*
Miscellaneous	*0*	*2*	*13*
Reject	*8*	*2*	*0*

ANGRY

		$\Sigma = 31$	59		24
Aggression of others		*69*	*33*		*4*
Against self		59	28		4
Physical	26		6	0	
Verbal	33		22	4	
Against others (verbal)		10	5		0

Category	Age groups		
	6–11	12–17	18+
Lack/loss of material object	*3*	*18*	*4*
Perversity of others	*10*	*9*	*25*
Disobedience	10	3	13
Behavior of political enemies	0	0	8
Others dirty room	0	3	0
Obstinacy of another in argument	0	3	4
Frustrations arising from Kibbutz living	*3*	*13*	*34*
Restrictions on desires (non-material)	3	5	13
Work irritations	0	0	13
Invasion of privacy	0	5	8
Interact with disliked person	0	3	0
Personal inadequacy	*6*	*6*	*0*
Failure in task	6	6	0
Group inadequacy	*3*	*12*	*25*
Group violates its own norms	3	12	25
Miscellaneous	*10*	*5*	*8*
Reject	*6*	*3*	*0*

AFRAID

	6–11	12–17	18+
Σ =	31	55	23
Physical environment	*41*	*57*	*47*
Animals	19	29	17
Wild	16	20	17
Domestic	3	9	0
Dark	10	22	4
Alone in fields	6	2	0
Physical danger (accident, drown, jump from high place, etc.)	6	4	26
Social environment: extra kibbutz	*26*	*17*	*21*
War	13	9	17
Doctor or dentist (pain)	13	2	0
Poor economic conditions in Israel	0	4	0
Alone in strange place	0	2	4
Social environment: kibbutz	*13*	*5*	*0*
Aggression	13	5	0
Self	*0*	*6*	*13*
Social responsibility or public performance	0	2	13
Discovered in wrong-doing	0	4	0
Miscellaneous	*10*	*5*	*9*
Reject	*10*	*11*	*9*

| | | Age groups | |
Category	6–11	12–17	18+
	BEST THING		
	$\Sigma = 28$	49	18
Property and possessions	*43*	*18*	*6*
Family	*4*	*2*	*6*
Obtain sibling	4	2	0
Obtain child	0	0	6
Pleasurable private experience	*36*	*38*	*45*
Travel	21	16	17
Work	7	0	0
Learn	4	16	22
Social privilege	4	2	0
Life	0	4	6
Achievement	*0*	*12*	*17*
Personal accomplishment	0	6	11
Prestige	0	2	6
Good chaver	0	4	0
Pleasurable experience for others	*7*	*16*	*12*
Peace	7	6	6
Welfare of group	0	10	6
Miscellaneous	*7*	*6*	*5*
Reject	*4*	*6*	*10*
	WORST THING		
	$\Sigma = 21$	44	18
Object of aggression	*5*	*2*	*0*
Physical	5	0	0
Verbal	0	2	0
Illness, injury, death	*47*	*44*	*45*
Illness and injury to self	19	13	11
Death of self	14	20	17
Death and injury of others	9	11	17
Wrong-doing (aggression)	*5*	*2*	*5*
Discovered in ignorance or wrong-doing	*0*	*7*	*0*
War	*19*	*4*	*11*
Separation	*0*	*15*	*11*
From parents	0	4	0
From group	0	11	11
Frustration of goal	*9*	*11*	*5*
Material object	9	2	0
Social desire	0	9	5
Miscellaneous	*19*	*4*	*0*
Reject	*0*	*10*	*22*

BAVELAS MORAL IDEALOGY TEST, IN PERCENTAGES (N-64)

VALUES

Category	Praised for adherence to, or conformity with			Blamed for violation or avoidance of			Total		
	Age groups			Age groups			Age groups		
	6–11	12–17	18+	6–11	12–17	18+	6–11	12–17	18+
Σ =	28	80	26	35	77	21	63	157	47
Competence	*26*	*48*	*66*	*14*	*38*	*34*	*20*	*44*	*51*
Intellectual	11	7	12	3	9	5	7	8	9
Artistic	4	15	4	0	3	0	2	9	2
Athletic	0	5	4	0	0	0	0	3	2
Work	11	20	31	11	17	24	11	19	28
Leadership	0	1	15	0	9	5	0	5	10
Self-restraint	*4*	*9*	*0*	*66*	*32*	*24*	*36*	*21*	*13*
Aggression	4	9	0	49	26	19	27	18	10
Destroy, steal property	0	0	0	17	6	5	9	3	3
Personal virtues	*0*	*7*	*4*	*0*	*12*	*10*	*0*	*9*	*7*
Good/bad character	0	7	4	0	12	10	0	9	7
Relation to authority	*0*	*0*	*0*	*11*	*3*	*10*	*6*	*1*	*5*
Obedient/disobedient	0	0	0	11	3	10	6	1	5
Regard for others	*50*	*19*	*12*	*3*	*8*	*15*	*27*	*14*	*14*
Generosity	50	19	12	0	5	5	25	12	9
Dirty room	0	0	0	3	3	0	2	2	0
Leave kibbutz	0	0	0	0	0	10	0	0	5
Service	*0*	*12*	*15*	*0*	*9*	*5*	*0*	*10*	*10*
Social participation	0	12	15	0	9	5	0	10	10
Miscellaneous	*14*	*4*	*4*	*3*	*0*	*2*	*8*	*2*	*2*
Reject	*7*	*0*	*0*	*3*	*0*	*0*	*4*	*0*	*0*

MORAL SURROGATES

Category	Praised Age groups			Blamed Age groups			Total Age groups		
	6–11	12–17	18+	6–11	12–17	18+	6–11	12–17	18+
	Σ = 33	102	23	35	98	22	68	200	45
Specific person/status	6	5	4	14	7	5	10	6	5
Recipient	0	3	4	0	7	5	0	5	5
Others	6	2	0	14	0	0	10	1	0
Parents	21	16	4	14	9	5	18	13	5
Parents	12	12	4	14	7	0	13	10	2
Father	0	4	0	0	2	5	0	3	3
Mother	9	0	0	0	0	0	5	0	0
"Educators"	21	13	0	43	27	0	32	20	0
Teacher	3	11	0	14	23	0	8	17	0
Nurse	18	2	0	29	4	0	24	3	0
Group	45	64	61	18	52	91	32	58	76
Kevutza	24	22	0	6	19	0	15	21	0
Chevrah	3	11	0	6	19	0	5	15	0
Special group	0	17	9	3	3	23	2	10	16
Kibbutz	18	14	52	3	11	68	10	12	60
Self	0	2	22	0	0	0	0	1	11
No One	0	1	4	0	0	0	0	1	2
Miscellaneous	6	0	4	11	4	0	8	2	2

INDEX

Abandonment, 433, 434, 435–437, 443

Abortions, 100

Abstract ability, 455

Adolescence, kibbutz and Western compared, 316, 326, 327–328, 336, 424, 425. *See also* High School

Adultery, 49

Adults, *see* Nurses; Parents; Teachers. For young adults, *see* Sabras.

Affection: physical displays of, 217, 230; distinguished from sex, 223; rejection of parental, 338; strong sabra need, 427–429, 435, 440–442, 445. *See also* Integration; Nurses; Parents

Aggression

in preschool: against nurses, 73, 76–77; definition, 152n, 162–163; tattling, 163–164; verbal, 164–165; physical, 165–168; instigations to, 90, 167–171, 214, 432; reactions to, 172–175, 213, 215; in Transitional Class; 179n; sanctions of, 181–182; ways of handling, 36–37, 183–192; bed-wetting as weapon, 208; sexual differences in, 247–248

in grammar school: forms of, 271–273, 274, 318; sexual differences in, 281

in high school: used for social control, 309, 310; forms of, 317–318; objects of, 317–326

among adult sabras: attitudes toward, 362; socialized throughout schooling, 409–413, 430–431; forms of, 416–422, 427–429; as cause of insecurity, 433–434, 435, 441–442, 451; as defense mechanism, 439–440

Agriculture, 5; training in, 210–211, 267, 288, 301, 302; sabra interest in, 371, 395

Alter-ego, 399, 406, 443

Ambitions: of sabras, 360, 448; sabra, for children, 394–397 *passim*

America: negativism toward, 257n–258n, 361, 363, 377, 380, 388; curiosity about, 262n

Animals, 241, 258, 273

Animism, 382–383

Anal training, *see* Toilet training

Anxiety: causes of, 409, 435–437, 444; responses to, 438, 440–441; castration anxiety, 235; "moral anxiety," 407, 416–422

Approval, need for, 219, 401–405, 413, 427–445 *passim*

Archeology, 395n

Architecture, 389

Army, service in, 345, 444, 449n

Art: training in preschool, 210, grammar school, 259, high school, 295; rejection of Jewish, 386, 389; sabra emphasis on, 394–398, 444, 454

Athletics, 143, 260n, 276, 288, 304–305

Authority: renunciation of paternal, 11–16; of teachers, 313; rejection of, 322–323, 382, 414; as cultural control, 399–400

Avoidance, 442, 445

Babies, *see* Nursery

Bathing: young children, 107, 211; high school, 329–330, 348

Beirur (clarification), 310

Ben Gurion, David, 381

Bialik, Haim Nachman, 385

Bible, 102, 340n; as textbook, 256–259 *passim*, 300, 383; attitudes toward, 385

Birthdays, 189n, 265

Birth control, 100

Birth rate, 99–100

Books, interest in: grammar school, 262; high school, 290, 299, 300; adult sabras, 389, 390, 395

Bowlby, John, 440n, 460